·Bartholomew·
MINI ATLAS
WORLD

• Bartholomew •

MINI ATLAS
WORLD

Bartholomew

An Imprint of HarperCollins*Publishers*

Bartholomew
An Imprint of HarperCollins*Publishers*
77-85 Fulham Palace Road, London, W6 8JB

Copyright © Bartholomew 1997
First published by Bartholomew 1991
Revised 1992, 1993, reprinted 1994
Revised 1994, 1996, reprinted 1996
Revised 1997

ISBN 0 7028 3352 5 (de luxe hardback)
ISBN 0 7028 3353 3 (paperback)

Printed in the UK by The Edinburgh Press Limited.

KH9466 (de luxe)
KH9537 (paperback)

CONTENTS

ix–xxiii	World Factfile
xxiv–xxv	World Physical
xxvi–xxvii	World Political
xxviii–xxix	World Time Zones
xxx–xxxi	World Environment
xxxii	Key to Symbols
1	Arctic Ocean
2–3	North America
4–5	Canada, West
6–7	Canada, East
8–9	USA, West
10–11	USA, East
12	USA, Alaska
13	Canada Pacific
14–15	Lower Canada, USA North-East
16	Washington – New York – Boston
17	USA, South-East
18–19	USA, South-Central
20	USA, Pacific NW
21	USA, Pacific S
22	San Francisco & Los Angeles
23	Central Mexico
24–25	Mexico & Central America
26–27	Caribbean
28	South America
29	South America, South
30	South America, Central
31	South America, NE

32–33	South America, North
34	Central Argentina
35	South-East Brazil
36–37	Europe
38–39	Scandinavia
40–41	British Isles
42–43	England & Wales
44	Scotland, North
45	Ireland
46	Paris – Brussels – Ruhr
47	Alps
48–49	France
50–51	Spain & Portugal
52–53	Italy
54–55	The Balkans
56–57	Germany & Austria
58–59	East-Central Europe
60–61	European Russia, Ukraine & Baltic States
62	North Asia
63	Russian Federation, East
64–65	Russian Federation, West
66–67	South Asia
68–69	East Asia
70–71	South-East Asia
72–73	Central China
74	Japan & Korea
75	Central Japan
76–77	Indo-China & Singapore

Index

WORLD FACTFILE

Abbreviations List

Eng.	English
Ital.	Italian
langs.	languages
Prot.	Protestant
R. Cath.	Roman Catholic
Trad. beliefs	Traditional beliefs
Austr. Dollar	Australian Dollar
CFA Franc	African Financial Community Franc
E. Carib. Dollar	Eastern Caribbean Dollar

The statistics on the following pages are from the latest available sources including UN data.

The Factfile shows capital city names in their English form. In the Atlas, capital city names are in the local form.

Flag	COUNTRY	Status	Area (sq km)	Population ('000)	Capital City
	Afghanistan	Republic	652 225	18 879	Kabul
	Albania	Republic	28 748	3 414	Tirana
	Algeria	Republic	2 381 741	27 325	Algiers
	Andorra	Principality	465	65	Andorra la Vella
	Angola	Republic	1 246 700	10 674	Luanda
	Antigua & Barbuda	Monarchy	442	65	St John's
	Argentina	Republic	2 766 889	34 180	Buenos Aires
	Armenia	Republic	29 800	3 548	Yerevan
	Australia	Federation	7 682 300	17 843	Canberra
	Austria	Republic	83 855	8 031	Vienna
	Azerbaijan	Republic	86 600	7 472	Baku
	The Bahamas	Monarchy	13 939	272	Nassau
	Bahrain	Monarchy	691	549	Manama
	Bangladesh	Republic	143 998	117 787	Dhaka
	Barbados	Monarchy	430	261	Bridgetown
	Belarus	Republic	207 600	10 355	Minsk
	Belgium	Monarchy	30 520	10 080	Brussels
	Belize	Monarchy	22 965	211	Belmopan
	Benin	Republic	112 620	5 246	Porto Novo
	Bhutan	Monarchy	46 620	1 614	Thimphu
	Bolivia	Republic	1 098 581	7 237	La Paz
	Bosnia-Herzegovina	Republic	51 130	3 527	Sarajevo
	Botswana	Republic	581 370	1 443	Gaborone
	Brazil	Republic	8 511 965	153 725	Brasília
	Brunei	Monarchy	5 765	280	Bandar Seri Begaw
	Bulgaria	Republic	110 994	8 443	Sofia
	Burkina	Republic	274 200	9 889	Ouagadougou

Main Languages	Main Religions	Currency
ari, Pushtu, Uzbek, Turkmen	Muslim	Afghani
lbanian , Greek	Muslim, Orthodox, R. Cath.	Lek
rabic, French, Berber	Muslim, Roman Catholic	Dinar
atalan, Spanish, French	Roman Catholic	Franc, Peseta
ortuguese, local langs.	R. Cath., Prot., Trad. beliefs	Kwanza
nglish, Creole	Protestant, Roman Catholic	E. Carib. Dollar
panish, Italian, Amerindian langs.	R. Cath., Prot., Jewish	Peso
rmenian, Azeri, Russian	Orthodox, R. Cath., Muslim	Dram
ng., Ital., Greek, Aboriginal langs.	Prot., R. Cath., Orthodox	Dollar
erman, Serbo-Croat , Turkish	Roman Catholic, Protestant	Schilling
zeri, Armenian, Russian, Lezgian	Muslim, Orthodox	Manat
nglish, Creole, French Creole	Protestant, Roman Catholic	Dollar
rabic, English	Muslim, Christian	Dinar
engali, Bihari, Hindi, Eng., local langs.	Muslim, Hindu, Buddhist, Christian	Taka
nglish, Creole	Protestant, Roman Catholic	Dollar
elorussian, Russian, Ukrainian	Orthodox, Roman Catholic	Rouble
utch , French, German , Italian	Roman Catholic, Protestant	Franc
nglish, Creole, Spanish, Mayan	R. Cath., Prot., Hindu	Dollar
ench, Fon, Yoruba, Adja, local langs.	Trad. beliefs, R. Cath., Muslim	CFA Franc
zongkha, Nepali, Assamese, English	Buddhist, Hindu, Muslim	Ngultrum
panish, Quechua, Aymara	R. Cath., Prot., Baha'i	Boliviano
erbo-Croat	Muslim, Orthodox, R. Cath., Prot.	Dinar
nglish, Setswana, Shona, local langs.	Trad. beliefs, Prot., R. Cath.	Pula
ortuguese, German, Japanese, Ital.	R. Cath., Spiritist, Prot.	Real
alay, English, Chinese	Muslim, Buddhist, Christian	Dollar (Ringgit)
ulgarian, Turkish, Romany	Orthodox, Muslim	Lev
ench, More, Fulani, local langs.	Trad. beliefs, Muslim, R. Cath.	CFA Franc

Flag	COUNTRY	Status	Area (sq km)	Population ('000)	Capital City
	Burundi	Republic	27 835	6 209	Bujumbura
	Cambodia	Monarchy	181 000	9 968	Phnom Penh
	Cameroon	Republic	475 442	12 871	Yaoundé
	Canada	Federation	9 970 610	29 248	Ottawa
	Cape Verde	Republic	4 033	381	Praia
	Central African Rep.	Republic	622 436	3 235	Bangui
	Chad	Republic	1 284 000	6 183	Ndjamena
	Chile	Republic	756 945	13 994	Santiago
	China	Republic	9 560 900	1 208 841	Beijing
	Colombia	Republic	1 141 748	34 520	Bogotá
	Comoros	Republic	1 862	630	Moroni
	Congo	Republic	342 000	2 516	Brazzaville
	Costa Rica	Republic	51 100	3 011	San José
	Côte d'Ivoire	Republic	322 463	13 695	Yamoussoukro
	Croatia	Republic	56 538	4 504	Zagreb
	Cuba	Republic	110 860	10 960	Havana
	Cyprus	Republic	9 251	734	Nicosia
	Czech Republic	Republic	78 864	10 333	Prague
	Denmark	Monarchy	43 075	5 205	Copenhagen
	Djibouti	Republic	23 200	566	Djibouti
	Dominica	Republic	750	71	Roseau
	Dominican Republic	Republic	48 442	7 769	Santo Domingo
	Ecuador	Republic	272 045	11 221	Quito
	Egypt	Republic	1 000 250	58 326	Cairo
	El Salvador	Republic	21 041	5 641	San Salvador
	Equatorial Guinea	Republic	28 051	389	Malabo
	Eritrea	Republic	117 400	3 437	Asmara

Main languages	Main Religions	Currency
Kirundi, French	R. Cath., Trad. beliefs, Prot.	Franc
Khmer, Vietnamese	Buddhist, R. Cath., Muslim	Riel
French, Eng., Fang, Bamileke	Trad. beliefs, R. Cath., Muslim	CFA Franc
Eng., French, Amerindian langs.	R. Cath., Prot., Orthodox, Jewish	Dollar
Portuguese, Portuguese Creole	R. Cath., Prot., Trad. beliefs	Escudo
French, Sango, Banda, Baya	Prot., R. Cath., Trad. beliefs	CFA Franc
Arabic, French, local langs.	Muslim, Trad. Beliefs, R. Cath.	CFA Franc
Spanish, Amerindian langs.	Roman Catholic, Protestant	Peso
Chinese, regional langs.	Confucian, Tao., Buddhist, Mus.	Yuan
Spanish, Amerindian langs.	Roman Catholic, Protestant	Peso
Comorian, French, Arabic	Muslim, Roman Catholic	Franc
French, Kongo, Monokutuba	R. Cath., Prot., Trad. beliefs	CFA Franc
Spanish	Roman Catholic, Protestant	Colón
French, Akan, Kru, Gur, local langs.	Trad. beliefs, Muslim, R. Cath.	CFA Franc
Serbo-Croat	R. Cath., Orthodox, Muslim	Kuna
Spanish	Roman Catholic, Protestant	Peso
Greek, Turkish, English	Orthodox, Muslim	Pound
Czech, Moravian, Slovak	Roman Catholic, Protestant	Koruna
Danish	Protestant, Roman Catholic	Krone
Somali, French, Arabic, Issa, Afar	Muslim, Roman Catholic	Franc
English, French Creole	Roman Catholic, Protestant	E. Carib. Dollar
Spanish, French Creole	Roman Catholic, Protestant	Peso
Spanish, Quechua, Amerindian langs.	Roman Catholic, Protestant	Sucre
Arabic, French	Muslim, Coptic	Pound
Spanish	Roman Catholic, Protestant	Colón
Spanish, Fang	R. Cath., Trad. beliefs	CFA Franc
Tigrinya, Arabic, Tigre, English	Muslim, Coptic	Ethiopian Birr

Flag	COUNTRY	Status	Area (sq km)	Population ('000)	Capital City
	Estonia	Republic	45 200	1 541	Tallinn
	Ethiopia	Republic	1 133 880	54 938	Addis Ababa
	Fiji	Republic	18 330	771	Suva
	Finland	Republic	338 145	5 095	Helsinki
	France	Republic	543 965	57 747	Paris
	Gabon	Republic	267 667	1 283	Libreville
	The Gambia	Republic	11 295	1 081	Banjul
	Georgia	Republic	69 700	5 450	Tbilisi
	Germany	Republic	357 868	81 410	Berlin
	Ghana	Republic	238 537	16 944	Accra
	Greece	Republic	131 957	10 426	Athens
	Grenada	Monarchy	378	92	St George's
	Guatemala	Republic	108 890	10 322	Guatemala City
	Guinea	Republic	245 857	6 501	Conakry
	Guinea-Bissau	Republic	36 125	1 050	Bissau
	Guyana	Republic	214 969	825	Georgetown
	Haiti	Republic	27 750	7 041	Port-au-Prince
	Honduras	Republic	112 088	5 770	Tegucigalpa
	Hungary	Republic	93 030	10 261	Budapest
	Iceland	Republic	102 820	266	Reykjavik
	India	Republic	3 287 263	918 570	New Delhi
	Indonesia	Republic	1 919 445	193 017	Jakarta
	Iran	Republic	1 648 000	59 778	Tehran
	Iraq	Republic	438 317	19 925	Baghdad
	Republic of Ireland	Republic	70 282	3 571	Dublin
	Israel	Republic	20 770	5 383	Jerusalem
	Italy	Republic	301 245	57 193	Rome

Main Languages	Main Religions	Currency
Estonian, Russian	Protestant, Orthodox	Kroon
Amharic, Oromo, local langs.	Orthodox, Muslim, Trad. beliefs	Birr
English, Fijian, Hindi	Prot., Hindu, R. Cath., Muslim	Dollar
Finnish, Swedish	Protestant, Orthodox	Markka
French, Fr. dialects, Arabic, German	R. Cath., Prot., Muslim	Franc
French, Fang, local langs.	R. Cath., Prot., Trad. beliefs	CFA Franc
English, Malinke, Fulani, Wolof	Muslim, Protestant	Dalasi
Georgian, Russian, Armenian, Azeri	Orthodox, Muslim	Lari
German, Turkish	Prot., R. Cath., Muslim	Mark
English, Hausa, Akan, local langs.	Prot., R. Cath., Muslim	Cedi
Greek, Macedonian	Orthodox, Muslim	Drachma
English, Creole	Roman Catholic, Protestant	E. Carib. Dollar
Spanish, Mayan langs.	Roman Catholic, Protestant	Quetzal
French, Fulani, Malinke, local langs.	Muslim, Trad. beliefs, R. Cath.	Franc
Portuguese, Port. Creole, local langs.	Trad. beliefs, Muslim, R. Cath.	Peso
Eng., Creole, Hindi, Amerindian langs.	Prot., Hindu, R. Cath., Muslim	Dollar
French, French Creole	R. Cath., Prot., Voodoo	Gourde
Spanish, Amerindian langs.	Roman Catholic, Protestant	Lempira
Hungarian, Romany, German, Slovak	Roman Catholic, Protestant	Forint
Icelandic	Roman Catholic, Protestant	Króna
Hindi, English, regional langs.	Hindu, Muslim, Sikh, Christian	Rupee
Indonesian, local langs.	Muslim, Prot., R. Cath., Hindu	Rupiah
Farsi, Azeri, Kurdish, regional langs.	Muslim, Baha'i, Christian	Rial
Arabic, Kurdish, Turkmen	Muslim, Roman Catholic	Dinar
English, Irish	Roman Catholic, Protestant	Punt
Hebrew, Arabic, Yiddish, English	Jewish, Muslim, Christian, Druze	Shekel
Italian, Italian dialects	Roman Catholic	Lira

Flag	COUNTRY	Status	Area (sq km)	Population ('000)	Capital City
	Jamaica	Monarchy	10 991	2 429	Kingston
	Japan	Monarchy	377 727	124 961	Tokyo
	Jordan	Monarchy	89 206	5 198	Amman
	Kazakhstan	Republic	2 717 300	17 027	Alma-Ata
	Kenya	Republic	582 646	27 343	Nairobi
	Kiribati	Republic	717	77	Bairiki
	Kuwait	Monarchy	17 818	1 620	Kuwait City
	Kyrgyzstan	Republic	198 500	4 596	Bishkek
	Laos	Republic	236 800	4 742	Vientiane
	Latvia	Republic	63 700	2 548	Riga
	Lebanon	Republic	10 452	2 915	Beirut
	Lesotho	Monarchy	30 355	1 996	Maseru
	Liberia	Republic	111 369	2 941	Monrovia
	Libya	Republic	1 759 540	5 225	Tripoli
	Liechtenstein	Monarchy	160	30	Vaduz
	Lithuania	Republic	65 200	3 721	Vilnius
	Luxembourg	Monarchy	2 586	401	Luxembourg
	Macedonia	Republic	25 713	2 142	Skopje
	Madagascar	Republic	587 041	14 303	Antananarivo
	Malawi	Republic	118 484	10 843	Lilongwe
	Malaysia	Federation	332 965	19 489	Kuala Lumpur
	Maldives	Republic	298	246	Male
	Mali	Republic	1 240 140	10 462	Bamako
	Malta	Republic	316	364	Valletta
	Marshall Islands	Republic	181	52	Dalap-Uliga-Darrit
	Mauritania	Republic	1 030 700	2 211	Nouakchott
	Mauritius	Republic	2 040	1 104	Port Louis

Main languages	Main Religions	Currency
English, Creole	Prot., R. Cath., Rastafarian	Dollar
Japanese	Shintoist, Buddhist, Christian	Yen
Arabic	Muslim, Christian, Muslim	Dinar
Kazakh, Russian, German, Ukrainian	Muslim, Orthodox, Prot.	Tanga
Swahili, English, local langs.	R. Cath., Prot., Trad. beliefs	Shilling
Kiribati, English	R. Cath., Prot., Baha'i, Mormon	Austr. Dollar
Arabic	Muslim, Christian, Hindu	Dinar
Kirghiz, Russian, Uzbek	Muslim, Orthodox	Som
Lao, local langs.	Buddhist, Trad. beliefs, R. Cath.	Kip
Latvian, Russian	Prot., R. Cath., Orthodox	Lat
Arabic, French, Armenian	Muslim, Prot., R. Cath.	Pound
Sesotho, English, Zulu	R. Cath., Prot., Trad. beliefs	Loti
English, Creole, local langs.	Trad. beliefs, Muslim, Prot.	Dollar
Arabic, Berber	Muslim, Roman Catholic	Dinar
German	Roman Catholic, Protestant	Swiss Franc
Lithuanian, Russian, Polish	R. Cath., Prot., Orthodox	Litas
Letzeburgish, German, French	Roman Catholic, Protestant	Franc
Macedonian, Albanian, Serbo-Croat	Orthodox, Muslim, R. Cath.	Denar
Malagasy, French	Trad. beliefs, R. Cath., Prot.	Franc
Eng., Chichewa, Lomwe, local langs.	Prot., R. Cath., Trad. beliefs	Kwacha
Malay, English, Chinese, Tamil	Muslim, Buddhist, Hindu	Dollar (Ringgit)
Divehi	Muslim	Rufiyaa
French, Bambara, local langs.	Muslim, Trad. beliefs, R. Cath.	CFA Franc
Maltese, English	Roman Catholic	Lira
Marshallese, English	Protestant, Roman Catholic	US Dollar
Arabic, French, local langs.	Muslim	Ouguiya
English, French Creole, Hindi	Hindu, R. Cath., Muslim, Prot.	Rupee

Flag	COUNTRY	Status	Area (sq km)	Population ('000)	Capital City
	Mexico	Republic	1 972 545	93 008	Mexico City
	Micronesia	Republic	701	121	Palikir
	Moldova	Republic	33 700	4 350	Chişinău
	Monaco	Monarchy	1.95	31	Monaco
	Mongolia	Republic	1 565 000	2 363	Ulan Bator
	Morocco	Monarchy	446 550	26 590	Rabat
	Mozambique	Republic	799 380	15 527	Maputo
	Myanmar	Republic	676 577	45 555	Rangoon
	Namibia	Republic	824 292	1 500	Windhoek
	Nauru	Republic	21	11	Yaren
	Nepal	Monarchy	147 181	21 360	Kathmandu
	Netherlands	Monarchy	41 526	15 380	Amsterdam
	New Zealand	Monarchy	270 534	3 493	Wellington
	Nicaragua	Republic	130 000	4 401	Managua
	Niger	Republic	1 267 000	8 846	Niamey
	Nigeria	Republic	923 768	108 467	Abuja
	North Korea	Republic	120 538	23 483	Pyongyang
	Norway	Monarchy	323 878	4 325	Oslo
	Oman	Monarchy	271 950	2 077	Muscat
	Pakistan	Republic	803 940	126 610	Islamabad
	Panama	Republic	77 082	2 563	Panama City
	Papua New Guinea	Monarchy	462 840	4 205	Port Moresby
	Paraguay	Republic	406 752	4 700	Asunción
	Peru	Republic	1 285 216	23 088	Lima
	Philippines	Republic	300 000	67 038	Manila
	Poland	Republic	312 683	38 544	Warsaw
	Portugal	Republic	88 940	9 830	Lisbon

Main Languages	Main Religions	Currency
Spanish, Amerindian langs.	Roman Catholic, Protestant	Peso
Eng., Trukese, Pohnpeian, local langs.	Protestant, Roman Catholic	US Dollar
Romanian, Russian, Ukrainian, Gagauz	Orthodox	Leu
French, Monegasque, Italian	Roman Catholic	Fr. Franc
Khalka, Kazakh, local langs.	Buddhist, Muslim, Trad. beliefs	Tugrik
Arabic, Berber, French, Spanish	Muslim, Roman Catholic	Dirham
Portuguese, Makua, Tsonga	Trad. beliefs, R. Cath., Muslim	Metical
Burmese, Shan, Karen, local langs.	Buddhist, Muslim, Prot., R. Cath.	Kyat
English, Afrikaans, German, Ovambo	Protestant, Roman Catholic	Dollar
Nauruan, Gilbertese, English	Protestant, Roman Catholic	Austr. Dollar
Nepali, Maithili, Bhojpuri, English	Hindu, Buddhist, Muslim	Rupee
Dutch, Frisian, Turkish	R. Cath., Prot., Muslim	Guilder
English, Maori	Protestant, Roman Catholic	Dollar
Spanish, Amerindian langs.	Roman Catholic, Protestant	Córdoba
French, Hausa, Fulani, local langs.	Muslim, Trad. beliefs	CFA Franc
English, Creole, Hausa, Yoruba, Ibo	Muslim, Prot., Roman Catholic	Naira
Korean	Trad. beliefs, Chondoist, Buddhist	Won
Norwegian	Protestant, Roman Catholic	Krone
Arabic, Baluchi, Farsi, Swahili	Muslim	Rial
Urdu, Punjabi, Sindhi, Pushtu, English	Muslim, Christian, Hindu	Rupee
Spanish, English Creole	R. Cath., Prot., Muslim, Baha'i	Balboa
English, Tok Pisin, local langs.	Prot., R. Cath., Trad. beliefs	Kina
Spanish, Guaraní	Roman Catholic, Protestant	Guaraní
Spanish, Quechua, Aymara	Roman Catholic, Protestant	Sol
English, Filipino, Cebuano, local langs.	R. Cath., Aglipayan, Muslim, Prot.	Peso
Polish, German	Roman Catholic, Orthodox	Złoty
Portuguese	Roman Catholic, Protestant	Escudo

Flag	COUNTRY	Status	Area (sq km)	Population ('000)	Capital City
	Qatar	Monarchy	11 437	540	Doha
	Romania	Republic	237 500	22 736	Bucharest
	Russian Federation	Republic	17 075 400	147 997	Moscow
	Rwanda	Republic	26 338	7 750	Kigali
	St Kitts & Nevis	Monarchy	261	41	Basseterre
	St Lucia	Monarchy	616	141	Castries
	St Vincent	Monarchy	389	111	Kingstown
	São Tomé & Príncipe	Republic	964	130	São Tomé
	Saudi Arabia	Monarchy	2 200 000	17 451	Riyadh
	Senegal	Republic	196 720	8 102	Dakar
	Seychelles	Republic	455	74	Victoria
	Sierra Leone	Republic	71 740	4 402	Freetown
	Singapore	Republic	639	2 930	Singapore
	Slovakia	Republic	49 035	5 347	Bratislava
	Slovenia	Republic	20 251	1 942	Ljubljana
	Solomon Islands	Monarchy	28 370	366	Honiara
	Somalia	Republic	637 657	9 077	Mogadishu
	South Africa	Republic	1 219 080	39 659	Pretoria/Cape Town
	South Korea	Republic	99 274	44 453	Seoul
	Spain	Monarchy	504 782	39 193	Madrid
	Sri Lanka	Republic	65 610	17 865	Colombo
	Sudan	Republic	2 505 813	27 361	Khartoum
	Surinam	Republic	163 820	418	Paramaribo
	Swaziland	Monarchy	17 364	879	Mbabane
	Sweden	Monarchy	449 964	8 794	Stockholm
	Switzerland	Federation	41 293	6 994	Bern
	Syria	Republic	185 180	13 844	Damascus

Main languages	Main Religions	Currency
rabic, Indian langs.	Muslim, Christian, Hindu	Riyal
omanian, Hungarian	Orthodox, R. Cath. protestant	Leu
ussian, Tatar, Ukrainian, local langs.	Orthodox, Muslim, Christian	Rouble
inyarwanda, French	R. Cath., Trad. beliefs, Prot.	Franc
nglish, Creole	Protestant, Roman Catholic	E. Carib. Dollar
nglish, French Creole	Roman Catholic, Protestant	E. Carib. Dollar
nglish, Creole	Protestant, Roman Catholic	E. Carib. Dollar
ortuguese, Portuguese Creole	Roman Catholic, Protestant	Dobra
rabic	Muslim	Riyal
rench, Wolof, Fulani, local langs.	Muslim, R. Cath., Trad. beliefs	CFA Franc
eychellois, English	Roman Catholic, Protestant	Rupee
nglish, Creole, Mende, Temne	Trad. beliefs, Muslim, Prot.	Leone
hinese, English, Malay, Tamil	Buddhist, Tao., Muslim, Christian	Dollar
lovak, Hungarian, Czech	R. Cath., Prot., Orthodox	Koruna
lovene, Serbo-Croat	Roman Catholic, Protestant	Tólar
ng., Solomon Is. Pidgin, local langs.	Protestant, Roman Catholic	Dollar
omali, Arabic	Muslim	Shilling
frikaans, English, local langs.	Prot., R. Cath., Muslim, Hindu	Rand
orean	Buddhist, Prot., R. Cath.	Won
panish, Catalan, Galician, Basque	Roman Catholic	Peseta
inhalese, Tamil, English	Buddhist, Hindu, Muslim, R. Cath.	Rupee
rabic, Dinka, Nubian, Beja, Nuer	Muslim, Trad. beliefs, R. Cath.	Dinar
utch, Surinamese, English, Hindi	Hindu, R. Cath., Prot., Muslim	Guilder
wazi, English	Prot., R. Cath., Trad. beliefs	Emalangeni
wedish	Protestant, Roman Catholic	Krona
erman, French, Italian, Romansch	Roman Catholic, Protestant	Franc
rabic, Kurdish, Armenian	Muslim, Christian	Pound

Flag	COUNTRY	Status	Area (sq km)	Population ('000)	Capital City
	Taiwan	Republic	36 179	21 074	Taipei
	Tajikistan	Republic	143 100	5 751	Dushanbe
	Tanzania	Republic	945 087	28 846	Dodoma
	Thailand	Monarchy	513 115	59 396	Bangkok
	Togo	Republic	56 785	3 928	Lomé
	Tonga	Monarchy	748	98	Nuku'alofa
	Trinidad & Tobago	Republic	5 130	1 257	Port of Spain
	Tunisia	Republic	164 150	8 733	Tunis
	Turkey	Republic	779 452	61 183	Ankara
	Turkmenistan	Republic	488 100	4 010	Ashkhabad
	Tuvalu	Monarchy	25	9	Funafuti
	Uganda	Republic	241 038	20 621	Kampala
	Ukraine	Republic	603 700	51 910	Kiev
	United Arab Emirates	Federation	77 700	1 861	Abu Dhabi
	United Kingdom	Monarchy	244 082	58 091	London
	United States	Republic	9 809 386	260 560	Washington
	Uruguay	Republic	176 215	3 167	Montevideo
	Uzbekistan	Republic	447 400	22 349	Tashkent
	Vanuatu	Republic	12 190	165	Port-Vila
	Venezuela	Republic	912 050	21 177	Caracas
	Vietnam	Republic	329 565	72 509	Hanoi
	Western Samoa	Monarchy	2 831	164	Apia
	Yemen	Republic	527 968	13 873	Sana
	Yugoslavia	Republic	102 173	10 515	Belgrade
	Zaire	Republic	2 345 410	42 552	Kinshasa
	Zambia	Republic	752 614	9 196	Lusaka
	Zimbabwe	Republic	390 759	11 150	Harare

Main Languages	Main Religions	Currency
...inese, local langs.	Buddhist, Taoist, Confucian	Dollar
...jik, Uzbek, Russian	Muslim	Rouble
...vahili, Eng., Nyamwezi, local langs.	R. Cath., Muslim, Trad. beliefs	Shilling
...ai, Lao, Chinese, Malay	Buddhist, Muslim	Baht
...ench, Ewe, Kabre, local langs.	Trad. beliefs, R. Cath., Muslim	CFA Franc
...ngan, English	Prot., R. Cath., Mormon	Pa'anga
...glish, Creole, Hindi	R. Cath., Hindu, Prot., Muslim	Dollar
...abic, French	Muslim	Dinar
...rkish	Muslim	Lira
...rkmen, Russian	Muslim	Manat
...valuan, English	Protestant	Dollar
...glish, Swahili, Luganda, local langs.	R. Cath., Prot., Muslim	Shilling
...krainian, Russian, regional langs.	Orthodox, Roman Catholic	Karbovanets
...rabic, English, Hindi, Urdu, Farsi	Muslim, Christian	Dirham
...glish, S. Indian langs., Chinese	Prot., R. Cath., Muslim, Sikh	Pound
...glish, Spanish, Amerindian langs.	Prot., R. Cath., Muslim, Jewish	Dollar
...panish	R. Cath., Prot., Jewish	Peso
...zbek, Russian, Tajik, Kazakh	Muslim, Orthodox	Som
...glish, Bislama, French	Prot., R. Cath., Trad. beliefs	Vatu
...panish, Amerindian langs.	Roman Catholic, Protestant	Bolívar
...etnamese, Thai, Khmer, Chinese	Buddhist, Taoist, Roman Catholic	Dong
...amoan, English	Prot., R. Cath., Mormon	Tala
...rabic	Muslim	Dinar, Rial
...erbo-Croat, Albanian, Hungarian	Orthodox, Muslim	Dinar
...ench, Lingala, Swahili, Kongo	R. Cath., Prot., Muslim	Zaïre
...glish, Bemba, Nyanja, Tonga	Prot., R. Cath., Trad. beliefs, Mus.	Kwacha
...nglish, Shona, Ndebele	Prot., R. Cath., Trad. beliefs	Dollar

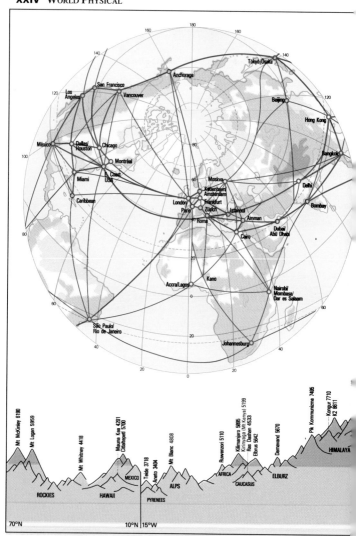

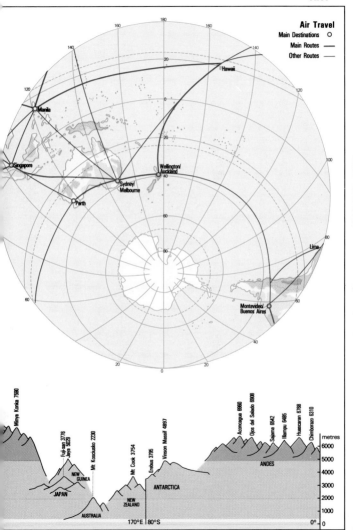

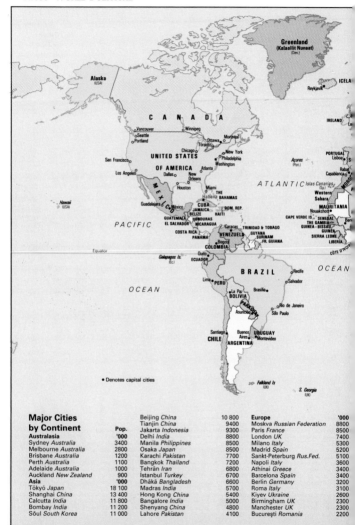

• Denotes capital cities

Major Cities		Beijing *China*	10 800	**Europe**	**'000**
by Continent	**Pop.**	Tianjin *China*	9400	Moskva *Russian Federation*	8800
Australasia	**'000**	Jakarta *Indonesia*	9300	Paris *France*	8500
Sydney *Australia*	3400	Delhi *India*	8800	London *UK*	7400
Melbourne *Australia*	2800	Manila *Philippines*	8500	Milano *Italy*	5300
Brisbane *Australia*	1200	Osaka *Japan*	8500	Madrid *Spain*	5200
Perth *Australia*	1100	Karachi *Pakistan*	7700	Sankt-Peterburg *Rus.Fed.*	5100
Adelaide *Australia*	1000	Bangkok *Thailand*	7200	Napoli *Italy*	3600
Auckland *New Zealand*	900	Tehrān *Iran*	6800	Athinai *Greece*	3400
Asia	**'000**	Istanbul *Turkey*	6700	Barcelona *Spain*	3400
Tōkyō *Japan*	18 100	Dhākā *Bangladesh*	6600	Berlin *Germany*	3200
Shanghai *China*	13 400	Madras *India*	5700	Roma *Italy*	3100
Calcutta *India*	11 800	Hong Kong *China*	5400	Kiyev *Ukraine*	2600
Bombay *India*	11 200	Bangalore *India*	5000	Birmingham *UK*	2300
Sŏul *South Korea*	11 000	Shenyang *China*	4800	Manchester *UK*	2300
		Lahore *Pakistan*	4100	Bucureşti *Romania*	2200

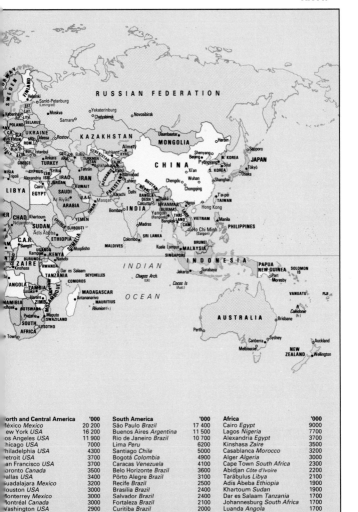

North and Central America	'000
México *Mexico*	20 200
New York *USA*	16 200
Los Angeles *USA*	11 900
Chicago *USA*	7000
Philadelphia *USA*	4300
Detroit *USA*	3700
San Francisco *USA*	3700
Toronto *Canada*	3500
Dallas *USA*	3400
Guadalajara *Mexico*	3200
Houston *USA*	3000
Monterrey *Mexico*	3000
Montréal *Canada*	3000
Washington *USA*	2900
Boston *USA*	2800

South America	'000
São Paulo *Brazil*	17 400
Buenos Aires *Argentina*	11 500
Rio de Janeiro *Brazil*	10 700
Lima *Peru*	6200
Santiago *Chile*	5000
Bogotá *Colombia*	4900
Caracas *Venezuela*	4100
Belo Horizonte *Brazil*	3600
Pôrto Alegre *Brazil*	3100
Recife *Brazil*	2500
Brasília *Brazil*	2400
Salvador *Brazil*	2400
Fortaleza *Brazil*	2100
Curitiba *Brazil*	2000
Guayaquil *Ecuador*	1700

Africa	'000
Cairo *Egypt*	9000
Lagos *Nigeria*	7700
Alexandria *Egypt*	3700
Kinshasa *Zaire*	3500
Casablanca *Morocco*	3200
Alger *Algeria*	3000
Cape Town *South Africa*	2300
Abidjan *Côte d'Ivoire*	2200
Tarábulus *Libya*	2100
Adis Abeba *Ethiopia*	1900
Khartoum *Sudan*	1900
Dar es Salaam *Tanzania*	1700
Johannesburg *South Africa*	1700
Luanda *Angola*	1700
Maputo *Mozambique*	1600

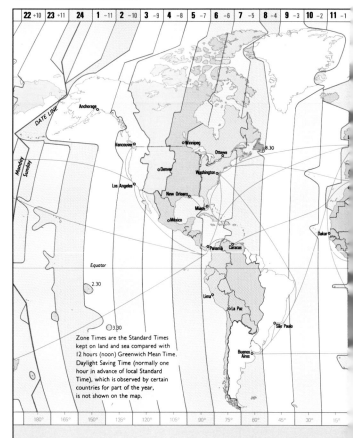

| 22 +10 | 23 +11 | 24 | 1 −11 | 2 −10 | 3 −9 | 4 −8 | 5 −7 | 6 −6 | 7 −5 | 8 −4 | 9 −3 | 10 −2 | 11 −1 |

DATE LINE

Monday / Sunday

Anchorage

Vancouver

Winnipeg

Ottawa

8.30

Denver

Washington

Los Angeles

New Orleans

Miami

Mexico

Dakar

Panama   Caracas

Equator

2.30

Lima

La Paz

São Paulo

3.30

Buenos Aires

Zone Times are the Standard Times kept on land and sea compared with 12 hours (noon) Greenwich Mean Time. Daylight Saving Time (normally one hour in advance of local Standard Time), which is observed by certain countries for part of the year, is not shown on the map.

| 180° | 165° | 150° | 135° | 120° | 105° | 90° | 75° | 60° | 45° | 30° | 15° |

Journey Times

Sail (via Cape)
164 days

Steam (via Cape)
43 days

Steam (via Suez)
30 days

Supertanker (via Cape)
28 days

Singapore ←

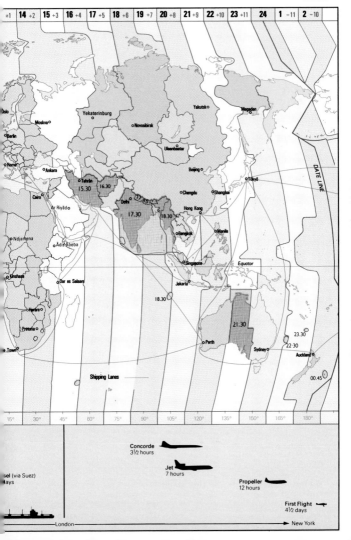

| +1 | **14** +2 | **15** +3 | **16** +4 | **17** +5 | **18** +6 | **19** +7 | **20** +8 | **21** +9 | **22** +10 | **23** +11 | **24** | **1** −11 | **2** −10 |

Oslo

Moskva

Berlin

Yekaterinburg

Yakutsk

Roma

Ankara

Novosibirsk

Magadan

Cairo

Tehrān
15.30

16.30

Ulaanbaatar

Ar Riyād

Delhi
17.45

Beijing

Tōkyō

17.30

18.30

Chengdu

Shanghai

Ndjamena

Ādīs Ābeba

Hong Kong

DATE LINE

Kinshasa

Dar es Salaam

Bangkok

Manila

Singapore

Equator

Jakarta

Harare

18.30

Pretoria

21.30

23.30

e Town

Perth

Sydney

22.30

Auckland

Shipping Lanes ———

00.45

| 15° | 30° | 45° | 60° | 75° | 90° | 105° | 120° | 135° | 150° | 165° | 180° |

Concorde
3½ hours

Jet
7 hours

Propeller
12 hours

First Flight ➡
4½ days

sel (via Suez)
days

London ——————————————————— New York

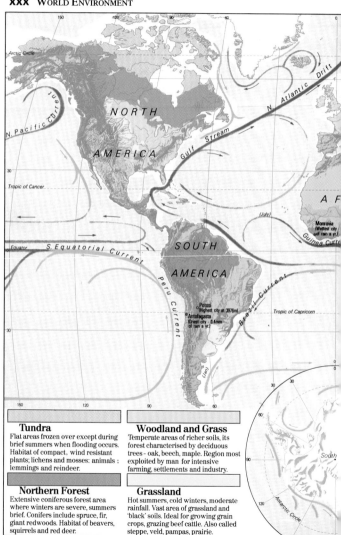

Arctic Circle

N. Pacific Current

N. Atlantic Drift

N O R T H

A M E R I C A

Gulf Stream

Tropic of Cancer

A F

Morrovia
(Wettest city
s of rain a yr.)

Guinea Current

Equator

S. Equatorial Current

S O U T H

A M E R I C A

Peru Current

Brazil Current

Potosi
(Highest city at 3976m)

Antofagasta
(Driest city - 0.4mm
of rain a yr.)

Tropic of Capricorn

(July)

(Jan)

South

Antarctic Circle

Tundra
Flat areas frozen over except during brief summers when flooding occurs. Habitat of compact, wind resistant plants; lichens and mosses; animals; lemmings and reindeer.

Northern Forest
Extensive coniferous forest area where winters are severe, summers brief. Conifers include spruce, fir, giant redwoods. Habitat of beavers, squirrels and red deer.

Woodland and Grass
Temperate areas of richer soils, its forest characterised by deciduous trees - oak, beech, maple. Region most exploited by man for intensive farming, settlements and industry.

Grassland
Hot summers, cold winters, moderate rainfall. Vast area of grassland and 'black' soils. Ideal for growing grain crops, grazing beef cattle. Also called steppe, veld, pampas, prairie.

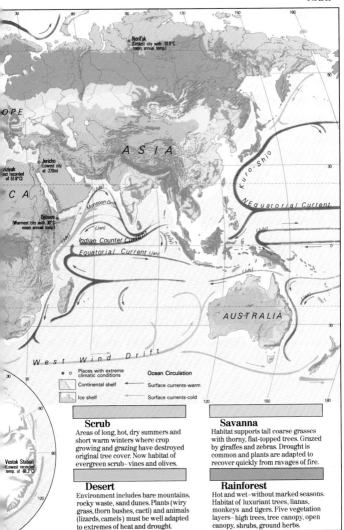

Noril'sk
(Coolest city with 10.9°C
mean annual temp.)

Jericho
(Lowest city
at -270m)

zziyah
est recorded
of 57.8°C)

Djibouti
(Warmest city with 30°C
mean annual temp.)

OPE

CA

ASIA

Kuro-Shio

N Equatorial Current

Monsoon Drift

(July)

(Jan)

Indian Counter Current

Equatorial Current (Jan)

(July)

(Jan)

(July)

AUSTRALIA

West Wind Drift

Vostok Station
(Lowest recorded
temp. of 88.3°C)

• ○ Places with extreme
climatic conditions

Continental shelf

Ice shelf

Ocean Circulation

→ Surface currents–warm

→ Surface currents–cold

Scrub
Areas of long, hot, dry summers and
short warm winters where crop
growing and grazing have destroyed
original tree cover. Now habitat of
evergreen scrub–vines and olives.

Desert
Environment includes bare mountains,
rocky waste, sand dunes. Plants (wiry
grass, thorn bushes, cacti) and animals
(lizards, camels) must be well adapted
to extremes of heat and drought.

Savanna
Habitat supports tall coarse grasses
with thorny, flat-topped trees. Grazed
by giraffes and zebras. Drought is
common and plants are adapted to
recover quickly from ravages of fire.

Rainforest
Hot and wet–without marked seasons.
Habitat of luxuriant trees, lianas,
monkeys and tigers. Five vegetation
layers– high trees, tree canopy, open
canopy, shrubs, ground herbs.

BOUNDARIES

	International
	International under Dispute
	Cease Fire Line
	Autonomous or State
	Administrative
	Maritime (National)

LETTERING STYLES

CANADA	Independent Nation
FLORIDA	State, Province or Autonomous Region
Gibraltar (U.K.)	Sovereignty of Dependent Territory
Lothian	Administrative Area
LANGUEDOC	Historic Region
Loire **Vosges**	Physical Feature or Physical Region

TOWNS AND CITIES

Square Symbols denote capital cities. Each settlement is given a symbol according to its relative importance, with type size to match.

▪	●	**New York**	Major City
▪	●	**Montréal**	City
▫	○	Ottawa	Small City
▪	●	**Québec**	Large Town
▫	○	St John's	Town
▫	○	Yorkton	Small Town
▫	○	Jasper	Village
			Built-up-area

LAKE FEATURES

	Permanent
	Seasonal

OTHER FEATURES

	River
	Seasonal River
=	Pass, Gorge
	Dam, Barrage
	Waterfall, Rapid
	Aqueduct
	Reef
▲ 4231	Summit, Peak
. 217	Spot Height, Depth
⌣	Well
▵ ••	Oil Field
▲	Gas Field
Gas / Oil	Oil / Natural Gas Pipeline
Gemsbok Nat. Pk.	National Park
∴UR	Historic Site
	Main Railway
	Other Railway
- - - - - - -	Under Construction
—+—+—	Rail Tunnel
- - - - - - -	Rail Ferry
	Canal
⊕	International Airport
✦	Other Airport

For pages 102-103, 104-105 only:

0	Sea Level
200m	
2000m	
4000m	
6000m	
	Depth

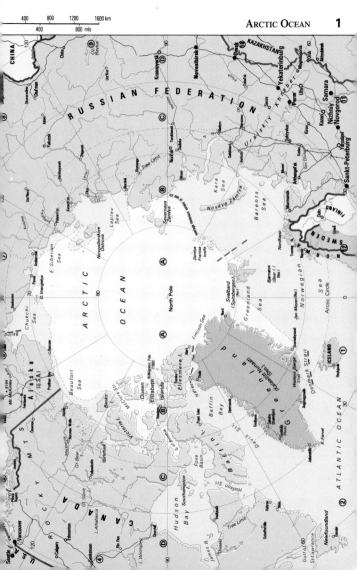

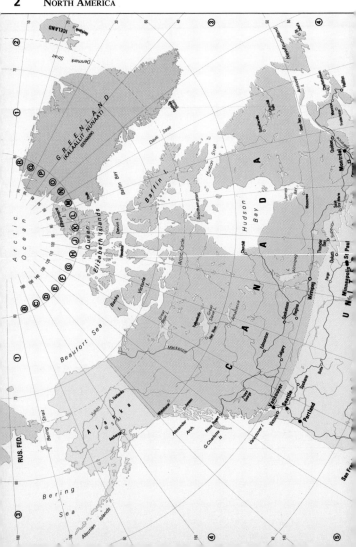

250 500 750 1000 1250 km
250 500 750 mls

⑤ ⑥ ⑦ ⑧

ATLANTIC OCEAN

New York
Philadelphia
Baltimore
Washington
Norfolk
Indianapolis
Charleston
Nashville
Atlanta
Jacksonville
Memphis
Birmingham
St Louis
Kansas City
Dallas
Fort Worth
New Orleans
Houston
San Antonio
Ohio
Mississippi
UNITED STATES OF AMERICA
El Paso
Chihuahua
Phoenix
Albuquerque
Los Angeles
San Diego

Bermuda Is. (U.K.)

THE BAHAMAS
Nassau
Miami
Tampa

CUBA
Habana
Guantánamo
HAITI
Kingston
JAMAICA
Port-au-Prince
DOMINICAN REP.
Sto Domingo
Puerto Rico (U.S.A.)
DOMINICA
ST LUCIA
ST VINCENT & THE GRENADINES
BARBADOS
GRENADA
TRINIDAD & TOBAGO
Netherlands Antilles

CARIBBEAN SEA

VENEZUELA
Caracas
Maracaibo
Medellín
Bogotá
COLOMBIA
Sta Marta
Barranquilla
Panama
PANAMA
BRAZIL
ECUADOR
Quito
PERU

BELIZE
Belmopan
GUATEMALA
Guatemala
EL SALVADOR
San Salvador
HONDURAS
Tegucigalpa
NICARAGUA
Managua
COSTA RICA
San José
L. de Coco (C.R.)

MÉXICO
Mérida
Veracruz
Tampico
Monterrey
Torreón
Mexico
Guadalajara
Acapulco
Mazatlán
Rio Grande
G. de California
Guadalupe (Mex.)
Is Revilla Gigedo (Mex.)
Clipperton (Fr.)
Galápagos Is. (Ecu.)

PACIFIC OCEAN

Tropic of Cancer
Equator

⑥ ⑦ ⑧ Ⓖ Ⓗ Ⓙ Ⓚ Ⓜ

ARCTIC OCEAN

Sverdrup Islands

PARRY ISLANDS

Prince of Wales Island

Bathurst Island

Melville Island

Banks Island

Victoria Island

McClure Strait

Viscount Melville Sound

McClintock Channel

Peel Sound

King William Island

Prince Albert Pen.

Wollaston Pen.

Amundsen Gulf

Coronation Gulf

Queen Maud Gulf

NORTHWEST TERRITORIES

Great Bear Lake

BEAUFORT SEA

Mackenzie Bay

Mackenzie Mountains

Selwyn Mountains

Richardson Mts

Brooks Range

Endicott Mts

ALASKA

YUKON TERRITORY

CANADA

Fairbanks

Anchorage

Cook Inlet

Mt McKinley

Gulf of Alaska

Kodiak Island

Bering Strait

RUS. FED.

St Lawrence I.

Norton Sound

Nome

Bristol Bay

Point Barrow

Wainwright

Prudhoe Bay

Whitehorse

St Elias Mts

Kenai Pen.

Alaska Range

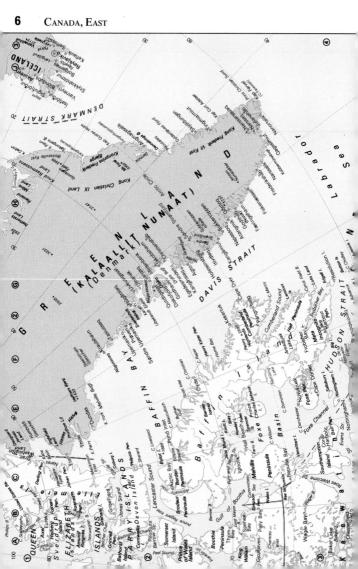

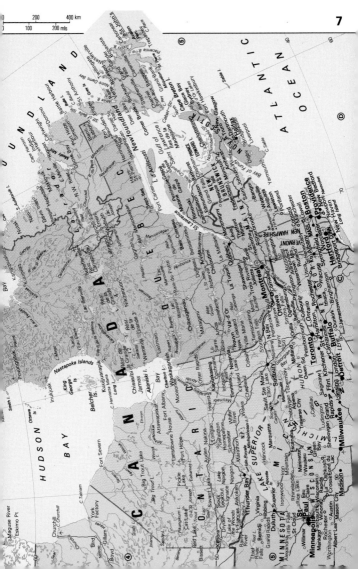

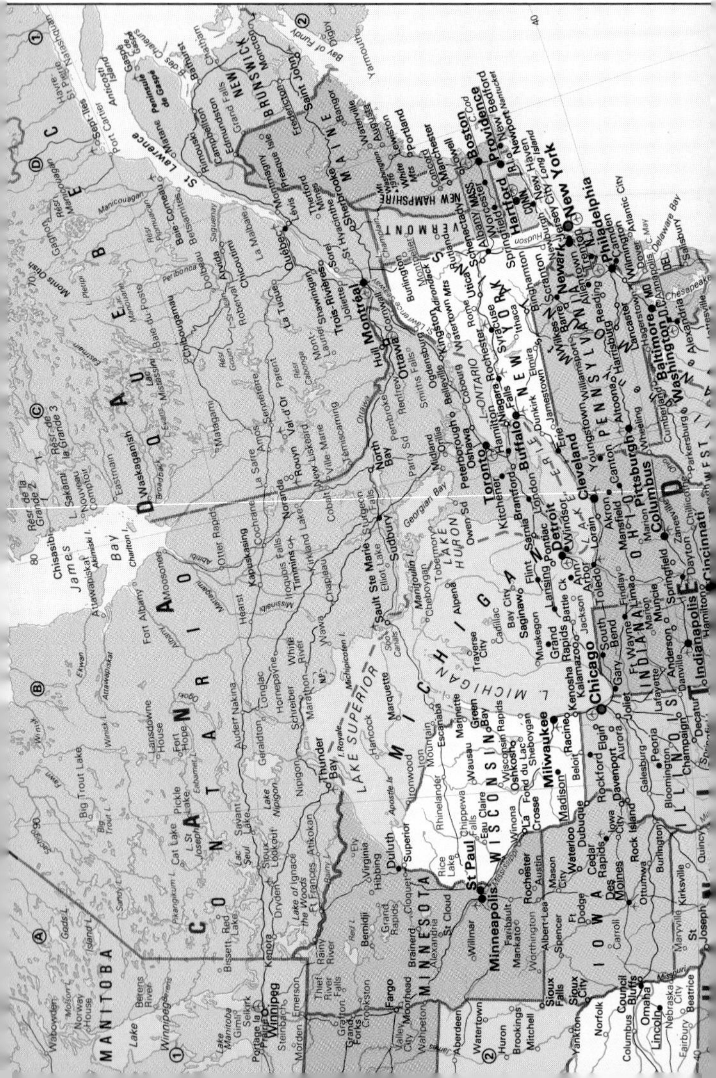

NEW BRUNSWICK

Bay of Fundy

MAINE

NEW HAMPSHIRE

VERMONT

St Lawrence

Québec

Montréal

Ottawa

Boston

Providence

Hartford

New York

Philadelphia

MASS.

ONTARIO

NEW YORK

Toronto

Buffalo

Rochester

Syracuse

PENNSYLVANIA

Baltimore

Washington

Pittsburgh

Cleveland

Columbus

Detroit

LAKE HURON

LAKE SUPERIOR

MICHIGAN

L. MICHIGAN

Sudbury

Georgian Bay

Chicago

INDIANA

Indianapolis

Milwaukee

WISCONSIN

Madison

ILLINOIS

Peoria

Springfield

Duluth

MINNESOTA

St Paul

Minneapolis

IOWA

Des Moines

CANADA

ONTARIO

MANITOBA

Winnipeg

James Bay

Hudson Bay

Fargo

Sioux Falls

Omaha

Lincoln

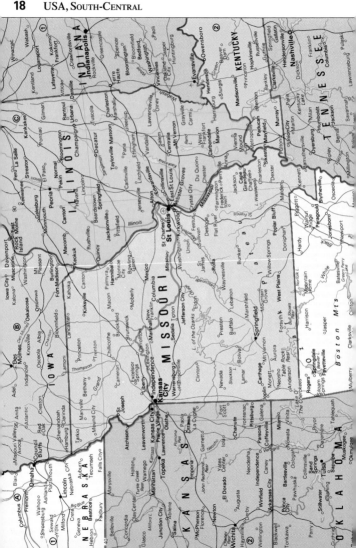

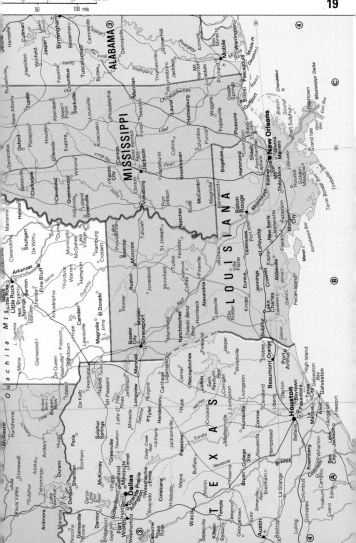

0   50   100   150   200 k
0   50   100 mils

CANADA

WASHINGTON

OREGON

CALIFORNIA

NEVADA

125

120

A

B

C

①

②

45

125

120

Parksville
Gibsons
Horseshoe Bay
Vancouver
Port Alberni
Nanaimo
Ladysmith
Barkley So.
Bamfield
Port Renfrew
Cowichan
Duncan
Sidney
Esquimalt
Victoria
Anacortes
San Juan I.
C. Flattery
Str. of Juan de Fuca
Forks
Olympic Nat. Park
Mt Olympus 2428
Port Angeles
Blaine
Ferndale
Bellingham
Mt Baker 3285
Burlington
Mt Vernon
Concrete
Ross L.
North Cascades Nat. Park
Mt Logan 2733
Hope
Princeton
Chilliwack
Agassiz
Skagit Mtn 2356
Abbotsford
Westm.

Okanagan
Keremeos
Osoyoos
Oliver
Oroville
Tonasket
Republic
Colville
Kettle River
Metaline Falls
Ione
Priest R.
Bonners Ferry
Castlegar
Grand Forks
Trail
Salmo
Creston

Marysville
Everett
Snohomish
Edmonds
Bellevue
Seattle
Bremerton
Port Orchard
Monroe
Renton
Kent
Tacoma
Auburn
Shelton
Olympia
Puyallup
Mt Rainier 4392
Mount Rainier Nat. Park
Snoqualmie Pass
Glacier Peak 3221
Chelan
L. Chelan
Wenatchee
Ephrata
Banks L.
Wilbur
Grand Coulee
Coulee
Medical Lake
Cheney
Spokane
Odessa
Ritzville
Moses Lake

Hoquiam
Aberdeen
Grays Harb.
South Bend
Raymond
Willapa B.
Chehalis
Centralia
Cowlitz
Naches
Yakima
Selah
Ellensburg
Othello
Toppenish
Sunnyside
Richland
Kennewick
Pasco
Dayton
Clarkston
Lewiston
Colfax
Pullman
Moscow
Kendrick
Potlatch

C. Disappointment
Astoria
Rainier
Seaside
St Helens
Longview
Kelso
Woodland
Mt St Helens 2950
Mt Adams 3751
Goldendale
Columbia
Arlington
Umatilla
Echo
Pendleton
Walla Walla
Blue Mountains
Wallowa
Enterprise

Tillamook
Portland
Hillsboro
Lake Oswego
Newberg
Gresham
Oregon City
Camas
Vancouver
White Salmon
Hood River
The Dalles
Mt Hood 3427
Condon
Ukiah
La Grande
Wallowa Mts
Sacajawea Pk 2997

McMinnville
Lincoln City
Newport
Corvallis
Albany
Salem
Stayton
Idanha
Mt Jefferson 3199
Madras
Mt Wilson 1707
John Day R.
Spray
Dayville
Long Creek
John Day
Unity
Baker

Yachats
Florence
Eugene
Springfield
Lebanon
Sweet Home
Lowell
Three Sisters 3156
Redmond
Prineville
Bend
Brothers
Canyon City
Reedsport
Cottage Grove
Oakridge
La Pine
Crescent
High Desert
Silver Lake
Burns
Drewsey
Crane
Harney Basin
Harney L.
Malheur L.

Coos Bay
N. Bend
Coos Bay
Myrtle Point
Oakland
Roseburg
Myrtle Creek
Canyonville
Mt Thielsen 2799
Chiloquin
Upper Klamath L.
Jordan Valley

C. Blanco
Port Orford
Gold Beach
Wolf Creek
Grants Pass
Central Point
Medford
Ashland
Prospect
Crater Nat. Pk.
Mt Scott 2721
Mt McLoughlin 2894
Bly
Valley Falls
Klamath Falls
Lakeview
Steens Mtn

Brookings
O'Brien
Hornbrook
Crescent City
Yreka
Dorris
Clear L. Resr
Willow Ranch
Goose L.
Denio
McDermitt

Pt St George
Klamath
Weed
Mt Shasta 4317
Mount Shasta
Canby
Adin
Middle Alturas Alkali L.
Upper L.
Warner Mts
Black Rock Desert
Santa Rosa Ra.
Winnemucca
Golconda

Humboldt Bay
Arcata
Eureka
Fortuna
Weaverville
Durismuir
Shasta L.
Project City
Burney
Redding
Lassen Nat. Pk.
Lassen Pk 3187
Eagle L.
Susanville
Rye Patch Resr
Imlay
Battle Mountain
Mt Tobin 2978

C. Mendocino

COAST RANGES
CASCADE RANGE
CASCADE RANGE
Klamath Mts
COLUMBIA PLATEAU
Snake

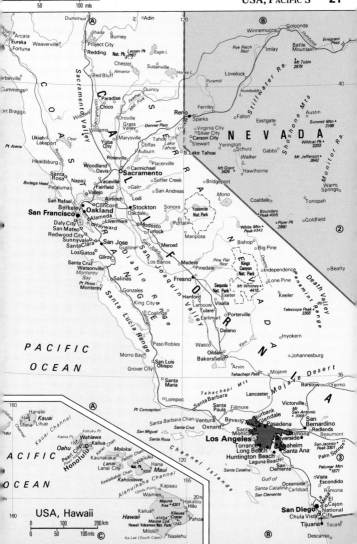

USA, Hawaii

200   400   600 km
100   200   300 mls

C. Fear

Ft Smith

Memphis Huntsville Chattanooga SOUTH
Little Rock   Gainesville Athens Florence Columbia CAROLINA
springs ARKANSAS   Gadsden Atlanta   Savannah Orangeburg
Pine   Tupelo   Augusta   Charleston
Bluff   Greenwood Columbus Birmingham   Macon
Greenville MISSISSIPPI Tuscaloosa ALABAMA
Monroe Jackson Meridian   Columbus GEORGIA Savannah
eveport   Montgomery Phenix   Albany
        Vicksburg   City   Waycross Brunswick
LOUISIANA Natchez Laurel Dothan Valdosta
Alexandria   Hattiesburg   Jacksonville
Lake   Baton   Mobile Tallahassee St. Augustine
Charles Rouge Biloxi Pensacola Panama City
Lafayette New Orleans   Gainesville Daytona Beach
eston   Ocala

C. Canaveral

                    Clearwater   Melbourne
GULF   OF   St Petersburg Tampa Ft Pierce Little Abaco
                    Tampa Bay Lake W Palm THE
                    Ft Myers Okeechobee Beach BAHAMAS②
MEXICO   Ft Lauderdale Lake Worth Gd Eleuthera
                    Hollywood   Berry Is. Cat San Salvador
                    The Everglades Miami Beach Nassau New Providence Exuma Sound
                    C. Sable   Andros   Long
                    Key West   Great Bahama Rum
                    Marquesas Keys   Bank Cay
                              Habana Matanzas
                              (Havana) Colón Sta Clara
Pinar del Río Cardenas Arch de
Guane Cienfuegos Camagüey Camro Romano
C. San Antonio G. de Batabanó Sancti Spíritus Moron Ciego de Ávila
G.de Campeche Progreso Pto CUBA Victoria de Banes
        Mérida Juárez Jardines las Tunas Holguín
        Tizimin de la Reina Manzanillo Bayamo Guantánamo
        Ticul Valladolid I. de G. de Guacanayabo C.Cruz Santiago
Campeche Peto Cozumel Little Cayman Cayman Brac de Cuba
        Yucatan B. de la Ascensión Grand Cayman
atzacoalcos Cd del Escárcega Chetumal (U.K.) Montego Bay Port
natlán Carmen Bco Chinchorro Spanish Town Antonio
I. de Términos Xpujil Ambergris Cay JAMAICA Kingston
Villahermosa Frontera Turneffe I. Pedro Cays
Ferrosquas   Belize Staan Creek (Jam.)
o San Cristóbal Flores BELIZE Honduras I. de Providencia
ntepec Tuxtla Pta Gorda de la Bahía (Col.)
O Gutiérrez Cobán Pto Trujillo I. de San Andrés
  Comitán Barrios L. de Caratasca (Col.)
Tonalá   GUATEMALA Pto Tela La Ceiba Serrana Bank
Huixtla S.de Sta Rosa HONDURAS (Hond. & Col.) Cayos Miskitos
Tapachula   Cortés Yoro   Juticalpa
Quezaltenango Guatemala Comayagua Tegucigalpa Pto Cabezas
Escuintla Sta Ana San Salvador Bonanza
San José S Miguel Matagalpa Prinzapolca
SonSonate EL SALVADOR La Unión León NICARAGUA
Chinandega G. de Fonseca Managua Bluefields
        Masaya L. de I. del Maíz
        Granada Nicaragua San Juan del Norte (Nic. & U.S.A.)
        San Juan San Juan del Norte
        G. de Papagayo COSTA
        Pen. de Puntarenas Alajuela
        Nicoya San José RICA Limón Colón Pta S. Blas
        G. de Nicoya Cartago G.de los La Chorrera Panamá
        Pto Cortés David Mosquitos PANAMA Arch. de
        Pen. de Osa Santiago Chitré las Perlas
        G.Dulce Pen. de Golfo
        Armuelles Azuero de Pta
                G. de Chiriquí Panamá Solano

30

① E

②

CARIBBEAN   SEA

③

10

④

90   D   E

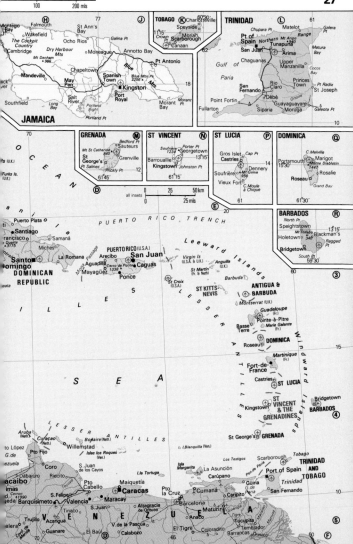

100   200   300   400 km
100   200 mils

H TOBAGO **K** Charlotteville
Montego Falmouth St Ann's Bay Speyside **TRINIDAD** **L** Galera Pt
Bay Wakefield Ocho Rios **Scarborough** Chupara Pt Matelot Range
Cambridge The Cockpit Moneague Crown Canaan Pt of Northern Mt Aripo 940
Country Dry Harbour Annotto Bay 62 Spain Tunapuna Matura
Mts Pt Antonio San Juan Arima Bay
Mt Denham 586 Chapeltown Chaguanas Upper Cocos
May Pen Spanish Blue Mtn Pk Manzanilla Bay
Mandeville Town 2256 18 Princes Pt Radix
Salt Kingston San Rio Town St Joseph
Southfield River Port Royal Fernando Claro
Long Portland Morant Point Fortin Débé Guayaguayare
Bay Bight Morant Bay Siparia Moruga Galeota Pt
JAMAICA Portland Pt Fullarton 10

GRENADA **M** **ST VINCENT** **N** **ST LUCIA** **P** **DOMINICA** **Q**
70 Bedford Pt Porter Pt C. Melville
St Mt Catherine Soufrière Georgetown Gros Islet Cap Pt Marigot
840 Sauteurs 13.15' Castries 14 Portsmouth Mt Diablotin
s (U.K.) St Grenville Barrouallie 19.30 1447
George's Kingstown Johnston Pt Soufrière Dennery Rosalie
Turks Is. St Salines Mt Gimie Roseau Grand Bay
(U.K.) Prickly Pt 12 61.15' 950 C. Moule 61.30'
61.45' Vieux Fort à Chique 61 20

BARBADOS **R**
0 25 50 km North Pt
all insets Speightstown 13.15
0 25 mils Holetown Mt Hillaby Blackman's
E 340 Ragged
Bridgetown Pt
South Pt 59.30
Puerto Plata PUERTO RICO TRENCH

ti Santiago **3**
francisco Samaná Leeward Islands
Santo Miches PUERTO RICO (U.S.A.) Virgin Is Anguilla
Domingo La Romana Arecibo San Juan (U.S.A. & U.K.) (U.K.)
DOMINICAN Mona Caguas St Martin Barbuda
REPUBLIC Passage Mayagüez Cerro de Punta (Fr. & Neth)
eata Ponce 1338 St Croix **ANTIGUA &**
L L E S (U.S.A.) **ST KITTS** **BARBUDA** **3**
I L S **NEVIS**
(U.K.) Montserrat Guadeloupe
Pointe-à-Pitre
Basse Marie Galante
Terre (Fr.)
DOMINICA
Roseau 15
Martinique
(Fr.)
Fort-de-
France
Castries **ST LUCIA**

S E A **VINCENT** Bridgetown
Kingstown **& THE** **BARBADOS**
GRENADINES
4
Windward Passage
St George's **GRENADA**

Aruba L E S S E R
(Neth) Bonaire (Neth) A N T I L L E S
to López Curaçao I.Blanquilla (Ven.)
G.de (Neth) Islas los Roques (Ven.) Los Testigos
ezuela Willemstad Scarborough Tobago
Coro S. Juan Isla La Asunción Pan de Paria **TRINIDAD**
de los Cayos Margarita **AND**
Pto I.la Tortuga Carúpano **TOBAGO**
acaibo Cabello Riecito Port of Spain
mas Maiquetía Pto Cumaná Güiria Trinidad
Cerro la Cruz Paria San Fernando
S. Felipe Maracay Barcelona Caripito 10
Barquisimeto Valencia **Caracas** Maturín
Tinaco S.Juan Anaco
lera V E N E Z U E L A Tigre Tucupita Temblador
Acarigua Altagracia El Tigre Coloradito Barrancas Orinoco
de Orituco **5**
Guanare El Baúl Calabozo Maturín **F**

Scale bars:
200   400   600 km
100   200   300 mls

BRAZIL
Cruz Alta
Sta Maria
Cachoeira
Ibicui
Sumampa
Reconquista
Goya
Mercedes
Iguazú
Paso de los Libres
Uruguaiana
Alegrete
São Livramento
Bagé
Rivera

Co. del Toro 6380
Grl Manuel Belgrano 6250
La Rioja
Rivadavia
Jachal
L. Mar Chiquita
Santa Fe
Paraná
Rafaela
S.Francisco
Concordia
Paysandú
Salto
Tacuarembó
Durazno
URUGUAY
Melo

La Serena
Coquimbo
Ovalle
6282 Olivares
Cruz del Eje
Córdoba
Va Dolores
Alta Gracia
Villa Maria
Bell Ville
Cdad de Gómez
P.de los Toros
Mercedes
Trinidad
Florida
Chur
Treinta y Tres

Punitaqui
Illapel
S.Juan
S.Juan
Mercedario
6770
Aconcagua
San Luis
Rio Cuarto
Rosario
San Nicolás
Canelones
Minas
Punta del Este
Rocha

Los Vilos
Quillota
Viña del Mar
Valparaíso
S.Antonio
S.Bernardo
Rancagua
Pichilemu
Santiago
Tupungato
6550
Vol.Maipo 5290
S.Fernando
Mendoza
S.Rafael
Mercedes
Córdoba
Venado Tuerto
Pergamino
Rufino
Junin
Lincoln
Chivilcoy
Buenos Aires
Avellaneda
La Plata
Colonia
Montevideo
Maldonado

Curicó
Talca
Linares
S.Carlos
Chillán
Vol.Petroa 6090
S.Alvar
Grl Pico
Pehuajó
Trenque Lauquen
Las Flores
Chascomús
Buenos Aires

Cauquenes
Mendoza
Bardas Blancas
Telén
Sta Rosa
Guaminí
Olavarría
Azul
Dolores
Ayacucho
Va Gesell

Tomé
Concepción
Coronel
Vol.Domuyo 4800
ARGENTINA
La Pampa
Carhue
Cnl Pringles
Tres Arroyos
Tandil
Balcarce
Mar del Plata
Miramar
Necochea

Lebu
Angol
Carahue
Temuco
Villarrica
Loncoquén
Zapala
Neuquén
Grl Roca
Choele Choel
Bahía Blanca
Punta Alta
Claromeco
Bahía Blanca

Tottén
Valdivia
La Unión
Osorno
Vol.Lanin 3776
Los Lagos
Río Negro
Viedma
Carmen de Patagones

Pto Varas
Puerto Montt
Ancud
Chiloé
Castro
Achao
Paso Limay
Nahuel Huapi
S.Carlos de Bariloche
El Bolsón
Valcheta
S.Antonio Oeste
Golfo San Matias

Maquinchao
Pto Pirámides

Chubut
Esquel
Las Plumas
Chubut
Trelew
Gaimán
Rawson
Pto Madryn

Pto Aisén
Coihaique
San Valentin 4058
L. Musters
L. Buenos Aires
Sarmiento
Caleta Olivia
Comodoro Rivadavia
Colonia Las Heras
Golfo San Jorge
Camarones
C.Dos Bahías

Lautaro 3380
Santa Cruz
Deseado
Deseado
C.Tres Puntas
Pta Médanos

ATLANTIC OCEAN

Patagonia
S.Martin
S.Julián
Viedma
S.Argentino
Calafate
Sta Cruz
Bahía Grande
Río Turbio
Río Gallegos

FALKLAND ISLANDS (ISLAS MALVINAS) U.K.
Jason Is
C. Dolphin
West Falkland
Weddell
East Falkland
Stanley
Beauchene Is
Falkland Sd

Pto Natales
Punta Arenas
Rio Grande
Isla Grande de Tierra del Fuego
Tierra del Fuego
San Diego
I. de los Estados
Ushuaia

at the same scale
Shag Rocks
South Georgia U.K.
C. Alexandra
C. Disappointment
Grytviken

Londonderry
Hoste
Navarino
Is Wollaston
C. de Hornos (C.Horn)
B. Diego Ramírez

200   400   600 km
100   200   300 mls

B   45   C   40   D   35   E

Equator

de Marajó
C. Maguariano
Salinópolis
Bragança
Capanema
Belém
Abaetetuba

de Marajó
Pará
B. de Marajó

São Luís
Alcântara
Pinheiro
Rosário
Parnaíba
Camocim
Acaraú

I. Fernando
de Noronha
Rocas

PARÁ   MARANHÃO
Monção
Chapadinha
Bacabal
Codó
Caxias
Piripiri
Campo Maior
Sobral
Sta Quitéria
Caninde
Itapipoca
Caucaia
Fortaleza (Ceará)

Marabá
Imperatriz
Teresina
Castelo
Crateus
Mombaça
Iguatu
Morada N
Russas
Quixadá
CEARÁ
Aracati
Areia Branca
Macau
Mossoró
Pto Calcanhar
Natal

Pto Franco
Grajaú
Carolina
Balsas
Floriano
Oeiras
Picos
J. do Norte
Crato
Taua
Acopiara
RIO GRANDE DO NORTE
Panu
Sousa
Patos
Caicó
Cabedelo
João Pessoa
Campina Grande
Barreiros

Araguaína
Araguaia
TOCANTINS
Balsas
PIAUI
S.Raimundo Nonato
Paulistana
Salgueiro
Ouricuri
PERNAMBUCO
Garanhuns
Palmeira dos
Caruaru
Limoeiro
Olinda
Recife
(Pernambuco)
Jaboatão

B R A Z I L
Palmas
Barra
Petrolina
Juazeiro
Cach.
PARAÍBA
Sen.do Bonfim
Jacobina
Serrinha
Aracajú
ALAGOAS
Penedo
Arapiraca
Propriá
SERGIPE
Maceió
Estância

Ilha do Bananal
Barreiras
Ibotirama
Iaçu
R.de Jacuipe
Feira de S.
Castro Alves
Cachoeira
Alagoinhas
Lagarto

Bom Jesus
da Lapa
BAHIA
Chapada Diamantina
Valença
Jequié
Salvador (Bahia)
B. de T. os Santos

GOIÁS
Uruaçu
Formosa
Jaraguá
Ceres
Aruanã
Caités
Ipiaú
Vitória da Conquista
Itabuna
Ilhéus

Pirenópolis
Brasília
São Francisco
Porteirinhas
Januária
Salinas
Canavieiras
Belmonte
ATLANTIC

Anápolis
Goiânia
Montes Claros
Araçuai
Sa do Chifre
Pôrto Seguro
OCEAN

Rio Verde
Caldas
Itumbiara
Paracatu
Pirapora
Teófilo Otôni
Itamaraju

Goiandira
Pinheiro
João
Corinto
Diamantina
Nanuque

São Simão
Barragem de
Catalão
Araguari
Curvelo
Patos de Minas
Valadares
Cnl Fabriciano
São Mateus

Uberlândia
Uberaba
Araxá
Itabira
MINAS GERAIS
ESPÍRITO
Linhares
Colatina

Ituiutaba
Barragem Água
Vermelha
Franca
Divinópolis
Belo Horizonte
Manhuaçu
Con.
Cariacica
SANTO
Vitória
Vila Velha

Rubinéia
Fernandópolis
S.JOSÉ
do R.PRêto
Barretos
Ribeirão Prêto
Passos
Lavras
S.João del Rei
Barbacena
Carangola
Ponte Nova
Lafaiete
Cachoeiro de Itapemirim
Itaperuna

Catanduva
SÃO PAULO
Araraquara
São Carlos
Poços de Caldas
Juiz de Fora
S.João da Barra
Campos

dente
sis.
Marília
Bauru
Piracicaba
Limeira
Jundiaí
Campinas
Volta Redonda
Barra Mansa
Nova/Friburgo
Petrópolis
Magé
Niterói

Jacareipba
carana
Itapeva
Itapetininga
Sorocaba
São Paulo
Santos
São Vicente
Itanhaém
Rio de Janeiro

Tropic of Capricorn

Castro
nta
arapuava
(Mafra)
Curitiba
Juquiá
Iguape
Paranaguá
São Francisco do Sul

0
1
2
5
3
10
4
15
5
20
6
25

Ⓐ 80 Ⓑ 75

I. de Perlas
NICARAGUA
Bluefields ①
S. Carlos
Pta Gallinas
Pen. de Guajira
Pto Fijo
Aruba / Curaçao / Bonaire
Neth.
Willemstad
Sta Marta Riohacha Maicao G. de Venezuela
Coro Riecito Pto Cabello
Barranquilla Ciénaga Machiques Cabimas Valencia Barquisimeto Marac
Cartagena Valledupar L. de Maracaibo Trujillo Acarigua San Ju
Heredia Limón Chinpó Sincelejo S. Jacinto Cd Ojeda Valera Cord. de Mér Guanare V. de la Pas
COSTA RICA San José Cartago David Santiago PANAMÁ Colón Panamá La Chorrera La Palma G. de Darién Turbo Barrancabermeja Mérida San Cristóbal Pamplona Cúcuta Bucaramanga Arauca Barinas N

Chitré G. de Panamá Quibdó Itagüí MEDELLÍN Bello Pto Berrio Yarumal Barbosa Sogamoso Málaga Tunja Chocontá Orocué Pto Carreño Pto Ay

Pen. de Azuero Buenaventura Manizales Pereira Cartago Armenia BOGOTÁ Girardot Villavicencio Granada Vichada

C. Corrientes Tuluá Ibagué Palmira CALI Neiva COLOMBIA Meta Pto Inírida Guaviare

Santander Popayán Vol. Puracé Pitalito Florencia Rico Calamar Guainía Cucuí

Tumaco El Diviso Pasto Mocoa Belén Caquetá Vaupés Mitú Icana

Esmeraldas S.Lorenzo Ipiales Tulcán Pto Asís Putumayo Salto Grande

Cojimíes Jama Otavalo Ibarra Lago Agrio Coca Leguízamo

Equator QUITO Cotopaxi Napo Japurá

Manta C. San Lorenzo Chone ECUADOR Tena

Jipijapa Ambato Guaranda Riobamba Macas Napo Iquitos Solimões Leticia Tabatinga A

GUAYAQUIL Babahoyo Milagro Azogues Gualaceo Pastaza Caxias S E L

La Libertad Puná Cuenca Gualaceo Marañón B

G. de Guayaquil Machala Loja Zamora L

Tumbes Zaruma Juruá

Talara Negritos Sullana Loja Elvira

Paita Piura Chulucanas Huancabamba Cruzeiro do Sul

Pta Aguja Catacaos Jaén Moyobamba

Lambayeque Ferreñafe Chachapoyas Tarapoto Feijó Bôca

Chiclayo Cajamarca ACRE Senã Madureira

Chepén Cajabamba Pucallpa

Pacasmayo Huamachuco Tingo María Rio Branco

Trujillo Otusco Pomabamba La Unión Brasiléia Porvenir

PACIFIC Huallanca Huánuco Bobijã Riba

OCEAN ⑤ Chimbote Huaraz Huascarán Madre de Dio

Casma La Oroya Oxapampa Pto Maldonado Pto Heath

Huarmey Barranca Cerro de Pasco Tarma La Merced

Pativilca Huacho Jauja Quillabamba BO

ISLAS GALÁPAGOS (ARCHIPIÉLAGO DO COLÓN) (Equ.) ⑦ Ancón Callao LIMA Huancayo Ayacucho MACHU PICCHU Cusco

Huancavelica Acobamba

Chincha Alta Pisco Andahuaylas Abancay Sicuani

Pen. de Paracas PERÚ Ayaviri

Nazca Ⓒ Ⓓ

at the same scale

0 200   400   600 km
100   200   300 mls

The Grenadines
I. de Margarita
GRENADA
St George's
La Asunción Peria
Carúpano Güiria
Cumaná Port of
uz Trinidad Spain
na Carípito G. de San Fernando
Paria
naco Maturín
vara Tigre
Cd Bolívar Orinoco
ZUELA Cd Guayana Upata
La Paragua Emb. de Guri
El Dorado Salto
del Angel
La Gran Roraima
Sabana 2180
Sta Elena
Sa Pacaraima
Bonfim Lethem
Boa Vista
RORAIMA
Caracaraí
rucuara Branco
Manaus Manacapuru
Careiro Itacoatiara
Tefé
A   Z   O   N   A   S
Manaus

TRINIDAD
AND
TOBAGO
Tobago

Mabaruma
Charity
Suddie Leguan I.
V-en-Hoop Georgetown
Bartica Linden New Amsterdam
GUYANA Nieuw
Nickerie
SURINAM
Julianatop
1280

ATLANTIC

OCEAN

Nieuw Amsterdam
Paramaribo Marienburg
Totness Albina
Blommesteinmeer
Sinnamary
I. du Diable (Devil's I.)
Kourou
Cayenne
FRENCH Cabo Orange
GUIANA Oiapoque

Serra Tumucumaque

AMAPÁ
Amapá
ilha de Maracá
Sa do Navio
Macapá Pto Santana
C. Maguarinho
I. de Marajó B. de Marajó
Salinópolis
Bragança
Park Capanema
Belém
Cametá Abaetetuba

Orixímina Óbidos Amazonas
Santarém Monte
Alegre
Altamira Tucuruí
P   A   R   Á

B   R   A   Z   I   L
Aveiro
Itaituba
Pimenta
Tapajós

Jacareacanga
S. Félix
Marabá Imperatriz
Pto
Franco
Araguaína Carolina

Lábrea Humaitá
Prainha
Serra do Cachimbo
Cachimbo
Pôrto Velho Ariquemia
C.do Araguaia
TOCANTINS
Palmas

RONDÔNIA
Serra dos Parecis
Vilhena
São Félix
ilha do Bananal

VIA
Trinidad Mato Grosso
MATO   GROSSO
Pto Artur

GOIÁS
Aruanã Uruaçu

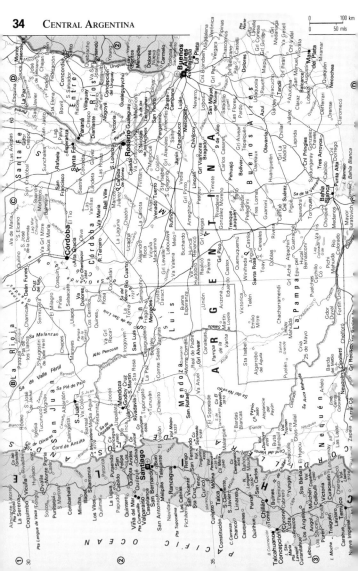

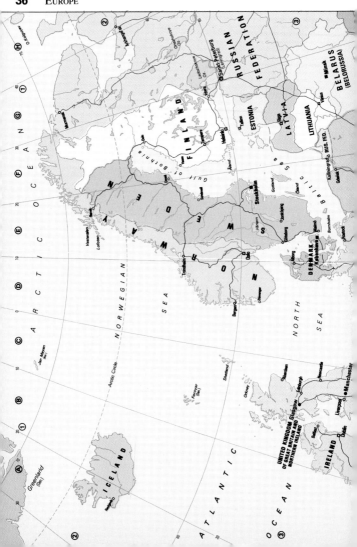

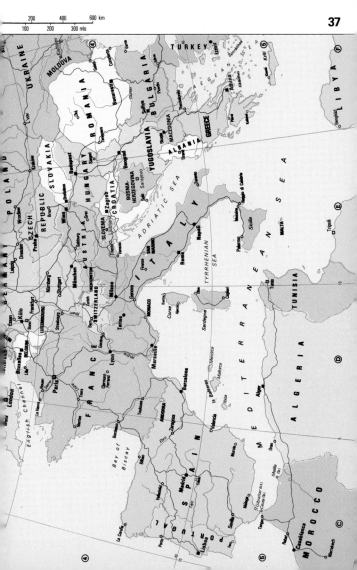

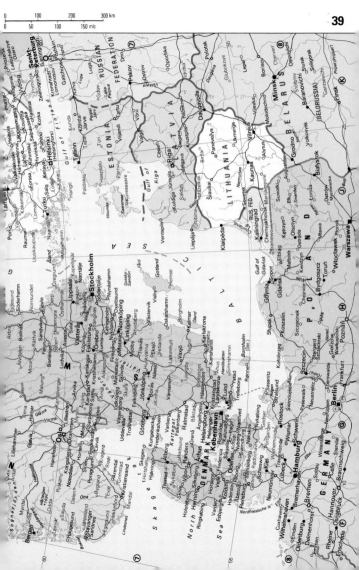

NORWAY

Bergen

Haugesund
Skudo
Lervika
Bomlo
Sumburgh Sкnd

Shetland

Herma Ness
Unst
Yell
Whalsay
Isbistero
St Magnus B.
Lerwick
Foula
Sumburgh Hd

Fair Isle

ORKNEY

Westray
Sanday
Rousay
Stronsay
Kirkwall
Stromness
Scapa Flow
Duncansby Hd
Holy

Suie Skerry
Stack Skerry

N. Rona

C. Wrath
Butt of Lewis

Sule Sgeir

Flannan Is.
Stornoway
Lewis
Harris

St Kilda

Outer Hebrides

N. Uist
Barra
S. Uist

Rum
Eigg
Coll
Tiree
Colonsay
Jura
Islay
Campbeltown
Rathlin I.

Malin Hd
Troy I.
Aran I.
Errigal
A 752
Londonderry

N. IRELAND
Ballymena
Coleraine

Thurso
Wick

Heimsdale
Dornoch Firth
Dornoch
Ben More
Assynt
Ben Hope
Dingwall
Ullapool
Kyle of Lochalsh
Portree
Skye
Mallaig
Fort William
Ben Nevis
1344
Oban
Mull
F. of Lorn
L. Lomond

Ben Macdui
4300
Braemar
Grampian
L. Ness
Ben
Fort
Augustus
Inverness

SCOTLAND

Elgin
Spey
Don
Dee

Fraserburgh
Peterhead
Buchan Ness
Aberdeen
Stonehaven
Montrose
F. of Tay
St Andrews
Pitlochry
Perth
Kirkcaldy
F. of Forth
Edinburgh
Stirling
Greenock
Paisley
Glasgow
Kilmarnock
Motherwell
Ayr
Irvine
F. of Clyde
Arran
Girvan
Merrick
842
Dumfries
Moffat
Nith
Hawick
Tweed
Galashiels

St Abbs Hd
Berwick-upon-Tweed

Holy I.
Morpeth
Blyth
Newcastle upon Tyne
Gateshead
S. Shields
Sunderland
Tyne
Carlisle

NORTH SEA

Stranraer

55

60

5

0

10

A

B

C

D

E

1

2

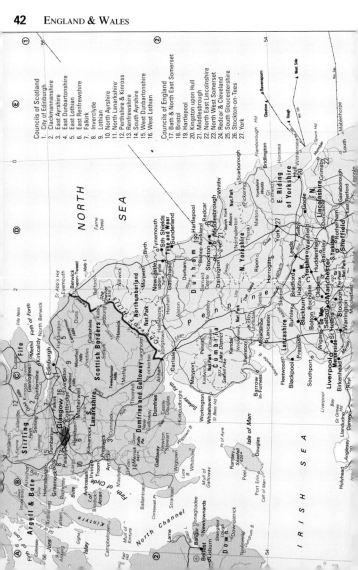

Councils of Scotland
1. City of Edinburgh
2. Clackmannanshire
3. East Ayrshire
4. East Dunbartonshire
5. East Lothian
6. East Renfrewshire
7. Falkirk
8. Inverclyde
9. Lothian
10. North Ayrshire
11. North Lanarkshire
12. Perthshire & Kinross
13. Renfrewshire
14. South Ayrshire
15. West Dunbartonshire
16. West Lothian

Councils of England
17. Bath & North East Somerset
18. Bristol
19. Hartlepool
20. Kingston upon Hull
21. Middlesbrough
22. North East Lincolnshire
23. North West Somerset
24. Redcar & Cleveland
25. South Gloucestershire
26. Stockton-on-Tees
27. York

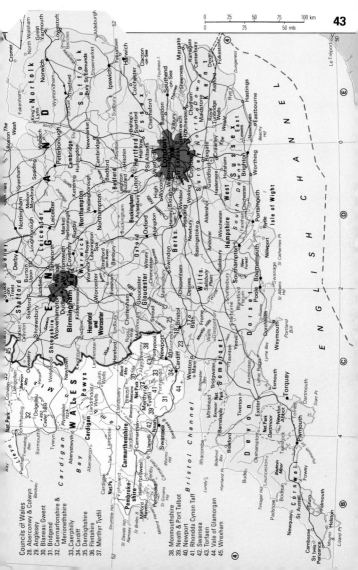

43

Councils of Wales
28. Aberconwy & Colwyn
29. Anglesey
30. Blaneau Gwent
31. Bridgend
32. Caernarfonshire & Merionethshire
33. Caerphilly
34. Cardiff
35. Denbighshire
36. Flintshire
37. Merthyr Tydfil

38. Monmouthshire
39. Neath & Port Talbot
40. Newport
41. Rhondda Cynon Taff
42. Swansea
43. Torfaen
44. Vale of Glamorgan
45. Wrexham

0 25 50 75 100 km
0 25 50 mls

(E) at the same scale

Councils of Scotland
1. Aberdeen City
2. City of Edinburgh
3. City of Glasgow
4. Clackmannanshire
5. Dundee City
6. East Dunbartonshire
7. East Lothian
8. East Renfrewshire
9. Falkirk
10. Inverclyde
11. Lothian
12. North Ayrshire
13. North Lanarkshire
14. Renfrewshire
15. South Lanarkshire
16. West Dunbartonshire
17. West Lothian

NORTH SEA

50   100   150   200 km
50   100 mls

France / Spain

Capbreton
Biarritz
stian
Irún
Tolosa
Pamplona
NAVARRA
Tafalla
ahorra
Alfaro
azona
Alagón
atayud
Daroca
Monreal
del C.
de Albarracín
Cuenca
uenca
Teruel
Penarroya
Sarrion
Segorbe
de
ción
Motilla
del P.
Utiel
Cabriel
Requena
Roda
Albacete
Almansa
URCIA
Villena
Hellin
Cieza
Caravaca
Orihuela
Totana
Lorca
Cartagena
cal
ra
Aguilas
Vera
de Gata

Mont-de-Marsan
Dax
Adour
Auch
Albi ©
Castres
s-T.A
Nîmes
Arles
Salon-d.-P.
D
Montpellier
Aix-en-Provence
Aubagne
Bayonne
Orthez
Toulouse
Tarn
Montmirat
Marseille
Oloron-Ste-Marie
Tarbes
Lourdes
St-Gaudens
Pamiers
Foix
Carcassonne
Narbonne
Béziers
Sète
Golfe du Lion
Toulon Hyères
FRANCE
Pyrénées
Quillan
Perpignan
ROUSSILLON
Vignemale
3290
P. de Aneto
3404
Viella
Montceny
2883
ANDORRA
Andorra-la-Vella
Bourg-Madame
C. de Creus
Costa Brava
Jaca
Sa de Guara
Huesca
Barbastro
Puigcerda
Figueras
(Figueres)
Gerona
(Girona)
San Feliu de G.
Zaragoza
Lérida
(Lleida)
Sabadell
Tarrasa
Granollers
Mataró
Badalona
Barcelona
Emb. de
Mequinenza
Valls
Villanueva-y-G.
(Vilanova i la Geltrú)
Caspe
Reus
Tarragona
Alcañiz
Tortosa
Golfo de
San Jorge
Amposta
C. de Tortosa
Vinaroz
Benicarló
Torreblanca
C. de Caballeria
40
Menorca
C. de Formentor
Ciudadela
Mahón
C. Binibeca
Villarreal
Castellon de la P.
Is Columbretes
Mallorca
Mayor
4445
Alcudia
Capdepera
Sagunto
Golfo de
Valencia
Valencia
Palma
de Mallorca
Manacor
Valencia
Santañy
Alcira
C. de Salinas
Cabrera
Játiva
Gandia
Ibiza
Onteniente
Denia
S. Antonio
Abad
Ibiza
ISLAS BALEARES
(BALEARIC ISLANDS)
(Sp.)
Alcoy
C. de la Nao
Benidorm
Formentera
Elda
Alicante
Elche
Costa Blanca
G. de
Mazarrón
C. de Palos

M E D I T E R R A N E A N   S E A

①

②

Alger
(Algiers)
Harrach
Dellys
Bejaia
(Bougie)
Cherchell
Boufarik
Tizi Ouzou
Djurdjura
Kherrata
Ténès
Blida
O. Isser
Bouira
Beni
Mansour
Sétif
Médéa
Bir Rabalou
Bj. bou
Arréridj
Miliana
Khemis
Dahra
Ech Cheliff
Ksar El
Boukhari
Mts du Hodna
M'Sila
Bosquet
Aïn
Oussera
er
Hadjel
Chott
el Hodna
Barika
C. Ferrat
Arzew
Mostaganem
A Massif de l'Ouarsenis
A L G E R I A
Bou Saâda
Mers el Kebir
Oran
O. Tlélat
Relizane
Mohammadia
Mascara
Mina
Tiaret
Ouassel
Plat. du Sersou
Z. Chergui
Monts des
Ouled Naïl
36
Beni-Saf
Aïn
Témouchent
Sidi-bel-Abbès
Frenda
© Z. Gharbi
③

① ②

Budapest
Nové Zámky
Komárno
Vác
Esztergom
Nitra
Talabanya
Székesfehérvár
Siófok
Baja
Apatin
Vukovar
Vinkovci
Osijek
Sarajevo
Goražde
Nikšić
Kotor
Budva

Wien
Mödling
Wr. Neustadt
Neunkirchen
Sopron
Győr
Pápa
Veszprém
Szombathely
Zalaegerszeg
Nagykanizsa
Dombóvár
Szekszárd
Pécs
Kaposvár
Daruvar
Našice
Pakrac
Slavonski Brod
Banja Luka
BOSNIA HERZEGOVINA
Zenica
Konjic
Mostar
Avtovac
Bileća
Trebinje
Dubrovnik

HUNGARY
CROATIA
Zagreb
Kapronca
Bjelovar
Sisak
Varaždin
Virovitica

St Pölten
Amstetten
Steyr
Eisenstadt
Bruck a.d. Mur
Mariazell
Leoben
Judenburg
Wolfsberg
Graz
Zagreb
Novo Mesto
Karlovac
Senj
Zadar
Šibenik
Split (Spalato)
Brač
Hvar
Korčula
Pelješac
Lastovo

Linz
Wels
Gmunden
Vöcklabruck
Bad Ischl
Radstadt
Salzburg
Bad Gastein
Spittal
Villach
Klagenfurt
Kranj
LJUBLJANA
Postojna
Rijeka (Fiume)
Cres
Krk
Rab
Pag
Velebit
Dugi O.
Kornat

AUSTRIA
SLOVENIA
Celje
Maribor
Jesenice
Trieste
Gorizia
Poreč
Rovinj
Pula

München
Rosenheim
Traunstein
Bad Tölz
Kitzbühel
Lienz
Cortina d'Ampezzo
Belluno
Udine
Gemona
Venezia (Venice)
Chioggia
Golfo di Venezia
Pescara
Chieti

GER.
Innsbruck
Brunico
Merano
Bolzano
Trento
Rovereto
Bassano
Treviso
Vicenza
Padova
Rovigo
Ferrara
Argenta
Ravenna
Ancona
Senigallia
Pesaro
Fano
Macerata
Ascoli Piceno
Teramo
L'Aquila

SWITZERLAND
LIECHTENSTEIN
Chur
St Moritz
Sondrio
Como
Lecco
Bergamo
Brescia
Verona
Mantova
Cremona
Parma
Reggio
Modena
Carpi
Bologna
Imola
Faenza
Forlì
Cesena
SAN MARINO
Rimini
Urbino
Città di Castello
Terni
Rieti

Milano (Milan)
Monza
Pavia
Lodi
Piacenza
Lecco
Varese
Como
Novara
Vercelli
Biella
Alessandria
Novi Ligure
Appno Ligure
Genova (Genoa)
Savona
La Spezia
Massa
Carrara
Lucca
Pistoia
Prato
Firenze (Florence)
Arezzo
Siena
Perugia
Foligno
Viterbo
Civitavecchia

Torino (Turin)
Asti
Mondovì
Cuneo
Aosta
Ivrea
Susa
Nice
Monte Carlo
San Remo
Imperia
Ventimiglia
Liguria Sea
Pisa
Livorno
Cecina
Piombino
Portoferraio
Elba
Grosseto
Orbetello
Montalto
Follonica

FRANCE
Briançon
Gap
Cannes
St Raphaël
St Tropez
Grasse
Côte d'Azur
Bastia
Calvi
Ajaccio
Corse (Corsica)
Ligurian Sea

A D R I A T I C   S E A

50 100 150 200 km
50 100 mils

A D R I A T I C   S E A

Manfredonia
Brindisi
Lecce
Maglie Otranto
C. Sta Maria
di Leuca

Monopoli
Molfetta
Bari
Le Murge
Altamura
Andria
Barletta
Matera
Manduria
Taranto
Gallipoli
Golfo di Taranto
IONIAN SEA

Potenza
Appno Lucano
Metaponto
Corigliano Calabro
Rossano
Crotone
Pra Alice

Campobasso
Avellino
Benevento
Sapri
Eboli
Castrovillari
La Sila
Mte Botte Donato 1928
Catanzaro
C. Rizzuto
G. di Squillace

Isernia
Cassino
Napoli (Naples)
Vesuvio
Sorrento
Torre del Greco
Salerno
Agropoli
G. di Policastro
Paola
Cosenza
Nicastro
Monte Cocuzzo 1541
Vibo Valentia
Pizzo
Paolano 1423
C. Spartivento

Formia
Pozzuoli
Capri
Ischia
Str. de Messina
Reggio di Calabria
C. dell'Armi
Palmi
Montalto 1955

Gaeta
Terracina
Latina
Anzio
I. Ponziane

TYRRHENIAN SEA

Stromboli
Isole Lipari
Vulcano
Messina
Giarre
Acireale
Catania
Barcellona
Mti Nebrodi
Patti
Cefalù
Lentini
Siracusa (Syracuse)
Noto
C. di Correnti

Salina
Filicudi
Alicudi
Panarea
Lipari
Palermo
Enna
Caltanissetta
Caltagirone
Modica
Ragusa
Vittoria
Comiso
Malta Channel

Ustica

SICILIA (SICILY)

Partinico
Castelvetrano
Alcamo
Sciacca
Licata
Gela
Agrigento

Trapani
Marsala
Mazara del Vallo
C. San Vito
Egadi
Favignana

Sicilian Channel

Pantelleria (It.)

M E D I T E R R A N E A N   S E A

MALTA
Gozo
Valletta
Marfa

C. Bon
Kelibia
Nabeul
Hammamet
Golfe de Hammamet
Sousse
Monastir
Mokhnine

C. Blanc
Bizerte
Halq el Oued
Menzel
Tunis
Enfida
M'saken
Kairouan

G. de Tunis

Matmata
Tabarka
Béja
Mejez el Bab
Teboursouk
Testour
Makthar
Kalaat Khasba
Thala
Kasserine

Annaba (Bône)
El Kala
Mte de la Medjerda
Souk Ahras
Guelma
Medjerda
Tébessa

TUNISIA

Dj. Zaghouan 1295

SARDEGNA (SARDINIA)

Bonifacio
Strait of Bonifacio
Sta Teresa
Olbia
Siniscola

Porto Torres
Sassari
Alghero
Nuoro
Gennargentu 1835
Arbatax
Muravera

Macomer
Oristano
G. di Oristano
Iglesias
Carbonia
Cagliari
G. di Cagliari
C. Teulada
C. Carbonara

S. Pietro
S. Antioco
C. Spartivento

Almanza

3

B

A

C

15

10

40

0   50   100   150   200 km
0   50   100   150 mls

UKRAINE

POLAND

SLOVAKIA

HUNGARY

ROMANIA

AUSTRIA

CROATIA

SLOVENIA

CZECH REP.

Budapest

Wien (Vienna)

Bratislava

Zagreb

Kraków

Wrocław

Praha (Prague)

Lublana

L'vov

Košice

Debrecen

Cluj-Napoca

Timişoara

Oradea

Subotica

Novi Sad

Graz

Linz

Maribor

Rijeka (Fiume)

Carpaţii Meridionali (Transylvanian Alps)

Mţii Apuseni

Beskidy Zachodnie

Podol'skaya Voz.

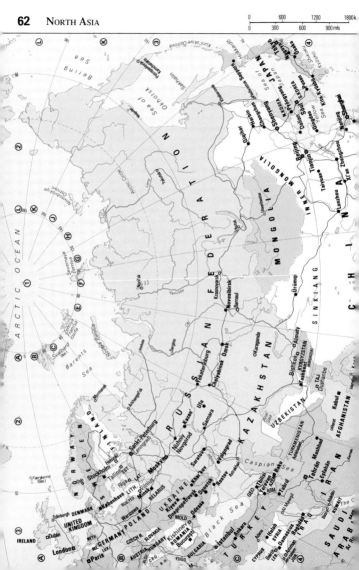

200   400   600   800 km
200   400 mls

GEORGIA
1 Abkhazia
2 Ajaria

AZERBAIJAN
3 Nakhichevan

RUSSIAN FEDERATION
First order administration
areas are only shown on
pages 60–61 due to scale.

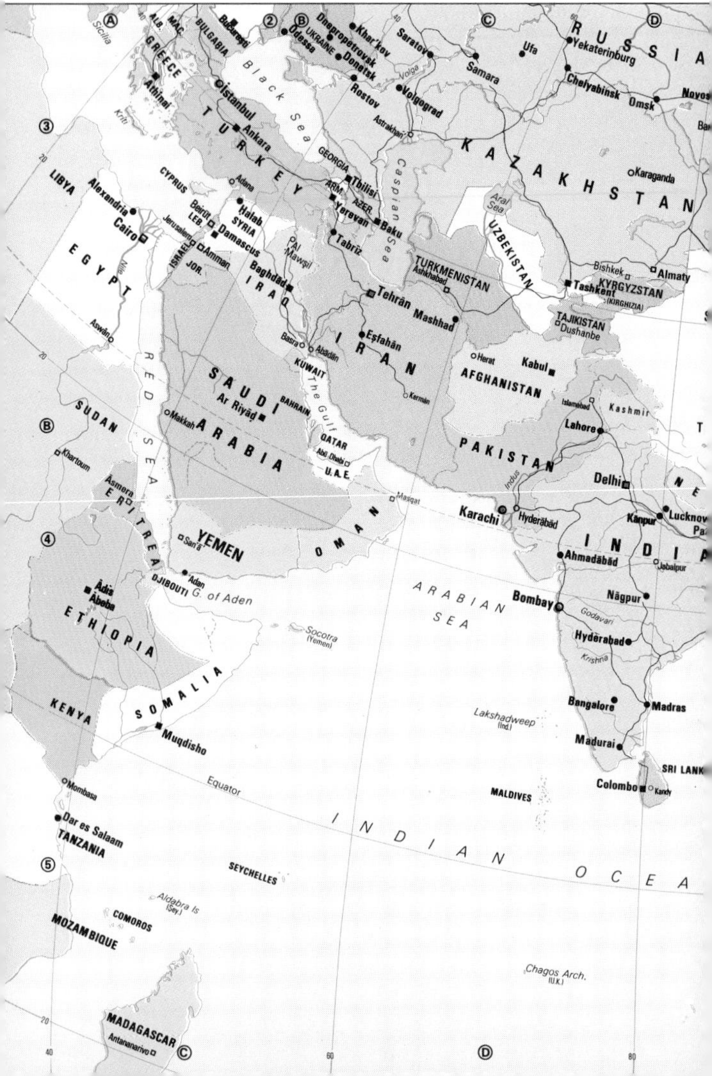

A   B   C   D

Scutra
GREECE
MAC.
Burgas
BULGARIA
Athínai
Krti

2

Dnepropetrovsk
Khar'kov
Saratov
UKRAINE
Donetsk
Rostov
Volga
Astrakhan'

Ufa
Yekaterinburg
Chelyabinsk
Omsk
Noves

RUSSIA

3

Black Sea
İstanbul
Ankara
TURKEY
GEORGIA
ARM.
Tbilisi
AZER.
Yerevan
Baku
Volgograd
Samara

KAZAKHSTAN

Karaganda

CYPRUS
Adana
Halab
Beirut
LEB.
Damascus
SYRIA
Al Mawsil
Tabriz

Caspian Sea
TURKMENISTAN
Aşgabat
Aral Sea

UZBEKISTAN
Bishkek
Almaty
Tashkent
(KIRGHIZIA)
KYRGYZSTAN

LIBYA
Alexandria
Cairo

EGYPT

ISR.
Jerusalem
JOR.
Amman
Baghdad
IRAQ
Basra
Abadan

Tehrān
Mashhad
TAJIKISTAN
Dushanbe

Esfahān
IRAN

Herat
Kabul
AFGHANISTAN
Islamabad
Kashmir

Aswân

SUDAN
RED SEA

Khartoum

SAUDI ARABIA
Ar Riyāḍ
Makkah

KUWAIT
BAHRAIN
The Gulf
QATAR
Abū Dhabi
U.A.E.

Kermān

PAKISTAN
Lahore

Delhi
INDIA
Kanpur
Lucknow
Pa
NE

B

Asmara
ERITREA
DJIBOUTI
YEMEN
Ṣan'ā'
Aden
G. of Aden

OMAN
Masqat

Karachi
Hyderābād

Ahmadābād

Karpur

4

Adīs Ababa
ETHIOPIA

ARABIAN
SEA

Bombay
Godavri
Nāgpur
Jabalpur
Hyderabad
Krishna

KENYA
SOMALIA
Socotra
(Yemen)

Muqdisho

Lakshadweep
(Ind.)

Bangalore
Madras
Madurai
SRI LANK
Colombo
Kandy

Mombasa

Equator

MALDIVES

INDIAN OCEA

Dar es Salaam
TANZANIA

5

Aldabra Is
(Sey.)

SEYCHELLES

COMOROS

MOZAMBIQUE

Chagos Arch.
(U.K.)

MADAGASCAR
Antananarivo

C   D

MONGOLIA

NEI MONGOL

Yin Shan

BO HAI

KOREA BAY

YELLOW SEA (HUANG HAI)

Major cities and places:

Changchun Jilin, Siping, Shenyang, Anshan, Fushun, Benxi, Liaoyang, Dandong, Jinzhou, Chaoyang, Beipiao, Chifeng, Dalian, Lüshun, Qinhuangdao, Tangshan, Tianjin (Tientsin), Beijing (Peking), Zhangjiakou, Xuanhua, Datong, Hohhot, Baotou, Wuhai, Yinchuan, Lanzhou, Linxia, Xining, Tianshui, Baoji, Xi'an (Sian), Xianyang, Hanzhong, Taiyuan, Yuci, Linfen, Houma, Shijiazhuang, Baoding, Xingtai, Handan, Anyang, Xinxiang, Zhengzhou, Luoyang, Sanmenxia, Nanyang, Jinan (Tsinan), Zibo, Weifang, Qingdao (Tsingtao), Yantai, Weihai, Jining, Xuzhou, Lianyungang, Bengbu, Kaifeng, Pingdingshan, Zhumadian, Xinyang

Provinces: Hebei, Shanxi, Shaanxi, Shandong, Henan, Ningxia, Qinghai, Jiangsu, Gansu

Qin Ling (mountains)

Tai Hang Shan

Huang He (Yellow River)

100   200   300   400 km
100   200 mls

SOUTH

CHINA

SEA

TAIWAN

FORMOSA

Chi-lung
T'ai-pei
Chang-hua
T'ai-chung
Chia-i
Nat. Pei Dinai
Tai-nan
Ping-tung
Kao-hsiung
Heng ch'un

Peng hu Liehtao
(Pescadores)

Dongsha Qundao
(Pratas)

Ningbo
Shaoxing
Wenling
Linhai
Huangyan
Hangzhou
Wenzhou

Zhejiang

Fuzhou
(Foochow)

Fujian

Sanming

Xiamen
Zhangzhou

Shantou
(Swatow)

Chao'an

Meizhou

Huizhou

Guangzhou
(Canton)
Kowloon
Hong Kong
Shenzhen
Foshan
Macau

Nanchang

Jiangxi

Changsha

Hunan

Zhuzhou
Xiangtan
Hengyang
Shaoyang

Guilin

Guangdong

Zhaoqing

Yangjiang
Maoming
Zhanjiang

Beihai

Hainan
Haikou

GULF
OF
TONGKING

Wuhan

Hubei

Huangshi

Chongqing

Guiyang

Guizhou

Anshun

Kunming

Yunnan

Chengdu

Sichuan

Nanning

Guangxi

Liuzhou

Wuzhou

Hanoi
Haiphong

VIETNAM

LAOS

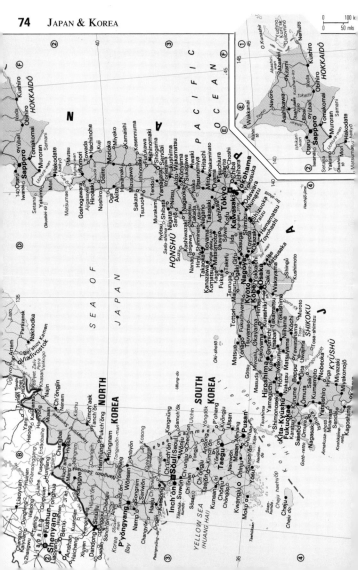

0 100 200 300 400 km
0 100 200 mils

S O U T H   C H I N A   S E A

B O R N E O

SARAWAK (Malaysia)
Kuching
Sambas
Singkawang
Pontianak
Kalimantan
I N D O N E S I A

M A L A Y S I A

PENINSULAR MALAYSIA
Kuala Lumpur
SINGAPORE
Johor Baharu
Melaka
Muar
Kelang
Port Dickson
Seremban
Kuantan
Kuala Trengganu
Kota Bharu

THAILAND
Vung Tau
Phu Vinh
Can Tho
Rach Gia
Long Xuyen
Khanh Hung
Vinh Loi
the Mekong
Mouths of

Ipoh
Butterworth
George Town
Penang
Taiping
Alor Setar
Hat Yai
Songkhla
Pattani
Yala
Narathiwat
Kuala Lipis
Gua Musang

Nakhon Si Thammarat
Surat Thani
Ranong
Phuket
Trang
Kantang

Medan
Binjei
Pematangsiantar
Tebingtinggi
Tanjungbalai
Rantauprapat
Padangsidempuan
Sibolga
Gunungsitoli
Nias

Pekanbaru
Bangkinang
Pakanbaru
Bukittinggi
Padangpanjang
Padang
Pariaman
Solok

Tanjungpinang
Kep. Riau
Kep. Lingga
Singkep
Jambi
Bangka
Pangkalpinang
Belinyu

NICOBAR ISLANDS (India)
Great Nicobar
Little Nicobar

Banda Aceh
Lhokseumawe
Sigli
Sabang
Meulaboh
Calang

Equator

Siberut

S U M A T E R A

Strait of Malacca

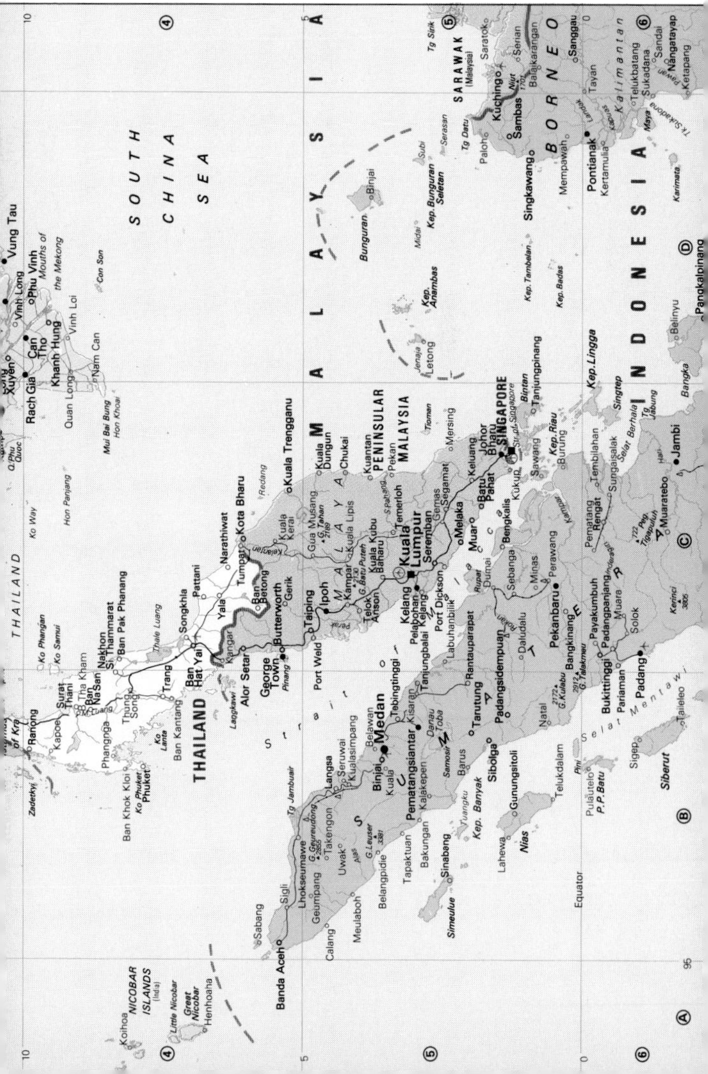

0 100 200 300 400 km
0 100 200 mls

Ⓐ 120 Ⓑ 125 Ⓒ

① *PACIFIC*

Dongsha
Qundao

Luzon
Strait
*Batan
Islands*
Basco

① *OCEAN*

20 20

Balintang Channel

Babuyan Islands

Babuyan Channel Cape Engaño

Cape Bojeador

Laoag
Aparri

② Banguod
Vigan
Tuguegarao
Ilagan

② *LUZON*

San
Fernando Mt Pulog 2929 Santiago
Solano
La Trinidad Bayombong
Baguio
Lingayen Dagupan San
San Carlos Jose Baler
Camiling
Tarlac Cabanatuan
Gapan
Angeles San Fernando Polillo
San Antonio Malolos Islands

SOUTH

Olongapo Manila Quezon City
Cavite Laguna Lamon

15 15

CHINA

Corregidor Santa Cruz Lucban
San Pablo Lucena Calagua Islands
SEA Lipa Jose Pañganiban
Batangas Sipocot Daet
Lubang Boac Catanduanes
Islands Naga

Calapan Iriga Mayon Virac
MINDORO Mt Halcon Legazpi
Sablayan Mt Baco Sorsogon
Marinduque Gubat
Busuanga Tablas Burias Bulan Catarman
Calamian Sibuyan
Group Romblon *Sea* Masbate
Culion Semirara Sibuyan Calbayog Oras
③ Linapacan Islands San Jose *Masbate* ③

El Nido Cuyo Pandan Roxas *Visayan* San Isidro Catbalogan
Taytay Islands *Sea* Baran *SAMAR*
Dalanganem Carigara Tacloban
Cleopatra Islands *PANAY* Cadiz Bogo Ormoc Guiuan
Needle Dumaran Iloilo Silay Escalante Baybay *Leyte* •10497
Roxas La Carlota Lapu-Lapu *Gulf* •10265
Puerto Binalbagan Bacolod Dinagat
Princesa Cagayan Cebu
Aborlan Islands Sipalay Bais *Bohol* Surigao Siargao

10 *Palawan Passage* Dumaguete Tagbilaran 10
Tubbataha Siaton Siquijor Butuan
Mt Reefs Lazi *Bohol Sea*
Mantalingajan Dipolog Dapitan Camiguin Gingoog
Dapitan Oroquieta Cagayan Dinagat Rio
Brooke's Mañukan de Oro Lianga
Point Liloy Mt Ozamiz Iligan
Balabac *SULU SEA* Tangub Malaybalay
Pagadian *MINDANAO* Bislig

Balabac Strait Zamboanga Illana Cotabato Tagum
Banggi Pen. Bay Malabang
Kudat Zamboanga Davao
Isabela Moro Digos
④ Mapin Parang *Gulf* Datu Mt Apo 2954 Mati ④

SABA H Jolo Cotabato General Lais
Malaysia Jolo Samales Santos Davao Gulf
Sandakan Group Cape San Agustin
Parang Tapul
Group Tawitawi Sibutu Sarangani
Group *Sulu Archipelago* Islands
Tawau *CELEBES*

120 *SEA* Kepulauan
Kawio
⑤ Ⓐ Ⓑ 125 Ⓒ Karakelong ⑤

KAZAKHSTAN

UZBEKISTAN

TURKMENISTAN

AFGHANISTAN

I R A N

I R A Q

SAUDI ARABIA

SYRIA

TURKEY

GEORGIA

ARMENIA

AZERBAIJAN

KUWAIT

BAHRAIN

QATAR

U.A.E.

JORDAN

ISRAEL

LEBANON

CYPRUS

E G Y P T

LIBYA

GREECE

BULGARIA

ROMANIA

MACEDONIA

ALBANIA

YUGOSLAVIA

BOSNIA HERZEGOVINA

CASPIAN SEA

BLACK SEA

MEDITERRANEAN SEA

The Gulf

Aral Sea (Aral'skoye More)

Tehrān

Baghdād

Damascus

Cairo

Al-Riyad

Ankara

İstanbul

Baku (Bakı)

Tbilisi

Yerevan

Tabriz

Eşfahān

Mashhad

Herat

Kuwait

Beirut

Amman

Jerusalem

Alexandria

Volgograd

Rostov-na-Donu

Donets'k

Odessa

Bucureşti

Sofia

Athína

İzmir

Halab

Hamadān

Shīrāz

Medina

0 200 400 600 800 km
0 200 400 mls

ARABIAN SEA

Carlsberg Ridge

O M A N

Rub' al Khālī

Nazwā
Sūr
Al Hadd
Maqšān
Gulf of
Masirah
Masirah
Ra's al Madrakah
Şalālah
Ra's Fartak
Ras Faruk

Somali Basin

A L   K H Ā L Ī

Layla
Al Lith
Al Qunfidhah
Najrān
Sa'dah
San'ā
Al Hudaydah
Ta'izz
Al Mukhā
Bāb al Mandab
Al Mukalla
Ash Shihr
Tarīm
Bir 'Ali
HADRAMAWT

YEMEN

Hadibah
(Soqatra)
Socotra
(Soqotra) Yemen
Abd al Kuri

Gulf of Aden

Adan
(Aden)
Djibouti
Berbera
Cerigaabo
Hobyo
Equator

DJIBOUTI

S O M A L I A

Muqdisho
(Mogadishu)
Marka
Baraawe

Port Sudan
Suakin
Mits'iwa
(Massawa)
Asmera
Ras Dashan
4533
ERITREA
Harēr
Diredawa
Jijiga
Shabele
Dolo
Odo
Kismaayo
Juba (Giuba)

Berber
Kassala
Gonder
Desē
Debre Markos
Nazret
Ginir
Batu
4307
Negēlē
Moyale
Tana

Omdurman
Khartoum
Wad Medani
Atbara
Merowe
Sennar
Blue Nile
L. Tana
Ādīs Ābeba
Jima
Gōbā
Gidolē

ETHIOPIA

KENYA

Nairobi
L. Turkana
Wajir
Garissa

Dongola
En Nahud
El Obeid
Kosti
Malakal
Sobat
Nimule
Juba

SUDAN

Ed Damer
Ed Dueim

White Nile
Rumbek

ZAIRE

UGANDA
Kampala
Jinja
Lake
Victoria

RWANDA
Kigali
BURUNDI
Bujumbura

TANZANIA

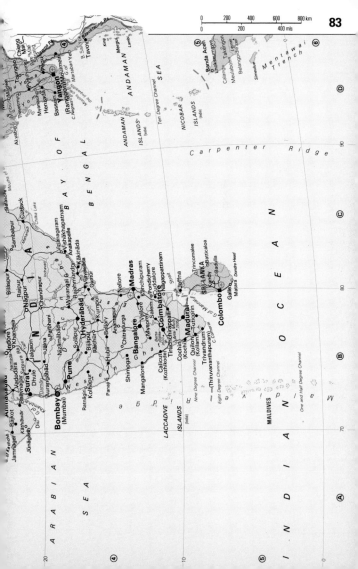

0 200 400 600 800 km
0 200 400 mls

A R A B I A N

S E A

I N D I A

Bombay (Mumbai)
Pune
Hyderabad
Bangalore
Madras
Coimbatore
Madurai
Tiruchirappalli

Cochin (Kochi)
Quilon (Kollam)
Trivandrum (Thiruvananthapuram)

LACCADIVE ISLANDS (India)

MALDIVES

I N D I A N   O C E A N

Nine Degree Channel
Eight Degree Channel
One and Half Degree Channel

SRI LANKA
Colombo
Galle
Jaffna
Trincomalee
Batticaloa
Kandy
Badulla

B A Y   O F   B E N G A L

ANDAMAN ISLANDS (India)

NICOBAR ISLANDS (India)

ANDAMAN SEA

Ten Degree Channel

Carpenter Ridge

Mentawai Trench

Banda Aceh

Cuttack
Sambalpur
Bilaspur
Raipur
Nagpur
Chandrapur
Indore
Surat
Vadodara
Rajkot
Jamnagar
Junagadh
Bhavnagar
Ahmadabad
Dhule
Jalgaon
Aurangabad
Sholapur
Bijapur
Kolhapur
Ratnagiri
Panaji
Mangalore
Shimoga
Chitradurga
Mysore
Salem
Nellore
Guntur
Vijayawada
Rajahmundry
Kakinada
Anakapalle
Vishakhapatnam
Vizianagaram
Warangal
Nizamabad
Parbhani
Raichur
Bellary
Hubli

Chiang Mai
Pegu
Yangon (Rangoon)
Bassein
Henzada
Myaungmya
Moulmein
Tavoy
Mergui

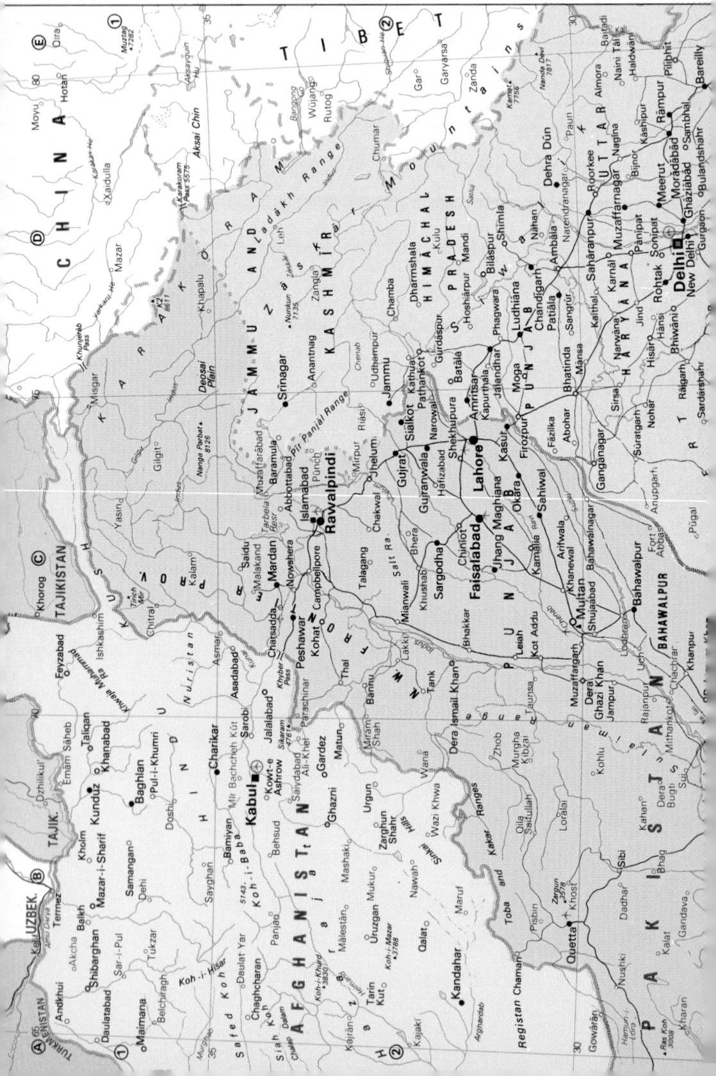

CHINA
TIBET
JAMMU AND KASHMIR
KARAKORAM
Ladakh Range
Pir Panjal Range
HIMACHAL PRADESH
PUNJAB
HARYANA
UTTAR
TAJIKISTAN
TAJIK.
UZBEK.
TURKMENISTAN
AFGHANISTAN
PAKISTAN
BAHAWALPUR
Hotan
Moyu
Xaidulla
Mazar
Aksai Chin
Karakoram Pass 5575
K2 8611
Khunjerab Pass
Deosai Plain
Nanga Parbat 8126
Gilgit
Misgar
Yasin
Chitral
Tirich Mir
Kalam
Saidu
Mardan
Nowshera
Campbellpore
Peshawar
Charsadda
Kohat
Thal
Bannu
Tank
Lakki
Mianwali
Talagang
Chakwal
Jhelum
Gujrat
Sialkot
Jammu
Srinagar
Anantnag
Baramula
Muzaffarabad
Abbottabad
Islamabad
Rawalpindi
Punch
Mirpur
Udhampur
Chamba
Dharmshala
Kulu
Mandi
Shimla
Bilaspur
Hoshiarpur
Pathankot
Gurdaspur
Batala
Amritsar
Kapurthala
Jalandhar
Phagwara
Ludhiana
Chandigarh
Patiala
Ambala
Nahan
Moga
Firozpur
Fazilka
Abohar
Bhatinda
Mansa
Sangrur
Kaithal
Narwana
Jind
Karnal
Panipat
Sonipat
Rohtak
Hansi
Hisar
Bhiwani
Delhi
New Delhi
Gurgaon
Ghaziabad
Meerut
Muzaffarnagar
Saharanpur
Roorkee
Dehra Dun
Moradabad
Rampur
Bareilly
Pilibhit
Haldwani
Naini Tal
Almora
Bijnor
Kashipur
Nagina
Sambhal
Bulandshahr
Lahore
Kasur
Shekhupura
Narowal
Gujranwala
Hafizabad
Sargodha
Chiniot
Faisalabad
Jhang Maghiana
Okara
Sahiwal
Kamalia
Arifwala
Bahawalnagar
Khanewal
Multan
Shujaabad
Bahawalpur
Lodhran
Muzaffargarh
Kot Addu
Leiah
Bhakkar
Dera Ismail Khan
Dera Ghazi Khan
Jampur
Rajanpur
Khanpur
Sadiqabad
Fort Abbas
Ganganagar
Suratgarh
Nohar
Sirsa
Anupgarh
Pugal
Raigarh
Sardarshahr
Kabul
Kowt-e Ashrow
Charikar
Sarobi
Jalalabad
Asadabad
Asmar
Khyber Pass
Parachinar
Gardez
Ghazni
Matun
Urgun
Zarghun Shahr
Wana
Wazi Khwa
Zhob
Murgha Kibzai
Qila Saifullah
Loralai
Kohlu
Dera Bugti
Sui
Kahan
Sibi
Bhag
Dadhar
Gandava
Kalat
Nushki
Quetta
Pishin
Khost
Zargun 3578
Chaman
Kandahar
Qalat
Maruf
Nawah
Mukur
Uruzgan
Tarin Kut
Malestan
Mashaki
Behsud
Panjao
Bamiyan
Saighan
Doshi
Pul-i-Khumri
Baghlan
Kunduz
Khanabad
Taliqan
Feyzabad
Ishkashim
Khorog
Emam Saheb
Kholm
Mazar-i-Sharif
Balkh
Termez
Samangan
Shibarghan
Akcha
Andkhui
Daulatabad
Maimana
Sar-i-Pul
Tukzar
Belchiragh
Daulat Yar
Chaghcharan
Kajaki
Gowaran
Kharan
Kandahar
Registan
Toba and Kakar Ranges
Sulaiman Range
Hindu Kush
Nuristan
Koh-i-Baba
Safed Koh
Salt Ra.
Indus
Chenab
Ravi
Sutlej
Zaskar
Kamet 7756
Nanda Devi 7817
Muztag 7282
Nunkun 7135
Zangla
Leh
Chumar
Wujang
Rutog
Gar
Garyarsa
Zanda

NORTH ATLANTIC OCEAN

AFGHANISTAN

KAZAKHSTAN

RUSSIAN FEDERATION

Nizhniy Novgorod
Sankt-Peterburg (Leningrad)
Helsinki
Moskva
Minsk
Kyiv
Warszawa
Berlin

FINLAND
Tallinn EST.
Riga LAT.
LITH.
BELARUS
POLAND
Kraków

NORWAY
Oslo
SWEDEN
Stockholm
DENMARK
København
Hamburg
NETH.
GERMANY
Praha
Wien
SLOVAKIA
Budapest
HUNGARY

UNITED KINGDOM
Dublin
IRELAND
London
Bruxelles
Luxembourg
Paris
FRANCE

North Sea
Baltic Sea

Caspian Sea

TURKMENISTAN
Aşgabat
UZBEKISTAN
Syr-Dar'ya
Amu-Dar'ya
Aral Sea

Mashhad
IRAN
Tehrān
Tabrīz
Baku
AZ.
GEORGIA Tbilisi
Yerevan
ARMENIA
Ankara
TURKEY
Istanbul

Black Sea

UKRAINE
MOLDOVA
Kishinev
Odessa
București
ROMANIA
BULGARIA
Beograd

Baghdad
IRAQ
Tigris
Euphrates
SYRIA
Damascus
Beirut
LEB.
Amman
JORDAN
ISR.
CYPRUS

SAUDI ARABIA
Ar Riyāḍ

KUWAIT
BAHRAIN
QATAR
UNITED ARAB EMIRATES
OMAN

Mecca
Medina
Red Sea

YEMEN
San'ā
Gulf of Aden
ERITREA
Asmera

SUDAN
Khartoum
El Obeid

EGYPT
Cairo
Alexandria
Nile
L. Nasser
Aswān
Port Said

LIBYA
Tripoli
Benghazi

CHAD
L. Chad

NIGER
NIGERIA

MALI
Tombouctou

MAURITANIA
Nouakchott

SENEGAL
Dakar
THE GAMBIA
GUINEA-BISSAU

BURKINA

ITALY
Roma
Napoli
Sicilia
Sardegna

GREECE
Athina
Tirana
ALB.
MAC.
Sarajevo
CROATIA
SLOV.
Adriatic Sea

SPAIN
Madrid
Barcelona
PORTUGAL
Lisboa

Mediterranean Sea

MOROCCO
Rabat
Casablanca
Marrakech
Tanger

ALGERIA
Alger
Oran

TUNISIA
Tunis
Constantine

SAHARA
Western Sahara

Bay of Biscay
Marseille
Lyon
Bordeaux

Corse

Tropic of Cancer

Azores (Port.)
Canaries
Madeira

400 800 1200 1600 km

400 800 mils

⑦ ⑧ ⑨ ⑩ ⑪

Ⓚ Ⓙ Ⓗ Ⓖ Ⓕ Ⓔ Ⓓ Ⓒ

Seychelles

Amirante Is
Aldabra Is

Tromelin (Fr.)

Réunion (Fr.)

SEYCHELLES

INDIAN OCEAN

Farquhar Is

Antsiranana

COMOROS

Mayotte (Fr.)

Mozambique Channel

MADAGASCAR

Antananarivo

Toliary

Toamasina

SOMALIA

Muqdisho

Kismaayo

ETHIOPIA

Mombasa

Zanzibar

Dar es Salaam

KENYA

Nairobi

Nakuru

Kisumu

Eldoret

Lake Turkana

UGANDA

Kampala

Entebbe

Jinja

Lake Victoria

Mwanza

Dodoma

TANZANIA

Tabora

Lake Tanganyika

RWANDA

Kigali

BURUNDI

Bujumbura

MALAWI

Lilongwe

Blantyre

Lake Nyasa (Lake Malawi)

Mzuzu

Nampula

MOZAMBIQUE

Beira

Zambezi

ZIMBABWE

Harare

Bulawayo

Mutare

Gweru

ZAMBIA

Lusaka

Kitwe

Ndola

Kabwe

Lake Kariba

Zambezi

CENTRAL AFRICAN REPUBLIC

Bangui

CAMEROON

Douala

Yaoundé

Ngaoundéré

ZAIRE

Kinshasa

Kananga

Mbuji-Mayi

Lubumbashi

Kisangani

Bukavu

Kindu

Zaire (Congo)

Kasai

CONGO

Brazzaville

Pointe-Noire

GABON

Libreville

Port-Gentil

EQUAT. GUINEA

Bioko

Malabo

SÃO TOMÉ & PRÍNCIPE

Gulf of Guinea

Matadi

Cabinda (Ang.)

ANGOLA

Luanda

Lobito

Benguela

Huambo

Malanje

Lubango

Cuanza

Cubango

Cunene

NAMIBIA

Windhoek

Walvis Bay

Keetmanshoop

Orange

BOTSWANA

Gaborone

Maun

Francistown

Okavango

SOUTH AFRICA

Johannesburg

Pretoria

Kimberley

Bloemfontein

SWAZILAND

Mbabane

LESOTHO

Maseru

Durban

East London

Port Elizabeth

Cape Town

Maputo

Inhambane

CÔTE D'IVOIRE

Yamoussoukro

Abidjan

LIBERIA

Monrovia

Buchanan

GHANA

Accra

Kumasi

Lagos

Ibadan

Porto Novo

Lomé

Cotonou

Port Harcourt

Ascension (U.K.)

St Helena (U.K.)

Tristan da Cunha (U.K.)

SOUTH ATLANTIC OCEAN

Equator

Tropic of Capricorn

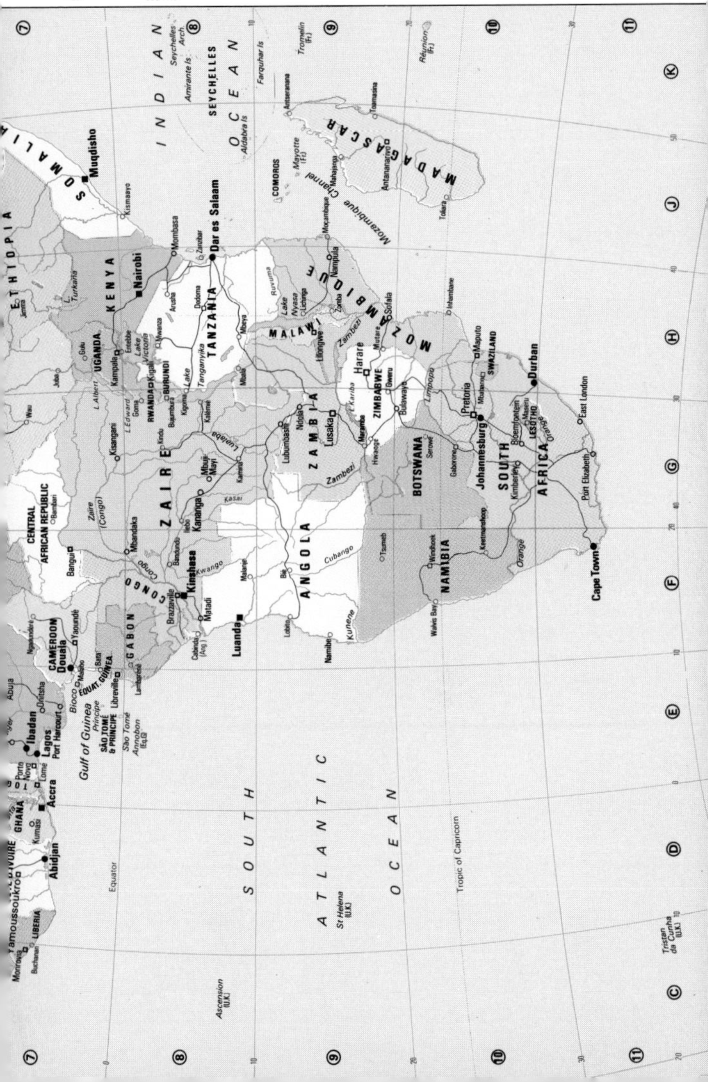

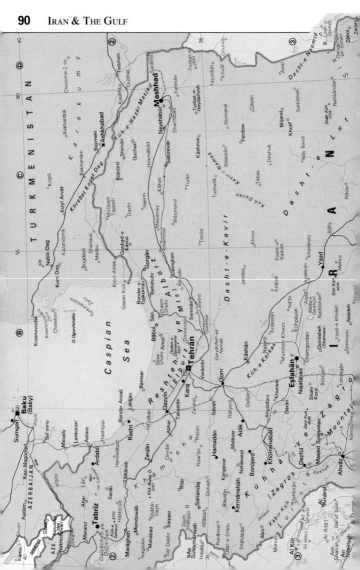

100 200 300 km
50 100 150 mls

CK SEA

Batumi
Ordu
Giresun Tirebolu Rize Çayeli
Trabzon Artvin Ardahan GEORGIA Rustavi
  Akhalkalaki Kumayri Kazakh
Gümüşhane Mescit D. Ardahan Akhalsikhe Mingechaurskoye Geokchay Shemakha
  3326 Kars Kirovakan Vkhr Vulkh
Refahiye Bayburt Sarıkamış Horasan Aragats Kamo AZERBAIJAN Sumgait
  2160 Erzurum Kağızman 6090 YerevaN ye Sevan Agdam Kazi Magomed Aliyat
Erzincan Aşkale Eleşkirt Ağrı ARMENIA Gyandzha Yevlakh
  Büyük Ararat Goris AZE. Iğdır Sal'yany
İvriği Tunceli Bingöl Doğubayazıt Ağrı 5165 Nakhichevan Masally
  Malazgirt Patnos Erciş Süphan D. Maku Kapydzhik 3900 Lenkoran Astara
Elazığ Palu 4058 Van Gölü 3500 Ahar Lari Ardabil
  Keban Muş Khvoy Marand 4821 Hashtpar
Malatya Ergani Silvan Bitlis Gevaş Van Salmas Daryachen-ye Tabriz Sarab Herowabad
  Adıyaman Diyarbakır Batman Siirt Pervari Mor 2715 Orümiyeh Küh-e 3710 Miäneh
ip Hilvan Siverek Midyat Şırnak Hakkâri 3810 Sahand Hashtrüd Zanjan
Şanlıurfa Mardin Nusaybin Zakho Amadiya Maragheh Miandowab Kirk Bulag D.
  Ceylanpınar Ra's al Al Qamishli Rawandiz Naqadeh Shahin 3707 Qeydar
Akçakale 'Ayn Al Hasakah Zalah Al Mawsil Dükan Mahabad Bijar Rowʼan
  J.Abd al Sinjar (Mosul) Sar Dasht Saqqez 35
abulus Buhayrat Adiz 920 Tall 'Afar Arbil Dezh. Sanandaj Razan
Manbij al Asad Ar Raqqah Al Badi As Sulaymaniyah Shahpur II. Qorveh IRAN
  As Sabkhah Al Hadr Ash Kirkük Halabja Alläbäd Hamadan Malayer
SYRIA Dayr az Mayadin Sharqat Tuz Khanaqin Qasr-e Shirin Bisotun Kangavar
  Zawr Baʼiji Khurmätü Ravänsar Kermanshah Nahavand
  As Sukhnah Tikrit Samarra Shähäbäd Borüjerd
Tudmur Al Bu Kamal Anah Miqdadiyah Khanaqin Ilam Khorramabad
  Al Qaʼim Al Khalis Mehran
iʼar Al Hadithah Hit Samarra Baʼqubah Luristan Kabir Kuh Dehloran
  Muhaywir W. al Wadian Hawr al Al Ramadi Baghdad Mehran Dezful
  Habbaniyah Al As Suwayrah Andimeshk
Badiyat Ar Rutbah Bahr al Milh Fallujah Al Kut Ali al Ahvaz
  ash Sham Al Musayyib Al Hayy Gharbi Amarah
  Karbala Al Hillah An Nuʼmaniyah Qalʼat Salih Khorram-
NA Turayf W. al Ubayyid Ad Diwaniyah Ar Rifaʼ shahr
  Al Jalamid Nukhayb Abu Sukhayr An Najaf Ash Al Qurnah Basra Abadan
  Badanah As Samawah Shatrah Hawr al Hammar Az Zubayr Safwan
  Al Harrah Ash Shabak As Salman An Nasiriyah KUWAIT Al Faw Bubiyan
  ʼIsawiyah Ma'niyah Süq ash Suyükh Al Ahmadi Minaʼ al
  Badanah Al Busayyah Al Haniyah kuwait Ahmadi
Ad Duwayd Sakakah Şahra al Hijarah Ad Dibdibah Al Ahmadi Al Watra
hayra Al Jawf Rafha al Widyan Nisab Hafar al Batin Al Mish'ab
  Al Jumaymah
SAUDI An Nafud Ar Tawsiyah Al Qaysamah Qaryat
Qalibah Jubbah ARABIA al Ulya
40 45

200   400   600km
100   200   300mls

Singai Desert

Yafo
Tel Aviv
Jerusalem
Amman
JORDAN
Gaza
El 'Arish
Suez
Port Said
Dumyât
El Mansûra
Damanhûr
Alexandria
Marsa Matrûh
Sîdi Barrâni
Tubruq (Tobruk)
Al Burdi
Banghâzi
Benghazi
Gulf of Sirte
Misrâtah
Tarhûnah
Tripoli
Al Khums
Zuwârah
TUNISIA
Gabes
Daraj
Ghadâmis
Nalût
Mizdah
Al Qaryah Ash Sharqiyah
Sirte Desert
As Sidrah
As Zahrah
Brak
Sabhâ
Marzûq
Ubari
Awbari
Idhan Murzûq
Al Qatrûn
Sardalas
In Amguel
Tafassasset
In Ezzine
Djanet
NIGER
Bilma
Agadem
Fachi
Ténéré du Tafassasset
Grand Erg de Bilma
Plateau du Tchigaï
Plateau du Djado
Plateau Mangueni
Séguédine
Dirkou
Aozou
Pic Toussidé 2266m
Tarso Emi Koussi 3415m
Tibesti
Erdi
Enedi
Ennedi
Depression du Mourdi
Ounianga Kébir
Faya (Largeau)
Borkou
Fada
Aïn Galakka
Koro Toro
Dikoa
Mao
Kanem
Nguigmi
CHAD
Moussoro
Salal
Ati
Oum Chalouba
Biltine
Ouaddaï
Abéché
Arada
Goz Beïda
Adré
SUDAN
El Fasher
Kutum
Umm Bell
Muhu
Sodiri
Bara
El Debba
Dongola
Merowe
Karima
Abu Hamed
Nubian Desert
Wadi Halfa
Selima Oasis
Bir Misaha
Jebel Abyad
'Atrun Oasis
'Uweinat
Ma'tan as Sarra
Rebiana Sand Sea
Al Kufrah Oasis
Al Jawf
Rebiana
Tâzirbû
Al Jaghbûb
Jâlû
Awjilah
Marâdah
Zaltan
Waddân
Hûn
Zillah
Al Fuqaha
Jabal as Sawda
Al Haruj al Aswad
Wâw al Kabîr
Wâw an Nâmûs
Serir Tibesti
Sîrte Desert
Great Sand Sea
Jârabûb
Sîwa
'Aqra
Qattâra Depression -133
Libyan Plateau
Marûh
Libyan Desert
Great Sand Sea
Gilf Kebir Plateau
Bir Tarfâwi
Bir Abu Husein
Kharga Oasis
El Khârga
Dâkhla Oasis
Mût
Baris
Aswân
Aswan High Dam
Lake Nasser
Kôm Ombo
Idfu
Esna
Luxor
Nile
Qena
Farâfra Oasis
Qasr Farâfra
Baharîya Oasis
Bawîti
El Fayûm
Beni Suef
Beni Mazâr
Maghâgha
El Minya
Mallawi
Asyût
Sohâg
Akhmîm
Baris
EGYPT
Shibin el Kôm
Cairo
El Qâhira
El Giza
Ismâ'îlîya
Zagâzig
Faiyûm
Gebel Shâyib 2187m
Ras Gharib
Gebel Gharib
G. Hamâta 1977
Hurghâda
Bur Safâga
El Quseir
Marsa 'Alam
Ras Banâs
Halâib
J. 'Asoteriba 2217m
Yanbu
Tropic of Cancer
Ras Abu Shagara
Port Sudan
Suakin
Tôkâr
Aqîq
Muhammad Qôl
Tawûd al Bahr
RED SEA
Tabûk
Al Jawf
Taymâ
Al Wajh
Aqaba
Mount Sinai
Gebel Katherîna 2642m
Gebel Mûsa
Nakhl
St Catherine's
Sharm el Sheikh
SAUDI ARABIA
Eritrea
Mitsiwa (Massawa)
Asmera
Adwa
Adi Ugri
Barentu
Nak'fa
Keren
Tesseney
Kassala
Khashm el Girba
Gedaref
Gala 'en Nahl
Sennar
Ed Damazin
Wad Medani
Sinja
El Geteina
Ed Dueim
Kosti
Rabak
White Nile
Blue Nile
Wad Medani
Khartoum North
Khartoum
Omdurman
El Geteina
Atbara
Ed Damer
Shendi
Berber
Kamlin
Singa

A   B   C
1   2   3

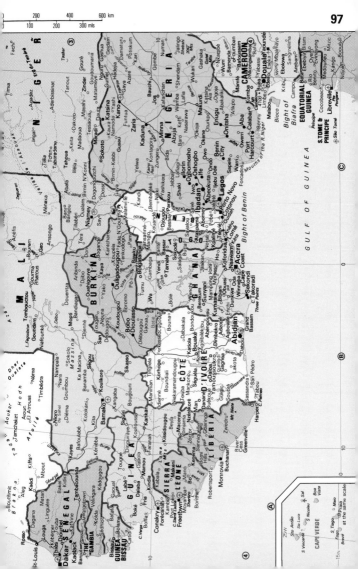

200   400   600 km
100   200   300 mils

SUDAN

ERITREA
Keren Mits'iwa 400 Massawa
Kassala Asmera
Adi Mersa
El Geteina Barentu Om Keru Fatma
Wad El Girba Hager
Medani Gedaref Adwa Mek'ele Ta'izz
El Gezira Qala'en Nahl Adigrat Aseb Al
El Hawata Ras Dashan Sek'ot'a Mukha Adan
Senar Singa Gonder 4533 3657 (Mochal) Uthman (Aden)
Kosti El Jebelein Dunkur Debre Debre Str. of Bab al Mandeb Gulf of Aden
El Obeid Renk Tana Tabor Weldiya Obock DJIBOUTI Tadjoura Djibouti
Umm Ruwaba Roseires Danglia Dese Biyo Kaboba Zeila
Rashad Belfodiyo Buye Markos Dire Dawa Guban Berbera Ceerigaabo
Kaka Paloich Fiche Birhan Harer Burao Hargeysa
Kodok Nejo Nek'emte Addis Awash Caynabo Laascaanood
Malakal Dembi Dolo Sodo Abeba Nazret Ahmar Mts Degeh Bur Damot
Bentiu Nasir Gore Koma Asela Golocha Aware Ogaden Warder Geladi Gaalkacyo
Akobo Jima Shashemene Goba Ginir Danan
Ayod Tor Abera Yirga Alem Mendebo Mts Haro Farina
Duk Mizan Gughe Arba Minch El Goran Sina Dhaqa Ceelbuur
Bor Pibor Post Teferi Maji Gidole Negelli Melka Guba Dolo Odo Xuddur Beled Weyne Dirri Meregh
Juba Mongalla Bako Mega Moyale Luuq Baydhabo Buulo Barde
Yei Moyo Lokichokio Lake Buna Baardheere Buur Hakaba Afgooye Marka Muqdisho (Mugadisho)
Nimule Kitgum Turkana Mt Kulal Marsabit Wajir Jilib Baraawe
Kinyeti Lodwar 2293 Jamaame Baraawe
Moroto Mt Nyiru Kangetet Afmadow Equator Kismaayo
UGANDA Soroti 2806 Maralal Gashi
Gulu Mbale Isiolo Nyahururu Garissa
Mubende Tororo Eldoret Nanyuki Mt Kenya
Kampala Jinja Kakamega Nakuru Nyeri Lamu
Entebbe Kisumu Kericho Embu Patta I.
RWANDA KENYA
Kigali Bukoba Lake Narok Thika Nairobi Tsavo Malindi
BURUNDI Victoria Musoma Kajiado Makindu Kilifi
Bujumbura Mwanza Ushashi Masai Voi Mombasa
Kibondo Nyakabindi Loolmalasin Kilimanjaro Kwale
Shinyanga Ngorongoro Crater Arusha Moshi Same Tanga Pemba I.
Kahama Nzega Mbulu Babati Korogwe Wete
Kaliua Tabora Singida Kondoa Kibaya Handeni Pangani
Uvinza TANZANIA Manyoni Dodoma Mpwapwa Zanzibar
Kigoma Mpanda Kitunda Kilosa Morogoro Bagamoyo
Kipili Rungwa Mikumi Dar es Salaam
Rukwa Iringa Ifakara Mahenge Kilwa Kivinje Mafia
Sumbawanga Chunya Sao Hill Mohoro Kilwa Kisiwani
Mbeya Rungwe Tukuyu Njombe Liwale Lindi Mtwara
Kasama Isoka Chilumba Marida Nachingwea Masasi Palma
Chinsali Rumphi Songea Newala Mocimboa da Praia
Mzuzu Mbamba Bay Tunduru Mueda Moroni COMOROS
Nkhata Bay Lupilichi Mecula Macomia Mutsamudu Anjouan
Lichinga Lupilichi Macaloge Metangula Mahéli

SOMALIA
at the same scale

Caluula Raas Caseyr
Qandala Boosaaso
Laasqoray Laz Xaafuun
Ceerigaabo Carcar Mts Ras Xaafuun
Qardho Bandarbeyla
Laascaanood Nugaal Eyl
Damot Jirriban
Gaalkacyo Dabaro
Hobyo

Aldabra Is
Assumption SEYCHELLES
Grande Is Glorieuses
Comore

G. Gauteng
M. Mpumalanga
K.-N. Kwazulu-Natal

at the same scale

Port Louis
Round I.
MAURITIUS
St Denis
Réunion
(Fr.)

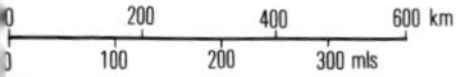

200   400   600 km
100   200   300 mls

Rukwa
Sumbawanga
Ruaha Nat.Pk.
Mikumi
Kilindoni
Kisiju
Mafia I.
Iringa
Ifakara
Mahenge
Kilwa Kivinje
Mohoro
Kilwa Kisiwani

SEYCHELLES

Aldabra Is
Assumption
Cosmoledo Is
Providence

Chunya
Rungwe 2959
Njombe
Sao Hill
Liwale
Lindi
Mtwara
C. Delgado
Mocimboa da Praia
Palma

Mbeya
Tukuyu
Karonga
Nachingwea
Masasi
Newala
Mueda
Mocimboa da Praia

Farquhar Is

Isoka
Chilumba
Nkhata Bay
Songea
Macomia
Ibo
Pemba

Is Glorieuses

Moroni
Grande Comore
Mutsamudu
COMOROS
Anjouan
Mahélé
Mayotte (Fr.)
Dzaoudzi

Tj. Babaomby
C. St Sébastien
Antseranana
Massif du Tsaratanana 2876
Vohimarina

MADAGASCAR
(MALAGASY REP.)

Antananarivo
(Tananarive)

Toamasina
(Tamatave)

Tropic of Capricorn

Mozambique Channel

Maputo
(Lourenço Marques)

SWAZILAND
Manzini
Mbabane

Pretoria
Johannesburg
Soweto
Germiston
Vereeniging
Klerksdorp

North West

Free State

LESOTHO
Maseru
Thaba Putsoa

Bloemfontein
Kimberley
Northern Cape

KwaZulu-Natal
Pietermaritzburg
Durban

Drakensberg

100 km
50 mls

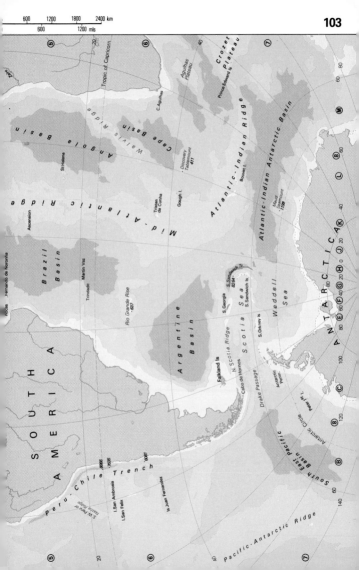

0 600 1200 1800 2400 km
0 600 1200 mls

NORTH AMERICA

Mendocino Seascarp
2826.
Murray Seascarp

Emperor Seamount Chain

16.
104·
Midway Is

1477.
id-Pacific Mountains

Hawaiian Islands

Tropic of Cancer

C.Falso

20

Is Revilla Gigedo

Clarion Fracture Zone

MARSHALL ISLANDS

P A C I F I C   O C E A N

P O L Y N E S I A

Line Is

Equator   0

NAURU

KIRIBATI

Phoenix Is

SOLOMON ISLANDS

TUVALU

6150.

Tokelau (N.Z.)

American Samoa

Ìs Marquises

ANUATU

Wallis & Futuna (Fr.)

W'BN SAMOA

FIJI

TONGA

Cook Is (N.Z.)

Niue

Samoa
Tahiti   Ìs de la Société   Ìs Tuamotu

French Polynesia

Cook Is

Ìs Gambier

Nouvelle Calédonie (Fr.)

Horizon Deep 10882

Ìs Tubuaï

Pitcairn (U.K.)

1344.   Sala y Gómez
I. de Pascua

S. Fiji Basin

10047.

Norfolk I. Ridge

Norfolk I.

Kermadec Trench

INTERNATIONAL DATE LINE

Tonga Trench

South West Pacific Basin

East Pacific Ridge

20

40

Rise

N.Cape

NEW ZEALAND

Chatham Is

New Zealand Plateau

ockland Is

Campbell I.

732.
Pacific-Antarctic Ridge

40

G   180   H   160   J   140   K   120   L   100   M

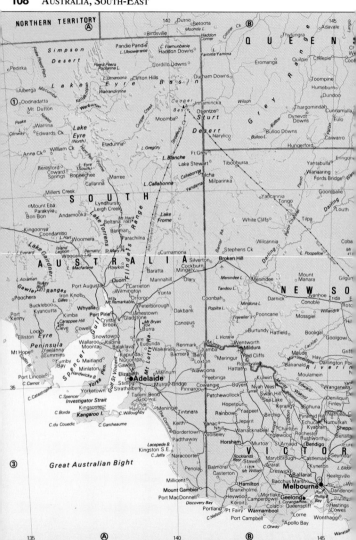

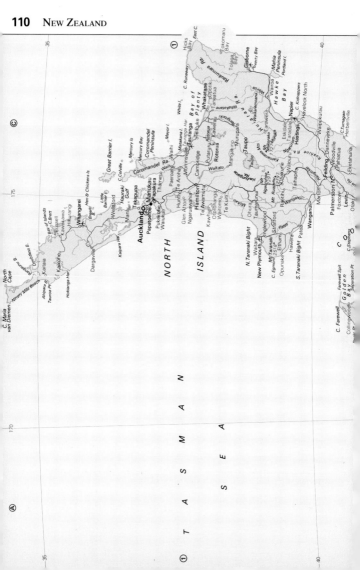

0 50 100 150 200km
0 50 100mls

② ③

Ⓒ

P A C I F I C

45

175

O C E A N

Ⓑ

Ⓐ

170

45

S O U T H

I S L A N D

SOUTHERN ALPS

C O O K   S T R A I T

Wellington
Upper Hutt
Lower Hutt
Tawa
Martinborough
C. Palliser
Palliser Bay
Mt. Ross
C. Campbell

Picton
Blenheim
Richmond
Nelson
Motueka
C. Foulwind

Karamea
Karamea Bight
Westport
Seddonville
Reefton
Greymouth
Runanga
Hokitika
Ross

Murchison
Victoria Ra.
Buller
Inangahua
Lyell
Lewis Pass
Maruia
Hanmer Springs
Waiau
Kaikoura
Kaikoura Pen.

Kahurangi Pt.
Richmond Ra.
Tasman Bay

Abut Hd.

Franz Josef Gl.

Jackson Bay

Cascade Pt.

Milford Sd.
Anita Pk.
McKerrow
Caswell Sd.
George Sd.
Secretary I.
Doubtful Sd.
Dusky Sd.
Breaksea Sd.
Resolution I.
Chalky Inlet
Preservation Inlet
Puysegur Pt.

Fiordland
Nat. Park

Te Anau
L. Te Anau
Manapouri
L. Manapouri
Mt. Aspiring
Mt. Earnslaw
Mt. Ward
Mt. Tutoko
Homer Tunnel
Te Aroha
Hollyford

Haast
Wanaka
L. Wanaka
L. Hawea
Mt. Cook
Mt. Tasman

Arrowtown
Queenstown
Cromwell
Kingston
Wanaka
Clyde
Alexandra
Roxburgh
Clutha

Mossburn
Winton
Wyndale
Te Anau
Wakatipu
L. Wakatipu
Ohai
Riverton
Invercargill
Bluff
Foveaux Strait

Otatara
Coalfish I.
Oban
Halfmoon Bay
Port Pegasus
Port Adventure
Stewart Island
Shelter Pt.

Solander I.

Gore
Mataura
Balclutha
Kaitangata
Milton
Lawrence
Clutha

Owaka

Balfour
Gore
Clinton

Heriot
Roxburgh
Ettrick
Waitahuna

Ranfurly
Naseby
St. Bathans
Lindis

Omarama
Kurow
Waimate

Aoraki
Mt. Cook
3754
Tekapo
L. Tekapo
L. Pukaki
L. Ohau
Fairlie
Twizel
Burkes Pass

Hawkdun Ra.
Dansey's Pass

Oamaru
Hampden
Palmerston
Waikouaiti
Port Chalmers
Dunedin
Otago Peninsula
Mosgiel
Taieri

Ashburton
Rakaia
Geraldine
Temuka
Timaru

Christchurch
Lyttelton
Akaroa
Banks Peninsula
Kaiapoi
Rangiora
Lincoln

Pegasus Bay
Canterbury Bight

Rakaia R.
Methven
Mt. Hutt

Amberley
Waipara
Cheviot

Mt. Travers
2338
Travers Ra.
Rotoiti
L. Rotoroa

SOUTH

ISLAND

② ③

| 0 | 400 | 800 | 1200 | 1600 km |
| 0 | 400 | 800 | 1600 mls |

Antarctic Research Stations
1 Artigas (Uruguay)
2 Teniente Rodolfo March Martin (Chile)
3 Bellingshausen (Rus. Fed.)
4 Chang Cheng (Great Wall) (China)
5 Comandante Ferraz (Brazil)
6 Henryk Arctowski (Poland)
7 Teniente Jubany (Arg.)
8 Great Britain (UK)
9 Capitán Arturo Prat (Chile)
10 General Bernardo O'Higgins (Chile)
11 Esperanza (Arg.)
12 Vicecomodoro Marambio (Arg.)
13 Palmer (USA)
14 Faraday (UK)
15 Rothera (UK)
16 General San Martín (Arg.)

In the index, the first number refers to the page, and the following letter
and number to the section of the map in which the index entry
can be found. For example, 48C2 **Paris** means that Paris can
be found on page 48 where column C and row 2 meet.

Abbreviations used in the index

Afghan	Afghanistan	Germ	Germany	Par	Paraguay	Arch	Archipelago
Alb	Albania	Hung	Hungary	Phil	Philippines	B	Bay
Alg	Algeria	Ind	Indonesia	Pol	Poland	C	Cape
Ant	Antarctica	Irish Rep	Ireland	Port	Portugal	Chan	Channel
Arg	Argentina	Leb	Lebanon	Rom	Romania	Gl	Glacier
Aust	Australia	Lib	Liberia	Russian Fed	Russian	Is(s)	Island(s)
Bang	Bangladesh	Liech	Liechtenstein		Federation	Lg	Lagoon
Belg	Belgium	Lux	Luxembourg	S Arabia	Saudi Arabia	L	Lake
Bol	Bolivia	Madag	Madagascar	Scot	Scotland	Mt(s)	Mountain(s)
Bulg	Bulgaria	Malay	Malaysia	Sen	Senegal	O	Ocean
Burk	Burkina	Maur	Mauritania	S Africa	South Africa	P	Pass
Camb	Cambodia	Mor	Morocco	Switz	Switzerland	Pen	Peninsula
Can	Canada	Mozam	Mozambique	Tanz	Tanzania	Plat	Plateau
CAR	Central African Republic	Myan	Myanmar	Thai	Thailand	Pt	Point
Den	Denmark	Neth	Netherlands	Turk	Turkey	Res	Reservoir
Div	Division	NZ	New Zealand	USA	United States	R	River
Dom Rep	Dominican Republic	Nic	Nicaragua		of America	S	Sea
El Sal	El Salvador	N Ire	Northern Ireland	Urug	Uruguay	Sd	Sound
Eng	England	Nig	Nigeria	Ven	Venezuela	Str	Strait
Eq Guinea	Equatorial Guinea	Nor	Norway	Viet	Vietnam	V	Valley
Eth	Ethiopia	Pak	Pakistan	Yugos	Yugoslavia		
Fin	Finland	PNG	Papua New Guinea	Zim	Zimbabwe		

A

57B2 **Aachen** Germany
46C1 **Aalst** Belg
38K6 **Ääneskoski** Fin
47C1 **Aarau** Switz
47B1 **Aare** R Switz
72A3 **Aba** China
97C4 **Aba** Nig
99D2 **Aba** Zaire
91A3 **Ābādān** Iran
90B3 **Ābādeh** Iran
96B1 **Abadla** Alg
35B1 **Abaeté** Brazil
35B1 **Abaeté** R Brazil
31B2 **Abaetetuba** Brazil
72D1 **Abagnar Qi** China
97C4 **Abakaliki** Nig
63B2 **Abakan** Russian Fed
97C3 **Abala** Niger
96C2 **Abalessa** Alg
32C6 **Abancay** Peru
90B3 **Abarqū** Iran
74E2 **Abashiri** Japan
74E2 **Abashiri-wan** B Japan
71F4 **Abau** PNG
99D2 **Abaya** L Eth
99D1 **Abbai** R Eth
99E1 **Abbe** L Eth
48C1 **Abbeville** France
19B4 **Abbeville** Louisiana, USA
17B1 **Abbeville** S Carolina, USA
45B2 **Abbeyfeale** Irish Rep
47C2 **Abbiategrasso** Italy
84C2 **Abbottabad** Pak
61H3 **Abdulino** Russian Fed
98C1 **Abéché** Chad
39F7 **Åbenrå** Den
97C4 **Abeokuta** Nig
43B3 **Aberaeron** Wales
43C3 **Aberconwy and**
Colwyn County
Wales
15C3 **Aberdeen** Maryland, USA
100B4 **Aberdeen** S Africa
44C3 **Aberdeen** Scot
8D2 **Aberdeen** S Dakota, USA
8A2 **Aberdeen**
Washington, USA
44C3 **Aberdeen City**
Division, Scotland
4J3 **Aberdeen** L Can
44C3 **Aberdeenshire**
Division, Scot
44C3 **Aberfeldy** Scot
43C4 **Abergavenny** Wales
43B3 **Aberystwyth** Wales
81C4 **Abhā** S Arabia
90A2 **Abhar** Iran
97B4 **Abidjan** Côte d'Ivoire
18A2 **Abilene** Kansas, USA
9D3 **Abilene** Texas, USA
43D4 **Abingdon** Eng
7B4 **Abitibi** R Can
7C5 **Abitibi,L** Can
61F5 **Abkhazia** Division,
Georgia
84C2 **Abohar** India
97C4 **Abomey** Benin
98B2 **Abong Mbang** Cam
79A4 **Aborlan** Phil
98B1 **Abou Deïa** Chad
91A4 **Abqaiq** S Arabia
50A2 **Abrantes** Port
95C2 **Abri** Sudan
106A3 **Abrolhos** Is Aust
8B2 **Absaroka Range** Mts USA
91B5 **Abū al Abyad** l UAE
91A4 **Abū 'Ali** l S Arabia
91B5 **Abu Dhabi** UAE
95C3 **Abu Hamed** Sudan
97C4 **Abuja** Nig
33D5 **Abuná** Brazil
32E6 **Abuná** R Bol
93D3 **Abū Sukhayr** Iraq

111B2 **Abut Head** C NZ
95C3 **Abu 'Urug** Well Sudan
99D1 **Abuye Meda** Mt Eth
99C1 **Abu Zabad** Sudan
90D2 **Abwong** Sudan
56B1 **Åby** Den
94B3 **Aby 'Aweigila** Well Egypt
99C2 **Abyei** Sudan
24B2 **Acambaro** Mexico
24B2 **Acaponeta** Mexico
24B3 **Acapulco** Mexico
31D2 **Acaraú** Brazil
32D2 **Acarigua** Ven
24C3 **Acatlán** Mexico
23B2 **Acatzingo** Mexico
97B4 **Accra** Ghana
85D4 **Achalpur** India
29B4 **Achao** Chile
47D1 **Achensee** L Austria
46E2 **Achern** Germany
41A3 **Achill** l Irish Rep
63B2 **Achinsk** Russian Fed
53C3 **Acireale** Italy
26C2 **Acklins** l
Caribbean S
32C6 **Acobamba** Peru
29B2 **Aconcagua** Mt Chile
31D3 **Acopiara** Brazil
88B4 **Açores** ls Atlantic O
A Coruña = La Coruña
47C2 **Acqui** Italy
108A2 **Acraman,L** Aust
Acre = 'Akko
32C5 **Acre** State, Brazil
22C3 **Acton** USA
23B1 **Actopan** Mexico
19A3 **Ada** USA
50B1 **Adaja** R Spain
91C5 **Adam** Oman
35A2 **Adamantina** Brazil
98B2 **Adamaoua** Region, Nig/Cam
47D1 **Adamello** Mt Italy
16C1 **Adams** USA

87B3 **Adam's Bridge** India/
Sri Lanka
13D2 **Adams L** Can
8A2 **Adams,Mt** USA
87C3 **Adam's Peak** Mt
Sri Lanka
81C4 **'Adan** Yemen
92C2 **Adana** Turk
60D5 **Adapazari** Turk
112B7 **Adare,C** Ant
108B1 **Adavale** Aust
47C2 **Adda** R Italy
91A4 **Ad Dahna'** Region, S Arabia
96A2 **Ad Dakhla** Mor
81C4 **Ad Dāli'** Yemen
91B4 **Ad Damman**
S Arabia
91A5 **Ad Dibdibah** Region, S Arabia
91A5 **Ad Dilam** S Arabia
91A5 **Ad Dir'iyah** S Arabia
93D3 **Ad Diwaniyah** Iraq
93D3 **Ad Duwayd** S Arabia
106C4 **Adelaide** Aust
4J3 **Adelaide Pen** Can
22D3 **Adelanto** USA
Aden = 'Adan
81C4 **Aden,G of** Yemen/
Somalia
97C3 **Aderbissinat** Niger
94C2 **Adhra** Syria
71E4 **Adi** l Indon
52B1 **Adige** R Italy
99D1 **Adigrat** Eth
85D5 **Adilābād** India
20B2 **Adin** USA
15D2 **Adirondack Mts** USA
99D2 **Ādis Ābeba** Eth
95C3 **Adi Ugri** Eritrea
93C2 **Adiyaman** Turk
54C1 **Adjud** Rom
4E4 **Admiralty I** USA
6B2 **Admiralty Inlet** B Can
87B1 **Adoni** India
48B3 **Adour** R France

96A2 Adrar Region, Maur
96C2 Adrar Mts Alg
96A2 Adrar Soutouf Region, Mor
98C1 Adré Chad
95A2 Adri Libya
47E2 Adria Italy
14B2 Adrian Michigan, USA
52B2 Adriatic S S Europe
99D1 Adwa Eth
61F5 Adygeya Division, Russian Fed
97B4 Adzopé Côte d'Ivoire
55B3 Aegean S Greece
80E2 Afghanistan Republic, Asia
99E2 Afgooye Somalia
97C4 Afikpo Nig
38G6 Afjord Nor
96C1 Aflou Alg
99E2 Afmadu Somalia
97A3 Afollé Region, Maur
94B2 Afula Israel
92B2 Afyon Turk
97C3 Agadez Niger
96B1 Agadir Mor
85D4 Agar India
62A2 Agartala India
20B1 Agassiz Can
97B4 Agboville Côte d'Ivoire
93E1 Agdam Azerbaijan
75B1 Agematsu Japan
48C3 Agen France
90A3 Agha Jari Iran
96A2 Aghwinit Well Mor
47C2 Agno R Italy
47E1 Agordo Italy
48C3 Agout R France
85D3 Agra India
93D2 Agri Turk
53C2 Agri R Italy
53B3 Agrigento Italy
55B3 Agrinion Greece
34A3 Agrio R Chile
53B3 Agropoli Italy
61H2 Agryz Russian Fed
6E3 Agto Greenland
27D3 Aguadilla Puerto Rico
24B1 Agua Prieta Mexico
24B2 Aguascalientes Mexico
23A1 Aguascalientes State, Mexico
35C1 Águas Formosas Brazil
50A1 Agueda Port
96A2 Aguelhok Mali
50B2 Águilas Spain
23A2 Aguililla Mexico
100B4 Agulhas,C S Africa
79C4 Agusan R Phil
93E2 Ahar Iran
110B1 Ahipara B NZ
85C4 Ahmadābād India
87B1 Ahmadnagar India
99E2 Ahmar Mts Eth
46D1 Ahr R Germany
46D1 Ahrgebirge Region, Germany
23A1 Ahuacatlán Mexico
23A1 Ahualulco Mexico
39G7 Åhus Sweden
90B2 Ahuvān Iran
90A3 Ahvāz Iran
26A4 Aiajuela Costa Rica
47B1 Aigle Switz
47B2 Aiguille d'Arves Mt France
47B2 Aiguille de la Grand Sassière Mt France
75B1 Aikawa Japan
17B1 Aiken USA
73A5 Ailao Shan Upland China
35C1 Aimorés Brazil
96B1 Ain Beni Mathar Mor
95B2 Ain Dalla Well Egypt
51C2 Ain el Hadjel Alg
95A3 Ain Galakka Chad

96B1 Ain Sefra Alg
92B4 'Ain Sukhna Egypt
75A2 Aioi Japan
96B2 Aioun Abd el Malek Well Maur
97B3 Aïoun El Atrouss Maur
30C2 Aiquile Bol
97C3 Air Desert Region Niger
13E2 Airdrie Can
48B1 Aire France
42D3 Aire R Eng
46C2 Aire R France
6C3 Airforce I Can
47C1 Airolo Switz
4E3 Aishihik Can
12G2 Aishihik L Can
46B2 Aisne Department, France
49C2 Aisne R France
71F4 Aitape PNG
58D1 Aiviekste R Latvia
72B2 Aixa Zuogi China
49D3 Aix-en-Provence France
47A2 Aix-les-Bains France
86B2 Aiyar Res India
55B3 Aiyion Greece
55B3 Aíyna I Greece
86C2 Aizawl India
100A3 Aizeb R Namibia
74E3 Aizu-Wakamatsu Japan
52A2 Ajaccio Corse
23B2 Ajalpan Mexico
65F5 Ajaria Division, Georgia
95B1 Ajdābiyā Libya
74E2 Ajigasawa Japan
94B2 Ajlūn Jordan
91C4 Ajman UAE
85C3 Ajmer India
9B3 Ajo USA
23A2 Ajuchitan Mexico
55C3 Ak R Turk
75B1 Akaishi-sanchi Mts Japan
87B1 Akalkot India
111B2 Akaroa NZ
75A2 Akashi Japan
61J3 Akbulak Russian Fed
93C2 Akçakale Turk
96A2 Akchar Watercourse Maur
55C3 Akdağ Mt Turk
98C2 Aketi Zaire
93D1 Akhalkalaki Georgia
93D1 Akhalsikhe Georgia
93D1 Akharnaí Greece
12D3 Akhiok USA
92A2 Akhisar Turk
58D1 Akhiste Latvia
95C2 Akhmim Egypt
61G4 Akhtubinsk Russian Fed
60D4 Akhtyrka Ukraine
75A2 Aki Japan
14B1 Akimiski I Can
74E3 Akita Japan
96A3 Akjoujt Maur
94B2 'Akko Israel
4E3 Aklavik Can
97B3 Aklé Aouana Desert Region Maur
99D2 Akobo Sudan
99D2 Akobo R Sudan
84B1 Akoha Afghan
85D4 Akola India
85D4 Akot India
6D3 Akpatok I Can
55B3 Akra Kafirévs C Greece
55B3 Ákra Maléa C Greece
38A2 Akranes Iceland
55C3 Ákra Sídheros C Greece
55B3 Ákra Spátha C Greece
55B3 Ákra Taínaron C Greece
10B2 Akron USA
94A1 Akrotiri B Cyprus

84D1 Aksai Chin Mts China
92B2 Aksaray Turk
61H3 Aksay Kazakhstan
84D1 Aksayquin Hu L China
92B2 Akşehir Turk
92B2 Akseki Turk
63D2 Aksenovo Zilovskoye Russian Fed
68D1 Aksha Russian Fed
82C1 Aksu China
61H5 Aktau Kazakhstan
65J5 Aktogay Kazakhstan
61J4 Aktumsyk Kazakhstan
65G4 Aktyubinsk Kazakhstan
38B1 Akureyri Iceland Akyab = Sittwe
65K5 Akzhal Kazakhstan
11B3 Alabama State, USA
11B3 Alabama R USA
17A1 Alabaster USA
92C2 Ala Dağları Mts Turk
61F5 Alagir Russian Fed
47B2 Alagna Italy
31D3 Alagoas State, Brazil
31D4 Alagoinhas Brazil
51B1 Alagón Spain
93E4 Al Ahmadī Kuwait
25D3 Alajuela Costa Rica
12B2 Alakanuk USA
38L5 Alakurtti Russian Fed
93E4 Al Amārah Iraq
21A2 Alameda USA
23B1 Alamo Mexico
9C3 Alamogordo USA
9C3 Alamosa USA
39H6 Åland I Fin
92B2 Alanya Turk
17B1 Alapaha R USA
65H4 Alapayevsk Russian Fed
92A2 Alaşehir Turk
68C3 Ala Shan Mts China
4C3 Alaska State, USA
4D4 Alaska,G of USA
12C3 Alaska Pen USA
4C3 Alaska Range Mts USA
52A2 Alassio Italy
47B1 Alatsee Italy
61G3 Alatyr' Russian Fed
108B2 Alawoona Aust
91C5 Al'Ayn UAE
82B2 Alayskiy Khrebet Mts Tajikistan
49D3 Alba Italy
92C2 Al Bāb Syria
51B2 Albacete Spain
50A1 Alba de Tormes Spain
93D2 Al Badi Iraq
54B1 Alba Iulia Rom
54A2 Albania Republic, Europe
106A4 Albany Aust
17B1 Albany Georgia, USA
15D2 Albany New York, USA
8A2 Albany Oregon, USA
7B4 Albany R Can
34B2 Albardón Arg
91C5 Al Bātinah Region, Oman
71F5 Albatross B Aust
95B1 Al Baydā Libya
50B1 Alberche R Spain
108A1 Alberga Aust
46B1 Albert France
5G4 Alberta Province, Can
99D2 Albert,L Uganda/Zaire
10A2 Albert Lea USA
99D2 Albert Nile R Uganda
49D2 Albertville France
48C3 Albi France
18B1 Albia USA
33G2 Albina Suriname
14B2 Albion Michigan, USA

15C2 Albion New York, USA
92C4 Al Bi'r S Arabia
91A5 Al Biyadh Region, S Arabia
50B2 Alborán I Spain
39G7 Ålborg Den
93D3 Al Bu Kamal Syria
47C1 Albula R Switz
9C3 Albuquerque USA
91C5 Al Buraymi Oman
94C1 Al Burayqah Libya
95A1 Al Burdi Libya
107D4 Albury Aust
93E3 Al Busayyah Iraq
50B1 Alcalá de Henares Spain
53B3 Alcamo Italy
51B1 Alcaniz Spain
31C2 Alcântara Brazil
50B2 Alcaraz Spain
50B2 Alcazar de San Juan Spain
51B2 Alcira Spain
35D1 Alcobaça Brazil
50B1 Alcolea de Pinar Spain
51B2 Alcoy Spain
51C2 Alcudia Spain
89J8 Aldabra Is Indian O
23B2 Aldan Russian Fed
63E2 Aldanskoye Nagor'ye Upland Russian Fed
43E3 Aldeburgh Eng
43E4 Alderney I UK
43D4 Aldershot Eng
97A3 Aleg Maur
30E4 Alegrete Brazil
34C2 Alejandro Roca Arg
30H6 Alejandro Selkirk I Chile
63G2 Aleksandrovsk Sakhalinskiy Russian Fed
65J4 Alekseyevka Kazakhstan
60E3 Aleksin Russian Fed
58B1 Alem Sweden
35C2 Alem Paraiba Brazil
49C2 Alençon France
21C4 Alenuihaha Chan Hawaiian Is Aleppo = Halab
6D1 Alert Can
49C3 Alès France
52A2 Alessandria Italy
64B3 Ålesund Nor
12C3 Aleutian Range Mts USA
4E4 Alexander Arch USA
100A3 Alexander Bay S Africa
17A1 Alexander City USA
112C3 Alexander I USA
111A3 Alexandra NZ
29G8 Alexandra,C South Georgia
6C2 Alexandra Fjord Can
95B1 Alexandria Egypt
11A3 Alexandria Louisiana, USA
10A2 Alexandria Minnesota, USA
10C3 Alexandria Virginia, USA
55C2 Alexandroúpolis Greece
13C2 Alexis Creek Can
94B2 Aley Leb
65K4 Aleysk Russian Fed
93D3 Al Fallūjah Iraq
51B1 Alfaro Spain
54C2 Alfatar Bulg
93E3 Al Fāw Iraq
35B2 Alfenas Brazil
55B3 Alfiós R Greece
47D2 Alfonsine Italy
35C2 Alfonzo Cláudio Brazil
35C2 Alfredo Chaves Brazil
61J4 Alga Kazakhstan
34B3 Algarrobo del Aguila Arg
50A2 Algeciras Spain

96C1 Alger Alg	91B5 Al Liwā' Region, UAE	33G4 Altamira Brazil	101D3 Amboasary Madag
96B2 Algeria Republic, Africa	109D1 Allora Aust	23B1 Altamira Mexico	101D2 Ambodifototra Madag
53A2 Alghero Sardegna	14B2 Alma Michigan, USA	53C2 Altamura Italy	101D3 Ambohimahasoa Madag
Algiers = Alger	Alma Ata = Almaty	68C1 Altanbulag Mongolia	71D4 Ambon Indon
15C1 Algonquin Park Can	71F2 Al Madinah = Medina	71F4 Altape PNG	101D3 Ambositra Madag
91C5 Al Hadd Oman	71F2 Almagan I Pacific O	24B2 Alta Vista Mexico	101D3 Ambovombe Madag
93D3 Al Hadithah Iraq	91B4 Al Manāmah Bahrain	47C1 Altdorf Switz	98B3 Ambriz Angola
92C3 Al Hadithah S Arabia	93D3 Al Ma'niyah Iraq	46D1 Altenkirchen Germany	98C1 Am Dam Chad
93D2 Al Hadr Iraq	21A1 Almanor,L USA	34B3 Altiplanicie del Payún Plat Arg	64H3 Amderma Russian Fed
91C5 Al Hajar al Gharbi Mts Oman	51B2 Almansa Spain	47B1 Altkirch France	24B2 Ameca Mexico
91C5 Al Hajar ash Sharqi Mts Oman	13B1 Alma Peak Mt Can	101C2 Alto Molócue Mozam	23B2 Amecacameca Mexico
93C3 Al Hamad Desert Region Jordan/S Arabia	91B5 Al Māriyyah UAE	10A3 Alton USA	34C2 Ameghino Arg
93E4 Al Haniyah Desert Region Iraq	95B1 Al Marj Libya	15C2 Altoona USA	56B2 Ameland I Neth
91A5 Al Hariq S Arabia	82B1 Almaty Kazakhstan	34B2 Alto Pencoso Mts Arg	16C2 Amenia USA
93C3 Al Harrah Desert Region S Arabia	93D2 Al Mawsil Iraq	35A1 Alto Sucuriú Brazil	112B10 American Highland Upland Ant
95A2 Al Harūj al Aswad Upland Libya	50B1 Almazán Spain	23B2 Altotonga Mexico	105H4 American Samoa Is Pacific O
91A4 Al Hasa Region, S Arabia	35C1 Almenara Brazil	23B2 Altoyac de Alvarez Mexico	17B1 Americus USA
93D2 Al Hasakah Syria	50B2 Almería Spain	82C2 Altun Shan Mts China	101C1 Amersfoort S Africa
93C4 Al Hawjā' S Arabia	61H3 Al'met'yevsk Russian Fed	20B2 Alturas USA	112C10 Amery Ice Shelf Ant
93E3 Al Hayy Iraq	56C1 Älmhult Sweden	9D3 Altus USA	55B3 Amfilokhía Greece
94C2 Al Hijānah Syria	93E3 Al Miqdādiyah Iraq	91B5 Al'Ubaylah S Arabia	55B3 Amfissa Greece
93D3 Al Hillah Iraq	112C3 Almirante Brown Base Ant	93C4 Al Urayq Desert Region S Arabia	63F1 Amga Russian Fed
91A5 Al Hillah S Arabia	34A1 Almirante Latorre Chile	91B5 Al'Uruq al Mu'taridah Region, S Arabia	63F1 Amga R Russian Fed
96B1 Al Hoceima Mor	55B3 Almirós Greece	9D2 Alva USA	69F2 Amgu Russian Fed
91A4 Al Hufūf S Arabia	91A4 Al Mish'āb S Arabia	23B2 Alvarado Mexico	69F1 Amgun' R Russian Fed
91B5 Al Humrah Region, UAE	50A2 Almodôvar Port	19A4 Alvarado USA	99D1 Amhara Region Eth
91C5 Al Huwatsah Oman	84D3 Almora India	39G6 Alvdalen Sweden	7D5 Amherst Can
90A2 Aliabad Iran	91A4 Al Mubarraz S Arabia	19A4 Alvin USA	16C1 Amherst Massachusetts, USA
91C4 Aliabad Iran	92C4 Al Mudawwara Jordan	38J5 Alvsbyn Sweden	Amherst = Kyaikkami
55B2 Aliákmon R Greece	91C5 Al Mudaybi Oman	80B3 Al Wajh S Arabia	87B2 Amhür India
93E3 Ali al Gharbi Iraq	91B4 Al Muharraq Bahrain	85D3 Alwar India	48C2 Amiens France
37B1 Alibag India	81C4 Al Mukallā Yemen	81C4 Al Widyān Desert Region Iraq/S Arabia	75B1 Amino Japan
51B2 Alicante Spain	81C4 Al Mukhā Yemen	72A2 Alxa Yougi China	94B1 Amioûn Leb
9D4 Alice Aust	93D3 Al Musayyib Iraq	93E2 Alyat Azerbaijan	89K8 Amirante Is Indian O
106C3 Alice Springs Aust	44B3 Alness Scot	39J8 Alytus Lithuania	86B1 Amlekhgan Nepal
53B3 Alicudi I Italy	93E3 Al Nu'māniyah Iraq	46E2 Alzey Germany	92C3 Amman Jordan
90A3 Aligūdarz Iran	77D4 Alor I Indon	23B2 Amacuzac R Mexico	38K6 Ämmänsaario Fin
84B2 Ali-Khel Afghan	77C4 Alor Setar Malay	99D2 Amadi Sudan	56B2 Ammersfoort Neth
55C3 Alimniá I Greece	Alost = Aalst	6C3 Amadjuak L Can	90B2 Amol Iran
86B1 Alipur Duār India	107E2 Alotau PNG	74D3 Amakusa-shotō I Japan	55C3 Amorgós I Greece
14B2 Aliquippa USA	106B3 Aloysius,Mt Aust	39G7 Amål Sweden	7C5 Amos Can
22B2 Alisal USA	34C3 Alpachiri Arg	63D2 Amalat R Russian Fed	Amoy = Xiamen
93C3 Al' Isawiyah S Arabia	14B1 Alpena USA	55B3 Amaliás Greece	101D3 Ampanihy Madag
100B4 Aliwal North S Africa	47B2 Alpes du Valais Mts Switz	85D4 Amalner India	35B2 Amparo Brazil
91C5 Al Jaghbūb Libya	52B1 Alpi Dolomitiche Mts Italy	74E4 Amami I Japan	51C1 Amposta Spain
93D3 Al Jālamid S Arabia	47B2 Alpi Graie Mts Italy	69E4 Amami gunto Arch Japan	85D4 Amravati India
95B2 Al Jawf Libya	9C3 Alpine Texas, USA	100C4 Amanzimtoti S Africa	85C4 Amreli India
93C4 Al Jawf S Arabia	63D2 Al Qaim Iraq	33G3 Amapá Brazil	84C2 Amritsar India
93D2 Al Jazirah Desert Region Syria/Iraq	47B2 Alpi Orobie Mts Italy	33G3 Amapá State, Brazil	56A2 Amsterdam Neth
50A2 Aljezur Port	47B2 Alpi Pennine Mts Italy	9C3 Amarillo USA	101H1 Amsterdam S Africa
91A4 Al Jubayl S Arabia	47C1 Alpi Retiche Mts Switz	60E5 Amasya Turk	15D2 Amsterdam USA
91C5 Al Kāmil Oman	47D1 Alpi Venoste Mts Italy	23A1 Amatlán Mexico	98C1 Am Tīman Chad
91A4 Al Khābūr R Syria	52A1 Alps Mts Europe	Amazonas = Solimões	88L3 Amu Darya R Uzbekistan
91C5 Al Khāburah Oman	95A1 Al Qaddāhiyah Libya	32D4 Amazonas State, Brazil	6A2 Amund Ringes I Can
93D3 Al Khālis Iraq	94C1 Al Qadmūs Syria	28A3 Amazonas R Brazil	4F2 Amundsen G Can
91C4 Al Khasab Oman	93D3 Al Qa'im Iraq	84D2 Ambala India	112B4 Amundsen S Ant
91A4 Al Khawr Qatar	91A5 Al Qaryah Ash Sharqiyah Libya	87C3 Ambalangoda Sri Lanka	80E Amundsen-Scott Base Ant
95A1 Al Khums Libya	92C3 Al Qaryatayn Syria	101D3 Ambalavao Madag	78D3 Amuntai Indon
91B5 Al Kidan Region, S Arabia	91A4 Al Qatif S Arabia	98B2 Ambam Cam	63E2 Amur R Russian Fed
94C2 Al Kiswah Syria	95A2 Al Qatrūn Libya	101D2 Ambanja Madag	33E2 Anaco Ven
56A2 Alkmaar Neth	91A4 Al Qaysūmah S Arabia	1C7 Ambarchik Russian Fed	8B2 Anaconda USA
95B2 Al Kufrah Oasis Libya	94C2 Al Quatayfah Syria	32B4 Ambato Ecuador	20B1 Anacortes USA
93E3 Al Kūt Iraq	50A2 Alqueva R Port	101D2 Ambato-Boeny Madag	55C3 Anáfi I Greece
92C2 Al Lādhiqiyah Syria	94C2 Al Qunayṭirah Syria	101D2 Ambatolampy Madag	93D3 'Anah Iraq
86A1 Allahābād India	81C4 Al Qunfidhah S Arabia	101D2 Ambatondrazaka Madag	21B3 Anaheim USA
94C2 Al Lajāh Mt Syria	93E3 Al Qurnah Iraq	57C3 Amberg Germany	87B2 Anaimalai Hills India
12D1 Allakaket USA	92C3 Al Quşayr Syria	25D3 Ambergris Cay I Belize	87C1 Anakapalle India
76B2 Allanmyo Myan	56B1 Als I Den	86A2 Ambikāpur India	12E1 Anaktuvuk P USA
95C2 'Allaqi Watercourse Egypt	49D2 Alsace Region, France	101D2 Ambilobe Madag	101D2 Analalava Madag
17B1 Allatoona L USA	57B2 Alsfeld Germany		92B2 Anamur Turk
15C2 Allegheny R USA	42C2 Alston Eng		75A2 Anan Japan
10C3 Allegheny Mts USA	38J5 Alta Nor		87B2 Anantapur India
17B1 Allendale USA	29D2 Alta Gracia Arg		84D2 Anantnag India
111A3 Allen,Mt NZ	27D5 Altagracia de Orituco Ven		31B5 Anápolis Brazil
15C2 Allentown USA	68A2 Altai Mts Mongolia		90C3 Anar Iran
87B3 Alleppey India	17B1 Altamaha R USA		90C3 Anarak Iran
49C2 Aller R France			9083 Anatahan I Pacific O
36C1 Allgäu Mts Germany			30D4 Añatuya Arg
8C2 Alliance USA			74B3 Anbyŏn N Korea
81C3 Al Līth S Arabia			22C4 Anacapa Is USA
			4D3 Anchorage USA
			30C2 Ancohuma Mt Bol
			32B6 Ancón Peru

Ancona

52B2 **Ancona** Italy
16C1 **Ancram** USA
29B4 **Ancud** Chile
34A3 **Andacollo** Arg
108A1 **Andado** Aust
32C6 **Andahuaylas** Peru
38F6 **Andalnes** Nor
50A2 **Andalucia** Region, Spain
17A1 **Andalusia** USA
83D4 **Andaman S** Myan
83D4 **Andaman S** Myan
108A2 **Andamooka** Aust
38H5 **Andenes** Nor
47C1 **Andermatt** Switz
57B2 **Andernach** Germany
14A2 **Anderson** Indiana, USA
18B2 **Anderson** Missouri, USA
17B1 **Anderson** S Carolina, USA
4F3 **Anderson** *R* Can
87B1 **Andhra Pradesh** State, India
55B3 **Andikithira** *I* Greece
65J5 **Andizhan** Uzbekistan
65H6 **Andkhui** Afghan
74B3 **Andong** S Korea
51C1 **Andorra** Principality, SW Europe
51C1 **Andorra-La-Vella** Andorra
43D4 **Andover** Eng
35A2 **Andradina** Brazil
12B2 **Andreafsky** USA
55B3 **Andreas,C** Cyprus
53C2 **Andria** Italy
11C4 **Andros** *I* The Bahamas
55B3 **Andros** *I* Greece
87A2 **Androth** *I* India
50B2 **Andújar** Spain
100A2 **Andulo** Angola
97C4 **Anécho** Togo
97A3 **Anéfis** Mali
34B3 **Añelo** Arg
63C2 **Angarsk** Russian Fed
38H6 **Ange** Sweden
24A2 **Angel de la Guarda** *I* Mexico
79B2 **Angeles** Phil
39G7 **Angelholm** Sweden
109C1 **Angellala Creek** *R* Aust
22B1 **Angels Camp** USA
71E4 **Angemuk** *Mt* Indon
48B2 **Angers** France
76C3 **Angkor** *Hist Site* Camb
41C3 **Anglesey** County Wales
41C3 **Anglesey** *I* Wales
19A4 **Angleton** USA
6G3 **Angmagssalik** Greenland
101D2 **Angoche** Mozam
29B3 **Angol** Chile
14B2 **Angola** Indiana, USA
100A2 **Angola** Republic, Africa
103H6 **Angola Basin** Atlantic O
12H3 **Angoon** USA
48C2 **Angoulême** France
96A1 **Angra do Heroísmo** Açores
35C2 **Angra dos Reis** Brazil
34C3 **Anguil** Arg
27E3 **Anguilla** *I* Caribbean S
26B2 **Anguilla Cays** *Is* Caribbean S
86B2 **Angul** India
99C3 **Angumu** Zaire
43A2 **Angus** Division, Scot
56C1 **Anholt** *I* Den
73C4 **Anhua** China
72D3 **Anhui** Province, China
12C2 **Aniak** USA
35B1 **Anicuns** Brazil
46B2 **Anizy-le-Château** France

4C3 **Anjak** USA
48B2 **Anjou** Region, France
101D2 **Anjouan** *I* Comoros
101D2 **Anjozorobe** Madag
74B3 **Anju** N Korea
72B3 **Ankang** China
92B2 **Ankara** Turk
101D2 **Ankaratra** *Mt* Madag
101D3 **Ankazoabo** Madag
101D2 **Ankazobe** Madag
56C2 **Anklam** Germany
76D3 **An Loc** Viet
73B4 **Anlong** China
73C3 **Anlu** China
18C2 **Anna** USA
96C1 **'Annaba** Alg
92C3 **An Nabk** S Arabia
92C3 **An Nabk** Syria
108A1 **Anna Creek** Aust
80C3 **An Nafud** *Desert* S Arabia
93D3 **An Najaf** Iraq
42C2 **Annan** Scot
15C3 **Annapolis** USA
86A1 **Annapurna** *Mt* Nepal
14B2 **Ann Arbor** USA
94C1 **An Näsirah** Syria
93D3 **An Näsiriyah** Iraq
47B2 **Annecy** France
47B1 **Annemasse** France
76D3 **An Nhon** Viet
73A5 **Anning** China
17A1 **Anniston** USA
89E8 **Annobon** *I* Eq Guinea
49C2 **Annonay** France
27J1 **Annotto Bay** Jamaica
73D3 **Anqing** China
72B2 **Ansai** China
57C3 **Ansbach** Germany
26C3 **Anse d'Hainault** Haiti
72E1 **Anshan** China
73B4 **Anshun** China
97C3 **Ansongo** Mali
14B3 **Ansted** USA
92C2 **Antakya** Turk
101E2 **Antalaha** Madag
92B2 **Antalya** Turk
92B2 **Antalya Körfezi** *B* Turk
101D2 **Antananarivo** Madag
112C1 **Antarctic Circle** Ant
112C3 **Antarctic Pen** Ant
50B2 **Antequera** Spain
96B2 **Anti-Atlas** *Mts* Mor
7D5 **Anticosti, I. d'** Can
27E3 **Antigua** *I* Caribbean S
Anti Lebanon = Jebel esh Sharqi
21A2 **Antioch** USA
19A3 **Antlers** USA
30B3 **Antofagasta** Chile
45C1 **Antrim** County, N Ire
45C1 **Antrim** N Ire
45C1 **Antrim Hills** N Ire
101D2 **Antseranana** Madag
101D2 **Antsirabe** Madag
101D2 **Antsohiny** Madag
76D3 **An Tuc** Viet
46C1 **Antwerpen** Belg
45C2 **An Uaimh** Irish Rep
84C3 **Anupgarh** India
87C3 **Anuradhapura** Sri Lanka
Anvers = Antwerpen
4B3 **Anvik** USA
63B3 **Anxi** China
72C2 **Anyang** China
72A3 **A'nyêmaqên Shan** *Upland* China
47C2 **Anza** *R* Italy
13E1 **Anzac** Can
65K4 **Anzhero-Sudzhensk** Russian Fed
53B2 **Anzio** Italy
74E2 **Aomori** Japan
52A1 **Aosta** Italy
97B3 **Aoukar** *Desert Region* Maur
96C2 **Aoulef** Alg
95A2 **Aozou** Chad
30E3 **Apa** *R* Brazil/Par

11B4 **Apalachee B** USA
17B2 **Apalachicola** USA
17A2 **Apalachicola B** USA
23B2 **Apan** Mexico
64E3 **Apatity** Russian Fed
32C3 **Apaporis** *R* Colombia
35A2 **Aparecida do Taboado** Brazil
79B2 **Aparri** Phil
54A1 **Apatin** Croatia
64E3 **Apatity** Russian Fed
24B3 **Apatzingan** Mexico
56B2 **Apeldoorn** Neth
87B2 **Apiai** Brazil
33F2 **Apoera** Surinam
108B3 **Apollo Bay** Aust
79C4 **Apo,Mt** *Mt* Phil
30F2 **Aporé** *R* Brazil
10A2 **Apostle Is** USA
10A2 **Apostle L** USA
23A1 **Apozol** Mexico
11B3 **Appalachian Mts** USA
52B2 **Appennino Abruzzese** *Mts* Italy
52A2 **Appennino Ligure** *Mts* Italy
53C2 **Appennino Lucano** *Mts* Italy
53B2 **Appennino Napoletano** *Mts* Italy
52B2 **Appennino Tosco-Emiliano** *Mts* Italy
52B2 **Appennino Umbro-Marchigiano** *Mts* Italy
47C1 **Appenzell** Switz
42C2 **Appleby** Eng
14A2 **Appleton** Wisconsin, USA
30F3 **Apucarana** Brazil
23B1 **Apulco** Mexico
32D2 **Apure** *R* Ven
32C6 **Apurímac** *R* Peru
92C4 **'Aqaba** Jordan
92B4 **'Aqaba,G of** Egypt/S Arabia
90B3 **'Aqdā** Iran
30E3 **Aquidauana** Brazil
23A2 **Aquila** Mexico
86A1 **Ara** India
17A1 **Arab** USA
81D4 **Arabian S** Asia/Arabian Pen
31D4 **Aracajú** Brazil
30E3 **Aracanguy, Mts de** Par
31D2 **Aracati** Brazil
30F3 **Araçatuba** Brazil
50A2 **Aracena** Spain
31C5 **Araçuaí** Brazil
94B3 **Arad** Israel
60B4 **Arad** Rom
98C1 **Arada** Chad
91B5 **'Arādah** UAE
106C1 **Arafura S** Indon/Aust
30F2 **Aragarças** Brazil
51B1 **Aragón** Region, Spain
50B1 **Aragón** *R* Spain
33G6 **Araguaia** *R* Brazil
31B3 **Araguaina** Brazil
31B5 **Araguari** Brazil
31B3 **Araguari** *R* Brazil
75B1 **Arai** Japan
96C2 **Arak** Alg
90A3 **Arāk** Iran
76A2 **Arakan Yoma** *Mts* Myan
87B2 **Arakkonam** India
65G5 **Aral Sea** Kazakhstan/Uzbekistan
80E1 **Aral'sk** Kazakhstan
Aral'skoye More = Aral S
40B2 **Aran** *I* Irish Rep
50B1 **Aranda de Duero** Spain
50B1 **Aranjuez** Spain
75A2 **Arao** Japan

97B3 **Araouane** Mali
29E2 **Arapey** *R* Urug
31D4 **Arapiraca** Brazil
35A2 **Araporgas** Brazil
30G4 **Ararangua** Brazil
31B6 **Araraquara** Brazil
35B2 **Araras** Brazil
107D4 **Ararat** Aust
93D2 **Ararat** Armenia
93C2 **Aras** *R* Azerbaijan
75C1 **Arato** Japan
32D2 **Arauca** *R* Ven
34A3 **Arauco** Chile
32C2 **Arauca** Colombia
85C4 **Aravalli Range** *Mts* India
31B5 **Araxá** Brazil
99D2 **Arba Minch** Eth
53A3 **Arbatax** Sardegna
93D2 **Arbil** Iraq
47A1 **Arbois** France
39H6 **Arbrå** Sweden
44C3 **Arbroath** Scot
47A1 **Arc** France
47B2 **Arc** *R* France
48B3 **Arcachon** France
17B2 **Arcadia** USA
20B2 **Arcata** USA
23A2 **Arcelia** Mexico
26B2 **Archipiélago de Camaguey** *Arch* Cuba
29B6 **Archipiélago de la Reina Adelaida** *Arch* Chile
29B4 **Archipiélago de las Chones** *Arch* Chile
32B2 **Archipiélago de las Perlas** *Arch* Panama
35B2 **Arcos** Brazil
50A2 **Arcos de la Frontera** Spain
6B2 **Arctic Bay** Can
1C1 **Arctic Circle**
4E3 **Arctic Red** Can
4E3 **Arctic Red** *R* Can
4D3 **Arctic Village** USA
54C2 **Arda** *R* Bulg
65F6 **Ardabil** Iran
93D1 **Ardahan** Turk
39F6 **Årdal** Nor
96C2 **Ardar des Iforas** *Upland* Alg/Mali
45C2 **Ardee** Irish Rep
90B2 **Ardekän** Iran
46C2 **Ardennes** Department, France
57A2 **Ardennes** Region, Belg
90B3 **Ardestan** Iran
45C2 **Ardh es Suwwan** *Desert Region* Jordan
50A2 **Ardila** *R* Port
109C2 **Ardlethan** Aust
9D3 **Ardmore** USA
44A3 **Ardnamurchan** *Pt* Scot
46A1 **Ardres** France
44B3 **Ardrishaig** Scot
42B2 **Ardrossan** Scot
27D3 **Arecibo** Puerto Rico
31D2 **Areia Branca** Brazil
21A2 **Arena,Pt** USA
39F7 **Arendal** Nor
30B2 **Arequipa** Peru
52B2 **Arezzo** Italy
52B2 **Argenta** Italy
49C2 **Argentan** France
46B2 **Argenteuil** France
28C7 **Argentina** Republic, S America
103F7 **Argentine Basin** Atlantic O
48C2 **Argenton-sur-Creuse** France
54C2 **Argeş** *R* Rom
84B2 **Arghadab** *R* Afghan
55B3 **Argolikós Kólpos** *G* Greece
46C2 **Argonne** Region, France
55B3 **Árgos** Greece
55B3 **Argostólion** Greece

4

22B3 Arguello,Pt USA
106B2 Argyle,L Aust
44B3 Argyll and Bute Division, Scot
56C1 Århus Den
100A3 Ariamsvlei Namibia
50B1 Arianzón R Spain
34C2 Arias Arg
97B3 Aribinda Burkina
30B2 Arica Chile
84C2 Arifwala Pak
  Ariha = Jericho
27L1 Arima Trinidad
35B1 Arinos Brazil
33F6 Arinos R Brazil
23A2 Ario de Rosales Mexico
27L1 Aripo,Mt Trinidad
33E5 Aripuana Brazil
33E5 Aripuaná R Brazil
44B3 Arisaig Scot
87B2 Ariskere India
13B2 Aristazabal I Can
34B3 Arizona Arg
9B3 Arizona State, USA
39G7 Ärjäng Sweden
61F3 Arkadak Russian Fed
19B3 Arkadelphia USA
65H4 Arkaly Kazakhstan
11A3 Arkansas State, USA
11A3 Arkansas R USA
18A2 Arkansas City USA
64F3 Arkhangel'sk Russian Fed
41B3 Arklow Irish Rep
47D1 Arlberg P Austria
49C3 Arles France
19A3 Arlington Texas, USA
15C3 Arlington Virginia, USA
20B1 Arlington Washington, USA
97C3 Arlit Niger
57B3 Arlon Belg
  Armageddon = Megiddo
45C1 Armagh County, N Ire
45C1 Armagh N Ire
61F5 Armavir Russian Fed
23A2 Armenia Mexico
32B3 Armenia Colombia
65F5 Armenia Republic, Europe
107E4 Armidale Aust
13D2 Armstrong Can
7C3 Arnaud R Can
92B2 Arnauti C Cyprus
56B2 Arnhem Neth
106C2 Arnhem,C Aust
106C2 Arnhem Land Aust
22B1 Arnold USA
15C1 Arnprior Can
46E1 Arnsberg Germany
100A3 Aroab Namibia
47C2 Arona Italy
12B2 Aropuk L USA
52A1 Arosa Switz
97A3 Arquipélago dos Bijagós Arch Guinea-Bissau
93D3 Ar Ramadi Iraq
42B2 Arran I Scot
93C2 Ar Raqqah Syria
95A2 Ar Raqubah Libya
49C1 Arras France
96A2 Arecife Canary Is
34C2 Arrecifes Arg
23A1 Arriaga Mexico
93E3 Ar Rifa'i Iraq
93E3 Ar Rihab Desert Region Iraq
91A5 Ar Riyad S Arabia
44B3 Arrochar Scot
111A2 Arrowtown NZ
23B1 Arroyo Seco Mexico
91B4 Ar Ru'ays Qatar
91C5 Ar Rustaq Oman
93D3 Ar Rutbah Iraq
49D2 Arsizio Italy
61G2 Arsk Russian Fed
55B3 Árta Greece

23A2 Arteaga Mexico
63B2 Artemovsk Russian Fed
63D2 Artemovskiy Russian Fed
9C3 Artesia USA
111B2 Arthur R NZ
112C2 Artigas Base Ant
29E2 Artigas Urug
4H3 Artillery L Can
48C1 Artois Region, France
112C2 Arturo Prat Base Ant
93D1 Artvin Turk
99D2 Aru Zaïre
33G6 Aruanã Brazil
27C4 Aruba I Caribbean S
86B1 Arun R Nepal
86C1 Arunāchal Pradesh Union Territory, India
87B3 Aruppukkottai India
99D3 Arusha Tanz
98C2 Aruwimi R Zaïre
68C2 Arvayheer Mongolia
47B2 Arve R France
7C5 Arvida Can
38H5 Arvidsjaur Sweden
39G7 Arvika Sweden
21B2 Arvin USA
94B1 Arwad I Syria
61F2 Arzamas Russian Fed
96B2 Asadabad Afghan
75A2 Asahi R Japan
74E2 Asahi dake Mt Japan
74E2 Asahikawa Japan
86B2 Asansol India
95A2 Asawanwah Well Libya
61K2 Asbest Russian Fed
103H5 Ascension I Atlantic O
57B3 Aschaffenburg Germany
56C2 Aschersleben Germany
52B2 Ascoli Piceno Italy
47C1 Ascona Switz
99E1 Aseb Eritrea
96C2 Asedjirad Upland Alg
99D2 Asela Eth
52B2 Asenovgrad Bulg
46C2 Asfeld France
61J2 Asha Russian Fed
111B2 Ashburn NZ
111B2 Ashburton NZ
106A3 Ashburton R Aust
92B3 Ashdod Israel
19B3 Ashdown USA
11B3 Asheville USA
109D1 Ashford Aust
43E4 Ashford Eng
  Ashgabat = Ashkhabad
74D3 Ashikaga Japan
75A2 Ashizuri-misaki Pt Japan
65G6 Ashkhabad Turkmenistan
10B3 Ashland Kentucky, USA
18A1 Ashland Nebraska, USA
14B2 Ashland Ohio, USA
8A2 Ashland Oregon, USA
109C1 Ashley Aust
16B2 Ashokan Res USA
94B3 Ashqelon Israel
93D3 Ash Shabakh Iraq
91C4 Ash Sha'm UAE
93D2 Ash Sharqat Iraq
93D3 Ash Shatrah Iraq
81C4 Ash Shihr Yemen
91A4 Ash Shumlul S Arabia
14B2 Ashtabula USA
7D4 Ashuanipi L Can
92C3 'Āsi R Syria
47D2 Asiago Italy
53A2 Asinara I Medit S

65K4 Asino Russian Fed
93D2 Aşkale Turk
39G7 Askersund Sweden
84C1 Āsmar Afghan
95A3 Asmera Eritrea
75A2 Aso Japan
99D1 Asosa Eth
111A2 Aspiring,Mt NZ
93C2 As Sabkhah Syria
91A5 As Salamiyah S Arabia
92C2 As Salmān Iraq
86C1 Assam State, India
93E3 As Samāwah Iraq
91B5 As Şanām Region, S Arabia
94C2 As Sanamayn Syria
56B1 Assen Neth
56B1 Assens Den
95A1 As Sidrah Libya
5H5 Assiniboia Can
5G4 Assiniboine,Mt Can
30F3 Assis Brazil
93C3 As Sukhnah Syria
93E2 As Sulaymānīyah Iraq
91A5 As Summan Region, S Arabia
99E3 Assumption I Seychelles
92C3 As Suwaydā' Syria
93D3 As Suwayrah Iraq
93E2 Astara Azerbaijan
52A2 Asti Italy
55C3 Astipálaia I Greece
50A1 Astorga Spain
8A2 Astoria USA
61G4 Astrakhan' Russian Fed
61G4 Astrakhan' Division, Russian Fed
50A1 Asturias Region, Spain
30E4 Asunción Par
99D2 Aswa R Uganda
80B3 Aswân Egypt
95C2 Aswân High Dam Egypt
95C2 Asyût Egypt
92C3 As Zilaf Syria
97C4 Atakpamé Togo
71D4 Atambua Indon
6E3 Atangmik Greenland
96A2 Atar Maur
65J5 Atasu Kazakhstan
95C3 Atatisk Baraji Res Turkmenistan
95C3 Atbara Sudan
65H4 Atbasar Kazakhstan
11A4 Atchafalaya B USA
10A3 Atchison USA
16B3 Atco USA
23A1 Atenguillo Mexico
52B2 Atessa Italy
46B1 Ath Belg
13E2 Athabasca Can
5H4 Athabasca R Can
4H5 Athabasca L Can
45B2 Athenry Irish Rep
  Athens = Athína
11B3 Athens Georgia, USA
14B3 Athens Ohio, USA
19A3 Athens Texas, USA
55B3 Athina Greece
41B3 Athlone Irish Rep
16C1 Athol USA
55B3 Áthos Mt Greece
45C2 Athy Irish Rep
98B1 Ati Chad
7A4 Atikoken Can
61F3 Atkarsk Russian Fed
18B2 Atkins USA
23B2 Atlacomulco Mexico
11B3 Atlanta Georgia, USA
14B2 Atlanta Michigan, USA
18A1 Atlantic USA
10C3 Atlantic City USA
16B2 Atlantic Highlands USA
103H6 Atlantic Indian Basin Atlantic O

103H7 Atlantic Indian Ridge Atlantic O
96C1 Atlas Saharien Mts Alg
4E4 Atlin Can
4E4 Atlin L Can
94B2 'Atlit Israel
23B2 Atlixco Mexico
11B3 Atmore USA
101D3 Atofinandrahana Madag
12D3 Atognak I USA
19A3 Atoka USA
23A1 Atotonilco Mexico
23B2 Atoyac R Mexico
32B2 Atrato R Colombia
91B5 Attaf Region, UAE
81C3 At Tā'if S Arabia
94C2 At Tall Syria
17A1 Attalla USA
7B4 Attauapiskat Can
7B4 Attauapiskat R Can
93D3 At Taysiyah Desert Region S Arabia
14A2 Attica Indiana, USA
46C2 Attigny France
15D2 Attleboro Massachusetts, USA
76D3 Attopeu Laos
92C4 At Tubayq Upland S Arabia
34B3 Atuel R Arg
39H7 Atvidaberg Sweden
22B2 Atwater USA
49D3 Aubagne France
46C2 Aube Department, France
49C3 Aubenas France
17A1 Auburn Alabama, USA
21A2 Auburn California, USA
14A2 Auburn Indiana, USA
18A1 Auburn Nebraska, USA
15C2 Auburn New York, USA
20B1 Auburn Washington, USA
48C3 Auch France
110B1 Auckland NZ
105G6 Auckland Is NZ
48C3 Aude R France
7B4 Auden Can
47B1 Audincourt France
109C1 Augathella Aust
57C3 Augsburg Germany
106A4 Augusta Aust
11B3 Augusta Georgia, USA
18A2 Augusta Kansas, USA
10D2 Augusta Maine, USA
12D3 Augustine I USA
58C2 Augustów Pol
106A3 Augustus,Mt Aust
46A2 Aumale France
85D3 Auraiya India
85D5 Aurangābād India
96C1 Aurès Mts Alg
48C3 Aurillac France
8C3 Aurora Colorado, USA
10B2 Aurora Illinois, USA
14B3 Aurora Indiana, USA
18B2 Aurora Mississippi, USA
100A3 Aus Namibia
14B2 Au Sable USA
10A2 Austin Minnesota, USA
21B2 Austin Nevada, USA
9D3 Austin Texas, USA
106C3 Australia Fed. State/ Monarchy
107D4 Australian Alps Mts Aust
37E4 Austria Federal Republic, Europe
46A1 Authie R France
24B3 Autlán Mexico
49C2 Autun France
49C2 Auvergne Region, France

Auxerre

49C2 **Auxerre** France
46B1 **Auxi-le-Châteaux**
       France
49C2 **Avallon** France
22C4 **Avalon** USA
7E5 **Avalon Pen** Can
35B2 **Avaré** Brazil
90D3 **Avaz** Iran
94B3 **Avedat** *Hist Site*
       Israel
33F4 **Aveiro** Brazil
50A1 **Aveiro** Port
29E2 **Avellaneda** Arg
53B2 **Avellino** Italy
46B1 **Avesnes-sur-Helpe**
       France
39H6 **Avesta** Sweden
52B2 **Avezzano** Italy
44C3 **Aviemore** Scot
111B2 **Aviemore,L** NZ
47B2 **Avigliana** Italy
49C3 **Avignon** France
50A1 **Avila** Spain
50A1 **Aviles** Spain
47D1 **Avisio** *R* Italy
108B3 **Avoca** *R* Aust
43D4 **Avon** *R* Dorset, Eng
43D3 **Avon** *R* Warwick,
       Eng
43C4 **Avonmouth** Wales
17B2 **Avon Park** USA
46B2 **Avre** *R* France
54A2 **Avtovac** Bosnia-
       Herzegovina
94C2 **A'waj** *R* Syria
74D4 **Awaji-shima** *B*
       Japan
99E2 **Awarē** Eth
111A2 **Awarua Pt** NZ
99E2 **Awash** Eth
99E2 **Awash** *R* Eth
75B1 **Awa-shima** *I* Japan
111B2 **Awatere** *R* NZ
95A2 **Awbārī** Libya
95D2 **Aweil** Sudan
98B2 **Awjilah** Libya
96A2 **Awserd** *Well* Mor
6A2 **Axel Heiburg I** Can
43C4 **Axminster** Eng
75B1 **Ayabe** Japan
29E3 **Ayacucho** Arg
32C6 **Ayacucho** Peru
65K5 **Ayaguz** Kazakhstan
82C2 **Ayakkum Hu** *L*
       China
50A2 **Ayamonte** Spain
63F2 **Ayan** Russian Fed
32C6 **Ayauiri** Peru
92A2 **Aydin** Turk
55C3 **Ayios Evstrátios** *I*
       Greece
43D4 **Aylesbury** Eng
13D2 **Aylmer,Mt** Can
94C2 **'Ayn al Fijah** Syria
93D2 **Ayn Zalah** Iraq
95B2 **Ayn Zuwayyah** *Well*
       Libya
99D2 **Ayod** Sudan
107D2 **Ayr** Aust
42B2 **Ayr** Scot
42B2 **Ayr** *R* Scot
42B2 **Ayre,Pt of** Eng
54C2 **Aytos** Bulg
76C3 **Ayutthaya** Thai
23A1 **Ayutla** Mexico
55C3 **Ayvacik** Turk
55C3 **Ayvalik** Turk
86A1 **Azamgarh** India
97B3 **Azaouad** *Desert
       Region* Mali
97D3 **Azare** Nig
92C2 **A'Zāz** Syria
       Azbine = Aïr
65F5 **Azerbaijan** Republic
       Asia
32B4 **Azogues** Ecuador
       Azores = Açores
98C1 **Azoum** *R* Chad
60E4 **Azov, Sea of**
       Russian Fed/Ukraine
       **Azovskoye More =
       Azov, Sea of**
96B1 **Azrou** Mor
34D3 **Azucena** Arg

32A2 **Azuero,Pen de**
       Panama
29E3 **Azul** Arg
94C2 **Az-Zabdānī** Syria
91C5 **Az Zāhirah** *Mts*
       Oman
95A2 **Az Zahra** Iraq
96A2 **Azzeffal** *R* Maur
93E3 **Az Zubayr** Iraq

B

94B2 **Ba'albek** Leb
92C3 **Ba'albek** Leb
94C2 **Ba'al Hazor** *Mt* Israel
99E2 **Baardheere** Somalia
54C2 **Babadag** Rom
92A1 **Babaeski** Turk
32B4 **Babahoyo** Ecuador
81C4 **Bāb al Mandab** *Str*
       Djibouti/Yemen
71D4 **Babar** *I* Indon
99D3 **Babati** Tanz
60E2 **Babayevo**
       Russian Fed
14B2 **Baberton** USA
13B1 **Babine** *R* Can
5F4 **Babine L** Can
90B2 **Bābol** Iran
79B2 **Babuyan Chan** Phil
79B2 **Babuyan Is** Phil
31C2 **Bacabal** Brazil
71D4 **Bacan** *I* Indon
60C4 **Bacau** Rom
76D1 **Bac Can** Viet
108B3 **Bacchus Marsh** Aust
82B2 **Bachu** China
4J3 **Back** *R* Can
12J2 **Backbone Ranges**
       Mts Can
76D1 **Bac Ninh** Viet
79B2 **Bacolod** Phil
79B3 **Baco,Mt** Phil
87B2 **Badagara** India
72A1 **Badain Jaran Shamo**
       Desert China
50A2 **Badajoz** Spain
51C1 **Badalona** Spain
93D3 **Badanah** S Arabia
46D2 **Bad Bergzabern**
       Germany
46D1 **Bad Ems** Germany
47C1 **Baden** Switz
57B3 **Baden-Baden**
       Germany
57B3 **Baden-Württemberg**
       State, Germany
57C3 **Badgastein** Austria
22C2 **Badger** USA
57B2 **Bad-Godesberg**
       Germany
57B2 **Bad Hersfeld**
       Germany
46D1 **Bad Honnef**
       Germany
85B4 **Badin** Pak
52B1 **Bad Ischl** Austria
93C3 **Badiyat ash Sham**
       Desert Region
       Jordan/Iraq
57B3 **Bad-Kreuznach**
       Germany
46D1 **Bad Nevenahr-
       Ahrweiler** Germany
47C1 **Bad Ragaz** Switz
57C3 **Bad Tolz** Germany
87C3 **Badulla** Sri Lanka
50B2 **Baena** Spain
97A3 **Bafata** Guinea-Bissau
4H2 **Baffin** *Region* Can
6C2 **Baffin B** Greenland/
       Can
6C2 **Baffin I** Can
98B2 **Bafia** Can
97A3 **Bafing** *R* Mali
97A3 **Bafoulabe** Mali
98B2 **Bafoussam** Cam
90C3 **Bafq** Iran
60E5 **Bafra Burun** *Pt* Turk
91C4 **Bāft** Iran
98B2 **Bafwasende** Zaïre
86A1 **Bagaha** India
87B1 **Bāgalkot** India
99D3 **Bagamoyo** Tanz
29F2 **Bagé** Brazil

93D3 **Baghdad** Iraq
86B2 **Bagherhat** Bang
91C3 **Bāghīn** Iran
84B1 **Baghlan** Afghan
49C3 **Bagnols-sur-Cèze**
       France
97B3 **Bagoé** *R* Mali
       Bagu = Pegu
79B2 **Baguio** Phil
86B1 **Bāhādurābād** India
11C4 **Bahamas,The** *Is*
       Caribbean S
86B2 **Baharampur** India
92A4 **Bahariya Oasis**
       Egypt
84C3 **Bahawalpur** Pak
84C3 **Bahawalpur**
       Province, Pak
85C3 **Bahawalnagar** Pak
       Bahia = Salvador
31C4 **Bahia** State, Brazil
29D3 **Bahia Blanca** Arg
29D3 **Bahia Blanca** *B* Arg
34A3 **Bahia Concepcion** *B*
       Chile
35C2 **Bahia da Ilha Grande**
       B Brazil
24B2 **Bahia de Banderas** *B*
       Mexico
24C2 **Bahia de Campeche**
       B Mexico
25D3 **Bahia de la Ascension**
       B Mexico
24B3 **Bahia de Petacalco** *B*
       Mexico
96A2 **Bahia de Rio de Oro**
       B Mor
35C2 **Bahia de Sepetiba** *B*
       Brazil
29C6 **Bahia Grande** *B* Arg
9B4 **Bahia Kino** Mexico
24A2 **Bahia Magdalena** *B*
       Mexico
24A2 **Bahia Sebastia
       Vizcaino** *B* Mexico
99D1 **Bahar Dar** Eth
86A1 **Baharaich** India
80D3 **Bahrain** Sheikdom,
       Arabian Pen
93D3 **Bahr al Milh** *L* Iraq
98C2 **Bahr Aouk** *R* Chad/
       CAR
       Bahrat Lut = Dead S
98C2 **Bahr el Arab**
       Watercourse Sudan
99D2 **Bahr el Ghazal** *R*
       Sudan
98B1 **Bahr el Ghazal**
       Watercourse Chad
101H1 **Baia de Maputo** *B*
       Mozam
31B2 **Baia de Marajó** *B*
       Brazil
101D2 **Baia de Pemba** *B*
       Mozam
31C2 **Baia de São Marcos**
       B Brazil
50A2 **Baia de Setúbal** *B*
       Port
31D4 **Baia de Todos os
       Santos** *B* Brazil
100A2 **Baia dos Tigres**
       Angola
60B4 **Baia Mare** Rom
98B2 **Baïbokoum** Chad
69E2 **Baicheng** China
101E2 **Baie Antongila** *B*
       Madag
7D5 **Baie-Comeau** Can
101D2 **Baie de Bombetoka**
       B Madag
101D2 **Baie de Mahajamba**
       B Madag
101D3 **Baie de St Augustin** *B*
       Madag
94B2 **Baie de St Georges** *B*
       Leb
10D2 **Baie des Chaleurs** *B*
       Can
7C4 **Baie-du-Poste** Can
72B3 **Baihe** China
72C3 **Bai He** *R* China
93D3 **Ba'iji** Iraq
86A2 **Baikunthpur** India

       **Baile Atha Cliath =
       Dublin**
54B2 **Băilesti** Rom
46B1 **Bailleul** France
72A3 **Baima** China
17B1 **Bainbridge** USA
12B2 **Baird Inlet** USA
4B3 **Baird Mts** USA
72D1 **Bairin Youqi** China
72D1 **Bairin Zuoqi** China
107D4 **Bairnsdale** Aust
79B4 **Bais** Phil
54A1 **Baja** Hung
9B3 **Baja California** State,
       Mexico
24A1 **Baja California** *Pen*
       Mexico
61J2 **Bakal** Russian Fed
98C2 **Bakala** CAR
97A3 **Bakel** Sen
8C2 **Baker** Montana,
       USA
8B2 **Baker** Oregon, USA
6A3 **Baker Foreland** *Pt*
       Can
4J3 **Baker L** Can
4J3 **Baker Lake** Can
8A2 **Baker,Mt** USA
9B3 **Bakersfield** USA
90C2 **Bakharden**
       Turkmenistan
90C2 **Bakhardok**
       Turkmenistan
60D3 **Bakhmach** Ukraine
38C1 **Bakkaflói** *B* Iceland
99D2 **Bako** Eth
99D2 **Bakouma** CAR
65F5 **Baku** Azerbaijan
       Baky = Baku
92B2 **Balâ** Turk
79A4 **Balabac** *I* Phil
70C3 **Balabac** *Str* Malay
78C2 **Balaikarangan** Indon
108A2 **Balaklava** Aust
61G3 **Balakovo**
       Russian Fed
86A2 **Balangir** India
61F3 **Balashov**
       Russian Fed
86B2 **Balasore** India
80A3 **Balat** Egypt
52C1 **Balaton** *L* Hung
29E3 **Balcarce** Arg
54C2 **Balchik** Bulg
111B3 **Balclutha** NZ
18B2 **Bald Knob** USA
17B1 **Baldwin** USA
9C3 **Baldy Peak** *Mt* USA
       **Balearic Is = Islas
       Baleares**
78C2 **Baleh** *R* Malay
79B2 **Baler** Phil
61H2 **Balezino** Russian Fed
106A1 **Bali** *I* Indon
92A2 **Balikesir** Turk
93C2 **Balikh** *R* Syria
78D3 **Balikpapan** Indon
79B2 **Balintang Chan** Phil
78C4 **Bali S** Indon
35A1 **Baliza** Brazil
84B1 **Balkh** Afghan
65J5 **Balkhash** Kazakhstan
44B3 **Balachulish** Scot
45B2 **Ballaghaderreen**
       Irish Rep
42B2 **Ballantrae** Scot
4G2 **Ballantyne Str** Can
87B2 **Ballapur** India
107D4 **Ballarat** Aust
42B2 **Ballater** Scot
112C7 **Balleny Is** Ant
86A1 **Ballia** India
109D1 **Ballina** Aust
41B3 **Ballina** Irish Rep
45B2 **Ballinasloe** Irish Rep
45B2 **Ballinrobe** Irish Rep
55A2 **Ballsh** Alb
45B1 **Ballycastle** Irish Rep
45C1 **Ballycastle** N Ire
45C1 **Ballymena** N Ire
45C1 **Ballymoney** N Ire
45B1 **Ballyshannon**
       Irish Rep

45B2 Ballyvaghan
Irish Rep
108B3 Balmoral Aust
34C2 Balnearia Arg
84B3 Balochistān Region,
Pak
100A2 Balombo Angola
109C1 Balonn R Aust
85C3 Balotra India
86A1 Balrāmpur India
107D4 Balranald Aust
31B3 Balsas Brazil
23B2 Balsas Mexico
24B3 Balsas R Mexico
60C4 Balta Ukraine
39H7 Baltic S N Europe
92B3 Baltim Egypt
45B3 Baltimore Irish Rep
10C3 Baltimore USA
86B1 Bālurghāt India
61H4 Balykshi Kazakhstan
91C4 Bam Iran
98B1 Bama Nig
97B3 Bamako Mali
96C2 Bambari CAR
17B1 Bamberg USA
57C3 Bamberg Germany
98C2 Bambili Zaire
35B2 Bamboi Brazil
98B2 Bamenda Can
13C3 Bamfield Can
98B2 Bamingui R CAR
98B2 Bamingui Bangoran
National Park CAR
84B2 Bamiyan Afghan
91D4 Bampūr Iran
91D4 Bampūr R Iran
98C2 Banalia Zaire
97B3 Banamba Mali
76C3 Ban Aranyaprathet
Thai
76C2 Ban Ban Laos
77C4 Ban Betong Thai
45C1 Banbridge N Ire
43D3 Banbury Eng
44C3 Banchory Scot
25D3 Banco Chinchorro Is
Mexico
15C1 Bancroft Can
86A1 Bānda India
70A3 Banda Aceh Indon
97B4 Bandama R Côte
d'Ivoire
91C4 Bandar Abbās Iran
90A2 Bandar Anzalī Iran
99F2 Bandarbeyla Somalia
91B4 Bandar-e Daylam
Iran
91B4 Bandar-e Lengheh
Iran
91B4 Bandar-e Māqām
Iran
91B4 Bandar-e Rig Iran
90B2 Bandar-e Torkoman
Iran
91A3 Bandar Khomeynī
Iran
78C2 Bandar Seri Begawan
Brunei
71D4 Banda S Indon
91C4 Band Boni Iran
35C2 Bandeira Mt Brazil
97B3 Bandiagara Mali
60C5 Bandirma Turk
45B3 Bandon Irish Rep
98B3 Bandundu Zaire
78B4 Bandung Indon
25E2 Banes Cuba
13D2 Banff Can
44C3 Banff Scot
5G4 Banff R Can
13D2 Banff Nat Pk Can
87B2 Bangalore India
98C2 Bangassou CAR
70C3 Banggi I Malay
95B1 Banghāzī Libya
76D2 Bang Hieng R Laos
78B3 Bangka I Indon
78A3 Bangko Indon
76C3 Bangkok Thai
82C3 Bangladesh
Republic, Asia
84D2 Bangong Co L China
10D2 Bangor Maine, USA

45D1 Bangor N Ire
16B2 Bangor
Pennsylvania, USA
42B3 Bangor Wales
78D3 Bangsalsembera
Indon
76B3 Bang Saphan Yai
Thai
79B2 Bangued Phil
98B2 Bangui CAR
100C2 Bangweulu L
Zambia
77C4 Ban Hat Yai Thai
76C2 Ban Hin Heup Laos
51C1 Ban Houei Sai Laos
76B3 Ban Hua Hin Thai
97B3 Bani R Mali
97C3 Bani Bangou Niger
95A1 Bani Walid Libya
92C2 Bāniyās Syria
94B2 Bāniyas Syria
52C2 Banja Luka Bosnia-
Herzegovina
78C3 Banjarmasin Indon
97A3 Banjul The Gambia
71B4 Ban Kantang Thai
76D2 Ban Khemmarat
Laos
77B4 Ban Khok Kloi Thai
71F5 Banks I Aust
5E4 Banks I British
Columbia, Can
4F2 Banks I Northwest
Territories, Can
20C1 Banks L USA
111B2 Banks Pen NZ
109C4 Banks Str Aust
86B2 Bankura India
76B2 Ban Mae Sariang
Thai
76B2 Ban Mae Sot Thai
76D3 Ban Me Thuot Viet
45C1 Bann R N Ire
77B4 Ban Na San Thai
84C2 Bannu Pak
34A3 Baños Maule Chile
76C2 Ban Pak Neun Laos
77C4 Ban Pak Phanang
Thai
76D3 Ban Ru Kroy Camb
76B3 Ban Sai Yok Thai
76C3 Ban Sattahip Thai
59B3 Banská Bystrica
Slovakia
85C4 Bānswāra India
77B4 Ban Tha Kham Thai
76D2 Ban Thateng Laos
76C2 Ban Tha Tum Thai
41B3 Bantry Irish Rep
41A3 Bantry B Irish Rep
76D3 Ban Ya Soup Viet
78C4 Banyuwangi Indon
72C3 Baofeng China
76C1 Bao Ha Viet
72B3 Baoji China
76D3 Bao Loc Viet
68B4 Baoshan China
72C1 Baotou China
87C1 Bāpatla India
46B1 Bapaume France
93D3 Ba'Qūbah Iraq
32J7 Baquerizo Moreno
Ecuador
54A2 Bar Montenegro,
Yugos
99D1 Bara Sudan
99E2 Baraawe Somalia
86A1 Barābanki India
66A1 Barabinsk
Russian Fed
65J4 Barabinsk
Russian Fed
65J4 Barabinskaya Step
Steppe Kazakhstan/
Russian Fed
50B1 Baracaldo Spain
26C2 Baracoa Cuba
94C2 Baradá R Syria
109C2 Baradine Aust
87A1 Bārāmati India
84C2 Bāramūla India
85D3 Bārān India
79B3 Barangas Phil
44C4 Baranof I USA
60C3 Baranovichi Belarus

108A2 Baratta Aust
86B1 Barauni India
31C6 Barbacena Brazil
27F4 Barbados I
Caribbean S
32C1 Barbastro Spain
84B2 Barberton S Africa
48B2 Barbezieux France
32C2 Barbosa Colombia
27E3 Barbuda I
Caribbean S
107D3 Barca = Al Marj
53C3 Barcellona Italy
51C1 Barcelona Spain
33E3 Barcelona Ven
107D3 Barcoo R Aust
34B3 Barda del Medio Arg
95A2 Bardaï Chad
29C3 Bardas Blancas Arg
86B2 Barddhamān India
59C3 Bardejov Slovakia
47C2 Bardi Italy
47B2 Bardonecchia Italy
43B3 Bardsey I Wales
84D3 Bareilly India
64D2 Barentseya I
Barents S
64E2 Barents S
Russian Fed
85A2 Barentu Eritrea
86A2 Bargarh India
47B2 Barge Italy
63D2 Barguzin
Russian Fed
63D2 Barguzin R
Russian Fed
86B2 Barhi India
53C2 Bari Italy
51D2 Bārika Alg
32C2 Barinas Ven
86B2 Baripāda India
84A1 Bari Sādri India
88C2 Barisal Bang
78C3 Barito R Indon
95A2 Barjuj Watercourse
Libya
73A3 Barkam China
18C2 Barkley,L USA
13B3 Barkley Sd Can
100B4 Barkly East S Africa
106C2 Barkly Tableland Mts
Aust
46C2 Bar-le-Duc France
106A3 Barlee,L Aust
106A3 Barlee Range Mts
Aust
53C2 Barletta Italy
85C3 Barmer India
108B2 Barmera Aust
43B3 Barmouth Wales
84D3 Barnard Castle Eng
65K4 Barnaul Russian Fed
16B3 Barnegat USA
16B3 Barnegat B USA
6C2 Barnes Icecap Can
17B1 Barnesville Georgia,
USA
14B3 Barnesville Ohio,
USA
42D3 Barnsley Eng
43B4 Barnstaple Eng
97C4 Baro Nig
32D1 Barquisimeto Ven
31C4 Barra Brazil
44A3 Barra I Scot
109D2 Barraba Aust
23A2 Barra de Navidad
Mexico
35C2 Barra de Piraí Brazil
35A1 Barragem de São
Brazil
35A1 Barra do Garças
Brazil
35B1 Barragem Agua
Vermelha R Brazil
50A2 Barragem do Castelo
do Bode R Brazil
50A2 Barragem do
Maranhão R Brazil
35A2 Barragem Três
Irmãos R Brazil
44A3 Barra Head Pt Scot

31C6 Barra Mansa Brazil
32B6 Barranca Peru
32C2 Barrancabermeja
Colombia
33E2 Barrancas Ven
30E4 Barranqueras Arg
32C1 Barranquilla
Colombia
33E2 Barras Colombia
16C1 Barre USA
34B2 Barreal Arg
31C4 Barreiras Brazil
50A2 Barreiro Port
31D3 Barreiros Brazil
107D5 Barren,C Aust
12D3 Barren Is USA
31B6 Barretos Brazil
13E2 Barrhead Can
14C2 Barrie Can
13C2 Barrière Can
108B2 Barrier Range Mts
Aust
107E4 Barrington,Mt Aust
27N2 Barrouaillie
St Vincent and the
Grenadines
4C2 Barrow USA
27A3 Barrow R Irish Rep
106C3 Barrow Creek Aust
106A3 Barrow I Aust
42C2 Barrow-in-Furness
Eng
4C2 Barrow,Pt USA
6A2 Barrow Str Can
15C1 Barry's Bay Can
87B1 Barsi India
9B3 Barstow USA
49C2 Bar-sur-Aube France
33F2 Bartica Guyana
92B1 Bartin Turk
107D2 Bartle Frere,Mt Aust
9D3 Bartlesville USA
10C3 Bartolomeu Dias
Mozam
58C2 Bartoszyce Pol
86B2 Barung I Indon
85D4 Barwāh India
85C4 Barwāni India
109C1 Barwon R Aust
61G3 Barysh Russian Fed
98B2 Basankusu Zaire
34D2 Basavilbaso Arg
79B1 Basco Phil
52A1 Basel Switz
53C2 Basento R Italy
79B1 Bashi Chan Phil
61H3 Bashkortostan
Division, Russian Fed
79B4 Basilan I Phil
43E4 Basildon Eng
43D4 Basingstoke Eng
8B2 Basin Region USA
93E3 Basra Iraq
46D2 Bas-Rhin
Department, France
76D3 Bassac R Camb
13E2 Bassano Can
52B1 Bassano Italy
47D2 Bassano del Grappa
Italy
97C4 Bassari Togo
101C3 Bassas da India I
Mozam Chan
76A2 Bassein Myan
27E3 Basse Terre
Guadeloupe
97C4 Bassila Benin
22C2 Bass Lake USA
107D4 Bass Str Aust
39G7 Båstad Sweden
84B3 Bastak Iran
86A1 Basti India
52A2 Bastia Corse
57B3 Bastogne Belg
19B3 Bastrop Louisiana,
USA
19A3 Bastrop Texas, USA
98A2 Bata Eq Guinea
78C3 Batakan Indon
84D2 Batala India
68B3 Batang China
88B2 Batangafo CAR

Batan Is

79B1	**Batan Is** Phil
35BJ2	**Batatais** Brazil
15C2	**Batavia** USA
109D3	**Batemans Bay** Aust
17B1	**Batesburg** USA
18B2	**Batesville** Arkansas, USA
19C3	**Batesville** Mississippi, USA
43C4	**Bath** Eng
15C2	**Bath** New York, USA
98B1	**Batha** *R* Chad
43C4	**Bath and North East Somerset** County Eng
107D4	**Bathurst** Aust
7D5	**Bathurst** Can
4F2	**Bathurst,C** Can
106C2	**Bathurst I** Aust
4H2	**Bathurst I** Can
4H3	**Bathurst Inlet** *B* Can
97B3	**Batié** Burkina
90B3	**Bátlāq-e-Gavkhūnī** *Salt Flat* Iran
109C3	**Batlow** Aust
93D2	**Batman** Turk
96C1	**Batna** Alg
11A3	**Baton Rouge** USA
94B1	**Batroun** Leb
76C3	**Battambang** Camb
87C3	**Batticaloa** Sri Lanka
13F2	**Battle** Can
10B2	**Battle Creek** USA
7E4	**Battle Harbour** Can
20C2	**Battle Mountain** USA
78D2	**Batukelau** Indon
65F5	**Batumi** Georgia
77C5	**Batu Pahat** Malay
78A3	**Baturaja** Indon
94B2	**Bat Yam** Israel
71D4	**Baubau** Indon
47B2	**Bauges** *Mts* France
7E4	**Bauld,C** Can
47B1	**Baumes-les-Dames** France
63D2	**Baunt** Russian Fed
31B6	**Bauru** Brazil
35A1	**Baus** Brazil
57C2	**Bautzen** Germany
78C4	**Bawean** Indon
95B2	**Bawiti** Egypt
97B3	**Bawku** Ghana
76B2	**Bawlake** Myan
108A2	**Bawlen** Aust
17B1	**Baxley** USA
25E2	**Bayamo** Cuba
78D4	**Bayan** Indon
68C2	**Bayandzürh** Mongolia
68B3	**Bayan Har Shan** *Mts* China
72A1	**Bayan Mod** China
52B1	**Bayan Obo** China
47A2	**Bayard** *F* France
12J3	**Bayard,Mt** Can
63D3	**Bayasgalant** Mongolia
79B3	**Baybay** Phil
93D1	**Bayburt** Turk
10B2	**Bay City** Michigan, USA
19A4	**Bay City** Texas, USA
92B2	**Bay Daglari** Turk
64H3	**Baydaratskaya Guba** *B* Russian Fed
99E2	**Baydhabo** Somalia
48B2	**Bayeux** France
47D1	**Bayerische Alpen** *Mts* Germany
57C3	**Bayern** State, Germany
92C3	**Bâyir** Jordan
63C2	**Baykalskiy Khrebet** *Mts* Russian Fed
63B1	**Baykit** Russian Fed
63B3	**Baylik Shan** *Mts* China/Mongolia
61J3	**Baymak** Russian Fed
79B2	**Bayombong** Phil
57C3	**Bayreuth** Germany
19C3	**Bay St Louis** USA
15D2	**Bay Shore** USA
15C1	**Bays,L of** Can
68A2	**Bayt Shan** *Mts* China
	Bayt Lahm = Bethlehem
19B4	**Baytown** USA
50B2	**Baza** Spain
59D3	**Bazaliya** Ukraine
48B3	**Bazas** France
73B3	**Bazhong** China
91D4	**Bazmān** Iran
94C1	**Echarre** Leb
16B3	**Beach Haven** USA
43E4	**Beachy Head** Eng
16C2	**Beacon** USA
101D2	**Bealanana** Madag
18B1	**Beardstown** USA
	Bear I = Bjørnøya
22B1	**Bear Valley** USA
8D2	**Beatrice** USA
44C2	**Beatrice** *Oilfield* N Sea
13C1	**Beatton** *R* Can
5F4	**Beatton River** Can
29E6	**Beauchene Is** Falkland Is
109D1	**Beaudesert** Aust
1B5	**Beaufort S** Can
100B4	**Beaufort West** S Africa
15D1	**Beauharnois** Can
44B3	**Beauly** Scot
21B3	**Beaumont** California, USA
11A3	**Beaumont** Texas, USA
49C2	**Beaune** France
48C2	**Beauvais** France
13F1	**Beauval** Can
12E1	**Beaver** Alaska, USA
13F2	**Beaver** *R* Saskatchewan, Can
4D3	**Beaver Creek** Can
12E1	**Beaver Creek** USA
18C2	**Beaver Dam** Kentucky, USA
13E2	**Beaverhill L** Can
14A1	**Beaver I** USA
18B2	**Beaver L** USA
13D1	**Beaverlodge** Can
85C3	**Beawar** India
34B2	**Beazly** Arg
35B2	**Bebedouro** Brazil
43E3	**Beccles** Eng
54B1	**Bečej** Serbia, Yugos
96B1	**Béchar** Alg
12C3	**Becharof L** USA
11B3	**Beckley** USA
43D3	**Bedford** County, Eng
43D3	**Bedford** Eng
14A3	**Bedford** Indiana, USA
27M2	**Bedford Pt** Grenada
42D2	**Beechey R** USA
109C3	**Beechworth** Aust
109D1	**Beenleigh** Aust
92B3	**Beersheba** Israel
	Beër Sheva = Beersheba
94B3	**Beér Sheva** *R* Israel
9D4	**Befale** Can
98C2	**Befale** Zaire
101D3	**Befandriana** Madag
109C3	**Bega** Aust
91B3	**Behbehãn** Iran
12H3	**Behm Canal** *Sd* USA
90B2	**Behshahr** Iran
90B2	**Behsud** Afghan
69E2	**Bei'an** China
73B5	**Beihai** China
72D2	**Beijing** China
76E1	**Beiliu** China
73B4	**Beipan Jiang** *R* China
72E1	**Beipiao** China
	Beira = Sofala
92C3	**Beirut** Leb
68B2	**Bei Shan** *Mts* China
94B2	**Beit ed Dine** Leb
94B3	**Beit Jala** Israel
50A2	**Beja** Port
96C1	**Béja** Tunisia
96C1	**Bejaia** Alg
50A1	**Béjar** Spain
90C3	**Bejestān** Iran
59C3	**Békéscsaba** Hung
101D3	**Bekily** Madag
86A1	**Bela** India
85B3	**Bela** Pak
78C2	**Belaga** Malay
16A3	**Bel Air** USA
87B1	**Belamoalli** India
71D3	**Belang** Indon
70A3	**Belangpidie** Indon
60C3	**Belarus** Republic, Europe
	Belau = Palau Is.
101C4	**Bela Vista** Mozam
70A3	**Belawan** Indon
61J2	**Belaya** *R* Ukraine
6A2	**Belcher Chan** Can
7C4	**Belcher Is** Can
84B1	**Belchiragh** Afghan
61H3	**Belebey** Russian Fed
99E2	**Beled Weyne** Somalia
31B2	**Belém** Brazil
32B3	**Belén** Colombia
34D2	**Belén** Urug
9C3	**Belen** USA
101D2	**Belfast** S Africa
101H1	**Belfast** N Ire
45D1	**Belfast Lough** *Estuary* N Ire
99D1	**Bélfodiyo** Eth
42D2	**Belford** Eng
49D2	**Belfort** France
87A1	**Belgaum** India
56A2	**Belgium** Kingdom, N W Europe
60E3	**Belgorod** Russian Fed
60E3	**Belgorod** Division, Russian Fed
60D4	**Belgorod Dnestrovskiy** Ukraine
	Belgrade = Beograd
95A2	**Bel Hedan** Libya
25D3	**Belize** Belize
25D3	**Belize** Republic, Cent America
48C2	**Belfry** France
5F4	**Bella Coola** Can
47C2	**Bellagio** Italy
19A4	**Bellaire** USA
47C1	**Bellano** Italy
87B1	**Bellary** India
109C1	**Bellata** Aust
47B2	**Belledonne** *Mts* France
8C2	**Belle Fourche** USA
49D2	**Bellegarde** France
7E4	**Belle I** France
7E4	**Belle Isle,Str of** Can
7C5	**Belleville** Can
18A2	**Belleville** Kansas, USA
20B1	**Bellevue** Washington, USA
109D2	**Bellingen** Aust
8A2	**Bellingham** USA
112C2	**Bellingshausen** *Base* Ant
112C3	**Bellingshausen S** Ant
52A1	**Bellinzona** Switz
32B2	**Bello** Colombia
107E3	**Bellona Reefs** Nouvelle Calédonie
22B1	**Bellota** USA
15D2	**Bellows Falls** USA
6B3	**Bell Pen** Can
52B1	**Belluno** Italy
29D2	**Bell Ville** Arg
31D5	**Belmonte** Brazil
25D3	**Belmopan** Belize
45B1	**Belmullet** Irish Rep
69E1	**Belogorsk** Russian Fed
101D3	**Beloha** Madag
31C5	**Belo Horizonte** Brazil
10B2	**Beloit** Wisconsin, USA
64E3	**Belomorsk** Russian Fed
61J3	**Beloretsk** Russian Fed
	Belorussia = Belarus
101D2	**Belo-Tsiribihina** Madag
64E3	**Beloye More** *S* Russian Fed
60E1	**Beloye Ozero** *L* Russian Fed
60E1	**Belozersk** Russian Fed
14B3	**Belpre** USA
108A2	**Beltana** Aust
19A3	**Belton** USA
59D3	**Bel'tsy** Moldova
16B2	**Belvidere** New Jersey, USA
98B3	**Bembe** Angola
97C3	**Bembéréke** Benin
10A2	**Bemidji** USA
39G6	**Bena** Nor
98C3	**Bena Dibele** Zaire
108C3	**Benalla** Aust
44B3	**Ben Attow** *Mt* Scot
50A1	**Benavente** Spain
44A3	**Benbecula** *I* Scot
106A4	**Bencubbin** Aust
8A2	**Bend** USA
44B3	**Ben Dearg** *Mt* Scot
60C4	**Bendery** Moldova
107D4	**Bendigo** Aust
57C3	**Benešov** Czech Republic
53B2	**Benevento** Italy
83C4	**Bengal,B of** Asia
96D1	**Ben Gardane** Tunisia
72D3	**Bengbu** China
78A2	**Bengkalis** Indon
78A3	**Bengkulu** Indon
100A2	**Benguela** Angola
92B3	**Benha** Egypt
44B2	**Ben Hope** *Mt* Scot
99C2	**Beni** Zaire
32D6	**Béni** *R* Bol
96B1	**Beni Abbes** Alg
51C1	**Benicarló** Spain
7A5	**Benidji** USA
51B2	**Benidorm** Spain
95C2	**Beni Mansour** Alg
95C2	**Beni Mazar** Egypt
96B1	**Beni Mellal** Mor
97C4	**Benin** Republic, Africa
97C4	**Benin City** Nig
95C2	**Beni Suef** Egypt
44B2	**Ben Kilbreck** *Mt* Scot
44B3	**Ben Lawers** *Mt* UK
109C4	**Ben Lomond** *Mt* Aust
44C3	**Ben Macdui** *Mt* Scot
44B2	**Ben More Assynt** *Mt* Scot
111B2	**Benmore,L** NZ
44B3	**Ben Nevis** *Mt* Scot
15D2	**Bennington** USA
94B2	**Bennt Jbail** Leb
98B2	**Bénoué** *R* Cam
9B3	**Benson** Arizona, USA
99C2	**Bentiu** Sudan
19B3	**Benton** Arkansas, USA
18C2	**Benton** Kentucky, USA
14A2	**Benton Harbor** USA
97C4	**Benue** *R* Nig
45B1	**Benwee Hd** *C* Irish Rep
44B3	**Ben Wyvis** *Mt* Scot
72E1	**Benxi** China
54B2	**Beograd** Serbia, Yugos
84C4	**Beohari** India
74C4	**Beppu** Japan
55A2	**Berat** Alb
99E1	**Berbera** Somalia
98B2	**Berberati** CAf
46A1	**Berck** France
60C4	**Berdichev** Ukraine
60E4	**Berdyansk** Ukraine
97B4	**Berekum** Ghana
22B2	**Berenda** USA

5J4 Berens R Can
5J4 Berens River Can
108A1 Beresford Aust
59C3 Berettyoujfalu Hung
58D2 Bereza Belarus
59C3 Berezhany Ukraine
65G4 Berezniki Russian Fed
60D4 Berezovo Ukraine
64H3 Berezovo Russian Fed
92A2 Bergama Turk
52A1 Bergamo Italy
39F6 Bergen Nor
46C1 Bergen op Zoom Neth
48C3 Bergerac France
46D1 Bergisch-Gladbach Germany
12F2 Bering Gl USA
1C6 Bering Str USA/Russian Fed
91C4 Berizak Iran
50B2 Berja Spain
8A3 Berkeley USA
112B2 Berkner I Ant
54B2 Berkovitsa Bulg
43D4 Berkshire County, Eng
16C1 Berkshire Hills USA
13D2 Berland R Can
56C2 Berlin Germany
56C2 Berlin State, Germany
15D2 Berlin New Hampshire, USA
30D3 Bermejo Bol
30D4 Bermejo R Arg
3M5 Bermuda I Atlantic O
52A1 Bern Switz
52B2 Bernardsville USA
34C3 Bernasconi Arg
56C2 Bernburg Germany
47B1 Berner Oberland Mts Switz
6B2 Bernier B Can
57C3 Berounka R Czech Republic
108B2 Berri Aust
96C1 Berriane Alg
48C2 Berry Region, France
22A1 Berryessa,L USA
11C4 Berry Is The Bahamas
98B2 Bertoua Cam
45B2 Bertraghboy B Irish Rep
15C2 Berwick USA
42C2 Berwick-upon-Tweed Eng
43C3 Berwyn Mts Wales
101D2 Besalampy Madag
49D2 Besançon France
59C3 Beskid Zachodnie Mts Pol
93C2 Besni Turk
94B3 Besor R Israel
11B3 Bessemer USA
101D2 Betafo Madag
50A1 Betanzos Spain
94B3 Bet Guvrin Israel
101G1 Bethal S Africa
100A3 Bethanie Namibia
18B1 Bethany Missouri, USA
18A2 Bethany Oklahoma, USA
4B3 Bethel Alaska, USA
16C2 Bethel Connecticut, USA
14B2 Bethel Park USA
15C2 Bethesda USA
94B3 Bethlehem Israel
101G1 Bethlehem S Africa
15C2 Bethlehem USA
48C1 Bethune France
101D3 Betioky Madag
108B1 Betoota Aust
98B2 Betou Congo
82A1 Betpak Dala Steppe Kazakhstan
101D3 Betroka Madag
7D5 Betsiamites Can
86A1 Bettiah India
12D1 Bettles USA

47C2 Béttola Italy
85D4 Betul India
85D3 Betwa R India
46D1 Betzdorf Germany
12C3 Beverley,L USA
16D1 Beverly USA
21B3 Beverly Hills USA
97B4 Beyla Guinea
87B2 Beypore India
92B1 Beyrouth = Beirut
92B2 Beysehir Turk
92B2 Beysehir Gölü L Turk
94B2 Beyt Shean Israel
47C1 Bezau Austria
60E2 Bezhetsk Russian Fed
49C3 Béziers France
90C2 Bezmein Turkmenistan
63C2 Beznosova Russian Fed
86B1 Bhadgaon Nepal
87C1 Bhadrachalam India
86B2 Bhadrakh India
87B2 Bhadra Res India
87B2 Bhadravati India
84B3 Bhag Pak
86B1 Bhagalpur India
84C2 Bhakkar Pak
82D3 Bhamo Myan
85D4 Bhandara India
85D3 Bharatpur India
85C4 Bharuch India
86B2 Bhatiápára Ghat Bang
84C2 Bhatinda India
87A2 Bhatkal India
86B2 Bhatpára India
85C4 Bhavnagar India
84C2 Bhera Pak
86A1 Bheri R Nepal
86A2 Bhilai India
85C3 Bhilwára India
87C1 Bhimavaram India
85D3 Bhind India
84D3 Bhiwáni India
87B1 Bhongir India
85D4 Bhopal India
86B2 Bhubaneshwar India
85B4 Bhuj India
85D4 Bhusáwal India
82C3 Bhutan Kingdom, Asia
71E4 Biak I Indon
58C2 Biala Podlaska Pol
58B2 Bialograd Pol
58C2 Bialystok Pol
38A1 Biargtangar C Iceland
90C2 Biarjmand Iran
48B3 Biarritz France
47C1 Biasca Switz
92B4 Biba Egypt
74E2 Bibai Japan
100A2 Bibala Angola
57B3 Biberach Germany
97B4 Bibiani Ghana
54C1 Bicaz Rom
97C4 Bida Nig
87B1 Bidar India
91C5 Bidbid Oman
43B4 Bideford Eng
43B4 Bideford B Eng
96C2 Bidon 5 Alg
58C2 Biebrza Pol
52A1 Biel Switz
59B2 Bielawa Pol
56B2 Bielefeld Germany
47B1 Bieler See L Switz
52A1 Biella Italy
58C2 Bielsk Podlaski Pol
76D3 Bien Hoa Viet
53B2 Biferno R Italy
72A1 Biga Turk
55C3 Bigadic Turk
19C3 Big Black R USA
18A1 Big Blue R USA
17B2 Big Cypress Swamp USA
4D3 Big Delta USA
49D2 Bigent Germany
13F2 Biggar Can
5H4 Biggar Kindersley Can

109D1 Biggenden Aust
12G3 Bigger,Mt Can
8C2 Bighorn R USA
76C3 Bight of Bangkok B Thai
97C4 Bight of Benin B W Africa
97C4 Bight of Biafra B Cam
6C3 Big I Can
47C1 Bignasco Switz
97A3 Bignona Sen
11B2 Big Pine USA
17B2 Big Pine Key USA
22C3 Big Pine Mt USA
14A2 Big Rapids USA
5H4 Big River Can
9C3 Big Spring USA
7A4 Big Trout L Can
7B4 Big Trout Lake Can
52C2 Bihać Bosnia-Herzegovina
86B1 Bihár India
86B2 Bihar State, India
99D3 Biharamulo Tanz
60B4 Bihor Mt Rom
87B1 Bijápur India
90A2 Bijár Iran
86A1 Bijauri Nepal
54A2 Bijeljina Bosnia-Herzegovina
73B4 Bijie China
84D3 Bijnor India
85C4 Bikáner India
94B2 Bikfaya Leb
69F2 Bikin Russian Fed
98B3 Bikoro Zaire
85C3 Bilara India
84D2 Bilaspur India
86A2 Bilaspur India
76B3 Bilauktaung Range Mts Thai
50B1 Bilbao Spain
Bilbo = Bilbao
59B3 Bilé R Czech Republic
54A2 Bileća Bosnia-Herzegovina
92B1 Bilecik Turk
98C2 Bili R Zaire
79B3 Biliran I Phil
8C2 Billings USA
95A3 Bilma Niger
11B3 Biloxi USA
81B4 Biltine Chad
85D4 Bina-Etawa India
79B3 Binalbagan Phil
101C2 Bindura Zim
100B2 Binga Zim
101C2 Binga Mt Zim
109D1 Bingara Aust
57B3 Bingen Germany
10C2 Binghamton USA
93D2 Bingöl Turk
72D3 Binhai China
78A2 Bintan I Indon
78A3 Bintuhan Indon
29B3 Bió Bió R Chile
102J4 Bioco I Atlantic O
87B1 Bir India
95B2 Bir Abu Husein Well Egypt
95B2 Bir'al Harash Well Libya
98C1 Birao CAR
86B1 Biratnagar Nepal
12E1 Birch Creek USA
108B3 Birchip Aust
5G4 Birch Mts Can
72A4 Bird Can
106C3 Birdsville Aust
106C2 Birdum Aust
86A1 Birganj Nepal
94A3 Bir Gifgáfa Well Egypt
94A3 Bir Hasana Well Egypt
35A2 Birigui Brazil
90C3 Birjand Iran
92B4 Birkat Qarun L Egypt

46D2 Birkenfeld Germany
42C3 Birkenhead Eng
60C4 Birlad Rom
94A3 Bir Lahfan Well Egypt
43C3 Birmingham Eng
11B3 Birmingham USA
95B2 Bir Misâha Well Egypt
96A2 Bir Moghrein Maur
97C3 Birnin Kebbi Nig
97C3 Birni N'Konni Nig
69F2 Birobidzhan Russian Fed
45C2 Birr Irish Rep
51C2 Bir Rabalou Alg
109C1 Birrie R Aust
44C2 Birsay Scot
61J2 Birsk Russian Fed
95B2 Bir Tarfâwi Well Egypt
63B2 Biryusa Russian Fed
39J7 Biržai Lithuania
96B2 Bir Zreigat Well Maur
48A2 Biscay,B of France/Spain
17B2 Biscayne B USA
46D2 Bischwiller France
73B4 Bishan China
82B1 Bishek Kyrgyzstan
8B3 Bishop USA
42D2 Bishop Auckland Eng
43E4 Bishop's Stortford Eng
86A2 Bishrámpur India
96C1 Biskra Alg
79C4 Bislig Phil
8C2 Bismarck USA
90A3 Bisotûn Iran
97A3 Bissau Guinea-Bissau
10A1 Bissett Can
5G4 Bistcho L Can
54C1 Bistrita R Rom
98B2 Bitam Gabon
57B3 Bitburg Germany
46D2 Bitche France
93D2 Bitlis Turk
55B2 Bitola Macedonia
56C2 Bitterfeld Germany
100A4 Bitterfontein S Africa
9283 Bittern Lake Can
8B2 Bitterroot Range Mts USA
74D3 Biwa-ko L Japan
99E1 Biyo Kaboba Eth
65K4 Biysk Russian Fed
96C1 Bizerte Tunisia
51C2 Bj bou Arréridj Alg
52C1 Bjelovar Croatia
96B2 Bj Flye Ste Marie Alg
64C2 Bjørnøya I Barents S
12F1 Black R USA
18B2 Black R USA
107D3 Blackall Aust
42C3 Blackburn Eng
4D3 Blackburn,Mt Can
13E2 Black Diamond Can
5H5 Black Hills USA
44B3 Black Isle Pen Scot
27R3 Blackman's Barbados
43C4 Black Mts Wales
43C3 Blackpool Eng
27H1 Black River Jamaica
8B2 Black Rock Desert USA
65E5 Black S Asia/Europe
45A1 Blacksod B Irish Rep
109D2 Black Sugarloaf Mt Aust
97B3 Black Volta R Ghana
41B3 Blackwater R Irish Rep
18A2 Blackwell USA
54B2 Blagoevgrad Bulg
63E2 Blagoveshchensk Russian Fed
20B1 Blaine USA
44C3 Blair Atholl Scot
44C3 Blairgowrie Scot
17B1 Blakely USA
108A1 Blanche,L Aust

34A2 Blanco *R* Arg
34B1 Blanco *R* Arg
8A2 Blanco,0 USA
7E4 Blanc Sablon Can
43C4 Blandford Forum Eng
43C4 Blaneau Gwent
County Wales
46A2 Blangy-sur-Bresle
France
46B1 Blankenberge Belg
101C2 Blantyre Malawi
48B2 Blaye France
109C2 Blayney Aust
111B2 Blenheim NZ
96C1 Blida Alg
- 14B1 Blind River Can
108A2 Blinman Aust
78C4 Blitar Indon
15D2 Block I USA
16D2 Block Island Sd USA
101G1 Bloemfontein
S Africa
101G1 Bloemhof S Africa
101G1 Bloemhof Dam *Res*
S Africa
33F3 Blommesteinmeer *L*
Surinam
38A1 Blonduós Iceland
45B1 Bloody Foreland *C*
Irish Rep
14A3 Bloomfield Indiana,
USA
18B1 Bloomfield Iowa,
USA
10B2 Bloomington Illinois,
USA
14A3 Bloomington
Indiana, USA
16A2 Bloomsburg USA
78C4 Blora Indon
6H3 Blosseville Kyst *Mts*
Greenland
57B3 Bludenz Austria
11B3 Bluefield USA
32A1 Bluefields Nic
26B3 Blue Mountain Peak
Mt Jamaica
16A2 Blue Mt USA
109D2 Blue Mts Aust
27J1 Blue Mts Jamaica
8A2 Blue Mts USA
Blue Nile = Bahr el
Azraq
99D1 Blue Nile *R* Sudan
4G3 Bluenose L Can
16A2 Blue Ridge Mts USA
13D2 Blue River Can
45B1 Blue Stack *Mt*
Irish Rep
111A3 Bluff NZ
106A4 Bluff Knoll *Mt* Aust
30G4 Blumenau Brazil
109D2 Blundez Austria
20B2 Bly USA
12E3 Blying Sd USA
9B3 Blythe USA
11B3 Blytheville USA
97A4 Bo Sierra Leone
79B3 Boac Phil
72D2 Boading China
14B2 Boardman USA
63C3 Boatou China
33E3 Boa Vista Brazil
97A4 Boa Vista *I* Cape
Verde
76E1 Bobai China
47C2 Bóbbio Italy
97B3 Bobo Dioulasso
Burkina
60C4 Bobruysk Belarus
17B2 Boca Chica Key *I*
USA
32D5 Bôca do Acre Brazil
35C1 Bocaiúva Brazil
98B2 Bocaranga CAR
17B2 Boca Raton USA
59C3 Bochnia Pol
56B2 Bocholt Germany
46D1 Bochum Germany
100A2 Bocoio Angola
98B2 Boda CAR
63D2 Bodaybo
Russian Fed

21A2 Bodega Head *Pt*
USA
95A3 Bodélé Region Chad
38J5 Boden Sweden
47C1 Bodensee *L* Switz/
Germany
87B1 Bodhan India
87B2 Bodinäyakkanür
India
43B4 Bodmin Eng
43B4 Bodmin Moor
Upland Eng
38G5 Bodø Nor
55C3 Bodrum Turk
98C3 Boende Zaïre
97A3 Boffa Guinea
76B2 Bogale Myan
19C3 Bogalusa USA
109C2 Bogan *R* Aust
97B3 Bogandé Burkina
8H3 Bogarnes Iceland
92C2 Bogaziyan Turk
61K2 Bogdanovich
Russian Fed
68A2 Bogda Shan *Mt*
China
100A3 Bogenfels Namibia
109D1 Boggabilla Aust
109C2 Boggabri Aust
45B2 Boggeragh Mts
Irish Rep
79B3 Bogo Phil
109C3 Bogong,Mt Aust
78B4 Bogor Indon
61H2 Bogorodskoye
Russian Fed
32C3 Bogotá Colombia
63A2 Bogotol Russian Fed
86B2 Bogra Bang
72D2 Bo Hai *B* China
46B2 Bohain-en-
Vermandois France
72D2 Bohai Wan *B* China
57C3 Böhmer-Wald
Upland Germany
79B4 Bohol *I* Phil
79B4 Bohol S Phil
35A1 Bois *R* Brazil
14B1 Bois Blanc I USA
8B2 Boise USA
96A2 Bojador,C Mor
79B2 Bojeador,C Phil
90C2 Bojnürd Iran
97A3 Boké Guinea
109C1 Bokhara *R* Aust
39F7 Boknafjord *Inlet* Nor
98B3 Boko Congo
76C3 Bokor Camb
98C3 Bokungu Zaïre
81C4 Bol Chad
23A1 Bolaños Mexico
97A3 Bolama Guinea-
Bissau
23A1 Bolanos *R* Mexico
48C2 Bolbec France
97B4 Bole Ghana
59B2 Boleslawiec Pol
97B3 Bolgatanga Ghana
60C4 Bolgrad Ukraine
34C3 Bolívar Arg
18B2 Bolívar Missouri,
USA
18C2 Bolívar Tennessee,
USA
30C2 Bolivia Republic,
S America
38H6 Bollnas Sweden
109C1 Bollon Aust
32C2 Bollón *Mt* Peru
52B2 Bologna Italy
60D2 Bologoye
Russian Fed
69F2 Bolon' Russian Fed
61G3 Bol'shoy Irgiz *R*
Russian Fed
74C2 Bol'shoy Kamen
Russian Fed
Bol'shoy Kavkaz
=Caucasus
61G4 Bol'shoy Uzen *R*
Kazakhstan
9C4 Bolson de Mapimi
Desert Mexico
43C3 Bolton Eng

92B1 Bolu Turk
38A1 Bolungarvik Iceland
52B1 Bolvadin Turk
98B3 Boma Zaïre
107D4 Bombala Aust
87A1 Bombay India
99D2 Bombo Uganda
35B1 Bom Despacho Brazil
86C1 Bomdila India
97A4 Bomi Hills Lib
31C4 Bom Jesus da Lapa
Brazil
63E2 Bomnak Russian Fed
99C2 Bomokandi *R* Zaïre
98C2 Bomu *R* CAR/Zaïre
27D4 Bonaire *I*
Caribbean S
12F2 Bona,Mt USA
25D3 Bonanza Nic
7E5 Bonavista Can
108A2 Bon Bon Aust
98C2 Bondo Zaïre
97B4 Bondoukou Côte
d'Ivoire
Bône = 'Annaba
33E3 Bonfim Guyana
98C2 Bongandanga Zaïre
98B1 Bongor Chad
19B3 Bonham USA
53A2 Bonifacio Corse
52A2 Bonifacio,Str of *Chan*
Medit S
Bonin Is = Ogasawara
Gunto
17B2 Bonita Springs USA
57B2 Bonn Germany
20C1 Bonners Ferry USA
12H1 Bonnet Plume *R* Can
13E2 Bonnyville Can
97A4 Bonthe Sierra Leone
99E1 Booaaso Somalia
108B2 Booligal Aust
99D1 Boonah Aust
15C2 Boonville USA
109C2 Boorowa Aust
6A2 Boothia,G of Can
6A2 Boothia Pen Can
98B3 Booué Gabon
108A1 Bopeechee Aust
99D2 Bor Sudan
92B2 Bor Turk
54B2 Bor Serbia, Yugos
8B2 Borah Peak *Mt* USA
39G7 Borås Sweden
91B4 Borãzjan Iran
108A3 Borda,C Aust
48B3 Bordeaux France
4G2 Borden I Can
6B2 Borden Pen Can
16B2 Bordentown USA
108B3 Bordertown Aust
96C2 Bordj Omar Dris Alg
8D1 Borens River Can
38A2 Borgarnes Iceland
9C3 Borger USA
39H7 Borgholm Sweden
47C2 Borgosia Italy
47D1 Borgo Valsugana
Italy
59C3 Borislav Ukraine
61F3 Borisoglebsk
Russian Fed
60C3 Borisov Belarus
60E3 Borisovka
Russian Fed
95A3 Borkou Region Chad
39H6 Borlänge Sweden
47C2 Bormida Italy
47D1 Bormio Italy
67F5 Borneo *I* Malay/
Indon
39H7 Bornholm *I* Den
55C3 Bornova Turk
98C2 Boro *R* Sudan
97B3 Boromo Burkina
60D2 Borovichi
Russian Fed
106C2 Borroloola Aust
54B1 Borsa Rom
90A3 Borüjed Iran
90B3 Borüjerd Iran
58B2 Bory Tucholskie
Region, Pol

63D2 Borzya Russian Fed
73B5 Bose China
101G1 Boshof S Africa
54A2 Bosna *R* Bosnia-
Herzegovina
37E4 Bosnia-Herzegovina
Republic, Europe
75C1 Bösö-hantö *B* Japan
Bosporus = Karadeniz
Boğazi
51C2 Bosquet Alg
98B2 Bossangoa CAR
98B2 Bossémbélé CAR
19B3 Bossier City USA
65K5 Bosten Hu *L* China
43D3 Boston Eng
10C2 Boston USA
11A3 Boston Mts USA
85C4 Botäd India
54B2 Botevgrad Bulg
101G1 Bothaville S Africa
64C3 Bothnia,G of
Sweden/Fin
100B3 Botletli *R* Botswana
60C4 Botosani Rom
100B3 Botswana Republic,
Africa
53C3 Botte Donato *Mt*
Italy
46D1 Bottrop Germany
35B2 Botucatu Brazil
7E5 Botwood Can
89D7 Bouaké Côte d'Ivoire
98B2 Bouar CAR
98B2 Bouca CAR
51C2 Boufarik Alg
Bougie = Bejaïa
97B3 Bougouni Mali
46C2 Bouillon France
96B2 Bou Izakarn Mor
46D2 Boulay-Moselle
France
8C2 Boulder Colorado,
USA
9B3 Boulder City USA
22A2 Boulder Creek USA
48C1 Boulogne France
98B2 Boumba *R* CAR
97B4 Bouna Côte d'Ivoire
8B3 Boundary Peak *Mt*
USA
97B4 Boundiali
Côte d'Ivoire
107F3 Bourail Nouvelle
Calédonie
97B3 Bourem Mali
49D2 Bourg France
49D2 Bourg de Péage
France
48C2 Bourges France
48C3 Bourg-Madame
France
49C2 Bourgogne Region,
France
47B2 Bourg-St-Maurice
France
108C2 Bourke Aust
43D4 Bournemouth Eng
96C1 Bou Saâda Alg
58B2 Bousso Chad
97A3 Boutilimit Maur
103J7 Bouvet I Atlantic O
34D2 Bovril Arg
13E2 Bow *R* Can
107D2 Bowen Aust
19A3 Bowie Texas, USA
13E2 Bow Island Can
11B3 Bowling Green
Kentucky, USA
18B2 Bowling Green
Missouri, USA
15C3 Bowling Green Ohio,
USA
15C3 Bowling Green
Virginia, USA
15C2 Bowmanville Can
109D2 Bowral Aust
54B1 Boxa Rom
90A3 Boxar Iran
72D3 Bo Xian China
72D2 Boxing China
92B1 Boyabat Turk
98B2 Boyali CAR
5J4 Boyd *S*

16B2 Boyertown USA
13E2 Boyle Can
41B3 Boyle Irish Rep
45C2 Boyne R Irish Rep
17B2 Boynton Beach USA
98C2 Boyoma Falls Zaïre
55C3 Bozca Ada I Turk
55C3 Boz Dağları Mts Turk
8B2 Bozeman USA
Bozen = Bolzano
98B2 Bozene CAR
98B2 Bozoum CAR
47B2 Bra Italy
52C2 Brač I Croatia
15C1 Bracebridge Can
95A2 Brach Libya
38H6 Bräcke Sweden
17B2 Bradenton USA
42D3 Bradford Eng
44E1 Brae Scot
44C3 Braemar Scot
50A1 Braga Port
34C3 Bragado Arg
50A1 Bragana Port
31B2 Bragança Brazil
35B2 Bragança Paulista Brazil
86C2 Brahman-Baria Bang
86B2 Brahmani R India
87E1 Brahmaputra R India
7E5 Braie Verte Can
60C4 Brăila Rom
10A2 Brainerd USA
97A3 Brakna Region, Maur
5F4 Brakne Can
14C2 Brampton Can
33E3 Bramon R Can
100A3 Brandberg Mt Namibia
56C2 Brandenburg Germany
56C2 Brandenburg State, Germany
101G1 Brandfort S Africa
8D2 Brandon Can
100B4 Brandvlei S Africa
57C2 Brandys nad Lebem Czech Republic
58B2 Braniewo Pol
10B2 Brantford Can
108B3 Branxholme Aust
7D5 Bras D'Or L Can
35C1 Brasila de Minas Brazil
32D6 Brasiléia Brazil
31B5 Brasília Brazil
54C1 Brasov Rom
78D1 Brassay Range Mts Malay
59B3 Bratislava Slovakia
63C2 Bratsk Russian Fed
15D2 Brattleboro USA
56C2 Braunschweig Germany
97A4 Brava I Cape Verde
9B3 Brawley USA
45C2 Bray Irish Rep
6C3 Bray I Can
13D2 Brazeau R Can
13D2 Brazeau,Mt Can
28D4 Brazil Republic, S America
103G5 Brazil Basin Atlantic O
9D3 Brazos R USA
98B3 Brazzaville Congo
57C3 Brdy Upland Czech Republic
111A3 Breaksea Sd NZ
110B1 Bream B NZ
78B4 Brebes Indon
44C3 Brechin Scot
46C1 Brecht Belg
59B3 Břeclav Czech Republic
43C4 Brecon Wales
43C4 Brecon Beacons Mts Wales
43B3 Brecon Beacons Nat Pk Wales
56A2 Breda Neth
100B4 Bredasdorp S Africa
38H6 Bredbyn Sweden

61J3 Bredy Russian Fed
15C2 Breezewood USA
47C1 Bregenz Austria
47C1 Bregenzer Ache R Austria
38A1 Breiðafjörður B Iceland
47C2 Brembo R Italy
17A1 Bremen USA
56B2 Bremen Germany
56B2 Bremerhaven Germany
20B1 Bremerton USA
19A3 Brenham USA
57C3 Brenner P Austria/Italy
47D2 Brenta Italy
47D2 Brenta R Italy
22B2 Brentwood Eng
52B1 Brescia Italy
Breslau = Wrocław
47D1 Bressanone Italy
44E1 Bressay I Scot
48B2 Bressuire France
58C2 Brest Belarus
48B2 Brest France
48B2 Bretagne Region, France
48B2 Breteuil France
46B2 Breton Woods USA
110B1 Brett,C NZ
109C1 Brewarrina Aust
16C2 Brewster New York, USA
20C1 Brewster Washington, USA
101G1 Breyten S Africa
52C1 Brežice Slovenia
98C2 Bria CAR
49D3 Briancon France
49C2 Briare France
43C4 Bridgend County Wales
21B2 Bridgeport California, USA
15D2 Bridgeport Connecticut, USA
19A3 Bridgeport Texas, USA
22C1 Bridgeport USA
16B3 Bridgeton USA
27F4 Bridgetown Barbados
7D5 Bridgewater Can
16D2 Bridgewater Eng
43C4 Bridgwater Eng
43C4 Bridgwater B Eng
42D2 Bridlington Eng
109C4 Bridport Aust
47B1 Brienzer See L Switz
46C2 Briey France
8B2 Brigham City USA
109C3 Bright Aust
43D4 Brighton Eng
46E1 Brilon Germany
55A2 Brindisi Italy
19B3 Brinkley USA
107E3 Brisbane Aust
15D2 Bristol Connecticut, USA
43C4 Bristol County Eng
43C4 Bristol Eng
15D2 Bristol Pennsylvania, USA
16D2 Bristol Rhode Island, USA
11B3 Bristol Tennessee, USA
11B3 Bristol B USA
43B4 Bristol Chan Eng/Wales
4D3 British Mts USA
5F4 British Columbia Province, Can
6B1 British Empire Range Mts Can
101G1 Brits S Africa
100B4 Britstown S Africa
48C2 Brive France
59B3 Brno Czech Republic
17B1 Broad R USA
7C4 Broadback R Can
44A2 Broad Bay Inlet Scot

44B3 Broadford Scot
5H4 Brochet Can
4G2 Brock I Can
15C2 Brockport USA
16D1 Brockton USA
15C2 Brockville Can
6B2 Brodeur Pen Can
42B2 Brodick Scot
58B2 Brodnica Pol
60C3 Brody Ukraine
19B3 Broken Bow USA
19B3 Broken Bow L USA
107D4 Broken Hill Aust
47C2 Broni Italy
38G5 Brønnøysund Nor
16C2 Bronx Borough, New York USA
79A4 Brooke's Point Phil
18B2 Brookfield Missouri, USA
11A3 Brookhaven USA
20B2 Brookings Oregon, USA
8D2 Brookings South Dakota, USA
16D1 Brookline USA
16C2 Brooklyn Borough, New York, USA
5G4 Brooks Can
12C3 Brooks,L USA
12A1 Brooks Mt USA
4C3 Brooks Range Mts USA
17B2 Brooksville USA
109D1 Brooloo Aust
106B2 Broome Aust
44C2 Brora Scot
20B2 Brothers USA
95A3 Broulkou Chad
13E3 Browning USA
9D4 Brownsville USA
9D3 Brownwood USA
46B1 Bruay-en-Artois France
106A3 Bruce,Mt Aust
14B1 Bruce Pen Can
59B3 Bruck an der Mur Austria
Bruges = Brugge
46B1 Brugge Belg
46D1 Brühl Germany
78C2 Brunei Sultanate, SE Asia
52B1 Brunico Italy
111B2 Brunner,L NZ
11B3 Brunswick Georgia, USA
18B2 Brunswick Mississippi, USA
29B6 Brunswick,Pen de Chile
109C4 Bruny I Aust
61F1 Brusenets Russian Fed
26A3 Bru Laguna Honduras
Brüssel = Bruxelles
56A2 Bruxelles Belg
108A2 Bryan,Mt Aust
60D3 Bryansk Russian Fed
60D3 Bryansk Division, Russian Fed
19B3 Bryant USA
59B2 Brzeg Pol
93E4 Būbiyan I Kuwait/Iraq
99D3 Bubu R Tanz
32C2 Bucaramanga Colombia
44D3 Buchan Oilfield N Sea
97A4 Buchanan Lib
44D3 Buchan Deep N Sea
6C2 Buchan G Can
40C2 Buchan Ness Pen Scot
7E5 Buchans Can
34C2 Buchardo Arg
Bucharest = Bucureşti
47C1 Buchs Switz
43D3 Buckingham Eng
12B1 Buckland R Can

12B1 Buckland R USA
108A2 Buckleboo Aust
98B3 Buco Zau Congo
54C2 Bucureşti Rom
59B3 Budapest Hung
84D3 Budaun India
43B4 Bude Eng
19B3 Bude USA
61F5 Budennovsk Russian Fed
54A2 Budva Montenegro, Yugos
98A2 Buéa Cam
22B3 Buellton USA
34B2 Buena Esperanza Arg
32B3 Buenaventura Colombia
23A2 Buenavista Mexico
29E2 Buenos Aires Arg
29D3 Buenos Aires State, Arg
18B2 Buffalo Mississippi, USA
10C2 Buffalo New York, USA
8C2 Buffalo South Dakota, USA
19A3 Buffalo Texas, USA
8C2 Buffalo Wyoming, USA
101H1 Buffalo R S Africa
13E2 Buffalo L Alberta, Can
5G3 Buffalo L Northwest Territories, Can
5H4 Buffalo Narrows Can
17B1 Buford USA
54C2 Buftea Rom
59B2 Bug R Pol/Ukraine
32B3 Buga Colombia
90B2 Bugdayli Turkmenistan
61H3 Bugulma Russian Fed
61H3 Buguruslan Russian Fed
93C2 Buhayrat al Asad Res Syria
41C3 Builth Wells Wales
34A2 Buin Chile
99C3 Bujumbura Burundi
98C3 Bukama Zaïre
99C3 Bukavu Zaïre
80E2 Bukhara Uzbekistan
78C2 Bukit Batubrok Mt Indon
70B4 Bukittinggi Indon
99D3 Bukoba Tanz
78D3 Buku Gandadiwata Mt Indon
71E4 Bula Indon
79B3 Bulan Phil
84D3 Bulandshahr India
100B3 Bulawayo Zim
58D4 Buldan Turk
68C2 Bulgan Mongolia
54B2 Bulgaria Republic, Europe
47B1 Bulle. Switz
111B2 Buller R NZ
109C3 Buller,Mt Aust
106A4 Bullfinch Aust
108B1 Bulloo R Aust
108B1 Bulloo Downs Aust
108B1 Bulloo L Aust
18B2 Bull Shoals Res USA
34A3 Bulnes Chile
108D1 Bulolo PNG
101G1 Bultfontein S Africa
98C2 Bumba Zaïre
76B2 Bumphal Dam Thai
99D3 Buna Kenya
106A4 Bunbury Aust
45C1 Buncrana Irish Rep
107E3 Bundaberg Aust
109D2 Bundarra Aust
85D3 Bundi India
45B1 Bundoran Irish Rep
109C1 Bungil R Aust
98B3 Bungo Angola
75A2 Bungo-suidō Str Japan
70B3 Bunguran I Ind

Bunia

99D2 **Bunia** Zaire
18B2 **Bunker** USA
19B3 **Bunkie** USA
17B2 **Bunnell** USA
78C3 **Buntok** Indon
71D3 **Buol** Indon
76C2 **Buraq** Syria
98C1 **Buram** Sudan
99E2 **Burao** Somalia
79B3 **Burauen** Phil
80C3 **Buraydah** S Arabia
21B3 **Burbank** USA
109C2 **Burcher** Aust
92B2 **Burdur** Turk
63F3 **Bureinskiy Khrebet**
  Mts Russian Fed
56C2 **Burg** Germany
54C2 **Burgas** Bulg
17C1 **Burgaw** USA
18T1 **Burgdorf** Switz
100B4 **Burgersdorp** S Africa
50B1 **Burgos** Spain
58B1 **Burgsvik** Sweden
55C3 **Burhaniye** Turk
87B1 **Burhanpur** India
79B3 **Burias** I Phil
76C2 **Buriram** Thai
35B1 **Buritis** Brazil
13B2 **Burke Chan** Can
106C2 **Burketown** Aust
97B3 **Burkina** Republic,
  Africa
15C1 **Burks Falls** Can
8B2 **Burley** USA
10A2 **Burlington** Iowa,
  USA
16B2 **Burlington** New
  Jersey, USA
10C2 **Burlington** Vermont,
  USA
20B1 **Burlington**
  Washington, USA
Burma = Myanmar
20B2 **Burney** USA
16A2 **Burnham** USA
107D5 **Burnie** Aust
42C3 **Burnley** Eng
20C2 **Burns** USA
5F4 **Burns Lake** Can
82C1 **Burqin** China
108A2 **Burra** Aust
109C2 **Burragorang,L** Aust
44C2 **Burray** I Scot
109C2 **Burren Junction**
  Aust
109C2 **Burrinjuck Res** Aust
60C5 **Bursa** Turk
80B3 **Bur Safâga** Egypt
  Bûr Sa'îd = Port Said
14B2 **Burton** USA
43D3 **Burton upon Trent**
  Eng
38J6 **Burtrask** Sweden
108B2 **Burtundy** Aust
71D4 **Buru** Indon
99C3 **Burundi** Republic,
  Africa
78A2 **Burung** Indon
99D1 **Burye** Eth
61H4 **Burynshik**
  Kazakhstan
43E3 **Bury St Edmunds**
  Eng
91B4 **Büshehr** Iran
98B3 **Busira** R Zaire
58C2 **Buskozdrój** Pol
94C2 **Busrá ash Shām**
  Syria
106A4 **Busselton** Aust
49D2 **Busto** Italy
52A1 **Busto Arsizio** Italy
79A3 **Busuanga** I Phil
34B3 **Buta Ranquil** Arg
99C3 **Butare** Rwanda
42B2 **Bute** I Scot
69E2 **Butha Qi** China
14C2 **Butler** USA
8B2 **Butte** USA
77C4 **Butterworth** Malay
40B2 **Butt of Lewis** I Scot
6D3 **Button Is** Can
79C4 **Butuan** Phil
71D4 **Butung** I Indon

C

61F3 **Buturlinovka**
  Russian Fed
86A1 **Butwal** Nepal
99E2 **Buulo Barde** Somalia
99E2 **Buur Hakaba**
  Somalia
61F2 **Buy** Russian Fed
72B1 **Buyant Ovvo**
  Mongolia
61G5 **Buynaksk**
  Russian Fed
63D3 **Buyr Nuur** L
  Mongolia
93D2 **Büyük Aǧri** Mt Turk
92A2 **Büyük Menderes** R
  Turk
54C1 **Buzău** Rom
54C1 **Buzău** R Rom
61H3 **Buzuluk** Russian Fed
16D2 **Buzzards B** USA
54B2 **Byala** Bulg
54B2 **Byala Slatina** Bulg
4H2 **Byam Martin** Chan
  Can
4H2 **Byam Martin I** Can
  Byblos = Jubail
94B1 **Byblos** Hist Site, Leb
58B2 **Bydgoszcz** Pol
39F7 **Bygland** Nor
62C1 **Bylot I** Can
109C2 **Byrock** Aust
22B2 **Byron** USA
109D1 **Byron,C** Aust
59B2 **Bytom** Pol

C

30E4 **Caacupé** Par
100A2 **Caàla** Angola
13B2 **Caamano Sd** Can
30E4 **Caazapá** Par
79B2 **Cabanatuan** Phil
31E3 **Cabedelo** Brazil
50A2 **Cabeza del Buey**
  Spain
34C3 **Cabildo** Arg
34A2 **Cabildo** Chile
32C1 **Cabimas** Ven
98B3 **Cabinda** Angola
98B3 **Cabinda** Province,
  Angola
27C3 **Cabo Beata** Dom Rep
51C2 **Cabo Binibeca** C
  Spain
53A3 **Cabo Carbonara** C
  Sardegna
34A3 **Cabo Carranza** C
  Chile
50A2 **Cabo Carvoeiro** C
  Port
9B3 **Cabo Colnett** C
  Mexico
32B2 **Cabo Corrientes** C
  Colombia
24B2 **Cabo Corrientes** C
  Mexico
26B3 **Cabo Cruz** C Cuba
50B1 **Cabo de Ajo** C Spain
51C1 **Cabo de Caballeria** C
  Spain
51C1 **Cabo de Creus** C
  Spain
50B2 **Cabo de Gata** C
  Spain
29C7 **Cabo de Hornos** C
  Chile
51C2 **Cabo de la Nao** C
  Spain
50A1 **Cabo de Peñas** C
  Spain
50A2 **Cabo de Roca** C Port
51C2 **Cabo de Salinas** C
  Spain
35C2 **Cabo de São Tomé** C
  Brazil
50A2 **Cabo de São Vicente**
  C Port
50A2 **Cabo de Sines** C
  Port
51C1 **Cabo de Tortosa** C
  Spain
29C4 **Cabo Dos Bahias** C
  Arg
50A2 **Cabo Espichel** C Port
9B4 **Cabo Falso** C Mexico

51B2 **Cabo Ferrat** C Alg
50A1 **Cabo Finisterre** C
  Spain
51C1 **Cabo Formentor** C
  Spain
35C2 **Cabo Frio** Brazil
35C2 **Cabo Frio** C Brazil
26A4 **Cabo Gracias á Dios**
  Honduras
31B2 **Cabo Maguarinho** C
  Brazil
50A2 **Cabo Negro** C Mor
109D1 **Caboolture** Aust
33G3 **Cabo Orange** C
  Mexico
21B3 **Cabo Punta Banda** C
  Mexico
101C2 **Cabora Bassa Dam**
  Mozam
24A1 **Caborca** Mexico
24B2 **Cabo Rojo** C Mexico
23B1 **Cabos** Mexico
29C6 **Cabo San Diego** C
  Arg
32A4 **Cabo San Lorenzo** C
  Ecuador
53A3 **Cabo Teulada** C
  Sardegna
50A2 **Cabo Trafalgar** C
  Spain
50B2 **Cabo Tres Forcas** C
  Mor
29C5 **Cabo Tres Puntas** C
  Arg
7D5 **Cabot Str** Can
50B2 **Cabra** Spain
50A1 **Cabreira** Mt Port
51C2 **Cabrera** I Spain
34A3 **Cabrero** Chile
51B2 **Cabriel** R Spain
23B2 **Cacahuamilpa**
  Mexico
54B2 **Čačak** Serbia, Yugos
23B2 **C A Carillo** Mexico
30E2 **Cáceres** Brazil
50A2 **Caceres** Spain
18B2 **Cache** USA
34C2 **Cache Creek** Can
30C4 **Cachi** Arg
33G5 **Cachimbo** Brazil
31D4 **Cachoeira** Brazil
35A1 **Cachoeira Alta** Brazil
31D3 **Cachoeira de Paulo
  Alfonso** Waterfall
  Brazil
29F2 **Cachoeira do Sul**
  Brazil
31C6 **Cachoeiro de
  Itapemirim** Brazil
22C3 **Cachuma,L** USA
100A2 **Cacolo** Angola
100A2 **Caconda** Angola
35A1 **Caçu** Brazil
100A2 **Caculuvar** R Angola
59B3 **Čadca** Slovakia
43C3 **Cader Idris** Mts
  Wales
10B2 **Cadillac** USA
79B3 **Cadiz** Phil
50A2 **Cadiz** Spain
50A2 **Cadiz** Spain
48B2 **Caen** France
42B3 **Caernarfon** Wales
43B3 **Caernarfon B** Wales
43C3 **Caernarfonshire and
  Merionethshire**
  County Wales
43C4 **Caerphilly** County
  Wales
94B2 **Caesarea** Hist Site
  Israel
31C4 **Caetité** Brazil
30C4 **Cafayate** Arg
92B2 **Caga Tepe** Turk
79P1 **Cagayan** R Phil
79B4 **Cagayan de Oro** Phil
79B4 **Cagayan Is** Phil
53A3 **Cagliari** Sardegna
27D3 **Caguas** Puerto Rico
45B3 **Caha Mts** Irish Rep
45A3 **Cahersiveen**
  Irish Rep
45C2 **Cahir** Irish Rep
45C2 **Cahore Pt** Irish Rep
48C3 **Cahors** France

101C2 **Caia** Mozam
100B2 **Caianda** Angola
35A1 **Caiapó** R Brazil
35A1 **Caiapónia** Brazil
31D3 **Caicó** Brazil
26C2 **Caicos Is** s
  Caribbean S
11C4 **Caicos Pass** The
  Bahamas
12C2 **Cairn Mt** USA
44C3 **Cairngorms** Mts
  Scot
107D2 **Cairns** Aust
92B3 **Cairo** Egypt
11B3 **Cairo** USA
108B1 **Caiwarro** Aust
32B5 **Cajabamba** Peru
32B5 **Cajamarca** Peru
27D5 **Calabozo** Ven
54B2 **Calafat** Rom
29B6 **Calafate** Arg
79B3 **Calagua Is** Phil
51B1 **Calahorra** Spain
48C1 **Calais** France
30C3 **Calama** Chile
32C3 **Calamar** Colombia
79A3 **Calamian Group** Is
  Phil
98B3 **Calandula** Angola
70A3 **Calang** Indon
95B2 **Calanscio Sand Sea**
  Libya
79B3 **Calapan** Phil
54C2 **Calarasi** Rom
51B1 **Calatayud** Spain
22B2 **Calaveras Res** USA
79B3 **Calbayog** Phil
19B4 **Calcasieu L** USA
86B2 **Calcutta** India
50A2 **Caldas da Rainha**
  Port
31B5 **Caldas Novas** Brazil
30B4 **Caldera** Chile
8B2 **Caldwell** USA
29C5 **Caleta Olivia** Arg
9B3 **Calexico** USA
5G4 **Calgary** Can
17B1 **Calhoun** USA
17B1 **Calhoun Falls** USA
32B3 **Cali** Colombia
87B2 **Calicut** India
8B3 **Caliente** Nevada,
  USA
8A3 **California** State, USA
22C3 **California Aqueduct**
  USA
87B2 **Calimere,Pt** India
34B2 **Calingasta** Arg
22A1 **Calistoga** USA
108B1 **Callabonna** R Aust
108A1 **Callabonna,L** Aust
15C1 **Callander** Can
44B3 **Callander** Scot
108A1 **Callanna** Aust
32B6 **Callao** Peru
13E1 **Calling L** Can
23B1 **Calnali** Mexico
17B2 **Caloosahatchee** R
  USA
109D1 **Caloundra** Aust
23B2 **Calpulalpan** Mexico
53B3 **Caltanissetta** Italy
98B3 **Caluango** Angola
100A2 **Calulo** Angola
100A2 **Caluquembe** Angola
99F1 **Caluula** Somalia
13B2 **Calvert I** Can
52A2 **Calvi** Corse
23A1 **Calvillo** Mexico
100A4 **Calvinia** S Africa
25E2 **Camagüey** Cuba
25E2 **Camagüey,Arch de** Is
  Cuba
30B2 **Camaná** Peru
30C3 **Camargo** Bol
22C3 **Camarillo** USA
29C4 **Camarones** Arg
20B1 **Camas** USA
98B3 **Camaxilo** Angola
98B3 **Cambatela** Angola
76C3 **Cambodia** Republic,
  S E Asia
43B4 **Camborne** Eng
49C1 **Cambrai** France

Cashel

43C3 Cambrian Mts Wales
14B2 Cambridge Can
43D3 Cambridge County, Eng
43E3 Cambridge Eng
27H1 Cambridge Jamaica
15C3 Cambridge Maryland, USA
15D2 Cambridge Massachussets, USA
110C1 Cambridge NZ
14B2 Cambridge Ohio, USA
4H3 Cambridge Bay Can
60E5 Cam Burun Pt Turk
11A3 Camden Arkansas, USA
109D2 Camden Aust
15D3 Camden New Jersey, USA
17B1 Camden South Carolina, USA
18B2 Cameron Missouri, USA
19A3 Cameron Texas, USA
4H2 Cameron I Can
111A2 Cameron Mts NZ
98A2 Cameroun Federal Republic, Africa
98A2 Cameroun Mt Cam
78B2 Cametá Brazil
79B4 Camiguin I Phil
79B2 Camiling Phil
17B1 Camilla USA
22B1 Camino USA
31C2 Camocim Brazil
98C3 Camissombo Angola
106C2 Camooweal Aust
34D2 Campana Arg
29A5 Campana I Chile
13B2 Campania I Can
111B2 Campbell,C NZ
13J2 Campbell I Can
111B2 Campbell I NZ
105G6 Campbell I NZ
4E3 Campbell,Mt Can
84C2 Campbellpore Pak
5F5 Campbell River Can
7D5 Campbellton Can
109D2 Campbelltown Aust
42B2 Campbeltown Scot
25C3 Campeche Mexico
108B3 Camperdown Aust
31D3 Campina Grande Brazil
31B6 Campinas Brazil
35B1 Campina Verde Brazil
98A2 Campo Cam
53B2 Campobasso Italy
35B2 Campo Belo Brazil
35B1 Campo Florido Brazil
30D4 Campo Gallo Arg
30F3 Campo Grande Brazil
31C2 Campo Maior Brazil
30F3 Campo Mourão Brazil
35C2 Campos Brazil
35B1 Campos Altos Brazil
47D1 Campo Tures Italy
5A Cam Ranh Viet
5G4 Camrose Can
100A2 Camucuio Angola
27K1 Canaan Tobago
16C1 Canaan USA
100A2 Canacupa Angola
2F3 Canada Dominion, N America
29D2 Cañada de Gomez Arg
9C3 Canadian R USA
60C5 Canakkale Turk
34B3 Canalejas Arg
13D2 Canal Flats Can
24A1 Cananea Mexico
102G3 Canary Isls Atlantic O
 Canary Is = Islas Canarias
23A2 Canas Mexico
24B2 Canatlán Mexico
11B4 Canaveral,C USA
31D5 Canavieiras Brazil
107D4 Canberra Aust

20B2 Canby California, USA
55C3 Çandarli Körfezi B Turk
16C2 Candlewood,L USA
29E2 Canelones Urug
18A2 Caney USA
100A2 Cangamba Angola
100B2 Cangombe Angola
72D2 Cangzhou China
7D4 Caniapiscau R Can
31D2 Canindé Brazil
92B1 Çankırı Turk
13D2 Canmore Can
44A3 Canna I Scot
87B2 Cannanore India
49D3 Cannes France
109C3 Cann River Aust
30F4 Canôas Brazil
13F1 Canoe L Can
9C3 Canon City USA
108B2 Canopus Aust
5H4 Canora Can
109C2 Canowindra Aust
13B2 Cantabria I Can
43E4 Canterbury Eng
111B2 Canterbury Bight B NZ
111B2 Canterbury Plains NZ
77D4 Can Tho Viet
 Canton = Guangzhou
19C3 Canton Mississippi, USA
18B1 Canton Missouri, USA
10B2 Canton Ohio, USA
12E2 Cantwell USA
20C2 Canyon City USA
12J2 Canyon Range Mts USA
20B2 Canyonville USA
23A2 Canzar Angola
76D1 Cao Bang Viet
31B2 Capanema Brazil
35B2 Capão Bonito Brazil
48B3 Capbreton France
24B2 Cap Corrientes C Mexico
52A2 Cap Corse C Corse
48B2 Cap de la Hague C France
15D1 Cap-de-la-Madeleine Can
6C3 Cap de Nouvelle-France C Can
51C2 Capdepera Spain
23A2 Cap de Tancitario C Mexico
109C4 Cape Barren I Aust
103J6 Cape Basin Atlantic O
7E5 Cape Breton I Can
97B4 Cape Coast Ghana
15D2 Cape Cod B USA
6C3 Cape Dorset Can
17C1 Cape Fear R USA
18C2 Cape Girardeau USA
6B3 Cape Henrietta Maria Can
 Cape Horn = Cabo de Hornos
104E3 Cape Johnston Depth Pacific O
35C1 Capelinha Brazil
4B3 Cape Lisburne USA
100A2 Capelongo Angola
15D3 Cape May USA
8A3 Cape Mendocino USA
98B3 Capenda Camulemba Angola
4F2 Cape Perry Can
7A4 Cape Tatnam Can
100A4 Cape Town S Africa
102G4 Cape Verde Is Atlantic O
102G4 Cape Verde Basin Atlantic O
12F3 Cape Yakataga USA
107D2 Cape York Pen Aust
46A1 Cap Gris Nez C France

26C3 Cap-Haïtien Haiti
31B2 Capim R Brazil
112C2 Capitán Arturo Prat Base Ant
27P2 Cap Moule à Chique C St Lucia
53C3 Capo Isola de Correnti C Italy
53C3 Capo Rizzuto C Italy
55A3 Capo Santa Maria di Leuca C Italy
53C3 Capo Spartivento C Italy
27P2 Cap Pt St Lucia
53B2 Capri I Italy
100B2 Caprivi Strip Region, Namibia
52A2 Cap Rosso C Corse
102H4 Cap Vert C Sen
32C4 Caquetá R Colombia
54B2 Caracal Rom
33E3 Caracaraí Brazil
32D1 Caracas Ven
35B2 Caraguatatuba Brazil
29B3 Carahue Chile
35C1 Caraí Brazil
35C2 Carandaí Brazil
31C6 Carangola Brazil
54B1 Caransebeş Rom
108A2 Carappee Hill Mt Aust
26A3 Caratasca Honduras
35C1 Caratinga Brazil
51B2 Caravaca Spain
35D1 Caravelas Brazil
18C2 Carbondale Illinois, USA
53A3 Carbonia Sardegna
7E5 Carborear Can
5G4 Carcaion Can
99E1 Carcar Mts Somalia
48C3 Carcassonne France
4E3 Carcross Can
23B2 Cardel Mexico
25D2 Cárdenas Cuba
23B1 Cárdenas Mexico
43C4 Cardiff Wales
43C4 Cardiff County Wales
43B3 Cardigan Wales
43B3 Cardigan B Wales
43B3 Cardiganshire County Wales
13E2 Cardston Can
54B1 Carei Rom
33F4 Careiro Brazil
34A2 Carén Chile
14B2 Carey USA
48B2 Carhaix-Plouguer France
29D3 Carhué Arg
31C6 Cariacica Brazil
5J4 Caribou Can
5G4 Caribou Mts Alberta, Can
5F4 Caribou Mts British Columbia, Can
79B3 Carigara Phil
48C2 Carignan France
33E1 Caripito Ven
15C1 Carleton Place Can
101G1 Carletonville S Africa
18C2 Carlinville USA
42C2 Carlisle Eng
14C2 Carlisle USA
34C3 Carlos Arg
35C1 Carlos Chagas Brazil
45C2 Carlow County, Irish Rep
45C2 Carlow Irish Rep
21B3 Carlsbad California, USA
9C3 Carlsbad New Mexico, USA
5H5 Carlyle Can
12G2 Carmacks Can
47B2 Carmagnola Italy
43B4 Carmarthen Wales
43B4 Carmarthen B Wales
43B4 Carmarthenshire County Wales
22B2 Carmel California, USA

16C2 Carmel New York, USA
94B2 Carmel,Mt Israel
34D2 Carmelo Urug
22B2 Carmel Valley USA
9B4 Carmen I Mexico
29D4 Carmen de Patagones Arg
18C2 Carmi USA
21A2 Carmichael USA
35B1 Carmo do Paranaíba Brazil
50A2 Carmona Spain
106A3 Carnarvon Aust
100B4 Carnarvon S Africa
35D1 Carncacá Brazil
45C1 Carndonagh Irish Rep
106B3 Carnegie,L Aust
98B2 Carnot CAR
108A2 Carnot,C Aust
17B2 Carol City USA
31B3 Carolina Brazil
101H1 Carolina S Africa
17C1 Carolina Beach USA
104F3 Caroline Is Pacific O
60B4 Carpathians Mts E Europe
59D3 Carpaţii Orientali Mts Rom
106C2 Carpentaria,G of Aust
83C5 Carpenter Ridge Indian O
49D3 Carpentras France
52B2 Carpi Italy
22C3 Carpinteria USA
17B2 Carrabelle USA
52B2 Carrara Italy
41B3 Garrauntoohil Mt Irish Rep
45C2 Carrickmacross Irish Rep
45B2 Carrick on Shannon Irish Rep
45C2 Carrick-on-Suir Irish Rep
108A2 Carrieton Aust
8D2 Carrington USA
50B1 Carrión R Spain
10A2 Carroll USA
17A1 Carrollton Georgia, USA
14A3 Carrollton Kentucky, USA
18B2 Carrollton Missouri, USA
18C2 Carruthersville USA
60E5 Carsamba Turk
92B2 Carsamba R Turk
8B3 Carson City USA
14B2 Carsonville USA
26B4 Cartagena Colombia
51B2 Cartagena Spain
32B3 Cartago Colombia
26A4 Cartago Costa Rica
11C2 Carterton NZ
18B2 Carthage Missouri, USA
15C2 Carthage New York, USA
19B3 Carthage Texas, USA
106B2 Cartier I Timor S
7E4 Cartwright Can
31D3 Caruaru Brazil
33E1 Carúpano Ven
46B1 Carvin France
34A2 Casablanca Chile
96B1 Casablanca Mor
35B2 Casa Branca Brazil
9B3 Casa Grande USA
52A1 Casale Monferrato Italy
47D2 Casalmaggiore Italy
34C3 Casares Arg
13C3 Cascade Mts Can/USA
111A2 Cascade Pt NZ
8A2 Cascade Range Mts USA
30F3 Cascavel Brazil
53B2 Caserta Italy
112C9 Casey Base Ant
45C2 Cashel Irish Rep

34C2 Casilda Arg
107E3 Casino Aust
32B5 Casma Peru
51B1 Caspe Spain
8C2 Casper USA
61G4 Caspian Lowland *Region* Kazakhstan
65G6 Caspian S Asia/Europe
14C3 Cass USA
100B2 Cassamba Angola
46B1 Cassel France
12J3 Cassiar Can
4E3 Cassiar Mts Can
35A1 Cassilândia Brazil
53B2 Cassino Italy
22C3 Castaic USA
34B2 Castaño R Arg
47D2 Castelfranco Italy
49D3 Castellane France
53B3 Castelli Arg
51B2 Castellon de la Plana Spain
31C3 Castelo Brazil
50A2 Castelo Branco Port
48C3 Castelsarrasin France
53B3 Castelvetrano Italy
108B3 Casterton Aust
50B2 Castilla La Nueva Region, Spain
50B1 Castilla La Vieja Region, Spain
41B3 Castlebar Irish Rep
44A3 Castlebay Scot
42C2 Castle Douglas Scot
20C1 Castlegar Can
45B2 Castleisland Irish Rep
108B3 Castlemaine Aust
45B2 Castlemaine Irish Rep
109C2 Castlereagh Aust
48C3 Castres-sur-l'Agout France
27E4 Castries St Lucia
29B4 Castro Arg
30F3 Castro Brazil
31D4 Castro Alves Brazil
53C3 Castrovillari Italy
22B2 Castroville USA
111A2 Caswell Sd NZ
25E2 Cat The Bahamas
79B3 Catabalogan Phil
32A5 Catacaos Peru
35C2 Cataguases Brazil
19B3 Catahoula L USA
35B1 Catalão Brazil
51C1 Cataluña Region, Spain
30C4 Catamarca Arg
30C4 Catamarca State, Arg
101C2 Catandica Mozam
79B3 Catanduanes I Phil
31B6 Catanduva Brazil
53C3 Catania Italy
53C3 Catanzaro Italy
79B3 Catarman Phil
108A2 Catastrophe,C Aust
26C5 Catatumbo R Ven
16A2 Catawissa USA
23B2 Catemaco Mexico
49D3 Cateri Corse
52A2 Cateraggio Corse
98B3 Catete Angola
97A3 Catio Guinea-Bissau
7A4 Cat Lake Can
13D3 Catlegar Can
107E3 Cato I Aust
25D2 Catoche,C Mexico
16A3 Catoctin Mt USA
15C3 Catonsville USA
34C3 Catrilo Arg
15D2 Catskill USA
15D2 Catskill Mts USA
32C2 Cauca R Colombia
31D2 Caucaia Brazil
32B2 Caucasia Colombia
65F5 Caucasus Mts Georgia
46B1 Caudry France
98B3 Caungula Angola
29B3 Cauquenes Chile
87B2 Cauvery R India
49D3 Cavaillon France
47D1 Cavalese Italy
97B4 Cavally R Lib

45C2 Cavan County, Irish Rep
45C2 Cavan Irish Rep
79B3 Cavite Phil
31C2 Caxias Brazil
32C4 Caxias Brazil
30F4 Caxias do Sul Brazil
98B3 Caxito Angola
17B1 Cayce USA
93D1 Çayeli Turk
33G3 Cayenne French Guiana
46A1 Cayeux-sur-Mer France
25E3 Cayman Brac I Caribbean S
26A3 Cayman Is Caribbean S
26A3 Cayman Trench Caribbean S
99E2 Caynabo Somalia
25E2 Cayo Romana I Cuba
25D3 Cayos Miskitos Is Nic
8A2 Cay Sal I Caribbean S
100B2 Cazombo Angola
Ceará = Fortaleza
31C3 Ceara State, Brazil
79B3 Cebu Phil
79B3 Cebu I Phil
16B3 Cecilton USA
52B2 Cecina Italy
8B3 Cedar City USA
19A3 Cedar Creek Res USA
5J4 Cedar L Can
10A2 Cedar Rapids USA
17A1 Cedartown USA
24A2 Cedros I Mexico
106C4 Ceduna Aust
99E2 Ceelbuur Somalia
99E2 Ceerigaabo Somalia
53B3 Cefalù Italy
59B3 Cegléd Hung
100A2 Cela Angola
24B2 Celaya Mexico
Celebes = Sulawesi
70C3 Celebes S S E Asia
14B2 Celina USA
52C1 Celje Slovenia
56C2 Celle Germany
71E4 Cendrawasih Pen Indon
47C2 Ceno R Italy
19B3 Center USA
16C2 Center Moriches USA
17A1 Center Point USA
47D2 Cento Italy
98B2 Central African Republic Africa
16D2 Central Falls USA
18C2 Centralia Illinois, USA
8A2 Centralia Washington, USA
20B2 Central Point USA
71F4 Central Range Mts PNG
16A3 Centreville Maryland, USA
78C4 Cepu Indon
71D4 Ceram Sea Indon
34C3 Cerdães Arg
31B5 Ceres Brazil
100A4 Ceres S Africa
22B2 Ceres USA
48C2 Cergy-Pontoise France
53C2 Cerignola Italy
60C5 Cernavodă Rom
9C4 Cerralvo I Mexico
23A1 Cerritos Mexico
34B2 Cerro Aconcagua Mt Arg
23B1 Cerro Azul Mexico
34A3 Cerro Campanario Mt Chile
34C2 Cerro Champaqui Mt Arg
23A2 Cerro Cuachaia Mt Mexico

23B1 Cerro de Astillero Mexico
34B2 Cerro de Olivares Mt Arg
32B6 Cerro de Pasco Peru
27D3 Cerro de Punta Mt Puerto Rico
23A2 Cerro El Cantado Mt Mexico
34B3 Cerro El Nevado Mt Arg
23A2 Cerro Grande Mt Mexico
34A2 Cerro Juncal Mt Arg/Chile
23A1 Cerro la Ardilla Mts Mexico
34B1 Cerro las Tortolas Mt Chile
23A2 Cerro Laurel Mt Mexico
34A2 Cerro Mercedario Mt Arg
34A3 Cerro Mora Mt Chile
27C4 Cerron Mt Ven
34B3 Cerro Payún Mt Arg
23B2 Cerro Penon del Rosario Mt Mexico
34B2 Cerro Sosneado Mt Arg
23A2 Cerro Teotepec Mt Mexico
34B2 Cerro Tupungato Mt Arg
23B2 Cerro Yucuyacau Mt Mexico
47C2 Cervo R Italy
52B2 Cesena Italy
60B2 Cēsis Latvia
59B3 České Budejovice Czech Republic
59B3 Českomoravská Vysocina Mts Czech Republic
55C3 Çeşme Turk
107E4 Cessnock Aust
52C2 Cetina R Croatia
96B1 Ceuta N W Africa
92C2 Ceyhan Turk
92C2 Ceyhan R Turk
92C2 Ceylanpinar Turk
Ceylon = Sri Lanka
63B2 Chaa-Khol Russian Fed
47B1 Chablais Region, France
34C2 Chacabuco Arg
32B5 Chachapoyas Peru
34B3 Chacharramendi Arg
84C3 Chachran Pak
30D4 Chaco State, Arg
98B1 Chad Republic, Africa
98B1 Chad L C Africa
34B3 Chadileuvu R Arg
8C2 Chadron USA
16C2 Chaffee USA
85A3 Chagai Pak
63F2 Chagda Russian Fed
84B2 Chaghcharan Afghan
104B4 Chagos Arch Indian O
27L1 Chaguanas Trinidad
91D4 Chāh Bahār Iran
76C2 Chai Badan Thai
76C3 Chaine des Cardamomes Mts Camb
98C4 Chaine des Mitumba Mts Zaire
76C2 Chaiyaphum Thai
34D2 Chajari Arg
84C2 Chakwal Pak
30B2 Chala Peru
100C2 Chalabesa Zambia
84A2 Chalap Dalam Mts Afghan
73C4 Chaling China
12F1 Chalkyitsik USA
46C2 Challerange France
46C2 Châlons en Champagne France
49C2 Chalon sur Saône France

57C3 Cham Germany
84B2 Chaman Pak
84D2 Chamba India
85D3 Chambal R India
8D3 Chamberlain USA
49D2 Chambéry France
46B2 Chambly France
85A3 Chambor Kalat Pak
90B3 Chamgordan Iran
34A2 Chamical Arg
47B2 Chamonix France
84B2 Champa India
49C2 Champagne Region, France
101G1 Champagne Castle Mt Lesotho
47A1 Champagnole France
10B2 Champaign USA
76D3 Champassak Laos
10C2 Champlain,L USA
87B2 Chāmrajnagar India
30B4 Chañaral Chile
34A3 Chanco Chile
4D3 Chandalar USA
4D3 Chandalar R USA
84D2 Chandigarh India
86C2 Chandpur Bang
85D5 Chandrapur India
91D4 Chānf Iran
101C2 Changara Mozam
74B2 Changbai China
69E2 Changchun China
73C4 Changde China
68E4 Chang-hua Taiwan
76D2 Changjiang China
73D3 Chang Jiang R China
74B2 Changjin N Korea
73C4 Changsha China
72E3 Changshu China
73C4 Changtu China
72B2 Changwu China
74B3 Changyön N Korea
73C4 Changzhi China
73E3 Changzhou China
48B2 Channel Is Europe
9B3 Channel Is UK
7E5 Channel Port-aux-Basques Can
76D2 Chanthaburi Thai
46B2 Chantilly France
18A2 Chanute USA
73D5 Chaoân China
73D3 Chao He R China
76C3 Chao Phraya R Thai
72E1 Chaoyang China
31C4 Chapada Diamantina Mts Brazil
31C2 Chapadinha Brazil
23A1 Chapala Mexico
23A1 Chapala,Lac de L Mexico
61H3 Chapayevo Kazakhstan
30F4 Chapecó Brazil
27H1 Chapeltown Jamaica
7B5 Chapleau Can
61E3 Chaplygin Russian Fed
112C3 Charcot I Ant
80E2 Chardzhou Turkmenistan
48C2 Charente R France
98B1 Chari R Chad
98B1 Chari Baguirmi Region, Chad
84B1 Charikar Afghan
18B1 Chariton R USA
33F2 Charity Guyana
84D3 Charkhari India
46C1 Charleroi Belg
18C2 Charleston Illinois, USA
18C2 Charleston Missouri, USA
11C3 Charleston S Carolina, USA
10B3 Charleston W Virginia, USA
98C3 Charlesville Zaire
107D3 Charleville Aust
49C2 Charleville-Mézières France
14A1 Charlevoix USA

14B2 **Charlotte** Michigan, USA
11B3 **Charlotte** N Carolina, USA
17B2 **Charlotte Harbor** B USA
10C3 **Charlottesville** USA
7D5 **Charlottetown** Can
27K1 **Charlotteville** Tobago
108B3 **Charlton** Aust
10C1 **Charlton I** Can
84C2 **Charsadda** Pak
107D3 **Charters Towers** Aust
48C2 **Chartres** France
29E3 **Chascomus** Arg
13D2 **Chase** Can
48B2 **Châteaubriant** France
48C2 **Châteaudun** France
48C2 **Châteaulin** France
48C2 **Châteauroux** France
46D2 **Château-Salins** France
49C2 **Château-Thierry** France
46C1 **Châtelet** Belg
48C2 **Châtellerault** France
43E4 **Chatham** Eng
7D5 **Chatham** New Brunswick, Can
16C1 **Chatham** New York, USA
14B2 **Chatham** Ontario, Can
13A2 **Chatham Sd** Can
12H3 **Chatham Str** USA
49C2 **Châtillon** France
47B2 **Châtillon** Italy
16B3 **Chatsworth** USA
17B1 **Chattahoochee** USA
17A1 **Chattahoochee** R USA
11B3 **Chattanooga** USA
76A1 **Chauk** Myan
49D2 **Chaumont** France
46C2 **Chauny** France
77D3 **Chau Phu** Viet
50A1 **Chaves** Port
61H2 **Chaykovskiy** Russian Fed
50B2 **Chazaouet** Alg
34C2 **Chazón** Arg
32C2 **Chcontá** Colombia
57C2 **Cheb** Czech Republic
65F4 **Cheboksary** Russian Fed
10B2 **Cheboygan** USA
61G5 **Chechnya** Division, Russian Fed
74B3 **Chech'on** S Korea
85C3 **Chechro** Pak
18A2 **Checotah** USA
76A2 **Cheduba** I Myan
108B1 **Cheepie** Aust
96B2 **Chegga** Maur
100C2 **Chegutu** Zim
20B1 **Chehalis** USA
74B4 **Cheju** S Korea
74B4 **Cheju do** I S Korea
74B4 **Cheju-haehyŏp** Str S Korea
63F2 **Chekunda** Russian Fed
20B1 **Chelan,L** USA
90B2 **Cheleken** Turkmenistan
34B3 **Chelforo** Arg
80D1 **Chelkar** Kazakhstan
59C2 **Chełm** Pol
58B2 **Chełmno** Pol
43E4 **Chelmsford** Eng
43C4 **Cheltenham** Eng
61K2 **Chelyabinsk** Russian Fed
61K3 **Chelyabinsk** Division, Russian Fed
101C2 **Chemba** Mozam
57C2 **Chemnitz** Germany
84D2 **Chenab** R India/Pak
96B2 **Chenachane** Alg
20C1 **Cheney** USA
18A2 **Cheney Res** USA

72D1 **Chengda** China
73A3 **Chengdu** China
72E2 **Chengshan Jiao** Pt China
73C4 **Chenxi** China
73C4 **Chen Xian** China
73D3 **Cheo Xian** China
32B5 **Chepen** Peru
34B2 **Chepes** Arg
48C2 **Cher** R France
23A2 **Cheran** Mexico
17C1 **Cheraw** USA
48B2 **Cherbourg** France
96C1 **Cherchell** Alg
63C2 **Cheremkhovo** Russian Fed
60E2 **Cherepovets** Russian Fed
60D4 **Cherkassy** Ukraine
61F5 **Cherkessk** Russian Fed
60D3 **Chernigov** Ukraine
60D3 **Chernobyl** Ukraine
60C4 **Chernovtsy** Ukraine
61J2 **Chernushka** Russian Fed
60B3 **Chernyakhovsk** Russian Fed
61G4 **Chernyye Zemli** Region, Russian Fed
18A2 **Cherokees,L o'the** USA
34A3 **Cherqueno** Chile
86C1 **Cherrapunji** India
60C3 **Cherven'** Belarus
59C2 **Chervonograd** Ukraine
10C3 **Chesapeake** B USA
42C3 **Cheshire** County, Eng
16C1 **Cheshire** USA
64F3 **Chëshskaya Guba** B Russian Fed
21A1 **Chester** California, USA
42C3 **Chester** Eng
18C2 **Chester** Illinois, USA
16C1 **Chester** Massachusets, USA
15C3 **Chester** Pennsylvania, USA
17B1 **Chester** S Carolina, USA
16A3 **Chester** USA
42D3 **Chesterfield** Eng
6A3 **Chesterfield Inlet** Can
14B3 **Chestertown** USA
25D3 **Chetumal** Mexico
13C1 **Chetwynd** Can
12A2 **Chevak** USA
111B2 **Cheviot** NZ
40C2 **Cheviots** Hills Eng/Scot
13D3 **Chewelah** USA
8C2 **Cheyenne** USA
83L1 **Chhapra** India
86C1 **Chhatak** Bang
85D4 **Chhatarpur** India
85D4 **Chhindwāra** India
73E5 **Chhuka** Bhutan
73E5 **Chi'ai** Taiwan
100A2 **Chiange** Angola
76C2 **Chiang Kham** Thai
76B2 **Chiang Mai** Thai
47C1 **Chiavenna** Italy
74E3 **Chiba** Japan
86B2 **Chibāsa** India
100A2 **Chibia** Angola
7C5 **Chibougamau** Can
101C2 **Chibuto** Mozam
10B2 **Chicago** USA
14A2 **Chicago Heights** USA
12G3 **Chichagof** I USA
43D4 **Chichester** Eng
75B1 **Chichibu** Japan
69G4 **Chichi-jima** I Japan
11B3 **Chickamauga L** USA
19C3 **Chickasawhay** R USA
9D3 **Chickasha** USA
12F2 **Chicken** USA
32A5 **Chiclayo** Peru

8A3 **Chico** USA
29C4 **Chico** R Arg
101C2 **Chicoa** Mozam
15D2 **Chicopee** USA
7C5 **Chicoutimi** Can
101C2 **Chicualacuala** Mozam
87B2 **Chidambaram** India
6D3 **Chidley,C** Can
17B2 **Chiefland** USA
99C3 **Chiengi** Zambia
47B2 **Chieri** Italy
46C2 **Chiers** R France
47C1 **Chiesa** R Italy
47D2 **Chiese** R Italy
52B2 **Chieti** Italy
72D1 **Chifeng** China
12C3 **Chiginagak,Mt** USA
23B2 **Chignahuapán** Mexico
12C3 **Chignik** USA
24B2 **Chihuahua** Mexico
24B2 **Chihuahua** Mexico
87B2 **Chik Ballāpur** India
87B2 **Chikmagalūr** India
12C2 **Chikuminuk L** USA
101C2 **Chikwawa** Malawi
76A1 **Chi-kyaw** Myan
87C1 **Chilakalūrupet** India
87B3 **Chilaw** Sri Lanka
28B6 **Chile** Republic
34B2 **Chilecito** Mendoza, Arg
100B2 **Chililabombwe** Zambia
86B2 **Chilka** L India
13C2 **Chilko** R Can
13C2 **Chilko L** Can
13C2 **Chilkotin** R Can
34A3 **Chillán** Arg
34D3 **Chillar** Arg
18B2 **Chillicothe** Missouri, USA
14B3 **Chillicothe** Ohio, USA
13C3 **Chilliwack** Can
86B1 **Chilmari** India
101C2 **Chilongozi** Zambia
100B2 **Chiloquin** USA
24C3 **Chilpancingo** Mexico
43D4 **Chiltern Hills** Upland Eng
14A2 **Chilton** USA
101C2 **Chilumba** Malawi
69E4 **Chi-lung** Taiwan
101C2 **Chilwa L** Malawi
46C1 **Chimay** Belg
65G5 **Chimbay** Uzbekistan
32B4 **Chimborazo** Mt Ecuador
32B5 **Chimbote** Peru
65H5 **Chimkent** Kazakhstan
101C2 **Chimoio** Mozam
67E3 **China** Republic, Asia
China National Republic = Taiwan
25D3 **Chinandega** Nic
32B6 **Chincha Alta** Peru
109D1 **Chinchilla** Aust
101C2 **Chinde** Mozam
86C2 **Chindwin** R Myan
100A2 **Chingola** Zambia
96A2 **Chinguetti** Maur
74B3 **Chinhae** S Korea
100C2 **Chinhoyi** Zim
84C2 **Chiniot** Pak
74B3 **Chinju** S Korea
98C2 **Chinko** R CAR
75B1 **Chino** Japan
101C2 **Chinsali** Zambia
52B1 **Chioggia** Italy
101C2 **Chipata** Zambia
101C2 **Chipinge** Zim
87A1 **Chiplūn** India
43C4 **Chippenham** Eng
10A2 **Chippewa Falls** USA
32A4 **Chira** R Peru
87C1 **Chirāla** India
101C3 **Chiredzi** Zim

95A2 **Chirfa** Niger
32A2 **Chiriquí** Mt Panama
54C2 **Chirpan** Bulg
32A2 **Chirripo Grande** Mt Costa Rica
100C2 **Chirundu** Zim
100B2 **Chisamba** Zambia
7C4 **Chisasibi** Can
73A4 **Chishui He** R China
Chişinău = Kishinev
47B2 **Chisone** R Italy
61H2 **Chistopol** Russian Fed
68D1 **Chita** Russian Fed
100A2 **Chitado** Angola
100A2 **Chitembo** Angola
12F2 **Chitina** USA
12F2 **Chitina** R USA
87B2 **Chitradurga** India
84C1 **Chitral** Pak
32A2 **Chitré** Panama
86C2 **Chittagong** Bang
85C4 **Chittaurgarh** India
87B2 **Chittoor** India
100B2 **Chiume** Angola
47D1 **Chiusa** Italy
47B2 **Chivasso** Italy
100C2 **Chivhu** Zim
29D2 **Chivilcoy** Arg
100C2 **Chivu** Zim
75A1 **Chizu** Japan
29C3 **Choele Choel** Arg
34C3 **Choique** Arg
24B2 **Choix** Mexico
48B2 **Chojnice** Pol
99D1 **Choke Mts** Eth
48B2 **Cholet** France
23B2 **Cholula** Mexico
100B2 **Choma** Zambia
100B2 **Chomo Yummo** Mt China/India
57C2 **Chomutov** Czech Republic
63C1 **Chona** R Russian Fed
74B3 **Ch'ŏnan** S Korea
76C3 **Chon Buri** Thai
32A4 **Chone** Ecuador
74B2 **Ch'ŏngjin** N Korea
74B3 **Ch'ŏngju** S Korea
74B3 **Ch'ŏngju** S Korea
100A2 **Chongoroi** Angola
73B4 **Chongqing** China
74B3 **Ch'ŏngup** S Korea
74B3 **Chŏnju** S Korea
86B1 **Chooyu** Mt China/Nepal
59D3 **Chortkov** Ukraine
74B3 **Ch'ŏrwŏn** N Korea
59B2 **Chorzow** Pol
34A3 **Chos-Malal** Arg
58B2 **Choszczno** Pol
86A2 **Chotanāgpur** Region, India
96C1 **Chott Melrhir** Alg
22B2 **Chowchilla** USA
63D3 **Choybalsan** Mongolia
6A3 **Chrantrey Inlet** B Can
111B2 **Christchurch** NZ
101G1 **Christiana** S Africa
6D2 **Christian,C** Can
12H3 **Christian Sd** Can
6E3 **Christianshab** Greenland
104D4 **Christmas I** Indian O
65J5 **Chu** Kazakhstan
65J5 **Chu, R** Kazakhstan
29C4 **Chubut** State, Arg
29C4 **Chubut** R Arg
60D2 **Chudovo** Russian Fed
Chudskoye Ozero = Peipus, Lake
12E2 **Chugiak** USA
75A1 **Chugoku-sanchi** Mts Japan
29F2 **Chuí** Brazil
29B3 **Chuillán** Chile
77C5 **Chukai** Malay
76D2 **Chu Lai** Viet

21B3 Chula Vista USA
12E2 Chulitna USA
63E2 Chulman Russian Fed
32A5 Chulucanas Peru
30C2 Chulumani Bol
65K4 Chulym Russian Fed
63A2 Chulym *R* Russian Fed
63B2 Chuma *R* Russian Fed
84D2 Chumar India
63F2 Chumikan Russian Fed
77B3 Chumphon Thai
74B3 Ch'unch'ŏn S Korea
86B2 Chunchura India
74B3 Ch'ungju S Korea
Chungking = Chongqing
99D3 Chunya Tanz
63C1 Chunya *R* Russian Fed
27L1 Chupara Pt Trinidad
30C3 Chuquicamata Chile
52A1 Chur Switz
86C2 Churāchāndpur India
7A4 Churchill Can
7D4 Churchill *R* Labrador, Can
7A4 Churchill *R* Manitoba, Can
7A4 Churchill,C Can
5H4 Churchill L Can
84C3 Churu India
23A2 Churumuco Mexico
61J2 Chusovoy
61G2 Chuvashia Division, Russian Fed
68B4 Chuxiong China
76D3 Chu Yang Sin *Mt* Viet
78A4 Cianjur Indon
47D2 Ciano d'Enza Italy
35A2 Cianorte Brazil
25E2 Ciego de Ávila Cuba
32C1 Ciénaga Colombia
25D2 Cienfuegos Cuba
59B3 Cieszyn Pol
51B2 Cieza Spain
92B2 Cihanbeyli Turk
23A2 Cihuatlán Mexico
78A4 Cijulang Indon
78B4 Cilacap Indon
54C1 Cimpina Rom
51C1 Cînca *R* Spain
52C2 Cinčer *Mt* Bosnia-Herzegovina
10B3 Cincinnati USA
54B1 Cindrelu *Mt* Rom
55C3 Cine *R* Turk
46C1 Ciney Belg
34B3 Cipolletti Arg
4D3 Circle Alaska, USA
14B3 Circleville USA
78B4 Cirebon Indon
43D4 Cirencester Eng
47D2 Citadella Italy
24C3 Citlaltepetl *Mt* Mexico
100A4 Citrusdal S Africa
52B2 Città del Vaticano Italy
52B2 Città di Castello Italy
24B2 Ciudad Acuña Mexico
23A2 Ciudad Altamirano Mexico
33E2 Ciudad Bolívar Ven
24B2 Ciudad Camargo Mexico
25C3 Ciudad del Carmen Mexico
23B1 Ciudad del Maíz Mexico
51C1 Ciudadela Spain
33E2 Ciudad Guayana Ven
24B3 Ciudad Guzman Mexico
23A2 Ciudad Hidalgo Mexico

24B1 Ciudad Juárez Mexico
9C4 Ciudad Lerdo Mexico
24C2 Ciudad Madero Mexico
23B2 Ciudad Mendoza Mexico
24B2 Ciudad Obregon Mexico
27C4 Ciudad Ojeda Ven
33E2 Ciudad Piar Ven
50B2 Ciudad Real Spain
50A1 Ciudad Rodrigo Spain
24C2 Ciudad Valles Mexico
24C2 Ciudad Victoria Mexico
52B2 Civitavecchia Italy
93D2 Cizre Turk
44C3 Clackmannanshire Division, Scot
43E4 Clacton-on-Sea Eng
43A2 Claire,L Can
14C2 Clairton USA
47A1 Clairvaux France
17A1 Clanton USA
100A4 Clanwilliam S Africa
45C2 Clara Irish Rep
34D3 Claraz Arg
45B2 Clare County, Irish Rep
14B2 Clare USA
45A2 Clare *I* Irish Rep
18A2 Claremore USA
45B2 Claremorris Irish Rep
109D1 Clarence *R* Aust
111B2 Clarence *R* NZ
106C2 Clarence Str Aust
12H3 Clarence Str USA
19B3 Clarendon USA
7E5 Claresholm Can
5G4 Clareshotm Can
18A1 Clarinda USA
15C2 Clarion Pennsylvania, USA
24A3 Clarion *I* Mexico
15C2 Clarion *R* USA
105J3 Clarion Fracture Zone Pacific O
11B3 Clark Hill Res USA
14B2 Clark,Pt Can
14B3 Clarksburg USA
11A3 Clarksdale USA
12C3 Clarks Point USA
20C1 Clarkston USA
18B2 Clarksville Arkansas, USA
35A1 Claro *R* Brazil
29D3 Claromecó Arg
18A2 Clay Center USA
44D2 Claymore Oilfield N Sea
13B3 Clayquot Sd Can
9C3 Clayton New Mexico, USA
15C2 Clayton New York, USA
41B3 Clear C Irish Rep
12E3 Cleare,C USA
13D1 Clear Hills *Mts* Can
21A2 Clear L USA
12E2 Clear Lake Res USA
13D2 Clearwater Can
11B4 Clearwater USA
13E1 Clearwater *R* Can
13C2 Clearwater L Can
9D3 Cleburne USA
42E2 Cleeton Oilfield North Sea
22B1 Clements USA
79A3 Cleopatra Needle *Mt* Phil
10D3 Clermont Aust
46B2 Clermont France
46C2 Clermont-en-Argonne France
49C2 Clermont-Ferrand France
46D1 Clervaux Germany
47D1 Cles Italy
108A2 Cleve Aust

19B3 Cleveland Mississippi, USA
10B2 Cleveland Ohio, USA
11B3 Cleveland Tennessee, USA
19A3 Cleveland Texas, USA
41B3 Clew B Irish Rep
45A2 Clifden Irish Rep
109D1 Clifton Aust
16B2 Clifton New Jersey, USA
13F3 Climax Can
18B2 Clinton Arkansas, USA
5F4 Clinton Can
16C2 Clinton Connecticut, USA
16D1 Clinton Massachusetts, USA
19B3 Clinton Mississippi, USA
18B2 Clinton Missouri, USA
16B2 Clinton New Jersey, USA
4H3 Clinton-Colden L Can
24B3 Clipperton *I* Pacific O
30C2 Cliza Bol
45B3 Clonakilty Irish Rep
107D3 Cloncurry Aust
45C1 Clones Irish Rep
45C2 Clonmel Irish Rep
10A2 Cloquet USA
12C2 Cloudy Mt USA
22C2 Clovis California, USA
9C3 Clovis New Mexico, USA
60B4 Cluj Rom
54B1 Cluj-Napoca Rom
47B1 Cluses France
47C2 Clusone Italy
111A3 Clutha *R* NZ
6D2 Clyde Can
111A3 Clyde NZ
42B2 Clyde *R* Scot

98A2 Cocobeach Gabon
27L1 Cocos B Trinidad
104C4 Cocos Is Indian O
23A1 Cocula Mexico
10C1 Cod,C USA
111A3 Codfish I NZ
7D4 Cod I Can
47E2 Codigoro Italy
31C2 Codó Brazil
47C2 Codogno Italy
8C2 Cody USA
56B2 Coesfeld Germany
8B2 Coeur d'Alene USA
9D3 Coffeyville USA
108A2 Coffin B Aust
109D2 Coff's Harbour Aust
23B2 Cofre de Perote *Mt* Mexico
48B2 Cognac France
15D2 Cohoes USA
108B3 Cohuna Aust
29B5 Coihaique Chile
32A3 Cojimies Ecuador
107D4 Colac Aust
31C5 Colatina Brazil
112B6 Colbeck,C Ant
43E4 Colchester Eng
16C2 Colchester USA
47B1 Col de la Faucille France
13E2 Cold L Can
52A1 Col du Grand St Bernard *P* Italy/Switz
47B2 Col du Lautaret *P* France
52A1 Col du Mont Cenis *P* France/Italy
14B2 Coldwater USA
12F1 Coleen *R* USA
14B2 Coleman Michigan, USA
45C1 Coleraine N Ire
111B2 Coleridge,L NZ
100B4 Colesberg S Africa
22C1 Coleville USA
22C2 Colfax California, USA
19B3 Colfax Louisiana, USA
20C1 Colfax Washington, USA
24B3 Colima Mexico
23A2 Colima State, Mexico
44A3 Coll I Scot
109C1 Collarenebri Aust
52A2 Colle de Tende *P* France/Italy
12F1 College USA
17B1 College Park Georgia, USA
16A3 College Park Washington, USA
19A3 College Station USA
106A4 Collie Aust
106B2 Collier B Aust
46A1 Collines de L'Artois *Mts* France
46B2 Collines De Thiérache France
14B2 Collingwood Can
110B2 Collingwood NZ
19C3 Collins Mississippi, USA
4H2 Collinson Pen Can
18C2 Collinsville Aust
17C2 Collinsville Illinois, USA
18A2 Collinsville Oklahoma, USA
34A3 Collipulli Chile
49D2 Colmar France
Cologne = Köln
35B2 Colômbia Brazil
32B3 Colombia Republic, S America
15C3 Colombia USA
87B3 Colombo Sri Lanka
25D2 Colon Cuba
32B2 Colón Panama
29E2 Colonia Urug

34D2 Colonia del Sacramento Urug
34B3 Colonia 25 de Mayo Arg
29C5 Colonia Las Heras Arg
44A3 Colonsay I Scot
23A1 Colontlán Mexico
27E5 Coloradito Ven
8C3 Colorado State, USA
9B3 Colorado R Arizona, USA
29D3 Colorado R Buenos Aires, Arg
8C3 Colorado R Texas, USA
9B3 Colorado Plat USA
8C3 Colorado Springs USA
22D3 Colton USA
16A3 Columbia Maryland, USA
19C3 Columbia Mississippi, USA
10A3 Columbia Missouri, USA
15C2 Columbia Pennsylvania, USA
11B3 Columbia S Carolina, USA
11B3 Columbia Tennessee, USA
13D2 Columbia R Can
8A2 Columbia R USA
5G4 Columbia,Mt Can
20C1 Columbia Plat USA
11B3 Columbus Georgia, USA
14A3 Columbus Indiana, USA
11B3 Columbus Mississippi, USA
8D2 Columbus Nebraska, USA
10B2 Columbus Ohio, USA
19A4 Columbus Texas, USA
20C1 Colville USA
4C3 Colville R USA
110C1 Colville,C NZ
4F3 Colville L Can
42C3 Colwyn Bay Wales
47E2 Comacchio Italy
22B1 Comanche Res USA
112C2 Comandante Ferraz Base Ant
25D3 Comayagua Honduras
34A2 Combarbalá Chile
45C2 Comeragh Mts Irish Rep
86C2 Comilla Bang
25B3 Comitán Mexico
49C2 Commentry France
683 Committees B Can
52A1 Como Italy
29C5 Comodoro Rivadavia Arg
23A1 Comonfort Mexico
87B3 Comorin,C India
101D2 Comoros Is Indian O
49C2 Compiègne France
49B2 Compostela Mexico
34B2 Comte Salas Arg
86C1 Cona China
97A4 Conakry Guinea
34B2 Concarán Arg
48B2 Concarneau France
35D1 Conceição da Barra Brazil
31B3 Conceição do Araguaia Brazil
35C1 Conceição do Mato Dentro Brazil
29B3 Concepción Arg
30E3 Concepción Par
29E2 Concepción R Par
24B2 Concepción del Oro Mexico
34D2 Concepcion del Uruguay Arg
9A3 Conception,Pt USA
35B2 Conchas Brazil
9C4 Conchos R Mexico

21A2 Concord California, USA
10C2 Concord New Hampshire, USA
29E2 Concordia Arg
8D3 Concordia USA
20B1 Concrete USA
109D1 Condamine Aust
107D4 Condobolin Aust
20B1 Condon USA
46C1 Condroz Mts Belg
17A1 Conecuh R USA
47E2 Conegliano Italy
89F8 Congo Republic, Africa
89F8 Congo R Congo, Congo,R = Zaire
14B1 Coniston Can
45B2 Connaught Region, Irish Rep
14B2 Conneaut USA
10C2 Connecticut State, USA
15D2 Connecticut R USA
15C2 Connellsville USA
45B2 Connemara,Mts of Irish Rep
14A3 Connersville USA
108B2 Conoble Aust
19A3 Conroe USA
35C2 Conselheiro Lafaiete Brazil
77D4 Con Son Is Viet
Constance,L = Bodensee
60C5 Constanta Rom
96C1 Constantine Alg
12C3 Constantine,C USA
29B3 Constitución Chile
13F3 Consul Can
47E2 Contarina Italy
31C4 Contas R Brazil
23B2 Contreras Mexico
4H3 Contuoyto L Can
11A3 Conway Arkansas, USA
15D2 Conway New Hampshire, USA
17C1 Conway South Carolina, USA
108A1 Conway,L Aust
42C3 Conwy Wales
106C3 Coober Pedy Aust
110B2 Cook Str NZ
13B2 Cook,C Can
4C3 Cook Inlet B USA
105H4 Cook Is Pacific O
111B2 Cook,Mt NZ
107D2 Cooktown Aust
109C2 Coolabah Aust
108C1 Cooladdi Aust
109C2 Coolah Aust
108B4 Coolgardie Aust
109C3 Cooma Aust
109C2 Coonabarabran Aust
108B2 Coonbah Aust
108G1 Coongoola Aust
87B2 Coonoor India
108B1 Cooper Basin Aust
108C3 Cooper Creek Aust
108B1 Cooper Creek R Aust
108A3 Coorong,The Aust
109D1 Cooroy Aust
20B2 Coos B USA
2082 Coos Bay USA
107D4 Cootamundra Aust
45C1 Cootehill Irish Rep
23B2 Copala Mexico
23B2 Copalillo Mexico
Copenhagen = København
30B4 Copiapó Chile
47D2 Copparo Italy
12F2 Copper R USA
4D3 Copper Centre USA
14B1 Copper Cliff Can
Coppermine = Qurlurtuuk
9A3 Coppermine,Pt Can

30B4 Coquimbo Chile
54B2 Corabia Rom
17B2 Coral Gables USA
6B3 Coral Harbour Can
107D2 Coral S Aust/PNG
104F4 Coral Sea Basin Pacific O
107E2 Coral Sea Island Territories Aust
108B3 Corangamite,L Aust
33F3 Corantijn R Surinam/Guyana
46B2 Corbeil-Essonnes France
50A1 Corcubion Spain
11B3 Cordele USA
26C3 Cordillera Central Mts Dom Rep
79B2 Cordillera Central Mts Phil
32B5 Cordillera de Ansita Mts Arg
32B5 Cordillera de los Andes Mts Peru
30C4 Cordillera del Toro Mt Arg
32C2 Cordillera de Mérida Ven
34A3 Cordillera de Viento Mts Arg
25D3 Cordillera Isabela Mts Nic
32B3 Cordillera Occidental Mts Colombia
32B3 Cordillera Oriental Mts Colombia
108B1 Cordillo Downs Aust
29D2 Córdoba Arg
24C3 Córdoba Mexico
50B2 Córdoba Spain
29D2 Córdoba State, Arg
4D3 Cordova USA
Corfu = Kérkira
109D2 Coricudgy,Mt Aust
53C3 Corigliano Calabro Italy
11B3 Corinth Mississippi, USA
31C5 Corinto Brazil
45B2 Cork County, Irish Rep
41B3 Cork Irish Rep
92A1 Çorlu Turk
35A2 Cornélio Procópio Brazil
7E5 Corner Brook Can
109C3 Corner Inlet B Aust
15C2 Corning USA
7C5 Cornwall Can
43B4 Cornwall County, Eng
43B4 Cornwall,C Eng
4H2 Cornwall I Can
6A2 Cornwallis I Can
32D1 Coro Ven
31C2 Coroatá Brazil
30C2 Coroico Bol
35B1 Coromandel Brazil
87C2 Coromandel Coast India
110C1 Coromandel Pen NZ
110C1 Coromandel Range Mts NZ
20A4 Corona California, USA
13E2 Coronation Can
4G3 Coronation G Can
34C2 Coronda Arg
29B3 Coronel Chile
34D3 Coronel Brandsen Arg
34C3 Coronel Dorrego Arg
35C1 Coronel Fabriciano Brazil
30E4 Coronel Oviedo Par
29D3 Coronel Pringles Arg
34C3 Coronel Suárez Arg
34D3 Coronel Vidal Arg
30B2 Coropuna Mt Peru
109C3 Corowa Aust
49D3 Corps France

9D4 Corpus Christi USA
9D4 Corpus Christi,L USA
79B3 Corregidor I Phil
35A1 Corrente R Mato Grosso, Brazil
30E4 Corrientes Arg
29B3 Corrientes State, Arg
19B3 Corrigan USA
106A4 Corrigin Aust
107E2 Corringe Is Aust
109C3 Corryong Aust
52A2 Corse I Medit S
42B2 Corsewall Pt Scot
Corsica = Corse
9D3 Corsicana USA
52A2 Corte Corse
9C3 Cortez USA
52B1 Cortina d'Ampezzo Italy
15C2 Cortland USA
23A2 Coruca de Catalan Mexico
93D1 Çoruh R Turk
60E5 Çorum Turk
30E2 Corumbá Brazil
35B1 Corumba R Brazil
35B1 Corumbaiba Brazil
20B2 Corvallis USA
96A1 Corvo I Açores
43C3 Corwen Wales
23B2 Coscomatopec Mexico
53C3 Cosenza Italy
101D1 Cosmoledo Is Seychelles
34C2 Cosquin Arg
51B2 Costa Blanca Region, Spain
51C1 Costa Brava Region, Spain
50B2 Costa de la Luz Region, Spain
50B2 Costa del Sol Region, Spain
22D4 Costa Mesa USA
25D3 Costa Rica Republic, Cent America
79B4 Cotabato Phil
30C3 Cotagaita Bol
49D3 Côte d'Azur Region, France
97B4 Côte d'Ivoire Republic, Africa
46C2 Côtes de Meuse Mts France
97C4 Cotonou Benin
32B4 Cotopaxi Mt Ecuador
43C4 Cotswold Hills Upland Eng
20B2 Cottage Grove USA
56C2 Cottbus Germany
108A3 Couedic,C du Aust
20C1 Couer d'Alene L USA
46B2 Coulommiers France
15C1 Coulonge R Can
22B2 Coulterville USA
4B3 Council USA
8D2 Council Bluffs USA
58C1 Courland Lagoon Lg Lithuania/Russian Fed
52B1 Courmayeur Italy
13B3 Courtenay Can
Courtrai = Kortrijk
48B2 Coutances France
43D3 Coventry Eng
50A1 Covilhã Spain
17B1 Covington Georgia, USA
19C3 Covington Louisiana, USA
109C2 Cowal,L Aust
108B3 Cowangie Aust
15D1 Cowansville Can
108A1 Coward Springs Aust
108A2 Cowell Aust
108C3 Cowes Aust
20B1 Cowichan L Can
20B1 Cowlitz R USA
109C2 Cowra Aust
30F2 Coxim Brazil
16C1 Coxsackie USA
86C2 Cox's Bazar Bang
22B2 Coyote USA

23A2 Coyuca de Benitez Mexico
59B2 Cracow Pol
100B4 Cradock S Africa
8C2 Craig USA
57C3 Crailsheim Germany
54B2 Craiova Rom
15D2 Cranberry L USA
5G5 Cranbrook Can
20C2 Crane Oregon, USA
16D2 Cranston USA
20B2 Crater L USA
20B2 Crater Lake Nat Pk USA
31C3 Crateus Brazil
31D3 Crato Brazil
14A2 Crawfordsville USA
17B1 Crawfordville USA
43D4 Crawley Eng
5H4 Cree L Can
46B2 Creil France
47C2 Crema Italy
52B1 Cremona Italy
46B2 Crépy-en-Valois France
52B2 Cres I Yugos
22D2 Crescent City USA
54C2 Crespo Arg
13D3 Creston Can
18B1 Creston USA
17A1 Crestview USA
108B3 Creswick Aust
47A1 Crêt de la Neige Mt France
　Crete = Kriti
18A1 Crete USA
55B3 Crete,S of Greece
48C2 Creuse R France
43C3 Crewe Eng
44B3 Crianlarich Scot
30G4 Criciuma Brazil
44A3 Crieff Scot
12C3 Crillon,Mt USA
35B1 Cristalina Brazil
52B1 Croatia Republic, Europe
78D1 Crocker Range Mts Malay
19A3 Crockett USA
106C2 Croker I Aust
44C3 Cromarty Scot
43E3 Cromer Eng
111A3 Cromwell NZ
11C4 Crooked I The Bahamas
13C2 Crooked R Can
8D2 Crookston USA
109C2 Crookwell Aust
109D1 Croppa Creek Aust
11A3 Crossett USA
12G3 Cross Sd USA
53C3 Crotone Italy
19B3 Crowley USA
27K1 Crown Pt Tobago
109D1 Crows Nest Aust
107D2 Croydon Aust
43D4 Croydon Eng
104B5 Crozet Basin Indian O
4F2 Crozier Chan Can
30F4 Cruz Alta Brazil
25E3 Cruz,C Cuba
29D2 Cruz del Eje Arg
35C2 Cruzeiro Brazil
32C5 Cruzeiro do Sul Brazil
13C1 Crysdale,Mt Can
108A2 Crystal Brook Aust
18B2 Crystal City Missouri, USA
14A1 Crystal Falls USA
101C2 Cuamba Mozam
100B2 Cuando R Angola
100A2 Cuangar Angola
100A2 Cuango,R = Kwango,R
34C2 Cuarto R Arg
24B2 Cuauhtémoc Mexico
23B2 Cuautla Mexico
25D2 Cuba Republic, Caribbean S
100A2 Cubango R Angola
100A2 Cuchi Angola
100A2 Cuchi R Angola
34C3 Cuchillo Có Arg

32D3 Cucui Brazil
32C2 Cúcuta Colombia
87B2 Cuddalore India
87B2 Cuddapah India
106A3 Cue Aust
32B4 Cuenca Ecuador
51B1 Cuenca Spain
24C3 Cuernavaca Mexico
19A4 Cuero USA
30E2 Cuiabá Brazil
30E2 Cuiabá R Brazil
23B2 Cuicatlan Mexico
35C1 Cuieté R Brazil
44A3 Cuillin Hills Mts Scot
99B3 Cuilo R Angola
100A2 Cuito R Angola
100A2 Cuito Cunavale Angola
23A2 Cuitzeo Mexico
77D3 Cu Lao Hon I Viet
109C1 Culcairn Aust
109C1 Culgoa R Aust
24B2 Culiacán Mexico
79A3 Culion I Phil
17A1 Cullman USA
47A2 Culoz France
15C3 Culpeper USA
32J7 Culpepper I Ecuador
17B2 Culter Ridge USA
111B2 Culverden NZ
33E1 Cumaná Ven
10C3 Cumberland Maryland, USA
11B3 Cumberland R USA
6D3 Cumberland Pen Can
34A3 Cumberland Sd Can
42C2 Cumbria Eng
21A2 Cummings USA
108A2 Cummins Aust
42B2 Cumnock Scot
34A3 Cunco Chile
100A2 Cunene R Angola/Namibia
52A2 Cuneo Italy
107D3 Cunnamulla Aust
44C3 Cupar Scot
54A2 Ćuprija Serbia, Yugos
27D4 Curaçao I Caribbean S
34A3 Curacautin Chile
34B3 Curaco R Arg
34A3 Curanilahue Chile
34A3 Curepto Chile
29B2 Curicó Chile
30G4 Curitiba Brazil
108A2 Curnamona Aust
100A2 Curoca R Angola
31C5 Curvelo Brazil
32C6 Cusco Peru
18A2 Cushing USA
13D2 Cutbank R Can
17B1 Cuthbert USA
34B3 Cutral-Có Arg
86B2 Cuttack India
100A2 Cuvelai Angola
56B2 Cuxhaven Germany
14B2 Cuyahoga Falls USA
79B3 Cuyo Is Phil
99C3 Cyangugu Zaïre
　Cyclades = Kikládhes
13F3 Cypress Hills Can
8J3 Cyprus Republic, Medit S
6D3 Cyrus Field B Can
59B3 Czech Republic Republic, Europe
59B2 Częstochowa Pol

D
76C1 Da R Viet
69E2 Da'an China
94C3 Dab'a Jordan
27C4 Dabajuro Ven
99E2 Dabaro Somalia
73B3 Daba Shan Mts China
99D1 Dabat Eth
85C4 Dabhoi India
72B3 Dabie Shan Mts China
97A3 Dabola Guinea
97B4 Dabou Côte d'Ivoire

59B2 Dabrowa Gorn Pol
57C3 Dachau Germany
57B3 Dachstein Mt Austria
73A3 Dada He R China
17B2 Dade City USA
84B3 Dadhar Pak
85B3 Dadu Pak
68C3 Dadu He R China
79B3 Daet Phil
73B3 Dafang China
76B2 Daga R Myan
99E2 Dagabur Eth
97A3 Dagana Sen
65G5 Dagestan Division, Russian Fed
79B2 Dagupan Phil
92B4 Dahab Egypt
63E3 Da Hinggan Ling Mts China
17B1 Dahlonega USA
85C4 Dahod India
86A1 Dailekh Nepal
34C3 Daireaux Arg
69F4 Daito Is Pacific O
106C3 Dajarra Aust
97A3 Dakar Sen
95B2 Dakhla Oasis Egypt
97C3 Dakoro Niger
54B2 Dakovica Serbia, Yugos
54A1 Dakovo Croatia
100B2 Dala Angola
97A3 Dalaba Guinea
72D1 Dalai Nur L China
68C2 Dalandzadgad Mongolia
79B3 Dalanganem Is Phil
76D3 Da Lat Viet
72A1 Dalay Mongolia
107E3 Dalby Aust
39F7 Dalen Nor
42C2 Dales,The Upland Eng
17A1 Daleville USA
9C3 Dalhart USA
4E2 Dalhousie,C Can
72E2 Dalian China
9D3 Dallas USA
20B1 Dalles,The USA
5E4 Dall I USA
85A3 Dalli Rajhara India
97C3 Dallol R Niger
97C3 Dallol Bosso R Niger
52C2 Dalmatia Region, Bosnia-Herzegovina
69F2 Dal'nerechensk Russian Fed
97B4 Daloa Côte d'Ivoire
73B4 Dalou Shan Mts China
86A2 Dāltenganj India
17B1 Dalton Georgia, USA
16C1 Dalton Massachusetts, USA
106C2 Daly R Aust
21A2 Daly City USA
78C3 Daly Waters Aust
79B4 Damaguete Phil
85C4 Daman India
92A3 Damanhûr Egypt
71D4 Damar I Indon
98B2 Damara CAR
92C3 Damascus Syria
16A3 Damascus USA
97D3 Damaturu Nig
90B2 Damavand Iran
98B3 Damba Angola
87C3 Dambulla Sri Lanka
90B2 Damghan Iran
85D4 Damoh India
99E2 Damot Eth
99E2 Damot Leb
106A3 Dampier Aust
94B3 Dana Jordan
22C2 Dana,Mt USA
97B4 Danané Lib
76D2 Da Nang Viet
79B3 Danao Phil
70A3 Danau Tobu L Indon
71D4 Danau Tuwuti L Indon
73A3 Danbu China
15D2 Danbury USA
86A1 Dandeldhura Nepal

87A1 Dandeli India
108C3 Dandenong Aust
74A2 Dandong China
100A4 Danger Pt S Africa
99D1 Dangila Eth
6D1 Danguard Jenson Land Region Can
7E4 Daniels Harbour Can
6G3 Dannebrogs Øy / Greenland
110C2 Dannevirke NZ
87C1 Dantewara India
　Danube = Donau
10B2 Danville Illinois, USA
11B3 Danville Kentucky, USA
10B2 Danville Pennsylvania, USA
11B3 Danville Virginia, USA
　Danzig = Gdansk
73C4 Dao Xian China
73B4 Daozhen China
79A3 Dapiak,Mt Phil
79B4 Dapitan Phil
68B3 Da Qaidam China
69E2 Daqing China
94C2 Dar'a Syria
91B4 Dārāb Iran
95A1 Daraj Libya
90B3 Dārān Iran
92C3 Dar'a Salkhad Syria
86B1 Darbhanga India
22C1 Dardanelle USA
18B2 Dardanelle,L USA
　Dar-el-Beïda = Casablanca
99D3 Dar es Salaam Tanz
110B1 Dargaville NZ
17B1 Darien USA
　Darjeeling = Därjiling
86B1 Därjiling India
107D4 Darling R Aust
109C1 Darling Downs Aust
6C1 Darling Pen Can
108B2 Darlington Aust
42D2 Darlington Eng
17C1 Darlington USA
57B3 Darmstadt Germany
95B1 Darnah Libya
4F3 Darnley B Ant
112C10 Darnley,C Ant
51B1 Daroca Spain
98C2 Dar Rounga Region, CAR
43C4 Dart R Eng
41C3 Dartmoor Moorland Eng
43C4 Dartmoor Nat Pk Eng
7D5 Dartmouth Can
43C4 Dartmouth Eng
107D1 Daru PNG
52C1 Daruvar Croatia
106C2 Darwin Aust
91B4 Daryācheh-ye Bakhtegan L Iran
90B3 Daryācheh-ye Maharlū L Iran
90B3 Daryācheh-ye Namak Salt Flat Iran
90D3 Daryācheh-ye-Sistan Salt L Iran/Afghan
91B4 Daryācheh-ye Tashk L Iran
80C2 Daryācheh-ye Orūmīyeh L Iran
91C4 Dārzin Iran
91B4 Das I UAE
73C3 Dashennonglia Mt China
80B1 Dasht Iran
90B3 Dasht-e Kavir Salt Desert Iran
90B3 Dasht-e Lut Salt Desert Iran
80B3 Dasht-e Naomid Desert Region Iran
85D3 Datia India
72A2 Datong China
72A2 Datong He R China
79B4 Datu Piang Phil
39K7 Daugava R Latvia

60C2 Daugavpils Latvia
6D1 Dauguard Jensen Land Greenland
84A1 Daulatabad Afghan
85D3 Daulpur India
46D1 Daun Germany
87A1 Daund India
5H4 Dauphin Can
16A2 Dauphin USA
49D2 Dauphiné Region, France
97C3 Daura India
85D3 Dausa India
87B2 Dävangere India
79C4 Davao Phil
79C4 Davao G Phil
22A2 Davenport California, USA
10A2 Davenport Iowa, USA
32A2 David Panama
4D3 Davidson Mts USA
21A2 Davis USA
112C10 Davis Base Ant
7D4 Davis Inlet Can
6E3 Davis Str Greenland/Can
61J3 Davlekanovo Russian Fed
47C1 Davos Switz
87B3 Dawa R Eth
73A4 Dawan China
84B2 Dawat Yar Afghan
Dawei = Tavoy
91B4 Dawhat Salwah B Qatar/S Arabia
76B2 Dawna Range Mts Myan
5J4 Dawson Can
17B1 Dawson Georgia, USA
107D3 Dawson R Aust
5F4 Dawson Creek Can
13D2 Dawson,Mt Can
12G2 Dawson Range Mts Can
73A3 Dawu China
73C3 Dawu China
48B3 Dax France
73B3 Daxian China
73B5 Daxin China
73A3 Daxue Shan Mts China
73C4 Dayong China
94C2 Dayr 'Ali Syria
94C1 Dayr 'Atiyah Syria
93D2 Dayr az Zawr Syria
10B3 Dayton Ohio, USA
19B4 Dayton Texas, USA
20C1 Dayton Washington, USA
11B4 Daytona Beach USA
73C4 Dayu China
78D3 Dayu Indon
72D2 Da Yunhe China
20C2 Dayville USA
73B3 Dazhu China
100B4 De Aar S Africa
26C2 Deadman's Cay The Bahamas
92C3 Dead S Israel/Jordan
46A1 Deal Eng
101G1 Dealesville S Africa
13B2 Dean C Eng
13B2 Dean Chan Can
34C2 Dean Funes Arg
14B2 Dearborn USA
4F3 Dease Arm B Can
4E4 Dease Lake Can
48C2 Death V USA
48C2 Deauville France
97B4 Debakala Côte d'Ivoire
12B2 Deban Mt USA
27L1 Débé Trinidad
59C2 Debica Pol
58C2 Dęblin Pol
97B3 Débo,L Mali
21K Debrecen Hung
99D2 Debre Birhan Eth
99D1 Debre Markos Eth
99D1 Debre Tabor Eth
11B3 Decatur Alabama, USA

17B1 Decatur Georgia, USA
10B3 Decatur Illinois, USA
14B2 Decatur Indiana, USA
48C3 Decazeville France
25B3 Deccan India
73A4 Dechang China
97B3 Dédougou Burkina
101C2 Dedza Malawi
42B2 Dee R Dumfries and Galloway, Scot
42C3 Dee R Eng/Wales
44C3 Dee R Grampian, Scot
15C1 Deep River Can
16C2 Deep River USA
109D1 Deepwater Aust
8B2 Deer Lake Can
8B2 Deer Lodge USA
34D3 Defferrari Arg
17A1 De Funiak Springs USA
68B3 Dêgê China
99E1 Degeh Bur Eth
106A3 De Grey R Aust
84D3 Deh Bid Iran
84B1 Dehi Afghan
96D1 Dehibat Tunisia
87B3 Dehiwala-Mt Lavinia Sri Lanka
90A3 Dehlorän Iran
84D2 Dehra Dün India
86A2 Dehri India
98C2 Deim Zubeir Sudan
94B2 Deir Abu Sa'id Jordan
94C1 Deir el Ahmar Leb
60B4 Dej Rom
19B3 De Kalb Texas, USA
63G2 De Kastri Russian Fed
54C2 Dekese Zaïre
98B2 Dekoa CAR
16B1 Dekusi Indon
9B3 Delano USA
10C3 Delaware State, USA
14B2 Delaware USA
15C2 Delaware R USA
15C2 Delaware B USA
109C3 Delegate Aust
47B1 Delemont Switz
101D2 Delgado C Mozam
84D3 Delhi India
15D2 Delhi New York, USA
92B1 Delice Turk
24B2 Delicias Mexico
90B3 Delijän Iran
47B1 Delle France
22D4 Del Mar USA
39F8 Delmenhorst Germany
4B3 De Long Mts USA
109C4 Deloraine Aust
5H5 Deloraine Can
17B2 Delray Beach USA
9C4 Del Rio USA
8B3 Delta USA
12E2 Delta R USA
12E2 Delta Junction USA
46D1 Demer R Belg
9C3 Deming USA
54C2 Demirköy Turk
49C1 Denain France
42C3 Denau Uzbekistan
42C3 Denbigh Wales
12B2 Denbigh,C USA
44C3 Denbighshire County Wales
78B3 Dendang Indon
46C1 Dendermonde Belg
99D2 Dendi Mt Eth
46B1 Dêndre R Belg
72B1 Dengkou China
72C3 Deng Xian China
Den Haag = 's-Gravenhage
27H1 Denham,Mt Jamaica
20H Den Helder Neth
51C2 Denia Spain
107D4 Deniliquin Aust
20C2 Denio USA
9D3 Denison Texas, USA
12D3 Denison,Mt USA

92A2 Denizli Turk
39F7 Denmark Kingdom, Europe
1C1 Denmark Str Greenland/Iceland
27P2 Dennery St Lucia
78D4 Denpasar Indon
16B3 Denton Maryland, USA
9D3 Denton Texas, USA
107E1 D'Entrecasteaux Is PNG
47B1 Dents du Midi Mt Switz
8C3 Denver USA
98B2 Déo R Cam
86B2 Deoghar India
86C2 Deoli India
84D1 Deosai Plain India
95B3 Dépression du Mourdi Chad
19B3 De Queen USA
84C3 Dera Pak
84B3 Dera Bugti Pak
84C2 Dera Ismail Khan Pak
106B2 Derby Aust
16C2 Derby Connecticut, USA
43D3 Derby County, Eng
43D3 Derby Eng
18A2 Derby Kansas, USA
60E3 Dergachi Ukraine
19B3 De Ridder USA
95C3 Derudeb Sudan
109C4 Derwent Bridge Aust
34B2 Desaguadero Arg
34B2 Desaguadero R Arg
30C2 Desaguadero R Bol
21E3 Deseanso Mexico
20B2 Deschutes R USA
99D1 Desê Eth
29C5 Deseado Arg
29C5 Deseado R Arg
47D2 Desenzano Italy
96A1 Deserta Grande I Medeira
30C4 Desierto de Atacama Desert Chile
18B2 Desloge USA
10A2 Des Moines Iowa, USA
60D3 Desna R Russian Fed
29B6 Desolación I Chile
14A2 Des Plaines USA
56C2 Dessau Germany
12G2 Destruction Bay Can
46A1 Desvres France
54B1 Deta Rom
100B2 Dete Zim
10B2 Detroit USA
76D3 Det Udom Thai
54B1 Deva Rom
56B2 Deventer Neth
44C3 Deveron R Scot
85C3 Devikot India
22C2 Devil Postpile Nat Mon USA
24C1 Devils Gate P USA
Devil's Island = Isla del Diablo
8D2 Devils Lake USA
12H3 Devils Paw Mt Can
43D4 Devizes Eng
85D3 Devli India
55B2 Devoll R Alb
43B4 Devon County, Eng
6A2 Devon I Can
107D5 Devonport Aust
86C1 Dewangiri Bhutan
85D4 Dewás India
101G1 Dewetsdorp S Africa
11B3 Dewey Res USA
19B3 De Witt USA
18C2 Dexter Missouri, USA

73A3 Deyang China
90C3 Deyhuk Iran
72D2 Dezhou China
90A2 Dezh Shähpür Iran
91B4 Dhahran S Arabia
86C2 Dhäkä Bang
87B2 Dhamavaram India

86A2 Dhamtari India
86B2 Dhanbäd India
86A1 Dhangarhi Nepal
86B1 Dhankuta Nepal
85D4 Dhär India
87B2 Dharmapuri India
84D2 Dharmshala India
97B3 Dhar Oualäta Desert Region Maur
86A1 Dhaulagiri Mt Nepal
86B2 Dhenkänäi India
94B3 Dhibah Jordan
55C3 Dhikti Óri Mt Greece
55C3 Dhodhekánisos Is Greece
55B3 Dhomokós Greece
87B1 Dhone India
85C4 Dhoraji India
85C4 Dhrängadhra India
86B1 Dhuburi India
85C4 Dhule India
22B2 Diablo,Mt USA
21A2 Diablo Range Mts USA
34C2 Diamante Arg
34B2 Diamante R Arg
31C5 Diamantina Brazil
107D3 Diamantina R Aust
86B2 Diamond Harbours India
22B1 Diamond Springs USA
91C4 Dibä UAE
98C3 Dibaya Zaïre
15C2 Dickson City USA
93D2 Dicle R Turk
13E2 Didsbury Can
85C3 Didwäna India
97B3 Diebougou Burkina
46D2 Diekirch Lux
97B3 Diéma Mali
76C1 Dien Bien Phu Viet
56B2 Diepholz Germany
48C2 Dieppe France
46C1 Diest Belg
46D2 Dieuze France
7D5 Digby Can
49D3 Digne-les-Bains France
49C2 Digoin France
79C4 Digos Phil
71E4 Digul R Indon
87A3 Dihang R India
Dijlah = Tigris
49C2 Dijon France
98B2 Dik Chad
99E1 Dikhil Djibouti
46B1 Diksmuide Belg
18I0 Dikson Russian Fed
84A2 Diläram Afghan
106B1 Dili Indon
76D3 Di Linh Viet
46E1 Dillenburg Germ
99C1 Dilling Sudan
12C3 Dillingham USA
8B2 Dillon USA
16A2 Dillsburg USA
100B2 Dilolo Zaïre
Dimashq = Damascus
98C3 Dimbelenge Zaïre
97B4 Dimbokro Côte d'Ivoire
54C2 Dimitrovgrad Bulg
61G3 Dimitrovgrad Russian Fed
94B3 Dimona Israel
86C1 Dimäpur India
79B3 Dinagat I Phil
86B1 Dinajpur India
48B2 Dinan France
46C1 Dinant Belg
92B2 Dinar Turk
99D1 Dinder R Sudan
87B2 Dindigul India
72B2 Dingbian China
86B1 Dinggyê China
41B3 Dingle Irish Rep
41A3 Dingle B Irish Rep
97A3 Dinguiraye Guinea
44B3 Dingwall Scot
72A2 Dingxi China
72D2 Ding Xian China

Dinh Lap

76D1 Dinh Lap Viet
22C2 Dinuba USA
97A3 Diouloulou Sen
86C1 Diphu India
99E2 Dire Dawa Eth
106A3 Dirk Hartog I Aust
95A3 Dirkou Niger
109C1 Dirranbandi Aust
99E2 Dirri Somalia
29G8 Disappointment,C
South Georgia
20B1 Disappointment,C
USA
106B3 Disappointment,L
Aust
108B3 Discovery B Aust
103J7 Discovery
Tablemount
Atlantic O
47C1 Disentis Muster
Switz
6E3 Disko Greenland
6E3 Disko Bugt B
Greenland
6E3 Diskorjord Greenland
58D1 Disna R Belarus
35B1 Distrito Federal
Federal District, Brazil
85C4 Diu India
79C4 Diuat Mts Phil
31C6 Divinópolis Brazil
61F4 Divnoye Russian Fed
93C2 Divriǧi Turk
22B1 Dixon California,
USA
5E4 Dixon Entrance Sd
Can/USA
13D1 Dixonville Can
93E3 Diyālā R Iraq
65F6 Diyarbakir Turk
90A3 Diz R Iran
98B2 Dja R Cam
71E4 Djadi R Alg
95A2 Djado,Plat du Niger
98B3 Djambala Congo
96C2 Djanet Alg
50A2 Djebel Bouhalla Mt
Mor
96C1 Djelfa Alg
98C2 Djéma CAR
97B3 Djenné Mali
91F3 Djibo Burkina
99E1 Djibouti Djibouti
99E1 Djibouti Republic, E
Africa
98C2 Djolu Zaire
97C4 Djougou Benin
99D2 Djúgu Zaire
38C2 Djúpivogur Iceland
51C2 Djurdjura Mts Alg
60E2 Dmitrov Russian Fed
Dnepr = Dnieper
60D4 Dneprodzerzhinsk
Ukraine
60E4 Dnepropetrovsk
Ukraine
60C3 Dneprovskaya
Nizmennost' Region,
Belarus
Dnestr = Dniester
60D4 Dnieper R Ukraine
60B4 Dniester R Ukraine
60D2 Dno Russian Fed
98B2 Doba Chad
58C1 Dobele Latvia
34C3 Doblas Arg
71E4 Dobo Indon
54A2 Doboj Bosnia-
Herzegovina
54B2 Dobreta-Turnu-
Severin Rom
54C2 Dobrich Bulg
60D3 Dobrush Belarus
31C5 Doce R Brazil
30D3 Doctor R P Peña Arg
87B2 Dod India
87B2 Doda Betta Mt India
9C3 Dodge City USA
99D3 Dodoma Tanz
75A1 Dōgo I Japan
97C3 Dogondoutchi Niger
93D2 Doğubayazit Turk

91B4 Doha Qatar
7C5 Dolbeau Can
49D2 Dôle France
43C3 Dolgellau Wales
47D1 Dolomitche Mts Italy
99E2 Dolo Odo Eth
29E3 Dolores Arg
34D2 Dolores Urug
23A1 Dolores Hidalgo
Mexico
4G3 Dolphin and Union
Str Can
29E6 Dolphin,C Falkland Is
71E4 Dom Mt Indon
65G4 Dombarovskiy
Russian Fed
38F6 Dombas Nor
46D2 Dombasle-sur-
Meurthe France
54A1 Dombóvár Hung
48B2 Domfront France
27E3 Dominica /
Caribbean S
27C3 Dominican Republic
Caribbean S
6C3 Dominion,C Can
7E4 Domino Can
68D1 Domna Russian Fed
52A1 Domodossola Italy
78D4 Dompu Indon
29B3 Domuyo Mt Arg
109D1 Domville,Mt Aust
44C3 Don R Scot
61F4 Don R Russian Fed
45C1 Donaghadee N Ire
57C3 Donau R Germany
57C3 Donauwörth
Germany
50A2 Don Benito Spain
42D3 Doncaster Eng
98B3 Dondo Angola
101C2 Dondo Mozam
87C3 Dondra Head C
Sri Lanka
45B1 Donegal County,
Irish Rep
40B3 Donegal Irish Rep
40B3 Donegal B Irish Rep
45B1 Donegal Mts
Irish Rep
60E4 Donetsk Ukraine
73C4 Dong'an China
106A3 Dongara Aust
73A4 Dongchuan China
76D2 Dongfang China
74B2 Dongfeng China
70C4 Donggala Indon
68B3 Dongji Cona L
China
74A3 Donggou China
73C5 Donghai Dao I China
72A1 Dong He R China
76D2 Dong Hoi Viet
73C5 Dong Jiang R China
95C3 Dongola Sudan
73D5 Dongshan China
73D5 Dongsha Qundao I
China
72C2 Dongsheng China
72E3 Dongtai China
73C4 Dongting Hu L China
73B5 Dongxing China
73D3 Dongzhi China
18B2 Doniphan USA
52C2 Donji Vakuf Bosnia-
Herzegovina
38G5 Dønna I Nor
21A2 Donner P USA
46D2 Donnersberg Mt
Germany
101G1 Donnybrook S Africa
Donostia = San
Sebastian
22B2 Don Pedro Res USA
12D1 Doonerak,Mt USA
79B4 Dopolong Phil
73A3 Do Qu R China
47B2 Dora Baltea R Italy
49D2 Dorbirn Austria
43C4 Dorchester Eng
6C3 Dorchester,C Can
48C2 Dordogne R France
56A2 Dordrecht Neth
13F2 Dore L Can

13F2 Dore Lake Can
97B3 Dori Burkina
57B3 Dornbirn Austria
44B3 Dornoch Scot
44B3 Dornoch Firth
Estuary Scot
38H6 Dorotea Sweden
109D2 Dorrigo Aust
20B2 Dorris USA
43C4 Dorset County, Eng
46D1 Dortmund Germany
56B2 Dortmund Germany
98C2 Doruma Zaire
63D2 Dosatuy Russian Fed
44B1 Doshi Afghan
22B2 Dos Palos USA
97C3 Dosso Niger
65G5 Dossor Kazakhstan
18D1 Dothan USA
49C1 Douai France
98A2 Douala Cam
109D1 Double Island Pt
Aust
49D2 Doubs R France
111A3 Doubtful Sd NZ
97B3 Douentza Mali
9C3 Douglas Arizona,
USA
42B2 Douglas Eng
17B1 Douglas Georgia,
USA
8C2 Douglas Wyoming,
USA
12A1 Douglas,C USA
13B2 Douglas Chan Can
12D3 Douglas,Mt USA
45B1 Douleens France
43D3 Doulting Eng
10C1 Doullens France
10C1 Doun County, N Ire
30F3 Dourados Brazil
50A1 Douro R Port
15C3 Dover Delaware, USA
43E4 Dover Eng
16B2 Dover New
Hampshire, USA
16B2 Dover New Jersey,
USA
14B2 Dover Ohio, USA
43D3 Dover R Eng
41D3 Dover,Str of UK/
France
71B5 Downington USA
42B2 Downpatrick N Ire
13C2 Downton,Mt USA
16B2 Doylestown USA
75A1 Dōzen I Japan
96A2 Dr'aa R Mor
35A2 Dracena Brazil
16D1 Dracut USA
49D3 Draguignan France
101C3 Drakensberg Mts
S Africa
101G1 Drakensberg Mt
S Africa
103E7 Drake Pass Pacific/
Atlantic O
55B2 Dráma Greece
39G7 Drammen Nor
38A1 Drangajökull Iceland
52C1 Drava R Slovenia
13D2 Drayton Valley Can
49C2 Dreaux France
57C2 Dresden Germany
48C2 Dreux France
20C2 Drewsey USA
54B2 Drin R Alb
54A2 Drina R Bosnia-
Herzegovina/Serbia
58D1 Drissa R Belarus
45C2 Drogheda Irish Rep
59C3 Drogobych Ukraine
112B12 Dronning Maud Land
Region, Ant
30D3 Dr P.P. Pena Par
5G4 Drumheller Can
14B1 Drummond I USA
15D1 Drummondville Can
58C2 Druskininksi
Lithuania
12G3 Dry B USA
7A5 Dryden Can
77H1 Dry Harbour Mts
Jamaica
76B3 Duang I Myan

91C4 Dubai UAE
5H3 Dubawnt R Can
4A3 Dubawnt L Can
107D4 Dubbo Aust
45C2 Dublin County,
Irish Rep
45C2 Dublin Irish Rep
17B1 Dublin USA
60E2 Dubna Russian Fed
60C3 Dubno Ukraine
15C2 Du Bois USA
13B2 Dubose,Mt Can
58D2 Dubrovica Ukraine
54A2 Dubrovnik Croatia
10A2 Dubuque USA
46C2 Dudelange Lux
1C10 Dudinka Russian Fed
43C3 Dudley Eng
97B4 Duekoué Côte
d'Ivoire
17F Duero R Spain
44C3 Dufftown Scot
52B2 Dugi Otok I Croatia
56B2 Duisburg Germany
93E3 Dükan Iraq
99D2 Duk Faiwil Sudan
91B4 Dukhān Qatar
73A4 Dukou China
68B3 Dulan China
34C2 Dulce R Arg
86C2 Dulit Range Mts
Malay
86C2 Dullabchara India
10A2 Duluth USA
94C2 Dūmā Syria
79A3 Dumaran I Phil
9D3 Dumas USA
94C2 Dumas USA
94C2 Dumayr Syria
42B2 Dumbarton Scot
42B2 Dumfries Scot
42B2 Dumfries and
Galloway Division,
Scot
86B2 Dumka India
15C1 Dumoine,L Can
112C8 Dumont d'Urville
Base Ant
95C1 Dumyat Egypt
54C2 Dunărea R Rom
45C2 Dunary Head Pt
Scot
54B2 Dunav R Bulg
59D3 Dunayevtsy Ukraine
13C3 Duncan Can
16A2 Duncannon USA
44C2 Duncansby Head Pt
Scot
45C1 Dundalk Irish Rep
16A3 Dundalk USA
45C1 Dundalk B Irish Rep
6D2 Dundas Greenland
4G2 Dundas Pen Can
71E5 Dundas Str Aust
44C3 Dundee S Africa
44C3 Dundee Scot
44C3 Dundee City
Division, Scot
108B1 Dundoo Aust
42B2 Dundrum B N Ire
111B3 Dunedin NZ
109C2 Dunedoo Aust
18B2 Dunfermline Scot
85C4 Dungarpur India
45C2 Dungarvan Irish Rep
43E4 Dungeness Eng
109D2 Dungog Aust
99D2 Dungu Zaire
95C2 Dunqunab Sudan
68B2 Dunhuang China
84B1 Dunkerque France
10A2 Dunkirk USA
99D1 Dunkur Eth
97B4 Dunkwa Ghana
41B3 Dun Laoghaire
Irish Rep
45B3 Dunmanway
Irish Rep
26B1 Dunmore Town
The Bahamas
44C2 Dunnet Head Pt Scot
42C2 Duns Scot
20B2 Dunsmuir USA

111A2 **Dunstan Mts** NZ
46C2 **Dun-sur-Meuse** France
72D1 **Duolun** China
18C2 **Du Quoin** USA
94B3 **Dura** Israel
49D3 **Durance** R France
24B2 **Durango** Mexico
50B1 **Durango** Spain
9C3 **Durango** USA
29E2 **Durano** Urug
9C3 **Durant** USA
94C1 **Duraykish** Syria
101H1 **Durban** S Africa
46D1 **Duren** Germany
86A2 **Durg** India
86B2 **Durgapur** India
42D2 **Durham** County, Eng
42D2 **Durham** Eng
11C3 **Durham** N Carolina, USA
16D1 **Durham** New Hampshire, USA
108B1 **Durham Downs** Aust
54A2 **Durmitor** Mt Montenegro, Yugos
44B2 **Durness** Scot
55A2 **Durrës** Alb
108B1 **Durrie** Aust
45A3 **Dursey** I Irish Rep
55C3 **Dursunbey** Turk
110B2 **D'Urville I** NZ
90D2 **Dushak** Turkmenistan
73B4 **Dushan** China
82A2 **Dushanbe** Tajikistan
111A3 **Dusky Sd** NZ
56B2 **Düsseldorf** Germany
73A4 **Duyun** China
92B1 **Düzce** Turk
60C2 **Dvina** R Latvia
85B4 **Dwarka** India
6D3 **Dyer,C** Can
11B3 **Dyersburg** USA
61F5 **Dykh Tau** Mt Russian Fed
108B1 **Dynevor Downs** Aust
68B2 **Dzag** Mongolia
63C3 **Dzamin Üüd** Mongolia
101D2 **Dzaoudzi** Mayotte
68C2 **Dzarnin Üüd** Mongolia
68B2 **Dzavhan Gol** R Mongolia
80E1 **Dzhezkazgan** Kazakhstan
61F2 **Dzerzhinsk** Russian Fed
63E2 **Dzhalinda** Russian Fed
65J5 **Dzhambul** Kazakhstan
60D4 **Dzhankoy** Ukraine
Dzharkent = Panfilov
65H4 **Dzhezkazgan** Kazakhstan
84B1 **Dzhilikul'** Tajikistan
65J5 **Dzhungarskiy Alatau** Mts Kazakhstan
59B2 **Dzierzoniow** Pol
63B3 **Dziuýl** Mongolia
82C1 **Dzungaria** Basin, China

E

7B4 **Eabamet L** Can
12F2 **Eagle** Alaska, USA
20B2 **Eagle L** California, USA
19A3 **Eagle Mountain L** USA
9C4 **Eagle Pass** USA
12E2 **Eagle Plain** Can
12E2 **Eagle River** USA
21B2 **Earlimart** USA
17B1 **Easley** USA
15C2 **East Aurora** USA
42B2 **East Ayrshire** Division, Scot
43E4 **Eastbourne** Eng
14A2 **East Chicago** USA
69E3 **East China Sea** China/Japan

100B4 **Eastern Cape** Province, S Africa
44B3 **East Dunbartonshire** Division, Scot
83B4 **Eastern Ghats** Mts India
29E6 **East Falkland I** Falkland Is
12E1 **East Fork** R USA
21B2 **Eastgate** USA
16C1 **Easthampton** USA
16C2 **East Hampton** USA
14A2 **East Lake** USA
14B2 **East Liverpool** USA
100B4 **East London** S Africa
44C3 **East Lothian** Division, Scot
7C4 **Eastmain** Can
7C4 **Eastmain** R Can
17B1 **Eastman** USA
15C3 **Easton** Maryland, USA
15C2 **Easton** Pennsylvania, USA
16B2 **East Orange** USA
105L4 **East Pacific Ridge** Pacific O
17B1 **East Point** USA
44B4 **East Renfrewshire** Division, Scot
42D3 **East Retford** Eng
42D3 **East Riding of Yorkshire** County Eng
11A3 **East St Louis** USA
1B7 **East Siberian S** Russian Fed
43E4 **East Sussex** County, Eng
17B1 **Eatonton** USA
10A2 **Eau Claire** USA
71F3 **Eauripik** I Pacific O
23B1 **Ebano** Mexico
98B2 **Ebebiyin** Eq Guinea
56C2 **Eberswalde** Germ
73A4 **Ebian** China
65K5 **Ebinur L** China
53C2 **Eboli** Italy
98B2 **Ebolowa** Cam
51B1 **Ebro** R Spain
92A1 **Eceabat** Turk
96C1 **Ech Cheliff** Alg
72D2 **Eching** China
20C1 **Echo** USA
4G3 **Echo Bay** Can
46D2 **Echternach** Lux
108B3 **Echuca** Aust
50A2 **Ecija** Spain
6B2 **Eclipse Sd** Can
32B4 **Ecuador** Republic, S America
99E1 **Ed** Eritrea
44C2 **Eday** I Scot
98C1 **Ed Da'ein** Sudan
99C3 **Ed Damer** Sudan
95C3 **Ed Debba** Sudan
44B2 **Eddrachillis B** Scot
99D1 **Ed Dueim** Sudan
109C4 **Eddystone Pt** Aust
98A2 **Edea** Cam
109C3 **Eden** Aust
42C2 **Eden** R Eng
101G1 **Edenburg** S Africa
111A3 **Edendale** NZ
46E2 **Edenkoben** Germany
46E1 **Eder** R Germany
6D3 **Edgell I** Can
64B2 **Edgeøya** I Barents S
16A3 **Edgewood** USA
94B3 **Edh Dhahiriya** Israel
55B2 **Edhessa** Greece
44C3 **Edinburgh** Scot
44C3 **Edinburgh, City of** Division, Scot
60C5 **Edirne** Turk
17B1 **Edisto** R USA
13D2 **Edith Cavell,Mt** Can
20B1 **Edmonds** USA
5G4 **Edmonton** Can
7D5 **Edmundston** Can
19A4 **Edna** USA
12H3 **Edna Bay** USA
52B1 **Edolo** Italy

94B3 **Edom** Region, Jordan
92A2 **Edremit** Turk
55C3 **Edremit Körfezi** B Turk
68B2 **Edrengiyn Nuruu** Mts Mongolia
5G4 **Edson** Can
34C3 **Eduardo Castex** Arg
12J2 **Eduni,Mt** USA
108B3 **Edward** R Aust
99C3 **Edward,L** Uganda/ Zaire
108A1 **Edwards Creek** Aust
9C3 **Edwards Plat** USA
18C2 **Edwardsville** USA
12H3 **Edziza,Mt** Can
12B2 **Eek** USA
46B1 **Eeklo** Belg
10B3 **Effingham** USA
6E3 **Egedesminde** Greenland
12C3 **Egegik** USA
59C3 **Eger** Hung
39F7 **Egersund** Nor
16B3 **Egg Harbor City** USA
4G2 **Eglinton I** Can
110B1 **Egmont,C** NZ
92B2 **Egridir Gölü** L Turk
95B2 **Egypt** Republic, Africa
50B1 **Eibar** Spain
49C2 **Eibeuf** France
46E1 **Eifel** Region, Germ
44A3 **Eigg** I Scot
83B5 **Eight Degree Chan** Indian O
106B2 **Eighty Mile Beach** Aust
108C3 **Eildon,L** Aust
56B2 **Eindhoven** Neth
47C1 **Einsiedeln** Switz
94B3 **Ein Yahav** Israel
57C2 **Eisenach** Germany
57C3 **Eisenerz** Austria
46D1 **Eitorf** Germany
72A1 **Ejin qi** China
23A2 **Ejutla** Mexico
110C2 **Eketahuna** NZ
65J4 **Ekibastuz** Kazakhstan
63F2 **Ekimchan** Russian Fed
92B3 **El Mahalla el Kubra** Egypt
39H7 **Eksjo** Sweden
10B1 **Ekwen** R Can
92A3 **El'Alamein** Egypt
92B3 **El'Arish** Egypt
92B4 **Elat** Israel
95B3 **El'Atrun Oasis** Sudan
93C2 **Elazig** Turk
93C3 **El Azraq** Jordan
52B2 **Elba** I Italy
95C2 **El Balyana** Egypt
32C2 **El Banco** Colombia
55B2 **Elbasan** Alb
27D5 **El Baúl** Ven
57C2 **Elbe** R Germany
94C1 **El Bega'a** R Leb
14A2 **Elberta** USA
8C3 **Elbert,Mt** USA
17B1 **Elberton** USA
92C2 **Elbistan** Turk
58B2 **Elblag** Pol
29E4 **El Bolson** Arg
61F5 **Elbrus** Mt Russian Fed
Elburz Mts = Reshteh-ye Alborz
21B3 **El Cajon** USA
19A4 **El Campo** USA
51B2 **Elche** Spain
51B2 **Elda** Spain
32B3 **El Diviso** Colombia
96B2 **El Djouf** Desert Region Maur
18B2 **Eldon** USA
11A3 **El Dorado** Arkansas, USA
35B2 **Eldorado** Brazil
9D3 **El Dorado** Kansas, USA
24B2 **El Dorado** Mexico
33E2 **El Dorado** Ven

99D2 **Eldoret** Kenya
22C1 **Eleanor,L** USA
96B2 **El Eglab** Region, Alg
50B1 **El Escorial** Spain
93D2 **Eleskirt** Turk
11C4 **Eleuthera** I The Bahamas
92B4 **El Faiyûm** Egypt
96B2 **El Farsia** Well Mor
98C1 **El Fasher** Sudan
92B4 **El Fashn** Egypt
50A1 **El Ferrol del Caudillo** Spain
99C1 **El Fula** Sudan
96C1 **El Gassi** Alg
99D1 **El Geteina** Sudan
99D1 **El Geziza** Region, Sudan
94B3 **El Ghor** V Israel/ Jordan
10B2 **Elgin** Illinois, USA
44C3 **Elgin** Scot
92B3 **El Giza** Egypt
96C1 **El Golea** Alg
99D2 **Elgon,Mt** Uganda/ Kenya
99E2 **El Goran** Eth
23A2 **El Grullo** Mexico
96B2 **El Guettara** Well Mali
96B2 **El Haricha** Desert Region Mali
92A4 **El Harra** Egypt
51C2 **El Harrach** Alg
99D1 **El Hawata** Sudan
23B1 **El Higo** Mexico
34A3 **El Huecu** Arg
92B4 **El'Igma** Desert Region Egypt
12B2 **Elim** USA
4H2 **Elira,C** Can
Elisabethville = Lubumbashi
39K6 **Eisenvaara** Fin
91 **El Iskandariya = Alexandria**
61F4 **Elista** Russian Fed
106C4 **Elizabeth** Aust
15D2 **Elizabeth** USA
11C3 **Elizabeth City** USA
17C1 **Elizabethtown** N Carolina, USA
16A2 **Elizabethtown** Pennsylvania, USA
96B1 **El Jadida** Mor
92C3 **El Jafr** Jordan
99D1 **El Jebelein** Sudan
96D1 **El Jem** Tunisia
58C2 **Elk** Pol
16B3 **Elk** R Maryland, USA
14B3 **Elk** R W Virginia, USA
14A2 **Elkhart** USA
96B2 **El Khenachich** Desert Region Mali
54C2 **Elkhovo** Bulg
14C3 **Elkins** USA
8B3 **Elko** USA
16B3 **Elkton** USA
92B3 **El Kuntilla** Egypt
99C1 **El Lagowa** Sudan
4H2 **Ellef Ringnes I** Can
8A2 **Ellensburg** USA
16B2 **Ellenville** USA
111B2 **Ellesmere,L** NZ
6B2 **Ellesmere I** Can
100B4 **Elliot** S Africa
7B5 **Elliot Lake** Can
94B3 **El Lisan** Pen Jordan
112B3 **Ellsworth Land** Region Ant
95B1 **El Maghra** L Egypt
92B3 **El Mansûra** Egypt
16B3 **Elmer** USA
96B3 **El Merelé** Desert Region Maur
34B2 **El Milagro** Arg

El Mīna

94B1 El Mîna Leb
92B4 El Minya Egypt
22B1 Elmira California, USA
10C2 Elmira New York, USA
96B2 El Mreitî Well Maur
56B2 Elmshorn Germany
98C1 El Muglad Sudan
96B2 El Mzereb Well Mali
79A3 El Nido Phil
99D1 El Obeid Sudan
23A2 El Oro Mexico
96C1 El Oued Alg
9C3 El Paso USA
21A2 El Porte USA
22C2 El Portal USA
50A2 El Puerto del Sta Maria Spain
El Qâhira = Cairo
El Quâs = Jerusalem
94B3 El Quseima Egypt
9D3 El Reno USA
25D3 El Salvador Republic, Cent America
22D4 Elsinore L USA
34B3 El Sosneade Arg
57C2 Elsterwerde Germany
El Suweis = Suez
50A1 El Teleno Mt Spain
110B1 Eltham NZ
33E2 El Tigre Ven
92B4 El Tîh Desert Region Egypt
34C2 El Tio Arg
20C1 Eltopia USA
92B4 El Tur Egypt
87C1 Elüru India
50A2 Elvas Port
32C5 Elvira Brazil
34A2 El Volcán Chile
14A2 Elwood USA
43E3 Ely Eng
14A2 Ely Minnesota, USA
8B3 Ely Nevada, USA
14B2 Elyria USA
90B2 Emämrüd Iran
84B1 Emäm Säheb Afghan
58B1 Eman R Sweden
61J4 Emba Kazakhstan
61J4 Emba R Kazakhstan
29C3 Embalse Cerros Colorados L Arg
51B2 Embalse de Alarcón Res Spain
50A2 Embalse de Alcántará Res Spain
50A1 Embalse de Almendra Res Spain
50A2 Embalse de Garcia de Sola Res Spain
33E2 Embalse de Guri L Ven
51B1 Embalse de Mequinenza Res Spain
50A1 Embalse de Ricobayo Res Spain
29E2 Embalse de Rio Negro Res Urug
29C3 Embalse El Chocón L Arg
29C4 Embalse Florentine Ameghino L Arg
50A1 Embalse Gabriel y Galan Res Spain
30D3 Embarcación Arg
5G4 Embarras Portage Can
47B2 Embrun France
99D3 Embu Kenya
56B2 Emden Germany
73A4 Emei China
107D3 Emerald Aust
70D4 Emeri Can
5J5 Emerson Can
21B1 Emigrant P USA
95A3 Emi Koussi Mt Chad
34B3 Emilio Mitre Arg
92B2 Emirdağ Turk
16B2 Emmaus USA
56B2 Emmen Neth

20C2 Emmett USA
16A3 Emmitsburg USA
12B2 Emmonak USA
9C4 Emory Peak Mt USA
24A2 Empalme Mexico
101H1 Empangeni S Africa
30E4 Empedrado Arg
105G1 Emperor Seamount Chain Pacific O
18A2 Emporia Kansas, USA
56B2 Ems R Germany
44B2 Enard B Scot
23A1 Encarnacion Mexico
30A4 Encarnación Par
97B4 Enchi Ghana
22D4 Encinitas USA
35C1 Encruzilhada Brazil
106B1 Endeh Indon
13D2 Enderby Pen L
112C11 Enderby Land Region, Ant
15C2 Endicott USA
12D1 Endicott Mts USA
47D1 Engadin Mts Switz
79B2 Engaño,C Phil
94B3 En Gedi Israel
57B2 Engelberg Switz
78A4 Enggano I Indon
41C3 England Country, UK
7E4 Englee Can
41C3 English Channel Eng/France
97B3 Enji Well Maur
39H7 Enkoping Sweden
53B3 Enna Italy
99C1 En Nahud Sudan
95B3 Ennedi Region Chad
109C1 Enngonia Aust
41B3 Ennis Irish Rep
19A3 Ennis Texas, USA
45C2 Enniscorthy Irish Rep
45C1 Enniskillen N Ire
45B2 Ennistimon Irish Rep
94B2 Enn Nâqoûra Leb
57C3 Enns R Austria
39F8 Enschede Neth
24A1 Ensenada Mexico
73B3 Enshi China
99D2 Entebbe Uganda
17A1 Enterprise Alabama, USA
20C1 Enterprise Oregon, USA
97C4 Enugu Nig
75B1 Enzan Japan
49C2 Epernay France
16A2 Ephrata Pennsylvania, USA
20C1 Ephrata Washington, USA
49D2 Épinal France
46A2 Epte R France
100A3 Epukiro Namibia
34C3 Epu pel Arg
90B3 Eqlid Iran
89D7 Equator
98A2 Equatorial Guinea Republic, Africa
47C2 Erba Italy
46D2 Erbeskopf Mt Germany
34A3 Ercilla Chile
93D2 Erciş Turk
92C2 Erciyas Daglari Mt Turk
74B2 Erdaobaihe China
72C1 Erdene Mongolia
68C2 Erdenet Mongolia
95B3 Erdi Region Chad
30F4 Erechim Brazil
92B1 Ereğli Turk
92B2 Ereğli Turk
68D2 Erenhot China
50B1 Eresma R Spain
57C2 Erft R Germany
57C2 Erfurt Germany
93C2 Ergani Turk
96B2 Erg Chech Desert Region Alg
95A3 Erg du Djourab Desert Chad
97D3 Erg Du Ténéré Desert Region Niger

92A1 Ergene R Turk
96B2 Erg Iguidi Region Alg
58D1 Ērgļi Latvia
98B1 Erguig R Chad
68D1 Ergun' R China/Russian Fed
63E2 Ergun Zuoqi China
95C3 Eriba Sudan
10C2 Erie USA
10B2 Erie,L Can/USA
42B2 Erin Port Eng
44A3 Eriskay I Scot
99D1 Eritrea Republic,Africa
46D1 Erkelenz Germany
57C3 Erlangen Germany
19B3 Erling,L USA
101G1 Ermelo S Africa
87B3 Ernäkulam India
87B2 Erode India
108B1 Eromanga Aust
96B1 Er Rachidia Mor
99D1 Er Rahad Sudan
101C2 Errego Mozam
40B2 Errigal Mt Irish Rep
41A3 Erris Head Pt Irish Rep
99D1 Er Roseires Sudan
94B2 Er Rummän Jordan
57C2 Erzgebirge Upland Germany
93C2 Erzincan Turk
93C2 Erzurum Turk
48C3 Esara R Spain
56B1 Esbjerg Den
9C4 Escalón Mexico
10B2 Escanaba USA
25C3 Escárcega Mexico
46C2 Esch Lux
21B3 Escondido USA
24B2 Escuinapa Mexico
25C3 Escuintla Guatemala
98B2 Eséka Cam
51C1 Esera R Spain
90B3 Eşfahän Iran
101H1 Eshowe S Africa
110C1 Eskdale NZ
38C1 Eskifjörður Iceland
39H7 Eskilstuna Sweden
4E3 Eskimo L Can
7A3 Eskimo Point Can
92B2 Eskisehir Turk
50A1 Esla R Spain
29A3 Esmeralda I Chile
32B3 Esmeraldas Ecuador
25B2 Esmerelda Cuba
49C3 Espalion France
14B1 Espanola Can
32J7 Española I Ecuador
106B4 Esperance Aust
34C2 Esperanza Arg
112C2 Esperanza Base Ant
35C1 Espirito Santo State, Brazil
101C3 Espungabera Mozam
29B4 Esquel Arg
20B1 Esquimalt Can
94C2 Esquina Jordan
94C2 Es Samra Jordan
96B1 Essaouira Mor
96A2 Es Semara Mor
56B2 Essen Germany
33F3 Essequibo R Guyana
43E4 Essex County, Eng
14B2 Essexville USA
57B3 Esslingen Germany
31D4 Estância Brazil
101G1 Estcourt S Africa
47D2 Este Italy
46B2 Esternay France
30D3 Esteros Par
5H5 Estevan Can
17B1 Estill USA
60B2 Estonia Republic, Europe
29B6 Estrecho de Magallanes Str Chile
50A2 Estremoz Port
59B3 Esztergom Hung
108A1 Etadunna Aust
46C2 Étain France

48C2 Étampes France
108A1 Etamunbanie,L Aust
46A1 Étaples France
85D3 Ètäwah India
99D2 Ethiopia Republic, Africa
23B2 Etla Mexico
53B3 Etna Mt Italy
12H3 Etolin I USA
12A2 Etolin Str USA
6C2 Eton Can
100A2 Etosha Nat Pk Namibia
100A2 Etosha Pan Salt L Namibia
17B1 Etowah USA
46D2 Ettelbruck Lux
109C2 Euabalong Aust
14B2 Euclid USA
109C3 Eucumbene,L Aust
108A2 Eudunda Aust
19A2 Eufala L USA
17A1 Eufaula USA
108C1 Eulo Aust
19B3 Eunice Louisiana, USA
46D1 Eupen Germany
93D3 Euphrates R Iraq
19C3 Eupora USA
48C2 Eure R France
20B2 Eureka California, USA
6B1 Eureka Can
8B3 Eureka Nevada, USA
6B2 Eureka Sd Can
8B2 Euroa Aust
109C1 Eurombah R Aust
101D3 Europa I Mozam Chan
57B2 Euskirchen Germany
13B2 Eutsuk L Can
13D2 Evansburg Can
7C4 Evans,L Can
6B3 Evans Str Can
14A2 Evanston Illinois, USA
8B2 Evanston Wyoming, USA
11B3 Evansville Indiana, USA
101G1 Evaton S Africa
106C4 Everard,L Aust
82C3 Everest,Mt China/Nepal
8A2 Everett Washington, USA
16C1 Everett,Mt USA
11B4 Everglades,The Swamp USA
43D3 Evesham Eng
98B2 Evinayong Eq Guinea
39F7 Evje Nor
47B1 Evolène Switz
50A2 Évora Port
48C2 Évreux France
53B3 Évvoia I Greece
98B3 Ewo Congo
22C1 Excelsior Mt USA
18B2 Excelsior Springs USA
21B2 Exeter California, USA
43C4 Exeter Eng
15D2 Exeter New Hampshire, USA
43C4 Exmoor Nat Pk Eng
43C4 Exmouth Eng
50A2 Extremadura Region, Spain
25E2 Exuma Sd The Bahamas
99D3 Eyasi L Tanz
42C2 Eyemouth Scot
6F2 Eyl Somalia
108B4 Eyre Aust
106C3 Eyre Creek R Aust
106C3 Eyre,L Aust
106C4 Eyre Pen Aust
5J6 Eyre I Phil
23A1 Eztatlan Mexico
55C3 Ezine Turk

F

4G3 Faber L Can
39E7 Fåborg Den
52B2 Fabriano Italy
95A3 Fachi Niger
95B3 Fada Chad
97C3 Fada N'Gourma Burkina
52B2 Faenza Italy
6E3 Faeringehavn Greenland
98B2 Fafa R CAR
99E2 Fafan R Eth
54B1 Făgăraş Rom
46C1 Fagnes Region, Belg
97B3 Faguibine,L Mali
91C5 Fahud Oman
96A1 Faiol I Açores
4D3 Fairbanks USA
14B3 Fairborn USA
8D2 Fairbury USA
16A3 Fairfax USA
21A2 Fairfield California, USA
16C2 Fairfield Connecticut, USA
14B3 Fairfield Ohio, USA
45C1 Fair Head Pt N Ire
40C2 Fair Isle I Scot
11B2 Fairlie NZ
14B3 Fairmont W Virginia, USA
13D1 Fairview Can
4E4 Fairweather,Mt USA
71F3 Fais I Pacific O
84C2 Faisalabad Pak
8C2 Faith USA
44L1 Faither,The Pen Scot
86A1 Faizäbäd India
43E3 Fakenham Eng
39G7 Fåköping Sweden
86C2 Falam Myan
24C2 Falcon Res Mexico/ USA
97A3 Faléme R Mali/Sen
39G7 Falkenberg Sweden
42C2 Falkirk Scot
44C3 Falkirk Division, Scot
29D6 Falkland Is Dependency, S Atlantic O
29E6 Falkland Sd Falkland Is
22D4 Fallbrook USA
8B3 Fallon USA
15D2 Fall River USA
18A1 Falls City USA
43B4 Falmouth Eng
27H1 Falmouth Jamaica
15D2 Falmouth Massachusetts, USA
100A4 False B S Africa
24A2 Falso,C Mexico
56C2 Falster I Den
54C1 Fălticeni Rom
39H6 Falun Sweden
92C2 Famagusta Cyprus
46C1 Famenne Region, Belg
76B2 Fang Thai
99D2 Fangak Sudan
73E5 Fang liao Taiwan
52B2 Fano Italy
112C3 Faraday Base Ant
99C2 Faradje Zaïre
101D3 Farafangana Madag
95B2 Farafra Oasis Egypt
80E2 Farah Afghan
71F2 Farallon de Medinilla I Pacific O
97A3 Faranah Guinea
71F3 Faraulep I Pacific O
43D4 Fareham Eng
Farewell,C = Kap Farvel
107G5 Farewell,C NZ
110B2 Farewell Spit Pt NZ
8D2 Fargo USA
94B2 Fari'a R Israel
10A2 Faribault USA
88B2 Faridpur Bang
90C2 Farīmān Iran

18B2 Farmington Missouri, USA
9C3 Farmington New Mexico, USA
22B2 Farmington Res USA
42D2 Farne Deep N Sea
13D2 Farnham,Mt Can
12H2 Faro Can
50A2 Faro Port
39H7 Fåro I Sweden
89K9 Farquhar Is Indian O
44B3 Farrar R Scot
14B2 Farrell USA
55B3 Fársala Greece
91B4 Fasä Iran
45B3 Fastnet Rock Irish Rep
60C3 Fastov Ukraine
86A1 Fatehpur India
13D1 Father Can
30F2 Fátima do Sul Brazil
101G1 Fauresmith S Africa
47B2 Faverges France
7B4 Fawn R Can
38H6 Fax R Sweden
38A2 Faxaflói B Iceland
95A3 Faya Chad
11A3 Fayetteville Arkansas, USA
11C3 Fayetteville N Carolina, USA
93E4 Faylakah I Kuwait
84C2 Fäzilka India
96A2 Fdérik Maur
11C3 Fear,C USA
24C2 Feather Middle Fork R USA
48C2 Fécamp France
52A1 Federación Arg
34D2 Federal Arg
71F3 Federated States of Micronesia Is Pacific O
56C2 Fehmarn I Germany
32C5 Feijó Brazil
73C5 Feilai Xai Bei Jiang R China
11C2 Feilding NZ
100C2 Feira Zambia
31D4 Feira de Santan Brazil
92C2 Feke Turk
57B3 Feldkirch Austria
34D2 Feliciano R Arg
41D3 Felixstowe Eng
47D1 Feltre Italy
38G6 Femund L Nor
74A2 Fengcheng China
73B4 Fengdu China
72D1 Fenging China
73B3 Fengjie China
72B3 Feng Xian China
72C1 Fengzhen China
72C2 Fen He R China
101D2 Fenoarivo Atsinanana Madag
60E5 Feodosiya Ukraine
90C3 Ferdow Iran
46B2 Fère-Champenoise France
82B2 Fergana Uzbekistan
45C1 Fermanagh County, N Ire
45B2 Fermoy Irish Rep
47D1 Fern Mt Austria
32J7 Fernandina I Ecuador
31D4 Fernandina Beach USA
103G5 Fernando de Noronha I / Atlantic O
35A2 Fernandópolis Brazil
20B1 Ferndale USA
21B2 Fernley USA
52B2 Ferrara Italy
32C6 Ferreñafe Peru
19B3 Ferriday USA
16S Fes Mor
18B2 Festus USA
54C2 Feteşti Rom
92A2 Fethiye Turk
61H5 Fetisovo Kazakhstan
44E1 Fetlar I Scot
84C1 Feyzäbad Afghan

101D3 Fianarantsoa Madag
99D2 Fiché Eth
101G1 Ficksburg S Africa
47D2 Fidenza Italy
55A2 Fier Alb
47D1 Fiera Di Primeiro Italy
44C3 Fife Region, Scot
44C3 Fife Ness Pen Scot
48C3 Figeac France
50A1 Figueira da Foz Port
51C1 Figueras Spain
Figueres = Figueras
96B1 Figuig Mor
105G4 Fiji Is Pacific O
30D3 Filadelfia Par
54B2 Filiaşi Rom
55B3 Filiatrá Greece
53B3 Filicudi I Italy
21B3 Fillmore California, USA
44B3 Findhorn R Scot
10B2 Findlay USA
13D2 Findlay,Mt Can
15C2 Finger Lakes USA
101C2 Fingoè Mozam
92B2 Finike Turk
106C3 Finke R Aust
108A1 Finke Flood Flats Aust
64D3 Finland Republic, N Europe
39J7 Finland,G of N Europe
5H4 Finlay R Can
5H4 Finlay Forks Can
108C3 Finley Aust
38H5 Finnsnes Nor
71F4 Finschhafen PNG
47C1 Finsteraarhorn Mt Switz
56C2 Finsterwalde Germany
45C1 Fintona N Ire
111A3 Fiordland Nat Pk NZ
94D2 Fiq Syria
93C2 Firat R Turk
22B2 Firebaugh USA
52B2 Firenze Italy
34C2 Firmat Arg
85D3 Firozäbäd India
84C2 Firozpur India
39H7 Firspäng Sweden
42B2 Firth of Clyde Estuary Scot
44A3 Firth of Lorn Estuary Scot
40C2 Firth of Tay Estuary Scot
91B4 Firüzäbäd Iran
100A3 Fish R Namibia
22C2 Fish Camp USA
16C2 Fishers I USA
6B3 Fisher Str Can
43B4 Fishguard Wales
6E3 Fiskenaesset Greenland
48B2 Fismes France
72D2 Fitchburg USA
44E2 Fitful Head Pt Scot
17B1 Fitzgerald USA
106B2 Fitzroy R Aust
106B2 Fitzroy Crossing Aust
11B1 Fitzwilliam I Can
99C3 Fizi Zaïre
9B3 Flagstaff USA
42D2 Flamborough Head C Eng
8C2 Flaming Gorge Res USA
12J2 Flat R Can
13E3 Flathead R USA
8B2 Flathead L USA
18B2 Flat River USA
84C2 Flattery,C USA
42C3 Fleetwood Eng
39F7 Flekkefjord Nor
69G4 Fleming Deep Pacific O
76B2 Flemington USA
56B2 Flensburg Germany

47B1 Fleurier Switz
106C4 Flinders I Aust
107D4 Flinders I Aust
106C2 Flinders R Aust
106C4 Flinders Range Mts Aust
5H4 Flin Flon Can
10B2 Flint USA
42C3 Flint Wales
11B3 Flint R USA
42C3 Flintshire County Wales
46B1 Flixecourt France
17A1 Florala USA
Florence = Firenze
11B3 Florence Alabama, USA
18A2 Florence Kansas, USA
20B2 Florence Oregon, USA
11C3 Florence S Carolina, USA
32B3 Florencia Colombia
46C1 Florenville Belg
96A1 Flores I Açores
106B1 Flores I Indon
34D3 Flores R Arg
70C4 Flores S Indon
31C3 Florianq Brazil
30G4 Florianópolis Brazil
29E2 Florida Urug
17B2 Florida State, USA
17B2 Florida City USA
107E1 Florida Is Solomon Is
11B4 Florida Keys Is USA
11B4 Florida,Strs of USA
55B2 Flórina Greece
38F6 Florø Nor
47D1 Fluchthorn Mt Austria
54C1 Focsani Rom
4A3 Fogo I Cape Verde
48C3 Foix France
6C3 Foley I Can
52B2 Foligno Italy
43E4 Folkestone Eng
52B2 Follonica Italy
22B1 Folsom USA
22B1 Folsom L, L USA
5H4 Fond-du-Lac Can
10B2 Fond du Lac USA
48C2 Fontainebleau France
48B2 Fontenac USA
48B2 Fontenay-le-Comte France
52C1 Fonyod Hung
Foochow = Fuzhou
12D2 Foraker,Mt USA
46D2 Forbach France
109C2 Forbes Aust
97C4 Forcados Nig
38F6 Forde Nor
108C1 Fords Bridge Aust
19B3 Fordyce USA
97A4 Forécariah Guinea
6G3 Forel,Mt Greenland
14B2 Forest Can
11B1 Forest Park USA
46A2 Forges-les-Eaux France
20B1 Forks USA
52B2 Forli Italy
51C2 Formentera I Spain
52B2 Formia Italy
96A1 Formigas I Açores
Formosa = Taiwan
30E4 Formosa Arg
31B5 Formosa Brazil
30D3 Formosa State, Arg
73D5 Formosa Str Taiwan/China
47D2 Fornovo di Taro Italy
38D3 Foroyar Is N Atlantic O
44C3 Forres Scot
106B4 Forrest Aust

11A3 **Forrest City** USA
107D2 **Forsayth** Aust
39J6 **Forssa** Fin
109D2 **Forster** Aust
18B2 **Forsyth** Missouri, USA
84C3 **Fort Abbas** Pak
7B4 **Fort Albany** Can
3102 **Fortaleza** Brazil
44B3 **Fort Augustus** Scot
100B4 **Fort Beaufort** S Africa
21A2 **Fort Bragg** USA
8C2 **Fort Collins** USA
15C1 **Fort Coulogne** Can
27E4 **Fort de France** Martinique
17A1 **Fort Deposit** USA
10A2 **Fort Dodge** USA
106A3 **Fortescue** R Aust
7A5 **Fort Frances** Can
4F3 **Fort Franklin** Can
4F3 **Fort Good Hope** Can
108B1 **Fort Grey** Aust
44B3 **Forth** R Scot
7B4 **Fort Hope** Can
3483 **Fortin Uno** Arg
4F3 **Fort Laird** Can
96C1 **Fort Lallemand** Alg
Fort Lamy = Ndjamena
11B4 **Fort Lauderdale** USA
4F3 **Fort Liard** Can
5G4 **Fort Mackay** Can
5G5 **Fort Macleod** Can
5G4 **Fort McMurray** Can
4E3 **Fort McPherson** Can
18B2 **Fort Madison** USA
8C2 **Fort Morgan** USA
11B4 **Fort Myers** USA
5F4 **Fort Nelson** Can
4F3 **Fort Norman** Can
17A1 **Fort Payne** USA
8C2 **Fort Peck Res** USA
11B4 **Fort Pierce** USA
4G3 **Fort Providence** Can
5G3 **Fort Resolution** Can
98B3 **Fort Rousset** Congo
5F4 **Fort St James** Can
13C1 **Fort St John** Can
13E2 **Fort Saskatchewan** Can
18B2 **Fort Scott** USA
4E3 **Fort Selkirk** Can
7B4 **Fort Severn** Can
61H5 **Fort Shevchenko** Kazakhstan
4F3 **Fort Simpson** Can
5G3 **Fort Smith** Can
4G3 **Fort Smith** Region, Can
11A3 **Fort Smith** USA
9C3 **Fort Stockton** USA
20B2 **Fortuna** California, USA ,
5G4 **Fort Vermillion** Can
17A1 **Fort Walton Beach** USA
10B2 **Fort Wayne** USA
44B3 **Fort William** Scot
9D3 **Fort Worth** USA
12F2 **Fortymile** R USA
12E1 **Fort Yukon** USA
73C5 **Foshan** China
47C2 **Fossano** Italy
12C3 **Foster,Mt** USA
98B3 **Fougamou** Gabon
48B2 **Fougères** France
44D1 **Foula** I Scot
43E4 **Foulness** I Eng
111B2 **Foulwind,C** NZ
98B2 **Foumban** Cam
49C1 **Fourmies** France
55C3 **Fournoi** I Greece
97A3 **Fouta Djallon** Mts Guinea
111B3 **Foveaux** Str NZ
43B4 **Fowey** Eng
13D2 **Fox Creek** Can
6B3 **Foxe Basin** G Can
6B3 **Foxe Chan** Can
6C3 **Foxe Pen** Can
110C2 **Foxton** NZ
13F2 **Fox Valley** Can

45B2 **Foynes** Irish Rep
100A2 **Foz de Cuene** Angola
30F4 **Foz do Iguaçu** Brazil
16A2 **Frackville** USA
34B2 **Fraga** Arg
16D1 **Framingham** USA
31B6 **Franca** Brazil
49C2 **France** Republic, Europe
12J2 **Frances** R Can
98B3 **Franceville** Gabon
49D2 **Franche Comté** Region, France
100B3 **Francistown** Botswana
13B2 **François L** Can
14A2 **Frankfort** Indiana, USA
11B3 **Frankfort** Kentucky, USA
101G1 **Frankfort** S Africa
57B2 **Frankfurt** Germany
46E1 **Frankfurt am Main** Germany
57C3 **Frankfurt-an-der-Oder** Germany
57C3 **Fränkischer Alb** Upland Germany
14A3 **Franklin** Indiana, USA
19B4 **Franklin** Louisiana, USA
16D1 **Franklin** Massachusetts, USA
16B2 **Franklin** New Jersey, USA
14C2 **Franklin** Pennsylvania, USA
4F2 **Franklin B** Can
20C1 **Franklin D Roosevelt** L USA
4F3 **Franklin Mts** Can
4J2 **Franklin Str** Can
111B2 **Franz Josef Glacier** NZ
Franz-Joseph-Land = Zemlya Frantsa Iosifa
5F5 **Fraser** R Can
44C3 **Fraserburgh** Scot
107E3 **Fraser** I Aust
13B2 **Fraser L** Can
47B1 **Frasne** France
47C1 **Frauenfeld** Switz
34D2 **Fray Bentos** Urug
40C2 **Frazerburgh** Scot
16B3 **Frederica** USA
56B1 **Fredericia** Den
15C3 **Frederick** Maryland, USA
15C3 **Fredericksburg** Virginia, USA
12H3 **Frederick Sd** USA
18B2 **Fredericktown** USA
7D5 **Fredericton** Can
6E3 **Frederikshåb** Greenland
39G7 **Frederikshavn** Den
15C2 **Fredonia** USA
39G7 **Fredrikstad** Nor
16B2 **Freehold** USA
26B1 **Freeport** The Bahamas
101G1 **Free State** Province S Africa
19A4 **Freeport** Texas, USA
97A4 **Freetown** Sierra Leone
57B3 **Freiburg** Germany
57C3 **Freistadt** Austria
106A4 **Fremantle** Aust
22B2 **Fremont** California, USA
18A1 **Fremont** Nebraska, USA
14B2 **Fremont** Ohio, USA
33G3 **French Guiana** Dependency, S America
109C4 **Frenchmans Cap** Mt Aust
105J4 **French Polynesia** Is Pacific O
24B2 **Fresnillo** Mexico

8B3 **Fresno** USA
22C2 **Fresno** R USA
47A1 **Fréteval** France
46B1 **Frévent** France
109C4 **Freycinet Pen** Aust
97A3 **Fria** Guinea
22C2 **Friant** USA
22C2 **Friant Dam** USA
52A1 **Fribourg** Switz
57B3 **Friedrichshafen** Germany
6D3 **Frobisher B** Can
6D3 **Frobisher Bay** Can
5H4 **Frobisher L** Can
61F4 **Frolovo** Russian Fed
43C4 **Frome** Eng
108A1 **Frome** R Aust
43C4 **Frome** R Eng
106C4 **Frome,L** Aust
25C3 **Frontera** Mexico
15C3 **Front Royal** USA
53B2 **Frosinone** Italy
73C5 **Fuchuan** China
73E4 **Fuding** China
24B2 **Fuerte** R Mexico
30E3 **Fuerte Olimpo** Par
96A2 **Fuerteventura** I Canary Is
72C2 **Fugu** China
68A2 **Fuhai** China
91C4 **Fujairah** UAE
75B1 **Fuji** Japan
73D4 **Fujian** Province, China
69F2 **Fujin** China
75B1 **Fujinomiya** Japan
74D3 **Fuji-san** Mt Japan
75B1 **Fujisawa** Japan
75B1 **Fuji-Yoshida** Japan
63A3 **Fukang** China
74C3 **Fukuchiyima** Japan
74D3 **Fukui** Japan
74C4 **Fukuoka** Japan
74C3 **Fukushima** Japan
74C4 **Fukuyama** Japan
57B2 **Fulda** Germany
57B2 **Fulda** R Germany
73B4 **Fuling** China
27L1 **Fullarton** Trinidad
22D4 **Fullerton** USA
18C2 **Fulton** Kentucky, USA
15C2 **Fulton** New York, USA
46C1 **Fumay** France
75C1 **Funabashi** Japan
96A1 **Funchal** Madeira
35C1 **Fundão** Brazil
7D5 **Fundy,B of** Can
101C3 **Funhalouro** Mozam
72D3 **Funing** China
73B5 **Funing** China
97C3 **Funtua** Nig
73D4 **Fuqing** China
101C2 **Furancungo** Mozam
91C4 **Furg** Iran
47C1 **Furka P** Switz
107D5 **Furneaux Group** Is Aust
56C2 **Fürstenwalde** Germany
57C3 **Fürth** Germany
74D3 **Furukawa** Japan
6B3 **Fury and Hecla St** Can
74A2 **Fushun** Liaoning, China
73A4 **Fushun** Sichuan, China
74B2 **Fusong** China
57C3 **Füssen** Germany
72E2 **Fu Xian** China
72E1 **Fuxin** China
72D3 **Fuyang** China
73A4 **Fuyuan** Yunnan, China
68A2 **Fuyun** China
73D4 **Fuzhou** China
56C1 **Fyn** I Den

G

99E2 **Gaalkacyo** Somalia

21B2 **Gabbs** USA
100A2 **Gabela** Angola
96D1 **Gabès** Tunisia
22B2 **Gabilan Range** Mts USA
98B3 **Gabon** Republic, Africa
100B3 **Gaborone** Botswana
54C2 **Gabrovo** Bulg
91B3 **Gach Sārān** Iran
17A1 **Gadsden** Alabama, USA
10A1 **Gads L** Can
53B2 **Gaeta** Italy
71F3 **Gaferut** I Pacific O
96C1 **Gafsa** Tunisia
60D2 **Gagarin** Russian Fed
97B4 **Gagnoa** Côte d'Ivoire
7D4 **Gagnon** Can
61F5 **Gagra** Georgia
86B1 **Gaibanda** India
29C4 **Gaimán** Arg
17B2 **Gainesville** Florida, USA
17B1 **Gainesville** Georgia, USA
19A3 **Gainesville** Texas, USA
42D3 **Gainsborough** Eng
108A2 **Gairdner,L** Aust
44B3 **Gairloch** Scot
16A3 **Gaithersburg** USA
87B1 **Gajendragarh** India
73D4 **Ga Jiang** R China
99D3 **Galana** R Kenya
103D5 **Galapagos** Is Pacific O
44C3 **Galashiels** Scot
54C1 **Galaţi** Rom
4C3 **Galena** Alaska, USA
18B2 **Galena** Kansas, USA
27L1 **Galeota Pt** Trinidad
27L1 **Galera Pt** Trinidad
10A2 **Galesburg** USA
15C2 **Galeton** USA
61F2 **Galich** Russian Fed
50A1 **Galicia** Region, Spain
Galilee,S of = Tiberias,L
27J1 **Galina Pt** Jamaica
98D1 **Gallabat** Sudan
47C2 **Gallarate** Italy
87C3 **Galle** Sri Lanka
51B1 **Gállego** R Spain
Gallipoli = Gelibolu
55A2 **Gallipoli** Italy
38J5 **Gällivare** Sweden
42B2 **Galloway** Region
42B2 **Galloway,Mull of** C Scot
8C3 **Gallup** USA
22B1 **Galt** USA
96A2 **Galtat Zemmour** Mor
25C2 **Galveston** USA
11A4 **Galveston B** USA
34C2 **Galvez** Arg
49D3 **Galvi** Corse
45B2 **Galway** County, Irish Rep
41B3 **Galway** Irish Rep
41B3 **Galway B** Irish Rep
86B1 **Gamba** China
97B3 **Gambaga** Ghana
4A3 **Gambell** USA
97A3 **Gambia** R The Gambia/Sen
97A3 **Gambia,The** Republic, Africa
105K6 **Gambier, Is** Pacific O
98B3 **Gamboma** Congo
100A2 **Gambos** Angola
87C3 **Gampola** Sri Lanka
99E2 **Ganale Dorya** R Eth
15C2 **Gananoque** Can
Gand = Gent
100A2 **Ganda** Angola
98C3 **Gandajika** Zaire
84B3 **Gandava** Pak
7E5 **Gander** Can
85C4 **Gāndhidhām** India
85C4 **Gāndhinagar** India
51B2 **Gandia** Spain
86B2 **Ganga** R India
85C3 **Ganganar** India

86C2 Gangaw Myan
72A2 Gangca China
82C2 Gangdise Shan Mts
China
Ganges = Ganga
86B1 Gangtok India
72B3 Gangu China
8C2 Gannett Peak Mt
USA
72B2 Ganquan China
108A3 Gantheaume C
Aust
39K8 Gantsevichi Belarus
73D4 Ganzhou China
97C3 Gao Mali
72A2 Gaolan China
72C2 Gaoping China
73B3 Gaoua Burkina
97A3 Gaoual Guinea
72D3 Gaoyou Hu L China
73C5 Gaozhou China
49D3 Gap France
79B2 Gapan Phil
84D2 Gar China
109C1 Garah Aust
31D3 Garanhuns Brazil
21A1 Garberville USA
35B2 Garça Brazil
35A2 Garcias Brazil
47D2 Garda Italy
9C3 Garden City USA
14A1 Garden Pen USA
34D3 Gardey Arg
84B2 Gardez Afghan
16C2 Gardiners I USA
16D1 Gardner USA
47D2 Gardone Italy
47D2 Gargano Italy
85D4 Garhakota India
61K2 Gari Russian Fed
100A4 Garies S Africa
99D3 Garissa Kenya
19A3 Garland USA
57C3 Garmisch-
Partenkirchen
Germany
90B2 Garmsar Iran
18A2 Garnett USA
8B2 Garnett Peak Mt
USA
48C3 Garonne R France
44B3 Garry R Scot
78B4 Garut Indon
86A2 Garwa India
14A2 Gary USA
82C2 Garyarsa China
4H3 Gary L Can
19A3 Garza-Little Elm Res
USA
90B2 Gasan Kuli
Turkmenistan
48B3 Gascogne Region,
France
18B2 Gasconade R USA
106A3 Gascoyne R Aust
98B2 Gashaka Nig
97D3 Gashua Nig
10D2 Gaspé Can
10D2 Gaspé,C. de Can
94A1 Gata,C Cyprus
60C2 Gatchina
Russian Fed
42D2 Gateshead Eng
19A3 Gatesville USA
15C1 Gatineau Can
15C1 Gatineau R Can
109D1 Gatton Aust
86C1 Gauhati India
58C1 Gauja R Latvia
86A1 Gauri Phanta India
100B3 Gauteng Province,
S Africa
22B3 Gaviota USA
39H6 Gävle Sweden
108A2 Gawler Ranges Mts
Aust
72A1 Gaxun Nur L China
86A2 Gaya India
97C3 Gaya Niger
14B1 Gaylord USA
109D1 Gayndah Aust
61H1 Gayny Russian Fed
60C4 Gaysin Ukraine
94B3 Gaza Israel

94B3 Gaza
Autonomous Region
S W Asia
92C2 Gaziantep Turk
97B4 Gbaringa Lib
58B2 Gdańsk Pol
58B2 Gdańsk,G of Pol
39K7 Gdov Russian Fed
58B2 Gdynia Pol
94A3 Gebel Halâl Mt
Egypt
92B4 Gebel Katherina Mt
Egypt
94A3 Gebel Libni Mt
Egypt
94A3 Gebel Maghâra Mt
Egypt
99D1 Gedaref Sudan
55C3 Gediz R Turk
56C1 Gedser Den
46C1 Geel Belg
108B3 Geelong Aust
109C4 Geevetson Aust
97D3 Geidam Nig
46D1 Geilenkirchen
Germany
99D3 Geita Tanz
73A5 Gejiu China
53B3 Gela Italy
99E2 Geladī Eth
46D1 Geldern Germany
55C2 Gelibolu Turk
92B2 Gelidonya Burun
Turk
46D1 Gelsenkirchen
Germany
39F8 Gelting Germany
77C5 Gemas Malay
46C1 Gembloux Belg
98B2 Gemena Zaïre
92C2 Gemerek Turk
92A1 Gemlik Turk
52B1 Gemona Italy
100B3 Gemsbok Nat Pk
Botswana
98C1 Geneina Sudan
34C3 General Acha Arg
34C3 General Alvear
Buenos Aires, Arg
34B2 General Alvear
Mendoza, Arg
34C2 General Arenales Arg
34D3 General Belgrano
Arg
112B2 General Belgrano
Base Ant
112C2 General Bernardo
O'Higgins Base Ant
30D3 General Conesa
Buenos Aires, Arg
30D3 General Eugenio A
Garay Par
34D3 General Guido Arg
34C3 General La Madrid
Arg
34C2 General Levalle Arg
30C4 General Manuel
Belgrano Mt Arg
34C3 General Paz
Buenos Aires, Arg
34C3 General Pico Arg
34D3 General Pinto Arg
34D3 General Pirán Arg
29C3 General Roca Arg
112C3 General San Martin
Base Ant
34C3 General Santos Phil
34C3 General Viamonte
Arg
34C3 General Villegas Arg
15C2 Genesee R USA
15C2 Geneseo USA
18A1 Geneva Nebraska,
USA
15C2 Geneva = Genève
Geneva,L of =
LacLéman
52A1 Genève Switz
50B2 Genil R Spain
Genoa = Genova
109C3 Genoa Aust
52A2 Genova Italy

32J7 Genovesa I Ecuador
46B1 Gent Belg
78B4 Genteng Indon
56C2 Genthin Germany
93E1 Geokchay Azerbaijan
7D4 George R Can
109C2 George,L Aust
17B2 George,L Florida,
USA
15D2 George,L New York,
USA
111A2 George Sd NZ
109C4 George Town Aust
15C3 Georgetown
Delaware, USA
33F2 Georgetown Guyana
14B3 Georgetown
Kentucky, USA
77C4 George Town Malay
27N2 Georgetown
St Vincent and the
Grenadines
17C1 Georgetown S
Carolina, USA
19A3 Georgetown Texas,
USA
93E2 Georgetown The
Gambia
112C8 George V Land
Region, Ant
65F6 Georgia Republic,
Europe
112C12 Georg Forster Base
Ant
17B1 Georgia State, USA
14B1 Georgian B Can
13C3 Georgia,Str of Can
106C3 Georgina R Aust
61F5 Georgiyevsk
Russian Fed
57C2 Gera Germany
111B2 Geraardsbergen Belg
31B2 Geral de Goiás
10A3 Geraldton Aust
10B2 Geraldton Can
94B3 Gerar R Israel
4C3 Gerdine,Mt USA
12E2 Gerdova Peak Mt
USA
77C4 Gerik Malay
60B4 Gerlachovský Štit Mt
Pol
13C1 Germansen Lodge
Can
56C2 Germany
Republic, Europe
101G1 Germiston S Africa
46D1 Gerolstein Germany
51C1 Gerona Spain
99E2 Gestro R Eth
50B1 Getafe Spain
16A3 Gettysburg
Pennsylvania, USA
93D2 Gevas Turk
55B2 Gevgelija Macedonia
47B1 Gex France
94C2 Ghabāghib Syria
96C1 Ghadamis Libya
90B2 Ghaem Shahr Iran
86A1 Ghāghara R India
97B4 Ghana Republic,
Africa
100B3 Ghanzi Botswana
96C1 Ghardaïa Alg
95A1 Gharyan Libya
95A2 Ghat Libya
84D3 Ghaziābād India
84C3 Ghazi Khan Pak
84B2 Ghazni Afghan
54C1 Gheorgheni Rom
88E4 Ghudamis Alg
90D3 Ghurian Afghan
95B2 Giado Libya
99E2 Giamame Somalia
53C3 Giarre Italy
100A3 Gibeon Namibia
50A2 Gibraltar Colony,
SW Europe
50A2 Gibraltar,Str of
Spain/Africa
106B3 Gibson Desert Aust
20B1 Gibsons Can

87B1 Giddalūr India
99D2 Gidole Eth
57B2 Giessen Germany
17B2 Gifford USA
74D3 Gifu Japan
42B2 Gigha I Scot
52B2 Giglio I Italy
50A1 Gijón Spain
10702 Gilbert R Aust
13C2 Gilbert,Mt Can
101C2 Gilé Mozam
94B2 Gilead Region,
Jordan
95B2 Gilf Kebir Plat Egypt
109C2 Gilgandra Aust
84C1 Gilgit Pak
84C1 Gilgit R Pak
108C2 Gilgunnia Aust
7A4 Gillam Can
108A2 Gilles L Aust
13L1 Gill I Can
14A1 Gills Rock USA
14A2 Gilman USA
22B2 Gilroy USA
8D1 Gimli Can
99H1 Gingindlovu S Africa
79C4 Gingoog Phil
99E1 Ginir Eth
5553 Gióna Mt Greece
109C3 Gippsland Mts Aust
14B2 Girard USA
32C3 Girardot Colombia
44C3 Girdle Ness Pen
Scot
93C1 Giresun Turk
85C4 Gir Hills India
98B2 Gïri R Zaïre
86B2 Giridih India
100A3 Giona = Genoa
48B2 Gironde R France
42B2 Girvan Scot
111C2 Gisborne NZ
46A2 Gisors France
99C3 Gitega Burundi
Giuba,R = Juba,R
52C2 Giurgiu Rom
46C1 Givet Belg
52C2 Gizycko Pol
55B2 Gjirokastër Alb
4J3 Gjoatlaven Can
39G6 Gjovik Nor
7D5 Glace Bay Can
12G3 Glacier Bat Nat Mon
USA
13E3 Glacier Nat Pk USA/
Can
20B1 Glacier Peak Mt
USA
6B2 Glacier Str Can
107E3 Gladstone
Queensland, Aust
108A2 Gladstone S Aust,
Aust
109C4 Gladstone Tasmania,
Aust
14A1 Gladstone USA
38A1 Glama Mt Iceland
39G6 Glåma R Nor
46D2 Glan R Germany
47C1 Glariner Mts Switz
47C1 Glarus Switz
18A2 Glasco USA
8C2 Glasgow Montana,
USA
42B2 Glasgow Scot
42B2 Glasgow, City of
Division, Scot
16B3 Glassboro USA
43C4 Glastonbury Eng
61H2 Glazov Russian Fed
59B3 Gleisdorf Austria
110C1 Glen Afton NZ
16A3 Glen Burnie USA
101H1 Glencoe S Africa
9B3 Glendale Arizona,
USA
22C3 Glendale California,
USA
12E2 Glenhallen USA
109D1 Glen Innes Aust
109C1 Glenmorgan Aust
109D2 Glenreagh Aust
16A3 Glen Rock USA
19A3 Glen Rose USA

Glenrothes

44C3 **Glenrothes** UK
15D2 **Glens Falls** USA
45B1 **Glenties** Irish Rep
19B3 **Glenwood** Arkansas, USA
8C3 **Glenwood Springs** USA
39F6 **Glittertind** Mt Nor
59B2 **Gliwice** Pol
9B3 **Globe** USA
58B2 **Głogów** Pol
38G5 **Glomfjord** Nor
109D2 **Gloucester** Aust
43C4 **Gloucester** Eng
16D1 **Gloucester** USA
100A3 **Glubczyce** Pol
60D3 **Glukhov** Russian Fed
59B3 **Gmünd** Austria
57C3 **Gmunden** Austria
58B2 **Gniezno** Pol
100A3 **Goabeb** Namibia
87A1 **Goa, Daman and Diu** Union Territory, India
86C1 **Goalpara** India
99D2 **Goba** Eth
100A3 **Gobabis** Namibia
34C2 **Gobernador Crespo** Arg
34B3 **Gobernador Duval** Arg
72B1 **Gobi** Desert China/Mongolia
75B2 **Gobo** Japan
87B1 **Godag** India
87C1 **Godavari** R India
14B2 **Goderich** Can
6E3 **Godhavn** Greenland
85C4 **Godhra** India
34B2 **Godoy Cruz** Arg
7A4 **Gods L** Can
6E3 **Godthåb** Greenland
Godwin Austen = K2
35B1 **Goiandira** Brazil
35B1 **Goianésia** Brazil
35B1 **Goiânia** Brazil
35A1 **Goiás** Brazil
31B4 **Goiás** State, Brazil
35A2 **Goio-Erê** Brazil
99D2 **Gojab** R Eth
55C2 **Gökçeada** / Turk
55C3 **Gökova Körfezi** B Turk
92C2 **Göksun** Turk
63C3 **Gol** R Mongolia
86C1 **Golaghat** India
92C2 **Gölbaşi** Turk
20C2 **Golconda** USA
20B2 **Gold Beach** USA
109D1 **Gold Coast** Aust
13D2 **Golden** B NZ
110B2 **Golden** B NZ
20B1 **Goldendale** USA
22A2 **Golden Gate** Chan USA
19B4 **Golden Meadow** USA
21B2 **Goldfield** USA
13B3 **Gold River** Can
56C2 **Goleniów** Pol
52A2 **Golfe d'Ajaccio** G Corse
96D1 **Golfe de Gabes** G Tunisia
Golfe de Gascogne = Biscay,Bay of
52A2 **Golfe de St Florent** G Corse
48B2 **Golfe de St-Malo** G France
49C3 **Golfe du Lion** G France
29B4 **Golfo Corcovado** G Chile
50B2 **Golfo de Almeria** G Spain
29B4 **Golfo de Ancud** G Chile
52D2 **Golfo de Batabano** G Cuba
50A2 **Golfo de Cadiz** G Spain
53A3 **Golfo de Cagliari** G Sardegna

24A1 **Golfo de California** G Mexico
25D4 **Golfo de Chiriqui** G Panama
25D3 **Golfo de Fonseca** Honduras
26B2 **Golfo de Guacanayabo** G Cuba
32A4 **Golfo de Guayaquil** G Ecuador
26B5 **Golfo del Darien** G Colombia/Panama
32A2 **Golfo de los Mosquitos** G Panama
25D3 **Golfo del Papagaya** G Nic
51B2 **Golfo de Mazarrón** G Spain
25D4 **Golfo de Nicoya** G Costa Rica
53A3 **Golfo de Oristano** G Sardegna
25E4 **Golfo de Panamá** G Panama
25D3 **Golfo de Papagayo** G Costa Rica
27E4 **Golfo de Paria** G Ven
29B5 **Golfo de Penas** G Chile
49D3 **Golfo de St Florent** Corse
51C1 **Golfo de San Jorge** G Spain
24C3 **Golfo de Tehuantepec** G Mexico
32B3 **Golfo de Torugas** G Colombia
32B2 **Golfo de Uraba** G Colombia
51C2 **Golfo de Valencia** G Spain
27C4 **Golfo de Venezuela** G Ven
52A2 **Golfo di Genova** G Italy
53C3 **Golfo di Policastro** G Italy
53C3 **Golfo di Squillace** B Italy
53C2 **Golfo di Taranto** G Italy
52A2 **Golfo di Venezia** G Italy
25D4 **Golfo Dulce** G Costa Rica
29C5 **Golfo San Jorge** G Arg
29D4 **Golfo San Matias** G Arg
68B3 **Golmud** China
99E2 **Golocha** Eth
12B2 **Golovin** USA
74F2 **Golovnino** Russian Fed
99C3 **Goma** Zaïre
97D3 **Gombe** Nig
90B3 **Gomel** Belarus
96A2 **Gomera** / Canary Is
24B2 **Gómez Palacio** Mexico
63E2 **Gonam** R
90C2 **Gonbad-e Kávús** Iran
86A1 **Gonda** India
85C4 **Gondal** India
99D1 **Gonder** Eth
92A1 **Gönen** Turk
55C3 **Gönen** R Turk
73A4 **Gongga Shan** Mt China
72A2 **Gonghe** China
97D3 **Gongola** R Nig
22B2 **Gonzales** California, USA
19A4 **Gonzales** Texas, USA
34C3 **Gonzalez Chaves** Arg
13C2 **Good Hope Mt** Can
8C2 **Goodland** USA
12B3 **Goodnews Bay** USA
109C1 **Goodooga** R Aust
42D3 **Goole** Eng

108C2 **Goolgowi** Aust
108A3 **Goolwa** Aust
106A4 **Goomalling** Aust
109C1 **Goombalie** Aust
109D1 **Goomeri** Aust
109D1 **Goondiwindi** Aust
7E4 **Goose Bay** Can
17C1 **Goose Creek** USA
20B2 **Goose L** USA
87B1 **Gooty** India
63C2 **Gora Munku Sardyk** Mt Mongolia/Russian Fed
64H3 **Gora Narodnaya** Mt Russian Fed
64G3 **Gora Tel'pos-iz** Russian Fed
54A2 **Goražde** Bosnia-Herzegovina
4D3 **Gordon** USA
13E1 **Gordon L** Can
15C3 **Gordonsville** USA
98B2 **Goré** Chad
99D2 **Goré** Eth
111A3 **Gore** NZ
63F2 **Gore Topko** Mt Russian Fed
45C2 **Gorey** Irish Rep
90B2 **Gorgan** Iran
93E2 **Goris** Armenia
52B1 **Gorizia** Italy
Gor'kiy = Nizniy Novgorod
61F2 **Gor'kovskoye Vodokhranilische** Res Russian Fed
57C2 **Görlitz** Germany
60E4 **Gorlovka** Ukraine
52C2 **Gorman** USA
54C2 **Gorna Orjahovica** Bulg
68A1 **Gorno-Altaysk** Russian Fed
69G2 **Gornozavodsk** Russian Fed
61F2 **Gorodets** Russian Fed
59C3 **Gorodok** Ukraine
59D3 **Gorodok** Ukraine
71F4 **Goroka** PNG
86A1 **Gorokhpur** India
71D3 **Gorontalo** Indon
61K2 **Goro Yurma** Mt Russian Fed
45B2 **Gort** Irish Rep
63C2 **Goryachinsk** Russian Fed
59D3 **Goryn'** R Ukraine
59C2 **Góry Świetokrzyskie** Upland Pol
64G3 **Gory Tel'pos-iz'** Mt Russian Fed
39H8 **Gorzów Wielkopolski** Pol
74E2 **Goshogawara** Japan
52C2 **Gospić** Croatia
54B2 **Gostivar** Macedonia
59D2 **Gostynin** Pol
39G7 **Göteborg** Sweden
98B2 **Gotel** Mts Nig
39H7 **Gotland** / Sweden
74B4 **Goto-retto** / Japan
39H7 **Gotska Sandön** / Sweden
74C3 **Götsu** Japan
98B1 **Goudoumaria** Niger
103H7 **Gough I** Atlantic O
109C2 **Goulburn** Aust
97B3 **Goumbou** Mali
97B3 **Goundam** Mali
98B1 **Gouré** Niger
97B3 **Gourma Rharous** Mali
46A2 **Gournay-en-Bray** France
98B2 **Gouro** Chad
71E5 **Gove Pen** Aust
60B4 **Goverla** Mt Ukraine
35C1 **Governador Valadares** Brazil
86A2 **Govind Ballabh Paht Ságar** L India

15C2 **Gowanda** USA
84B3 **Gowárán** Afghan
30E4 **Goya** Arg
98C1 **Goz-Beida** Chad
53B3 **Gozo** I Medit S
95C3 **Goz Regeb** Sudan
100B4 **Graaff-Reinet** S Africa
15C1 **Gracefield** Can
109D1 **Grafton** Aust
8D2 **Grafton** N Dakota, USA
14B3 **Grafton** W Virginia, USA
5E4 **Graham I** Can
13C1 **Graham** R Can
13E1 **Graham L** Can
100B4 **Grahamstown** S Africa
31B3 **Grajaú** Brazil
58C2 **Grajewo** Pol
55B2 **Grámmos** Mt Greece/Alb
44B3 **Grampian** Mts Scot
32C3 **Granada** Colombia
25D3 **Granada** Nic
50B3 **Granada** Spain
15D1 **Granby** Can
96A2 **Gran Canaria** / Canary Is
30D4 **Gran Chaco** Region Arg
14A2 **Grand** R Michigan, USA
18B1 **Grand** R Missouri, USA
27Q2 **Grand B** Dominica
11C4 **Grand Bahama** / The Bahamas
102F2 **Grand Banks** Atlantic O
97B4 **Grand Bassam** Côte d'Ivoire
9B3 **Grand Canyon** USA
26A3 **Grand Cayman** / Caribbean S
13E2 **Grand Centre** Can
20C1 **Grand Coulee** USA
34B3 **Grande** R Arg
31C4 **Grande** R Bahia, Brazil
35B1 **Grande** R Minas Gerais/São Paulo, Brazil
13D2 **Grande Cache** Can
47A2 **Grande Chartreuse** Region, France
101D2 **Grande Comore** / Comoros
13D1 **Grande Prairie** Can
19A3 **Grande Prairie** USA
95A3 **Grand Erg de Bilma** Desert Niger
96B2 **Grand erg Occidental** Mts Alg
96C2 **Grand erg Oriental** Mts Alg
7C4 **Grande Rivière de la Baleine** R Can
20C1 **Grande Ronde** R USA
7D5 **Grand Falls** New Brunswick, Can
7E5 **Grand Falls** Newfoundland, Can
20C1 **Grand Forks** Can
8D2 **Grand Forks** USA
16B1 **Grand Gorge** USA
14A2 **Grand Haven** USA
19C3 **Grand Isle** USA
19B4 **Grand L** USA
15D2 **Grand Mère** Can
50A2 **Grândola** Port
5J4 **Grand Rapids** Can
14A2 **Grand Rapids** Michigan, USA
10A2 **Grand Rapids** Minnesota, USA
47B2 **Grand St Bernard** P Italy/Switz
8B2 **Grand Teton** Mt USA

8B2 **Grand Teton Nat Pk** USA
46A2 **Grandvilliers** France
25D1 **Grangebung** USA
51C1 **Granollérs** Spain
52A1 **Gran Paradiso** *Mt* Italy
47D1 **Gran Pilastro** *Mt* Austria/Italy
43D3 **Grantham** Eng
21B2 **Grant,Mt** USA
44C2 **Grantown-on-Spey** Scot
9C3 **Grants** USA
20B2 **Grants Pass** USA
44B2 **Granville** France
5H4 **Granville L** Can
35C1 **Grão Mogol** Brazil
49D3 **Grasse** France
21A2 **Grass Valley** USA
5H5 **Gravelbourg** Can
46B1 **Gravelines** France
100C3 **Gravelotte** S Africa
15C2 **Gravenhurst** Can
109D1 **Gravesend** Aust
12H3 **Gravina I** USA
12B2 **Grayling** USA
20B1 **Grays Harbor** *B* USA
14B3 **Grayson** USA
18C2 **Grayville** USA
59B3 **Graz** Austria
27H1 **Great** *R* Jamaica
11C4 **Great Abaco** *I* The Bahamas
106B4 **Great Australian Bight** *G* Aust
16B3 **Great B** New Jersey, USA
25E2 **Great Bahama Bank** The Bahamas
110C1 **Great Barrier I** NZ
107D2 **Great Barrier Reef** *Is* Aust
16C1 **Great Barrington** USA
4F3 **Great Bear L** Can
9D2 **Great Bend** USA
107D3 **Great Dividing Range** *Mts* Aust
42D2 **Great Driffield** Eng
16B3 **Great Egg Harbor** *B* USA
112B10 **Greater Antarctic** Region, Ant
26B2 **Greater Antilles** *Is* Caribbean S
43D4 **Greater London** Metropolitan County, Eng
43C3 **Greater Manchester** County, Eng
25E2 **Great Exuma** *I* The Bahamas
8B2 **Great Falls** USA
44B3 **Great Glen** *V* Scot
86B1 **Great Himalayan Range** *Mts* Asia
11C4 **Great Inagua** *I* The Bahamas
100B4 **Great Karroo** *Mts* S Africa
109C4 **Great L** Aust
100A3 **Great Namaland** Region, Namibia
42C3 **Great Ormes Head** *C* Wales
11C4 **Great Ragged** *I* The Bahamas
99D3 **Great Ruaha** *R* Tanz
15D2 **Great Sacandaga L** USA
8B2 **Great Salt L** USA
95B2 **Great Sand Sea** Libya/Egypt
106B3 **Great Sandy Desert** Aust
8A2 **Great Sandy Desert** USA
  Great Sandy I = Fraser I
4G3 **Great Slave L** Can
16C2 **Great South B** USA
106B3 **Great Victoria Desert** Aust

112C2 **Great Wall** *Base* Ant
72B2 **Great Wall** China
43E3 **Great Yarmouth** Eng
94B1 **Greco,C** Cyprus
55B3 **Greece** Republic, Europe
15C2 **Greece** USA
8C2 **Greeley** USA
6B1 **Greely Fjord** Can
14A1 **Green B** USA
14A2 **Green Bay** USA
14A3 **Greencastle** Indiana, USA
16C1 **Greenfield** Massachusetts, USA
14A2 **Greenfield** Wisconsin, USA
13F2 **Green Lake** Can
6F2 **Greenland** Dependency, N Atlantic O
102H1 **Greenland Basin** Greenland S
1B1 **Greenland S** Greenland
42B2 **Greenock** Scot
16C2 **Greenport** USA
16B3 **Greensboro** Maryland, USA
11C3 **Greensboro** N Carolina, USA
15C2 **Greensburg** Pennsylvania, USA
44B3 **Greenstone Pt** Scot
18C2 **Greenup** USA
17A1 **Greenville** Alabama, USA
97B4 **Greenville** Lib
19B3 **Greenville** Mississippi, USA
16D1 **Greenville** N Hampshire, USA
14B2 **Greenville** Ohio, USA
17B1 **Greenville** S Carolina, USA
19A3 **Greenville** Texas, USA
43E4 **Greenwich** Eng
16C2 **Greenwich** USA
16B3 **Greenwood** Delaware, USA
19B3 **Greenwood** Mississippi, USA
17B1 **Greenwood** S Carolina, USA
18B2 **Greers Ferry L** USA
108A1 **Gregory,L** Aust
107D2 **Gregory Range** *Mts* Aust
56C2 **Greifswald** Germany
64F3 **Gremikha** Russian Fed
56C1 **Grenå** Den
19C3 **Grenada** USA
27E4 **Grenada** *I* Caribbean S
109C2 **Grenfell** Aust
49D2 **Grenoble** France
27M2 **Grenville** Grenada
107D2 **Grenville,C** Aust
20B1 **Gresham** USA
78C4 **Gresik** Jawa, Indon
78A3 **Gresik** Sumatera, Indon
19B4 **Gretna** USA
111B2 **Grey** *R* NZ
12G2 **Grey Hunter Pk** *Mt* Can
7E4 **Grey Is** Can
16C1 **Greylock,Mt** USA
111B2 **Greymouth** NZ
107D3 **Grey Range** *Mts* Aust
45C2 **Greystones** Irish Rep
101H1 **Greytown** S Africa
101F1 **Griekwastad** S Africa
17B1 **Griffin** USA
108C2 **Griffith** Aust
107D5 **Grim,C** Aust
15C2 **Grimsby** Can
42D3 **Grimsby** Eng
38B1 **Grimsey I** Iceland
13D1 **Grimshaw** Can
39F7 **Grimstad** Nor

47C1 **Grindelwald** Switz
6A2 **Grinnell Pen** Can
6B2 **Grise Fjord** Can
61H1 **Griva** Russian Fed
39J7 **Grobina** Latvia
58C2 **Grodno** Belarus
86A1 **Gromati** *R* India
56B2 **Groningen** Neth
106C2 **Groote Eylandt** *I* Aust
100A2 **Grootfontein** Namibia
100B3 **Grootvloer** *Salt L* S Africa
27P2 **Gros Islet** St Lucia
46E1 **Grosser Feldberg** *Mt* Germany
52B2 **Grosseto** Italy
46E2 **Gross-Gerau** Germany
57C3 **Grossglockner** *Mt* Austria
47E1 **Gross Venediger** *Mt* Austria
12C3 **Grosvenor,L** USA
22B2 **Groveland** USA
21A2 **Grover City** USA
15D2 **Groveton** USA
61G5 **Groznyy** Russian Fed
58B2 **Grudziadz** Pol
100A3 **Grünau** Namibia
44E2 **Grutness** Scot
61E3 **Gryazi** Russian Fed
61E2 **Gryazovets** Russian Fed
29G8 **Grytviken** South Georgia
45A2 **Gt Blasket** *I* Irish Rep
35C2 **Guaçui** Brazil
23A1 **Guadalajara** Mexico
50B1 **Guadalajara** Spain
107E1 **Guadalcanal** *I* Solomon Is
50B2 **Guadalimar** *R* Spain
50B1 **Guadalope** *R* Spain
50B2 **Guadalqivir** *R* Spain
24B2 **Guadalupe** Mexico
3G6 **Guadalupe** *I* Mexico
48B2 **Guadeloupe** *I* Caribbean S
50B2 **Guadian** *R* Spain
50A2 **Guadiana** *R* Port
50B2 **Guadix** Spain
32D6 **Guajará Mirim** Brazil
32C6 **Guajira,Pen de** Colombia
32B4 **Gualaceo** Ecuador
34D2 **Gualeguay** Arg
34D2 **Gualeguaychú** Arg
71F2 **Guam** *I* Pacific O
34C3 **Guamini** Arg
77C5 **Gua Musang** Malay
23A1 **Guanajuato** Mexico
23A1 **Guanajuato** State, Mexico
32D2 **Guanare** Ven
25D2 **Guane** Cuba
73A3 **Guangdong** Province, China
72C3 **Guanghua** China
73A4 **Guangmao Shan** *Mt* China
73B5 **Guangnan** China
72B3 **Guangyuan** China
73D4 **Guangze** China
67F3 **Guangzhou** China
35C1 **Guanhães** Brazil
32D3 **Guania** *R* Colombia
27E5 **Guanica** P Rico
26B2 **Guantánamo** Cuba
72D1 **Guanting Shuiku** *Res* China
73B5 **Guanxi** Province, China
73A3 **Guan Xian** China
32B2 **Guapa** Colombia
33E6 **Guaporé** *R* Brazil/Bol
30C2 **Guaqui** Bol
32B4 **Guaranda** Ecuador
30F4 **Guarapuava** Brazil
35B2 **Guaratinguetá** Brazil
50A1 **Guarda** Port

35B1 **Guarda Mor** Brazil
9C4 **Guasave** Mexico
47D2 **Guastalla** Italy
25C3 **Guatemala** Guatemala
25C3 **Guatemala** Republic, Cent America
34C3 **Guatraché** Arg
32C3 **Guaviare** *R* Colombia
35B2 **Guaxupé** Brazil
27L1 **Guayaguayare** Trinidad
32A4 **Guayaquil** Ecuador
24A2 **Guaymas** Mexico
34D2 **Guayquiraró** *R* Arg
100B2 **Guba** Zaïre
99E2 **Guban** *Region* Somalia
79B3 **Gubat** Phil
56C2 **Gubin** Pol
87B2 **Güdür** India
14B2 **Guelph** Can
26A2 **Guanabacoa** Cuba
98C1 **Guéréda** Chad
48C2 **Guéret** France
48B2 **Guernsey** *I* UK
23A2 **Guerrero** State, Mexico
99D2 **Gughe** *Mt* Eth
63E2 **Gugigu** China
71F2 **Guguan** *I* Pacific O
109C2 **Guiargambone** Aust
73C4 **Guidong** China
97B4 **Guiglo** Côte d'Ivoire
73C5 **Gui Jiang** *R* China
43D4 **Guildford** Eng
73C4 **Guilin** China
47B2 **Guillestre** France
72A2 **Guinan** China
97A3 **Guinea** Republic, Africa
104H4 **Guinea Basin** Atlantic O
97A3 **Guinea-Bissau** Republic, Africa
97C4 **Guinea,G of** W Africa
26A2 **Güines** Cuba
97B3 **Guir** *Well* Mali
84C2 **Guiranwala** Pak
33E1 **Gūiria** Ven
46B2 **Guise** France
79C3 **Guiuan** Phil
73B5 **Gui Xian** China
73B4 **Guiyang** China
73B4 **Guizhou** Province, China
85C4 **Gujarāt** State, India
84C2 **Gujrat** Pak
87B1 **Gulbarga** India
58D1 **Gulbene** Latvia
87B1 **Guledagudda** India
80D3 **Gulf,The** S W Asia
109C2 **Gulgong** Aust
73A4 **Gulin** China
12E2 **Gulkana** *L* USA
12E2 **Gulkana** USA
13E2 **Gull L** Can
13F2 **Gull Lake** Can
55C3 **Güllük Körfezi** *B* Turk
99D2 **Gulu** Uganda
109C1 **Guluguba** Aust
99D2 **Gumel** Nig
46D1 **Gummersbach** Germany
86A2 **Gumpla** India
93C1 **Gümüşhane** Turk
86B3 **Guna** India
86B2 **Guna** India
109C3 **Gundagai** Aust
98B3 **Gungu** Zaïre
6H3 **Gunnbjørn Fjeld** *Mt* Greenland
109D2 **Gunnedah** Aust
87B1 **Guntakal** India
17A1 **Guntersville** USA
17A1 **Guntersville L** USA
87C1 **Guntūr** India
77C5 **Gunung Batu Putch** *Mt* Malay
78D3 **Gunung Besar** *Mt* Indon

Gunung Bulu

78D2 Gunung Bulu Mt Indon
78A3 Gunung Gedang Mt Indon
78A3 Gunung Lawit Mt Malay
78C4 Gunung Lawu Mt Indon
78D2 Gunung Menyapa Mt Indon
78D2 Gunung Niapa Mt Indon
78A3 Gunung Patah Mt Indon
78C4 Gunung Raung Mt Indon
78A3 Gunung Resag Mt Indon
78D3 Gunung Sarempaka Mt Indon
78C4 Gunung Sumbing Mt Indon
77C5 Gunung Tahan Mt Malay
78A2 Gunung Talakmau Mt Indon
100A2 Gunza Angola
72D3 Guoyang China
84C2 Gurdaspur India
84D3 Gurgaon India
86A1 Gurkha Nepal
92C2 Gürün Turk
31B2 Gurupi R Brazil
100C2 Guruve Zim
71A4 Gurvan Sayhan Uul Upland Mongolia
61H4 Gur'yev Kazakhstan
97C3 Gusau Nig
58C2 Gusev Russian Fed
74A3 Gushan China
61F2 Gus'khrustalnyy Russian Fed
12G3 Gustavus USA
22B2 Gustine USA
11B3 Guston USA
56B2 Gütersloh Germany
18C2 Guthrie Kentucky, USA
18C2 Guthrie Oklahoma, USA
23B1 Gutiérrez Zamora Mexico
33F3 Guyana Republic, S America
102F4 Guyana Basin Atlantic O
72C1 Guyang China
48B3 Guyenne Region, France
9C3 Guyra Aust
109D2 Guyra Aust
72B2 Guyuan China
109C2 Gwabegar Aust
85D3 Gwalior India
100B3 Gwanda Zim
98C2 Gwane Zaire
82A3 Gwardar Pak
45B1 Gweebarra B Irish Rep
89G9 Gwelo Zim
100B2 Gweru Zim
109C1 Gwydir R Aust
65F5 Gyandzha Azerbaijan
86B1 Gyangzê China
68B3 Gyaring Hu L China
64J2 Gydanskiy Poluostrov Pen Russian Fed
86B1 Gyirong China
81 Gyldenløves Greenland
109D1 Gympie Aust
59B3 Gyöngyös Hung
59B3 Györ Hung

H

38K6 Haapajärvi Fin
60B2 Haapsalu Estonia
56A2 Haarlem Neth
46D1 Haarstrang Region, Germany
25D2 Habana Cuba
86C2 Habiganj Bang
74D4 Hachijo-jima I Japan
75B1 Hachiman Japan

74E2 Hachinohe Japan
75B1 Hachioji Japan
16B2 Hackettstown USA
108A2 Hack,Mt Mt Aust
42C2 Haddington Scot
108B1 Haddon Corner Aust
108B1 Haddon Downs Aust
97D3 Hadejia Nig
97C3 Hadejia R Nig
94B2 Hadera Israel
56B1 Haderslev Den
81D4 Hadiboh Socotra
4H2 Hadley B Can
73B5 Hadong Vietnam
81C4 Hadramawt Region, Yemen
56C1 Hadsund Den
74B3 Haeju N Korea
91A4 Hafar al Bātin S Arabia
6J2 Haffners Bjerg Mt Greenland
84C2 Hafizabad Pak
86C1 Häflong India
38A2 Hafnafjördur Iceland
12B3 Hagemeister I USA
56B2 Hagen Germany
15C3 Hagerstown USA
75A2 Hagi Japan
73A5 Ha Giang Vietnam
46D2 Hagondange France
45B2 Hags Hd R Irish Rep
46D2 Haguenau France
66A3 Hagunia Well Mor
69C4 Haha-jima I Japan
68B3 Hah Xil Hu L China
74A2 Haicheng China
76D1 Hai Duong Viet
94B2 Haifa Israel
94B2 Haifa,B of Israel
72D2 Hai He R China
73C5 Haikang China
76E1 Haikou China
80C3 Ha'il S Arabia
86C2 Hailākāndi India
63D3 Hailar China
74B2 Hailong China
69E2 Hailun China
38J5 Hailuoto I Fin
76D2 Hainan I China
12G3 Haines USA
12G2 Haines Junction Can
59B3 Hainfeld Austria
73B5 Haiphong Vietnam
26C3 Haiti Republic, Caribbean S
95C3 Haiya Sudan
72A2 Haiyan China
72B2 Haiyuan China
73D2 Haizhou Wan B China
59C3 Hajdúböszörmény Hung
75B1 Hajiki-saki Pt Japan
96C2 Haka Myan
21C4 Hakalau Hawaiian Is
93D2 Hakkâri Turk
74E2 Hakodate Japan
Hakwa = Haka
75B1 Hakui Japan
75B1 Haku-san Mt Japan
92C2 Halab Syria
93E3 Halabja Iraq
95C2 Halaib Sudan
94C1 Halba Leb
68B2 Halban Mongolia
56C2 Halberstadt Germany
79B3 Halcon,Mt Phil
39G7 Halden Nor
86B2 Haldia India
84D3 Haldwāni India
13C1 Halfway R Can
7D5 Halifax Can
42D3 Halifax Eng
6D1 Hall Basin Sd Can
6B3 Hall Beach Can
46C1 Halle Belg
56C2 Halle Germany
112B1 Halley Base Ant
39F6 Hallingdal R Nor
56D2 Hall Pen Can
108B2 Hall's Creek Aust
71D3 Halmahera I Indon

39G7 Halmstad Sweden
56B2 Haltern Germany
38J5 Halti Mt Nor
42C2 Haltwhistle Eng
91B4 Halul I Qatar
94B3 Haluza Hist Site Israel
75A2 Hamada Japan
96C2 Hamada de Tinrhert Desert Region Alg
96B2 Hamada du Dra Upland Alg
90A3 Hamadān Iran
96B2 Hamada Tounassine Region, Alg
92C2 Hamāh Syria
75B2 Hamamatsu Japan
39G6 Hamar Nor
87C3 Hambantota Sri Lanka
19B3 Hamburg Arkansas, USA
18A1 Hamburg Iowa, USA
16B2 Hamburg Pennsylvania, USA
56B2 Hamburg Germany
16C2 Hamden USA
39J6 Hämeenlinna Fin
106A3 Hamersley Range Aust
74B2 Hamgyong Sanmaek Mts N Korea
74D3 Hamhŭng N Korea
68B2 Hami China
94B1 Hamīdīyah Syria
108B3 Hamilton Aust
14C2 Hamilton Can
110C1 Hamilton NZ
15C3 Hamilton Ohio, USA
42B2 Hamilton Scot
22B2 Hamilton,Mt USA
38K6 Hamina Fin
86A1 Hamīrpur India
56B2 Hamm Germany
95A2 Hammādah al Hamra Upland Libya
38H6 Hammerdal Sweden
38J4 Hammerfest Nor
14A2 Hammond Illinois, USA
19B3 Hammond Louisiana, USA
16B3 Hammonton USA
111B3 Hampden NZ
43D4 Hampshire County, Eng
19B3 Hampton Arkansas, USA
91C4 Hāmūn-e Jaz Mūrian L Iran
84B3 Hamun-i-Lora Salt L Pak
21C4 Hana Hawaiian Is
21C4 Hanalei Hawaiian Is
74E2 Hanamaki Japan
72C2 Hancheng China
72C3 Hanchuan China
15C3 Hancock Maryland, USA
10B2 Hancock Michigan, USA
75B1 Handa Japan
72C2 Handan China
99D3 Handeni Tanz
72B2 Hanggin Qi China
39J7 Hangö Fin
73E3 Hangzhou China
73E3 Hangzhou Wan B China
111B2 Hanmer Springs NZ
13E2 Hanna Can
18B2 Hannibal USA
56B2 Hannover Germany
39G7 Hanöbukten B Sweden
76D1 Hanoi Viet
16A3 Hanover USA
29B6 Hanover I Chile
72B3 Han Shui China
73C3 Han Shui R China
85D3 Hānsi India
68C2 Hantay Mongolia
72B3 Hanzhong China
86B2 Hāora India

38J5 Haparanda Sweden
86C1 Hāpoli India
92C4 Haql S Arabia
91A5 Harad S Arabia
99E2 Hara Fanna Eth
75C1 Haramachi Japan
101C2 Harare Zim
98C1 Haraze Chad
18B2 Harbor Beach USA
85D4 Harda India
39F6 Hardangerfjord Inlet Nor
46D2 Hardt Germany
108A2 Hardwicke B Aust
18B2 Hardy USA
99E2 Harēr Eth
99E2 Hargeysa Somalia
94B3 Har Hakippa Mt Israel
68B3 Har Hu L China
78A3 Hari R Indon
75A2 Harima-nada B Japan
56B2 Harlingen Neth
9D4 Harlingen USA
43E4 Harlow Eng
94B2 Har Meron Mt Israel
20C2 Harney Basin USA
20C2 Harney L USA
38H6 Härnösand Sweden
63B3 Har Nuur L Mongolia
97B4 Harper Lib
12F2 Harper,Mt USA
15C3 Harpers Ferry USA
94B3 Har Ramon Mt Israel
7C4 Harricanaw R Can
16B3 Harrington USA
7E4 Harrington Harbour Can
44A3 Harris District Scot
18C2 Harrisburg Illinois, USA
16A2 Harrisburg Pennsylvania, USA
101G1 Harrismith S Africa
18A2 Harrison Arkansas, USA
13C2 Harrison,C Can
13C3 Harrison L Can
18B2 Harrisonville USA
44A3 Harris,Sound of Chan Scot
14B2 Harrisville USA
42D3 Harrogate Eng
94B3 Har Saggi Mt Israel
38H5 Harstad Nor
12G2 Hart R Can
39F6 Härteigen Mt Nor
16C2 Hartford Connecticut, USA
14A2 Hartford Michigan, USA
38G6 Hartkjølen Mt Nor
108A2 Hart,L Aust
43B4 Hartland Pt Eng
42D2 Hartlepool Eng
42D2 Hartlepool County Eng
19A3 Hartshorne USA
17B1 Hartwell Res USA
101F1 Hartz R S Africa
68B2 Har Us Nuur L Mongolia
43E4 Harwich Eng
8D2 Haryana State, India
94B3 Hāsā Jordan
94B2 Hāsbaiya Leb
43D4 Haselmere Eng
75B2 Hashimoto Japan
90A2 Hashtpar Iran
90A2 Hashtrūd Iran
87B2 Hassan India
56B2 Hasselt Belg
96C2 Hassi Inifel Alg
54B3 Hassi Mdakane Well Alg
96C1 Hassi Messaoud Alg
108C3 Hastings Aust
43E4 Hastings Eng
8D2 Hastings Nebraska, USA

110C1 Hastings NZ
108B2 Hatfield Aust
12B1 Hatham Inlet USA
85D3 Hathira India
76D2 Ha Tinh Viet
108B2 Hattah Aust
11C3 Hatteras,C USA
19C3 Hattiesburg USA
59B3 Hatvan Hung
76D3 Hau Bon Viet
99E2 Haud Region, Eth
39F7 Haugesund Nor
110C1 Hauhungaroa Range Mts NZ
13F1 Haultain R Can
110B1 Hauraki G NZ
11A3 Hauroko,L NZ
47C1 Hausstock Mt Switz
96B1 Haut Atlas Mts Mor
98C2 Haute Kotto Region, CAR
46C1 Hautes Fagnes Belg
46B1 Hautmont Belg
96B1 Hauts Plateaux Alg
90D3 Hauzdar Iran
18B1 Havana USA
Havana = Habana
87B3 Havankulam Sri Lanka
110C1 Havelock North NZ
43B4 Haverfordwest Wales
16D1 Haveri India
87B2 Häveri India
16C2 Haverstraw USA
59B3 Havlíčkúv Brod Czech Republic
8C2 Havre USA
16A3 Havre de Grace USA
7D4 Havre-St-Pierre Can
54C2 Havsa Turk
21C4 Hawaii I Hawaiian Is
21C4 Hawaii Volcanoes Nat Pk Hawaiian Is
111A2 Hawea,L NZ
110B1 Hawera NZ
42C2 Hawick Scot
111A2 Hawkdun Range Mts NZ
110C1 Hawke B NZ
110D1 Hawke,C Aust
108A2 Hawker Aust
76B1 Hawng Luk Myan
93D3 Hawr al Habbaniyah L Iraq
93D3 Hawr al Hammár L Iraq
21B2 Hawthorne USA
108B2 Hay Aust
5G3 Hay R Can
4G2 Hayange France
4B3 Haycock USA
7A4 Hayes R Can
6D2 Hayes Halvø Region Greenland
12E2 Hayes,Mt USA
5G3 Hay River Can
18A2 Haysville USA
22A2 Hayward California, USA
86B2 Hazárībāg India
46B1 Hazebrouck France
46B3 Hazelhurst USA
4G2 Hazel Str Can
5F4 Hazelton Can
13B1 Hazelton Mts Can
6C1 Hazen L Can
94B3 Hazeva Israel
16B2 Hazleton USA
22A1 Healdsburg USA
108C3 Healesville Aust
12E2 Healy USA
104B6 Heard I Indian O
19A3 Hearne USA
10B2 Hearst Can
72D2 Hebei Province, China
109C1 Hebel Aust
72C2 Hebi China
72C2 Hebian China
7D4 Hebron Can
94B3 Hebron Israel

18A1 Hebron Nebraska, USA
5E4 Hecate Str Can
12H3 Heceta I USA
73B5 Hechi China
4G2 Hecla and Griper B Can
111C2 Hector,Mt NZ
38G6 Hede Sweden
39H6 Hedemora Sweden
20C1 He Devil Mt USA
56B2 Heerenveen Neth
46C1 Heerlen Neth
Hefa = Haifa
73D3 Hefei China
73B4 Hefeng China
69F2 Hegang China
73B5 Hegura-jima I Japan
94B3 Heidan R Jordan
56B2 Heide Germany
101G1 Heidelberg Transvaal, S Africa
57B3 Heidelberg Germany
63E2 Heihe China
101G1 Heilbron S Africa
57B3 Heilbronn Germany
56C2 Heiligenstadt Germany
38K6 Heinola Fin
72B2 Heiang China
6J3 Hekla Mt Iceland
76C1 Hekou Viet
73A5 Hekou Yaozou Zizhixian China
72B2 Helan China
72B2 Helan Shan Mt China
19B3 Helena Arkansas, USA
8B2 Helena Montana, USA
22D3 Helendale USA
71E3 Helen Reef I Pacific O
42C2 Helensburgh Scot
91B4 Helleh R Iran
51B2 Hellin Spain
20C1 Hells Canyon R USA
56B2 Hellweg Region, Germany
22B2 Helm USA
80E2 Helmand R Afghan
100A3 Helmeringhausen Namibia
46C1 Helmond Neth
44C2 Helmsdale Scot
74B2 Helong China
39G7 Helsingborg Sweden
Helsingfors = Helsinki
46C1 Helsingør Den
38J6 Helsinki Fin
43B4 Helston Eng
92B4 Helwân Egypt
19A3 Hempstead USA
39H7 Hemse Sweden
72A3 Henan China
72D3 Henan Province, China
110B1 Hen and Chicken Is NZ
14A3 Henderson Kentucky, USA
9B3 Henderson Nevada, USA
19B3 Henderson Texas, USA
73E5 Heng-ch'un Taiwan
68B4 Hengduan Shan Mts China
56B2 Hengelo Neth
72B2 Hengshan China
72D2 Hengshui China
76D1 Heng Xian China
73C4 Hengyang China
77A4 Henhoaha Nicobar Is
43D4 Henley-on-Thames Eng
16B3 Henlopen,C USA
7B4 Henrietta Maria,C Can
19A2 Henryetta USA
112C2 Henryk Arctowski Base Ant
6D3 Henry Kater Pen Can

68C2 Hentiyn Nuruu Mts Mongolia
76B2 Henzada Myan
73B5 Hepu China
80E2 Herat Afghan
5H4 Herbert Can
72E1 Herberville NZ
46E1 Herborn Germany
26A4 Heredia Costa Rica
43C3 Hereford Eng
43C3 Hereford & Worcester County, Eng
46B1 Herentals Belg
47B1 Héricourt France
18A2 Herington USA
11A3 Heriot NZ
47C1 Herisau Switz
44E1 Herma Ness Pen Scot
109C2 Hermidale Aust
111B2 Hermitage NZ
Hermon,Mt = Jebel ash Shaykh
24A2 Hermosillo Mexico
16A2 Herndon Pennsylvania, USA
22C2 Herndon California, USA
46D1 Herne Germany
56B1 Herning Den
90A2 Herowäbad Iran
50A2 Herrera del Duque Spain
16A2 Hershey USA
43D4 Hertford County, Eng
94B2 Herzliyya Israel
46C1 Hesbaye Region, Belg
46B1 Hesdin France
72B2 Heshui China
22D3 Hesperia USA
12H2 Hess R Can
57B2 Hessen State, Germ
22C2 Hetch Hetchy Res USA
42C2 Hexham Eng
73C5 He Xian China
72C2 Heyuan China
108B3 Heywood Aust
72D2 Heze China
73C4 Hialeah USA
10A2 Hibbing USA
110C1 Hicks Bay NZ
109C3 Hicks,Pt Aust
23B1 Hidalgo State, Mexico
24B2 Hidalgo del Parral Mexico
35B1 Hidrolândia Brazil
96A2 Hierro I Canary Is
75C1 Higashine Japan
74C4 Higashi-suidō Str Japan
20B2 High Desert USA
19B4 High Island USA
44B3 Highland Division, Scot
22D3 Highland USA
22C1 Highland Peak Mt USA
16B2 Highlands Falls USA
11B3 High Point USA
13D1 High Prairie Can
5G4 High River Can
17B2 High Springs USA
16B2 Hightstown USA
43D4 High Wycombe Eng
39J7 Hiiumaa I Estonia
80B3 Hijaz Region, S Arabia
75B2 Hikigawa Japan
75B1 Hikone Japan
110B1 Hikurangi NZ
9C4 Hildago Mexico
24B2 Hidalgo del Parral Mexico
56B2 Hildesheim Germany
27R3 Hillaby,Mt Barbados
56C1 Hillerød Den
14B3 Hillsboro Ohio, USA
20B1 Hillsboro Oregon, USA
19A3 Hillsboro Texas, USA
108C2 Hillston Aust

44E1 Hillswick Scot
21C4 Hilo Hawaiian Is
93C2 Hilvan Turk
56B1 Hilversum Neth
84D2 Himachal Pradesh State, India
82B3 Himalaya Mts Asia
85C4 Himatnagar India
74C4 Himeji Japan
74D3 Himi Japan
92C3 Hims Syria
12E1 Hinchinbrook Entrance USA
12E2 Hinchinbrook I USA
85D3 Hindaun India
84B1 Hindu Kush Mts Afghan
87B2 Hindupur India
13D1 Hines Creek Can
87B2 Hinganghät India
69E2 Hinggan Ling Upland China
85B3 Hingol R Pak
85D5 Hingoli India
38H5 Hinnøya I Nor
16C1 Hinsdale USA
13D2 Hinton Can
86A2 Hipolito Itrogoyen Arg
86A2 Hirakud Res India
87B2 Hirfanli Baraji Res Turk
87B2 Hirihar India
74E2 Hirosaki Japan
74C4 Hiroshima Japan
46C2 Hirson France
54B1 Hirşova Rom
38J4 Hirtshals Den
26C3 Hispaniola I Caribbean S
94C1 Hisyah Syria
93D3 Hit Iraq
74E2 Hitachi Japan
75C1 Hitachi-Ota Japan
43D4 Hitchin Eng
38F6 Hitra I Nor
75A2 Hiuchi-nada B Japan
75A2 Hiwasa Japan
74B3 Hjørring Den
76B1 Hka R Myan
97C4 Ho Ghana
76D1 Hoa Binh Viet
76D3 Hoa Da Viet
109C4 Hobart Aust
9C3 Hobbs USA
56B1 Hobro Den
13C2 Hobson L Can
99E2 Hobyo Somalia
76D3 Ho Chi Minh Viet
54B3 Hochkonig Mt Austria
54B1 Hódmező'hely Hung
59B3 Hodonin Czech Republic
74B2 Hoeryong N Korea
57C2 Hof Germany
38B2 Hofsjökull Mts Iceland
74C4 Hōfu Japan
96C2 Hoggar Upland Alg
46D1 Hohe Acht Mt Germany
70C1 Hohhot China
6J3 Hohn Iceland
68B3 Hoh Sai Hu L China
82C2 Hoh Xil Shan Mts China
99D2 Hoima Uganda
86C1 Hojäi India
75A2 Hojo Japan
110B1 Hokianga Harbour B NZ
111B2 Hokitika NZ
74E2 Hokkaidō Japan
90C2 Hokmäbäd Iran
9B3 Holbrook USA
19A2 Holdenville USA
87B2 Hole Narsipur India
27R3 Holetown Barbados
26B2 Holguín Cuba
11B2 Holitika NZ
12C1 Holitna R USA

Hollabrunn

59B3 Hollabrunn Austria
14A2 Holland USA
22B2 Hollister USA
19C3 Holly Springs USA
22C3 Hollywood California, USA
17B2 Hollywood Florida, USA
4G2 Holman Island Can
38J6 Holmsund Sweden
94B2 Holon Israel
56B1 Holstebro Den
6E3 Holsteinborg Greenland
14B2 Holt USA
18A2 Holton USA
12C2 Holy Cross USA
42B3 Holyhead Wales
42D2 Holy I Eng
43B3 Holy I Wales
16C1 Holyoke Massachusetts, USA
86C2 Homalin Myan
6D3 Home B Can
12D3 Homer Alaska, USA
19B3 Homer Louisiana, USA
111A2 Homer Tunnel NZ
17B1 Homerville USA
17B2 Homestead USA
17A1 Homewood USA
87B1 Homnäbäd India
101C3 Homoine Mozam
25D3 Hondo R Mexico
25D3 Honduras Republic, Cent America
25D3 Honduras,G of Honduras
39G6 Honefoss Nor
15C2 Honesdale USA
21A1 Honey L USA
76C1 Hong R Viet
76D1 Hon Gai Viet
73A4 Hongguo China
73C4 Hong Hu L China
72B2 Honghui China
73C4 Hongjiang China
73C5 Hong Kong China
68D2 Hongor Mongolia
73B5 Hongshui He R China
72A3 Hongyuan China
73D2 Hongze Hu L China
107E1 Honiara Solomon Is
77C4 Hon Khoai I Camb
76D3 Hon Lan I Viet
38K4 Honningsvåg Nor
21C4 Honolulu Hawaiian Is
77C4 Hon Panjang I Viet
74D3 Honshu I Japan
20B1 Hood,Mt USA
20B1 Hood River USA
45C2 Hook Head I Irish Rep
12G3 Hoonah USA
12A2 Hooper Bay USA
101G1 Hoopstad S Africa
56A2 Hoorn Neth
9B3 Hoover Dam USA
12E2 Hope Alaska, USA
19B3 Hope Arkansas, USA
13C3 Hope USA
7D4 Hopedale Can
64D2 Hopen I Barents S
6J3 Hopes Advance,C Can
108B3 Hopetoun Aust
100B3 Hopetown S Africa
18C2 Hopkinsville USA
20B1 Hoquiam USA
93D1 Horasan Turk
99F1 Hordiyo Somalia
47C1 Horgen Switz
105H5 Horizon Depth Pacific O
91C4 Hormuz,Str of Oman/ Iran
59B3 Horn Austria
6H3 Horn C Iceland
38H5 Hornavan L Sweden
19B3 Hornbeck USA
42D2 Hornbrook USA
111B2 Hornby NZ

7B5 Hornepayne Can
4F3 Horn Mts Can
42D3 Hornsea Eng
72B1 Horn Uul Mt Mongolia
30E3 Horqueta Par
15C2 Horseheads USA
56C1 Horsens Den
108B3 Horsham Aust
43D4 Horsham Eng
39G7 Horten Nor
4F3 Horton R Can
78C2 Hose Mts Malay
85D4 Hoshangäbäd India
84D2 Hoshiarpur India
87B1 Hospet India
29C7 Hoste I Chile
82B2 Hotan China
19B3 Hot Springs Arkansas, USA
8C2 Hot Springs S. Dakota, USA
4G3 Hottah Can
46A2 Houdan France
72C2 Houma France
19B4 Houma USA
16C2 Housatonic R USA
13B2 Houston USA
19C3 Houston Mississippi, USA
19A4 Houston Texas, USA
106A3 Houtman Is Aust
68B2 Hovd Mongolia
68C1 Hövsgol Nuur L Mongolia
14A2 Howard City USA
12C1 Howard P USA
109C3 Howe,C Aust
101H1 Howick S Africa
44C2 Hoy I Scot
39F6 Høyanger Nor
59B2 Hradec-Králové Czech Republic
59A2 Hranice Czech Republic
59B3 Hron R Slovakia
73E5 Hsin-chu Taiwan
73E5 Hsüeh Shan Mt Taiwan
72B2 Huachi China
32B6 Huacho Peru
72D3 Huade China
72D1 Huade China
72D3 Huaibin China
72D3 Huai He R China
73C4 Huaihua China
73C5 Huaiji China
72D3 Huainan China
69E4 Hua-lien Taiwan
32B5 Huallaga R Peru
32B5 Huallanca Peru
32B5 Huamachuco Peru
100A2 Huambo Angola
30C2 Huanay Bol
32B5 Huancabamba Peru
32B6 Huancavelica Peru
32B6 Huancayo Peru
72D2 Huangchuan China
Huang Hai = Yellow S
72B2 Huang He R China
72B2 Huangling China
73C3 Huangpi China
73D4 Huangshan China
73D3 Huangshi China
34C3 Huanguelén Arg
73E4 Huangyan China
74B2 Huanren China
30C2 Huanuni Bol
72B2 Huan Xian China
32B5 Huaráz Peru
32B6 Huarmey Peru
32B5 Huascarán Mt Peru
30B4 Huasco Chile
23B2 Huatusco Mexico
23B1 Huauchinango Mexico
23B2 Huautla Mexico
72C2 Hua Xian China
24B2 Huayapan R Mexico
73C3 Hubei Province, China

87B1 Hubli India
34C3 Hucal Arg
74B2 Huch'ang N Korea
42D3 Huddersfield Eng
39H6 Hudiksvall Sweden
17B2 Hudson Florida, USA
14B2 Hudson Michigan, USA
16C1 Hudson New York, USA
16C1 Hudson R USA
7B4 Hudson B Can
5H4 Hudson Bay Can
13C1 Hudson's Hope Can
6C3 Hudson Str Can
73D1 Hue Viet
50A2 Huelva Spain
23A2 Hueramo Mexico
51B2 Huércal Overa Spain
51B1 Huesca Spain
23B2 Huexotla Hist Site Mexico
107D3 Hughenden Aust
12D1 Hughes USA
86B2 Hugli R India
19A3 Hugo USA
73D4 Hui'an China
110C1 Huiarau Range Mts NZ
74B2 Huich'on N Korea
74B2 Huifa He R China
32B3 Huila Mt Colombia
73D5 Huilai China
73A4 Huili China
74B2 Huinan China
34C2 Huinca Renancó Arg
25C3 Huixtla Mexico
73A4 Huize China
73C5 Huizhou China
23B2 Hujuápan de Léon Mexico
69F2 Hulin China
15C1 Hull Can
42D3 Hull Eng
58B1 Hultsfred Sweden
63D3 Hulun Nur L China
69E1 Huma China
33E5 Humaita Brazil
100B4 Humansdorp S Africa
42D3 Humber R Eng
5H4 Humboldt Can
20C2 Humboldt R USA
20B2 Humboldt B USA
21B2 Humboldt L USA
21B2 Humboldt Gletscher Gl Greenland
108C1 Humeburn Aust
109C3 Hume,L Aust
100A2 Humpata Angola
32C2 Humphreys USA
38A1 Húnaflóri B Iceland
73C4 Hunan Province, China
72C2 Hunchun China
13C2 Hundred Mile House Can
54B1 Hunedoara Rom
59B3 Hungary Republic, Europe
108B1 Hungerford Aust
74B3 Húngnam N Korea
74B2 Hunjiang China
46D2 Hunsrück Mts, Germany
109D2 Hunter R Aust
13B2 Hunter I Can
109C4 Hunter Is Aust
12D2 Hunter,Mt USA
14A3 Huntingburg USA
43D3 Huntingdon Eng
14A2 Huntingdon Indiana, USA
14B3 Huntington W Virginia, USA
22C4 Huntington Beach USA
22C2 Huntington L USA
110C1 Huntly NZ
44C3 Huntly Scot
12J2 Hunt,Mt Can
108A1 Hunt Pen Aust
17A1 Huntsville Alabama, USA

15C1 Huntsville Can
19A3 Huntsville Texas, USA
76D2 Huong Khe Viet
71F4 Huon Peninsula Pen PNG
109C4 Huonville Anst
14B1 Hurd,C Can
80B3 Hurghada Egypt
8D2 Huron S. Dakota, USA
14B1 Huron,L Can/USA
34A2 Hurtado Chile
111B2 Hurunui R NZ
38B1 Husavik Iceland
54C1 Husi Rom
39G7 Husskvarna Sweden
12C1 Huslia USA
94B2 Husn Jordan
56B2 Husum Germany
109C2 Hutton,Mt Aust
72D2 Hutuo He R China
46C1 Huy Belg
72A2 Huzhu China
52C2 Hvar I Croatia
100B2 Hwange Zim
100B2 Hwange Nat Pk Zim
15D2 Hyannis USA
68B2 Hyargas Nuur L Mongolia
5E4 Hydaburg USA
110B2 Hyde Park USA
87B1 Hyderäbäd India
85B3 Hyderabad Pak
49D3 Hyères France
12J2 Hyland R Can
8B2 Hyndman Peak Mt USA
38K6 Hyrynsalmi Fin
13D1 Hythe Can
74C4 Hyuga Japan
39J6 Hyvikää Fin

I

31C4 Iacu Brazil
54C2 Ialomita R Rom
54C1 Iasi Rom
97C4 Ibadan Nig
32B3 Ibagué Colombia
54B2 Ibar R (Montenegro/ Serbia, Yugos
32B3 Ibarra Ecuador
35B1 Ibiá Brazil
30E4 Ibicui R Brazil
34D2 Ibicuy Arg
51C2 Ibiza Spain
51C2 Ibiza I Spain
101D2 Ibo Mozam
31C4 Ibotirama Brazil
91C5 'Ibri Oman
32B6 Ica Peru
32B4 Icá R Brazil
32D3 Icana Brazil
38A1 Iceland Republic, N Atlantic O
13C2 Ice Mt Can
87A1 Ichalkaranji India
74E3 Ichihara Japan
75B1 Ichinomiya Japan
74E3 Ichinoseki Japan
12F3 Icy B USA
4B2 Icy C USA
19B3 Idabell USA
18D2 Idaho Falls USA
20B2 Idanha USA
46D2 Idar Oberstein Germany
95A2 Idehan Marzūg Desert Libya
95A2 Idehan Ubari Desert Libya
96C2 Idelès Alg
68B2 Iderlym Gol R Mongolia
95C2 Idfu Egypt
55B3 Ídhi Óros Mt Greece
55B3 Ídhra I Greece
98B3 Idiofa Zaire
12C2 Iditarod R USA
92C2 Idlib Syria
39K7 Idritsa Russian Fed
100B4 Idutywa S Africa
55C3 Ierápetra Greece
46B1 Ieper Belg

63D2 Iet Oktyobr'ya Russian Fed
99D3 Ifakara Tanz
71F3 Ifalik I Pacific O
101D3 Ifanadiana Madag
97C4 Ife Nig
97C3 Iférouane Niger
78C2 Igan Malay
35B2 Igarapava Brazil
93E2 Igdir Iran
39H6 Iggesund Sweden
34B2 Iglesia Arg
53A3 Iglesias Sardegna
6B3 Igloolik Can
10A2 Ignace Can
55B2 Igoumenitsa Greece
61H2 Igra Russian Fed
23B2 Iguala Mexico
35B2 Iguape Brazil
35B2 Iguatama Brazil
31D3 Iguatu Brazil
98A3 Iguéla Gabon
101D3 Ihosy Madag
74D3 Iida Japan
75B1 Iide-san Mt Japan
39K6 Iisalmi Fin
75A2 Iizuka Japan
97C4 Ijebu Ode Nig
56C3 IJsselmeer S Neth
55C3 Ikaria I Greece
74E2 Ikeda Japan
98C3 Ikela Zaire
54E2 Ikhtiman Bulg
12D3 Ikolik,C USA
10D2 Ikopa R Madag
79B2 Ilagan Phil
90A3 Ilam Iran
47C1 Ilanz Switz
13F1 Île a la Crosse Can
13F1 Île a la Crosse,L Can
89G8 Ilebo Zaire
96D1 Île de Jerba I Tunisia
48B2 Île de Noirmoutier I France
48B2 Île de Ré I France
107F3 Île des Pins I Nouvelle Calédonie
48A2 Île d'Ouessant I France
48B2 Île d'Yeu I France
61J3 Ilek R Russian Fed
107F2 Îles Bélep Nouvelle Calédonie
107E2 Îles Chesterfield Nouvelle Calédonie
49D3 Îles d'Hyères Is France
43B4 Ilfracombe Eng
92B1 Ilgaz Dağlari Mts Turk
101C3 Ilha Bazaruto I Mozam
35B2 Ilha De Maracá I Brazil
33G4 Ilha de Marajó I Brazil
35B2 Ilha de São Sebastião I Brazil
33G6 Ilha do Bananal Region Brazil
35C2 Ilha Grande I Brazil
35B2 Ilha Santo Amaro I Brazil
96A1 Ilhas Selvegens I Atlantic O
35A2 Ilha Solteira Dam I Brazil
31D4 Ilhéus Brazil
12C3 Iliamna L USA
12D2 Iliamna V USA
79B4 Iligan Phil
63C2 Ilim R Russian Fed
12H1 Ilim Russian Fed
63G3 Il'inskiy Russian Fed
55B3 Iliodhrómia I Greece
79B4 Illana B Phil
34A2 Illapel Chile
34A2 Illapel R Chile
97C3 Illéla Niger
47D1 Iller R Germany
4C4 Illiamna L USA
10A2 Illinois State, USA
10A2 Illinois R USA
18B2 Illinois R USA
96C2 Illizi Alg

30B2 Ilo Peru
79B3 Iloilo Phil
38L6 Ilomantsi Fin
97C4 Ilorin Nig
75B1 Imabari Japan
60C1 Imatra Fin
30C4 Imbituba Brazil
99E2 Imi Eth
20C2 Imlay USA
47D1 Immenstadt Germany
52B2 Imola Italy
31B3 Imperatriz Brazil
52A2 Imperia Italy
98B2 Impfondo Congo
86C2 Imphal India
47D1 Imst Austria
12B1 Imuruk L USA
71B1 Ina Japan
96C2 In Afaleleh Well Alg
75B2 Inamba-jima I Japan
96C2 In Amenas Alg
38K5 Inari Fin
38K5 Inarijärvi L Fin
75A1 Inawashiro-ko L Japan
50E5 Ince Burun Pt Turk
92B2 Incekum Burun Pt Turk
74B3 Inch'ŏn S Korea
96B2 In Dagouber Well Mali
35B1 Indaia R Brazil
38H6 Indals R Sweden
21B2 Independence California, USA
18A2 Independence Kansas, USA
18B2 Independence Missouri, USA
78A3 Inderagiri R Indon
61H4 Inderborskly Kazakhstan
83B3 India Federal Republic, Asia
14A2 Indiana State, USA
15C2 Indiana USA
104C6 Indian-Antarctic Ridge Indian O
14A3 Indianapolis USA
7E4 Indian Harbour Can
104B4 Indian O
10B1 Indianola Iowa, USA
19B3 Indianola Mississippi, USA
35B1 Indianópolis Brazil
76D2 Indo China Region, S E Asia
70C3 Indonesia Republic, S E Asia
85D4 Indore India
78B4 Indramayu Indon
48C2 Indre R France
85B3 Indus R Pak
60B5 Inebolu Turk
96C2 In Ebeggi Well Alg
96C2 In Ecker Alg
92A1 Inegöl Turk
71E6 In Ezzane Alg
97C3 Ingal Niger
14B2 Ingersoll Can
107D2 Ingham Aust
6D2 Inglefield Land Region Can
110B1 Inglewood NZ
109D1 Inglewood Queensland, Aust
22C4 Inglewood USA
108B3 Inglewood Victoria, Aust
38B2 Ingólfshöfdi I Iceland
57C3 Ingolstadt Germany
86B2 Ingraj Bāzār India
96C3 In-Guezzam Well Alg
101C3 Inhambane Mozam
101C3 Inharrime Mozam
35B1 Inhumas Brazil
32D3 Inírida R Colombia
45A2 Inishbofin I Irish Rep

45A1 Inishkea I Irish Rep
45B1 Inishmaan I Irish Rep
45B2 Inishmore I Irish Rep
45B1 Inishmurray I Irish Rep
45C1 Inishowen District, Irish Rep
45B1 Inishshark I Irish Rep
45B1 Inishturk I Irish Rep
12H3 Inklin Can
12H3 Inklin R Can
12C1 Inland L USA
47D1 Inn R Austria
108B1 Innamincka Aust
68C2 Inner Mongolia Autonomous Region, China
107D2 Innisfail Aust
12C2 Innoko R USA
57C3 Innsbruck Austria
98B3 Inongo Zaire
96C2 In Salah Alg
47B1 Interlaken Switz
24C3 Intexpec Mexico
54C2 Intra Italy
78D3 Intu Indon
75C1 Inubo-saki C Japan
7C4 Inukjuak Can
4E3 Inuvik Can
4E3 Inuvik Region Can
44B3 Inveraray Scot
111A3 Invercargill NZ
4B4 Inverclyde Division, Scot
109D1 Inverell Aust
13D2 Invermere Can
44B3 Inverness Scot
44A3 Inverurie Scot
108A3 Investigator Str Aust
68A1 Inya Russian Fed
21B2 Inyokern USA
98B3 Inzia R Zaire
18A2 Iola USA
44B3 Iona I Scot
100A2 Iôna Nat Pk Angola
20C1 Ione USA
Ionian Is = Ioníoi Nísoi
55B3 Ionian S Italy/Greece
55B3 Ioníoi Nísoi Is
55C3 Ios I Greece
10A2 Iowa State, USA
10A2 Iowa City USA
35B1 Ipameri Brazil
35C1 Ipanema Brazil
61F4 Ipatovo Russian Fed
32B3 Ipiales Colombia
77C5 Ipoh Malay
30F2 Iporá Brazil
55C2 Ipsala Turk
109D1 Ipswich Aust
43E3 Ipswich Eng
16D1 Ipswich USA
30B3 Iquique Chile
32C4 Iquitos Peru
55C3 Iráklion Greece
80D2 Iran Republic, S W Asia
91D4 Iranshahr Iran
23A1 Irapuato Mexico
93D3 Iraq Republic, S W Asia
95A2 Ira Wan Watercourse Libya
94B2 Irbid Jordan
61K2 Irbit Russian Fed
36C3 Ireland Republic, NW Europe
33F3 Ireng R Guyana
74B3 Iri S Korea
71E4 Irian Jaya Province, Indon
21B3 Iriba Chad
99D3 Iringa Tanz
71J4 Iriomote I Japan
33G5 Iriri R Brazil
42B3 Irish S Eng/Irish Rep
12D1 Irkillik R USA

63C2 Irkutsk Russian Fed
65J4 Irlysh R Kazakhstan
108A2 Iron Knob Aust
14A1 Iron Mountain USA
107D2 Iron Range Aust
14A1 Iron River USA
14B3 Irontown USA
10A2 Ironwood USA
10B2 Iroquois Falls Can
75B2 Iro-zaki C Japan
67A7 Irrawaddy,Mouths of the Myan
65H4 Irtysh R Russian Fed
51B1 Irun Spain
42B2 Irvine Scot
19A3 Irving USA
79B4 Isabela Phil
32J7 Isabela I Ecuador
4H2 Isachsen Can
4H2 Isachsen,C Can
6H3 Isafjördur Iceland
74C4 Isahaya Japan
98C2 Isangi Zaire
47D1 Isar R Germany
47D1 Isarco R Italy
44E1 Isbister Scot
47D1 Ischgl Austria
53A3 Ischia I Italy
75B2 Ise Japan
47D2 Iseo Italy
46D1 Iserlohn Germany
53B2 Isernia Italy
75B2 Ise-wan B Japan
60E4 Ishigaki I Japan
74E2 Ishikari R Japan
74E2 Ishikari-wan B Japan
64H4 Ishim Russian Fed
65H4 Ishim R Kazakhstan
74E3 Ishinomaki Japan
75C1 Ishioka Japan
84C1 Ishkashim Afghan
14A1 Ishpeming USA
65J4 Isil'kul Russian Fed
99D2 Isiolo Kenya
98C2 Isiro Zaire
92C2 Iskenderun Turk
92C2 Iskenderun Körfezi B Turk
92B1 Iskilip Turk
65K4 Iskitim Russian Fed
54B2 Iskur R Bulg
12H3 Iskut R Can/USA
23B2 Isla Mexico
34C3 Isla Bermejo I Arg
71A4 Isla Blanquilla Ven
32A2 Isla Coiba I Panama
9B4 Isla de Cedros I Mexico
29B4 Isla de Chiloé I Chile
25D2 Isla de Cozumel I Mexico
26C3 Isla de la Gonâve Cuba
26A2 Isla de la Juventud I Cuba
34D2 Isla de las Lechiguanas I Arg
3K8 Isla del Coco I Costa Rica
25D3 Isla del Maíz I Caribbean S
23B1 Isla de Lobos I Mexico
29D6 Isla de los Estados I Arg
28E2 Isla de Marajó I
105L5 Isla de Pascua I Pacific O
26A4 Isla de Providencia I Caribbean S
26A4 Isla de San Andres I Caribbean S
30G4 Isla de Santa Catarina I Brazil
33G2 Isla du Diable I French Guiana
31E2 Isla Fernando de Noronha I Brazil
29C6 Isla Grande de Tierra del Fuego I Arg/Chile
27D4 Isla la Tortuga I Ven
84C2 Islamabad Pak

24A2 **Isla Magdalena** *I* Mexico
27E4 **Isla Margarita** Ven
34A3 **Isla Mocha** Chile
1782 **Islamorada** USA
10A1 **Island L** Can
108A2 **Island Lg** Aust
110B1 **Islands,B** of NZ
32A4 **Isla Puná** *I* Ecuador
103D6 **Isla San Ambrosia** *I* Pacific O
103D6 **Isla San Felix** *I* Pacific O
24A2 **Isla Santa Margarita** *I* Mexico
34A3 **Isla Santa Maria** *I* Chile
51C2 **Islas Baleares** *Is* Spain
96A2 **Islas Canarias** *Is* Atlantic O
51C2 **Islas Columbretes** *Is* Spain
25D3 **Islas de la Bahia** *Is* Honduras
26A4 **Islas del Maíz** *Is* Caribbean S
33E1 **Islas de Margarita** *Is* Chile
29C7 **Islas Diego Ramirez** *Is* Chile
32J7 **Islas Galapagos** *Is* Pacific O
30H6 **Islas Juan Fernández** Chile
32D1 **Islas los Roques** *Is* Ven
Islas Malvinas = **Falkland Is**
105L3 **Islas Revilla Gigedo** *Is* Pacific O
29C7 **Islas Wollaston** *Is* Chile
97A3 **Isla Tidra** *I* Maur
29B5 **Isla Wellington** *I* Chile
48C2 **Isle R** France
104B5 **Isle Amsterdam** *I* Indian O
43D4 **Isle of Wight** *I* Eng
10B2 **Isle Royale** *I* USA
104B5 **Isle St Paul** *I* Indian O
104A6 **Isles Crozet** *I* Indian O
105J4 **Isles de la Société** Pacific O
105K5 **Isles Gambier** *Is* Pacific O
101D2 **Isles Glorieuses** *Is* Madag
104B6 **Isles Kerguelen** *Is* Indian O
105K4 **Isles Marquises** *Is* Pacific O
105J4 **Isles Tuamotu** *Is* Pacific O
105J5 **Isles Tubai** *Is* Pacific O
22B1 **Isleton** USA
92B3 **Ismâ'îliya** Egypt
101D3 **Isoanala** Madag
101C2 **Isoka** Zambia
53B3 **Isola Egadi** *I* Italy
52B2 **Isola Ponziane** *I* Italy
53B3 **Isole Lipari** *I* Italy
52C2 **Isole Tremiti** *Is* Italy
75B1 **Isosaki** Japan
92B2 **Isparta** Turk
94B2 **Israel** Republic, S W Asia
51C2 **Ister** *R* Alg
48C2 **Issoire** France
49C2 **Issoudun** France
92A1 **Istanbul** Turk
55B3 **Istiáia** Greece
25C3 **Istmo de Tehuantepec** *Isthmus* Mexico
17B2 **Istokpoga,L** USA
52B1 **Istra** *Pen* Croatia
35B1 **Itaberai** Brazil
35C1 **Itabira** Brazil
35C2 **Itabirito** Brazil

31D4 **Itabuna** Brazil
33F4 **Itacoatiara** Brazil
32B2 **Itagui** Colombia
33F4 **Itaituba** Brazil
30G4 **Itajaí** Brazil
35B2 **Itajubá** Brazil
52B2 **Italy** Republic, Europe
35D1 **Itamaraju** Brazil
35C1 **Itamarandiba** Brazil
35C1 **Itambacuri** Brazil
35C1 **Itambé** *Mt* Brazil
86C1 **Itânagar** India
35B2 **Itanhém** Brazil
35C1 **Itanhém** *R* Brazil
35C1 **Itaobim** Brazil
35B2 **Itapecerica** Brazil
35C2 **Itaperuna** Brazil
31C5 **Itapetinga** Brazil
35B2 **Itapetininga** Brazil
35B2 **Itapeva** Brazil
31D2 **Itapipoca** Brazil
35B1 **Itapuranga** Brazil
30E4 **Itaqui** Brazil
35C1 **Itarantim** Brazil
35B2 **Itararé** Brazil
35B2 **Itararé** *R* Brazil
35C2 **Itaúna** Brazil
33E6 **Iténez** *R* Brazil/Bol
15C2 **Ithaca** USA
98C2 **Itimbiri** *R* Zaire
55C1 **Itinga** Brazil
6E3 **Itivdleq** Greenland
75B2 **Ito** Japan
74D3 **Itoigawa** Japan
33E6 **Itonomas** *R* Bol
35B1 **Itu** Brazil
35B1 **Itumbiara** Brazil
35A1 **Iturama** Brazil
30C3 **Iturbe** Arg
35B2 **Iturutaba** Brazil
56B2 **Itzehoe** Germany
56D2 **Ivacevichi** Belarus
35A2 **Ivai** *R* Brazil
38K5 **Ivalo** Fin
54A2 **Ivangrad** Montenegro, Yugos
108B2 **Ivanhoe** Aust
59C3 **Ivano-Frankovsk** Ukraine
61F2 **Ivanovo** Russian Fed
61F2 **Ivanovo** Division, Russian Fed
65H3 **Ivdel'** Russian Fed
98B2 **Ivindo** *R* Gabon
101D3 **Ivohibe** Madag
101D2 **Ivongo Soanierana** Madag
Ivory Coast = **Côte d'Ivoire**
52A1 **Ivrea** Italy
6C3 **Ivujivik** Can
74E3 **Iwaki** Japan
74C4 **Iwakuni** Japan
74E2 **Iwanai** Japan
97C4 **Iwo** Nig
69G4 **Iwo** Jima
23A2 **Ixmiquilpan** Mexico
23A1 **Ixtlán** Mexico
75A2 **Iyo** Japan
75A2 **Iyo-nada** *B* Japan
62K3 **Izhevsk** Russian Fed
64G3 **Izhma** Russian Fed
91C5 **Izki** Oman
60C4 **Izmail** Ukraine
92A1 **Izmir** Turk
55C3 **Izmir Körfezi** *B* Turk
92A1 **Izmit** Turk
55C2 **Iznik Gölü** *L* Turk
94C2 **Izra'** Syria
23B2 **Izúcar de Matamoros** Mexico
75B2 **Izumi-sano** Japan
75A1 **Izumo** Japan
74D4 **Izu-shotō** *Is* Japan

J

95B1 **Jabal al Akhdar** *Mts* Libya
94C2 **Jabal al 'Arab** Syria
95A2 **Jabal as Sawdā** *Mts* Libya

91B5 **Jabal az Zannah** UAE
94C1 **Jabal Halimah** *Mt* Leb/Syria
83B3 **Jabalpur** India
59B2 **Jablonec nad Nisou** Czech Republic
31D3 **Jaboatāo** Brazil
35B2 **Jaboticabal** Brazil
51B1 **Jaca** Spain
23B1 **Jacala** Mexico
33F5 **Jacareacanga** Brazil
35B2 **Jacareí** Brazil
30F3 **Jacinto** Brazil
29C2 **Jáchal** Arg
13F2 **Jackfish L** Can
109C1 **Jackson** Aust
22B1 **Jackson** California, USA
14B2 **Jackson** Michigan, USA
19B3 **Jackson** Mississippi, USA
18C2 **Jackson** Missouri, USA
14B3 **Jackson** Ohio, USA
11B3 **Jackson** Tennessee, USA
111B2 **Jackson,C** NZ
111A2 **Jackson Head** *Pt* NZ
19B3 **Jacksonville** Arkansas, USA
17B1 **Jacksonville** Florida, USA
18B2 **Jacksonville** Illinois, USA
17C1 **Jacksonville** N Carolina, USA
19A3 **Jacksonville** Texas, USA
17B1 **Jacksonville Beach** USA
26C3 **Jacmel** Haiti
84B3 **Jacobabad** Pak
31C4 **Jacobina** Brazil
23A2 **Jacona** Mexico
Jadotville = Likasi
32B5 **Jaén** Peru
50B2 **Jaén** Spain
Jaffa = Tel Aviv Yafo
94A3 **Jaffa,C** Aust
87B3 **Jaffna** Sri Lanka
86B2 **Jagannathganj Ghat** Bang
87C1 **Jagdalpur** India
91C4 **Jagin** *R* Iran
87B1 **Jagtial** India
29F2 **Jaguarāo** *R* Brazil
35B1 **Jahrom** Iran
85D6 **Jaina** India
72A2 **Jainca** China
85D3 **Jaipur** India
85C3 **Jaisalmer** India
52C2 **Jajce** Bosnia-Herzegovina
78B4 **Jakarta** Indon
6E3 **Jakobshavn** Greenland
38J6 **Jakobstad** Fin
23B2 **Jalaca** Mexico
84B2 **Jalal-Kut** Afghan
84B2 **Jalandhar** India
23B2 **Jalapa** Mexico
35A2 **Jales** Brazil
86B1 **Jaleswar** Nepal
85B4 **Jalgaon** India
97D4 **Jalingo** Nig
51B1 **Jalón** *R* Spain
85C3 **Jālor** India
23A1 **Jalostotitlan** Mexico
85B4 **Jalpāiguri** India
23B1 **Jalpan** Mexico
95B2 **Jālū Oasis** Libya
32A4 **Jama** Ecuador
26B3 **Jamaica** *I* Caribbean S
26B3 **Jamaica Chan** Caribbean S
86B2 **Jamalpur** Bang
78A3 **Jambi** Indon
86C4 **Jambusar** India
7B4 **James B** Can
5J5 **Jameston** USA

108A2 **Jamestown** Aust
8D2 **Jamestown** N. Dakota, USA
15C2 **Jamestown** New York, USA
16D2 **Jamestown** Rhode Island, USA
23B2 **Jamiltepec** Mexico
87B1 **Jamkhandi** India
84C2 **Jammu** India
84D2 **Jammu and Kashmir** State, India
85B4 **Jamnagar** India
84C3 **Jampur** Pak
38K6 **Jämsä** Fin
86B2 **Jamshedpur** India
86B1 **Janakpur** Nepal
35C1 **Janaúba** Brazil
90B3 **Jandaq** Iran
109J1 **Jandowae** Aust
1B1 **Jan Mayen** *I* Norwegian S
35C1 **Januária** Brazil
85D4 **Jaora** India
51 **Japan** Empire, E Asia
74C3 **Japan,S of** S E Asia
104F2 **Japan Trench** Pacific O
32D4 **Japurá** Brazil
93C2 **Jarābulus** Syria
35B1 **Jaraguá** Brazil
50B1 **Jarama** *R* Spain
84B2 **Jarān** Jordan
30E3 **Jardim** Brazil
51B2 **Jardin** *R* Spain
26B2 **Jardines de la Reina** *Is* Cuba
Jargalant = Hovd
33G3 **Jari** *R* Brazil
86C1 **Jaria Jhánjail** Bang
46C2 **Jarny** France
58B2 **Jarocin** Pol
59C2 **Jaroslaw** Pol
38G6 **Järpen** Sweden
72B2 **Jartai** China
85C4 **Jasdan** India
97C4 **Jasikan** Ghana
91C4 **Jāsk** Iran
59C3 **Jaslo** Pol
29D6 **Jason Is** Falkland Is
18B2 **Jasper** Arkansas, USA
13D2 **Jasper** Can
17B1 **Jasper** Florida, USA
14A3 **Jasper** Indiana, USA
19B3 **Jasper** Texas, USA
13D2 **Jasper Nat Pk** Can
58B2 **Jastrowie** Pol
35A1 **Jataí** Brazil
51B2 **Játiva** Spain
35B2 **Jau** Brazil
32B6 **Jauja** Peru
86A1 **Jaunpur** India
33A3 **Java** *I* Indon
87B2 **Javadi Hills** India
Javari = Yavari
70B4 **Java S** Indon
104D4 **Java Trench** Indon
78B4 **Java** *I* Indon
71F4 **Jayapura** Indon
94C2 **Jayrūd** Syria
96B2 **Jbel Ouarkziz** *Mts* Mor
96B1 **Jbel Sarhro** *Mt* Mor
19B4 **Jeanerette** USA
97C4 **Jebba** Nig
93D2 **Jebel 'Abd al 'Aziz** *Mt* Syria
95B3 **Jebel Abyad** Sudan
91C5 **Jebel Akhdar** Sudan
92C4 **Jebel al Lawz** *Mt* S Arabia
94B2 **Jebel ash Shaykh** *Mt* Syria
95C2 **Jebel Asoteriba** *Mt* Sudan
94B3 **Jebel Ed Dabab** *Mt* Jordan
94B3 **Jebel el Ata'ita** *Mt* Jordan
92C3 **Jebel esh Sharqi** *Mts* Leb/Syria

94C3 Jebel Ithrīyat *Mt* Jordan
91C5 Jebel Ja'lan *Mt* Oman
94B2 Jebel Liban *Mts* Leb
94C2 Jebel Ma'lūlā *Mt* Syria
98C1 Jebel Marra *Mt* Sudan
94C3 Jebel Mudeisisat *Mt* Jordan
95C2 Jebel Oda *Mt* Sudan
94B3 Jebel Qasr ed Deir *Mt* Jordan
94B2 Jebel Um ed Daraj *Mt* Jordan
95B2 Jebel Uweinat *Mt* Sudan
42C2 Jedburgh Scot
Jedda = Jiddah
59C2 Jedrzejów Pol
19B3 Jefferson Texas, USA
11A3 Jefferson City USA
8B3 Jefferson Mt, USA
14A3 Jeffersonville USA
60C2 Jekabpils Latvia
59B2 Jelena Gora Pol
60B2 Jelgava Latvia
78C4 Jember Indon
57C2 Jena Germany
78B2 Jenaja *I* Indon
47D1 Jenbach Austria
94B2 Jenin Israel
19B3 Jennings USA
59B2 Jenseniky *Upland* Czech Republic
6F3 Jensen Nunatakker *Mt* Greenland
6B3 Jens Munk *I* Can
108B3 Jeparit Aust
31D4 Jequie Brazil
35C1 Jequitaí *R* Brazil
35C1 Jequitinhonha Brazil
31C5 Jequitinhonha *R* Brazil
50A2 Jerez de la Frontera Spain
50A2 Jerez de los Caballeros Spain
94B3 Jericho Israel
108C3 Jerilderie Aust
48B2 Jersey *I* UK
10C2 Jersey City USA
15C2 Jersey Shore USA
92C3 Jerusalem Israel
109D3 Jervis B Aust
13C2 Jervis Inlet *Sd* Can
52B1 Jesenice Slovenia
86B2 Jessore Bang
11B3 Jesup USA
34C2 Jesus Maria Arg
16D2 Jewett City USA
54A2 Jezerce *Mt* Alb
58C2 Jezioro Mamry *L* Pol
13D2 Jezioro Śniardwy *L* Pol
94B2 Jezzine Leb
85D4 Jhábua India
84C2 Jhang Maghiana Pak
85D3 Jhánsi India
86A2 Jhársuguda India
84C2 Jhelum Pak
84C2 Jhelum *R* Pak
11C3 J H Kerr L USA
84D3 Jhunjhunūn India
69F2 Jiamusi China
73C4 Ji'an Jiangxi, China
74B2 Ji'an Jilin, China
73D4 Jiande China
73D4 Jiang'an China
73D4 Jiangbiancun China
73B3 Jiangcheng China
73B3 Jiang Jiang *R* China
72D5 Jiangmen China
73D3 Jiangsu Province, China
73C4 Jiangxi Province, China
73A3 Jiangyou China
72D1 Jianping China
73A5 Jianshui China

73D4 Jian Xi *R* China
73D4 Jianyang China
72E2 Jiaonan China
72E2 Jiao Xian China
72E2 Jiaozhou Wan *B* China
72C2 Jiaozuo China
73E3 Jiaxiang China
68B3 Jiayuguan China
81B3 Jiddah S Arabia
72D3 Jiexiu China
72C2 Jiexiu China
72A3 Jigzhi China
59B3 Jihlava Czech Republic
99E2 Jilib Somalia
69E2 Jilin China
51B1 Jiloca *R* Spain
99D2 Jima Eth
9C4 Jiménez Coahuila, Mexico
72C2 Jinan China
84D3 Jind India
72B2 Jingbian China
73D4 Jingdezhen China
76C1 Jinghong China
73C3 Jingmen China
72B2 Jingning China
73B4 Jing Xiang China
73D4 Jinhua China
72C1 Jining Nei Monggol, China
72D2 Jining Shandong, China
99D2 Jinja Uganda
76C1 Jinping China
73A4 Jinsha Jiang *R* China
72A3 Jinshi China
72E1 Jinxi China
72E2 Jin Xian China
72E1 Jinzhou China
33E5 Jiparaná *R* Brazil
32A4 Jipijapa Ecuador
23A2 Jiquilpan Mexico
91C4 Jīroft Iran
99E2 Jirriban Somalia
73B4 Jishou China
92C3 Jisr ash Shughūr Syria
54B2 Jiu *R* Rom
73D4 Jiujiang China
73A4 Jiulong China
73D4 Jiulong Jiang *R* China
69F2 Jixi China
83D4 Jiza Jordan
81C4 Jizan S Arabia
97A3 Joal Sen
35C1 João Monlevade Brazil
31E3 João Pessoa Brazil
35B1 João Pirheiro Brazil
34B2 Jocoli Arg
63A5 Jodhpur India
38K6 Joensuu Fin
46C2 Joeuf France
13D2 Joffre,Mt Can
86B1 Jogbani India
87A2 Jog Falls India
101G1 Johannesburg S Africa
21B2 Johannesburg USA
6C2 Johan Pen Can
12D1 John H USA
20C2 John Day USA
20B1 John Day *R* USA
44C2 John O'Groats Scot
18A2 John Redmond Res USA
11B3 Johnson City Tennessee, USA
17B1 Johnston USA
27N2 Johnston Pt St Vincent and the Grenadines
15C2 Johnstown Pennsylvania, USA
77C5 Johor Bharu Malay
49C2 Joigny France
30G4 Joinville Brazil
61H3 Jok *R* Russian Fed
38H5 Jokkmokk Sweden
93E2 Jolfa Iran
10B2 Joliet USA

7C5 Joliette Can
79B4 Jolo Phil
79B4 Jolo *I* Phil
82D2 Jomda China
58C1 Jonava Lithuania
72A3 Jonê China
11A3 Jonesboro Arkansas, USA
19B3 Jonesboro Louisiana, USA
26B2 Jones Sd Can
58C1 Joniskis Lithuania
39G7 Jönköping Sweden
11A3 Joplin USA
92C3 Jordan Kingdom, S W Asia
94B2 Jordan *R* Israel
20C2 Jordan Valley USA
86C1 Jorhat India
38J5 Jörn Sweden
78C3 Jorong Indon
39F7 Jerpeland Nor
79B3 Jose Pañganiban Phil
106B2 Joseph Bonaparte G Aust
46B2 Josselin France
94B2 Jotunheimen *Mt* Nor
94B2 Jouai'ya Leb
94B2 Jounié Leb
88C1 Jowai India
99E2 Jowhar Somalia
12H2 Joy,Mt Can
5F5 Juan de Fuca,Str of Can/USA
101D2 Juan de Nova *I* Mozam Chan
34D3 Juárez Arg
31C3 Juàzeiro Brazil
31D3 Juazeiro do Norte Brazil
99D2 Juba Sudan
99E2 Juba *R* Somalia
94B1 Jubail Leb
93D3 Jubbah S Arabia
96A2 Juby,C Mor
51B2 Jucar *R* Spain
23B2 Juchatengo Mexico
23A1 Juchipila *R* Mexico
23A1 Juchitan Mexico
57C3 Judenburg Austria
80B3 Juilaca Peru
73C4 Juiling Shan *Hills* - China
16C6 Juiz de Fora Brazil
30C3 Jujuy State, Arg
30C2 Juli Peru
33F3 Julianator *Mt* Surinam
6F3 Julianehab Greenland
46D1 Jülich Germany
81A4 Jumla Nepal
94B3 Jum Suwwána *Mt* Jordan
85C4 Jūnágadh India
72D2 Junan China
9D3 Junction City USA
31B6 Jundiaí Brazil
4E4 Juneau USA
22C2 June Lake USA
52A1 Jungfrau *Mt* Switz
16A2 Juniata *R* USA
29D2 Junin Arg
29D2 Junin Peru
31B6 Juquiá Brazil
99C2 Jur *R* Sudan
42B2 Jura *I* Scot
49D2 Jura *Mts* France
44B3 Jura,Sound of *Chan* Scot
94B3 Jurf ed Darāwish Jordan
65K4 Jugra Russian Fed
60B2 Jūrmala Latvia
32D4 Juruá *R* Brazil
33C4 Juruena *R* Brazil
94C1 Jūsiyah Syria
34D3 Justo Daract Arg
31D4 Jutaí *R* Brazil
25D3 Juticalpa Honduras
Jutland = Jylland
90C3 Jūymand Iran
88K6 Juzur al Halanīyat *Is* Oman

56B1 Jylland *Pen* Den
38K6 Jyväskylä Fin

K

82B2 K2 *Mt* China/India
90C2 Kaakhka Turkmenistan
101H1 Kaapmuiden S Africa
71D4 Kabaena *I* Indon
97A4 Kabala Sierra Leone
99D3 Kabale Uganda
98C3 Kabalo Zaire
98C3 Kabambare Zaire
61F5 Kabardino-Balkariya Division, Russian Fed
99D2 Kabarole Uganda
98C3 Kabinda Zaire
90A3 Kabir Kuh *Mts* Iran
100B2 Kabompo Zambia
100B2 Kabompo *R* Zambia
98C3 Kabongo Zaire
84B2 Kabul Afghan
85B4 Kachchh,G of India
61J2 Kachkanar Russian Fed
63C2 Kachug Russian Fed
76B3 Kadan Myan
78D3 Kadapongan *I* Indon
85C4 Kadi India
108A2 Kadina Aust
72B2 Kadinhahi Turk
60E4 Kadiyevka Ukraine
100B2 Kadoma Zim
99C1 Kadugli Sudan
97C3 Kaduna Nig
72A3 Kaduna *R* Nig
87B2 Kadūr India
97A3 Kaédi Maur
97A3 Kaena Pt Hawaiian Is
74B3 Kaesong N Korea
97C4 Kafanchan Nig
94C1 Kafrīne Sen
94C1 Kafrūn Bashūr Syria
100B2 Kafue Zambia
100B2 Kafue *R* Zambia
100B2 Kafue Nat Pk Zambia
74D3 Kaga Japan
65H6 Kagan Kazakhstan
90D3 Kagizman Turk
74C4 Kagoshima Japan
90C2 Kāhak Iran
99D3 Kahama Tanz
84B3 Kahan Pak
78C3 Kahayan *R* Indon
98B3 Kahemba Zaire
46E1 Kahler Asten *Mt* Germany
91C4 Kahnūj Iran
18B1 Kahoka USA
21C4 Kahoolawe *I* Hawaiian Is
92C2 Kahramanmaraş Turk
21C4 Kahuku Pt Hawaiian Is
111B2 Kaiapoi NZ
33F2 Kaieteur Fall Guyana
72C3 Kaifeng China
111B2 Kaikohe NZ
111B2 Kaikoura NZ
111B2 Kaikoura Pen NZ
111B2 Kaikoura Range *Mts* NZ
73B4 Kaili China
21C4 Kailua Hawaiian Is
71E4 Kaimana Indon
75B2 Kainan Japan
97C3 Kainji Res Nig
110B1 Kaipara Harbour *B* NZ
73C5 Kaiping China
72C4 Kairouan Tunisia
22C2 Kaiser Peak *Mt* USA
57B3 Kaiserslautern Germ
58B2 Kaishantun China
58D2 Kaisiadorys Lithuania
110B1 Kaitaia NZ
111A3 Kaitangata NZ
84D3 Kaithal India
21C4 Kaiwi Chan Hawaiian Is

73B3 **Kai Xian** China
73A5 **Kaiyuan** Liaoning, China
74A2 **Kaiyuan** Yunnan, China
12C2 **Kaiyuh Mts** USA
38K6 **Kajaani** Fin
84B2 **Kajaki** Afghan
99D3 **Kajiado** Kenya
84B2 **Kajrān** Afghan
99D1 **Kaka** Sudan
99D2 **Kakamega** Kenya
75A2 **Kake** Japan
12H3 **Kake** USA
12D3 **Kakhonak** USA
65E5 **Kakhovskoye Vodokhranilishche** *Res* Ukraine
91B4 **Kākī** Iran
87C1 **Kakinada** India
75A2 **Kakogawa** Japan
4D2 **Kaktovik** USA
75C1 **Kakuda** Japan
Kalaallit Nunaat = Greenland
55B3 **Kalabáka** Greece
78D1 **Kalabakan** Malay
100B2 **Kalabo** Zambia
61F3 **Kalach** Russian Fed
61F4 **Kalach-na-Donu** Russian Fed
86C2 **Kaladan** *R* Myan
21C4 **Ka Lae** *C* Hawaiian Is
100B3 **Kalahari Desert** Botswana
38J6 **Kalajoki** Fin
63D2 **Kalakan** Russian Fed
70A3 **Kalakepen** Indon
84C1 **Kalam** Pak
55B3 **Kalámai** Greece
10B2 **Kalamazoo** USA
84B3 **Kalat** Pak
92B1 **Kalecik** Turk
78D3 **Kalembau** *I* Indon
98C3 **Kalémié** Zaire
38L5 **Kalevala** Russian Fed
86C2 **Kalewa** Myan
12D2 **Kalgin I** USA
106B4 **Kalgoorlie** Aust
87B2 **Kalianda** Indon
79B3 **Kalibo** Phil
98C3 **Kalima** Zaire
78C3 **Kalimantan** Province, Indon
55C3 **Kálimnos** *I* Greece
86B1 **Kālimpang** India
60B3 **Kaliningrad** Russian Fed
60C3 **Kalinkovichi** Belarus
8B2 **Kalispell** USA
58B2 **Kalisz** Pol
99D3 **Kaliua** Tanz
38J5 **Kalix** *R* Sweden
100A3 **Kalkfeld** Namibia
100A3 **Kalkfonti** Namibia
108A1 **Kallakoopah** *R* Aust
38K6 **Kallávesi** *L* Fin
55C3 **Kallonís Kólpos** *B* Greece
39H7 **Kalmar** Sweden
61G4 **Kalmykia-Khalmg Tangch** Division, Russian Fed
100B2 **Kalomo** Zambia
18B1 **Kalona** USA
13B2 **Kalone Peak** *Mt* Can
87A2 **Kalpeni** *I* India
85D3 **Kālpi** India
53A3 **Kalsat Khasba** Tunisia
12B2 **Kalskag** USA
12C2 **Kaltag** USA
60E3 **Kaluga** Russian Fed
60E3 **Kaluga** Division, Russian Fed
39G7 **Kalundborg** Den
59C3 **Kalush** Ukraine
87B2 **Kalyandurg** India
60E2 **Kalyazin** Russian Fed
61H1 **Kama** *R* Russian Fed
74E3 **Kamaishi** Japan
84C2 **Kamalia** Pak
110C1 **Kamanawa Mts** NZ
100A2 **Kamanjab** Namibia

84D2 **Kamat** *Mt* India
87B3 **Kamban** India
61H2 **Kambarka** Russian Fed
97A4 **Kambia** Sierra Leone
61F3 **Kamenka** Russian Fed
65K4 **Kamen-na-Obi** Russian Fed
61K2 **Kamensk-Ural'skiy** Russian Fed
5H3 **Kamilukuak** *L* Can
98C3 **Kamina** Zaire
7A3 **Kaminak** *L* Can
75C1 **Kaminoyama** Japan
5F4 **Kamloops** Can
93E1 **Kamo** Armenia
75C1 **Kamogawa** Japan
99D2 **Kampala** Uganda
77C5 **Kampar** Malay
78A2 **Kampar** *R* Indon
56B2 **Kampen** Neth
76B2 **Kamphaeng Phet** Thai
77C3 **Kampot** Camb
91D4 **Kamsaptar** Iran
61J2 **Kamskoye Vodokhranilishche** *Res* Russian Fed
85D4 **Kāmthi** India
61G3 **Kamyshin** Russian Fed
61K2 **Kamyshlov** Russian Fed
7C4 **Kanaaupscow** *R* Can
98C3 **Kananga** Zaire
61G2 **Kanash** Russian Fed
75B1 **Kanayama** Japan
74D3 **Kanazawa** Japan
4C3 **Kanbisha** USA
87B2 **Kānchipuram** India
84D2 **Kandahar** Afghan
64E3 **Kandalaksha** Russian Fed
38L5 **Kandalakshskaya Guba** *B* Russian Fed
97C3 **Kandi** Benin
109C2 **Kandos** Aust
87C3 **Kandy** Sri Lanka
15C2 **Kane** USA
6C1 **Kane Basin** *B* Can
98B1 **Kanem** Desert Region Chad
97B3 **Kangaba** Mali
92C2 **Kangal** Turk
6E3 **Kangâmiut** Greenland
91B4 **Kangān** Iran
77C4 **Kangar** Malay
106C4 **Kangaroo I** Aust
6E3 **Kangâtsiaq** Greenland
90A3 **Kangavar** Iran
72C1 **Kangbao** China
86B1 **Kangchenjunga** *Mt* China/Nepal
73A4 **Kangding** China
6G3 **Kangerdlugssuaq** *B* Greenland
6G3 **Kangerdlugssvatsaiq** *B* Greenland
99D2 **Kangetet** Kenya
74B2 **Kanggye** N Korea
7D4 **Kangiqsualujjuaq** Can
6C3 **Kangiqsujuaq** Can
7C3 **Kangirsuk** Can
74B3 **Kangnŭng** S Korea
98B2 **Kango** Gabon
68B4 **Kangto** *Mt* China
72B3 **Kang Xian** China
77D4 **Kanh Hung** Viet
98C3 **Kaniama** Zaire
87B1 **Kani Giri** India
39J6 **Kankaanpää** Fin
14A2 **Kankakee** USA
14A2 **Kankakee** *R* USA
97B3 **Kankan** Guinea
86A2 **Känker** India
87B3 **Kanniyākumari** India
97C3 **Kano** Nig

74C4 **Kanoya** Japan
86A1 **Kanpur** India
9D3 **Kansas** State, USA
18A2 **Kansas** *R* USA
10A3 **Kansas City** USA
73C3 **Kanshi** China
63B2 **Kansk** Russian Fed
97C3 **Kantchari** Burkina
86B2 **Kanthi** India
12D2 **Kantishna** USA
12D2 **Kantishna** *R* USA
108B3 **Kanye** Botswana
68D6 **Kao-hsiung** Taiwan
100A2 **Kaoka Veld** *Plain* Namibia
97A3 **Kaolack** Senegal
100B2 **Kaoma** Zambia
21C4 **Kapaau** Hawaiian Is
98C3 **Kapanga** Zaire
6F3 **Kap Cort Adelaer** *C* Greenland
6F3 **Kap Dalton** *C* Greenland
39H7 **Kapellskär** Sweden
6F3 **Kap Farvel** *C* Greenland
6G3 **Kap Gustav Holm** *C* Greenland
100B2 **Kapiri** Zambia
78C2 **Kapit** Malay
19B3 **Kaplan** USA
57C3 **Kaplice** Czech Republic
77B4 **Kapoe** Thai
99C3 **Kapona** Zaire
52C1 **Kaposvár** Hung
6C2 **Kap Parry** *C* Can
6H3 **Kap Ravn** *C* Greenland
71E4 **Kapuas** *R* Indon
108A2 **Kapunda** Aust
84D2 **Kapurthala** India
7B5 **Kapuskasing** Can
109D2 **Kaputar** *Mt* Aust
93E2 **Kapydzhik** *Mt* Armenia
6D2 **Kap York** *C* Greenland
92B1 **Karabük** Turk
55C2 **Karacabey** Turk
61F5 **Karachevo-Cherkesiya** Division, Russian Fed
85B4 **Karachi** Pak
87A1 **Karād** India
60E5 **Kara Daglari** *Mt* Turk
54C5 **Karadeniz Boğazi** *Sd* Turk
68D1 **Karaftit** Russian Fed
65J5 **Karaganda** Kazakhstan
65J5 **Karagayly** Kazakhstan
87B2 **Kāraikāl** India
90B2 **Karaj** Iran
92C3 **Karak** Jordan
65G5 **Kara Kalpakskaya Respublika,** Uzbekistan
84D1 **Karakax He** China
71D3 **Karakelong** *I* Indon
84D1 **Karakoram** *Mts* India
84D1 **Karakoram P** India
97A3 **Karakoro** *R* Maur/Sen
65G6 **Karakumy** Desert Russian Fed
94B3 **Karama** Jordan
92B2 **Karaman** Turk
65K5 **Karamay** China
111B2 **Karamea** NZ
111B2 **Karamea Bight** *B* NZ
85D4 **Kāranja** India
92B2 **Karapinar** Turk
64G2 **Kara S** Russian Fed
100A3 **Karasburg** Namibia
38K5 **Karasjok** Nor
65J4 **Karasuk** Russian Fed
92C2 **Karataş** Turk
65H5 **Kara Tau** *Mts* Kazakhstan
76B3 **Karathuri** Myan
74B4 **Karatsu** Japan

91B4 **Karāz** Iran
93D3 **Karbalā'** Iraq
59C3 **Karcag** Hung
55B3 **Kardhítsa** Greece
38J5 **Karesvando** Sweden
96B2 **Karet** *Desert Region* Maur
65K4 **Kargasok** Russian Fed
97D3 **Kari** Nig
100B2 **Kariba** Zim
100B2 **Kariba** *L* Zim/Zambia
100B2 **Kariba Dam** Zim/Zambia
95C3 **Karima** Sudan
78B3 **Karimata** *I* Indon
86C2 **Karimganj** Bang
87B1 **Karīmnagar** India
99E1 **Karin** Somalia
39J6 **Karis** Fin
99C3 **Karishimbe** *Mt* Zaire
55B3 **Káristos** Greece
87A2 **Kārkal** India
71F4 **Karkar I** PNG
91A3 **Karkheh** *R* Iran
60D4 **Karkinitskiy Zaliv** *B* Ukraine
63B3 **Karlik Shan** *Mt* China
58B2 **Karlino** Pol
52C2 **Karlobag** Croatia
52C1 **Karlovac** Croatia
54B2 **Karlovo** Bulg
57C2 **Karlovy Vary** Czech Republic
39G7 **Karlshamn** Sweden
39G7 **Karlskoga** Sweden
39H7 **Karlskrona** Sweden
57B3 **Karlsruhe** Germany
39G7 **Karlstad** Sweden
12D3 **Karluk** USA
87A1 **Karnātaka** State, India
54C2 **Karnobat** Bulg
100B2 **Karoi** Zim
99C3 **Karonga** Malawi
95C3 **Karora** Sudan
78D3 **Karossa** Indon
55C3 **Kárpathos** *I* Greece
6E3 **Karrats Fjord** Greenland
93D1 **Kars** Turk
65H4 **Karsakpay** Kazakhstan
58D1 **Kārsava** Latvia
80E2 **Karshi** Uzbekistan
38J6 **Karstula** Fin
94B1 **Kartaba** Leb
54C2 **Kartal** Turk
61K3 **Kartaly** Russian Fed
90A3 **Kārün** *R* Iran
86A1 **Karwa** India
87A2 **Kārwār** India
61K2 **Karymskoye** Russian Fed
98B3 **Kasai** *R* Zaire
100B2 **Kasaji** Zaire
101C2 **Kasama** Zambia
100B2 **Kasane** Zambia
87A2 **Kāsaragod** India
5H3 **Kasba** *L* Can
100B2 **Kasempa** Zambia
100B2 **Kasenga** Zaire
99D2 **Kasese** Uganda
90B3 **Kāshān** Iran
12C2 **Kashegelok** USA
82B2 **Kashi** China
74D3 **Kāshīpur** India
74D3 **Kashiwazaki** Japan
66D3 **Kashmir** State, India
61F3 **Kasimov** Russian Fed
18C2 **Kaskaskia** *R* USA
38J6 **Kaskinen** Fin
61K2 **Kasli** Russian Fed
5G5 **Kaslo** Can
98C3 **Kasonga** Zaire
98B3 **Kasongo-Lunda** Zaire
55C3 **Kásos** *I* Greece
Kaspiyskiy = Lagan'
95C3 **Kassala** Sudan
56B2 **Kassel** Germany

96C1 **Kasserine** Tunisia
100A2 **Kassinga** Angola
92B1 **Kassmooa** Turk
55B3 **Kastélli** Greece
92A2 **Kastéllorizon** /
 Greece
55B2 **Kastória** Greece
55C3 **Kástron** Greece
74D3 **Kasugai** Japan
75A1 **Kasumi** Japan
101C2 **Kasungu** Malawi
4C2 **Kasur** Pak
100B2 **Kataba** Zambia
98C3 **Katako-kombe** Zaïre
4D3 **Katalla** USA
63G2 **Katangli** Russian Fed
106A4 **Katanning** Aust
55B2 **Katerini** Greece
5E4 **Kates Needle** Mt
 Can/USA
82D3 **Katha** Myan
106C2 **Katherine** Aust
85C4 **Käthiäwär** Pen India
86B1 **Kathmandu** Nepal
84D2 **Kathua** India
86B1 **Katihär** India
100B2 **Katima Mulilo**
 Namibia
4C4 **Katmai,Mt** USA
12D3 **Katmai Nat Mon**
 USA
86A2 **Katni** India
109D2 **Katoomba** Aust
35D9 **Katowice** Pol
39H7 **Katrinehölm** Sweden
97C3 **Katsina** Nig
97C4 **Katsina Ala** Nig
75C1 **Katsuta** Japan
75C1 **Katsuura** Japan
75B1 **Katsuya** Japan
65H6 **Kattakurgan**
 Uzbekistan
39G7 **Kattegat** Str Den/
 Sweden
21C4 **Kauai** / Hawaiian Is
21C4 **Kauai Chan** Hawaiian
 Is
21C4 **Kaulakahi Chan**
 Hawaiian Is
21C4 **Kaunakaki** Hawaiian
 Is
60B3 **Kaunas** Lithuania
97C3 **Kaura Namoda** Nig
38J5 **Kautokeino** Nor
55B2 **Kavadarci** Macedonia
55C2 **Kavajë** Alb
87B2 **Kavali** India
55B2 **Kaválla** Greece
85B4 **Kávda** India
75B1 **Kawagoe** Japan
75B1 **Kawaguchi** Japan
110B1 **Kawakawa** NZ
99C3 **Kawambwa** Zambia
86A2 **Kawardha** India
15C2 **Kawartha Lakes** Can
74D3 **Kawasaki** Japan
110C1 **Kawerau** NZ
110B1 **Kawhia** NZ
97B3 **Kaya** Burkina
12F3 **Kayak I** USA
78D2 **Kayan** R Indon
87B3 **Käyankulam** India
97A3 **Kayes** Mali
92C2 **Kayseri** Turk
1B8 **Kazach'ye**
 Russian Fed
93E1 **Kazakh** Azerbaijan
65G5 **Kazakhstan** Republic,
 Asia
61G2 **Kazan'** Russian Fed
54C2 **Kazanlük** Bulg
69G4 **Kazan Retto** /s
 Japan
91B4 **Käzerün** Iran
61H1 **Kazhim** Russian Fed
93E1 **Kazi Magomed**
 Azerbaijan
59C3 **Kazincbarcika** Hung
55B3 **Kéa** / Greece
21C4 **Kealaikahiki Chan**
 Hawaiian Is
8D2 **Kearney** USA
93C2 **Keban Baraji** Res
 Turk

97A3 **Kébémer** Sen
97C1 **Kebili** Tunisia
94C1 **Kebir** R Leb/Syria
38H5 **Kebnekaise** Mt
 Sweden
59B3 **Kecskemét** Hung
58C1 **Kedainiai** Lithuania
97A3 **Kédougou** Sen
12J2 **Keele** R Can
12H2 **Keele Pk** Mt Can
21B2 **Keeler** USA
15D2 **Keene** New
 Hampshire, USA
100A3 **Keetmanshoop**
 Namibia
18C1 **Keewanee** USA
6A3 **Keewatin** Region
 Can
55B3 **Kefallinía** / Greece
94B2 **Kefar Sava** Israel
97C4 **Keffi** Nig
38A2 **Keflavík** Iceland
5G4 **Keg River** Can
76B1 **Kehsi Mansam**
 Myan
108B3 **Keith** Aust
44C3 **Keith** Scot
4F3 **Keith Arm** B Can
85D3 **Kekri** India
77C5 **Kelang** Malay
77C4 **Kelantan** R Malay
84B1 **Kelif** Turkmenistan
92A1 **Kelkit** R Turk
98B3 **Kéllé** Congo
4F2 **Kellet,C** Can
20C1 **Kellogg** USA
64D3 **Kelloselka** Fin
45C2 **Kells** Irish Rep
42B2 **Kells Range** Hills
 Scot
58C1 **Kelme** Lithuania
55C3 **Kelowna** Can
5F4 **Kelsey Bay** Can
42C2 **Kelso** Scot
20B1 **Kelso** USA
64E3 **Kem'** Russian Fed
38L6 **Kem'** R Russian Fed
97B3 **Ke Macina** Mali
13B2 **Kemano** Can
65K4 **Kemerovo**
 Russian Fed
38J5 **Kemi** Fin
38K5 **Kemi** R Fin
38K5 **Kemijärvi** Fin
46C1 **Kempen** Region, Belg
26B2 **Kemps Bay**
 The Bahamas
109D2 **Kempsey** Aust
57C3 **Kempten** Germany
12D3 **Kenai** USA
12D3 **Kenai Mts** USA
12D2 **Kenai Pen** USA
99D2 **Kenamuke Swamp**
 Sudan
42C2 **Kendal** Eng
109D2 **Kendall** Aust
71D4 **Kendari** Indon
78C3 **Kendawangan** Indon
86B2 **Kendräpära** India
20C1 **Kendrick** USA
97A4 **Kenema** Sierra Leone
98B3 **Kenge** Zaïre
76B1 **Kengtung** Myan
100B3 **Kenhardt** S Africa
97A3 **Kéniéba** Mali
96B1 **Kénitra** Mor
45B3 **Kenmare** Irish Rep
45B3 **Kenmare** R Irish Rep
19B4 **Kenner** USA
18C2 **Kennett** USA
16B3 **Kennett Square** USA
20C1 **Kennewick** USA
5F4 **Kenny Dam** Can
7A5 **Kenora** Can
10B2 **Kenosha** USA
43E4 **Kent** County, Eng
20B1 **Kent** Washington,
 USA
14A2 **Kentland** USA
14B2 **Kenton** USA
4A2 **Kent Pen** Can
11B3 **Kentucky** State, USA
11B3 **Kentucky L** USA

19B3 **Kentwood** Louisiana,
 USA
14A2 **Kentwood** Michigan,
 USA
99D2 **Kenya** Republic,
 Africa
Kenya,Mt = Kirinyaga
18B1 **Keokuk** USA
86A2 **Keonchi** India
86B2 **Keonjhargarh** India
71E4 **Kepaluan Tanimbar**
 Indon
6H3 **Keplavik** Iceland
59B2 **Kepno** Pol
78B2 **Kepulauan Anambas**
 Indon
71E4 **Kepulauan Aru** Arch
 Indon
78B2 **Kepulauan Badas** /s
 Indon
71E4 **Kepulauan Banda**
 Indon
71D4 **Kepulauan Banggai** /
 Indon
78B2 **Kepulauan Bunguran
 Seletan** Arch Indon
71E4 **Kepulauan Kai** Arch
 Indon
71D4 **Kepulauan Leti** /
 Indon
78A3 **Kepulauan Lingga** /s
 Indon
70A4 **Kepulauan Mentawi**
 Arch Indon
78A2 **Kepulauan Riau** Arch
 Indon
78D4 **Kepulauan Sabalana**
 Arch Indon
71D3 **Kepulauan Sangihe**
 Arch Indon
71D4 **Kepulauan Sula** /
 Indon
71D3 **Kepulauan Talaud**
 Arch Indon
78B2 **Kepulauan Tambelan**
 /s Indon
71E4 **Kepulauan Tanimbar**
 / Indon
71D4 **Kepulauan Togian** /
 Indon
71D4 **Kepulauan
 Tukambesi** /s Indon
87B2 **Kerala** State, India
108B3 **Kerang** Aust
39K6 **Kerava** Fin
60E4 **Kerch'** Ukraine
71F4 **Kerema** PNG
20C1 **Keremeps** Can
95C3 **Keren** Eritrea
104B6 **Kerguelen Ridge**
 Indian O
99D3 **Kericho** Kenya
70B4 **Kerinci** Mt Indon
99D2 **Kerio** R Kenya
80E2 **Kerki** Turkmenistan
55A3 **Kérkira** Greece
55A3 **Kérkira** / Greece
91C3 **Kerman** Iran
22B2 **Kerman** USA
90A3 **Kermänshäh** Iran
21B2 **Kern** R USA
13F2 **Kerrobert** Can
45B2 **Kerry** County,
 Irish Rep
17B1 **Kershaw** USA
78B3 **Kertamulia** Indon
63D3 **Kerulen** R
 Mongolia
96B2 **Kerzaz** Alg
55C2 **Keşan** Turk
74E3 **Kesennuma** Japan
38L5 **Kesten 'ga**
 Russian Fed
42C2 **Keswick** Eng
65K4 **Ket** R Russian Fed
97C4 **Kéta** Ghana
78D3 **Ketapang** Indon
5E4 **Ketchikan** USA
97C3 **Ketia** Niger
85B4 **Keti Bandar** Pak
58C2 **Ketrzyn** Pol
14B3 **Kettering** Eng
14B3 **Kettering** USA
20C1 **Kettle** R Can

20C1 **Kettle River Range**
 Mts USA
7C3 **Kettlestone B** Can
90C3 **Kevir-I Namak** Salt
 Flat Iran
14A2 **Kewaunee** USA
14B1 **Key Harbour** Can
17B2 **Key Largo** USA
11B4 **Key West** USA
63C2 **Kezhma** Russian Fed
54A1 **K'Eleghäza** Hung
12B2 **Kgun L** USA
94C2 **Khabab** Syria
62H3 **Khabarovsk**
 Russian Fed
85B3 **Khairpur** Pak
85B3 **Khairpur** Region, Pak
100B3 **Khakhea** Botswana
55C3 **Khálki** / Greece
55B2 **Khalkidhikí** Pen
 Greece
55B3 **Khalkis** Greece
61G2 **Khalturin**
 Russian Fed
85C4 **Khambhät,G of** India
85D4 **Khämgaon** India
76C2 **Kham Keut** Laos
87C1 **Khammam** India
84B1 **Khänabäd** Afghan
93F3 **Khänaqin** Iraq
85D4 **Khandwa** India
84C2 **Khanewal** Pak
94C3 **Khan ez Zabib**
 Jordan
77D4 **Khanh Hung** Viet
55B3 **Khaniá** Greece
84C3 **Khanpur** Pak
65H3 **Khanty-Mansiysk**
 Russian Fed
94B3 **Khan Yunis** Egypt
84D1 **Khapalu** India
68C2 **Khapcheranga**
 Russian Fed
61G4 **Kharabali**
 Russian Fed
86B2 **Kharagpur** India
91C4 **Khärän** Iran
84B3 **Kharan** Pak
90B3 **Kharänaq** Iran
91R4 **Kharg** /s Iran
95C2 **Khârga Oasis**
 Egypt
85D4 **Khargon** India
60E4 **Khar'kov** Ukraine
54C2 **Kharmanli** Bulg
61F2 **Kharovsk**
 Russian Fed
95C3 **Khartoum** Sudan
95C3 **Khartoum North**
 Sudan
74C2 **Khasan** Russian Fed
95C3 **Khashm el Girba**
 Sudan
86C1 **Khasi-Jaintia Hills**
 India
54C2 **Khaskovo** Bulg
1B9 **Khatanga**
 Russian Fed
76B3 **Khawsa** Myan
76C2 **Khe Bo** Viet
84B4 **Khed Brahma** India
51C2 **Khemis** Alg
96B1 **Khenifra** Mor
51D2 **Kherrata** Alg
60D4 **Kherson** Ukraine
63D2 **Khilok** Russian Fed
55C3 **Khíos** Greece
55C3 **Khíos** / Greece
60C4 **Khmel'nitskiy**
 Ukraine
59C3 **Khodorov** Ukraine
84B1 **Kholm** Afghan
76D3 **Khong** Laos
91B4 **Khong** Iran
69F2 **Khor** Russian Fed
91B4 **Khonj** Iran
91B5 **Khor Duwayhin** B
 UAE
84C1 **Khorog** Tajikistan
90A3 **Khorramäbäd** Iran
90C3 **Khost** Iran
84B2 **Khost** Pak

60C4 **Khotin** Ukraine
12C2 **Khotol** *Mt* USA
60C3 **Khoynitski** Belarus
63F2 **Khrebet Dzhugdzhur** *Mts* Russian Fed
90C2 **Khrebet Kopet Dag** *Mts* Turkmenistan
64H3 **Khrebet Pay-khoy** Russian Fed
82C1 **Khrebet Tarbagatay** *Mts* Kazakhstan
63E2 **Khrebet Tukuringra** *Mts* Russian Fed
82A1 **Khudzhand** Tajikistan
86B2 **Khulna** Bang
84D1 **Khunjerab P** China/India
90B3 **Khunsar** Iran
91A4 **Khurays** S Arabia
86B2 **Khurda** India
84D3 **Khurja** India
94B2 **Khushab** Pak
94B2 **Khushniyah** Syria
59C3 **Khust** Ukraine
99C1 **Khuwei** Sudan
85B3 **Khuzdar** Pak
90D3 **Khvaf** Iran
61G3 **Khvalynsk** Russian Fed
90C3 **Khvor** Iran
93D2 **Khvoy** Iran
84C1 **Khwaja Muhammad** *Mts* Afghan
84C2 **Khyber P** Afghan/Pak
99C3 **Kiambi** Zaire
19A3 **Kiamichi** *R* USA
12B1 **Kiana** USA
98B3 **Kibangou** Congo
99C3 **Kibaya** Tanz
98C3 **Kibombo** Zaire
99D3 **Kibondo** Tanz
99D3 **Kibungu** Rwanda
55B2 **Kičevo** Macedonia
5C4 **Kicking Horse P** Can
97C3 **Kidal** Mali
43C3 **Kidderminster** Eng
97A3 **Kidira** Sen
110C1 **Kidnappers,C** NZ
59C2 **Kiel** Germany
59C2 **Kielce** Pol
56C2 **Kieler Bucht** *B* Germany
Kiev = Kiyev
80E2 **Kifab** Uzbekistan
97A3 **Kiffa** Maur
89H8 **Kigali** Rwanda
12A2 **Kigluaik Mts** USA
99C3 **Kigoma** Tanz
75B2 **Kii-sanchi** *Mts* Japan
74C4 **Kii-suidō** *B* Japan
54B1 **Kikinda** Serbia, Yugos
55B3 **Kikládhes** *Is* Greece
71F4 **Kikori** PNG
98B3 **Kikwit** Zaire
21C4 **Kilauea Crater** *Mt* Hawaiian Is
4C3 **Kilbuck Mts** USA
74B2 **Kilchu** N Korea
109D1 **Kilcoy** Aust
45C2 **Kildare** County, Irish Rep
45C2 **Kildare** Irish Rep
19B3 **Kilgore** USA
99D3 **Kilifi** Kenya
99D3 **Kilimanjaro** *Mt* Tanz
99D3 **Kilindoni** Tanz
92C2 **Kilis** Turk
45C2 **Kilkee** Irish Rep
45C2 **Kilkenny** County, Irish Rep
45C2 **Kilkenny** Irish Rep
45B2 **Kilkieran B** Irish Rep
55B2 **Kilkis** Greece
45B1 **Killala B** Irish Rep
45B2 **Killaloe** Irish Rep
109D1 **Killarney** Aust
41B3 **Killarney** Irish Rep
19A3 **Killeen** USA
12D1 **Killik** *R* USA
44B3 **Killin** Scot
55B3 **Killini** *Mt* Greece

45B1 **Killybegs** Irish Rep
42B2 **Kilmarnock** Scot
61H2 **Kil'mez** Russian Fed
99D3 **Kilosa** Tanz
41B3 **Kilrush** Irish Rep
99C3 **Kilwa** Zaire
99D3 **Kilwa Kisivani** Tanz
99D3 **Kilwa Kivinje** Tanz
108A2 **Kimba** Aust
12F2 **Kimball,Mt** USA
13D3 **Kimberley** Can
101F1 **Kimberley** S Africa
106B2 **Kimberley Plat** Aust
74B2 **Kimch'aek** N Korea
74B3 **Kimch'ŏn** S Korea
55B3 **Kími** Greece
60E2 **Kimry** Russian Fed
70C3 **Kinabalu** *Mt* Malay
78D1 **Kinabatangan** *R* Malay
14B2 **Kincardine** Can
13B1 **Kincolith** Can
19B3 **Kinder** USA
13F2 **Kindersley** Can
97A3 **Kindia** Guinea
98C3 **Kindu** Zaire
61H3 **Kinel'** Russian Fed
61F2 **Kineshma** Russian Fed
109D1 **Kingaroy** Aust
21A2 **King City** Aust
5G4 **Kingcome Inlet** Can
7C4 **King George Is** Can
107D4 **King I** Aust
13B2 **King I** Can
106B2 **King Leopold Range** *Mts* Aust
9B3 **Kingman** USA
98C3 **Kingombe** Zaire
108A2 **Kingoonya** Aust
22C2 **Kingsburg** USA
21B2 **Kings Canyon Nat Pk** USA
108A3 **Kingscote** Aust
106B2 **King Sd** Aust
112C2 **King Sejong** *Base* Ant
14A1 **Kingsford** USA
17B1 **Kingsland** USA
43E3 **King's Lynn** Eng
16C2 **Kings Park** USA
8B2 **Kings Peak** *Mt* USA
107C4 **Kingston** Aust
7C5 **Kingston** Can
25E3 **Kingston** Jamaica
15D2 **Kingston** New York, USA
111A3 **Kingston** NZ
42D3 **Kingston upon Hull** County Eng
27E4 **Kingstown** St Vincent and the Grenadines
9D4 **Kingsville** USA
44B3 **Kingussie** Scot
4J3 **King William I** Can
100B4 **King William's Town** S Africa
98B3 **Kinkala** Congo
39G7 **Kinna** Sweden
44D3 **Kinnairds Head** *Pt* Scot
75B1 **Kinomoto** Japan
44C3 **Kinross** Scot
45B3 **Kinsale** Irish Rep
98B3 **Kinshasa** Zaire
78D3 **Kintap** Indon
42B2 **Kintyre** Pen Scot
13D1 **Kinuso** Can
99D2 **Kinyeti** *Mt* Sudan
55B3 **Kiparissía** Greece
55B3 **Kiparissiakós Kólpos** *G* Greece
15C1 **Kipawa,L** Can
99D3 **Kipili** Tanz
45C2 **Kippure** *Mt* Irish Rep
100B2 **Kipushi** Zaire
63C2 **Kirensk** Russian Fed
Kirghizia = Kyrgyzstan
82B1 **Kirgizskiy Khrebet** *Mts* Kyrgyzstan
98B3 **Kiri** Zaire

105G4 **Kiribati** *Is* Pacific O
92B2 **Kırıkkale** Turk
99D3 **Kirinyaga** *Mt* Kenya
60D2 **Kirishi** Russian Fed
85B3 **Kirthar Range** *Mts* Pak
55C3 **Kirkağaç** Turk
90A2 **Kirk Bulāg Dāgh** *Mt* Iran
42C2 **Kirkby** Eng
44C3 **Kirkcaldy** Scot
42B2 **Kirkcudbright** Scot
38K5 **Kirkenes** Nor
14B2 **Kirkland Lake** Can
12A2 **Kirkpatrick,Mt** Ant
10A2 **Kirksville** USA
93D2 **Kirkūk** Iraq
44C2 **Kirkwall** Scot
18B2 **Kirkwood** USA
60D3 **Kirov** Russian Fed
61G2 **Kirov** Russian Fed
61G2 **Kirov Division,** Russian Fed
93D1 **Kirovakan** Armenia
61J2 **Kirovgrad** Russian Fed
60D4 **Kirovograd** Ukraine
61H2 **Kirs** Russian Fed
92B2 **Kirşehir** Turk
56C2 **Kiruna** Sweden
75B1 **Kiryū** Japan
98C2 **Kisangani** Zaire
75B1 **Kisarazu** Japan
86B1 **Kishanganj** India
85C3 **Kishangarh** India
60C4 **Kishinev** Moldova
75B2 **Kishiwada** Japan
99D3 **Kisii** Kenya
99D3 **Kisiju** Tanz
59C3 **Kiskunhalas** Hung
65F5 **Kislovodsk** Russian Fed
99E3 **Kismaayo** Somalia
75B1 **Kiso-sammyaku** *Mts* Japan
97A4 **Kissidougou** Guinea
17B2 **Kissimmee,L** USA
99D3 **Kisumu** Kenya
59C3 **Kisvárda** Hung
97B3 **Kita** Mali
65H6 **Kitab** Uzbekistan
75C1 **Kitakata** Japan
74C4 **Kita-Kyūshū** Japan
99D2 **Kitale** Kenya
69G4 **Kitalo** *I* Japan
74E2 **Kitami** Japan
7B5 **Kitchener** Can
99D2 **Kitgum** Uganda
55B3 **Kíthira** *I* Greece
55B3 **Kíthnos** *I* Greece
94A1 **Kiti,C** Cyprus
4H3 **Kitikmeot** *Region* Can
13B2 **Kitimat** Can
38L5 **Kitnen** *R* Fin
75A2 **Kitsuki** Japan
15C2 **Kittanning** USA
38J5 **Kittilä** Fin
99D3 **Kitunda** Tanz
100B2 **Kitwe** Zambia
57C3 **Kitzbühel** Austria
47E1 **Kitzbühler Alpen** *Mts* Austria
57C3 **Kitzingen** Germany
98C3 **Kiumbi** Zaire
12B1 **Kivalina** USA
59D2 **Kivercy** Ukraine
99C3 **Kivu,L** Zaire/Rwanda
4B3 **Kiwalik** USA
60D3 **Kiyev** Ukraine
61J2 **Kizel** Russian Fed
92C2 **Kizil** *R* Turk
80D2 **Kizyl-Arvat** Turkmenistan
90B2 **Kizyl-Atrek** Turkmenistan
57C2 **Kladno** Czech Republic
57C3 **Klagenfurt** Austria
60B2 **Klaipėda** Lithuania
8A2 **Klamath** *R* USA
20B2 **Klamath** *R* USA
8A2 **Klamath Falls** USA

20B2 **Klamath Mts** USA
57C3 **Klatovy** Czech Republic
12H3 **Klawak** USA
94B1 **Kleiat** Leb
101G1 **Klerksdorp** S Africa
60E2 **Klin** Russian Fed
58B1 **Klintehamn** Sweden
60D3 **Klintsy** Russian Fed
52C2 **Ključ** Bosnia-Herzegovina
59B2 **Kłodzko** Pol
12G2 **Klondike** *R* Can/USA
4D3 **Klondike Plat** Can/USA
59B3 **Klosterneuburg** Austria
12G2 **Kluane** *R* Can
12G2 **Kluane L** Can
12G2 **Kluane Nat Pk** Can
59B2 **Kluczbork** Pol
12G3 **Klukwan** USA
12E2 **Klutina L** USA
12E2 **Knight I** USA
43C3 **Knighton** Wales
52C2 **Knin** Croatia
106A4 **Knob,C** Aust
46B1 **Knokke-Heist** Belg
112C9 **Knox Coast** Ant
11B3 **Knoxville** Tennessee, USA
6H3 **Knud Ramsussens Land** *Region* Greenland
78B3 **Koba** Indon
6F3 **Kobbermirebugt** Greenland
74D4 **Kobe** Japan
56C1 **København** Den
57B2 **Koblenz** Germany
60B3 **Kobrin** Russian Fed
71E4 **Kobroör** *I* Indon
12C1 **Kobuk** *R* USA
54B2 **Kočani** Macedonia
76C3 **Ko Chang** *I* Thai
86B1 **Koch Bihar** India
47D1 **Kochel** Germany
6C3 **Koch I** Can
Kochi = Cochin
74C4 **Kōchi** Japan
12D3 **Kodiak** USA
12D3 **Kodiak I** USA
87B2 **Kodiyakkari** India
99D2 **Kodok** Sudan
100A3 **Koes** Namibia
101G1 **Koffiefontein** S Africa
97B4 **Koforidua** Ghana
74D3 **Kōfu** Japan
75B1 **Koga** Japan
39G7 **Køge** Den
84C2 **Kohat** Pak
84B2 **Koh-i-Baba** *Mts* Afghan
84B1 **Koh-i-Hisar** *Mts* Afghan
84B2 **Koh-i-Khurd** *Mt* Afghan
86C1 **Kohima** India
84B1 **Koh-i-Mazar** *Mt* Afghan
84B3 **Kohlu** Pak
60C2 **Kohtla Järve** Estonia
75B1 **Koide** Japan
12F2 **Koidern** Can
77A4 **Koihoa** *Is* Nicobar Is
74B3 **Köje-do** *I* S Korea
65H4 **Kokchetav** Kazakhstan
39J6 **Kokemaki** *L* Fin
38J6 **Kokkola** Fin
107D1 **Kokoda** PNG
14A2 **Kokomo** USA
71E4 **Kokonau** Indon
65K5 **Kokpekty** Kazakhstan
7D4 **Koksoak** *R* Can
100A4 **Kokstad** S Africa
76C3 **Ko Kut** *I* Thai
38L5 **Kola** Russian Fed
71D4 **Kolaka** Indon
77B4 **Ko Lanta** *I* Thai
Kolam = Quilon
87B2 **Kolar** India
87B2 **Kolar Gold Fields** India

97A3 Kolda Sen
39F7 Kolding Den
87A1 Kolhāpur India
12C3 Kolianek USA
59B2 Kolín Czech Republic
57B2 Köln Germany
58B2 Kolo Pol
52C1 Kolobrzeg Pol
97B3 Kolokani Mali
60E2 Kolomna
      Russian Fed
60C4 Kolomyya Ukraine
65K4 Kolpashevo
      Russian Fed
55B2 Kólpos Merabéllou B
      Greece
55B2 Kólpos Singitikós G
      Greece
55B2 Kólpos Strimonikós
      G Greece
55B2 Kólpos Toronaíos G
      Greece
38L5 Kol'skiy Poluostrov
      Pen Russian Fed
38G6 Kolvereid Nor
100B2 Kolwezi Zaire
  1C7 Kolyma R
      Russian Fed
54B2 Kom Mt Bulg/Serbia,
      Yugos
99D2 Koma Eth
97D3 Komaduga Gana R
      Nig
59B3 Komárno Slovakia
101H1 Komati R S Africa
74D3 Komatsu Japan
75A2 Komatsushima
      Japan
64G3 Komi Division,
      Russian Fed
61H2 Komi-Permyak
      Division,
      Russian Fed
70C4 Komodo I Indon
71E4 Komoran I Indon
75B1 Komoro Japan
55C2 Komotiní Greece
76D3 Kompong Cham
      Camb
76C3 Kompong Chhnang
      Mts Camb
77C3 Kompong Som
      Camb
76C3 Kompong Thom
      Camb
76D3 Kompong Trabek
      Camb
63F2 Komsomol'sk na
      Amure Russian Fed
65H4 Konda R
      Russian Fed
99D3 Kondoa Tanz
87B1 Kondūkūr India
  6G3 Kong Christian IX
      Land Region
      Greenland
  6F3 Kong Frederik VI Kyst
      Mts Greenland
  6E3 Kong Håkon VII Ant
64C2 Kong Karls Land Is
      Barents S
78D2 Kongkemul Mt
      Indon
98C3 Kongolo Zaire
39F7 Kongsberg Den
39G6 Kongsvinger Nor
      Königsberg =
      Kaliningrad
58B2 Konin Pol
54A2 Konjic Bosnia-
      Herzegovina
61F1 Konosha Russian Fed
75B1 Konosu Japan
60D3 Konotop Ukraine
59C2 Kónskie Pol
49D2 Konstanz Germany
97C3 Kontagora Nig
76D3 Kontum Viet
92B2 Konya Turk
13D3 Kootenay R Can
85C5 Kopargaon India
  6J3 Köpasker Iceland
38A2 Kópavogur Iceland
52B1 Koper Slovenia

80D2 Kopet Dag Mts Iran/
      Turkmenistan
61K2 Kopeysk Russian Fed
77C4 Ko Phangan I Thai
77B4 Ko Phuket I Thai
39H7 Köping Sweden
87B1 Koppal India
52C1 Koprivnica Croatia
85B4 Korangi Pak
87C1 Koraput India
86A2 Korba India
57B2 Korbach Germany
  4B3 Korbuk R USA
55B2 Korçë Alb
52C2 Korčula I Croatia
72E2 Korea B China/Korea
74B4 Korea Str S Korea/
      Japan
59D2 Korec Ukraine
92B1 Körğlu Tepesi Mt
      Turk
97B4 Korhogo Côte d'Ivoire
85B4 Kori Creek India
55B3 Korinthiakós Kólpos
      G Greece
55B3 Kórinthos Greece
74E3 Kōriyama Japan
61K3 Korkino Russian Fed
92B2 Korkuteli Turk
52C1 Korla China
52C2 Kornat I Croatia
60D5 Köroğlu Tepesi R
      Turk
99D3 Korogwe Tanz
108B3 Koroit Aust
71E3 Koror Palau Is,
      Pacific O
59C3 Körös R Hung
60D5 Korosten Ukraine
95A3 Koro Toro Chad
12B3 Korovin I USA
69G2 Korsakov Russian Fed
39G7 Korsør Den
46B1 Kortrijk Belg
55C3 Kós I Greece
77C4 Ko Samui I Thai
58B2 Koscierzyna Pol
PN07D4 Kosciusko Mt Aust
12H3 Kosciusko I USA
74B4 Koshikijima-retto I
      Japan
59C3 Košice Slovakia
74B3 Kosong N Korea
54B2 Kosovo Aut Republic,
      Serbia, Yugos
54B2 Kosovska Mitrovica
      Serbia, Yugos
97B4 Kossou L Côte
      d'Ivoire
101G1 Koster S Africa
99D1 Kosti Sudan
59D2 Kostopol' Ukraine
61F2 Kostroma
      Russian Fed
61E2 Kostroma Division,
      Russian Fed
56C2 Kostrzyn Pol
39H8 Koszalin Pol
85D3 Kota India
78A4 Kotaagung Indon
78C3 Kotabaharu Indon
78D3 Kotabaru Indon
77C4 Kota Bharu Malay
78A3 Kotabum Indon
24C2 Kot Addu Pak
78D1 Kota Kinabalu Malay
87C1 Kotapad India
61G2 Kotel'nich
      Russian Fed
61F4 Kotel'nikovo
      Russian Fed
39K6 Kotka Fin
64F3 Kotlas Russian Fed
12B2 Kotlik USA
54A2 Kotor Montenegro,
      Yugos
60C4 Kotovsk Ukraine
85B3 Kotri Pak
87C1 Kottagüdem India
87B3 Kottayam India
98C2 Kotto R CAR
87B2 Kottūru India
12B1 Kotzebue USA
  4B3 Kotzebue Sd USA

97C3 Kouande Benin
98C2 Kouango CAR
97B3 Koudougou Burkina
98B3 Koulamoutou Gabon
97B3 Koulikoro Mali
97B3 Koupéla Burkina
33G2 Kourou French
      Guiana
97B3 Kouroussa Guinea
98B1 Kousséri Cam
39K6 Kouvola Fin
38L5 Kovdor Russian Fed
60B3 Kovel' Ukraine
      Kovno = Kaunas
61J2 Kovrov Russian Fed
61F3 Kovylkino
      Russian Fed
60E1 Kovzha R
      Russian Fed
77C4 Ko Way I Thai
73C5 Kowloon Hong Kong
84B2 Kowt-e-Ashrow
      Afghan
92A2 Köyceğiz Turk
38L5 Koydor Russian Fed
67A3 Koyna Res India
12B2 Koyuk USA
12B1 Koyuk R USA
12C2 Koyukuk USA
12C1 Koyukuk R USA
92C2 Kozan Turk
55B2 Kozáni Greece
      Kozhikode = Calicut
61G2 Koz'modemyansk
      Russian Fed
75B2 Közu-shima I Japan
39F7 Krageró Nor
54B2 Kragujevac Serbia,
      Yugos
77B3 Kra,Isthmus of Myan/
      Malay
      Krakatau = Rakata
94C1 Krak des Chevaliers
      Hist Site Syria
      Kraków = Cracow
54B2 Kraljevo Serbia,
      Yugos
60E4 Kramatorsk Ukraine
38H6 Kramfors Sweden
52B1 Kranj Slovenia
61G1 Krasavino
      Russian Fed
64G2 Krasino Russian Fed
59C2 Kraśnik Pol
61G3 Krasnoarmeysk
      Russian Fed
60E5 Krasnodar
      Russian Fed
60F3 Krasnodar Division,
      Russian Fed
61J2 Krasnokamsk
      Russian Fed
61K2 Krasnotur'insk
      Russian Fed
61J2 Krasnoufimsk
      Russian Fed
61J3 Krasnousol'-skiy
      Russian Fed
65G3 Krasnovishersk
      Russian Fed
65G5 Krasnovodsk
      Turkmenistan
63B2 Krasnoyarsk
      Russian Fed
59C2 Krasnystaw Pol
61G3 Krasnyy Kut
      Russian Fed
60E4 Krasnyy Luch
      Ukraine
61G4 Krasnyy Yar
      Russian Fed
76D3 Kratie Camb
  6E2 Kraulshavn
      Greenland
56B2 Krefeld Germany
60D4 Kremenchug Ukraine
60D4 Kremenchugskoye
      Vodokhranilische
      Res Ukraine
59D2 Kremenets Ukraine
98A2 Kribi Cam
60D3 Krichev Belarus
47E1 Krimml Austria
87B1 Krishna R India

87B2 Krishnagiri India
86B2 Krishnangar India
39F7 Kristiansand Nor
39G7 Kristianstad Sweden
64B3 Kristiansund Nor
39G7 Kristinehamn
      Sweden
38J6 Kristiinankaupunki
      Fin
55B3 Kriti I Greece
60D4 Krivoy Rog Ukraine
52B1 Krk I Croatia
  6G3 Kronpris Frederik
      Bjerge Mts
      Greenland
39K7 Kronshtadt
      Russian Fed
101G1 Kroonstad S Africa
65F5 Kropotkin
      Russian Fed
101G1 Krugersdorp S Africa
78A4 Krui Indon
55A2 Kruje Alb
58D2 Krupki Belarus
12B1 Krusenstern,C USA
54B2 Kruševac Serbia,
      Yugos
39K7 Krustpils Latvia
12G3 Kruzof I USA
65F5 Krym Pen Ukraine
60E5 Krymsk Russian Fed
58B2 Krzyz Pol
96C1 Ksar El Boukhari Alg
96B1 Ksar el Kebir Mor
70A3 Kuala Indon
77C5 Kuala Dungun Malay
77C4 Kuala Kerai Malay
77C5 Kuala Kubu Baharu
      Malay
77C5 Kuala Lipis Malay
77C5 Kuala Lumpur Malay
77C4 Kuala Trengganu
      Malay
78D1 Kuamut Malay
74A2 Kuandian China
77C5 Kuantan Malay
93E1 Kuba Azerbaijan
71F4 Kubar PNG
78C2 Kuching Malay
70C3 Kudat Malay
78C4 Kudus Indon
61H2 Kudymkar
      Russian Fed
57C3 Kufstein Austria
90C3 Kuh Duren Upland
      Iran
91C4 Küh e Bazmān Mt
      Iran
90B3 Kūh-e Dinar Mt Iran
90C2 Kūh-e-Hazār Masjed
      Iran
91C4 Küh-e Jebāl Barez
      Mts Iran
90B3 Kūh-e Karkas Mts
      Iran
91C4 Küh-e Laleh Zar Mt
      Iran
90A2 Küh-e Sahand Mt
      Iran
91D4 Kuh e Taftān Mt Iran
90A2 Kūhhaye Sabalan
      Mts Iran
90A3 Kūhhā-ye Zāgros Mts
      Iran
38K6 Kuhmo Fin
90B3 Kūhpāyeh Iran
90C3 Kūhpāyeh Iran
91C4 Küh ye Bashākerd
      Mts Iran
90A2 Kūh ye Sabalan Mt
      Iran
100A3 Kuibis Namibia
  4B4 Kuigillingok USA
100A2 Kuito Angola
12H3 Kuiu I USA
74E2 Kuji Japan
75A2 Kuju-san Mt Japan
12C3 Kukaklek L USA
54B2 Kukës Alb
77C5 Kukup Malay
91C4 Kul R Iran
55C3 Kula Turk
61J4 Kulaksti Kazakhstan
99D2 Kulal,Mt Kenya

Kulata

55B2 Kulata Bulg
60B2 Kuldiga Latvia
61H4 Kul'sary Kazakhstan
84D2 Kulu India
92B2 Kulu Turk
65J4 Kulunda Russian Fed
108B2 Kulwin Aust
61G5 Kuma R Russian Fed
75B1 Kumagaya Japan
78C3 Kumai Indon
74C4 Kumamoto Japan
75B2 Kumano Japan
54B2 Kumanovo Macedonia
63E2 Kumara China
97B4 Kumasi Ghana
65F5 Kumayri Armenia
98A2 Kumba Cam
87B2 Kumbakonam India
61J3 Kumertau Russian Fed
74B3 Kümhwa S Korea
39H7 Kumla Sweden
87A2 Kumta India
82C1 Kümüx China
84C2 Kunar R Afghan
39K7 Kunda Estonia
87A2 Kundapura India
85C4 Kundla India
84B1 Kunduz Afghan
89F9 Kunene R Angola
39G7 Kungsbacka Sweden
61J2 Kungur Russian Fed
76B1 Kunhing Myan
82B2 Kunlun Shan Mts China
73A4 Kunming China
74B3 Kunsan S Korea
38K6 Kuopio Fin
61E3 Kupa Division, Russian Fed
52C1 Kupa R Croatia/ Bosnia-Herzegovina
106B2 Kupang Indon
107D2 Kupiano PNG
12H3 Kupreanof I USA
60L4 Kupyansk Ukraine
82C1 Kuqa China
75B1 Kurabe Japan
74C4 Kurashiki Japan
74A1 Kurayoshi Japan
54C2 Kürdzhali Bulg
74C4 Kure Japan
60B2 Kuressaare Estonia
63A1 Kureyka R Russian Fed
65H4 Kurgan Russian Fed
38J6 Kurikka Fin
Kuril Is = Kuril'skoye Osrova
69H2 Kuril'skiye Ostrova Russian Fed
87B1 Kurnool India
75C1 Kuroiso Japan
111B2 Kurow NZ
109D2 Kurri Kurri Aust
60E3 Kursk Russian Fed
Kurskiy Zaliv = Courland Lagoon
68A2 Kuruktag R China
100B3 Kuruman S Africa
74C4 Kurume Japan
87C3 Kurunegala Sri Lanka
65K5 Kurunktag R China
61J2 Kusa Russian Fed
55C3 Kuşadasi Körfezi B Turk
55C2 Kus Golü T Turk
74C4 Kushimoto Japan
74E2 Kushiro Japan
86B2 Kushtia Bang
61H3 Kushum R Kazakhstan
80E2 Kushva R Russian Fed
65G4 Kushva Russian Fed
12B2 Kuskokwim R USA
12B3 Kuskokwim B USA
12C2 Kuskokwim Mts USA
86A1 Kusma Nepal
74E2 Kussharo-ko L Japan
65H4 Kustanay Kazakhstan
92A2 Kütahya Turk

78D3 Kutai R Indon
59B3 Grená Hora Czech Republic
58B2 Kutno Pol
98B3 Kutu Zaire
86C2 Kutubdia I Bang
98C1 Kutum Sudan
7C4 Kuujjuaq Can
7C4 Kuujjuarapidu Can
38K5 Kuusamo Fin
61J3 Kuvandyk Russian Fed
93E4 Kuwait Kuwait
80C3 Kuwait Sheikdom, S W Asia
75B1 Kuwana Japan
Kuybyshev = Samara
65J4 Kuybyshev Russian Fed
61G3 Kuybyshevskoye Vodokhranilishche Res Russian Fed
63C2 Kuytun Russian Fed
60E5 Kuzey Anadolu Daglari Mts Turk
61G3 Kuznetsk Russian Fed
38J4 Kvaenangen Sd Nor
12C3 Kvichak USA
12C3 Kvichak R USA
12C3 Kvichak B USA
38G5 Kvigtind Mt Nor
38H5 Kvikkjokk Sweden
99D3 Kwale Kenya
74B3 Kwangju S Korea
98B3 Kwango R Zaire
100C3 Kwazulu-Natal Province, S Africa
100B2 Kwekwe Zim
12B2 Kwethluk USA
12B2 Kwethluk R USA
12B2 Kwidzyn Pol
71E4 Kwoka Mt Indon
108C3 Kyabram Aust
76B2 Kyaikkami Myan
76B2 Kyaikto Myan
68C1 Kyakhta Russian Fed
108A2 Kyancutta Aust
76B1 Kyaukme Myan
76B1 Kyauk-padaung Myan
76A2 Kyaukpyu Myan
40B2 Kyle of Lochalsh Scot
46D1 Kyll R Germany
108B3 Kyneton Aust
99D2 Kyoga L Uganda
109D1 Kyogle Aust
74B3 Kyōngju S Korea
74D3 Kyoto Japan
65J5 Kyrgyzstan Republic, Asia
65H4 Kyshtym Russian Fed
74C4 Kyúshú I Japan
104E3 Kyushu-Palau Ridge Pacific O
54B2 Kyustendil Bulg
68B1 Kyzyl Russian Fed
65H5 Kyzylkum Desert Kazakhstan
65H5 Kyzl Orda Kazakhstan

L

99E2 Laascaanood Somalia
46E1 Laasphe Germany
99E1 Laasqoray Somalia
96A2 Laâyoune Mor
23A1 La Barca Mexico
97A3 Labé Guinea
59B2 Labe R Czech Republic
15D1 Labelle Can
17B2 La Belle USA
12G2 Laberge,L Can
13E2 La Biche,L Can
61F5 Labinsk Russian Fed
94C1 Laboué Leb
34C2 Labrador Region Can
7D4 Labrador City Can

7E4 Labrador S Greenland/Can
23A1 Lábrea Brazil
78D1 Labuan Malay
78D1 Labuan I Malay
78B4 Labuhan Indon
76A2 Labutta Myan
65H3 Labytnangi Russian Fed
7C4 Lac á L'eau Claire Can
46B2 La Capelle France
34C2 La Carlota Arg
79B3 La Carlota Phil
1C4 Lac Belot L Can
7C4 Lac Bienville L Can
83B4 Laccadive Is India
47B2 Lac d'Annecy L France
4G3 Lac de Gras L Can
47B1 Lac de Joux L Switz
47B1 Lac de Neuchâtel L Switz
23A2 Lac de Patzcuaro L Mexico
23A2 Lac de Sayula L Mexico
4F3 Lac des Bois L Can
47A2 Lac du Bourget L France
25D3 La Ceiba Honduras
108A3 Lacepede B Aust
48C2 La Châtre France
47B1 La-Chaux-de-Fonds Switz
94B3 Lachish Hist Site Israel
107D4 Lachlan R Aust
32B2 La Chorrera Panama
15D1 Lachute Can
7D4 Lac Joseph L Can
15C2 Lackawanna USA
5G4 Lac la Biche Can
4G3 Lac la Martre L Can
5H4 Lac la Ronge L Can
52A1 Lac Léman L Switz/ France
10C1 Lac Manouane L Can
15D1 Lac Megantic Can
7C4 Lac Mistassini L Can
13E2 Lacombe Can
15D2 Laconia USA
50A1 La Coruña Spain
10A2 La Crosse USA
5A4 La Cruces USA
7A4 Lac Seul L Can
18B2 La Cygne USA
84D2 Ladákh Range India
73B5 Ladong China
60D1 Ladozhskoye Ozero L Russian Fed
6B2 Lady Ann Str Can
101G1 Ladybrand S Africa
13C3 Ladysmith Can
101G1 Ladysmith S Africa
71F4 Lae PNG
76C3 Laem Ngop Thai
56C1 Laesø I Den
10B2 Lafayette Indiana, USA
11A3 Lafayette Louisiana, USA
46B2 La Fère France
46B2 La-Ferté-sous-Jouarre France
97C4 Lafia Nig
97C4 Lafiagi Nig
48B2 La Flèche France
96C1 La Galite I Tunisia
56C1 Lagan R Sweden
31D4 Lagarto Brazil
96C1 Laghouat Alg
35C2 Lagoa de Araruama Brazil
29F2 Lagoa dos Patos L Brazil
52A2 Lagoa Feia Brazil
32B4 Lago Agrio Ecuador
35C1 Lagoa Juparaná L Brazil

29D2 Lagoa mar Chiguita L Arg
29F2 Lagoa Mirim L Brazil/Urug
29B6 Lago Argentino L Arg
29B5 Lago Buenos Aires L Arg
29B5 Lago Cochrane L Arg/Chile
29C5 Lago Colhué Huapí L Arg
24B2 Lago de Chapala L Mexico
32A2 Lago de Chiriquí L Panama
23A2 Lago de Cuitzeo L Mexico
29B3 Lago de la Laja L Chile
53A2 Lago del Coghinas L Sardegna
32C2 Lago de Maracaibo L Ven
25D3 Lago de Nicaragua L Nic
32A1 Lago de Perlas L Nic
52B2 Lago di Bolsena L Italy
52B2 Lago di Bracciano L Italy
47B2 Lago di Como L Italy
47D2 Lago d'Idro L Italy
47C2 Lago di Garda L Italy
47C2 Lago di Lecco L Italy
47C2 Lago di Lugano L Italy
47D2 Lago d'Iseo L Italy
47D2 Lago d'Orta L Italy
29B5 Lago General Carrera L Chile
52A1 Lago Maggiore L Italy
29C5 Lago Musters L Arg
48B3 Lagon France
29B4 Lago Nahuel Haupí L Arg
29B5 Lago O'Higgins L Chile
53A2 Lago Omodeo L Sardegna
30C2 Lago Poopó L Bol
29B4 Lago Ranco L Chile
32D6 Lago Raguaado L Bol
97C4 Lagos Nig
50A2 Lagos Port
29B5 Lago San Martin L Arg/Chile
24B2 Lagos de Moreno Mexico
30C2 Lago Titicaca Bol/ Peru
29B5 Lago Viedma L Arg
48B3 Lagrande Spain
106B2 Lagrange Aust
11B3 La Grange Georgia, USA
14A3 La Grange Kentucky, USA
19A4 La Grange Texas, USA
33E2 La Gran Sabana Mts Ven
48B3 Lagronño Spain
34A1 Laguna Argentina L Arg
21B3 Laguna Beach USA
34C3 Laguna Colorada Grande L Arg
79B3 Laguna de Bay L Phil
25D3 Laguna de Caratasca Lg Honduras
25D4 Laguna de Chiriquí L Panama
25D3 Laguna de Managua L Nic
25D3 Laguna de Nicaragua L Nic
26A4 Laguna de Perlas Lg Nic

23B1 Laguna de Pueblo Viejo *L* Mexico
24C2 Laguna de Tamiahua *Lg* Mexico
25C3 Laguna de Términos *Lg* Mexico
23A1 Laguna de Yuriria *L* Mexico
23B1 Laguna la Altamira Mexico
24C2 Laguna Madre *Lg* Mexico
34C2 Laguna Mar Chiquita *L* Arg
29B4 Laguna Nahuel Huapi *L* Arg
34C2 Laguna Paiva Arg
29B4 Laguna Ranco Chile
9C4 Laguna Seca Mexico
23B1 Laguna Tortugas *L* Mexico
70C3 Lahad Datu Malay
78A3 Lahat Indon
38J6 Lahia Fin
90B2 Lāhījān Iran
46D1 Lahn *R* Germany
46D1 Lahnstein Germany
44E2 Lahore Pak
39K6 Lahti Fin
23A2 La Huerta Mexico
98B2 Lai Chad
73B5 Laibin China
76C1 Lai Chau Viet
100B4 Laingsburg S Africa
44B2 Lairg Scot
78A3 Lais Indon
79C4 Lais Phil
72E2 Laiyang China
72D2 Laizhou Wan *B* China
34A3 Laja *R* Chile
30F4 Lajes Brazil
22D4 La Jolla USA
9C3 La Junta USA
109C2 Lake Cargelligo Aust
11A3 Lake Charles USA
17B1 Lake City Florida, USA
17C1 Lake City S Carolina, USA
42C2 Lake District Region, Eng
22D4 Lake Elsinore USA
109C3 Lake Eyre Basin Aust
15C2 Lakefield Can
6D3 Lake Harbour Can
22C3 Lake Hughes USA
16B2 Lakehurst USA
19A4 Lake Jackson USA
13E2 Lake la Biche Can
17B2 Lakeland USA
7A5 Lake of the Woods Can
20B1 Lake Oswego USA
21A2 Lakeport USA
19B3 Lake Providence USA
111B2 Lake Pukaki NZ
109C3 Lakes Entrance Aust
22C2 Lakeshore USA
108B1 Lake Stewart Aust
15C1 Lake Traverse Can
8A2 Lakeview USA
20B1 Lakeview Mt USA
19B2 Lake Village USA
17B2 Lake Wales USA
16B2 Lakewood New Jersey, USA
14B2 Lakewood Ohio, USA
17B2 Lake Worth USA
86A1 Lakhimpur India
85B4 Lakhpat India
84C2 Lakki Pak
55B3 Lakonikós Kólpos *G* Greece
97B4 Lakota Côte d'Ivoire
38K4 Lakselbord Inlet Nor
38K4 Lakselv Nor
34C2 La Laguna Arg
32A4 La Libertad Ecuador
34A2 La Ligua Chile

50A2 La Linea Spain
85D4 Lalitpur India
5H4 La Loche Can
13F1 la Loche,L Can
46C1 La Louvière Belg
26A4 La Luz Nic
7C5 La Malbaie Can
23B2 La Malinche *Mt* Mexico
50B2 La Mancha Region, Spain
9C3 Lamar Colorado, USA
18B2 Lamar Missouri, USA
19A4 La Marque USA
98B3 Lambaréné Gabon
32A5 Lambayeque Peru
112B10 Lambert Gl Ant
16B2 Lambertville USA
42B1 Lamblon,C Can
47C2 Lambro *R* Italy
76C2 Lam Chi *R* Thai
50A1 Lamego Port
47B2 La Meije *Mt* France
32B6 La Merced Peru
21B3 La Mesa USA
55B3 Lamía Greece
42C2 Lammermuir Hills Scot
39G7 Lammhult Sweden
79B3 Lamon *B* Phil
18B1 Lamoni USA
71F3 Lamotrek *I* Pacific O
43B3 Lampeter Wales
99E3 Lamu Kenya
47D1 Lana Italy
21C4 Lanaʻi *I* Hawaiian Is
21C4 Lanaʻi City Hawaiian Is
42C2 Lanark Scot
76B3 Lanbi *I* Myan
76C1 Lancang *R* China
42C3 Lancashire County, Eng
21B3 Lancaster California, USA
18B1 Lancaster Eng
15D2 Lancaster New Hampshire, USA
10C3 Lancaster Ohio, USA
16A2 Lancaster Pennsylvania, USA
17B1 Lancaster S Carolina, USA
6B2 Lancaster Sd Can
78B3 Landak *R* Indon
46E2 Landau Germany
57C3 Landeck Austria
8C2 Lander USA
34C2 Landeta Arg
57C3 Landsberg Germany
4F2 Lands End *C* Can
43B4 Land's End *Pt* Eng
57C3 Landshut Germany
39G7 Landskrona Sweden
17A1 Lanett USA
56B2 Langenhagen Germany
57B2 Langenthal Switz
42C2 Langholm Scot
38A2 Langjökull *Mts* Iceland
77B4 Langkawi *I* Malay
13C3 Langley Can
108C1 Langlo *R* Aust
47B1 Langnau Switz
49D2 Langres France
70A3 langsa Indon
72B3 Lang Shan *Mts* China
68C2 Langtou China
76D1 Lang Son Viet
48C3 Languedoc Region, France
29B3 Lanin *Mt* Chile
79B4 Lanoa,L *L* Phil
11B3 Lansdale USA
7B4 Lansdowne House Can
21D3 Lansford USA
10B2 Lansing USA
47B2 Lanslebourg France

96A2 Lanzarote *I* Canary Is
72A2 Lanzhou China
47B2 Lanzo Torinese Italy
79B2 Laoag Phil
76C1 Lao Cai Viet
72D1 Laoha He *R* China
45C2 Laois County, Irish Rep
46B2 Laon France
32B6 La Oroya Peru
76C2 Laos Republic, S E Asia
49C2 Lapalisse France
32B2 La Palma Panama
96A2 La Palma *I* Canary Is
34C2 La Pampa State, Arg
33E2 La Paragua Ven
29E2 La Paz Arg
34B2 La Paz Arg
30C2 La Paz Bol
24A2 La Paz Mexico
69G2 La Perouse Str Japan/Russian Fed
23A1 La Piedad Mexico
20B2 La Pine USA
19B3 Laplace USA
23A2 la Placita Mexico
29E2 La Plata Arg
11C4 La Plonge,L Can
14A2 La Porte USA
39K6 Lappeenranta Fin
38H5 Lappland *Region* Sweden/Fin
34C3 Laprida Arg
1B8 Laptev S Russian Fed
38J6 Lapua Fin
79B3 Lapu-Lapu Phil
9B4 La Purisima Mexico
95B2 Laqiya Arba'in *Well* Sudan
30C3 La Quiaca Arg
52B2 L'Aquila Italy
91B4 Lār Iran
96B1 Larache Mor
8C2 Laramie USA
8C2 Laramie Range *Mts* USA
50B2 Larca Spain
9D4 Laredo USA
91B4 Larestan Region, Iran
Largeau = Faya
17C1 L'Argentière France
17B2 Largo USA
42B2 Largs Scot
90A2 Lārī Iran
51B2 La Rioja Spain
30C4 La Rioja State, Arg
55B3 Lárisa Greece
85B3 Larkana Pak
92B3 Larnaca Greece
94A1 Larnaca B Cyprus
45D1 Larne N Ire
50A1 La Robla Spain
46C1 La Roche-en-Ardenne Belg
48B2 La Rochelle France
48B2 La Roche-sur-Foron France
48B2 La Roche-sur-Yon France
51B2 La Roda Spain
27D3 La Romana Dom Rep
5H4 La Ronge Can
5H4 La Ronge,L Can
44C2 Larvik Nor
65J3 Laryak Russian Fed
50B2 La Sagra *Mt* Spain
15D1 La Salle Can
18C1 La Salle USA
7C5 La Sarre Can
34C1 Las Avispas Arg
34A2 Las Cabras Chile
9C3 Las Cruces USA
26C3 La Selle *Mt* Haiti
72B2 Lasengmia China
30B4 La Serena Chile
34A2 La Sila *Mts* Italy
90B2 Lāsjerd Iran
34A3 Las Lajas Chile

50A2 Las Marismas *Marshland* Spain
96A2 Las Palmas de Gran Canaria Canary Is
52A2 La Spezia Italy
29C4 Las Plumas Arg
34C2 Las Rosas Arg
20B2 Lassen Peak *Mt* USA
20B2 Lassen Volcanic Nat Pk USA
23B2 las Tinaí Mexico
98B3 Lastoursville Gabon
52C2 Lastovo *I* Croatia
24B2 Las Tres Marías *Is* Mexico
34C2 Las Varillas Arg
9C3 Las Vegas USA
Latakia = Al Ladhiqiyah
53B2 Latina Italy
32D1 La Toma Arg
32D1 La Tortuga *I* Ven
79B2 La Trinidad Phil
109C4 Latrobe Aust
94B3 Latrun Israel
7C5 La Tuque Can
87B1 Lātūr India
60B2 Latvia Republic, Europe
107D5 Launceston Aust
43B4 Launceston Eng
54A3 La Unión Chile
25D3 La Unión El Salvador
23A2 La Unión Mexico
32B5 La Unión Peru
107D2 Laura Aust
15C3 Laurel Delaware, USA
16A3 Laurel Maryland, USA
11B3 Laurel Mississippi, USA
10A2 Laurel Montana, USA
10C3 Laurens USA
17C1 Laurinburg USA
52A1 Lausanne Switz
78D3 Laut *I* Indon
29B5 Lautaro *Mt* Chile
46D2 Lauterecken Germany
15D1 Laval Can
48B2 Laval France
22B2 Laveaga Peak *Mt* USA
47C2 Laveno Italy
31B6 Lavras Brazil
4A3 Lavrentiya Russian Fed
101H1 Lavumisa Swaziland
78D3 Laut *I* Indon
76B1 Lawksawk Myan
18A2 Lawrence Kansas, USA
15D2 Lawrence Massachusetts, USA
111A3 Lawrence NZ
14A3 Lawrenceville Illinois, USA
9D3 Lawton USA
91A5 Layla S Arabia
99D2 Laylo Sudan
23A2 Lázaro Cárdenas Mexico
99E1 Laz Daua Somalia
79B4 Lazi Phil
8C2 Lead USA
12C1 Leader Can
84B2 Leavenworth USA
58B2 Leba Pol
18B2 Lebanon Missouri, USA
20B2 Lebanon Oregon, USA
15C2 Lebanon Pennsylvania, USA
92C3 Lebanon Republic, S W Asia
101C3 Lebombo *Mts* Mozam/S Africa/Swaziland
58B2 Lebork Pol
47A2 Le Bourg-d'Oisans France
47B1 Le Brassus Switz
29B3 Lebu Chile

Le Buet

47B1 Le Buet Mt France
46B1 Le Cateau France
55A2 Lecce Italy
52A1 Lecco Italy
47D1 Lech R Austria
47D1 Lechtaler Alpen Mts Austria
49C2 Le Creusot France
43C3 Ledbury Eng
32E2 Leduc Can
16C1 Lee USA
45B3 Lee R Irish Rep
41C3 Leeds Eng
43C3 Leek Eng
56B2 Leer Germany
17B2 Leesburg Florida, USA
16A3 Leesburg Virginia, USA
19B3 Leesville USA
109C2 Leeton Aust
56B2 Leeuwarden Neth
106A4 Leeuwin,C Aust
22C2 Lee Vining USA
27E3 Leeward Is Caribbean S
94A1 Lefkara Cyprus
79B3 Legazpi Phil
47D2 Legnago Italy
59B2 Legnica Pol
33F2 Leguan Inlet Guyana
32C4 Leguizamo Colombia
84D2 Leh India
48C2 Le Havre France
16B2 Lehigh R USA
16B2 Lehighton USA
84C2 Leiah Pak
59B3 Leibnitz Austria
43D3 Leicester Eng
107C2 Leichhardt R Aust
56A2 Leiden Neth
46B1 Leie R Belg
106C4 Leigh Creek Aust
43D4 Leighton Buzzard Eng
56B2 Leine R Germany
50A2 Leinster Region, Irish Rep
39F7 Leirvik Nor
57C2 Leipzig Germany
50A2 Leiria Port
73C4 Leiyang China
73B5 Leizhou Bandao Pen China
73C5 Leizhou Wan B China
56A2 Lek R Neth
96C1 Le Kef Tunisia
19B3 Leland USA
54A2 Lelija Mt Bosnia-Herzegovina
49C2 Le Locle France
48C2 Le Mans France
6D3 Lemieux Is Can
8C2 Lemmon USA
21B2 Lemoore USA
49C2 Lempdes France
76B2 Lemro R Myan
52C2 Le Murge Region, Italy
63C2 Lena R Russian Fed
38L6 Lendery Russian Fed
73C4 Lengshujiang China
 Leningrad = Sankt-Peterburg
60C2 Leningrad Division, Russian Fed
112B7 Leningradskaya Base Ant
61H3 Leninogorsk Tatarstan, Russian Fed
68A1 Leninogorsk Kazakhstan
65K4 Leninsk-Kuznetskiy Russian Fed
69F2 Leninskoye Russian Fed
65F6 Lenkoran' Azerbaijan
46E1 Lenne R Germany

46B1 Lens France
63D1 Lensk Russian Fed
53B3 Lentini Italy
52B1 Lenya R Myan
52B1 Leoben Austria
43C3 Leominster Eng
16D1 Leominster USA
24B2 Leon Mexico
25D3 León Nic
50A1 León Region, Spain
50A1 León Spain
100A3 Leonardville Namibia
106B3 Leonora Aust
35C2 Leopoldina Brazil
 Léopoldville = Kinshasa
60C3 Lepel Belarus
73D4 Leping China
49C2 Le Puy-en-Velay France
98B2 Léré Chad
101G1 Leribe Lesotho
47C2 Lerici Italy
51C1 Lérida Spain
23A1 Lerma R Mexico
47D1 Lermoos Austria
55C3 Léros I Greece
44E1 Lerwick Scot
46A2 Les Andelys France
26C3 Les Cayes Haiti
47B2 Les Écrins Mt France
73A4 Leshan China
54B2 Leskovac Serbia, Yugos
48B3 Les Landes Region, France
101G1 Leslie S Africa
61H2 Lesnoy Russian Fed
63B2 Lesosibirsk Russian Fed
101G1 Lesotho Kingdom, S Africa
69F2 Lesozavodsk Russian Fed
48B2 Les Sables-d'Olonne France
112A Lesser Antarctica Region, Ant
27D4 Lesser Antilles Is Caribbean S
65F5 Lesser Caucasus Mts Azerbaijan/Georgia
13E1 Lesser Slave L Can
55C3 Lesvos I Greece
58B2 Leszno Pol
42C2 Letha Range Mts Myan
5G5 Lethbridge Can
33F3 Lethem Guyana
59D3 Letichev Ukraine
63D2 Let Oktyobr'ya Russian Fed
78B2 Letong China
46A1 Le Touquet-Paris-Plage France
76B2 Letpadan Myan
48C1 Le Tréport France
47B1 Leuk Switz
57A2 Leuven Belg
55B3 Levádhia Greece
38G6 Levanger Nor
47B2 Levanna Mt Italy
71D5 Lévêque,C Aust
46D1 Leverkusen Germany
59B3 Levice Slovakia
47C1 Levico Italy
110C2 Levin NZ
7C5 Lévis Can
15D2 Levittown USA
53B3 Levka Óri Mt Greece
55B3 Levkás Greece
55B3 Levkás I Greece
106B2 Lévêque,C Aust
54C2 Levski Bulg
43E4 Lewes Eng
40B2 Lewis I Scot
21C4 Lewisburg USA
111B2 Lewis P NZ
8B2 Lewis Range Mts USA
8B2 Lewiston Idaho, USA
10C2 Lewiston Maine, USA

8C2 Lewistown Montana, USA
15C2 Lewistown Pennsylvania, USA
19B3 Lewisville USA
11B3 Lexington Kentucky, USA
18B2 Lexington Missouri, USA
15C3 Lexington Park USA
79C3 Leyte G Phil
54A2 Lezhe Alb
82D3 Lhasa China
86C1 Lhazê China
70A3 Lhokseumawe Indon
86C1 Lhozhag China
68B4 Lhunze China
 Liancourt Rocks = Tok-do
79C4 Lianga Phil
72B3 Lianjiang China
73C5 Lianjiang China
73C5 Lian Xian China
72D3 Lianyungang China
72E1 Liaodong Bandao Pen China
72E1 Liaodong Wan B China
72E1 Liao He R China
72E1 Liaoning Province, China
72E1 Liaoyang China
74B2 Liaoyuan China
4F3 Liard R Can
4F4 Liard River Can
46C2 Liart France
98B2 Libenge Zaïre
9C3 Liberal USA
57C2 Liberec Czech Republic
97A4 Liberia Republic, Africa
18B2 Liberty Missouri, USA
15D2 Liberty New York, USA
19B3 Liberty Texas, USA
48B3 Libourne France
98A2 Libreville Gabon
95A2 Libya Republic, Africa
95B2 Libyan Desert Libya
95B1 Libyan Plat Egypt
53B3 Licata Italy
43D3 Lichfield Eng
101C2 Lichinga Mozam
101G1 Lichtenburg S Africa
14B3 Licking R USA
22B2 Lick Observatory USA
60C3 Lida Belarus
39G7 Lidköping Sweden
52B2 Lido di Ostia Italy
58B2 Liechtenstein Principality, Europe
57B2 Liège Belg
58C1 Lielupe R Latvia
57C3 Lienart Zaïre
60B2 Liepāja Latvia
46C1 Lier Belg
47B1 Liestal Switz
15C1 Lièvre R Can
45C2 Liffey R Irish Rep
45C1 Lifford Irish Rep
107F3 Lifu / Nouvelle Calédonie
109C1 Lightning Ridge Aust
46C2 Ligny-en-Barrois France
101C2 Ligonha R Mozam
47C2 Liguria Region, Italy
52A2 Ligurian S Italy
21C4 Lihue Hawaiian Is
102D4 Likasi Zaïre
49C1 Lille France
39G6 Lillehammer Nor
46B1 Lillers France
39G7 Lillestøm Nor
13C2 Lillooet Can

13C2 Lillooet R Can
101C2 Lilongwe Malawi
79B4 Liloy Phil
54A2 Lim R Montenegro/Serbia, Yugos
32B6 Lima Peru
50A1 Lima Spain
10B2 Lima USA
92B3 Limassol Cyprus
45C1 Limavady N Ire
34B3 Limay R Arg
34B3 Limay Mahuida Arg
18B2 Lime Cam
101C2 Limbe Malawi
57B2 Limburg W Gem
31B6 Limeira Brazil
45B2 Limerick County, Irish Rep
41B3 Limerick Irish Rep
56B1 Limfjorden L Den
106C2 Limmen Bight B Aust
55C3 Límnos I Greece
31D3 Limoeiro Brazil
48C2 Limoges France
25D4 Limón Costa Rica
8C3 Limón USA
48C2 Limousin Region, France
73A3 Linapacan Str Phil
29B3 Linares Chile
9D4 Linares Mexico
50B2 Linares Spain
68B4 Lincang China
29D2 Lincoln Arg
18A1 Lincoln California, USA
42D3 Lincoln County, Eng
42D3 Lincoln Eng
18C1 Lincoln Illinois, USA
8D2 Lincoln Nebraska, USA
5D2 Lincoln New Hampshire, USA
111B2 Lincoln NZ
80A Lincoln S Greenland
20B2 Lincoln City USA
14B2 Lincoln Park USA
52A2 L'Incudina Mt Corse
57B3 Lindau Germany
33F2 Linden Guyana
39F7 Lindesnes C Nor
99D3 Lindi Tanz
61F3 Lindi R Zaïre
101G1 Lindley S Africa
55C3 Lindos Greece
15C2 Lindsay Can
105J3 Line Is Pacific O
61C2 Linfen China
76D2 Lingao China
79B2 Lingayen Phil
56B2 Lingen Germany
73B5 Lingshan China
72C2 Lingshi China
97A3 Linguère Sen
73E4 Linhai Rhejiang, China
31D5 Linhares Brazil
72B1 Linhe China
74B2 Linjiang China
39H7 Linköping Sweden
72D2 Linqing China
35B2 Lins Brazil
72A2 Lintao China
47C1 Linthal Switz
68D2 Linxi China
72A2 Linxia China
57C3 Linz Austria
79B3 Lipa Phil
61E3 Lipari Russian Fed
60E3 Lipetsk Division, Russian Fed
54B1 Lipova Rom
56B2 Lippe R Germany
46E1 Lippstadt Germany
99D2 Lira Uganda
98B3 Liranga Congo
50A2 Lisboa Port
 Lisbon = Lisboa
45C1 Lisburn N Ire
45B2 Liscannor B Irish Rep

73D4 Lishui China
73C4 Li Shui *R* China
60E4 Lisichansk Ukraine
48C2 Lisieux France
60E3 Liski Russian Fed
46B2 L'Isle-Adam France
47B1 L'Isle-sur-le-Doubs
France
107E3 Lismore Aust
45B2 Listowel Irish Rep
73B5 Litang China
94B2 Litani *R* Leb
33C3 Litani *R* Surinam
18C2 Litchfield USA
107E4 Lithgow Aust
60B2 Lithuania Republic,
Europe
16A2 Lititz USA
69F2 Litovko Russian Fed
11A3 Little *R* USA
11C4 Little Abaco /
The Bahamas
110C1 Little Barrier I NZ
13E2 Little Bow *R* Can
25D3 Little Cayman /
Caribbean S
16B3 Little Egg Harbor *B*
USA
26C2 Little Inagua /
Caribbean S
77A4 Little Nicobar /
Nicobar Is
11A3 Little Rock USA
22D3 Littlerock USA
13D2 Little Smoky Can
13D2 Little Smoky *R* Can
16A3 Littlestown USA
15D2 Littleton New
Hampshire, USA
74B2 Liuhe China
73B5 Liuzhou China
55B3 Livanátais Greece
60E1 Līvāni Latvia
12E1 Livengood USA
17B1 Live Oak USA
21A2 Livermore USA
7D5 Liverpool Can
42C3 Liverpool Eng
4E2 Liverpool *B* Can
42C3 Liverpool *R* Can
6C2 Liverpool,C Can
109D2 Liverpool Range *Mts*
Aust
8B2 Livingston Montana,
USA
19B3 Livingston Texas,
USA
44C4 Livingston UK
Livingston =
Maramba
19A3 Livingston,L USA
52C2 Livno Bosnia-
Herzegovina
60E3 Livny Russian Fed
14B2 Livonia USA
52C2 Livorno Italy
99D3 Liwale Tanz
52B1 Ljubljana Slovenia
38G6 Ljungan *R* Sweden
39H6 Ljungby Sweden
39H6 Ljusdal Sweden
38H6 Ljusnan *R* Sweden
43C4 Llandeilo Wales
43C4 Llandovery Wales
43C3 Llandrindod Wells
Wales
43C3 Llandudno Wales
43B4 Llanelli Wales
43C3 Llangollen Wales
9C3 Llano Estacado *Plat*
USA
32C2 Llanos Region,
Colombia/Ven
30D2 Llanos de Chiquitos
Region, Bol
Lleida = Lérida
50A2 Llerena Spain
43B3 Lleyn *Pen* Wales
89F7 Lloró Colombia
5H4 Lloydminster Can
30C3 Llullaillaco *Mt* Arg/
Chile
30C3 Loa *R* Chile
9C2 Loan France

98B3 Loange *R* Zaire
100B3 Lobatse Botswana
98B3 Lobaye *R* CAR
34D3 Löbau Germany
100A2 Lobito Angola
34D3 Lobos Arg
47C2 Locano Italy
71C1 Locarno Switz
44B3 Loch Awe *L* Scot
44A3 Lochboisdale Scot
44B3 Loch Bracadale Inlet
Scot
44B3 Loch Broom Estuary
Scot
42B2 Loch Doon *L* Scot
44B3 Loch Earn *L* Scot
44B2 Loch Eriboll Inlet
Scot
44B3 Loch Erisht *L* Scot
48C2 Loches France
44B3 Loch Etive Inlet Scot
44B3 Loch Ewe Inlet Scot
44B3 Loch Fyne Inlet Scot
44B3 Loch Hourn Inlet
Scot
44B3 Lochinver Scot
44B3 Loch Katrine *L* Scot
44C3 Loch Leven *L* Scot
44B3 Loch Linnhe Inlet
Scot
44B3 Loch Lochy *L* Scot
44B3 Loch Lomond *L* Scot
44B3 Loch Long Inlet Scot
44A3 Lochmaddy Scot
44B3 Loch Maree *L* Scot
44B3 Loch Morar *L* Scot
44C3 Lochnagar *Mt* Scot
44B3 Loch Ness *L* Scot
44B3 Loch Rannoch *L*
Scot
44A2 Loch Roag Inlet Scot
44B3 Loch Sheil *L* Scot
44B3 Loch Shin *L* Scot
44A3 Loch Snizort Inlet
Scot
44B3 Loch Tay *L* Scot
44B3 Loch Torridon Inlet
Scot
108A2 Lock Aust
42C2 Lockerbie Scot
15C2 Lock Haven USA
15C2 Lockport USA
76D3 Loc Ninh Viet
53C3 Locri Italy
94B3 Lod Israel
108B3 Loddon *R* Aust
60D1 Lodeynoye Pole
Russian Fed
84C3 Lodhran Pak
52A1 Lodi Italy
21A2 Lodi USA
98C3 Lodja Zaire
47B1 Lods France
99D2 Lodwar Kenya
58B2 Łódź Pol
38G5 Lofoten Is Nor
8B2 Logan Utah, USA
4D3 Logan,Mt Can
14A2 Logansport Indiana,
USA
19B3 Logansport
Louisiana, USA
50B1 Logroño Spain
86A2 Lohārdaga India
39J6 Lohja Fin
76B2 Loikaw Myan
39J6 Loimaa Fin
48C2 Loir *R* France
49C2 Loire *R* France
32B4 Loja Ecuador
50B2 Loja Spain
38K5 Lokan Tekojärvi *Res*
Fin
46B1 Lokeren Belg
99D2 Lokitaung Kenya
58D1 Loknya Russian Fed
98C3 Lokolo *R* Zaire
98C3 Lokoro *R* Zaire
6D3 Loks Land / Can
56C2 Lolland / Den
54B2 Lom Bulg
98C3 Lomami *R* Zaire

97A4 Loma Mts Sierra
Leone/Guinea
47C2 Lombardia Region,
Italy
71D4 Lomblen / Indon
78D4 Lombok / Indon
97C4 Lomé Togo
98C3 Lomela Zaire
98C3 Lomela *R* Zaire
60C2 Lomonosov
Russian Fed
47B1 Lomont Region,
France
21A3 Lompoc USA
58B2 Łomża Pol
87A1 Lonāvale India
29B3 Loncoche Chile
78S London Can
43D4 London Eng
45C1 Londonderry County,
N Ire
45C1 Londonderry N Ire
29B7 Londonderry / Chile
106B2 Londonderry,C Aust
30C4 Londres Arg
30D3 Londrina Brazil
21B2 Lone Pine USA
11C4 Long / The Bahamas
71F4 Long / PNG
78C2 Long Akah Malay
47E1 Longarone Italy
34A3 Longavi *Mt* Chile
27H2 Long B Jamaica
17C1 Long B USA
9B3 Long Beach
California, USA
15D2 Long Beach New
York, USA
15D2 Long Branch USA
73D5 Longchuan China
20C2 Long Creek USA
109C4 Longford Aust
45C2 Longford County,
Irish Rep
45C2 Longford Irish Rep
44D3 Long Forties *Region*
N Sea
72D1 Longhua China
7C4 Long I Can
10C2 Long I USA
16C2 Long Island Sd USA
55B3 Longlac Can
73B5 Longlin China
8C2 Longmont USA
78D2 Longnawan Indon
29B3 Longquimay Chile
107D3 Longreach Aust
72A3 Longshou Shan
Upland China
42C2 Longtown USA
16D1 Longueuil Can
34A3 Longuimay Chile
46C2 Longuyon France
11A3 Longview Texas,
USA
8A2 Longview
Washington, USA
46C2 Longwy France
72A3 Longxi China
73D4 Long Xuyen Viet
73D4 Longyan China
73B5 Longzhou China
47D2 Lonigo Italy
49D2 Lons-le-Saunier
France
11C3 Lookout,C USA
99D3 Loolmalasin *Mt* Tanz
13D1 Loon *R* Can
45B2 Loop Hd C Irish Rep
76C3 Lop Buri Thai
98A3 Lopez *C* Gabon
68B2 Lop Nur *L* China
50A2 Lora del Rio Spain
71D2 Lorain USA
84B2 Loralai Pak
90B3 Lordegān Iran
107E4 Lord Howe / Aust
105G5 Lord Howe Rise
Pacific O
6A3 Lord Mayor B Can
9C3 Lordsburg USA
35B2 Lorena Brazil
47E2 Loreo Italy
23A1 Loreto Mexico

48B2 Lorient France
108B3 Lorne Aust
57B3 Lörrach Germany
49D2 Lorraine Region
France
9C3 Los Alamos USA
34A2 Los Andes Chile
29B3 Los Angeles Chile
9B3 Los Angeles USA
21A2 Los Banos USA
34B2 Los Cerrillos Arg
21A2 Los Gatos USA
52B2 Lošinj / Croatia
29B3 Los Lagos Chile
24B2 Los Mochis Mexico
22B3 Los Olivos USA
34A3 Los Sauces Chile
44C3 Lossiemouth Scot
27E4 Los Testigos *Is* Ven
29B2 Los Vilos Chile
48C3 Lot *R* France
34A3 Lota Chile
42C2 Lothian Region, Scot
99D2 Lotikipi Plain Sudan/
Kenya
47B1 Lötschberg Tunnel
Switz
38K5 Lotta *R* Fin/
Russian Fed
48B2 Loudéac France
97A3 Louga Sen
41B3 Lough Allen *L*
Irish Rep
45C2 Lough Boderg *L*
Irish Rep
43D3 Loughborough Eng
45C2 Lough Bowna *L*
Irish Rep
45C1 Lough Carlingford *L*
N Ire
41B3 Lough Conn *L*
Irish Rep
41B3 Lough Corrib *L*
Irish Rep
41B3 Lough Derg *L*
Irish Rep
45C2 Lough Derravaragh *L*
Irish Rep
4H2 Loughead I Can
45C2 Lough Ennell *L*
Irish Rep
41B3 Lough Erne *L* N Ire
40B2 Lough Foyle Estuary
N Ire/Irish Rep
40B3 Lough Neagh *L* N Ire
45C1 Lough Oughter *L*
Irish Rep
45B2 Loughrea Irish Rep
45C2 Lough Ree *L*
Irish Rep
45C2 Lough Sheelin *L*
Irish Rep
42B2 Lough Strangford *L*
Irish Rep
45C1 Lough Swilly Estuary
Irish Rep
14B3 Louisa USA
70C3 Louisa Reef /
S E Asia
12E2 Louise,L USA
107E2 Louisiade Arch
Solomon Is
11A3 Louisiana State, USA
17B1 Louisville Georgia,
USA
11B3 Louisville Kentucky,
USA
38L5 Loukhi Russian Fed
48B3 Lourdes France
108C2 Louth Aust
45C2 Louth County,
Irish Rep
42D3 Louth Eng
Louvain = Leuven
48C2 Louviers France
60D2 Lovat *R* Russian Fed
54B2 Loveč Bulg
21B1 Lovelock USA
52B1 Lóvere Italy
9C3 Lovington USA
38L5 Lovozero
Russian Fed
6B3 Low,C Can

Lowell

10C2 **Lowell** Massachusetts, USA
20B2 **Lowell** Oregon, USA
16D1 **Lowell** USA
111B2 **Lower Hutt** NZ
43E3 **Lowestoft** Eng
58B2 **Lowicz** Pol
108B2 **Loxton** Aust
5F4 **Loyd George,Mt** Can
54A2 **Loznica** Serbia, Yugos
23A2 **Loz Reyes** Mexico
65H3 **Lozva** R Russian Fed
100B2 **Luacano** Angola
98C3 **Luachimo** Angola
98C3 **Lualaba** R Zaire
100B2 **Luampa** Zambia
100B2 **Luân** Angola
73D3 **Lu'an** China
98B3 **Luanda** Angola
100A2 **Luando** R Angola
100B2 **Luanginga** R Angola
76C1 **Luang Namtha** Laos
76C2 **Luang Prabang** Laos
98B3 **Luangue** R Angola
100C2 **Luangwa** R Zambia
72D1 **Luan He** R China
72D1 **Luanping** China
100B2 **Luanshya** Zambia
100B2 **Luapula** R Zaire
50A1 **Luarca** Spain
98B3 **Lubalo** Angola
58D2 **L'uban** Belarus
98B3 **Lubang Is** Phil
100A2 **Lubango** Angola
9C3 **Lubbock** USA
56C2 **Lübeck** Germany
58B2 **Lubefu** Zaire
98C3 **Lubefu** R Zaire
98C3 **Lubero** Zaire
98C3 **Lubilash** R Zaire
52C2 **Lublin** Pol
60D3 **Lubny** Ukraine
78C2 **Luboń Antia** Malay
98C3 **Lubudi** Zaire
98C3 **Lubudi** R Zaire
78A3 **Lubuklinggau** Indon
100B2 **Lubumbashi** Zaire
98C3 **Lubutu** Zaire
79B3 **Lucban** Phil
52B2 **Lucca** Italy
42B2 **Luce B** Scot
19C3 **Lucedale** USA
79B3 **Lucena** Phil
59B3 **Lucenec** Slovakia
Lucerne = Luzern
73C5 **Luchuan** China
56C2 **Luckenwalde** Germany
101F1 **Luckhoff** S Africa
86A1 **Lucknow** India
100B2 **Lucusse** Angola
46D1 **Lüdenscheid** Germany
100A3 **Lüderitz** Namibia
84D2 **Ludhiana** India
14A2 **Ludington** USA
43C3 **Ludlow** Eng
54C2 **Ludogorie** Upland Bulg
17B1 **Ludowici** USA
54B1 **Luduş** Rom
39H6 **Ludvika** Sweden
57B3 **Ludwigsburg** Germany
57B3 **Ludwigshafen** Germany
56C2 **Ludwigslust** Germany
98C3 **Luebo** Zaire
98C3 **Luema** R Zaire
98C3 **Luembe** R Angola
100A2 **Luena** Angola
100B2 **Luene** R Angola
72B3 **Lüeyang** China
73D5 **Lufeng** China
11A3 **Lufkin** USA
60C2 **Luga** Russian Fed
60C2 **Luga** R Russian Fed
52A1 **Lugano** Switz
101C2 **Lugela** Mozam
101C2 **Lugenda** R Mozam
50A1 **Lugo** Spain

54B1 **Lugoj** Rom
72A3 **Luhuo** China
98B3 **Lui** R Angola
100B2 **Luiana** Angola
100B2 **Luiana** R Angola
Luichow Peninsula = Leizhou Bandao
47C2 **Luino** Italy
98B2 **Luionga** R Zaire
72B2 **Luipan Shan** Upland China
100B2 **Luishia** China
68B4 **Luixi** China
98C3 **Luiza** Zaire
34B2 **Luján** Arg
34D2 **Luján** Arg
73D3 **Lujiang** China
98B3 **Lukenie** R Zaire
64E4 **Luki** Russian Fed
98B3 **Lukolela** Zaire
58C2 **Lukov** Pol
98C3 **Lukuga** R Zaire
100B2 **Lukulu** Zambia
38J5 **Lule** R Sweden
38J5 **Luleå** Sweden
54C2 **Lüleburgaz** Turk
72C2 **Lüliang Shan** Mts China
19A4 **Luling** USA
98C2 **Lulonga** R Zaire
Luluabourg = Kananga
100B2 **Lumbala Kaquengue** Angola
11C3 **Lumberton** USA
78D1 **Lumbis** Indon
86C1 **Lumding** India
100B2 **Lumeje** Angola
111A3 **Lumsden** NZ
39G7 **Lund** Sweden
101C2 **Lundazi** Zambia
43B4 **Lundy** I Eng
42C2 **Lune** R Eng
56C2 **Lüneburg** Germany
46D2 **Lunéville** France
100B2 **Lunga** R Zambia
86C2 **Lunglei** India
100A2 **Lungue Bungo** R Angola
58D2 **Luninec** Belarus
98B3 **Luobomo** Congo
73B5 **Luocheng** China
73C5 **Luoding** China
72C3 **Luohe** China
72C3 **Luo He** R Henan, China
72B2 **Luo He** R Shaanxi, China
73C4 **Luoxiao Shan** Hills China
72C3 **Luoyang** China
98B3 **Luozi** Zaire
100B2 **Lupane** Zim
101C2 **Lupilichi** Mozam
Lu Qu = Tao He
30E4 **Luque** Par
45C1 **Lurgan** N Ire
101C2 **Lurio** R Mozam
90A3 **Luristan** Region, Iran
100B2 **Lusaka** Zambia
98C3 **Lusambo** Zaire
55A2 **Lushnje** Alb
99D3 **Lushoto** Tanz
68B4 **Lushui** China
72E2 **Lushun** China
43D4 **Luton** Eng
60C3 **Lutsk** Ukraine
99E2 **Luuq** Somalia
99D3 **Luvua** R Zaire
99D3 **Luwegu** R Tanz
100C2 **Luvingu** Zambia
71D4 **Luwuk** Indon
46D2 **Luxembourg** Grand Duchy, N W Europe
49D2 **Luxembourg** Lux
73A5 **Luxi** China
95C2 **Luxor** Egypt
61G1 **Luza** Russian Fed
61G1 **Luza** R Russian Fed
52A1 **Luzern** Switz
73B5 **Luzhai** China
73B4 **Luzhi** China
73B4 **Luzhou** China
35B1 **Luziânia** Brazil
79B2 **Luzon** I Phil

79B1 **Luzon Str** Phil
59C3 **L'vov** Ukraine
12B3 **Lybster** Scot
38H6 **Lycksele** Sweden
100B3 **Lydenburg** S Africa
8B3 **Lyell,Mt** USA
16A2 **Lykens** USA
43C4 **Lyme B** Eng
43C4 **Lyme Regis** Eng
11C3 **Lynchburg** USA
108A2 **Lyndhurst** Aust
15D2 **Lynn** USA
12G3 **Lynn Canal** Sd USA
17A1 **Lynn Haven** USA
5H4 **Lynn Lake** Can
5H3 **Lynx L** Can
49C2 **Lyon** France
12G3 **Lyon Canal** Sd USA
17B1 **Lyons** Georgia, USA
106A3 **Lyons** R Aust
47B2 **Lys** R Italy
61J2 **Lys'va** Russian Fed
111B2 **Lyttelton** NZ
13C2 **Lytton** Can
22A1 **Lytton** USA
58D2 **Lyubeshov** Ukraine
60E2 **Lyublino** Russian Fed

M

76C1 **Ma** R Viet
94B2 **Ma'agan** Jordan
94B2 **Ma'alot Tarshiha** Israel
92C3 **Ma'an** Jordan
73D3 **Ma'anshan** China
92C2 **Ma'arrat an Nu'mān** Syria
46C1 **Maas** R Neth
46C1 **Maaseik** Belg
79B3 **Maasin** Phil
57B2 **Maastricht** Neth
101C3 **Mabalane** Mozam
33F2 **Mabaruma** Guyana
42E3 **Mablethorpe** Eng
101C3 **Mabote** Mozam
58C2 **Mabrita** Belarus
58D2 **M'adel** Belarus
35C2 **Macaé** Brazil
9D3 **McAlester** USA
9D4 **McAllen** USA
101C2 **Macaloge** Mozam
33G3 **Macapá** Brazil
35C1 **Macarani** Brazil
32B4 **Macas** Ecuador
31D3 **Macaú** Brazil
73C5 **Macau** Dependency, China
98C2 **M'Bari** R CAR
13C2 **McBride** Can
12F2 **McCarthy** USA
13A2 **McCauley I** Can
42C3 **Macclesfield** Eng
6B1 **McClintock B** Can
4H2 **McClintock Chan** Can
4C2 **McClure** USA
22B2 **McClure,L** USA
4G2 **McClure Str** Can
19B3 **McComb** USA
8C2 **McCook** USA
6C2 **Macculloch,C** Can
13C1 **McCusker,Mt** Can
4F4 **McDame** Can
20C2 **McDermitt** USA
13E2 **Macdonald** R Can
106C3 **Macdonnell Ranges** Mts Aust
50A1 **Macedo de Cavaleiros** Port
55B2 **Macedonia** Republic, Europe
31D3 **Maceió** Brazil
97B4 **Macenta** Guinea
52B2 **Macerata** Italy
108A2 **Macfarlane,L** Aust
19B3 **McGehee** USA
45B3 **MacGillycuddys Reeks** Mts Irish Rep
4C3 **McGrath** USA
35B2 **Machado** Brazil
101C3 **Machaila** Mozam
99D3 **Machakos** Kenya
32B4 **Machala** Ecuador
101C3 **Machaze** Mozam
87B1 **Mācherla** India

94B2 **Machgharab** Leb
87C1 **Machilipatnam** India
32C1 **Machiques** Ven
32C6 **Machu-Picchu** Hist Site Peru
101C3 **Macia** Mozam
109C1 **MacIntyre** R Aust
107D3 **Mackay** Aust
106B3 **Mackay,L** Aust
14C2 **McKeesport** USA
13C1 **Mackenzie** Can
4F3 **Mackenzie** R Can
4G2 **Mackenzie B** Can
4G2 **Mackenzie King I** Can
4E3 **Mackenzie Mts** Can
14B1 **Mackinac,Str of** USA
14B1 **Mackinaw City** USA
12D2 **McKinley,Mt** USA
19A3 **McKinney** USA
6C2 **Mackinson Inlet** B Can
100B2 **Macksville** Aust
20B2 **Mclaoughlin,Mt** USA
100D1 **Maclean** Aust
100B4 **Maclear** S Africa
5G4 **McLennan** Can
13D2 **McLeod** R Can
4G3 **McLeod B** Can
4G3 **McLeod,L** Aust
13C1 **McLeod Lake** Can
4E3 **Macmillan** R Can
12H2 **Macmillan P** Can
20B2 **McMinnville** Oregon, USA
112B7 **McMurdo** Base Ant
12D2 **McNaughton L** Can
18B1 **Macomb** USA
53A2 **Macomer** Sardegna
101C2 **Macomia** Mozam
49C2 **Mâcon** France
11B3 **Macon** Georgia, USA
18B2 **Macon** Missouri, USA
100B2 **Macondo** Angola
18A2 **McPherson** USA
104F6 **Macquarie Is** Aust
109C2 **Macquarie** R Aust
109C4 **Macquarie Harbour** B Aust
109D2 **Macquarie,L** Aust
17B1 **McRae** USA
112B11 **Mac. Robertson Land** Region, Ant
45B3 **Macroom** Irish Rep
96C1 **M'Sila** Alg
4G3 **McTavish Arm** B Can
14D1 **Macumba** R Aust
47C2 **Macunaga** Italy
4F3 **McVicar Arm** B Can
59B3 **M'yardvár** Hung
94B3 **Mādabā** Jordan
95A3 **Madadi** Well Chad
89J10 **Madagascar** I Indian O
95A2 **Madama** Niger
71F4 **Madang** PNG
97C3 **Madaoua** Niger
86C2 **Madaripur** Bang
90B2 **Madau** Turkmenistan
15C1 **Madawaska** R Can
96A1 **Madeira** I Atlantic O
33E5 **Madeira** R Brazil
7D5 **Madeleine, Isle de la** Can
24B2 **Madera** Mexico
21A2 **Madera** USA
87A1 **Madgaon** India
86B1 **Madhubani** India
86A2 **Madhya Pradesh** State, India
87B2 **Madikeri** India
98B3 **Madimba** Zaire
98B3 **Madingo Kayes** Congo
98B3 **Madingou** Congo
10B3 **Madison** Indiana, USA
10B2 **Madison** Wisconsin, USA
18C2 **Madisonville** Kentucky, USA
19A3 **Madisonville** Texas, USA

78C4	**Madiun** Indon
99D2	**Mado Gashi** Kenya
47D1	**Madonna Di Campiglio** Italy
87C2	**Madras** India
20B2	**Madras** USA
29A6	**Madre de Dios** *I* Chile
32D6	**Madre de Dios** *R* Bol
50B1	**Madrid** Spain
50B2	**Madridejos** Spain
78C4	**Madura** *I* Indon
87B3	**Madurai** India
75B1	**Maebashi** Japan
76B3	**Mae Khlong** *R* Thai
77B4	**Mae Nam Lunang** *R* Thai
76C2	**Mae Nam Mun** *R* Thai
76B2	**Mae Nam Ping** *R* Thai
101D2	**Maevatanana** Madag
101G1	**Mafeteng** Lesotho
109C3	**Maffra** Aust
99D3	**Mafia** *I* Tanz
101G1	**Mafikeng** S Africa
30G4	**Mafra** Brazil
92C3	**Mafraq** Jordan
32C2	**Magangué** Colombia
34D3	**Magdalena** Arg
24A1	**Magdalena** Mexico
26C4	**Magdalena** *R* Colombia
78D1	**Magdalena,Mt** Malay
56C2	**Magdeburg** Germany
31C6	**Magé** Brazil
78C4	**Magelang** Indon
47C1	**Maggia** *R* Switz
92B4	**Maghâgha** Egypt
45C1	**Magherafelt** N Ire
55A2	**Maglie** Italy
61J3	**Magnitogorsk** Russian Fed
19B3	**Magnolia** USA
101C2	**Magoé** Mozam
15D1	**Magog** Can
23B1	**Magozal** Mexico
13E2	**Magrath** Can
7A3	**Maguse River** Can
76B1	**Magwe** Myan
90A2	**Mahābād** Iran
86B1	**Mahabharat Range** *Mts* Nepal
87A1	**Mahad** India
85D4	**Mahadeo Hills** India
101D2	**Mahajanga** Madag
100B3	**Mahalapye** Botswana
86A2	**Mahanadi** *R* India
101D2	**Mahanoro** Madag
16A2	**Mahanoy City** USA
87A1	**Maharashtra** State, India
86A2	**Mähäsamund** India
76C2	**Maha Sarakham** Thai
101D2	**Mahavavy** *R* Madag
87B1	**Mahbubnagar** India
96D1	**Mahdia** Tunisia
87B2	**Mahe** India
85D4	**Mahekar** India
87A1	**Mahé** *I* Comoros
86A2	**Mahendragarh** India
99D3	**Mahenge** Tanz
85C4	**Maheshana** India
110C1	**Mahia Pen** NZ
85D3	**Mahoba** India
51C2	**Mahon** Spain
12J1	**Mahony L** Can
96D1	**Mahrès** Tunisia
85C4	**Mahuva** India
32C1	**Maicao** Colombia
47B1	**Maiche** France
43E4	**Maidstone** Eng
98B1	**Maiduguri** Nig
86A2	**Maihar** India
86C2	**Maijdi** Bang
76B3	**Mail Kyun** *I* Myan
84A1	**Maimana** Afghan
14B1	**Main Chan** Can
98B3	**Mai-Ndombe** *L* Zaire
10D2	**Maine** State, USA
48B2	**Maine** *Region* France
44C2	**Mainland** *I* Scot
85D3	**Mainpuri** India
46A2	**Maintenon** France
101D2	**Maintirano** Madag
57B2	**Mainz** Germany
97A4	**Maio** *I* Cape Verde
29C2	**Maipó** *Mt* Arg/Chile
34D3	**Maipú** Arg
32D1	**Maiquetia** Ven
47B2	**Maira** *R* Italy
86C1	**Mairābāri** India
86C2	**Maiskhal** *I* Bang
107E4	**Maitland** New South Wales, Aust
108A2	**Maitland** S Australia, Aust
112C12	**Maitri** *Base* Ant
74D3	**Maizuru** Japan
70C4	**Majene** Indon
30B2	**Majes** *R* Peru
99D2	**Maji** Eth
72D2	**Majia He** *R* China
	Majunga = Mahajanga
70C4	**Makale** Indon
86B1	**Makalu** *Mt* India/ Nepal
98B2	**Makanza** Zaire
52C2	**Makarska** Croatia
61F2	**Makaryev** Russian Fed
	Makassar = Ujung Pandang
78D3	**Makassar Str** Indon
61H4	**Makat** Kazakhstan
97A4	**Makeni** Sierra Leone
60E4	**Makeyevka** Ukraine
100B3	**Makgadikgadi** *Salt Pan* Botswana
61G5	**Makhachkala** Russian Fed
99D3	**Makindu** Kenya
88H5	**Makkah** S Arabia
7C4	**Makkovik** Can
59C3	**Makó** Hung
98B2	**Makokou** Gabon
110C1	**Makorako,Mt** NZ
98B2	**Makoua** Congo
85C3	**Makrāna** India
85A3	**Makran Coast Range** *Mts* Pak
96C1	**Makthar** Tunisia
93D2	**Mākū** Iran
98C3	**Makumbi** Zaire
74C4	**Makurazaki** Japan
97C4	**Makurdi** Nig
79B4	**Malabang** Phil
87A2	**Malabar Coast** India
89E7	**Malabo** Bioko
77C5	**Malacca,Str of** S E Asia
32C2	**Málaga** Colombia
50B2	**Málaga** Spain
101D3	**Malaimbandy** Madag
99D2	**Malakal** Sudan
84C2	**Malakand** Pak
78C4	**Malang** Indon
98B3	**Malange** Angola
97C3	**Malanville** Benin
39H7	**Mälaren** *L* Sweden
34B3	**Malargüe** Arg
12F3	**Malaspina Gl** USA
93C2	**Malatya** Turk
101C2	**Malawi** Republic, Africa
	Malawi,L = Nyasa,L
79C4	**Malaybalay** Phil
90A3	**Malāyer** Iran
70B3	**Malaysia** Federation, S E Asia
93D2	**Malazgirt** Turk
58B2	**Malbork** Pol
56C2	**Malchin** Germany
18C2	**Malden** USA
83B5	**Maldives** *Is* Indian O
104B4	**Maldives Ridge** Indian O
29F2	**Maldonado** Urug
47D1	**Male** Italy
85C4	**Malegaon** India
59B3	**Malé Karpaty** *Upland* Slovakia
101C2	**Malema** Mozam
84B2	**Mālestān** Afghan
38H5	**Malgomaj** *L* Sweden
95B3	**Malha** *Well* Sudan
20C2	**Malheur L** USA
97B3	**Mali** Republic, Africa
78D1	**Malinau** Indon
99E3	**Malindi** Kenya
	Malines = Mechelen
40B2	**Malin Head** *Pt* Irish Rep
45A1	**Malkalka Range** *Mts* India
85D4	**Malkäpur** India
55C2	**Malkara** Turk
54C2	**Malko Tûrnovo** Bulg
44B3	**Mallaig** Scot
95C2	**Mallawi** Egypt
47D1	**Mälles Venosta** Italy
51C2	**Mallorca** *I* Spain
45B2	**Mallow** Irish Rep
38G6	**Malm** Nor
38J5	**Malmberget** Sweden
46D1	**Malmédy** Germany
43C4	**Malmesbury** Eng
100A4	**Malmesbury** S Africa
39G7	**Malmö** Sweden
61G2	**Malmyzh** Russian Fed
79B3	**Malolos** Phil
15D2	**Malone** USA
101G1	**Maloti** *Mts* Lesotho
38F6	**Måløy** Nor
28A2	**Malpelo** *I* Colombia
34A2	**Malpo** *R* Chile
85D3	**Mālpura** India
8C2	**Malta** Montana, USA
53B3	**Malta Chan** Malta/ Italy
53B3	**Malta** *I* Medit S
100A3	**Maltahöhe** Namibia
42D2	**Malton** Eng
39G6	**Malung** Sweden
87A1	**Mälvan** India
19B3	**Malvern** USA
61G4	**Malwa Plat** India
63D2	**Mama** Russian Fed
61H2	**Mamadysh** Russian Fed
99C2	**Mambasa** Zaire
71E4	**Mamberamo** *R* Indon
98B2	**Mambéré** *R* CAR
98A2	**Mamfé** Cam
33D6	**Mamoré** *R* Bol
97A3	**Mamou** Guinea
101D2	**Mampikony** Madag
97B4	**Mampong** Ghana
94B3	**Mamshit** *Hist Site* Israel
100B3	**Mamuno** Botswana
34B2	**Man** Côte d'Ivoire
21C4	**Mana** Hawaiian Is
101D3	**Manabo** Madag
33E4	**Manacapuru** Brazil
51C2	**Manacor** Spain
70D3	**Manado** Indon
25D3	**Managua** Nic
101D3	**Manakara** Madag
101D2	**Mananara** Madag
111A3	**Manapouri** NZ
111A3	**Manapouri,L** NZ
86C1	**Manas** Bhutan
82C1	**Manas** China
65K5	**Manas Hu** *L* China
86A1	**Manaslu** *Mt* Nepal
16B2	**Manasquan** USA
33E3	**Manaus** Brazil
92B2	**Manavgat** Turk
93C2	**Manbij** Syria
42B2	**Man,Calf of** *I* Eng
87B1	**Mancheral** India
	Manchester = Manchester Connecticut, USA
42C3	**Manchester** Eng
10C2	**Manchester** New Hampshire, USA
16A2	**Manchester** Pennsylvania, USA
69E2	**Manchuria** *Hist Region,* China
9184	**Mand** *R* Iran
101C2	**Manda** Tanz
35A2	**Mandaguari** Brazil
39F7	**Mandal** Nor
76B1	**Mandalay** Myan
68C2	**Mandalgovi** Mongolia
8C2	**Mandan** USA
14A2	**Mandelona** USA
28B3	**Mandera** Eth
26B3	**Mandeville** Jamaica
101C2	**Mandimba** Mozam
86A2	**Mandla** India
101D2	**Mandritsara** Madag
101D2	**Mandvi** India
53C2	**Manduria** Italy
85B4	**Mändvi** India
87B2	**Mandya** India
58D2	**Manevichi** Ukraine
42D3	**Manfield** Eng
53C2	**Manfredonia** Italy
98B1	**Manga** *Desert Region* Niger
110C1	**Mangakino** NZ
54C2	**Mangalia** Rom
98B1	**Mangalmé** Chad
87A2	**Mangalore** India
68B3	**Mangnai** China
101C2	**Mangoche** Malawi
101D3	**Mangoky** *R* Madag
71D4	**Mangole** *I* Indon
85B4	**Mängral** India
63E2	**Mangui,** China
8D3	**Manhattan** USA
31C6	**Manhuaçu** Brazil
11A4	**Manicoré** Brazil
7D5	**Manicouagan** *R* Can
91A4	**Manifah** S Arabia
79B3	**Manila** Phil
109D2	**Manilla** Aust
97B3	**Maninian** Côte d'Ivoire
86C2	**Manipur** State, India
86C2	**Manipur** *R* Myan
92A2	**Manisa** Turk
41C3	**Man,Isle of** Irish S
14A2	**Manistee** USA
14A2	**Manistee** USA
14A1	**Manistique** USA
5H4	**Manitoba** Province, Can
13F2	**Manito,L** Can
14A1	**Manitou Is** USA
7B5	**Manitoulin** *I* Can
14A2	**Manitowoc** USA
32B2	**Manizales** Colombia
101D3	**Manja** Madag
106A4	**Manjimup** Aust
87B1	**Mänjra** *R* India
10A2	**Mankato** USA
97A4	**Mankono** Côte d'Ivoire
12D2	**Manley Hot Springs**
110B1	**Manly** NZ
85C4	**Manmäd** India
78A3	**Manna** Indon
14A2	**Mannahill** Aust
87B3	**Mannar** Sri Lanka
87B3	**Mannar,G of** India
87B2	**Mannärgudi** India
57B3	**Mannheim** Germany
13D1	**Manning** Can
17B1	**Manning** USA
108A2	**Mannum** Aust
97A4	**Mano** Sierra Leone
98C3	**Manono** Zaire
76B3	**Manoron** Myan
75B1	**Mano-wan** *B* Japan
74B2	**Manp'o** N Korea
10B2	**Mansa** India
100B2	**Mansa** Zambia
6B3	**Mansel I** Can
19B2	**Mansfield** Arkansas, USA
108C3	**Mansfield** Aust
19B3	**Mansfield** Louisiana, USA
10B2	**Mansfield** Massachusetts, USA
10B2	**Mansfield** Ohio, USA

Mansfield

44

15C2	**Mansfield** Pennsylvania, USA
71E2	**Mansfield Deep** Pacific O
32A4	**Manta** Ecuador
79A4	**Mantalingajan,Mt** Phil
32B6	**Mantaro** *R* Peru
22B2	**Manteca** USA
48C2	**Mantes** France
52B1	**Mantova** Italy
38J6	**Mantta** Fin
61F2	**Manturovo** Russian Fed
35A2	**Manuel Ribas** Brazil
79B4	**Manukan** Phil
110B1	**Manukau** NZ
71F4	**Manus** *r I* Pacific O
50B2	**Manzanares** Spain
25E2	**Manzanillo** Cuba
24B3	**Manzanillo** Mexico
63D3	**Manzhouli** China
94C3	**Manzil** Jordan
101C3	**Manzini** Swaziland
98B1	**Mao** Chad
72A2	**Maomao Shan** *Mt* China
73C5	**Maoming** China
101C3	**Mapai** Mozam
71E3	**Mapia** *Is* Pacific O
79A4	**Mapin** *r I* Phil
5H5	**Maple Creek** Can
101H1	**Maputo** Mozam
101H1	**Maputo** *R* Mozam
	Ma Qu = Huange He
72A3	**Maqu** China
86B1	**Maquan He** *R* China
98B3	**Maquela do Zombo** Angola
29C4	**Maquinchao** Arg
31B3	**Marabá** Brazil
32C1	**Maracaibo** Ven
32D1	**Maracay** Ven
95A2	**Marádah** Libya
97C3	**Maradi** Niger
90A2	**Marágheh** Iran
99D2	**Maralal** Kenya
107F1	**Maramasike** *I* Solomon Is
100B2	**Maramba** Zambia
90A2	**Marand** Iran
31B2	**Maranhão** State, Brazil
109C1	**Maranoa** *R* Aust
32B4	**Marañón** *R* Peru
1TB2	**Marathon** Florida, USA
78D2	**Maratua** *I* Indon
23A2	**Maravatio** Mexico
79B4	**Marawi** Phil
34B2	**Marayes** Arg
50B2	**Marbella** Spain
106A3	**Marble Bar** Aust
108B3	**Marblehall** S Africa
16D1	**Marblehead** USA
57B2	**Marburg** Germany
57B2	**Marche** Belg
50A2	**Marchean** Spain
46C1	**Marche-en-Famenne** Belg
32J7	**Marchena** *I* Ecuador
17B2	**Marco** USA
34C2	**Marcos Juárez** Arg
12E2	**Marcus Baker,Mt** USA
15D2	**Marcy,Mt** USA
84C2	**Mardan** Pak
29E3	**Mar del Plata** Arg
93D2	**Mardin** Turk
99D1	**Mareb** *R* Eritrea/Eth
16B1	**Margaretville** USA
43E4	**Margate** Eng
54B1	**Marghita** Rom
109C4	**Maria I** Aust
13E1	**Mariana Lake** Can
104F3	**Marianas Trench** Pacific O
86C1	**Mariani** India
19B3	**Marianna** Arkansas, USA
17A1	**Marianna** Florida, USA

7G4	**Maria Van Diemen,C** NZ
59B3	**Mariazell** Austria
52C1	**Maribor** Slovenia
99C2	**Maridi** Sudan
112B5	**Marie Byrd Land** Region, Ant
27E3	**Marie Galante** *I* Caribbean S
39H6	**Mariehamn** Fin
46C1	**Mariembourg** Belg
33G2	**Marienburg** Surinam
100A3	**Mariental** Namibia
39G7	**Mariestad** Sweden
17B1	**Marietta** Georgia, USA
14B3	**Marietta** Ohio, USA
19A3	**Marietta** Oklahoma, USA
27Q2	**Marigot** Dominica
60B3	**Marijampole** Lithuania
31B6	**Marília** Brazil
98B3	**Marimba** Angola
79B3	**Marinduque** *I* Phil
10B2	**Marinette** USA
30F3	**Maringá** Brazil
98C2	**Maringa** *R* Zaire
18B2	**Marion** Arkansas, USA
18C2	**Marion** Illinois, USA
10B2	**Marion** Indiana, USA
10B2	**Marion** Ohio, USA
17C1	**Marion** S Carolina, USA
11B3	**Marion,L** USA
107E2	**Marion Reef** Aust
22B2	**Mariposa** USA
22B2	**Mariposa** *R* USA
22B2	**Mariposa Res** USA
60C5	**Marira** *R* Bulg
60E4	**Mariupol'** Ukraine
61G2	**Mari El** Division, Russian Fed
94B2	**Marjayoun** Leb
58D2	**Marjina Gora** Belarus
94B3	**Marka** Jordan
99E2	**Marka** Somalia
56C1	**Markaryd** Sweden
43C3	**Market Drayton** Eng
43D3	**Market Harborough** Eng
112A	**Markham,Mt** Ant
22C1	**Markleeville** USA
16D1	**Marlboro** Massachusetts, USA
107D3	**Marlborough** Aust
46B2	**Marle** France
43A3	**Marlin** USA
48C3	**Marmande** France
55C2	**Marmara,Adi** *I* Turk
92A1	**Marmara,S of** Turk
55C3	**Marmaris** Turk
14B3	**Marmet** USA
52B1	**Marmolada** *Mt* Italy
12D3	**Marmot B** USA
47A1	**Marnay** France
46B2	**Marne** Department, France
46B2	**Marne** *R* France
98B2	**Maro** Chad
101D2	**Maroantsetra** Madag
101C2	**Marodera** Zim
33G3	**Maroni** *R* French Guiana
109D1	**Maroochydore** Aust
98B1	**Maroua** Cam
101D2	**Marovoay** Madag
118B4	**Marquesas Keys** *Is* USA
10B2	**Marquette** USA
46A1	**Marquise** France
109C2	**Marra** *R* Aust
101H1	**Marracuene** Mozam
96B1	**Marrakech** Mor
106C3	**Marree** Aust
19B4	**Marrero** USA
101C2	**Marromeu** Mozam
101C2	**Marrupa** Mozam
95C2	**Marsa Alam** Egypt
99D2	**Marsabit** Kenya

53B3	**Marsala** Italy
49D3	**Marseille** France
12B2	**Marshall** Alaska, USA
14A3	**Marshall** Illinois, USA
14B2	**Marshall** Michigan, USA
18B2	**Marshall** Missouri, USA
11A3	**Marshall** Texas, USA
105G3	**Marshall Is** Pacific O
18B2	**Marshfield** Missouri, USA
26B1	**Marsh Harbour** The Bahamas
19B4	**Marsh I** USA
12H2	**Marsh L** Can
76B2	**Martaban,G of** Myan
78A3	**Martapura** Indon
78C3	**Martapura** Indon
15D2	**Martha's Vineyard** *I* USA
49D2	**Martigny** Switz
59B3	**Martin** Slovakia
111C2	**Martinborough** NZ
34B3	**Martin de Loyola** Arg
23B1	**Martinez de la Torre** Mexico
27E4	**Martinique** *I* Caribbean S
17A1	**Martin,L** USA
15C3	**Martinsburg** USA
14B2	**Martins Ferry** USA
103G6	**Martin Vaz** *I* Atlantic O
49D3	**Martiques** France
110C2	**Marton** NZ
50B2	**Martos** Spain
78D1	**Marudi** Malay
84B2	**Maruf** Afghan
75A2	**Marugame** Japan
85C3	**Mārwār** India
65H6	**Mary** Turkmenistan
107E3	**Maryborough** Queensland, Aust
108B3	**Maryborough** Victoria, Aust
5F4	**Mary Henry,Mt** Can
10C3	**Maryland** State, USA
42C2	**Maryport** Eng
21A2	**Marysville** California, USA
18A2	**Marysville** Kansas, USA
20B1	**Marysville** Washington, USA
10A2	**Maryville** Iowa, USA
18B1	**Maryville** Missouri, USA
95A2	**Marzuq** Libya
94B2	**Mas'adah** Syria
99D3	**Masai Steppe** Upland Tanz
99D3	**Masaka** Uganda
93E2	**Masally** Azerbaijan
74B3	**Masan** S Korea
101C2	**Masasi** Tanz
25D3	**Masaya** Nic
79B3	**Masbate** Phil
79B3	**Masbate** *I* Phil
96C1	**Mascara** Alg
23A1	**Mascota** Mexico
35D1	**Mascote** Brazil
101G1	**Maseru** Lesotho
66C3	**Mashad** Iran
84B2	**Mashaki** Afghan
90C2	**Mashhad** Iran
98B3	**Masi-Manimba** Zaire
99D2	**Masindi** Uganda
99C3	**Masisi** Zaire
90A3	**Masjed Soleyman** Iran
101E2	**Masoala** *C* Madag
10A2	**Mason City** USA
91C5	**Masqat** Oman
52B2	**Massa** Italy
10C2	**Massachusetts** State, USA
15D2	**Massachusetts B** USA
98B1	**Massakori** Chad
101C3	**Massangena** Mozam

	Massawa = Mits'iwa
15D2	**Massena** USA
98A2	**Masseya** Chad
14B1	**Massey** Can
49C2	**Massif Central** *Mts* France
98B2	**Massif de l'Adamaoua** *Mts* Cam
26C3	**Massif de la Hotte** *Mts* Haiti
101D3	**Massif de l'Isalo** Upland Madag
98C2	**Massif des Bongo** Upland CAR
49D2	**Massif du Pelvoux** *Mts* France
101D2	**Massif du Tsaratanana** *Mt* Madag
14B2	**Massillon** USA
97B3	**Massina** Region, Mali
101C3	**Massinga** Mozam
101C3	**Massingir** Mozam
	Massoukou = Franceville
61H4	**Masteksay** Kazakhstan
111C2	**Masterton** NZ
74C4	**Masuda** Japan
101C3	**Masvingo** Zim
92C2	**Maşyāf** Syria
98B3	**Matadi** Zaire
25D3	**Matagalpa** Nic
7C4	**Matagami** Can
9D4	**Matagorda B** USA
110C1	**Matakana I** NZ
100A2	**Matala** Angola
87C3	**Matale** Sri Lanka
97A3	**Matam** Sen
97C3	**Matameye** Niger
24C2	**Matamoros** Mexico
95B2	**Ma'tan as Sarra** *Well* Libya
7D5	**Matane** Can
25D2	**Matanzas** Cuba
34A2	**Mataquito** *R* Chile
87C3	**Matara** Sri Lanka
106A1	**Mataram** Indon
30B2	**Matarani** Peru
51C1	**Mataró** Spain
111A3	**Mataura** NZ
24B2	**Matehuala** Mexico
27L1	**Matelot** Trinidad
53C2	**Matera** Italy
59C3	**Mátészalka** Hung
85D3	**Mathura** India
79C4	**Mati** Phil
78D3	**Matisiri** *I* Indon
43D3	**Matlock** Eng
33F6	**Mato Grosso** Brazil
33F6	**Mato Grosso** State, Brazil
30E2	**Mato Grosso do Sul** State, Brazil
101H1	**Matola** Mozam
91C5	**Matrah** Oman
92A3	**Matrûh** Egypt
74C3	**Matsue** Japan
74E2	**Matsumae** Japan
74C3	**Matsumoto** Japan
74D4	**Matsusaka** Japan
74C4	**Matsuyama** Japan
7B5	**Mattagami** *R* Can
15C1	**Mattawa** Can
52A1	**Matterhorn** *Mt* Italy/ Switz
26C2	**Matthew Town** The Bahamas
16C2	**Mattituck** USA
18C2	**Mattoon** USA
84B2	**Matun** Afghan
27L1	**Matura B** Trinidad
33E2	**Maturín** Ven
86A1	**Mau** India
101C2	**Maúa** Mozam
49C1	**Maubeuge** France
108B2	**Maude** Aust
103J8	**Maud Seamount** Atlantic O
21C4	**Maui** *I* Hawaiian Is
34A3	**Maule** *R* Chile
14B2	**Maumee** USA
14B2	**Maumee** *R* USA
100B2	**Maun** Botswana

21C4 **Mauna Kea** *Mt* Hawaiian Is
21C4 **Mauna Loa** *Mt* Hawaiian Is
4F3 **Maunoir,L** Can
4F3 **Maunoir,L** Can
48C2 **Maurac** France
96A2 **Mauritania** Republic, Africa
100E3 **Mauritius** *I* Indian O
100B2 **Mavinga** Angola
86C2 **Mawlaik** Myan
**Mawlamyine =
Moulmein**
112C10 **Mawson** *Base* Ant
98B3 **Maxixe** Mozam
63F2 **Maya** *R* Russian Fed
93D2 **Mayādīn** Syria
11C4 **Mayaguana** *I* The Bahamas
27D3 **Mayagüez** Puerto Rico
97C3 **Mayahi** Niger
98B3 **Mayama** Congo
90C2 **Mayamey** Iran
42B2 **Maybole** Scot
10C3 **May,C** USA
109C4 **Maydena** Aust
46D1 **Mayen** Germany
48B2 **Mayenne** France
13D2 **Mayerthorpe** Can
18C2 **Mayfield** USA
61E5 **Maykop** Russian Fed
65H6 **Maymaneh** Afghan
76B1 **Maymyo** Myan
4E3 **Mayo** Can
45B2 **Mayo** County, Irish Rep
16A3 **Mayo** USA
45B1 **Mayo,Mts of** Irish Rep
79B3 **Mayon** *Mt* Phil
51C2 **Mayor** *Mt* Spain
34C3 **Mayor Buratovich** Arg
110C1 **Mayor I** NZ
30D2 **Mayor P Lagerenza** Par
101D2 **Mayotte** *I* Indian O
27H2 **May Pen** Jamaica
79B3 **May Point,C** USA
47D1 **Mayrhofen** Austria
16B3 **Mays Landing** USA
14B3 **Maysville** USA
98B3 **Mayumba** Gabon
10D2 **Mazabuka** Zambia
84D1 **Mazar** China
94B3 **Mazār** Jordan
53B3 **Mazara del Vallo** Italy
84B1 **Mazar-i-Sharif** Afghan
24B2 **Mazatlán** Mexico
60B2 **Mazeikiai** Lithuania
94B3 **Mazra** Jordan
10C3 **Mbabane** Swaziland
98B2 **Mbaïki** CAR
99D3 **Mbala** Zambia
100B3 **Mbalabala** Zim
99D2 **Mbale** Uganda
98B2 **Mbalmayo** Cam
98B2 **Mbam** *R* Cam
101C2 **Mbamba Bay** Tanz
98B2 **Mbandaka** Zaïre
98B3 **Mbanza Congo** Angola
98B3 **Mbanza-Ngungu** Zaïre
99D3 **Mbarara** Uganda
98B2 **Mbenza** Congo
98B2 **Mbére** *R* Cam
99D3 **Mbeya** Tanz
98B3 **Mbinda** Congo
97A3 **Mbout** Maur
98C3 **Mbuji-Mayi** Zaïre
99D3 **Mbulu** Tanz
96B2 **Mcherrah** Region, Alg
101C2 **Mchinji** Malawi
9B3 **Mead,L** USA
5H4 **Meadow Lake** Can
14B2 **Meadville** USA
7E4 **Mealy Mts** Can
109C1 **Meandarra** Aust
5G4 **Meander River** Can

45C2 **Meath** County, Irish Rep
49C2 **Meaux** France
16C1 **Mechanicville** USA
56A2 **Mechelen** Belg
96B1 **Mecheria** Alg
56C2 **Mecklenburg-Vorpommern** *State* Germany
56C2 **Mecklenburger Bucht** *B* Germany
101C2 **Meconta** Mozam
101C2 **Mecubari** Mozam
101D2 **Mecufi** Mozam
101C2 **Mecula** Mozam
70A3 **Medan** Indon
34C3 **Médanos** Arg
34D2 **Médanos** Arg
13E2 **Medecine Hat** Can
32B2 **Medellín** Colombia
96D1 **Medenine** Tunisia
8A2 **Medford** USA
54C2 **Medgidia** Rom
34D3 **Media Agua** Arg
54B1 **Mediaş** Rom
20C1 **Medical Lake** USA
5G5 **Medicine Hat** Can
35C1 **Medina** Brazil
80B3 **Medina** S Arabia
50B1 **Medinaceli** Spain
50B1 **Medina del Campo** Spain
50A1 **Medina de Rio Seco** Spain
86B2 **Medinipur** India
88E4 **Mediterranean S** Europe
13F2 **Medley** Can
61J3 **Mednogorsk** Russian Fed
86D1 **Mêdog** China
98B2 **Médouneu** Gabon
61F3 **Medvedica** *R* Russian Fed
64E3 **Medvezh'yegorsk** Russian Fed
106A3 **Meekatharra** Aust
84D3 **Meerut** India
99D2 **Méga** Eth
55B3 **Megalópolis** Greece
55B3 **Mégara** Greece
86C1 **Meghálaya** *State,* India
86C2 **Meghna** *R* Bang
94B2 **Megiddo** *Hist Site* Israel
91B4 **Mehran** *R* Iran
90B3 **Mehriz** Iran
35B1 **Meia Ponte** *R* Brazil
88B2 **Meiganga** Cam
76B1 **Meiktila** Myan
47C1 **Meiringen** Switz
73A4 **Meishan** China
57C2 **Meissen** Germany
73D5 **Mei Xian** China
73D5 **Meizhou** China
30B3 **Mejillones** Chile
98B2 **Mekambo** Gabon
99D1 **Mek'elé** Eth
96B1 **Meknès** Mor
76D3 **Mekong** *R* Viet
97C3 **Mekrou** *R* Benin
77C5 **Melaka** Malay
104F4 **Melanesia** *Region* Pacific O
78C3 **Melawi** *R* Indon
107D4 **Melbourne** Aust
11B4 **Melbourne** USA
Melchor Múzquiz Mexico
61J3 **Meleuz** Russian Fed
98B1 **Melfi** Chad
5H4 **Melfort** Can
96B1 **Melilla** N W Africa
29B4 **Melimoyu** *Mt* Chile
34C2 **Melincué** Arg
34C2 **Melipilla** Chile
60E4 **Melitopol'** Ukraine
6D2 **Melville Bugt** *B* Greenland
99D2 **Melka Guba** Eth
101H1 **Melmoth** S Africa
34C2 **Melo** Urug
29F2 **Melo** Urug

22B2 **Melones Res** USA
12D1 **Melozitna** *R* USA
47C1 **Mels** Switz
43D3 **Melton Mowbray** Eng
49C2 **Melun** France
5H4 **Melville** Can
27D2 **Melville,C** Dominica
4F3 **Melville Hills** *Mts* Can
106C2 **Melville I** Aust
4G2 **Melville I** Can
7E4 **Melville,L** Can
6B3 **Melville Pen** Can
45B1 **Melvin,L** Irish Rep
101B2 **Memba** Mozam
106A1 **Memboro** Indon
57C3 **Memmingen** Germany
78B2 **Mempawah** Indon
11B3 **Memphis** Tennessee, USA
19B3 **Mena** USA
43B3 **Menai Str** Wales
97C3 **Menaka** Mali
14A2 **Menasha** USA
78C3 **Mendawai** *R* Indon
49C3 **Mende** France
99D2 **Mendebo Mts** Eth
43C4 **Mendip Hills** *Upland* Eng
20B2 **Mendocino,C** USA
105J2 **Mendocino Seascarp** Pacific O
22B2 **Mendota** California, USA
29C2 **Mendoza** Arg
29C2 **Mendoza** *State,* Arg
55C3 **Menemen** Turk
46B1 **Menen** Belg
72D3 **Mengcheng** China
78B3 **Menggala** Indon
78B1 **Menghai** China
73A5 **Mengla** China
76B1 **Menglian** China
73A5 **Mengzi** China
107D4 **Meninde** Aust
108B2 **Meninde L** Aust
108A3 **Meningie** Aust
14A1 **Menominee** USA
14A2 **Menomonee Falls** USA
100A2 **Menongue** Angola
51C1 **Menorca** *I* Spain
12F2 **Mentasta Mts** USA
78B3 **Mentok** Indon
14B2 **Mentor** USA
46B2 **Menton** France
72A2 **Menyuan** China
61H2 **Menzelinsk** Russian Fed
56B2 **Meppen** Germany
78D2 **Merah** Indon
18B2 **Meramec** *R* USA
52B1 **Merano** Italy
71F4 **Merauke** Indon
8A3 **Merced** USA
22B2 **Merced** *R* USA
29B2 **Mercedario** *Mt* Chile
29C2 **Mercedes** Buenos Aires, Arg
30E4 **Mercedes** Corrientes, Arg
29E2 **Mercedes** Urug
110C1 **Mercury B** NZ
110C1 **Mercury Is** NZ
4F2 **Mercy Bay** Can
4F2 **Mercy,C** Can
99E2 **Meregh** Somalia
76B3 **Mergui** Myan
76B3 **Mergui Arch** Myan
50A2 **Mérida** Spain
32C2 **Mérida** Ven
11B3 **Meridian** USA
109C3 **Merimbula** Aust
42B2 **Merrick** *Mt* Scot
14A2 **Merrillville** USA
13C2 **Merritt** Can
17B2 **Merritt Island** USA
109D2 **Merriwa** Aust

99E1 **Mersa Fatma** Eritrea
51B2 **Mers el Kebir** Alg
42C3 **Mersey** *R* Eng
42C3 **Merseyside** Metropolitan County, Eng
92B2 **Mersin** Turk
77C5 **Mersing** Malay
85C3 **Merta** India
43C4 **Merthyr Tydfil** Wales
43C4 **Merthyr Tydfil** County Wales
50A2 **Mertola** Port
99D3 **Meru** *Mt* Tanz
92C1 **Merzifon** Turk
46D2 **Merzig** Germany
9B3 **Mesa** USA
46E1 **Meschede** Germany
93D1 **Mescit Dağ** *Mt* Turk
12C3 **Meshik** USA
99C2 **Meshra Er Req** Sudan
47C1 **Mesocco** Switz
55B3 **Mesolóngion** Greece
19A3 **Mesquite** Texas, USA
101C2 **Messalo** *R* Mozam
53C3 **Messina** Italy
100B3 **Messina** S Africa
55B3 **Messini** Greece
55B3 **Messiniakós Kólpos** *G* Greece
54B2 **Meta** *R* Bulg
52B1 **Mestre** Italy
32C3 **Meta** *R* Colombia
60D2 **Meta** *R* Ven
32D2 **Meta** *R* Ven
6C3 **Meta Incognito Pen** Can
19B4 **Metairie** USA
20C1 **Metaline Falls** USA
84B1 **Metan** Arg
101C2 **Metangula** Mozam
53C2 **Metaponto** Italy
44C3 **Methil** Scot
16D1 **Methuen** USA
11B2 **Methven** NZ
12H3 **Metlakatla** USA
18C2 **Metropolis** USA
87B2 **Mettür** India
49D2 **Metz** France
70A3 **Meulaboh** Indon
46A2 **Meulan** France
46C2 **Meuse** Department, France
49D2 **Meuse** *R* France
19A3 **Mexia** USA
24A1 **Mexicali** Mexico
24B2 **Mexico** Federal Republic, Cent America
24C3 **México** Mexico
23A2 **México** State, Mexico
18B2 **Mexico** USA
24C2 **México,G of** Cent America
94B3 **Mezada** *Hist Site* Israel
23B2 **Mezcala** Mexico
64F3 **Mezen'** Russian Fed
64G2 **Mezhdusharskiy, Ostrov** *I* Russian Fed
85D4 **Mhow** India
23B2 **Miahuatlán** Mexico
11B4 **Miami** Florida, USA
18B2 **Miami** Oklahoma, USA
11B4 **Miami Beach** USA
90A2 **Miandowâb** Iran
101D2 **Miandrivazo** Madag
90A2 **Miâneh** Iran
84C2 **Mianwali** Pak
73A3 **Mianyang** China
73C3 **Mianyang** China
73A3 **Mianyang** China
72E2 **Miaodao Qundao** *Arch* China
73B4 **Miao Ling** *Upland* China
61K3 **Miass** Russian Fed
59C3 **Michalovce** Slovakia
27D3 **Miches** Dom Rep
10B2 **Michigan** State, USA
14A2 **Michigan City** USA

10B2	**Michigan,L** USA
7B5	**Michipicoten I** Can
23A2	**Michoacan** State, Mexico
54C2	**Michurin** Bulg
61F3	**Michurinsk** Russian Fed
104F3	**Micronesia** *Region* Pacific O
78B2	**Midai** *I* Indon
102F4	**Mid Atlantic Ridge** Atlantic O
46B1	**Middelburg** Neth
20B2	**Middle Alkali L** USA
16D2	**Middleboro** USA
100B4	**Middleburg** Cape Province, S Africa
16A2	**Middleburg** Pennsylvania, USA
101G1	**Middleburg** Transvaal, S Africa
16B1	**Middleburgh** USA
15D2	**Middlebury** USA
11B3	**Middlesboro** USA
42D2	**Middlesbrough** Eng
42D2	**Middlesbrough** County Eng
16C2	**Middletown** Connecticut, USA
16B3	**Middletown** Delaware, USA
15D2	**Middletown** New York, USA
14B3	**Middletown** Ohio, USA
16A2	**Middletown** Pennsylvania, USA
96B1	**Midelt** Mor
104B4	**Mid Indian Basin** Indian O
104B4	**Mid Indian Ridge** Indian O
7C5	**Midland** Can
14B2	**Midland** Michigan, USA
9C3	**Midland** Texas, USA
101D3	**Midongy Atsimo** Madag
105G2	**Mid Pacific Mts** Pacific O
20C2	**Midvale** USA
105H2	**Midway Is** Pacific O
18A2	**Midwest City** USA
93D2	**Midyat** Turk
54B2	**Midžor** *R* Serbia, Yugos
59B2	**Mielec** Pol
54C1	**Miercurea-Ciuc** Rom
50A1	**Mieres** Spain
16A2	**Mifflintown** USA
72D1	**Mijun Shuiku** *Res* China
54B2	**Mikhaylovgrad** Bulg
61F3	**Mikhaylovka** Russian Fed
65J4	**Mikhaylovskiy** Russian Fed
38K6	**Mikkeli** Fin
55C3	**Mikonos** *I* Greece
59B3	**Mikulov** Czech Republic
99D3	**Mikumi** Tanz
74D3	**Mikuni-sammyaku** *Mts* Japan
75B2	**Mikura-jima** *I* Japan
32B4	**Milagro** Ecuador
	Milan = **Milano**
51C2	**Milana** Alg
101C2	**Milange** Mozam
52A1	**Milano** Italy
92A2	**Milas** Turk
107D4	**Mildura** Aust
73A5	**Mile** China
93D3	**Mileh Tharthār** *L* Iraq
107E3	**Miles** Aust
8C2	**Miles City** USA
16C2	**Milford** Connecticut, USA
15C3	**Milford** Delaware, USA
15D2	**Milford** Massachusetts, USA
18A1	**Milford** Nebraska, USA
16B2	**Milford** Pennsylvania, USA
43B4	**Milford Haven** Wales
43B4	**Milford Haven** Wales
18A2	**Milford L** USA
111A2	**Milford Sd** NZ
13E2	**Milk River** Can
49C3	**Millau** France
16C2	**Millbrook** USA
17B1	**Milledgeville** USA
12F2	**Miller,Mt** USA
61F4	**Millerovo** Russian Fed
16A2	**Millersburg** USA
108A1	**Millers Creek** Aust
16C1	**Millers Falls** USA
22C2	**Millerton** USA
108B3	**Millicent** Aust
109D1	**Millmerran** Aust
45B2	**Milltown Malbay** Irish Rep
22A2	**Mill Valley** USA
15D3	**Millville** USA
6H2	**Milne Land** *I* Greenland
21C4	**Milolii** Hawaiian Is
55B3	**Milos** *I* Greece
107D3	**Milparinka** Aust
16A2	**Milroy** USA
111A3	**Milton** NZ
16A2	**Milton** Pennsylvania, USA
10B2	**Milwaukee** USA
51C2	**Mina** *R* Alg
93E4	**Minā' al Aḥmadī** Kuwait
91C4	**Mināb** Iran
74C4	**Minamata** Japan
78A2	**Minas** Indon
29E2	**Minas** Urug
31B5	**Minas Gerais** State, Brazil
35C1	**Minas Novas** Brazil
25C3	**Minatitlan** Mexico
76A1	**Minbu** Myan
76A1	**Minbya** Myan
34A2	**Mincha** Chile
44A3	**Minch,Little** *Sd* Scot
44A2	**Minch,North** *Sd* Scot
40B2	**Minch,The** *Sd* Scot
12D2	**Minchumina,L** USA
47D2	**Mincio** *R* Italy
79B4	**Mindanao** *I* Phil
19B3	**Minden** Louisiana, USA
56B2	**Minden** Germany
108B2	**Mindona L** Aust
79B3	**Mindoro** *I* Phil
79B3	**Mindoro Str** Phil
45C3	**Mine Hd** *C* Irish Rep
43C4	**Minehead** Eng
30F2	**Mineiros** Brazil
19A3	**Mineola** USA
23B1	**Mineral de Monte** Mexico
16A2	**Minersville** USA
108B2	**Mingary** Aust
72A2	**Minhe** China
87A3	**Minicoy** *I* India
73D4	**Min Jiang** *R* Fujian, China
73A4	**Min Jiang** *R* Sichuan, China
22C2	**Minkler** USA
108A2	**Minlaton** Aust
72A2	**Minle** China
97C4	**Minna** Nig
10A2	**Minneapolis** USA
5J4	**Minnedosa** Can
10A2	**Minnesota** State, USA
50A1	**Miño** *R* Spain
8C2	**Minot** USA
72A2	**Minqin** China
72A3	**Min Shan** *Upland* China
60C3	**Minsk** Belarus
58C2	**Minsk Mazowiecki** Pol
12E2	**Minto** USA
4G2	**Minto Inlet** *B* Can
7C4	**Minto,L** Can
63D2	**Minusinsk** Russian Fed
72A3	**Min Xian** China
7E5	**Miquelon** Can
22D3	**Mirage L** USA
87A1	**Miraj** India
29E3	**Miramar** Arg
84B2	**Miram Shah** Pak
50B1	**Miranda de Ebro** Spain
47D2	**Mirandola** Italy
84B2	**Mir Bachāh Küt** Afghan
78D1	**Miri** Malay
96A3	**Mirik,C** Mali
63A1	**Mirnoye** Russian Fed
63O1	**Mirnyy** Russian Fed
112C9	**Mirnyy** *Base* Ant
84C2	**Mirpur** Pak
85B3	**Mirpur Khas** Pak
55B3	**Mirtoan S** Greece
74B3	**Miryang** S Korea
86A1	**Mirzäpur** India
23B2	**Misantla** Mexico
84C1	**Misgar** Pak
14A2	**Mishawaka** USA
12B1	**Misheguk Mt** USA
75A2	**Mi-shima** *I* Japan
107E2	**Misima I** Solomon Is
30F4	**Misiones** State, Arg
59C3	**Miskolc** Hung
94C2	**Mismiyah** Syria
71E4	**Misoöl** *I* Indon
95A1	**Misrätah** Libya
7B5	**Missinaibi** *R* Can
20B1	**Mission City** Can
15C2	**Mississauga** Can
11A3	**Mississippi** *R* State, USA
19C3	**Mississippi Delta** USA
8B2	**Missoula** USA
96B1	**Missour** Mor
11A3	**Missouri** State, USA
10A2	**Missouri** *R* USA
10C1	**Mistassini,L** Can
30B2	**Misti** *Mt* Peru
109C1	**Mitchell** Aust
8D2	**Mitchell** USA
107D2	**Mitchell** *R* Aust
11B3	**Mitchell,Mt** USA
45B2	**Mitchelstown** Irish Rep
84C3	**Mithankot** Pak
55C3	**Mitilini** Greece
23B2	**Mitla** Mexico
32C3	**Mitú** Colombia
99C3	**Mitumbar** *Mts* Zaire
98C3	**Mitwaba** Zaire
98B3	**Mitzic** Gabon
75B1	**Miura** Japan
72C3	**Mi Xian** China
69F3	**Miyake** *I* Japan
75B2	**Miyake-jima** *I* Japan
74C4	**Miyakonojo** Japan
74C4	**Miyazaki** Japan
75B1	**Miyazu** Japan
72D1	**Miyun** China
99D2	**Mizan Teferi** Eth
95A1	**Mizdah** Libya
45B3	**Mizen Hd** *C* Irish Rep
54C1	**Mizil** Rom
86C2	**Mizo Hills** India
86C2	**Mizoram** Union Territory, India
94B3	**Mizpe Ramon** Israel
112B11	**Mizuho** *Base* Ant
74E3	**Mizusawa** Japan
39H7	**Mjolby** Sweden
100B2	**Mkushi** Zambia
101H1	**Mkuzi** S Africa
57C2	**Mladá Boleslav** Czech Republic
58C2	**Mława** Pol
52C2	**Mljet** *I* Croatia
100B3	**Mmabatho** S Africa
84D2	**Mnadi** India
97A4	**Moa** *R* Sierra Leone
94B3	**Moab** Region, Jordan
9C3	**Moab** USA
98B3	**Moanda** Congo
98B3	**Moanda** Gabon
99C3	**Moba** Zaire
99D3	**Mobaye** CAR
98C2	**Mobayi** Zaire
10A3	**Moberly** USA
11B3	**Mobile** USA
11B3	**Mobile B** USA
8C2	**Mobridge** USA
101D2	**Moçambique** Mozam
76C1	**Moc Chau** Viet
100B3	**Mochudi** Botswana
101D2	**Mocimboa da Praia** Mozam
32B3	**Mocoa** Colombia
35B2	**Mococa** Brazil
34D2	**Mocoreta** *R* Arg
23B1	**Moctezuma** *R* Mexico
101C2	**Mocuba** Mozam
47B2	**Modane** France
101G1	**Modder** *R* S Africa
52B2	**Modena** Italy
49D2	**Moder** *R* France
8A3	**Modesto** USA
22B2	**Modesto Res** USA
53B3	**Modica** Italy
59B3	**Mödling** Austria
107D4	**Moe** Aust
47C1	**Moesa** *R* Switz
42C2	**Moffat** Scot
84D2	**Moga** India
35B2	**Mogi das Cruzes** Brazil
60C3	**Mogilev** Belarus
60C4	**Mogilev Podolskiy** Ukraine
35B2	**Mogi-Mirim** Brazil
101D2	**Mogincual** Mozam
47E2	**Mogliano** Italy
34B2	**Mogna** Arg
68D1	**Mogocha** Russian Fed
65K4	**Mogochin** Russian Fed
50A2	**Moguer** Spain
110C1	**Mohaka** *R* NZ
86C2	**Mohanganj** Bang
15D2	**Mohawk** *R* USA
99D3	**Mohoro** Tanz
65J5	**Mointy** Kazakhstan
38G5	**Mo i Rana** Nor
48C3	**Moissac** France
21B2	**Mojave** USA
22D3	**Mojave** *R* USA
9B3	**Mojave Desert** USA
78C4	**Mojokerto** Indon
86B1	**Mokama** India
110B1	**Mokau** *R* NZ
22B1	**Mokelumne Aqueduct** USA
22B1	**Mokelumne Hill** USA
22B1	**Mokelumne North Fork** *R* USA
101G1	**Mokhotlong** Lesotho
96D1	**Moknine** Tunisia
86C1	**Mokokchung** India
98B1	**Mokolo** Cam
74B4	**Mokpo** S Korea
61F3	**Moksha** *R* Russian Fed
23B1	**Molango** Mexico
55B3	**Molaoi** Greece
60B4	**Moldavia** = **Moldova**
38F6	**Molde** Nor
60C4	**Moldova** Republic, Europe
54B1	**Moldoveanu** *Mt* Rom
100B3	**Molepolole** Botswana
53A3	**Molfetta** Italy
34A3	**Molina** Chile
30B2	**Mollendo** Peru
60C3	**Molodechno** Belarus
112C11	**Molodezhnaya** *Base* Ant

21C4 **Molokai** *I* Hawaiian Is
61G2 **Moloma** *R* Russian Fed
99C2 **Molong** Aust
100B3 **Molopo** *R* Botswana
98B2 **Moloundu** Cam
8D1 **Molson L** Can
71D4 **Molucca S** Indon
71D4 **Moluccas** *Is* Indon
101C2 **Moma** Mozam
31C3 **Mombaça** Brazil
99D3 **Mombasa** Kenya
98C2 **Mompono** Zaire
56C2 **Mon** *I* Den
44A3 **Monach** *I* Scot
49D3 **Monaco**
Principality, Europe
44B3 **Monadhliath** *Mts* Scot
45C1 **Monaghan** County, Irish Rep
45C1 **Monaghan** Irish Rep
27D3 **Mona Pass** Caribbean S
13B2 **Monarch Mt** Can
5G4 **Monashee Mts** Can
41B3 **Monastereven** Irish Rep
45C1 **Moncalieri** Italy
31B2 **Monção** Brazil
38L5 **Monchegorsk** Russian Fed
56B2 **Mönchen-gladbach** Germany
24B2 **Monclova** Mexico
7D5 **Moncton** Can
9C4 **Monctova** Mexico
50A1 **Mondego** *R* Port
52A2 **Mondovi** Italy
27H1 **Moneague** Jamaica
14C2 **Monessen** USA
18B2 **Monett** USA
52B1 **Monfalcone** Italy
50A1 **Monforte de Lemos** Spain
98C2 **Monga** Zaire
98C2 **Mongala** *R* Zaire
76D1 **Mongala** Sudan
99D2 **Mongalla** Sudan
76D1 **Mong Cai** Viet
99D2 **Mongo** Chad
68B2 **Mongolia** Republic, Asia
100B2 **Mongu** Zambia
21B2 **Monitor Range** *Mts* USA
98C3 **Monkoto** Zaire
43C4 **Monmouth** Wales
18B1 **Monmouth** USA
13C2 **Monmouth,Mt** USA
43C4 **Monmouthshire** County Wales
97C4 **Mono** *R* Togo
21C2 **Mono L** USA
53C2 **Monopoli** Italy
51B1 **Monreal del Campo** Spain
19B3 **Monroe** Louisiana, USA
14B2 **Monroe** Michigan, USA
20B1 **Monroe** Washington, USA
18B2 **Monroe City** USA
97A4 **Monrovia** Lib
20D3 **Monrovia** USA
56A2 **Mons** Belg
47D2 **Monselice** Italy
58B1 **Monsterás** Sweden
101D2 **Montagne d'Ambre** *Mt* Madag
96C1 **Montagnes des Ouled Nail** *Mts* Alg
12E3 **Montague I** USA
49C3 **Mont Aigoual** *Mt* France
48B2 **Montaigu** France
53C3 **Montalto** *Mt* Italy
88B2 **Montana** State, USA
50A1 **Montañas de León** *Mts* Spain
49C2 **Montargis** France
48C3 **Montauban** France

15D2 **Montauk** USA
15D2 **Montauk Pt** USA
49D2 **Montbéliard** France
52A1 **Mont Blanc** *Mt* France/Italy
49C2 **Montceau les Mines** France
51C1 **Montceny** *Mt* Spain
49D3 **Mont Cinto** *Mt* Corse
46C2 **Montcornet** France
48B3 **Mont-de-Marsan** France
49C2 **Montdidier** France
30D2 **Monteagudo** Bol
33G4 **Monte Alegre** Brazil
52A2 **Monte Amiata** *Mt* Italy
47D2 **Monte Baldo** *Mt* Italy
15C1 **Montebello** Can
106A3 **Monte Bello Is** Aust
47E2 **Montebelluna** Italy
49D3 **Monte Carlo** Monaco
35B1 **Monte Carmelo** Brazil
34D2 **Monte Caseros** Arg
52B2 **Monte Cimone** *Mt* Italy
52A2 **Monte Cinto** *Mt* Corse
34B2 **Monte Coman** Arg
52B2 **Monte Corno** *Mt* Italy
27C3 **Montecristi** Dom Rep
52B2 **Montecristo** *I* Italy
23A1 **Monte Escobedo** Mexico
53C2 **Monte Gargano** *Mt* Italy
26B3 **Montego Bay** Jamaica
47D2 **Monte Grappa** *Mt* Italy
47C2 **Monte Lesima** *Mt* Italy
49C3 **Montélimar** France
53B2 **Monte Miletto** *Mt* Italy
50A2 **Montemo-o-Novo** Port
24C2 **Montemorelos** Mexico
26B5 **Montená** Colombia
54A2 **Montenegro** Republic, Yugos
31D3 **Monte Pascoal** *Mt* Brazil
34A2 **Monte Patria** Chile
53C3 **Monte Pollino** *Mt* Italy
101C2 **Montepuez** Mozam
8A3 **Monterey** California, USA
15C3 **Monterey** Virginia, USA
8A3 **Monterey B** USA
32B2 **Montería** Colombia
30D2 **Montero** Bol
24B2 **Monterrey** Mexico
31C5 **Montes Claros** Brazil
50B1 **Montes de Toledo** *Mts* Spain
29E2 **Montevideo** Urug
52A2 **Monte Viso** *Mt* Italy
27P2 **Mont Gimie** *Mt* St Lucia
11B3 **Montgomery** Alabama, USA
96C2 **Mont Gréboun** Niger
46C2 **Monthermé** France
47D1 **Monthey** Switz
19B3 **Monticello** Arkansas, USA
15C2 **Monticello** New York, USA
9C3 **Monticello** Utah, USA
53A2 **Monti del Gennargentu** *Mt* Sardegna
47D2 **Monti Lessini** *Mts* Italy

53B3 **Monti Nebrodi** *Mts* Italy
7C5 **Mont-Laurier** Can
48C2 **Montluçon** France
7C5 **Montmagny** Can
46C2 **Montmédy** France
49C3 **Mont Mézenc** *Mt* France
48C2 **Montmirail** France
50B2 **Montoro** Spain
49D3 **Mont Pelat** *Mt* France
14B2 **Montpelier** Ohio, USA
10C2 **Montpelier** Vermont, USA
49C3 **Montpellier** France
7C5 **Montréal** Can
48C1 **Montreuil** France
52A1 **Montreux** Switz
47B1 **Mont Risoux** *Mt* France
8C3 **Montrose** Colorado, USA
40C2 **Montrose** Scot
48B2 **Mont-St-Michel** France
96B1 **Monts des Ksour** *Mts* Alg
51C3 **Monts des Ouled Neil** *Mts* Alg
51C2 **Monts du Hodna** *Mts* Alg
27E3 **Montserrat** *I* Caribbean S
10C1 **Monts Otish** *Mts* Can
12B1 **Monument Mt** USA
9B3 **Monument V** USA
98C2 **Monveda** Zaire
76B1 **Monywa** Myan
52A1 **Monza** Italy
100B2 **Monze** Zambia
47C1 **Mooi** *R* S Africa
101G1 **Mooi River** S Africa
108B1 **Moomba** Aust
109D2 **Moonda Range** *Mts* Aust
108B1 **Moonda L** Aust
109D1 **Moonie** Aust
109C1 **Moonie** *R* Aust
108A2 **Moonta** Aust
106A4 **Moora** Aust
106A3 **Moore,L** Aust
42C2 **Moorfoot Hills** Scot
8D2 **Moorhead** USA
22C3 **Moorpark** USA
7B4 **Moose** *R* Can
5H4 **Moose Jaw** Can
5H4 **Moosomin** Can
7B4 **Moosonee** Can
16D2 **Moosup** USA
101C2 **Mopeia** Mozam
97B3 **Mopti** Mali
30B2 **Moquegua** Peru
39G6 **Mora** Sweden
31D3 **Morada** Brazil
84D3 **Morādābād** India
52A1 **Monte Rosa** *Mt* Italy/Switz
24B2 **Monterrey** Mexico
101D2 **Morafenobe** Madag
101D2 **Moramanga** Madag
27J2 **Morant Bay** Jamaica
27J2 **Morant Pt** Jamaica
87B3 **Moratuwa** Sri Lanka
59B3 **Morava** *R* Austria/Slovakia
54B2 **Morava** *R* Serbia, Yugos
90C3 **Moraveh Tappeh** Iran
44C3 **Moray** Division, Scot
44C3 **Moray Firth** *Estuary* Scot
47C1 **Morbegno** Italy
85C4 **Morbi** India
93D2 **Mor Dağ** *Mt* Turk
5J4 **Morden** Can
61F3 **Mordoviya** Division, Russian Fed
42C2 **Morecambe** Eng
42C2 **Morecambe B** Eng
107D3 **Moree** Aust
14B3 **Morehead** USA
47C1 **Mörel** Switz

24B3 **Morelia** Mexico
23B2 **Morelos** State, Mexico
85D3 **Morena** India
5E4 **Moresby I** Can
109D1 **Moreton I** Aust
98B2 **Moreuil** France
47B1 **Morez** France
19B4 **Morgan City** USA
22B2 **Morgan Hill** USA
14C3 **Morgantown** USA
101G1 **Morgenzon** S Africa
47B1 **Morges** Switz
46D2 **Morhange** France
74E2 **Mori** Japan
27K1 **Moriatio** Tobago
13B2 **Morice L** Can
13E2 **Morinville** Can
74E3 **Morioka** Japan
109D2 **Morisset** Aust
63D1 **Morkoka** *R* Russian Fed
48B2 **Morlaix** France
27Q2 **Morne Diablotin** *Mt* Dominica
106C2 **Morninton I** Aust
85B3 **Moro** Pak
96B2 **Morocco** Kingdom, Africa
79B4 **Moro G** Phil
99D3 **Morogoro** Tanz
23A1 **Moroleon** Mexico
101D3 **Morombe** Madag
26B2 **Morón** Cuba
101D3 **Morondava** Madag
50A2 **Moron de la Frontera** Spain
101D2 **Moroni** Comoros
71D3 **Morotai** *I* Indon
99D2 **Moroto** Uganda
61F4 **Morozovsk** Russian Fed
42D2 **Morpeth** Eng
19B2 **Morrilton** USA
35B1 **Morrinhos** Brazil
110C1 **Morrinsville** NZ
16B2 **Morristown** New Jersey, USA
15C2 **Morristown** New York, USA
16B2 **Morrisville** Pennsylvania, USA
21A2 **Morro Bay** USA
23A2 **Morro de Papanoa** Mexico
23A2 **Morro de Petatlán** Mexico
101C2 **Morrumbala** Mozam
101C3 **Morrumbene** Mozam
61F3 **Morshansk** Russian Fed
47C2 **Mortara** Italy
34C2 **Morteros** Arg
33G6 **Mortes** *R* Mato Grosso, Brazil
35C2 **Mortes** *R* Minas Gerais, Brazil
108B3 **Mortlake** Aust
27L1 **Moruga** Trinidad
109D3 **Moruya** Aust
109C1 **Morven** Aust
44B3 **Morvern** *Pen* Scot
109C3 **Morwell** Aust
76B3 **Moscos Is** Myan
 Moscow = **Moskva**
20C1 **Moscow** Idaho, USA
56B2 **Mosel** *R* Germany
46D2 **Moselle** Department, France
46D2 **Moselle** *R* France
20C1 **Moses Lake** USA
111B3 **Mosgiel** NZ
99D3 **Moshi** Tanz
38G5 **Mosjøen** Nor
62G2 **Moskal'vo** Russian Fed
60E2 **Moskva** Russian Fed
60E2 **Moskva** Division, Russian Fed
35C1 **Mosquito** *R* Brazil
39G7 **Moss** Nor
98B3 **Mossaka** Congo
100A4 **Mossel Bay** S Africa
98B3 **Mossendjo** Congo

108B2 **Mossgiel** Aust
31D3 **Mossoro** Brazil
57C2 **Most** Czech Republic
96C1 **Mostaganem** Alg
54A2 **Mostar** Bosnia-Herzegovina
58C2 **Mosty** Belarus
39H7 **Mosul = Al Mawşil**
42C2 **Motala** Sweden
86A1 **Motherwell** Scot
51B2 **Motihari** India
50B2 **Motilla del Palancar** Spain
11B2 **Motril** Spain
11B2 **Motueka** NZ
11B2 **Motueka** R NZ
47B1 **Moudon** Switz
98B3 **Mouila** Gabon
108B2 **Moulamein** Aust
4G2 **Mould Bay** Can
49C2 **Moulins** France
76B2 **Moulmein** Myan
96B1 **Moulouya** R Mor
17B1 **Moultrie** USA
17C1 **Moultrie,L** USA
18C2 **Mound City** Illinois, USA
18A1 **Mound City** Missouri, USA
98B2 **Moundou** Chad
14B3 **Moundsville** USA
12J1 **Mountain** R Can
17A1 **Mountain Brook** USA
18B2 **Mountain Grove** USA
18B2 **Mountain Home** Arkansas, USA
22A2 **Mountain View** USA
12B2 **Mountain Village** USA
16A3 **Mount Airy** Maryland, USA
16A2 **Mount Carmel** USA
108A1 **Mount Dutton** Aust
108A2 **Mount Eba** Aust
108B3 **Mount Gambier** Aust
16B3 **Mount Holly** USA
16A2 **Mount Holly Springs** USA
108A2 **Mount Hope** Aust
106C3 **Mount Isa** Aust
108A2 **Mount Lofty Range** Mts Aust
12D2 **Mount McKinley Nat Pk** USA
106A3 **Mount Magnet** Aust
108B2 **Mount Manara** Aust
107E3 **Mount Morgan** Aust
19B3 **Mount Pleasant** Texas, USA
20B1 **Mount Rainier Nat Pk** USA
43B4 **Mounts B** Eng
20B2 **Mount Shasta** USA
11B3 **Mount Vernon** Illinois, USA
19A3 **Mount Vernon** Kentucky, USA
20B1 **Mount Vernon** Washington, USA
45C1 **Mourne Mts** N Ire
98B1 **Moussoro** Chad
86B2 **Mouths of the Ganga** India/Bang
85B4 **Mouths of the Indus** Pak
77D4 **Mouths of the Mekong** Viet
97C4 **Mouths of the Niger** Nig
47B1 **Moutier** Switz
47B2 **Moûtiers** France
96C2 **Mouydir** Mts Alg
98B3 **Mouyondzi** Congo
46C2 **Mouzon** France
59B3 **M'óvár** Hung
23A1 **Moyahua** Mexico
99D2 **Moyale** Kenya
97A4 **Moyamba** Sierra Leone
96B1 **Moyen Atlas** Mts Mor
100B4 **Moyeni** Lesotho
99D2 **Moyo** Uganda

32B5 **Moyobamba** Peru
84D1 **Moyu** China
101C3 **Mozambique** Republic, Africa
101C3 **Mozambique Chan** Mozam/Madag
61H2 **Mozhga** Russian Fed
60C3 **Mozyr'** Belarus
99D3 **Mpanda** Tanz
101C2 **Mpika** Zambia
99D3 **Mporokosa** Zambia
100B2 **Mposhi** Zambia
101G1 **Mpulungu** Zambia
101G1 **Mpumalanga** Province S Africa
99D3 **Mpwapwa** Tanz
60E3 **Mtsensk** Russian Fed
101H1 **Mtubatuba** S Africa
101D2 **Mtwara** Tanz
76C2 **Muang Chainat** Thai
76C2 **Muang Chiang Rai** Thai
76C2 **Muang Kalasin** Thai
76C2 **Muang Khon Kaen** Thai
76B2 **Muang Lampang** Thai
76B2 **Muang Lamphun** Thai
76C2 **Muang Loei** Thai
76C2 **Muang Lom Sak** Thai
76C2 **Muang Nakhon Phanom** Thai
76B2 **Muang Nakhon Sawan** Thai
76C2 **Muang Nan** Thai
76C2 **Muang Phayao** Thai
76C2 **Muang Phetchabun** Thai
76C2 **Muang Phichit** Thai
76C2 **Muang Phitsanulok** Thai
76C2 **Muang Phrae** Thai
76C2 **Muang Roi Et** Thai
76C2 **Muang Sakon Nakhon** Thai
76C3 **Muang Samut Prakan** Thai
76C2 **Muang Uthai Thani** Thai
76C2 **Muang Yasothon** Thai
77C5 **Muar** Malay
78C2 **Muara** Brunei
70B4 **Muara** Indon
78A3 **Muaralakitan** Indon
78A3 **Muaratebo** Indon
78C3 **Muaratewah** Indon
78A3 **Muarenim** Indon
76A2 **Muaungmaya** Myan
99D2 **Mubende** Uganda
100C2 **Muchinga** Mts Zambia
44A3 **Muck** / Scot
109C1 **Muckadilla** Aust
100B2 **Muconda** Angola
35D1 **Mucuri** Brazil
35C1 **Mucuri** R Brazil
100B2 **Mucusso** Angola
69E2 **Mudanjiang** China
76B2 **Mudon** Myan
101C2 **Mueda** Mozam
107F3 **Mueo** Nouvelle Calédonie
100B2 **Mufulira** Zambia
73C4 **Mufu Shan** Hills China
Mugadishu = Muqdisho
93C4 **Mughayra** S Arabia
92A2 **Muğla** Turk
65G5 **Mugodzhary** Mts Kazakhstan
73A3 **Muguaping** China
73A3 **Muhaywir** Iraq
57C3 **Mühldorf** Germany
57C2 **Mühlhausen** Germany
38K6 **Muhos** Fin
77C4 **Mui Bai Bung** C Camb
45C2 **Muine Bheag** Irish Rep

100B2 **Mujimbeji** Zambia
59C3 **Mukachevo** Ukraine
78C2 **Mukah** Malay
69G4 **Muko-jima** / Japan
86A1 **Muktinath** Nepal
84B2 **Mukur** Afghan
18B2 **Mulberry** USA
12C2 **Mulchatna** R USA
34A3 **Mulchén** Chile
56C2 **Mulde** R Germany
71F5 **Mulgrave I** Aust
50B2 **Mulhacén** Mt Spain
46D1 **Mülheim** Germany
49D2 **Mulhouse** France
73A4 **Muli** China
44B3 **Mull** / Scot
87C3 **Mullaitvu** Sri Lanka
109C2 **Mullaley** Aust
106A3 **Mullewa** Aust
16B3 **Mullica** R USA
45C2 **Mullingar** Irish Rep
42B2 **Mull of Kintyre** Pt Scot
45C1 **Mull of Oa** C Scot
109D1 **Mullumbimby** Aust
100B2 **Mulobezi** Zambia
84C2 **Multan** Pak
Mumbai = Bombay
100B2 **Mumbwa** Zambia
61G4 **Mumra** Russian Fed
71D4 **Muna** / Indon
57C3 **München** Germany
14A2 **Muncie** USA
15C2 **Muncy** USA
56B2 **Münden** Germany
109D1 **Mundubbera** Aust
109C1 **Mungallala** Aust
109C1 **Mungallala** R Aust
99C2 **Mungbere** Zaïre
86A2 **Mungeli** India
86B1 **Munger** India
109C1 **Mungindi** Aust
Munich = München
14A1 **Munising** USA
29B6 **Muñoz Gomero,Pen** Chile
Münster Region, Irish Rep
47C1 **Münster** Switz
56B2 **Münster** Germany
54B1 **Muntii Apuseni** Mts Rom
54B1 **Muntii Cǎlimanilor** Mts Rom
54B1 **Muntii Carpatii Meridionali** Mts Rom
54B1 **Muntii Rodnei** Mts Rom
54B1 **Muntii Zarandului** Mts Rom
100B2 **Munyati** R Zim
93C2 **Munzur Silsilesi** Mts Turk
64D3 **Muomio** Fin
76C1 **Muong Khoua** Laos
76D3 **Muong Man** Viet
76D2 **Muong Nong** Laos
76C1 **Muong Ou Neua** Laos
76C2 **Muong Sen** Viet
76C1 **Muong Sing** Laos
76C1 **Muong Son** Laos
38J5 **Muonio** Fin
38J5 **Muonio** R Sweden/Fin
99E2 **Muqdisho** Somalia
52B1 **Mur** R Austria
74D3 **Murakami** Japan
29B5 **Murallón** Mt Arg/Chile
61G2 **Murashi** Russian Fed
93D2 **Murat** R Turk
53A3 **Muravera** Sardegna
75C1 **Murayama** Japan
90B3 **Murcheh Khvort** Iran
111B2 **Murchison** NZ
106A3 **Murchison** R Aust
51B2 **Murcia** Region, Spain
51B2 **Murcia** Spain
54B1 **Mureş** R Rom
46E2 **Murg** R Germany
65H6 **Murgab** R Turkmenistan
84B2 **Murgha Kibzai** Pak

109D1 **Murgon** Aust
86B2 **Muri** India
35C2 **Muriaé** Brazil
98C3 **Muriege** Angola
64E3 **Murmansk** Russian Fed
61F2 **Murom** Russian Fed
74E2 **Muroran** Japan
74C4 **Muros** Spain
74C4 **Muros** Japan
75A2 **Muroto-zaki** C Japan
20C2 **Murphy** Idaho, USA
22B1 **Murphys** USA
18C2 **Murray** Kentucky, USA
108B2 **Murray** R Aust
13C2 **Murray** R Can
108A3 **Murray Bridge** Aust
71F4 **Murray,L** PNG
17B1 **Murray,L** USA
105J2 **Murray Seacarp** Pacific O
108B2 **Murrumbidgee** R Aust
109C2 **Murrumburrah** Aust
109D2 **Murrurundi** Aust
47B1 **Murten** Switz
108B3 **Murtoa** Aust
110C1 **Murupara** NZ
86A2 **Murwara** India
109D1 **Murwillimbah** Aust
93D2 **Muş** Turk
54B2 **Musala** Mt Bulg
74B2 **Musan** N Korea
91C4 **Musandam** Pen Oman
Muscat = Masqat
91C5 **Muscat** Region, Oman
106C3 **Musgrave Range** Mts Aust
98B3 **Mushie** Zaïre
14A2 **Muskegon** USA
14A2 **Muskegon** R USA
14A2 **Muskogee** USA
15C2 **Muskoka,L** Can
95C3 **Musmar** Sudan
99D3 **Musoma** Tanz
8C2 **Musselshell** R USA
100A2 **Mussende** Angola
48C2 **Mussidan** France
55C2 **Mustafa-Kemalpasa** Turk
86A1 **Mustang** Nepal
70D2 **Muswellbrook** Aust
Mut Egypt
101C2 **Mutarara** Mozam
101C2 **Mutare** Zim
101C2 **Mutoko** Zim
101D2 **Mutsamudu** Comoros
100B2 **Mutshatsha** Zaïre
74E2 **Mutsu** Japan
74E2 **Mutsu-wan** B Japan
45B2 **Mutton** / Irish Rep
72B2 **Mu Us Shamo** Desert China
100A2 **Muxima** Angola
63D2 **Muya** Russian Fed
38L6 **Muyezerskiy** Russian Fed
99D3 **Muyinga** Burundi
99D3 **Muyumba** Zaïre
82A1 **Muyun Kum** Desert Kazakhstan
84C2 **Muzaffarābad** Pak
84C2 **Muzaffargarh** Pak
84D3 **Muzaffarnagar** India
86B1 **Muzaffarpur** India
64H3 **Muzhi** Russian Fed
82C2 **Muztag** Mt China
82B2 **Muztagata** Mt China
100C2 **Mvuma** Zim
99D3 **Mwanza** Tanz
98C3 **Mwanza** Zaïre
98C3 **Mweka** Zaïre
98C3 **Mwene Ditu** Zaïre
100C3 **Mwenezi** Zim
99C3 **Mwenga** Zaïre
100C2 **Mweru** L Zambia
100B2 **Mwinilunga** Zambia
83D4 **Myanaung** Myan
83D3 **Myanmar** Republic, Asia

Nechako

86D2 Myingyan Myan
76B1 Myingyao Myan
76B3 Myinmoletkat *Mt* Myan
82D3 Myitkyina Myan
76B3 Myitta Myan
86C2 Mymensingh Bang
69F3 Myojin *I* Japan
39F6 Myrdal Nor
38B2 Myrdalsjökur *Ice Cap* Iceland
17C1 Myrtle Beach USA
20B2 Myrtle Creek USA
39G7 Mysen Nor
56C2 Mysliborz Pol
64F3 Mys Kanin Nos *C* Russian Fed
59B3 Myslenice Pol
69H1 Mys Lopatka *C* Russian Fed
87B2 Mysore India
60D5 Mys Sarych *C* Ukraine
16D2 Mystic USA
61H5 Mys Tyub-Karagan *Pt* Kazakhstan
63G2 Mys Yelizavety *C* Russian Fed
64H2 Mys Zhelaniya *C* Russian Fed
77D3 My Tho Viet
20B2 Mytle Point USA
101C2 Mzimba Malawi
101C2 Mzuzu Malawi

N

21C4 Naalehu Hawaiian Is
39J6 Naantali Fin
45C2 Naas Irish Rep
75B2 Nabari Japan
61H2 Naberezhnye Chelny Russian Fed
12F2 Nabesna *R* USA
96D1 Nabeul Tunisia
94B2 Nablus Israel
101C2 Nacala Mozam
20B1 Naches USA
101C2 Nachingwea Tanz
19B3 Nacogdoches USA
76A3 Nacondam *I* Indian O
24B1 Nacozari Mexico
85C4 Nadiad India
60B3 Nador Mor
90B3 Nadushan Iran
59C3 Nadvornaya Ukraine
56C1 Naestved Den
95B2 Näfürah Libya
75A2 Nagahama Japan
82D3 Naga Hills Myan
75B1 Nagai Japan
86C1 Nägäland State, India
74D3 Nagano Japan
74D3 Nagaoka Japan
86C1 Nagaon India
87B2 Nägappattinam India
85C4 Nagar Parkar Pak
74E4 Nagasaki Japan
75B2 Nagashima Japan
75A2 Nagato Japan
85C3 Nägaur India
87B3 Nagercoil India
85B3 Nagha Kalat Pak
84D3 Nagina India
74D3 Nagoya Japan
85D4 Nagpur India
82D2 Nagqu China
59B3 Nagykanizsa Hung
59B3 Nagykörös Hung
69E4 Naha Japan
8A2 Nahaimo Can
84D2 Nahan India
4F3 Nahanni Butte Can
94B2 Nahariya Israel
90A3 Nahävand Iran
46D2 Nahe *R* Germany
72D2 Nahpu China
72E1 Naimen Qi China
72C2 Nain Can
90B3 Nä'in Iran
84D3 Naini Tal India
44C3 Nairn Scot
44C3 Nairn *R* Scot
43C2 Nairobi Kenya

90B3 Najafābād Iran
74C2 Najin N Korea
75A2 Nakama Japan
74E3 Nakaminato Japan
75A2 Nakamura Japan
75B1 Nakano Japan
75A1 Nakano-shima *I* Japan
74C4 Nakatsu Japan
75B2 Nakatsu-gawa Japan
95C3 Nak' fa Eritrea
93E2 Nakhichevan Azerbaijan
93E2 Nakhichevan Division, Azerbaijan
92B4 Nakhl Egypt
74C2 Nakhodka Russian Fed
76C3 Nakhon Pathom Thai
76C3 Nakhon Ratchasima Thai
77C4 Nakhon Si Thammarat Thai
12H3 Nakina Can
7B4 Nakina Ontario, Can
12C3 Naknek USA
12C3 Naknek *L* USA
4C4 Nakrek USA
39G8 Nakskov Den
99D3 Nakuru Kenya
13D2 Nakusp Can
61F5 Nal'chik Russian Fed
87B1 Nalgonda India
87B1 Nallamala Range *Mts* India
95A1 Nalūt Libya
101H1 Namaacha Mozam
65G6 Namak *L* Iran
90C3 Namak-e Shadad *Salt Flat* Iran
65J5 Namangan Uzbekistan
101C2 Namapa Mozam
100A4 Namaqualand Region, S Africa
109D1 Nambour Aust
109D2 Nambucca Heads Aust
77D4 Nam Can Viet
82D2 Nam Co *L* China
76D1 Nam Dinh Viet
101C2 Nametil Mozam
74B4 Namhae-do *I* S Korea
100A2 Namib Desert Namibia
100A2 Namibe Angola
100A3 Namibia Republic, Africa
82D3 Namjagbarwa Feng *Mt* China
71D4 Namlea Indon
109C2 Namoi *R* Aust
13D1 Nampa Can
20C2 Nampa USA
97B3 Nampala Mali
76B1 Nam Phong Thai
74B3 Namp'o N Korea
101C2 Nampula Mozam
38G6 Namsos Nor
76B1 Namton Myan
86D2 Namtu Myan
13B2 Namu Can
101C2 Namuno Mozam
46C1 Namur Belg
100A2 Namutoni Namibia
74B3 Namwŏn S Korea
13C3 Nanaimo Can
74B2 Nanam N Korea
109D1 Nanango Aust
74D3 Nanao Japan
74D3 Nanatsu-jima *I* Japan
73B3 Nanbu China
73D4 Nanchang China
73B3 Nanchong China
49D2 Nancy France
87B2 Nänded India
109D2 Nandewar Range *Mts* Aust
85C4 Nandurbar India
87B1 Nandyāl India
98B2 Nanga Eboko Cam

84C1 Nanga Parbat *Mt* Pak
74C3 Nangapinoh Indon
78C3 Nangatayap Indon
74B2 Nangnim Sanmaek *Mts* N Korea
86C1 Nang Xian China
67F3 Nangzhou China
87B2 Nanjangüd India
72D3 Nanjing China
Nanking = Nanjing China
75A2 Nankoku Japan
73C4 Nan Ling Region, China
73B5 Nanning China
6F3 Nanortalik Greenland
73A5 Nanpan Jiang *R* China
86A1 Nänpära India
73D4 Nanping China
6A1 Nansen Sd Can
99D3 Nansio Tanz
48B2 Nantes France
72E3 Nantong China
35C1 Nanuque Brazil
72C3 Nanyang China
72D2 Nanyang Hu *L* China
99D2 Nanyuki Kenya
74D3 Naoetsu Japan
85B4 Naokot Pak
22A1 Napa USA
12B2 Napaiskak USA
75C2 Napanee Can
65K4 Napas Russian Fed
6E3 Napassoq Greenland
76D2 Nape Laos
110C1 Napier NZ
Naples = Napoli
17B2 Naples Florida, USA
19B3 Naples Texas, USA
73B5 Napo China
32C4 Napo *R* Peru/Ecuador
53B2 Napoli Italy
90A2 Naqadeh Iran
94C2 Naqb Ishtar Jordan
75B2 Nara Japan
97B3 Nara Mali
107D4 Naracoorte Aust
23B1 Naranjos Mexico
77C4 Narathiwat Thai
86C2 Narayanganj Bang
87B1 Narayenpet India
49C3 Narbonne France
87B2 Narendranagar India
6C2 Nares Str Can
58C2 Narew *R* Pol
75C1 Narita Japan
85C4 Narmada *R* India
84D3 Narnaul India
60E2 Naro Fominsk Russian Fed
99D3 Narok Kenya
84C2 Narowal Pak
107D4 Narrabri Aust
109C1 Narran *L* Aust
109C2 Narrandera Aust
106A4 Narrogin Aust
109C2 Narromine Aust
85D4 Narsimhapur India
87C1 Narsipatnam India
6F3 Narssaq Greenland
6F3 Narssarssuaq Greenland
75C1 Narugo Japan
75A2 Naruto Japan
60C2 Narva Russian Fed
38H5 Narvik Nor
84D3 Narwāna India
64G3 Nar'yan Mar Russian Fed
108B1 Narylico Aust
65J5 Naryn Kyrgyzstan
97C4 Nasarawa Nig
103D5 Nasca Ridge Pacific O
16D1 Nashua USA

19B3 Nashville Arkansas, USA
11B3 Nashville Tennessee, USA
54A1 Našice Croatia
85D4 Näsik India
99D1 Nasir Sudan
13B1 Nass *R* Can
26B1 Nassau The Bahamas
16C1 Nassau USA
95C2 Nasser,L Egypt
39G7 Nässjö Sweden
10C3 Nastapoka Is Can
100B3 Nata Botswana
31D3 Natal Brazil
70A3 Natal Indon
90B3 Natanz Iran
7D4 Natashquan Can
7D4 Natashquan *R* Can
19B3 Natchez USA
19B3 Natchitoches USA
108C3 Nathalia Aust
6H2 Nathorsts Land Region Greenland
13C1 Nation *R* Can
21B3 National City USA
75C1 Natori Japan
99D3 Natron *L* Tanz
106A4 Naturaliste,C Aust
47D1 Nauders Austria
56C2 Nauen Germany
16C2 Naugatuck USA
57C2 Naumburg Germany
94B3 Naur Jordan
105G4 Nauru *I* Pacific O
63C2 Naushki Russian Fed
22B1 Nautla Mexico
9C3 Navajo Res USA
50A1 Navalmoral de la Mata Spain
29C7 Navarino *I* Chile
51B1 Navarra Province, Spain
34D3 Navarro Arg
19A3 Navasota USA
19A3 Navasota *R* USA
50A1 Navia *R* Spain
34A2 Navidad Chile
50C4 Navlakhi India
60D3 Navlya Russian Fed
24B2 Navojoa Mexico
55B3 Navpaktos Greece
55B3 Návplion Greece
48C2 Navsári India
86B2 Nawāda India
84B2 Nawah Afghan
85B3 Nawrabshah Pak
23A1 Naxi China
55C3 Náxos *I* Greece
23A1 Nayar Mexico
90C3 Näy Band Iran
91B4 Näy Band Iran
74E2 Nayoro Japan
94B2 Nazareth Israel
48B2 Nazay France
32C6 Nazca Peru
92A2 Nazilli Turk
63B2 Nazimovo Russian Fed
7D4 Nazko *R* Can
99D2 Nazret Eth
91C5 Nazwa Oman
65J4 Nazyvayevsk Russian Fed
100A2 Ndalatando Angola
98C2 Ndélé CAR
98B3 Ndende Gabon
98B1 Ndjamena Chad
98B3 Ndjolé Gabon
100B2 Ndola Zambia
10C2 Neabul Aust
108A1 Neales *R* Aust
55B3 Neápolis Greece
43C4 Neath Wales
43C4 Neath and Port Talbot County Wales
109C1 Nebine *R* Aust
65G6 Nebit Dag Turkmenistan
8C2 Nebraska State, USA
18A1 Nebraska City USA
13C2 Nechako *R* Can

19A3	Neches *R* USA
34D3	Necochea Arg
86C1	Nédong China
9B3	Needles USA
14A2	Neenah USA
5J4	Neepawa Can
46C1	Neerpelt Belg
63C2	Neftelensk Russian Fed
99D2	Negele Eth
94B3	Negev *Desert* Israel
60B4	Negolu *Mt* Rom
87B3	Negombo Sri Lanka
76A2	Negrais,C Myan
32A4	Negritos Peru
33E4	Negro *R* Amazonas, Brazil
29C4	Negro *R* Arg
34D2	Negro *R* Urug
79B4	Negros *l* Phil
54C2	Negru Voda Rom
90D3	Nehbändan Iran
73B4	Neijiang China
72B1	Nei Monggol Autonomous Region, China
32B3	Neiva Colombia
99D2	Nejo Eth
99D2	Nek'emte Eth
60D2	Nelidovo Russian Fed
87B2	Nellore India
69F2	Nel'ma Russian Fed
13D3	Nelson Can
11B2	Nelson NZ
7A4	Nelson *R* Can
108B3	Nelson,C Aust
12B2	Nelson *l* USA
97B3	Néma Maur
72A1	Nemagt Uul *Mt* Mongolia
58C1	Neman *R* Lithuania
54C1	Nemira *Mt* Rom
74F2	Nemuro Japan
63E3	Nen *R* China
41B3	Nenagh Irish Rep
12E2	Nenana USA
12E2	Nenana *R* USA
43D3	Nene *R* Eng
69E2	Nenjiang China
18A2	Neodesha USA
18B2	Neosho USA
63C2	Nepa Russian Fed
82C3	Nepal Kingdom, Asia
84A1	Nepalganj Nepal
45B1	Nephin *Mt* Irish Rep
94B3	Neqarot *R* Israel
34A3	Nequén State, Arg
68D1	Nerchinsk Russian Fed
52C2	Neretva *R* Bosnia-Herzegovina/Croatia
71F2	Nero Deep Pacific O
38C1	Neskaupstaður Iceland
46B2	Nesle France
7E5	Nesleyville Can
55B2	Néstos *R* Greece
94B2	Netanya Israel
16B2	Netcong USA
56B2	Netherlands Kingdom, Europe
3M7	Netherlands Antilles *Is* Caribbean S
86C2	Netrakona Bang
6C3	Nettilling *L* Can
56C2	Neubrandenburg Germany
47B1	Neuchâtel Switz
46C2	Neufchâteau Belg
48C2	Neufchâtel France
46A2	Neufchâtel-en-Bray France
56B2	Neumünster Germany
52C1	Neunkirchen Austria
46D2	Neunkirchen Germany
34B3	Neuquén Arg
29B4	Neuquén State, Arg
34B3	Neuquén *R* Arg
56C2	Neuruppin Germany
46D1	Neuss Germany
46E2	Neustadt Germany
56C2	Neustadt Germany
56C2	Neustrelitz Germany
46D1	Neuwied Germany
8B3	Nevada State, USA
18B2	Nevada USA
34A3	Nevada de Chillán *Mts* Arg/Chile
23A2	Nevada de Collima Mexico
23B2	Nevada de Toluca *Mt* Mexico
94B3	Nevatim Israel
60C2	Nevel' Russian Fed
49C2	Nevers France
109C2	Nevertire Aust
27E3	Nevis *l* Caribbean S
58D2	Nevis *R* Belarus/Lithuania
92B2	Nevşehir Turk
61K2	Nev'yansk Russian Fed
101C2	Newala Tanz
14A3	New Albany Indiana, USA
19C3	New Albany Mississippi, USA
33F2	New Amsterdam Guyana
109C1	New Angledool Aust
15C3	Newark Delaware, USA
10C2	Newark New Jersey, USA
14B2	Newark Ohio, USA
43D3	Newark-upon-Trent Eng
15D2	New Bedford USA
13B2	New Bella Bella Can
20B1	Newberg USA
11C3	New Bern USA
17B1	Newberry USA
26B2	New Bight The Bahamas
14B3	New Boston USA
9D4	New Braunfels USA
16C2	New Britain USA
7D5	New Brunswick Province, Can
16B2	New Brunswick USA
16B2	New Brunswick USA
43D4	Newbury Eng
16D1	Newburyport USA
16C2	New Canaan USA
109D2	Newcastle Aust
14A3	New Castle Indiana, USA
42B2	Newcastle N Ire
14B2	New Castle Pennsylvania, USA
101G1	Newcastle S Africa
8C2	Newcastle Wyoming, USA
42D2	Newcastle upon Tyne Eng
106C2	Newcastle Waters Aust
45B2	Newcastle West Irish Rep
84D3	New Delhi India
109D2	New England Range *Mts* Aust
12B3	Newenham,C USA
43D4	New Forest,The Eng
7D4	Newfoundland Province, Can
7E5	Newfoundland *l* Can
102F2	Newfoundland Basin Atlantic O
18B2	New Franklin USA
42B2	New Galloway Scot
107E1	New Georgia *l* Solomon Is
7D5	New Glasgow Can
71F4	New Guinea SE Asia
12D3	Newhalen USA
22C3	Newhall USA
10C2	New Hampshire State, USA
101H1	New Hanover *l* S Africa
43E4	Newhaven Eng
15D2	New Haven USA
13B1	New Hazelton Can
19B3	New Iberia USA
10C2	New Jersey State, USA
7C5	New Liskeard Can
10C2	New London USA
106J3	Newman Aust
22B2	Newman USA
43E3	Newmarket Eng
45B2	Newmarket Irish Rep
15C3	New Market USA
9C3	New Mexico State, USA
16C2	New Milford USA
17B1	Newnan USA
109C4	New Norfolk Aust
11A3	New Orleans USA
16B2	New Paltz USA
14B2	New Philadelphia USA
110B1	New Plymouth NZ
18B2	Newport Arkansas, USA
43D4	Newport Eng
14B3	Newport Kentucky, USA
20B2	Newport Oregon, USA
16A2	Newport Pennsylvania, USA
15D2	Newport Rhode Island, USA
15D2	Newport Vermont, USA
43C4	Newport Wales
43C4	Newport County Wales
20C1	Newport Washington, USA
22D4	Newport Beach USA
11C3	Newport News USA
27E3	New Providence *l* Caribbean S
43B4	Newquay Eng
6C3	New Quebec Crater Can
45C2	New Ross Irish Rep
45C1	Newry N Ire
17B2	New Smyrna Beach USA
107D4	New South Wales State, Aust
12C3	New Stuyahok USA
18A2	Newton Kansas, USA
16D1	Newton Massachusetts, USA
19C3	Newton Mississippi, USA
16B2	Newton New York, USA
43C4	Newton Abbot Eng
44C2	Newton Stewart N Ire
42B2	Newton Stewart Scot
43C3	Newtown Wales
42B2	Newtownards N Ire
16A2	Newville USA
10C2	New Westminster Can
10C2	New York State, USA
10C2	New York USA
110	New Zealand Dominion, SW Pacific O
105G6	New Zealand Plat Pacific O
61F2	Neya Russian Fed
91B4	Neyriz Iran
90C2	Neyshäbūr Iran
60D3	Nezhin Russian Fed
98B3	Ngabé Congo
100B3	Ngami *L* Botswana
110C1	Ngaruawahia NZ
110C1	Ngaruroro *R* NZ
110C1	Ngauruhoe,Mt NZ
98B3	Ngo Congo
76D2	Ngoc Linh *Mt* Viet
98B2	Ngoko *R* Cam
68B3	Ngoring Hu *L* China
99D3	Ngorongoro Crater Tanz
98B3	N'Gounié *R* Gabon
98B1	Nguigmi Niger
71E3	Ngulu *l* Pacific O
97D3	Nguru Nig
76D3	Nha Trang Viet
108B3	Nhill Aust
101H1	Nhlangano Swaziland
76D2	Nhommarath Laos
106C2	Nhulunbuy Aust
97B3	Niafounké Mali
14A1	Niagara USA
15C2	Niagara Falls Can
15C2	Niagara Falls USA
10C3	Niah Malay
97B4	Niakaramandougou Côte d'Ivoire
97C3	Niamey Niger
99C2	Niangara Zaire
98C2	Nia Ke Zaire
70A3	Nias *l* Indon
25D3	Nicaragua Republic, Cent America
53C3	Nicastro Italy
49D3	Nice France
26B1	Nicholl's Town The Bahamas
83D5	Nicobar Is Indian O
92B2	Nicosia Cyprus
25D3	Nicoya,Pen de Costa Rica
58C2	Nidzica Pol
46D2	Niederbronn France
56B2	Niedersachsen State, Germany
99C3	Niemba Zaire
56B2	Nienburg Germany
46D1	Niers *R* Germany
97B4	Niete,Mt Lib
33F2	Nieuw Amsterdam Surinam
33F2	Nieuw Nickerie Surinam
46B1	Nieuwpoort Belg
92B2	Niğde Turk
97C3	Niger Republic, Africa
97C4	Niger *R* Nig
97C4	Nigeria Federal Republic, Africa
55B2	Nigrita Greece
75C1	Nihommatsu Japan
74D3	Niigata Japan
74C4	Niihama Japan
75B2	Nii-jima *l* Japan
75A2	Niimi Japan
74D3	Niitsu Japan
94B3	Nijil Jordan
56B2	Nijmegen Neth
64E3	Nikel' Russian Fed
97C3	Nikki Bénin
74D3	Nikko Japan
60D4	Nikolayev Ukraine
61H2	Nikolayevsk Russian Fed
63G2	Nikolayevsk-na-Amure Russian Fed
61G2	Nikol'sk Russian Fed
61G3	Nikol'sk Russian Fed
60D4	Nikopol' Ukraine
92C1	Niksar Turk
91D4	Nikshahr Iran
54A2	Nikšić Montenegro, Yugos
71D4	Nila *l* Indon
80B3	Nile *R* N E Africa
94A3	Niles USA
87B2	Nilgiri Hills India
46C2	Nîmach India
49C3	Nîmes France
109C3	Nimmitabel Aust
90C2	Nimule Sudan
83B5	Nine Degree Chan Indian O
104C4	Ninety-East Ridge Indian O
109C3	Ninety Mile Beach Aust
73D4	Ningde China
73D4	Ningdu China
68B3	Ningjing Shan *Mts* China

76D1	Ningming China
73A4	Ningnan China
72B2	Ningxia Province, China
72B2	Ning Xian China
73B5	Ninh Binh Vietnam
107D1	Ninigo Is PNG
12D2	Ninilchik USA
8D2	Niobrara R USA
98B3	Nioki Zaire
97B3	Nioro du Sahel Mali
48B2	Niort France
5H4	Nipawin Can
7B5	Nipigon Can
7B5	Nipigon,L Can
7B5	Nipissing R Can
14B1	Nipissing,L Can
87B1	Nirmal India
86B1	Nirmāli India
54B2	Niš Serbia, Yugos
81C4	Nişāb Yemen
69F4	Nishino-shima / Japan
75A1	Nishino-shima / Japan
75A2	Nishiwaki Japan
12D2	Nishtún R Can
12H2	Nisutlin R Can
7C4	Nitchequon Can
31C6	Niterói Brazil
11R	Nith R Scot
59B3	Nitra Slovakia
14B3	Nitro USA
78C2	Niut Mt Malay
46C1	Nivelles Belg
49C2	Nivernais Region, Belg
38L5	Nivskiy Russian Fed
87B1	Nizāmābād India
94B3	Nizana Hist Site Israel
61J2	Nizhniye Sergi Russian Fed
61F2	Nizhniy Novgorod Russian Fed
61F2	Nizhniy Novgorod Division, Russian Fed
61F3	Nizhniy Lomov Russian Fed
65G4	Nizhniy Tagil Russian Fed
63B1	Nizhnyaya Tunguska R Russian Fed
93C2	Nizip Turk
100B2	Njoko R Zambia
99D3	Njombe Tanz
98B2	Nkambe Cam
101C2	Nkhata Bay Malawi
98B2	Nkongsamba Cam
97C3	N'Konni Niger
86C2	Noakhali Bang
12C1	Noatak R USA
74C4	Nobeoka Japan
47D1	Noce R Italy
23A1	Nochistlán Mexico
23B2	Nochixtlán Mexico
19A3	Nocona USA
24A1	Nogales Sonora, Mexico
9B3	Nogales USA
23B2	Nogales Veracruz, Mexico
47D2	Nogara Italy
75A2	Nogata Japan
60E2	Noginsk Russian Fed
34D2	Nogoyá Arg
34D2	Nogoyá R Arg
84C3	Nohar India
75B2	Nojima-saki C Japan
98B2	Nola CAR
61G2	Nolinsk Russian Fed
16D2	Nomans Land / USA
12A2	Nome USA
46D2	Nomeny France
72B1	Nomgon Mongolia
5H3	Nonacho L Can
74C2	Nong Khai Thai
101H1	Nongoma S Africa
12B1	Noorvik USA
13B3	Nootka Sd Can
98B3	Noqui Angola
7C5	Noranda Can

46B1	Nord Department, France
64D2	Nordaustlandet / Barents S
13D2	Nordegg Can
38F6	Nordfjord Inlet Nor
39F8	Nordfriesische Is Germany
56C2	Nordhausen Germ
56B2	Nordrhein Westfalen State, Germany
38J4	Nordkapp C Nor
6E3	Nordre Greenland
38H5	Nord Stronfjället Mt Sweden
1B9	Nordvik Russian Fed
45C2	Nore R Irish Rep
43E3	Norfolk County, Eng
8D2	Norfolk Nebraska, USA
11C3	Norfolk Virginia, USA
107F3	Norfolk I Aust
18B2	Norfolk L USA
105G5	Norfolk Ridge Pacific O
1C10	Noril'sk Russian Fed
18C1	Normal USA
19A2	Norman USA
48B2	Normandie Region, France
107D2	Normanton Aust
12J1	Norman Wells Can
4B3	Norme USA
15C2	Norristown USA
39H7	Norrköping Sweden
39H6	Norrsundet Sweden
39H7	Norrtälje Sweden
106B4	Norseman Aust
63F2	Norsk Russian Fed
102J2	North S N W Europe
106A4	Northam Aust
102E3	North American Basin Atlantic O
106A3	Northampton Aust
43D3	Northampton County, Eng
43D3	Northampton Eng
15D2	Northampton USA
4G3	North Arm R Can
17B1	North Augusta USA
6D4	North Batavisk I Can
42B2	North Ayrshire Division, Scot
13F2	North Battleford Can
7C5	North Bay Can
20B2	North Bend USA
42C2	North Berwick Scot
7D5	North,C Can
7G4	North,C NZ
11B3	North Carolina State, USA
20B1	North Cascade Nat Pk USA
14B1	North Chan Can
42B2	North Chan Ire/Scot
8C2	North Dakota State, USA
43C4	North Downs Eng
14C2	North East USA
102H2	North East Atlantic Basin Atlantic O
4B3	Northeast C USA
42D3	Northeast Lincolnshire County Eng
100B3	Northern Cape Province, S Africa
40B3	Northern Ireland UK
104F3	Northern Mariana Is Pacific O
100B3	Northern Province Province, S Africa
27L1	Northern Range Mts Trinidad
106C2	Northern Territory Aust
44C3	North Esk R Scot
16C1	Northfield Massachusetts, USA
12D2	North Fork R USA
110B1	North I NZ
74B3	North Korea Republic, S E Asia

42C2	North Lanarkshire Division, Scot
	North Land = Severnaya Zemlya
43D3	North Lincolnshire County Eng
19B3	North Little Rock USA
1B4	North Magnetic Pole Can
17B2	North Miami USA
17B2	North Miami Beach USA
8C2	North Platte USA
8C2	North Platte R USA
27R3	North Pt Barbados
14B1	North Pt USA
40B2	North Rona I Scot
44C2	North Ronaldsay I Scot
13F2	North Saskatchewan R Can
40D2	North Sea N W Europe
40D2	North Slope Region USA
109D1	North Stradbroke I Aust
110B1	North Taranaki Bight B NZ
9C3	North Truchas Peak Mt USA
44A3	North Uist I Scot
42C2	Northumberland County, Eng
107E3	Northumberland Is Aust
7D5	Northumberland Str Can
20B1	North Vancouver Can
43E3	North Walsham Eng
12F2	Northway USA
100B3	North West Province, S Africa
106A3	North West C Aust
84C2	North West Frontier Province, Pak
7D4	North West River Can
43C4	North West Somerset County Eng
4F3	North West Territories Can
42D2	North York Moors Nat Pk Eng
12B2	Norton B USA
12B2	Norton Sd USA
112B1	Norvegia,C Ant
16C2	Norwalk Connecticut, USA
14B2	Norwalk Ohio, USA
39F6	Norway Kingdom, Europe
5J4	Norway House Can
6A2	Norwegian B Can
102H1	Norwegian Basin Norwegian S
64A3	Norwegian S N W Europe
16C2	Norwalk Connecticut, USA
43E3	Norwich Eng
16D1	Norwood Massachusetts, USA
14B3	Norwood Ohio, USA
54C2	Nos Emine C Bulg
74D2	Noshiro Japan
54C2	Nos Kaliakra C Bulg
44E1	Noss I Scot
91D4	Nostrābād Iran
101D2	Nosy Barren I Madag
101D2	Nosy Be I Madag
101E2	Nosy Boraha I Madag
101D3	Nosy Varika Madag
87B2	Notéč R Pol
5G4	Notikeuin Can
53C3	Noto Italy
39F7	Notodden Nor
75B1	Noto-hantō Pen Japan
7E5	Notre Dams B Can
43D3	Nottingham County, Eng
43D3	Nottingham Eng

6C3	Nottingham I Can
6C3	Nottingham Island Can
96A2	Nouadhibou Maur
97A3	Nouakchott Maur
107F3	Nouméa Nouvelle Calédonie
97B3	Nouna Burkina
107F3	Nouvelle Calédonie / S W Pacific O
98B3	Nova Caipemba Angola
35A2	Nova Esparança Brazil
35C2	Nova Friburgo Brazil
100A2	Nova Gaia Angola
35B2	Nova Granada Brazil
35B2	Nova Horizonte Brazil
35C1	Nova Lima Brazil
	Nova Lisboa = Huambo
35A2	Nova Londrina Brazil
101C3	Nova Mambone Mozam
47C2	Novara Italy
7D5	Nova Scotia Province, Can
22A1	Novato USA
35C1	Nova Venécia Brazil
60D4	Novaya Kakhovka Ukraine
64G2	Novaya Zemlya / Barents S
54C2	Nove Zagora Bulg
31C2	Nove Russas Brazil
54A1	Nové Zámky Slovakia
60D2	Novgorod Russian Fed
60D2	Novgorod Division, Russian Fed
47C2	Novi Ligure Italy
54C2	Novi Pazar Bulg
54B2	Novi Pazar Serbia, Yugos
54A1	Novi Sad Serbia, Yugos
61J3	Novoalekseyevka Kazakhstan
61F3	Novoanninskiy Russian Fed
61E4	Novocherkassk Russian Fed
60C3	Novograd Volynskiy Ukraine
58D2	Novogrudok Ukraine
30F4	Novo Hamburgo Brazil
65H5	Novokazalinsk Kazakhstan
65K4	Novokuznetsk Russian Fed
112B12	Novolazarevskaya Base Ant
52C1	Novo Mesto Slovenia
60E3	Novomoskovsk Russian Fed
60E5	Novorossiysk Russian Fed
65K4	Novosibirsk Russian Fed
1B8	Novosibirskiye Ostrova / Russian Fed
61J3	Novotroitsk Russian Fed
61G3	Novo Uzensk Russian Fed
59C2	Novovolynsk Ukraine
61G2	Novo Vyatsk Russian Fed
60D3	Novozybkov Russian Fed
58C2	Novy Dwór Mazowiecki Pol
61K2	Novyy Lyalya Russian Fed
61H5	Novyy Port Russian Fed
61H5	Novyy Uzen Kazakhstan

Nowa Sól

58B2 Nowa Sól Pol
18A2 Nowata USA
Nowgong = Nagaon
12D2 Nowitna R USA
99D2 Nowra Aust
90B2 Now Shahr Iran
84C2 Nowshera Pak
59C3 Nowy Sącz Pol
12H3 Noyes I USA
46B2 Noyon France
97B4 Nsawam Ghana
99D1 Nuba Mts Sudan
81B3 Nubian Desert Sudan
34A3 Nuble R Chile
9D4 Nueces R USA
5J3 Nueltin L Can
26A2 Nueva Gerona Cuba
34A3 Nueva Imperial Chile
9C4 Nueva Laredo
Mexico
24B2 Nueva Palmira Urug
24B2 Nueva Rosita Mexico
26B2 Nuevitas Cuba
24B1 Nuevo Casas Grandes
Mexico
24C2 Nuevo Laredo
Mexico
99E2 Nugaal Region,
Somalia
6E2 Nûgâtsiaq Greenland
6E2 Nugssuaq Pen
Greenland
6E2 Nûgussaq I
Greenland
108A2 Nukey Bluff Mt Aust
93D3 Nukhayb Iraq
65G5 Nukus Uzbekistan
12C2 Nulato USA
106B4 Nullarbor Plain Aust
97D4 Numan Nig
75B1 Numata Japan
98C2 Numatinna R Sudan
74D3 Numazu Japan
71E4 Numfoor I Indon
108C3 Numurkah Aust
12B2 Nunapitchuk USA
84D2 Nunkun Mt India
53A2 Nuoro Sardegna
91B3 Nurābād Iran
47C2 Nure R Italy
108A2 Nuriootpa Aust
84C1 Nuristan Upland
Afghan
61H3 Nurlat Russian Fed
38K6 Nurmes Fin
57C3 Nürnberg Germany
108C2 Nurri,Mt Aust
93D2 Nusaybin Turk
12C3 Nushagak R USA
12C3 Nushagak B USA
12C3 Nushagak Pen USA
84B3 Nushki Pak
7D4 Nutak Can
12F2 Nutzotin Mts USA
Nuuk = Godthåb
86A1 Nuwakot Nepal
87C3 Nuwara-Eliya
Sri Lanka
6C3 Nuyukjuak Can
16C2 Nyack USA
99D2 Nyahururu Kenya
108B3 Nyah West Aust
4C3 Nyai USA
68B3 Nyainqentanglha
Shan Mts China
99D3 Nyakabindi Tanz
5U1 Nyala Sudan
68B1 Nyalam China
98C2 Nyamlell Sudan
64F3 Nyandoma
Russian Fed
100C2 Nyanga Zim
98B3 Nyanga R Gabon
101C2 Nyasa L Malawi/
Mozam
76B2 Nyaunglebin Myan
61J2 Nyazepetrovsk
Russian Fed
39G7 Nyborg Den
39H7 Nybro Sweden
64J3 Nyda Russian Fed
6D1 Nyeboes Land
Region Can
99D3 Nyeri Kenya

101C2 Nyimba Zambia
82D3 Nyingchi China
59C3 Nyiregyháza Hung
99D2 Nyiru,Mt Kenya
38J6 Nykarleby Fin
39F7 Nykøbing Den
39G8 Nykøbing Den
39H7 Nyköping Sweden
100B3 Nylstroom S Africa
109C2 Nymagee Aust
39H7 Nynäshamn Sweden
109C2 Nyngan Aust
47B1 Nyon Switz
49D3 Nyons France
59B2 Nysa Pol
20C2 Nyssa USA
63D1 Nyurba Russian Fed
99D3 Nzega Tanz
97B4 Nzérékore Guinea
98B3 N'zeto Angola

O

6F3 Oaggsimiut
Greenland
8C2 Oahe Res USA
21C4 Oahu I Hawaiian Is
108B2 Oakbank Aust
22B2 Oakdale USA
109D1 Oakey Aust
21A2 Oakland California,
USA
20B2 Oakland Oreg,
USA
14A3 Oakland City USA
14A2 Oak Lawn USA
22B2 Oakley California,
USA
20B2 Oakridge USA
14C2 Oakville Can
111B3 Oamaru NZ
109C4 Oatlands Aust
23B2 Oaxaca Mexico
23B2 Oaxaca State,
Mexico
65J3 Ob' R Russian Fed
75B1 Obama Japan
111A3 Oban NZ
74E3 Obanazawa Japan
47D1 Oberammergau
Germany
46D1 Oberhausen
Germany
47D1 Oberstdorf Germany
71D4 Obi I Indon
33F4 Obidos Brazil
74E2 Obihiro Japan
98C2 Obo CAR
99E1 Obock Djibouti
58B2 Oborniki Pol
60E3 Oboyan Russian Fed
20B2 O'Brien USA
61H3 Obshchiy Syrt
Russian Fed
64J3 Obskava Guba B
Russian Fed
97B4 Obuasi Ghana
17B2 Ocala USA
32C2 Ocana Colombia
50B2 Ocaña Spain
12G3 Ocean I USA
15C3 Ocean City
Maryland, USA
16B3 Ocean City New
Jersey, USA
5F4 Ocean Falls Can
22D4 Oceanside USA
19C3 Ocean Springs USA
61H2 Ocher Russian Fed
44C3 Ochil Hills Scot
17B1 Ochlockonee R USA
27H1 Ocho Rios Jamaica
17B1 Ocmulgee R USA
17B1 Oconee R USA
14A2 Oconto USA
23A1 Ocotlán Jalisco,
Mexico
23B2 Ocotlán Oaxaca,
Mexico
97B4 Oda Ghana
75A1 Oda Japan

38B2 Ódáðahraun Region,
Iceland
74E2 Odate Japan
74D3 Odawara Japan
39F6 Odda Nor
50A2 Odemira Port
55C3 Ödemiş Turk
101G1 Odendaalsrus
S Africa
39G7 Odense Den
56C2 Oder R Pol/Germany
9C3 Odessa Texas, USA
60D4 Odessa Ukraine
20C1 Odessa Washington,
USA
97B4 Odienné Côte
d'Ivoire
59B2 Odra R Pol
31C3 Oeiras Brazil
53C2 Ofanto R Italy
94B3 Ofaqim Israel
45C2 Offaly County,
Irish Rep
49D1 Offenbach Germany
49D2 Offenburg Germany
74D3 Oga Japan
99E2 Ogaden Region, Eth
74D3 Ogaki Japan
8C2 Ogallala USA
69G4 Ogasawara Gunto Is
97C4 Ogbomosho Nig
8B2 Ogden Utah, USA
15C2 Ogdensburg USA
17B1 Ogeechee R USA
12G1 Ogilvie Can
4E3 Ogilvie Mts Can
17B1 Oglethorpe,Mt USA
47D2 Oglio R Italy
47B1 Ognon R France
97C4 Ogoja Nig
98A3 Ogooué R Gabon
58C1 Ogre Latvia
96B2 Ogulet Khenachich
Well Mali
52C1 Ogulin Croatia
111A3 Ohai NZ
110C1 Ohakune NZ
96C2 Ohanet Alg
111A2 Ohau,L NZ
10B2 Ohio State, USA
14A3 Ohio R USA
100A2 Ohopoho Namibia
57C2 Ohre R
Czech Republic
55B2 Ohrid Macedonia
55B2 Ohridsko Jezero L
Macedonia/Alb
110B1 Ohura NZ
33G3 Oiapoque French
Guiana
68B2 Oijiaojing China
14C2 Oil City USA
21B2 Oildale USA
46B2 Oise Department,
France
49C2 Oise R France
74C4 Oita Japan
22C3 Ojai USA
24B2 Ojinaga Mexico
23B2 Ojitlán Mexico
75B1 Ojiya Japan
30C4 Ojos del Salado Mt
Arg
23A1 Ojueloz Mexico
60E3 Oka R Russian Fed
100A3 Okahandja Namibia
20C1 Okanagan Falls
Can
13D2 Okanagan L Can
20C1 Okanogan USA
20C1 Okanogan R USA
20B1 Okanogan Range
Mts Can/USA
84C2 Okara Pak
100A2 Okavango R Angola/
Namibia
100B2 Okavango Delta
Marsh Botswana
74D3 Okaya Japan
74C4 Okayama Japan
75B2 Okazaki Japan
17B2 Okeechobee USA
17B2 Okeechobee,L USA

17B1 Okefenokee Swamp
USA
97C4 Okene Nig
84A Okha India
69G1 Okha Russian Fed
86B1 Okhaldunga Nepal
62J3 Okhotsk,S of
Russian Fed
69E4 Okinawa I Japan
69E4 Okinawa gunto Arch
Japan
74C3 Oki-shoto Is Japan
9D3 Oklahoma State, USA
18A2 Oklahoma City USA
18A2 Okmulgee USA
98B3 Okondja Gabon
98B3 Okoyo Congo
97C4 Okpara R Nig
84A2 Oktyabr'sk
Kazakhstan
61H3 Oktyabr'skiy
Russian Fed
74D2 Okushiri-tō I Japan
38A2 Ólafsvik Iceland
39H7 Oland I Sweden
108B2 Olary Aust
18D2 Olathe USA
29D3 Olavarria Arg
53A2 Olbia Sardegna
12G1 Old Crow Can
56B2 Oldenburg
Niedersachsen,
Germany
56C2 Oldenburg
Schleswig-Holstein,
Germany
15C2 Old Forge USA
42C3 Oldham Eng
12D3 Old Harbor USA
41B3 Old Head of Kinsale
Irish Rep
16C2 Old Lyme USA
13E2 Olds Can
72D1 Oldziyt Mongolia
15C2 Olean USA
63E2 Olekma R
Russian Fed
63D1 Olekminsk
Russian Fed
38L5 Olenegorsk
Russian Fed
60D1 Olevsk Ukraine
69F2 Ol'ga Russian Fed
100A3 Olifants R Namibia
55B2 Ólimbos Mt Greece
35B2 Olímpia Brazil
23B2 Olinala Mexico
31E3 Olinda Brazil
34C2 Oliva Arg
29C2 Olivares Mt Arg
35C2 Oliveira Brazil
33D3 Oliver Can
30C3 Ollague Chile
30C3 Ollague Mt Bol
18C2 Olney USA
68E1 Olochi Russian Fed
39J7 Olofstrom Sweden
99B3 Olombo Congo
59B3 Olomouc
Czech Republic
60D1 Olonets Russian Fed
79B3 Olongapa Phil
48B3 Oloron Ste Marie
France
100A2 Olovyannaya
Russian Fed
46D1 Olpe Germany
58C2 Olsztyn Pol
54B2 Olt R Rom
47B1 Olten Switz
20B1 Olympia USA
20B1 Olympic Nat Pk USA
Olympus = Ólimbos
20B1 Olympus,Mt USA
65L4 Om' R Russian Fed
75B1 Omachi Japan
75B2 Omae-zaki C Japan
45C1 Omagh N Ire
18A1 Omaha USA
20C1 Omak USA
91C5 Oman Sultanate,
Arabian Pen
91C4 Oman,G of UAE
98A3 Omboué Gabon

99D1 Omdurman Sudan
23B2 Ometepec Mexico
99D1 Om Häjer Eritrea
13B1 Omineca R Can
13B1 Omineca Mts Can
75B1 Omiya Japan
12H3 Ommaney,C USA
4H2 Ommaney R Can
99D2 Omo R Eth
65J4 Omsk Russian Fed
74B4 Omura Japan
74C4 Omuta Japan
61H2 Omutninsk Russian Fed
78D3 Onang Indon
14B1 Onanga L Gabon
100A2 Oncócua Angola
100A2 Ondangua Namibia
59C3 Ondava R Slovakia
68D2 Öndörhaan Molgolia
83B5 One and Half Degree Chan Indian O
64E3 Onega Russian Fed
64E3 Onega R Russian Fed
15C2 Oneida L USA
8D2 O'Neill USA
69H2 Onekotan I Russian Fed
98C3 Onema Zaire
15D2 Oneonta USA
54C1 Onești Rom
64E3 Onezhskoye Ozero L Russian Fed
100A2 Ongiva Angola
74B3 Ongjin N Korea
72D1 Ongniud Qi China
87C1 Ongole India
15C2 Onieda L USA
101D3 Onilahy R Madag
97C4 Onitsha Nig
68C2 Onjüül Mongolia
75B1 Ono Japan
75B2 Onohara-jima I Japan
74C4 Onomichi Japan
106A3 Onslow Aust
17C1 Onslow B USA
75B1 Ontake-san Mt Japan
22D3 Ontario California, USA
20C2 Ontario Oregon, USA
7A4 Ontario Province, Can
15C2 Ontario L Can/USA
51B2 Onteniente Spain
106C3 Oodnadatta Aust
106C4 Ooldea Aust
18A2 Oologah L USA
46B1 Oostende Belg
46B1 Oosterschelde Estuary Neth
87B2 Ootacamund India
13B2 Ootsa L Can
69H1 Opala Russian Fed
98C3 Opala Zaire
87C3 Opanake Sri Lanka
61G2 Oparino Russian Fed
59B3 Opava Czech Republic
17A1 Opelika USA
19B3 Opelousas USA
12C2 Ophir USA
58D1 Opochka Russian Fed
59B2 Opole Pol
Oporto = Porto
110C1 Opotiki NZ
17A1 Opp USA
38F6 Oppdal Nor
110B1 Opunake NZ
54B1 Oradea Rom
38B2 Oraefajökull Mts Iceland
85D3 Orai India
96B1 Oran Alg
30D3 Orán Arg
109C2 Orange Aust
22D4 Orange California, USA
49C3 Orange France
19B3 Orange Texas, USA
100A3 Orange R S Africa

17B1 Orangeburg USA
17B1 Orange Park USA
14B2 Orangeville Can
56C2 Oranienburg Ger
79C3 Oras Phil
54B1 Orăștie Rom
54B1 Oravița Rom
52B2 Orbetello Italy
109C3 Orbost Aust
46B1 Orchies France
47B2 Orco R Italy
106B2 Ord R Aust
106B2 Ord,Mt Aust
93C1 Ordu Turk
39H7 Örebro Sweden
8A2 Oregon State, USA
14B2 Oregon City USA
20B1 Oregon City USA
39H6 Öregrund Sweden
60E2 Orekhovo Zuyevo Russian Fed
60E3 Orel Russian Fed
60E3 Orel Division Russian Fed
61H3 Orenburg Russian Fed
61H3 Orenburg Division Russian Fed
34D3 Orense Arg
50A1 Orense Spain
56C1 Oresund Str Den/Sweden
111A3 Oreti R NZ
55C3 Orhaneli R Turk
68C2 Orhon Gol R Mongolia
32E2 Orinoco R Ven
86A2 Orissa State, India
53A3 Oristano Sardegna
38K6 Orivesi I Fin
33F4 Oriximiná Brazil
23B2 Orizaba Mexico
35B1 Orkney I Scot
35B2 Orlândia Brazil
17B2 Orlando USA
48C2 Orléanais Region France
48C2 Orléans France
63B2 Orlik Russian Fed
82A3 Ormara Pak
79B3 Ormoc Phil
17B2 Ormond Beach USA
46C2 Ornain R France
47B1 Ornans France
48B2 Orne R France
38H6 Örnsköldsvik Sweden
32C3 Orocue Colombia
94B3 Oron Israel
Orontes = 'Aşi
79B4 Oroquieta Phil
59C3 Oroshaza Hung
21A2 Oroville California, USA
20C1 Oroville Washington, USA
47B1 Orsières Switz
65G4 Orsk Russian Fed
38F6 Ørsta Nor
48B3 Orthez France
50A1 Ortigueira Spain
47D1 Ortles Mts Italy
27L1 Ortoire R Trinidad
93E2 Orūmīyeh Iran
30C2 Oruro Bol
61J2 Osa Russian Fed
18B2 Osage R USA
75B1 Osaka Japan
25D4 Osa,Pen de Costa Rica
18C2 Osceola Arkansas, USA
18B1 Osceola Iowa, USA
20C2 Osgood Mts USA
15C2 Oshawa Can
75B2 O-shima I Japan
10B2 Oshkosh USA
97C4 Oshogbo Nig

7B5 Oshosh USA
98B3 Oshwe Zaïre
54A1 Osijek Croatia
65K5 Osinniki Russian Fed
58D2 Osipovichi Belarus
18B1 Oskaloosa USA
60A2 Oskarshamn Sweden
39G7 Oslo Nor
92C2 Osmaniye Turk
56B2 Osnabrück Germany
30F4 Osório Brazil
29B4 Osorno Chile
50B1 Osorno Spain
20C1 Osoyoos Can
13C1 Ospika R Can
107D5 Ossa,Mt Aust
16C2 Ossining USA
60D2 Ostashkov Russian Fed
Ostend = Oostende
38G6 Østerdalen V Nor
38G6 Östersund Sweden
56B2 Ostfriesische Inseln Is Germany
39H6 Östhammar Sweden
53B2 Ostia Italy
47D2 Ostiglia Italy
59B3 Ostrava Czech Republic
58B2 Ostróda Pol
58B2 Ostroleka Pol
60C2 Ostrov Russian Fed
64J2 Ostrov Belyy I Russian Fed
64H1 Ostrov Greem Bell I Barents S
64F3 Ostrov Kolguyev I Russian Fed
74F2 Ostrov Kunashir I Russian Fed
64F2 Ostrov Mechdusharskiy I Barents S
90B2 Ostrov Ogurchinskiy I Turkmenistan
64G1 Ostrov Rudol'fa I Barents S
64G2 Ostrov Vaygach I Russian Fed
1B7 Ostrov Vrangelya I Russian Fed
58B2 Ostrów Wlkp. Pol
59C2 Ostrowiec Pol
58C2 Ostrów Mazowiecka Pol
50A2 Osuna Spain
15C2 Oswego USA
15C2 Oswego R USA
43C3 Oswestry Eng
59B2 Oświęcim Pol
75B1 Ota Japan
111A3 Otago Pen NZ
110C2 Otaki NZ
74E2 Otaru Japan
32B3 Otavalo Ecuador
100A2 Otavi Namibia
75C1 Otawara Japan
20C1 Othello USA
55B3 Óthris Mt Greece
16C1 Otis Massachusetts, USA
16B2 Otisville USA
100A3 Otjiwarongo Namibia
72B2 Otog Qi China
110C1 Otorohanga NZ
55A2 Otranto Italy
55A2 Otranto,Str of Chan Italy/Alb
14A2 Otsego USA
75B1 Otsu Japan
39F6 Otta Nor
39F7 Otta R Nor
15C1 Ottawa Can
18A2 Ottawa Kansas, USA
15C1 Ottawa R Can
7B4 Ottawa Is Can
6B1 Otter Rapids Can
6B1 Otto Fjord Can
101G1 Ottosdal S Africa
18B1 Ottumwa USA
46D2 Ottweiler Germany
97C4 Oturkpo Nig

32B5 Otusco Peru
108B3 Otway,C Aust
58C2 Otwock Pol
47D1 Ötz Austria
47D1 Ötztal Mts Austria
76C1 Ou R Laos
19B3 Ouachita R USA
19B3 Ouachita,L USA
19B3 Ouachita Mts USA
96A2 Ouadane Maur
98C2 Ouadda CAR
98C1 Ouaddaï Desert Region Chad
97B3 Ouagadougou Burkina
97B3 Ouahigouya Burkina
98C2 Ouaka CAR
97B3 Oualam Niger
96C2 Oualen Alg
98C2 Ouanda Djallé CAR
96A2 Ouarane Region, Maur
96C1 Ouargla Alg
98C2 Ouarra R CAR
96B1 Ouarzazate Mor
51C2 Ouassel R Alg
98B2 Oubangui R Congo
46B1 Oudenaarde Belg
100B4 Oudtshoorn S Africa
51B2 Oued Tlélat Alg
96B1 Oued Zem Mor
98B2 Ouesso Congo
96B1 Ouezzane Mor
98B2 Ouham R Chad
97C4 Ouidah Benin
97B3 Oujda Mor
38J6 Oulainen Fin
38K5 Oulu Fin
38K6 Oulu R Fin
38K6 Oulujärvi L Fin
38K5 Oum Chalouba Chad
98B1 Oum Hadjer Chad
98B3 Oum Haouach Watercourse Chad
38K5 Ounas R Fin
95B3 Ounianga Kébir Chad
46D1 Our R Germany
46B2 Ourcq R France
Ourense = Orense
31C3 Ouricuri Brazil
35B2 Ourinhos Brazil
35C2 Ouro Prêto Brazil
46C1 Ourthe R Belg
42E3 Ouse R Eng
43E3 Ouse R Eng
40B2 Outer Hebrides Is Scot
22C4 Outer Santa Barbara Chan USA
100A3 Outjo Namibia
38K6 Outokumpu Fin
108B3 Ouyen Aust
47C2 Ovada Italy
34A2 Ovalle Chile
100A2 Ovamboland Region, Namibia
61H5 Ova Tyuleni Is Kazakhstan
38J5 Overtorneå Sweden
50A1 Oviedo Spain
60C3 Ovruch Ukraine
63E2 Ovsyanka Russian Fed
111A3 Owaka NZ
75B2 Owase Japan
11B3 Owensboro USA
21B2 Owens L USA
14B2 Owen Sound Can
107D1 Owen Stanley Range Mts PNG
97C4 Owerri Nig
97C4 Owo Nig
14B2 Owosso USA
20C2 Owyhee R USA
20C2 Owyhee Mts USA
32B6 Oxapampa Peru
39H7 Oxelösund Sweden
43D4 Oxford Eng
43D4 Oxford County, Eng
16D1 Oxford Massachusetts, USA
19C3 Oxford Mississippi, USA
45B1 Ox Mts Irish Rep

Oxnard

22C3 Oxnard USA
74D3 Oyama Japan
13E2 Oyen Can
98B2 Oyem Gabon
44B3 Oykel R Scot
39F6 Øyre Nor
109C4 Oyster B Aust
79B4 Ozamiz Phil
17A1 Ozark USA
18B2 Ozark Plat USA
18B2 Ozarks,L of the USA
59C3 Ozd Hung
65K5 Ozero Alakol L
 Kazakhstan/
 Russian Fed
65J5 Ozero Balkhash L
 Kazakhstan
63C2 Ozero Baykal L
 Kazakhstan
65J4 Ozero Chany L
 Russian Fed
69F1 Ozero
 Chukchagirskoye
 Russian Fed
69F1 Ozero Evoron
 Russian Fed
 Ozero Chudskoye =
 Peipus,L
60D2 Ozero Il'men L
 Russian Fed
38L5 Ozero Imandra L
 Russian Fed
82B1 Ozero Issyk Kul' L
 Kyrgyzstan
69F2 Ozero Khanka L
 China/Russian Fed
38L5 Ozero Kovdozero L
 Russian Fed
38L5 Ozero Kuyto L
 Russian Fed
38L5 Ozero Pyaozero L
 Russian Fed
65H4 Ozero Tengiz L
 Kazakhstan
38L5 Ozero Topozero L
 Russian Fed
65K5 Ozero Zaysan L
 Kazakhstan
23B1 Ozuluama Mexico

P

100A4 Paarl S Africa
44A3 Pabay I Scot
58B2 Pabianice Pol
86B2 Pabna Bang
58D2 Pabrade Lithuania
32B5 Pacasmayo Peru
23B1 Pachuca Mexico
105K6 Pacific-Antarctic
 Ridge Pacific O
22B2 Pacific Grove USA
84C2 Pacitan Indon
35C1 Pacui R Brazil
70B4 Padang Indon
56B2 Paderborn Germany
53C3 Padlei Can
86C2 Padma R Bang
47D2 Padova R Italy
9D4 Padre I USA
43B4 Padstow Eng
108B3 Padthaway Aust
 Padua = Padova
14A3 Paducah Kentucky,
 USA
11B3 Paducah USA
38L5 Padunskoye More L
 Russian Fed
74A3 Paengnyóng-do I S
 Korea
110C1 Paeroa NZ
100C3 Pafuri Mozam
52B2 Pag I Croatia
79B4 Pagadian Phil
79B4 Pagai Selatan I Indon
70B4 Pagai Utara I Indon
71F2 Pagan I Pacific O
78D3 Pagatan Indon
55C3 Pagondhas Greece
21C4 Pahala USA
21C4 Pahoa Hawaiian Is
17B2 Pahokee USA
39K6 Päijänne L Fin
21C4 Pailola Chan
 Hawaiian Is

14B2 Painesville USA
9B3 Painted Desert USA
42B2 Paisley Scot
32A5 Paita Peru
38J5 Pajala Sweden
80E3 Pakistan Republic,
 Asia
76C2 Pak Lay Laos
86D2 Pakokku Myan
13E2 Pakowki L Can
52C1 Pakrac Croatia
76C2 Paks Hung
76C2 Pak Sane Laos
76D2 Pakse Laos
99D2 Pakwach Uganda
98B2 Pala Chad
52C2 Palagruza I Croatia
46B2 Palaiseau France
 Palakhat = Palghat
78C3 Palangkaraya Indon
78A3 Palembang Indon
50B1 Palencia Spain
94A1 Paleokhorio Cyprus
53B3 Palermo Italy
17D4 Palestine USA
98C2 Paletwa Myan
87B2 Pälghät India
85C3 Päli India
85C4 Pälitana India
 Palk Str India/
 Sri Lanka
61G3 Pallasovka
 Russian Fed
38J5 Pallastunturi Mt Fin
111B2 Palliser B NZ
111C2 Palliser,C NZ
101D2 Palma Mozam
51C2 Palma de Mallorca
 Spain
31D3 Palmares Brazil
26A5 Palmar Sur Costa
 Rica
31B4 Palmas Brazil
97B4 Palmas,C Lib
26B2 Palma Soriano Cuba
17B2 Palm Bay USA
17B2 Palm Beach USA
22C3 Palmdale USA
31D3 Palmeira dos Indos
 Brazil
12E2 Palmer USA
112C3 Palmer Base Ant
112C3 Palmer Arch Ant
112B3 Palmer Land Region
 Ant
111B3 Palmerston NZ
110C2 Palmerston North NZ
16B2 Palmerton USA
17B2 Palmetto USA
53C3 Palmi Italy
32B3 Palmira Colombia
107D2 Palm Is Aust
21B3 Palm Springs USA
18B2 Palmyra Missouri,
 USA
16A2 Palmyra
 Pennsylvania, USA
86B2 Palmyras Pt India
22A2 Palo Alto USA
78B2 Paloh Indon
99D1 Paloich Sudan
21B3 Palomar Mt USA
70D4 Palopo Indon
70A4 Palu Indon
93C2 Palu Turk
84D3 Palwal India
97C3 Pama Burkina
78C4 Pamekasan Indon
78B4 Pameungpeuk Indon
48C3 Pamiers France
82B2 Pamir Mts China
65J6 Pamir R Russian Fed
11C3 Pamlico Sd USA
9C3 Pampa USA

34B2 Pampa de la Salinas
 Salt pan Arg
34B3 Pampa de la Varita
 Plain Arg
32C2 Pamplona Colombia
50B1 Pamplona Spain
12C2 Pana USA
54B2 Panagyurishte Bulg
87A1 Panaji India
32B2 Panamá Panama
32A2 Panama Republic,
 Cent America
26B5 Panama Canal
 Panama
17A1 Panama City USA
21B2 Panamint Range Mts
 USA
21B2 Panamint V USA
47D2 Panaro R Italy
79B3 Panay I Phil
54B2 Pancevo Serbia,
 Yugos
79B3 Pandan Phil
87B1 Pandharpur India
86C2 Pandie Pandie Aust
58C1 Panevezys Lithuania
65K5 Panfilov Kazakhstan
76B1 Pang R Myan
99D3 Pangani Tanz
99D3 Pangani R Tanz
98C3 Pangi Zaire
78B3 Pangkalpinang Indon
6D3 Pangnirtung Can
76B1 Pangtara Myan
79B4 Pangutaran Group Is
 Phil
84D3 Panipat India
84B2 Panjao Afghan
74B3 P'anmunjóm N Korea
86A2 Panna India
35A2 Panorama Brazil
53B3 Pantelleria I Medit S
32B1 Pantepec Mexico
23B1 Panuco Mexico
23B1 Pánuco R Mexico
73A4 Pan Xian China
53C3 Paola Italy
18B2 Paola USA
14A3 Paoli USA
59B3 Pápa Hung
110B1 Papakura NZ
23B2 Papaloapan R
 Mexico
112A Papantla Mexico
44E1 Papa Stour I Scot
110C1 Papatoetoe NZ
44C2 Papa Westray I Scot
107D1 Papua,G of PNG
107D1 Papua New Guinea
 Republic, S E Asia
34A2 Papudo Chile
76B2 Papun Myan
33G4 Para State, Brazil
31B2 Pará R Brazil
106A3 Paraburdoo Aust
32B6 Paracas,Pen de Peru
35B1 Paracatu Brazil
35B1 Paracatu R Brazil
108A2 Parachilna Aust
84C2 Parachinar Pak
54B2 Paracin Serbia,
 Yugos
35C1 Pará de Minas Brazil
21A2 Paradise California,
 USA
18B2 Paragould USA
33E6 Paraguá R Bol
33E2 Paragua R Ven
32B2 Paraguai R Brazil
30E4 Paraguari Par
30E3 Paraguay Republic,
 S America
30E3 Paraguay R Par
31D3 Paraíba State, Brazil
35B2 Paraíba R Brazil
35C2 Paraíba do Sul R
 Brazil
97C4 Parakou Benin
108A2 Parakylia Aust
87B3 Paramakkudi India
33F2 Paramaribo Surinam
69H1 Paramushir I
 Russian Fed
30F3 Paraná State, Brazil

34C2 Paraná Urug
29E2 Paraná R Arg
31B4 Paraná R Brazil
35A2 Paraná R Brazil
35A2 Paranaguá Brazil
35A1 Paranaiba Brazil
35A1 Paranaiba R Brazil
35A2 Paranapanema R
 Brazil
35A2 Paranavai Brazil
79A4 Parang Phil
35C1 Paraope R Brazil
110B2 Paraparaumu NZ
87B1 Parbhani India
94B2 Pardes Hanna Israel
35A3 Pardo R Bahia, Brazil
35D1 Pardo R Brazil
35A2 Pardo R Mato
 Grosso do Sul, Brazil
35B1 Pardo R Minas
 Gerais, Brazil
35B2 Pardo R Sao Paulo,
 Brazil
59B2 Pardubice
 Czech Republic
69F4 Parece Vela Reef
 Pacific O
10C2 Parent Can
70C4 Parepare Indon
34C3 Parera Arg
70B4 Pariaman Indon
33E1 Paria,Pen de Ven
48C2 Paris France
74S5 Paris Kentucky, USA
19A3 Paris Texas, USA
14B3 Parkersburg USA
109C2 Parkes Aust
16B3 Parkesburg USA
14A2 Park Forest USA
20B1 Parksville Can
87B1 Parli India
14B2 Parma Italy
14B2 Parma USA
31C2 Parnaiba Brazil
31C2 Parnaiba R Brazil
55B3 Párnon Oros Mts
 Greece
60B2 Pärnu Estonia
86B1 Paro Bhutan
108B1 Paroo R Aust
108B2 Paroo Channel R
 Aust
55C3 Páros I Greece
47B2 Parpaillon Mts
 France
34A3 Parral Chile
109D2 Parramatta Aust
9C4 Parras Mexico
6B3 Parry B Can
4G2 Parry Is Can
7C5 Parry Sd Can
14B1 Parry Sound Can
57C3 Parsberg Germany
5F4 Parsnip R Can
18A2 Parsons Kansas, USA
14C3 Parsons West
 Virginia, USA
48B2 Parthenay France
53B3 Partinico Italy
74C2 Partizansk
 Russian Fed
33G4 Paru R Brazil
101G1 Parys S Africa
19A4 Pasadena Texas,
 USA
22C3 Pasadena California,
 USA
78D3 Pasangkayu Indon
76B2 Pasawing Myan
19C3 Pascagoula USA
54C1 Pascani Rom
20C1 Pasco USA
46B1 Pas-de-Calais
 Department, France
39G8 Pasewalk Germany
91C4 Pashū'iyeh Iran
106B4 Pasley,C Aust
29E2 Paso de los Toros
 Urug
29B4 Paso Limay Arg
21A2 Paso Robles USA
45B3 Passage West
 Irish Rep
16B2 Passaic USA

57C3 Passau Germany
30E4 Passo de los Libres Arg
47D1 Passo di Stelvio Mt Italy
30F4 Passo Fundo Brazil
35B2 Passos Brazil
47B2 Passy France
32B4 Pastaza R Peru
34C3 Pasteur Arg
5H4 Pas,The Can
32B3 Pasto Colombia
12B2 Pastol B USA
47D2 Pasubio Mt Italy
3286 Pativilca Peru
58C1 Pasvalys Lithuania
85C4 Pätan India
108B3 Patchewollock Aust
10B1 Patea NZ
111B2 Patea R NZ
53B3 Paterno Italy
16B2 Paterson USA
111A3 Paterson Inlet B NZ
84D2 Pathankot India
Pathein = Bassein
84D2 Patiäla India
53C5 Patiala = Bassein
55C3 Pátmos I Greece
86B1 Patna India
93D2 Patnos Turk
63D2 Patomskoye Nagor'ye Upland Russian Fed
31D3 Patos Brazil
35B1 Patos de Minas Brazil
34B2 Patquia Arg
55B3 Pátrai Greece
35B1 Patrocinio Brazil
99E3 Patta I Kenya
78D4 Pattallasang Indon
77C4 Pattani Thai
22B2 Patterson California, USA
19B4 Patterson Louisiana, USA
12H2 Patterson,Mt Can
22C2 Patterson Mt USA
13B1 Pattullo,Mt Can
31D3 Patu Brazil
86C2 Patuakhali Bang
25D3 Patuca R Honduras
23A2 Patzcuaro Mexico
48B3 Pau France
4F3 Paulatuk Can
31C3 Paulistana Brazil
101H1 Paulpietersburg S Africa
19A3 Pauls Valley USA
76B2 Paungde Myan
84D2 Pauri India
38H5 Pauskie Nor
35C1 Pavão Brazil
47C2 Pavia Italy
65J4 Pavlodar Kazakhstan
61J2 Pavlovka Russian Fed
61F2 Pavlovo Russian Fed
61F3 Pavlovsk Russian Fed
78C3 Pawan R Indon
18A2 Pawhuska USA
16D2 Pawtucket USA
47B1 Payerne Switz
20C2 Payette USA
7C4 Payne,L Can
34D2 Paysandu Urug
46A2 Pays-de-Bray Region, France
54B2 Pazardzhik Bulg
13D1 Peace R Can
17B2 Peace R USA
13D1 Peace River Can
43D3 Peak District Nat Pk Eng
108A1 Peake R Aust
109C2 Peak Hill Aust
71E4 Peak Mandala Mt Indon
42D3 Peak,The Mt Eng
19B3 Pearl R USA
21C4 Pearl City Hawaiian Is

21C4 Pearl Harbor Hawaiian Is
4H2 Peary Chan Can
101C2 Pebane Mozam
66C1 Peć Serbia, Yugos
35C1 Peçanha Brazil
19B4 Pecan Island USA
38L5 Pechenga Russian Fed
64F3 Pechora R Russian Fed
64G3 Pechorskoye More S Russian Fed
53C2 Pecoraro Mt Italy
9C3 Pecos USA
9C3 Pecos R USA
59B3 Pécs Hung
108A1 Pedirka Aust
26B3 Pedro Azul Brazil
35B2 Pedroguiho Brazil
26B3 Pedro Cays Is Caribbean S
17C1 Pee Dee R USA
16C2 Peekskill USA
42B2 Peel Eng
12H1 Peel R Can
4J2 Peel Sd Can
108A1 Peera Peera Poolanna L Aust
13E1 Peerless L Can
71E4 Peg Arfak Mt Indon
111B2 Pegasus B NZ
83D4 Pegu Myan
78A3 Pegunungan Barisan Mts Indon
78C2 Pegunungan Iran Mts Malay/Indon
71E4 Pegunungan Maoke Mts Indon
78D3 Pegunungan Meratus Mts Indon
78C2 Pegunungan Muller Mts Indon
78C3 Pegunungan Schwaner Mts Indon
78A3 Pegunungan Tigapuluh Mts Indon
76B2 Pegu Yoma Mts Myan
34C3 Pehuajó Arg
Péipsi Järve = Peipus,L
39K7 Peipus, Lake Estonia/ Russian Fed
35A2 Peixe R Sao Paulo, Brazil
72D3 Pei Xian China
78A4 Pekalongan Indon
77C5 Pekan Malay
78A2 Pekanbaru Indon
18C1 Pekin USA
Peking = Beijing
77C5 Pelabohan Kelang Malay
78D4 Pelau Pelau Kangean Is Indon
78C4 Pelau Pelau Karimunjawa Arch Indon
78D4 Pelau Pelau Postilyon Is Indon
54B1 Peleaga Mt Rom
63D2 Peleduy Russian Fed
14B2 Pelee I Can
71D4 Peleng I Indon
12G3 Pelican USA
69F1 Peliny Osipenko Aust
34C3 Pellegrini Arg
38J5 Pello Fin
12H2 Pelly R Can
6A3 Pelly Bay Can
12G2 Pelly Crossing Can
12H2 Pelly Mts Can

30F5 Pelotas Brazil
30F4 Pelotas R Brazil
47B2 Pelvoux Region, France
78B4 Pemalang Indon
78A3 Pematang Indon
101D2 Pemba Mozam
99D3 Pemba I Tanz
13C2 Pemberton Can
13D2 Pembina R Can
15C1 Pembroke Can
17B1 Pembroke Can
43B4 Pembroke Wales
43B4 Pembrokeshire County Wales
34A3 Pemuco Chile
78D2 Penambo Range Mts Malay
26A5 Penápolis Brazil
50A2 Peñarroya Spain
51B1 Penarroya Mt Spain
50A1 Peña Trevina Mt Spain
98B2 Pende R Chad
12J3 Pendelton,Mt Can
20C1 Pendleton USA
20C1 Pend Oreille R USA
31D4 Penedo Brazil
14B2 Penetanguishene Can
73D5 P'eng-hu Lieh-tao Is Taiwan
72E2 Penglai China
73B4 Pengzi China
71E4 Pengunungan Maoke Mts Indon
26C4 Península de la Guajiri Pen Colombia
27E4 Península de Paria Pen Ven
Peninsular Malaysia = Malay
10D2 Peninsule de Gaspé Pen Can
21A1 Penjamo Mexico
87B2 Penner R India
42C2 Pennine Chain Mts Eng
16B3 Penns Grove USA
10C2 Pennsylvania State, USA
6D3 Penny Highlands Mts Can
33C3 Penola Aust
106C4 Penong Aust
42C2 Penrith Eng
11B3 Pensacola USA
112A Pensacola Mts Ant
78D1 Pensiangan Malay
35A3 Penticton Can
44C2 Pentland Firth Chan Scot
44C3 Pentland Hills Scot
61G3 Penza Division Russian Fed
43B4 Penzance Eng
78A3 Perabumulih Indon
77C5 Perak R Malay
78A2 Perawang Indon
81B4 Percira Colombia
35A3 Pereira Barreto Brazil
61F4 Perelazovskiy Russian Fed
12D3 Perenosa B USA
54B2 Pernik Bulg
18A2 Perote Mexico
23B2 Perote Mexico
49C3 Perpignan France
22D4 Perris USA
17B1 Perry Florida, USA

17B1 Perry Georgia, USA
18A2 Perry Oklahoma, USA
4H3 Perry River Can
14B2 Perrysburg USA
12C3 Perryville Alaska, USA
18C2 Perryville Missouri, USA
17H Perth Aust
15C2 Perth Can
44C3 Perth Scot
16B2 Perth Amboy USA
44C3 Perthshire and Kinross Division, Scot
32C6 Peru Republic, S America
18C1 Peru USA
103E5 Peru-Chile Trench Pacific O
52B2 Perugia Italy
52C2 Prušic Croatia
39D2 Pervari Turk
61F3 Pervomaysk Russian Fed
60D4 Pervomaysk Ukraine
61J2 Pervoural'sk Russian Fed
52B2 Pesaro Italy
22A2 Pescadero = P'eng-hu Lieh-tao
52R? Pescara Italy
47D2 Peschiera Italy
84C2 Peshawar Pak
56B2 Pesqu Bolb Alb
14A1 Peshtigo USA
60E2 Pestovo Russian Fed
94B2 Petah Tiqwa Israel
46C2 Pétange Lux
23A2 Petatlán Mexico
101C2 Petauke Zambia
108A2 Peterborough Aust
15C2 Peterborough Can
43D3 Peterborough Eng
44D3 Peterhead Scot
6D1 Petermann Gletscher Gl Greenland
106B3 Petermann Range Mts Aust
29B3 Peteroa Mt Arg/Chile
13F1 Peter Pond L Can
12H3 Petersburg Alaska, USA
85C4 Petläd India
23B2 Petlalcingo Mexico
25D2 Peto Mexico
63D2 Petomskoye Nagor'ye Upland Russian Fed
34A2 Petorca Chile
14B1 Petoskey USA
31C3 Petrolina Brazil
65H4 Petropavlovsk Kazakhstan
25C2 Petrópolis Brazil
61G3 Petrovsk Russian Fed
68C1 Petrovsk Zabaykal'skiy Russian Fed
64E3 Petrozavodsk Russian Fed
101G1 Petrus S Africa
101G1 Petrusburg S Africa
46D2 Pfälzer Wald Region, Germany
57B3 Pforzheim Germany
84D2 Phagwara India
85C3 Phalodi India
46D2 Phalsbourg France
87A1 Phaltan India
77B4 Phangnga Thai
76C3 Phanom Dang Mts Camb
76D3 Phan Rang Viet
76D3 Phan Thiet Viet
17D1 Phenix City USA
76D3 Phet Buri Thai
76D3 Phiafay Laos
19C3 Philadelphia Mississippi, USA
17B1 Perry Florida, USA

16B2 **Philadelphia** Pennsylvania, USA
Philippeville = Skikda
46C1 **Philippeville** Belg
71D2 **Philippine S** *Pacific O*
71D2 **Philippines** Republic, S E Asia
104E3 **Philippine Trench** *Pacific O*
15C2 **Philipsburg** Pennsylvania, USA
12E1 **Philip Smith Mts** USA
79B2 **Phillipine S** Phil
6B1 **Phillips B** Can
16B2 **Phillipsburg** New Jersey, USA
62B3 **Philpots Pen** Can
76C3 **Phnom Penh** Camb
9B3 **Phoenix** Arizona, USA
76C1 **Phoenixville** USA
76C1 **Phong Saly** Laos
Phra Nakhon = Bangkok
76C2 **Phu Bia** *Mt* Laos
76D3 **Phu Cuong** Viet
77C4 **Phuket** Thai
86A2 **Phulbani** India
76C2 **Phu Miang** *Mt* Thai
76D2 **Phu Set** *Mt* Laos
76D1 **Phu Tho** Viet
77D4 **Phu Vinh** Viet
47C2 **Piacenza** Italy
109C2 **Pian** *R* Aust
7A2 **Pianosa** *I* Italy
52C2 **Pianosa** *I* Italy
58C2 **Piaseczno** Pol
54C1 **Piatra-Neamţ** Rom
31C3 **Piauí** State, Brazil
47E2 **Piave** *R* Italy
99D2 **Pibor** *R* Sudan
99D2 **Pibor Post** Sudan
48B1 **Picardie** Region, France
19C3 **Picayune** USA
47B2 **Pic de Rochebrune** *Mt* France
34A2 **Pichilemu** Chile
34C3 **Pichi Mahuida** Arg
42D2 **Pickering** Eng
7A4 **Pickle Lake** Can
96A1 **Pico** *I* Açores
47C1 **Pico Bernina** *Mt* Switz
51C1 **Pico de Anito** *Mt* Spain
24B3 **Pico del Infiernillo** *Mt* Mexico
27C3 **Pico Duarte** *Mt* Dom Rep
31C3 **Picos** Brazil
50B1 **Picos de Europa** *Mt* Spain
109D2 **Picton** Aust
111B2 **Picton** NZ
95A2 **Pic Toussidé** *Mt* Chad
35B2 **Piedade** Brazil
22C2 **Piedra** USA
24B2 **Piedras Negras** Mexico
38K6 **Pieksämäki** Fin
38K6 **Pielinen** *L* Fin
47B2 **Piemonte** Region, Italy
8C2 **Pierre** USA
59B3 **Piešťany** Slovakia
101H1 **Pietermaritzburg** S Africa
100B3 **Pietersburg** S Africa
101H1 **Piet Retief** S Africa
60B4 **Pietrosu** *Mt* Rom
47E1 **Pieve di Cadore** Italy
13E2 **Pigeon L** Can
18B2 **Piggott** USA
34C3 **Piguë** Arg
7A4 **Pikangikum L** Can
8C3 **Pikes Peak** USA
100A4 **Piketberg** S Africa
6F3 **Pikiutaleq** Greenland
82B2 **Pik Kommunizma** *Mt* Tajikistan
98B2 **Pikounda** Congo

82C1 **Pik Pobedy** *Mt* China/Kyrgyzstan
34D3 **Pila** Arg
58B2 **Piła** Pol
30E4 **Pilar** Par
30D3 **Pilcomayo** *R* Arg/Par
84D3 **Pilibhit** India
59B2 **Pilica** *R* Pol
109C4 **Pillar,C** Aust
55B3 **Pílos** Greece
12C3 **Pilot Point** USA
12B2 **Pilot Station** USA
19C3 **Pilottown** USA
33F4 **Pimenta** Brazil
77C4 **Pinang** *I* Malay
26A2 **Pinar del Río** Cuba
34B2 **Pinas** Arg
46C1 **Pinche** Belg
13E2 **Pincher Creek** Can
31B2 **Pindaré** *R* Brazil
55B3 **Píndhos** *Mts* Greece
19B3 **Pine Bluff** USA
106C2 **Pine Creek** Aust
22C1 **Pinecrest** USA
22C2 **Pinedale** California, USA
22C2 **Pine Flat Res** USA
64F3 **Pinega** *R* Russian Fed
16A2 **Pine Grove** USA
17B2 **Pine Hills** USA
17B2 **Pine I** USA
19B3 **Pineland** USA
17B2 **Pinellas Park** USA
5G3 **Pine Point** Can
47B2 **Pinerolo** Italy
19B3 **Pines,L o'the** USA
19B3 **Pineville** USA
72C3 **Pingdingshan** China
73B5 **Pingguo** China
72C2 **Pingliang** China
72B2 **Pingliang** China
73D4 **Pingtan Dao** *I* China
73E5 **P'ing tung** Taiwan
72A3 **Pingwu** China
73B5 **Pingxiang** Guangxi, China
73B4 **Pingxiang** Jiangxi, China
31B2 **Pinheiro** Brazil
70A3 **Pini** *I* Indon
55B3 **Piniós** *R* Greece
106A4 **Pinjarra** Aust
13C1 **Pink Mountain** Can
108B3 **Pinnaroo** Aust
Pinos,I de, I = Isla de la Juventud
21A2 **Pinos,Pt** USA
23B2 **Pinotepa Nacional** Mexico
70C1 **Pinrang** Indon
60C3 **Pinsk** Belarus
32J7 **Pinta** *I* Ecuador
61G1 **Pinyug** Russian Fed
9B3 **Pioche** USA
52B2 **Piombino** Italy
59B2 **Piórsá** Iceland
59B2 **Piotrków Trybunalski** Pol
44E2 **Piper** *Oilfield* N Sea
21B2 **Piper Peak** *Mt* USA
10C2 **Pipmuacan Res** Can
14B2 **Piqua** USA
35B1 **Piracanjuba** Brazil
35B2 **Piracicaba** Brazil
35B2 **Piraçununga** Brazil
35B2 **Piraí do Sul** Brazil
55B3 **Piraiévs** Greece
35B2 **Pirajuí** Brazil
35A1 **Piranhas** Brazil
35C1 **Pirapora** Brazil
35B1 **Pirenópolis** Brazil
35B1 **Pires do Rio** Brazil
55B3 **Pírgos** Greece
Pirineos = Pyrénées
31C2 **Piripiri** Brazil
46D2 **Pirmasens** Germany
54B2 **Pirot** Serbia, Yugos
84C2 **Pir Panjäl Range** *Mt* Pak
71D4 **Piru** Indon
22C3 **Piru Creek** *R* USA
49E3 **Pisa** Italy
32B6 **Pisco** Peru

57C3 **Pisek** Czech Republic
84B2 **Pishin** Pak
30C4 **Pissis** *Mt* Arg
49E3 **Pistoia** Italy
50B1 **Pisuerga** *R* Spain
20B2 **Pit** *R* USA
32B3 **Pitalito** Colombia
105K5 **Pitcairn I** Pacific O
38H5 **Pite** *R* Sweden
38J5 **Piteå** Sweden
54B2 **Piteşti** Rom
63B2 **Pit Gorodok** Russian Fed
38L6 **Pitkyaranta** Russian Fed
44C3 **Pitlochry** Scot
34A3 **Pitrutquén** Chile
13B2 **Pitt I** Can
22B1 **Pittsburg** California, USA
18B2 **Pittsburg** Kansas, USA
14C2 **Pittsburgh** USA
18B2 **Pittsfield** Illinois, USA
16C1 **Pittsfield** Massachusetts, USA
109D1 **Pittsworth** Aust
86A1 **Piuthan** Nepal
47D1 **Pizzo Redorta** *Mt* Italy
38B2 **Pjórsá** Iceland
32A5 **Pjura** Peru
7E5 **Placentia B** Can
22B1 **Placerville** USA
46B1 **Plaine des Flandres** France
96C2 **Plaine du Tidikelt** *Desert Region*
9C3 **Plainview** Texas, USA
22B2 **Planada** USA
30F2 **Planalto de Mato Grosso** *Plat* Brazil
31D3 **Planalto do Borborema** *Plat* Brazil
32A1 **Planalto do Mato Grosso** *Mts* Brazil
19A3 **Plano** USA
17B2 **Plantation** USA
17B2 **Plant City** USA
50A1 **Plasencia** Spain
61K3 **Plast** Russian Fed
69F2 **Plastun** Russian Fed
96C2 **Plateau du Tademait** Alg
48C2 **Plateau Lorrain** *Plat* France
48C2 **Plateaux de Limousin** *Plat* France
51C2 **Plateau du Sersou** *Plat* Alg
26C5 **Plato** Colombia
8C2 **Platte** *R* USA
15D2 **Plattsburgh** USA
18B1 **Plattsmouth** USA
57C2 **Plauen** Germany
60E3 **Plavsk** Russian Fed
23A2 **Playa Azul** Mexico
32A4 **Playas** Ecuador
23B2 **Playa Vicente** Mexico
50A1 **Plaza de Moro Almanzor** *Mt* Spain
22B2 **Pleasanton** California, USA
16B3 **Pleasantville** USA
14A3 **Pleasure Ridge Park** USA
76D3 **Pleiku** Viet
110C1 **Plenty,B of** NZ
58B2 **Pleszew** Pol
7C4 **Pletipi,L** Can
54B2 **Pleven** Bulg
54A2 **Pljevlja** Montenegro, Yugos
52C2 **Ploče** Croatia
58B2 **Płock** Pol
48B2 **Ploërmel** France
54C2 **Ploieşti** Rom
60B3 **Płońsk** Pol
54B2 **Plovdiv** Bulg
20C1 **Plummer** USA
12C2 **Plummer,Mt** USA

100B3 **Plumtree** Zim
22B1 **Plymouth** California, USA
43B4 **Plymouth** Eng
14A2 **Plymouth** Indiana, USA
16D2 **Plymouth** Massachusetts, USA
15C2 **Plymouth** Pennsylvania, USA
43B4 **Plymouth Sd** Eng
43C3 **Plynlimon** *Mt* Wales
57C3 **Plzeň** Czech Republic
58B2 **Pniewy** Pol
38K6 **Pnyäselkä** *L* Fin
97B3 **Pô** Burkina
47E2 **Po** *R* Italy
97C4 **Pobé** Benin
69G2 **Pobedino** Russian Fed
15C2 **Pocatello** USA
15C3 **Pocomoke City** USA
35B2 **Pocos de Caldas** Brazil
54A2 **Podgorica** Montenegro, Yugos
47D2 **Po di Volano** *R* Italy
63B1 **Podkamennaya** *R* Russian Fed
60E2 **Podol'skaya Vozvyshennost'** *Upland* Ukraine
59D3 **Podporozh'ye** Russian Fed
61F1 **Podyuga** Russian Fed
100A3 **Pofadder** S Africa
74B3 **P'ohang** S Korea
112C9 **Poinsett,C** Ant
108C2 **Point** Aust
27H1 **Pointe-à-Pitre** Guadeloupe
48B2 **Pointe de Barfleur** *Pt* France
98B3 **Pointe Noire** Congo
98A2 **Pointe Pongara** *Pt* Gabon
108B3 **Point Fairy** Aust
27L1 **Point Fortin** Trinidad
4B3 **Point Hope** USA
4G3 **Point L** Can
12B1 **Point Lay** USA
16B2 **Point Pleasant** New Jersey, USA
14B3 **Point Pleasant** W Virginia, USA
47B2 **Point St Bernard** *Mt* France
48C2 **Poitiers** France
48B2 **Poitou** Region, France
46A2 **Poix** France
85C3 **Pokaran** India
109C1 **Pokataroo** Aust
61G3 **Pokrovsk** Russian Fed
63E1 **Pokrovsk** Russian Fed
58B2 **Poland** Republic, Europe
92B2 **Polath** Turk
78D3 **Polewali** Indon
47A1 **Poligny** France
55B2 **Poliyiros** Greece
87B2 **Pollachi** India
79B3 **Pololo Is** Phil
57B2 **Polonnye** Ukraine
61E2 **Polotsk** Russian Fed
60D4 **Poltava** Russian Fed
64F3 **Poluostrov Kanin** *Pen* Russian Fed
61H5 **Poluostrov Mangyshlak** *Pen* Kazakhstan
38L5 **Poluostrov Rybachiy** *Pen* Russian Fed
64H2 **Poluostrov Yamal** *Pen* Russian Fed
38L5 **Polyarnyy** Murmansk, Russian Fed

1B8 Polyarnyy Yakutskaya, Russian Fed
105H3 Polynesia Region Pacific O
32B5 Pomabamba Peru
35C2 Pomba R Brazil
22D3 Pomona USA
18A2 Pomona Res USA
17B2 Pompano Beach USA
16B2 Pompton Lakes USA
18A2 Ponca City USA
27D3 Ponce Puerto Rico
17B2 Ponce de Leon B USA
87B2 Pondicherry India
6C2 Pond Inlet Can
50A1 Ponferrade Spain
98C2 Pongo R Sudan
101H1 Pongola R S Africa
87B2 Ponnani India
86C2 Ponnyadoung Range Mts Myan
13E2 Ponoka Can
64F3 Ponoy Russian Fed
48B2 Pons France
35D1 Ponta da Baleia Brazil
96A1 Ponta Delgada Açores
98B3 Ponta do Padrão Pt Angola
35C2 Ponta dos Búzios Pt Brazil
30F4 Ponta Grossa Brazil
35B2 Pontal Brazil
46D2 Pont-à-Mousson France
30E3 Ponta Pora Brazil
49D2 Pontarlier France
19B3 Pontchartrain,L USA
52B2 Pontedera Italy
52A2 Ponte Lecca Corse
50A1 Pontevedra Spain
18C1 Pontiac Illinois, USA
14B2 Pontiac Michigan, USA
78B3 Pontianak Indon
48B2 Pontivy France
48B2 Pontoise France
19C3 Pontotoc USA
43C4 Pontypool Wales
43C4 Pontypridd Wales
43D4 Poole Eng
108B2 Pooncarie Aust
108B2 Poopelloe,L L Aust
12C2 Poorman USA
32B3 Popayán Colombia
46B1 Poperinge Belg
13B2 Popilta,L Aust
18B2 Poplar Bluff USA
19C3 Poplarville USA
107D1 Popndetta PNG
23B2 Popocatepetl Mt Mexico
98B3 Popokabaka Zaïre
71F4 Popondetta PNG
13A2 Porcher I Can
12F1 Porcupine R Can/USA
52B1 Poreč Croatia
35A2 Porecatu Brazil
39J6 Pori Fin
111B2 Porirua NZ
38H5 Porjus Sweden
69G2 Poronaysk Russian Fed
47B1 Porrentruy Switz
38K4 Porsangen Inlet Nor
39F7 Porsgrunn Nor
45C1 Portadown N Ire
8D2 Portage la Prairie Can
13C3 Port Alberni Can
50A2 Portalegre Port
9C3 Portales USA
100B4 Port Alfred S Africa
13B2 Port Alice Can

19B3 Port Allen USA
20B1 Port Angeles USA
26B3 Port Antonio Jamaica
45C2 Portarlington Irish Rep
19B4 Port Arthur USA
108A2 Port Augusta Aust
26C3 Port-au-Prince Haiti
14B2 Port Austin USA
108B3 Port Campbell Aust
86B2 Port Canning India
7D5 Port Cartier Can
111B3 Port Chalmers NZ
17B2 Port Charlotte USA
16C2 Port Chester USA
15C2 Port Colborne Can
15C2 Port Credit Can
100C4 Port Davey B Aust
26C3 Port-de-Paix Haiti
77C5 Port Dickson Malay
100C4 Port Edward S Africa
35C1 Porteirinha Brazil
14B2 Port Elgin Can
100B4 Port Elizabeth S Africa
27N2 Port Elizabeth St Vincent and the Grenadines
21B2 Porterville USA
107D4 Port Fairy Aust
98A3 Port Gentil Gabon
19B3 Port Gibson USA
12D3 Port Graham USA
20B1 Port Hammond Can
89E7 Port Harcourt Nig
13B2 Port Hardy Can
7D5 Port Hawkesbury Can
106A3 Port Hedland Aust
Port Heiden = Meshik
7D4 Port Hope Can
43B3 Porthmadog Wales
7E4 Port Hope Simpson Can
22C3 Port Hueneme USA
14B2 Port Huron USA
50A2 Portimão Port
109D2 Port Jackson B Aust
16C2 Port Jefferson USA
16B2 Port Jervis USA
109D2 Port Kembla Aust
14B2 Portland Indiana, USA
10C2 Portland Maine, USA
109C2 Portland New South Wales, Aust
20B1 Portland Oregon, USA
108B3 Portland Victoria, Aust
27H2 Portland Bight B Jamaica
43C4 Portland Bill Pt Eng
109C4 Portland,C Aust
13A1 Portland Canal Can/USA
110C1 Portland I NZ
27H2 Portland Pt Jamaica
45C2 Port Laoise Irish Rep
108A2 Port Lincoln Aust
97A4 Port Loko Sierra Leone
101E3 Port Louis Mauritius
108B3 Port MacDonnell Aust
13B2 Port McNeill Can
109D2 Port Macquarie Aust
12B3 Port Moller USA
107D1 Port Moresby PNG
100A3 Port Nolloth S Africa
16B3 Port Norris USA
89E7 Porto Novo Benin
50A1 Porto Port
30F5 Pôrto Alegre Brazil
33F6 Pôrto Artur Brazil
30F3 Pôrto E Cunha Brazil
52B2 Portoferraio Italy
27E4 Port of Spain Trinidad
47D2 Portomaggiore Italy
97C4 Porto Novo Benin
20B1 Port Orchard USA
20B2 Port Orford USA
96A1 Porto Santo I Medeira

31D5 Pôrto Seguro Brazil
53A2 Porto Torres Sardegna
53A2 Porto Vecchio Corse
33E5 Porto Velho Brazil
111A3 Port Pegasus B NZ
108B3 Port Phillip B Aust
108A2 Port Pirie Aust
44A3 Portree Scot
20B1 Port Renfrew Can
27J2 Port Royal Jamaica
17B1 Port Royal Sd USA
45C1 Portrush N Ire
92B3 Port Said Egypt
17A2 Port St Joe USA
100B4 Port St Johns S Africa
7E4 Port Saunders Can
100C4 Port Shepstone S Africa
13A2 Port Simpson Can
27Q2 Portsmouth Dominica
43D4 Portsmouth Eng
14B3 Portsmouth Ohio, USA
11C3 Portsmouth Virginia, USA
109D2 Port Stephens B Aust
95C3 Port Sudan Sudan
19C3 Port Sulphur USA
38K5 Porttipahan Tekojärvi Res Fin
50A2 Portugal Republic, Europe
14A2 Port Washington USA
77C5 Port Weld Malay
32D6 Porvenir Bol
39K6 Porvoo Fin
30E4 Posadas Arg
50B2 Posadas Spain
47D1 Poschiavo Switz
6B2 Posheim Pen Can
90C3 Posht-e Badam Iran
71D4 Poso Indon
58D1 Postavy Belarus
14B2 Port Clinton USA
100B3 Postmasburg S Africa
52B1 Postojna Slovenia
74C2 Pos'yet Russian Fed
101G1 Potchefstroom S Africa
19B3 Poteau USA
53C2 Potenza Italy
100B3 Potgietersrus S Africa
97D3 Potiskum Nig
20C1 Potlatch USA
15C3 Potomac R USA
30C2 Potosí Bol
30C4 Potrerillos Chile
56C2 Potsdam Germany
16B2 Pottstown USA
16A2 Pottsville USA
16C2 Poughkeepsie USA
35B2 Pouso Alegre Brazil
110C1 Poverty B NZ
61F3 Povorino Russian Fed
7C4 Povungnituk Can
8C2 Powder R USA
106C2 Powell Creek Aust
9B3 Powell,L USA
13C3 Powell River Can
43C3 Powys County, Wales
73D4 Poyang Hu L China
92B2 Pozanti Turk
23B1 Poza Rica Mexico
58B2 Poznań Pol
50B2 Pozoblanco Spain
53B2 Pozzuoli Italy
97B4 Pra R Ghana
76C3 Prachin Buri Thai
76B3 Prachuap Khiri Khan Thai
59B2 Praděd Mt Czech Republic
49C3 Pradelles France
35D1 Prado Brazil

Prague = Praha
57C2 Praha Czech Republic
97A4 Praia Cape Verde
33E5 Prainha Brazil
18B2 Prairie Village USA
76C3 Prakhon Chai Thai
35B1 Prata Brazil
35B1 Prata R Brazil
Prates = Dongsha Qundao
49E3 Prato Italy
16B1 Prattsville USA
17A1 Prattville USA
48B1 Prawle Pt Eng
78D4 Praya Indon
47D1 Predazzo Italy
63B2 Predivinsk Russian Fed
58C2 Pregolyu R Russian Fed
76D3 Prek Kak Camb
56C2 Prenzlau Germany
76A3 Preparis I Myan
76A2 Preparis North Chan Myan
59B3 Přerov Czech Republic
23A2 Presa del Infiernillo Mexico
9B3 Prescott Arizona, USA
19B3 Prescott Arkansas, USA
15C2 Prescott Can
30D4 Presidencia Roque Sáenz Peña Arg
35A2 Presidente Epitácio Brazil
112C2 Presidente Frei Base Ant
23A2 Presidente Miguél Aleman L Mexico
35A2 Presidente Prudente Brazil
35B2 Presidente Venceslau Brazil
59C3 Prešov Slovakia
55B2 Prespansko Jezero L Macedonia, Yugos
10D2 Presque Isle USA
42C3 Preston Eng
8B2 Preston Idaho, USA
18B2 Preston Missouri, USA
42B2 Prestwick Scot
31B6 Prêto R Brazil
35B1 Prêto R Brazil
101G1 Pretoria S Africa
55B3 Préveza Greece
76D3 Prey Veng Camb
8B3 Price USA
13B2 Price I Can
60D4 Prichernomorskaya Nizmennost' Lowland Ukraine
60D3 Priluki Ukraine
34C2 Primero R Arg
39K6 Primorsk Russian Fed
60E4 Primorsko-Akhtarsk Russian Fed
13F2 Primrose L Can
5H4 Prince Albert Can
4F2 Prince Albert,C Can
4G2 Prince Albert Pen Can
5E4 Prince Albert Sd Can
6C3 Prince Charles I Can
112B10 Prince Charles Mts Ant
7D5 Prince Edward I Can
13C2 Prince George Can
4H2 Prince Gustaf Adolp S Can
5E4 Prince of Wales I USA

Prince of Wales I

71F5 **Prince of Wales I** Aust
4H2 **Prince of Wales I** Aust
4G2 **Prince of Wales Str** Can
4F2 **Prince Patrick I** Can
6A2 **Prince Regent Inlet** Str Can
13A2 **Prince Rupert** Can
107D2 **Princess Charlotte B** Aust
13B2 **Princess Royal I** Can
27L1 **Princess Town** Trinidad
13C3 **Princeton** Can
18C2 **Princeton** Kentucky, USA
18B1 **Princeton** Missouri, USA
16B2 **Princeton** New Jersey, USA
4D3 **Prince William** USA
12E2 **Prince William Sd** USA
97C4 **Príncipe** I W Africa
20B2 **Prineville** USA
12E1 **Pringle,Mt** USA
61F3 **Prins Christian Sund** Sd Greenland
112B12 **Prinsesse Astrid Kyst** Region, Ant
112B12 **Prinsesse Ragnhild Kyst** Region, Ant
64B2 **Prins Karls Forland** I Barents S
25D3 **Prinzapolca** Nic
58D2 **Pripet** R Belarus
Pripyat' = Pripet
54B2 **Priština** Serbia, Yugos
56C2 **Pritzwalk** Germany
61F3 **Privolzhskaya Vozvyshennost'** Upland Russian Fed
54B2 **Prizren** Serbia, Yugos
78C4 **Probolinggo** Indon
5G5 **Procatello** USA
87B2 **Proddatūr** India
72C2 **Progreso** Mexico
20B2 **Project City** USA
61F5 **Prokhladnyy** Russian Fed
65K4 **Prokop'yevsk** Russian Fed
61F4 **Proletarskaya** Russian Fed
64G2 **Proliv Karskiye Vorota** Str Russian Fed
Prome = Pyè
31D4 **Propriá** Brazil
20B2 **Prospect** Oregon, USA
107D3 **Proserpine** Aust
59B3 **Prostějov** Czech Republic
6E2 **Prøven** Greenland
49D3 **Provence** Region, France
16D2 **Providence** USA
15D2 **Provincetown** USA
49C2 **Provins** France
8B2 **Provo** USA
13E2 **Provost** Can
4D2 **Prudhoe Bay** USA
6E2 **Prudhoe Land** Greenland
58C2 **Pruszkow** Pol
60C4 **Prut** R Romania/Moldova
60C4 **Prutul** R Romania
58C2 **Pruzhany** Belarus
18A2 **Pryor** USA
59C3 **Przemyśl** Pol
55C3 **Psará** I Greece
60C2 **Pskov** Russian Fed
60C2 **Pskov** Division, Russian Fed
58D2 **Ptich** R Belarus
55B2 **Ptolemaís** Greece
32C5 **Pucallpa** Peru
73D4 **Pucheng** China
34A3 **Pucón** Chile

38K5 **Pudasjärvi** Fin
87B2 **Pudukkottai** India
23B2 **Puebla** Mexico
23B2 **Puebla** State, Mexico
50A1 **Puebla de Sanabria** Spain
50A1 **Puebla de Trives** Spain
9C2 **Pueblo** USA
34B3 **Puelches** Arg
34B3 **Puelén** Arg
23A2 **Puente Ixbapa** Mexico
34B2 **Puente del Inca** Arg
32A5 **Puerta Aguja** Peru
30B2 **Puerta Coles** Peru
34B2 **Puerta de los Llanos** Arg
31D3 **Puerta do Calcanhar** Pt Brazil
32C1 **Puerta Gallinas** Colombia
23B2 **Puerta Maldonado** Pt Mexico
32A2 **Puerto Mariato** Panama
29C5 **Puerta Médanosa** Pt Arg
23A2 **Puerta Mongrove** Mexico
25E4 **Puerto San Blas** Pt Panama
23A2 **Puerta San Telmo** Mexico
29B5 **Puerto Aisén** Chile
25D4 **Puerto Armuelles** Panama
33F6 **Puerto Artur** Brazil
32B3 **Puerto Asis** Colombia
32D2 **Puerto Ayacucho** Ven
25D3 **Puerto Barrios** Guatemala
32C2 **Puerto Berrio** Colombia
32D1 **Puerto Cabello** Ven
25D3 **Puerto Cabezas** Nic
32D2 **Puerto Carreño** Colombia
25D4 **Puerto Cortes** Costa Rica
25D3 **Puerto Cortés** Honduras
96A2 **Puerto del Rosario** Canary Is
30F3 **Puerto E Cunha** Brazil
32C1 **Puerto Fijo** Ven
31B3 **Puerto Franco** Brazil
32D6 **Puerto Heath** Bol
25D2 **Puerto Juarez** Mexico
33E1 **Puerto la Cruz** Ven
50B2 **Puertollano** Spain
27C4 **Puerto López** Colombia
29D4 **Puerto Madryn** Arg
32D6 **Puerto Maldonado** Peru
23B2 **Puerto Marquez** Mexico
29B4 **Puerto Montt** Chile
30E3 **Puerto Murtinho** Brazil
29B6 **Puerto Natales** Chile
24A1 **Puerto Peñasco** Mexico
29D4 **Puerto Pirámides** Arg
27C3 **Puerto Plata** Dom Rep
79A4 **Puerto Princesa** Phil
32B3 **Puerto Rico** Colombia
27D3 **Puerto Rico** I Caribbean S
27D3 **Puerto Rico Trench** Caribbean S
23A2 **Puerto San Juan de Lima** Mexico
33G4 **Puerto Santana** Brazil
30E2 **Puerto Suárez** Bol

24B2 **Puerto Vallarta** Mexico
29B4 **Puerto Varas** Chile
30D2 **Puerto Villarroel** Bol
61G3 **Pugachev** Russian Fed
84C3 **Pugal** India
51C1 **Puigcerdá** Spain
111B2 **Pukaki,L** NZ
74B2 **Pukch'ŏng** N Korea
110B1 **Pukekohe** NZ
111B2 **Puketeraki Range** Mts NZ
52B2 **Pula** Croatia
15C2 **Pulaski** New York, USA
71E4 **Pulau Kolepom** I Indon
70A4 **Pulau Pulau Batu** Is Indon
58C2 **Puławy** Pol
87C2 **Pulkat,L** India
84B1 **Pul-i-Khumri** Afghan
87B3 **Puliyangudi** India
20C1 **Pullman** USA
71E3 **Pulo Anna Merir** I Pacific O
79B2 **Pulog,Mt** Phil
38L5 **Pulozero** Russian Fed
58C2 **Pułtusk** Pol
30C4 **Puna de Atacama** Arg
86B1 **Punakha** Bhutan
84C2 **Punch** Pak
87A1 **Pune** India
23A2 **Punepeo** Mexico
98C3 **Punia** Zaire
34A2 **Punitaqui** Chile
86A2 **Punjab** Province, Pak
84D2 **Punjab** State, India
30B2 **Puno** Peru
24A2 **Punta Abreojos** Pt Mexico
53C3 **Punta Alice** Pt Italy
34C3 **Punta Alta** Arg
29B6 **Punta Arenas** Chile
24A2 **Punta Baja** Pt Mexico
34A2 **Punta Curaumilla** Pt Chile
100A2 **Punta da Marca** Pt Angola
101C3 **Punta de Barra Falsa** Pt Mozam
74C2 **Punta del Este** Urug
24A2 **Punta Eugenia** Pt Mexico
25D3 **Punta Gorda** Belize
17B2 **Punta Gorda** USA
34A3 **Punta Lavapié** Pt Chile
34A2 **Punta Lengua de Vaca** Pt Chile
53B2 **Punta Licosa** Pt Italy
34A1 **Punta Poroto** Pt Chile
9B4 **Punta San Antonio** Pt Mexico
34A2 **Punta Topocalma** Chile
53C4 **Punta Stilo** Pt Italy
64J3 **Pur** R Russian Fed
19A2 **Purcell** USA
12C1 **Purcell Mt** USA
13D2 **Purcell Mts** Can
34A3 **Purén** Chile
86B2 **Puri** India
87B1 **Pūrna** India
86B1 **Pūrnia** India
76C3 **Pursat** Camb
23A1 **Puruándiro** Mexico
33E4 **Purus** R Brazil
19C3 **Purvis** USA
78B4 **Purwokerto** Indon
78C4 **Purworejo** Indon
85D5 **Pusad** India
74B3 **Pusan** S Korea
60D2 **Pushkin** Russian Fed
58D1 **Pustoshka** Russian Fed
82D3 **Puta** Myan
34A2 **Putaendo** Chile
110C1 **Putaruru** NZ
73D4 **Putian** China

16D2 **Putnam** USA
87B3 **Puttalam** Sri Lanka
56C2 **Puttgarden** Germany
32B4 **Putumayo** R Ecuador
78C2 **Putussibau** Indon
38K6 **Puulavesi** L Fin
20B1 **Puyallup** USA
49C2 **Puy de Sancy** Mt France
111A3 **Puysegur Pt** NZ
99C3 **Pweto** Zaire
43B3 **Pwllheli** Wales
76B2 **Pyapon** Myan
61F5 **Pyatigorsk** Russian Fed
76B2 **Pyè** Myan
74B3 **P'yŏngyang** N Korea
108B3 **Pyramid Hill** Aust
21B1 **Pyramid L** USA
111A2 **Pyramid,Mt** NZ
48B3 **Pyrénées** Mts France
58D1 **Pytalovo** Russian Fed
76B2 **Pyu** Myan

Q

94B2 **Qabatiya** Israel
94C3 **Qa'el Hafira** Mud Flats Jordan
94C3 **Qa'el Jinz** Mud Flats Jordan
68B3 **Qaidam Pendi** Salt Flat China
94C2 **Qa Khanna** Salt Marsh Jordan
99D1 **Qala'en Nahl** Sudan
84B2 **Qalat** Afghan
94C1 **Qal'at al Hisn** Syria
81C3 **Qal'at Bishah** S Arabia
93E3 **Qal'at Sālih** Iraq
68B3 **Qamdo** China
99E1 **Qandala** Somalia
99E2 **Qardho** Somalia
95B2 **Qara** Egypt
90A3 **Qare Shirin** Iran
91A4 **Qaryat al Ulyā** S Arabia
94C3 **Qasr el Kharana** Jordan
91D4 **Qasr-e-Qand** Iran
95B2 **Qasr Farafra** Egypt
94C2 **Qatana** Syria
91A4 **Qatar** Emirate, Arabian Pen
94C3 **Qatrāna** Jordan
95B2 **Qattâra Depression** Egypt
90C3 **Qāyen** Iran
90A2 **Qazvin** Iran
95C2 **Qena** Egypt
90A2 **Qeydar** Iran
91B4 **Qeys** I Iran
94B3 **Qeziot** Israel
73B5 **Qian Jiang** R China
72E1 **Qian Shan** Upland China
72E3 **Qidong** China
73B4 **Qijiang** China
84B2 **Qila Saifullah** Pak
72A2 **Qilian** China
68B3 **Qilian Shan** China
72E2 **Qingdao** China
72A2 **Qinghai** Province, China
68B3 **Qinghai Hu** L China
72D3 **Qingjiang** Jiangsu, China
73D4 **Qingjiang** Jiangxi, China
72B3 **Qing Jiang** R China
72C2 **Qingshuihe** China
72B2 **Qingshui He** R China
72B2 **Qingtonxia** China
72B2 **Qingyang** China
74B2 **Qingyuan** Liaoning, China
73D4 **Qingyuan** Zhejiang, China
82C2 **Qing Zang** Upland China
73D5 **Qinjiang** China
72B3 **Qin Ling** Mts China

73B5 Qinzhou China
76E2 Qionghai China
73A3 Qionglai Shan Upland China
76D1 Qiongzhou Haixia Str China
69E2 Qiqihar China
94B2 Qiryat Ata Israel
94B3 Qiryat Gat Israel
94B2 Qiryat Shemona Israel
94B2 Qiryat Yam Israel
94B2 Qishon R Israel
63A3 Qitai China
73C4 Qiyang China
72B1 Qog Qi China
90B2 Qoïleh-ye Damavand Mt Iran
90B3 Qom Iran
90B3 Qomisheh Iran
94C1 Qomolangma Feng = Everest,Mt
6E3 Qórnoq Greenland
90A2 Qorveh Iran
91C4 Qotābad Iran
16C1 Quabbin Res USA
16B2 Quakertown USA
77C3 Quam Phu Quoc I Viet
76D2 Quang Ngai Viet
76D2 Quang Tri Viet
77D4 Quan Long Viet
73D5 Quanzhou Fujian, China
73C4 Quanzhou Guangxi, China
5H4 Qu' Appelle R Can
91C5 Quarayyāt Oman
13B2 Quatsino Sd Can
90C2 Quchan Iran
109C3 Queanbeyan Aust
7C1 Québec Can
7C4 Quebec Province, Can
35B1 Quebra-Anzol R Brazil
34D2 Quebracho Urug
30F4 Quedas do Iguaçu Brazil/Arg
16A3 Queen Anne USA
13B2 Queen Bess,Mt Can
5E4 Queen Charlotte Is Can
13B2 Queen Charlotte Sd Can
13B2 Queen Charlotte Str Can
4H1 Queen Elizabeth Is Can
112B9 Queen Mary Land Region, Ant
4H3 Queen Maud G Can
112A Queen Maud Mts Ant
16C2 Queens Borough, New York, USA
108B3 Queenscliff Aust
107D3 Queensland State, Aust
109C4 Queenstown Aust
111A3 Queenstown NZ
100B4 Queenstown S Africa
16A3 Queenstown USA
98B3 Quela Angola
101C2 Quelimane Mozam
34C3 Quemuquemú Arg
13C2 Quensel L Can
34D3 Quequén R Arg
23A1 Querétaro Mexico
23A1 Querétaro State Mexico
13C2 Quesnel Can
84B2 Quetta Pak
25C3 Quezaltenango Guatemala
79B3 Quezon City Phil
100A2 Quibala Angola
98B3 Quibaxe Angola
32B2 Quibdó Colombia
48B2 Quiberon France
98B3 Quicama Nat Pk Angola

73A4 Quijing China
34A2 Quilima Chile
34C2 Quilino Arg
32C6 Quillabamba Peru
30C2 Quillacollo Bol
48C3 Quillan France
5H4 Quill L Can
5H4 Quill Lakes Can
34A2 Quillota Chile
87B3 Quilon India
108B1 Quilpie Aust
34C2 Quilpué Chile
98B3 Quimbele Angola
48B2 Quimper France
48B2 Quimperlé France
21A2 Quincy California, USA
10A3 Quincy Illinois, USA
16D1 Quincy Massachusetts, USA
34B2 Quines Arg
12B3 Quinhagak USA
76D3 Qui Nhon Viet
50B2 Quintanar de la Orden Spain
34A2 Quintero Chile
34C2 Quinto R Arg
34A3 Quirihue Chile
100A2 Quirima Angola
109D2 Quirindi Aust
101D2 Quissanga Mozam
101C3 Quissico Mozam
32B4 Quito Ecuador
31D2 Quixadá Brazil
108A2 Quorn Aust
4G3 Qurlurtuuq Can
95C2 Quseir Egypt
6E3 Qutdligssat Greenland
73B3 Qu Xian Sichuan, China
73D4 Qu Xian Zhejiang, China
76D2 Quynh Luu Viet
72C2 Quzhou China
86C1 Qüzü China

R

38J6 Raahe Fin
44A3 Raasay I Scot
44A3 Raasay,Sound of Chan Scot
99F1 Raas Caseyr C Somalia
52B2 Rab I Croatia
78D4 Raba Indon
59B3 Rába R Hung
96B1 Rabat Mor
94B3 Rabba Jordan
80B3 Rabigh S Arabia
47B2 Racconigi Italy
7E5 Race,C Can
76D3 Rachaya Leb
57C3 Rachel Mt Germany
76D3 Rach Gia Viet
14A2 Racine USA
59D3 Rădăuţi Rom
85C4 Radhanpur India
27L1 Radix,Pt Trinidad
58C2 Radom Pol
59B2 Radomsko Pol
58C1 Radviliskis Lithuania
4G3 Rae Can
86A1 Rae Bareli India
4G3 Rae Isthmus Can
110C1 Raetihi NZ
34C2 Rafaela Arg
94B3 Rafah Egypt
98C2 Rafai CAR
93D3 Rafhā Al Jumaymah S Arabia
91C3 Rafsanjan Iran
98C2 Raga Sudan
27R3 Ragged Pt Barbados
53B3 Ragusa Italy
99D1 Rahad R Sudan
84C3 Rahimyar Khan Pak
90B3 Rähjerd Iran
34D2 Raíces Arg
87B1 Räichur India
86A2 Raigarh India
108B3 Rainbow Aust

17A1 Rainbow City USA
20B1 Rainier USA
20B1 Rainier,Mt USA
10A2 Rainy L Can
12D2 Rainy P USA
10A2 Rainy River Can
86A2 Raipur India
87C1 Rájahmundry India
78C2 Rajang R Malay
84C3 Rajanpur Pak
87B3 Rajapalaiyam India
84C3 Rajasthan State, India
84C3 Rájgarh India
85D4 Rajgarh State, India
85C4 Rajkot India
86B2 Rájmahál Hills India
86A2 Raj Nändgaon India
85C4 Räjpipla India
86B2 Rajshahi Beng
85B3 Rajur India
111B2 Rakaia R NZ
78B4 Rakata I Indon
82C3 Raka Zangbo R China
59D3 Rakhov Ukraine
100B3 Rakops Botswana
58D2 Rakov Belarus
11C3 Raleigh USA
7A5 Ralny L Can
94B2 Rama Israel
94B3 Ramallah Israel
87B3 Rämanäthapuram India
69G3 Ramapo Deep Pacific O
94B2 Ramat Gan Israel
46A2 Rambouillet France
86B2 Rämgarh Bihar, India
85C3 Rämgarh Rajosthan, India
90A3 Rämhormoz Iran
94B3 Ramla Israel
91C5 Ramlat Al Wahibah Region, Oman
21B3 Ramona USA
84D3 Rämpur India
85D4 Rämpura India
90B2 Rämsar Iran
42B2 Ramsey Eng
14A2 Ramsey I Wales
43E4 Ramsgate Eng
94C2 Ramtha Jordan
71F4 Ramu R PNG
34A2 Rancagua Chile
86B2 Ränchi India
86A2 Ränchi Plat India
101G1 Randburg S Africa
39G7 Randers Den
101G1 Randfontein S Africa
15D2 Randolph Vermont, USA
111B3 Ranfurly NZ
86C2 Rangamati Bang
111B2 Rangiora NZ
110C1 Rangitaiki R NZ
110C1 Rangitikei R NZ
109B2 Rangoon = Yangon
86B1 Rangpur India
87B2 Räninennur India
8A2 Ranier,Mt USA
86B2 Ränigänj India
109C2 Rankins Springs Aust
6A3 Ranklin Inlet Can
85B4 Rann of Kachchh India
77B4 Ranong Thai
70A3 Rantauparapat Indon
18C1 Rantoul USA
49D3 Rapallo Italy
62E2 Rapel R Chile
8C2 Rapid City USA
14A1 Rapid River USA
15C3 Rappahannock R USA
47C1 Rapperswil Switz
16B2 Raritan B USA
95C2 Ras Abu Shagara C Sudan
93D2 Ra's al 'Ayn Syria

91C5 Ra's al Hadd C Oman
91C4 Ras al Kaimah UAE
91C4 Ras-al-Kuh C Iran
81D4 Ra's al Madrakah C Oman
91A4 Ra's az Zawr C S Arabia
95C2 Räs Bânas C Egypt
94A3 Ras Burûn C Egypt
99D1 Ras Dashan Mt Eth
91A4 Ra's-e-Barkan C Iran
92A3 Räs el Kenâyis Pt Egypt
81D4 Ra's Fartak C Yemen
95C2 Räs Ghârib Egypt
99D1 Rashad Sudan
91B4 Rashädiya Jordan
92B3 Rashid Egypt
90A2 Rasht Iran
91C5 Ra's Jibish C Oman
94B3 Ras Khanzira C Somalia
84B3 Ras Koh Mt Pak
95C2 Räs Muhammad C Egypt
96A2 Ras Nouadhibou C Maur
69H2 Rasshua I
61F3 Rasskazovo Russian Fed
91A4 Ra's Tanäqib C S Arabia
91B4 Ra's Tannürah S Arabia
57B3 Rastatt Germany
Ras Uarc = Cabo Tres Forcas
99F1 Ras Xaafuun C Somalia
84C3 Ratangarh India
76B3 Rat Buri Thai
85D3 Rath India
56C2 Rathenow Germany
45B2 Rathkeale Irish Rep
45C1 Rathlin I N Ire
45B2 Räth Luirc Irish Rep
85D4 Ratlam India
87A1 Ratnägiri India
58C2 Ratnapura Sri Lanka
47D1 Rattenberg Austria
39H6 Rättvik Sweden
12H3 Ratz,Mt Can
34D3 Rauch Arg
110C1 Raukumara Range Mts NZ
35C2 Raul Soares Brazil
39J6 Rauma Fin
86A2 Raurkela India
90A3 Ravänsar Iran
90C3 Rävar Iran
59C2 Rava Russkaya Ukraine
16C1 Ravenna USA
57B3 Ravenna Italy
57B3 Ravensburg Germany
107D2 Ravenshoe Aust
42E2 Ravenspurn Oilfield N Sea
84C2 Ravi R Pak
84C2 Rawalpindi Pak
93D2 Rawändiz Iraq
58B2 Rawicz Pol
106B4 Rawlinna Aust
8C2 Rawlins USA
29C4 Rawson Arg
78C3 Raya Mt Indon
87B2 Räyadurg India
94C2 Rayak Leb
7E5 Ray,C Can
22C2 Räymen Iran
22C2 Raymond California, USA
20B1 Raymond Washington, USA
109D2 Raymond Terrace Aust
12D1 Ray Mts USA
23B1 Rayon Mexico
90A2 Razan Iran
54C2 Razgrad Bulg

Razim

54C2 Razim L Rom
43D4 Reading Eng
16B2 Reading USA
4G3 Read Island Can
16C1 Readsboro USA
34B2 Real de Padre Arg
34C3 Realicó Arg
95B2 Rebiana Well Libya
95B2 Rebiana Sand Sea Libya
38L6 Reboly Russian Fed
106B4 Recherche,Arch of the Is Aust
31E3 Recife Brazil
107F2 Recifs D'Entrecasteaux Nouvelle Calédonie
46D1 Recklinghausen Germany
30E4 Reconquista Arg
19B3 Red R USA
77C4 Redang I Malay
16B2 Red Bank New Jersey, USA
21A1 Red Bluff USA
42D2 Redcar Eng
42D2 Redcar and Cleveland County Eng
13E2 Redcliff Can
109D1 Redcliffe Aust
108B2 Red Cliffs Aust
13E2 Red Deer Can
13E2 Red Deer R Can
20B2 Redding USA
10A2 Red L USA
7C4 Red Lake Can
16A3 Red Lion USA
20B2 Redmond USA
18A1 Red Oak USA
48B2 Redon France
22C4 Redondo Beach USA
12D2 Redoubt V USA
73B5 Red River Delta Vietnam
80B3 Red Sea Africa/Arabian Pen
52B2 Redwater Can
22A2 Redwood City USA
14A2 Reed City USA
22C2 Reedley USA
20B2 Reedsport USA
47C1 Refahiye Turk
93C2 Refahiye Turk
35D1 Regência Brazil
57C3 Regensburg Germany
96C2 Reggane Alg
53C3 Reggio di Calabria Italy
47D2 Reggio Nell'Emilia Italy
54B1 Reghin Rom
5H4 Regina Can
100A3 Rehoboth Namibia
15C3 Rehoboth Beach USA
94B3 Rehovot Israel
32D1 Reicito Ven
43D4 Reigate Eng
46C2 Reims France
5H4 Reindeer R Can
50B1 Reinosa Spain
16A3 Reisterstown USA
101G1 Reitz S Africa
Reliance Can
108A2 Remarkable,Mt Aust
78C4 Rembang Indon
91C4 Remeshk Iran
46D1 Remscheid Germany
18C2 Rend,L USA
56B2 Rendsburg Germany
15C1 Renfrew Can
42B2 Renfrewshire Division Scot
78A3 Rengat Indon
34A2 Rengo Chile
59D3 Reni Ukraine
99D1 Renk Sudan
6H2 Renland Pen Greenland
108B2 Renmark Aust
107F2 Rennell I Solomon Is
48B2 Rennes France

21B2 Reno USA
47D2 Reno R Italy
15C2 Renovo USA
16C1 Rensselaer USA
20B1 Renton USA
70D4 Reo Indon
35B2 Reprêsa de Furnas Dam Brazil
30E3 Reprêsa Ilha Grande Dam Brazil
38L6 Reprêsa Itaipu Dam Brazil
35A2 Reprêsa Porto Primavera Dam Brazil
35B1 Reprêsa Três Marias Dam Brazil
20C1 Republic USA
41B3 Republic of Ireland NW Europe
Repulse Bay Can
15C1 Réservoir Baskatong Res Can
10C1 Réservoir de la Grande 2 Res Can
10C1 Réservoir de la Grande 3 Res Can
7C4 Réservoir de la Grande 4 Res Can
7C5 Réservoir Cabonga Res Can
7D4 Réservoir Caniapiscau Res Can
7C5 Réservoir Gouin Res Can
10D1 Réservoir Manicouagan Res Can
90B2 Reshteh-ye Alborz Mts Iran
72D2 Reshui China
30E4 Resistencia Arg
54B1 Resita Rom
6A2 Resolute Can
11A3 Resolution I NZ
6D3 Resolution Island Can
101H1 Ressano Garcia Mozam
34B2 Retamito Arg
46C2 Rethel France
55B3 Réthimnon Greece
89K10 Reunion I Indian O
51C1 Reus Spain
47C1 Reuss R Switz
47D1 Reutte Austria
61K3 Revda Russian Fed
13D2 Revelstoke Can
24A3 Revillagigedo Is Mexico
12H3 Revillagigedo I USA
46C2 Revin France
94B3 Rewiwim Israel
86A2 Rewa India
84D3 Rewari India
8B2 Rexburg USA
38A2 Reykjavik Iceland
24C2 Reynosa Mexico
48B2 Rezé France
52B1 Rezekne Latvia
61K2 Rezh Russian Fed
47C1 Rhätikon Mts Austria/Switz
94B1 Rhazir Republic, Leb
56B2 Rhein R W Europe
56B2 Rheine Germany
47B1 Rheinfelden Switz
49D2 Rheinland Pfalz Region, Germany
47C1 Rheinwaldhorn Mt Switz
Rhine = Rhein
10B2 Rhinelander USA
47C2 Rho Italy
15D2 Rhode Island State, USA
16D2 Rhode Island Sd USA
55B3 Rhodes = Ródhos
Rhondda Cynon Taff County Wales
49C3 Rhône R France
43C3 Rhyl Wales

31D4 Riachão do Jacuipe Brazil
50A1 Ria de Arosa B Spain
50A1 Ria de Betanzos B Spain
50A1 Ria de Corcubion B Spain
50A1 Ria de Lage R Spain
50A1 Ria de Sta Marta B Spain
84C2 Riasi Pak
50A1 Ribadeo Spain
35A2 Ribas do Rio Pardo Brazil
101C2 Ribaué Mozam
42C3 Ribble R Eng
35B2 Ribeira Brazil
35B2 Ribeirão Prêto Brazil
32D6 Riberalta Bol
15C2 Rice L Can
10A2 Rice Lake USA
101H1 Richard's Bay S Africa
19A3 Richardson USA
12G1 Richardson Mts Can
8B3 Richfield USA
20C1 Richland USA
22A2 Richmond California, USA
101H1 Richmond Natal, S Africa
109D2 Richmond New South Wales, Aust
111B2 Richmond NZ
107D3 Richmond Queensland, Aust
15C3 Richmond Virginia, USA
111B2 Richmond Range Mts NZ
15C2 Rideau,L Can
17B1 Ridgeland USA
15C2 Ridgway USA
27D4 Riecito Ven
47D1 Rienza R Italy
57C2 Riesa Germany
29B6 Riesco I Chile
101F1 Riet R S Africa
52B2 Rieti Italy
50B2 Rif Mts Mor
58C1 Riga Latvia
58C1 Riga,G of Estonia/Latvia
91C4 Rigan Iran
20C1 Riggins USA
7E4 Rigolet Can
39J6 Riihimaki Fin
52B1 Rijeka Croatia
13E2 Rimbey Can
39H7 Rimbo Sweden
52B2 Rimini Italy
54C1 Rimnicu Sărat Rom
54B1 Rimnicu Vilcea Rom
10D2 Rimouski Can
23A1 Rincón de Romos Mexico
39F7 Ringkøbing Den
98A2 Rio Benito Eq Guinea
32D5 Rio Branco Brazil
23B1 Rio Bravo del Norte R Mexico/USA
32C1 Riochacha Colombia
35B2 Rio Claro Brazil
27L1 Rio Claro Trinidad
34C3 Rio Colorado Arg
34C2 Rio Cuarto Arg
31D4 Rio de Jacuipe Brazil
35C2 Rio de Janeiro Brazil
35C2 Rio de Janeiro State, Brazil
29E3 Rio de la Plata Est Arg/Urug
29C6 Rio Gallegos Arg
29C6 Rio Grande Arg
30F5 Rio Grande Brazil
26A4 Rio Grande Nic
25D3 Rio Grande R Nic
23A1 Rio Grande de Santiago Mexico

31D3 Rio Grande do Norte State, Brazil
30F4 Rio Grande do Sul State, Brazil
103G6 Rio Grande Rise Atlantic O
26C4 Riohacha Colombia
49C2 Riom France
32B4 Riombamba Ecuador
30C2 Rio Mulatos Bol
29C3 Rio Negro State, Arg
30F4 Rio Pardo Brazil
34C2 Rio Tercero Arg
33E6 Rio Theodore Roosevelt R Brazil
29B6 Rio Turbio Arg
35A1 Rio Verde Brazil
23A1 Rio Verde Mexico
14B3 Ripley Ohio, USA
14B3 Ripley West Virginia, USA
42D2 Ripon Eng
22B2 Ripon USA
94B3 Rishon le Zion Israel
16A3 Rising Sun USA
39F7 Risør Norway
6H3 Ritenbek Greenland
22C2 Ritter,Mt USA
20C1 Ritzville USA
34B2 Rivadavia Arg
34A1 Rivadavia Chile
34C3 Rivadavia Gonzalez Moreno Arg
52B2 Riva de Garda Italy
34C3 Rivera Arg
34C3 Rivera Urug
22B2 Riverbank USA
97B4 River Cess Lib
16C2 Riverhead USA
108B3 Riverina Aust
111A3 Riversdale NZ
22D4 Riverside USA
13B2 Rivers Inlet Can
111A3 Riverton NZ
8C2 Riverton USA
17B2 Riviera Beach USA
7C4 Rivière aux Feuilles R Can
7D4 Rivière de la Baleine R Can
7D4 Rivière du Petit Mécatina R Can
46C2 Rivigny-sur-Ornain France
93D1 Rize Turk
72D2 Rizhao China
Rizhskiy Zaliv =Riga,G of
39F7 Rjukan Nor
6B2 Roanes Pen Can
49C2 Roanne France
17A1 Roanoke Alabama, USA
11C3 Roanoke Virginia, USA
11C3 Roanoke R USA
45B3 Roaringwater B Irish Rep
38J6 Robertsforz Sweden
19B2 Robert S Kerr Res USA
97A4 Robertsport Lib
7C5 Roberval Can
30H6 Robinson Crusoe I Chile
108B2 Robinvale Aust
13D2 Robson,Mt Can
24A3 Roca Partida I Mexico
103G5 Rocas I Atlantic O
31E2 Rocas I Brazil
29F2 Rocha Urug
42C3 Rochdale Eng
48B2 Rochefort France
5G3 Rocher River Can
108B3 Rochester Aust
7C5 Rochester Can
43E4 Rochester Eng
10A2 Rochester Minnesota, USA
15D2 Rochester New Hampshire, USA
10C2 Rochester New York, USA

10B2 **Rockford** USA
11B3 **Rock Hill** USA
10A2 **Rock Island** USA
10B3 **Rocklands Res** Aust
17B2 **Rockledge** USA
8C2 **Rock Springs** Wyoming, USA
11D2 **Rocks Pt** NZ
109C3 **Rock,The** Aust
16C2 **Rockville** Connecticut, USA
14A3 **Rockville** Indiana, USA
16A3 **Rockville** Maryland, USA
14B1 **Rocky Island L** Can
13E2 **Rocky Mountain House** Can
8B1 **Rocky Mts** Can/USA
12B2 **Rocky Pt** USA
56C2 **Rødbyhavn** Den
34B2 **Rodeo** Arg
49C3 **Rodez** France
55C3 **Ródhos** Greece
55C3 **Ródhos** *I* Greece
52C2 **Rodi Garganico** Italy
54B2 **Rodopi Planina** *Mts* Bulg
106A3 **Roebourne** Aust
46C1 **Roermond** Neth
46C1 **Roeselare** Belg
6B3 **Roes Welcome Sd** Can
18D2 **Rogers** USA
16C2 **Rogers City** USA
20B2 **Rogue** *R* USA
85B3 **Rohri** Pak
84D3 **Rohtak** India
58C1 **Roja** Latvia
30A3 **Rolândia** Brazil
18B2 **Rolla** USA
109C1 **Roma** Aust
52B2 **Roma** Italy
47C2 **Romagnano** Italy
17C1 **Romain,C** USA
54C1 **Roman** Rom
103H5 **Romanche Gap** Atlantic O
71D4 **Romang** *I* Indon
60B4 **Romania** Republic, E Europe
17B2 **Romano,C** USA
49D2 **Romans sur Isère** France
79B3 **Romblon** Phil
Rome = Roma
17A1 **Rome** Georgia, USA
15C2 **Rome** New York, USA
49C2 **Romilly-sur-Seine** France
15C3 **Romney** USA
60D3 **Romny** Ukraine
56B1 **Rømø** *I* Den
47B1 **Romont** Switz
48B2 **Romorantin** France
50A2 **Ronda** Spain
33E6 **Rondônia** Brazil
24F6 **Rondônia** State, Brazil
30F2 **Rondonópolis** Brazil
73B4 **Rong'an** China
73B4 **Rongcheng** China
72E2 **Rongcheng** China
73B4 **Rongjiang** China
73B4 **Rong Jiang** *R* China
76A1 **Rongklang Range** *Mts* Myan
39G7 **Rønne** Den
39H7 **Ronneby** Sweden
112B2 **Ronne Ice Shelf** Ant
46B1 **Ronse** Belg
46A1 **Ronthieu** Region, France
9C3 **Roof Butte** *Mt* USA
84D3 **Roorkee** India
46C1 **Roosendaal** Neth
112B6 **Roosevelt I** Ant
106C2 **Roper** *R* Aust
33E3 **Roraima** *Mt* Brazil
33E2 **Roraime** *Mt* Ven
38G6 **Røros** Nor
47C1 **Rorschach** Switz
38G6 **Rørvik** Nor

27Q2 **Rosalie** Dominica
22C3 **Rosamond L** USA
34C2 **Rosario** Arg
31C2 **Rosário** Brazil
34D2 **Rosario del Tala** Arg
48B2 **Roscoff** France
45B2 **Roscommon** County, Irish Rep
41B3 **Roscommon** Irish Rep
45C2 **Roscrea** Irish Rep
27E3 **Roseau** Dominica
109C4 **Rosebery** Aust
20B2 **Roseburg** USA
19A4 **Rosenberg** USA
57C3 **Rosenheim** Germany
13F2 **Rosetown** Can
58E2 **Roşiori de Vede** Rom
39G7 **Roskilde** Den
60D3 **Roslavl'** Russian Fed
61E2 **Roslyatino** Russian Fed
111B2 **Ross** NZ
12H2 **Ross** *R* Can
40B3 **Rossan** *Pt* Irish Rep
53C3 **Rossano** Italy
19C3 **Ross Barnett Res** USA
15C1 **Rosseau L** Can
107E2 **Rossel I** Solomon Is
112A **Ross Ice Shelf** Ant
20B1 **Ross L** USA
13D3 **Rossland** Can
45C2 **Rosslare** Irish Rep
111C2 **Ross,Mt** NZ
97A3 **Rosso** Maur
43C4 **Ross-on-Wye** Eng
60E4 **Rossosh** Russian Fed
4E3 **Ross River** Can
112B6 **Ross S** Ant
91B4 **Rostāq** Iran
56C2 **Rostock** Germany
Rostov = Rostov-na-Donu
61E4 **Rostov-na-Donu** Russian Fed
17B1 **Roswell** Georgia, USA
9C3 **Roswell** New Mexico, USA
71F2 **Rota** Pacific O
56B2 **Rotenburg** Niedersachsen, Germany
46E1 **Rothaar-Geb** Region Germany
112C3 **Rothera** *Base* Ant
42D3 **Rotherham** Eng
42B2 **Rothesay** Scot
71D5 **Roti** *I* Indon
108C2 **Roto** Aust
111B2 **Rotoiti,L** NZ
110C1 **Rotorua** NZ
110C1 **Rotorua,L** NZ
56A2 **Rotterdam** Neth
46B1 **Roubaix** France
48C2 **Rouen** France
42E3 **Roulers** = Roeselare
101E3 **Round I** Mauritius
109D2 **Round Mt** Aust
8C2 **Roundup** USA
44C2 **Rousay** *I* Scot
48C3 **Roussillon** Region, France
10C2 **Rouyn** Can
38K5 **Rovaniemi** Fin
47D2 **Rovereto** Italy
47D2 **Rovigo** Italy
52B1 **Rovinj** Croatia
59D2 **Rovno** Ukraine
90A2 **Row'ān** Iran
109C1 **Rowena** Aust
6C3 **Rowley I** Can
106A2 **Rowley Shoals** Aust
79A3 **Roxas** Palawan, Phil
79B3 **Roxas** Panay, Phil
111A3 **Roxburgh** NZ
45C2 **Royal Canal** Irish Rep
43D3 **Royal Leamington Spa** Eng
14B2 **Royal Oak** USA
43E3 **Royal Tunbridge Wells** Eng

48B2 **Royan** France
46B2 **Roye** France
43D3 **Royston** Eng
59C3 **Rožňava** Slovakia
46B2 **Rozoy** France
61F2 **Rtishchevo** Russian Fed
99D3 **Ruaha Nat Pk** Tanz
110C1 **Ruahine Range** *Mts* NZ
110C1 **Ruapehu,Mt** NZ
65D3 **Rub al Khāli** *Desert* S Arabia
44A3 **Rubha Hunish** Scot
35A2 **Rubinéia** Brazil
65K4 **Rubtsovsk** Russian Fed
12C2 **Ruby** USA
91C4 **Rūdan** Iran
90A2 **Rūdbār** Iran
69F2 **Rudnaya Pristan'** Russian Fed
54B2 **Rudoka Planina** *Mt* Macedonia
72E3 **Rudong** China
14B1 **Rudyard** USA
46A1 **Rue** France
48C2 **Ruffec** France
99D3 **Rufiji** *R* Tanz
34C2 **Rufino** Arg
100A3 **Rufisque** Sen
100B2 **Rufunsa** Zambia
43D3 **Rugby** Eng
39G8 **Rügen** *I* Germany
56B2 **Ruhr** *R* Germany
73D4 **Rui'an** China
54C1 **Rujen** *Mt* Bulg/Macedonia
99D3 **Rukwa** *L* Tanz
44A3 **Rum** *I* Scot
54A1 **Ruma** Serbia, Yugos
91A4 **Rumāh** S Arabia
98C2 **Rumbek** Sudan
26C2 **Rum Cay** *I* Caribbean Is
47A2 **Rumilly** France
106C2 **Rum Jungle** Aust
101C2 **Rumphi** Malawi
110C1 **Runanga** NZ
110C1 **Runaway,C** NZ
100C3 **Rundi** *R* Zim
100A2 **Rundu** Namibia
99D3 **Rungwa** Tanz
99D3 **Rungwa** *R* Tanz
99D3 **Rungwe** *Mt* Tanz
82C2 **Ruoqiang** China
68C2 **Ruo Shui** *R* China
54C1 **Rupea** Rom
7C4 **Rupert** *R* Can
46D1 **Rur** *R* Germany
32D6 **Rurrenabaque** Bol
101C2 **Rusape** Zim
54C2 **Ruse** Bulg
10B3 **Rushville** Illinois, USA
108B3 **Rushworth** Aust
19A3 **Rusk** USA
17B2 **Ruskin** USA
110B1 **Russell** NZ
18B2 **Russellville** Arkansas, USA
18C2 **Russellville** Kentucky, USA
21A2 **Russian** *R* USA
62C3 **Russian Fed** Asia/Europe
93E1 **Rustavi** Georgia
101G1 **Rustenburg** S Africa
19B3 **Ruston** USA
99C3 **Rutana** Burundi
46E1 **Rüthen** Germany
23B2 **Rutla** Mexico
15D2 **Rutland** USA
84D2 **Rutog** China
Ruvu = Pangani
101D2 **Ruvuma** *R* Tanz/Mozam
99D2 **Ruwenzori Range** *Mts* Uganda/Zaire
101C2 **Ruya** *R* Zim
59B3 **Ružomberok** Slovakia
99C3 **Rwanda** Republic, Africa

60E3 **Ryazan'** Russian Fed
60E3 **Ryazan'** Division, Russian Fed
61F3 **Ryazhsk** Russian Fed
60E2 **Rybinsk** Russian Fed
60E2 **Rybinskoye Vodokhranilishche** *Res* Russian Fed
13D1 **Rycroft** Can
43D4 **Ryde** Eng
43E4 **Rye** Eng
20C2 **Rye Patch Res** USA
60D3 **Ryl'sk** Russian Fed
61G4 **Ryn Peski** *Desert* Kazakhstan
74D3 **Ryōtsu** Japan
59D3 **Ryskany** Moldova
69E4 **Ryukyu Retto** *Arch* Japan
59C2 **Rzeszów** Pol
60D2 **Rzhev** Russian Fed

S

91B3 **Sa'ādatābād** Iran
56C2 **Saale** *R* Germany
47B1 **Saanen** Switz
46D2 **Saar** *R* Germany
46D2 **Saarbrücken** Germany
46D2 **Saarburg** Germany
39J7 **Saaremaa** *I* Estonia
46D2 **Saarland** State, Germany
46D2 **Saarlouis** Germany
34C3 **Saavedra** Arg
54A2 **Šabac** Serbia, Yugos
51C1 **Sabadell** Spain
75B1 **Sabae** Japan
78D1 **Sabah** State, Malay
26C4 **Sabanalarga** Colombia
70A3 **Sabang** Indon
87C1 **Sabari** *R* India
94B2 **Sabastiya** Israel
30C2 **Sabaya** Bol
93C3 **Sab'Bi'ār** Syria
94C2 **Sabhā** Jordan
95A2 **Sabhā** Libya
24B2 **Sabinas** Mexico
24B2 **Sabinas Hidalgo** Mexico
19A3 **Sabine** *R* USA
19B4 **Sabine L** USA
91B5 **Sabkhat Matti** *Salt Marsh* UAE
94A3 **Sabkhet El Bardawil** *Lg* Egypt
79B3 **Sablayan** Phil
7D5 **Sable,C** Can
17B2 **Sable,C** USA
7D5 **Sable I** Can
90C2 **Sabzevār** Iran
20C1 **Sacajawea Peak** USA
10A1 **Sachigo** *R* Can
57C2 **Sachsen** State, Germany
56C2 **Sachsen-Anhalt** State, Germany
47F1 **Säckingen** Germany
22B1 **Sacramento** USA
21A1 **Sacramento** *R* USA
21A1 **Sacramento** *V* USA
9C3 **Sacramento Mts** USA
81C4 **Sa'dah** Yemen
54B2 **Sadanski** Bulg
82D3 **Sadiya** India
50A2 **Sado** *R* Portugal
74D3 **Sado-shima** *I* Japan
85C3 **Sādri** India
Safad = Zefat
84A2 **Safed Koh** *Mts* Afghan
52C3 **Säffle** Sweden
94B3 **Saft** Jordan
96B1 **Safi** Mor
90D3 **Safīdābeh** Iran
94C1 **Şāfītā** Syria
60E2 **Safonovo** Russian Fed
75A2 **Saga** Japan
76B1 **Sagaing** Myan
75B2 **Sagami-nada** *B* Japan

Sāgar

85D4 **Sāgar** India
16C2 **Sag Harbor** USA
14B2 **Saginaw** USA
14B2 **Saginaw B** USA
26B2 **Sagua de Tánamo** Cuba
26B2 **Sagua la Grande** Cuba
51B2 **Saguenay** R Can
49C3 **Sagunto** Spain
94C3 **Sahāb** Jordan
50A1 **Sahagún** Spain
96C2 **Sahara** Desert N Africa
84D3 **Saharanpur** India
84C2 **Sahiwal** Pak
93D3 **Sahrā al Hijarah** Desert Region Iraq
23A1 **Sahuayo** Mexico
107D1 **Saibai I** Aust
96C1 **Saïda** Alg
94B2 **Sāïda** Leb
91C4 **Sa'idabad** Iran
51B2 **Sāidia** Mor
86B1 **Saidpur** India
84C2 **Saidu** Pak
75A1 **Saigō** Japan
  Saigon = Ho Chi Minh
86C2 **Saiha** India
68D2 **Saihan Tal** China
75A2 **Saijo** Japan
74C4 **Saiki** Japan
42C2 **St Abb's Head** Pt Scot
43D4 **St Albans** Eng
15D2 **St Albans** Vermont, USA
14B3 **St Albans** West Virginia, USA
43C4 **St Albans Head** C Eng
13E2 **St Albert** Can
46B1 **St Amand-les-Eaux** France
48C2 **St Amand-Mont Rond** France
17A2 **St Andrew B** USA
44C3 **St Andrews** Scot
17B1 **St Andrew Sd** USA
27H1 **St Ann's Bay** Jamaica
7E4 **St Anthony** Can
108B3 **St Arnaud** Aust
17B2 **St Augustine** USA
46D2 **St-Avold** France
42C2 **St Bees Head** Pt Eng
47B2 **St-Bonnet** France
42B4 **St Brides B** Wales
48B2 **St-Brieuc** France
15C2 **St Catharines** Can
27M2 **St Catherine,Mt** Grenada
17B1 **St Catherines I** USA
43D4 **St Catherines Pt** Eng
49C2 **St Chamond** France
18B2 **St Charles** Missouri, USA
47B1 **St Clair** Can
14B2 **St Clair,L** Can/USA
14B2 **St Clair Shores** USA
49D2 **St Claud** France
10A2 **St Cloud** USA
47B1 **Ste Croix** Switz
27E3 **St Croix** I Caribbean S
42B4 **St Davids Head** Pt Wales
46B2 **St Denis** France
101E3 **St Denis** Réunion
46C2 **St Dizier** France
12F2 **St Elias,Mt** USA
12G2 **St Elias Mts** Can
48B2 **Saintes** France
47B2 **St Étienne** France
18B2 **St Francis** R USA
100B4 **St Francis,C** S Africa
47C1 **St Gallen** Switz
48C3 **St-Gaudens** France
109C1 **St George** Aust
17B1 **St George** South Carolina, USA
9B3 **St George** Utah, USA

17B2 **St George I** Florida, USA
20B2 **St George,Pt** USA
15D1 **St-Georges** Can
27E4 **St George's** Grenada
45C3 **St George's Chan** Irish Rep/Wales
47B2 **St Germain-en-Laye** France
47C1 **St-Gervais** France
47C1 **St Gotthard** P Switz
43B4 **St Govans Head** Pt Wales
22A1 **St Helena I**
103H5 **St Helena I** Atlantic O
100A4 **St Helena B** S Africa
17B1 **St Helena Sd** USA
109C4 **St Helens** Aust
42C3 **St Helens** Eng
20B1 **St Helens** USA
20B1 **St Helens,Mt** USA
43B4 **St Helier** Jersey
47B1 **St Hippolyte** France
46C1 **St-Hubert** Belg
7C5 **St-Hyacinthe** Can
14B1 **St Ignace** USA
43B4 **St Ives** Eng
18B2 **St James** Missouri, USA
5E4 **St James,C** Can
15D1 **St Jean** Can
48B2 **St Jean-d'Angely** France
47B2 **St-Jean-de-Maurienne** France
10C2 **St Jean,L** Can
15D1 **St-Jérôme** Can
20C1 **St Joe** USA
7D5 **Saint John** Can
7E5 **St John's** Can
14B2 **St Johns** Michigan, USA
17B2 **St Johns** R USA
15D2 **St Johnsbury** USA
19B3 **St Joseph** Louisiana, USA
14A2 **St Joseph** Michigan, USA
18B2 **St Joseph** Missouri, USA
27L1 **St Joseph** Trinidad
14B2 **St Joseph** R USA
14B1 **St Joseph,L** Can
7A4 **St Joseph,L** Can
47B1 **St Julien** France
48C2 **St-Junien** France
46B2 **St-Just-en-Chaussée** France
40B2 **St Kilda** I Scot
27E3 **St Kitts-Nevis** Is Caribbean S
47A1 **St-Laurent** France
7D5 **St Lawrence** R Can
7D5 **Saint Lawrence,G of** Can
4A3 **St Lawrence I** USA
15C2 **St Lawrence Seaway** Can/USA
48B2 **St Lô** France
97A3 **St Louis** Sen
11A3 **St Louis** USA
27E4 **St Lucia** I Caribbean S
101H1 **St Lucia,L** S Africa
44E1 **St Magnus B** Scot
48B2 **St Malo** France
20C1 **St Maries** USA
27E3 **St Martin** I Caribbean S
108A2 **St Mary Peak** Mt Aust
109C4 **St Marys** Aust
15C2 **St Marys** Aust
17B1 **St Marys** USA
46C2 **Ste-Menehould** France
12B2 **St Michael** USA
16A3 **St Michaels** USA
47B2 **St-Michel** France
46C2 **St-Mihiel** France
47C1 **St Moritz** Switz
48B2 **St-Nazaire** France

46C1 **St-Niklaas** Belg
46B1 **St-Omer** France
13E2 **St Paul** Can
10A2 **St Paul** Minnesota, USA
97A4 **St Paul** R Lib
17B2 **St Petersburg** USA
7E5 **St Pierre** Can
15D1 **St Pierre,L** Can
46B1 **St-Pol-Sur-Ternoise** France
59B3 **St Pölten** Austria
46B2 **St Quentin** France
49D3 **St Raphaël** France
101D2 **St Sébastien** C Madag
17B1 **St Simons I** USA
17B1 **St Stephen** USA
14B2 **St Thomas** Can
49D3 **St-Tropez** France
46C1 **St Truiden** Belg
46A1 **St-Valéry-sur-Somme** France
27E4 **St Vincent and the Grenadines** Is Caribbean S
108A2 **St Vincent,G** Aust
46D1 **St-Vith** Germany
46D2 **St Wendel** Germany
71F2 **Saipan** Pacific O
84B2 **Saydabad** Afghan
30C2 **Sajama** Mt Bol
74D4 **Sakai** Japan
75A2 **Sakaidi** Japan
75A1 **Sakaiminato** Japan
93C4 **Sakākah** S Arabia
10C1 **Sakami,L** Can
100B2 **Sakania** Zaire
101D3 **Sakaraha** Madag
60D5 **Sakarya** R Turk
58C1 **Sakasleja** Latvia
74D3 **Sakata** Japan
97C4 **Sakété** Benin
69G1 **Sakhalin** I Russian Fed
69E4 **Sakishima gunto** Is Japan
97A4 **Sal** I Cape Verde
61F4 **Sal** R Russian Fed
58A3 **Sala** Sweden
34D3 **Saladillo** Arg
34C2 **Saladillo** R Arg
34D3 **Salado** R Buenos Aires, Arg
34B3 **Salado** R Mendoza/San Luis, Arg
30D4 **Salado** R Sante Fe, Arg
97B4 **Salaga** Ghana
76C3 **Sala Hintoun** Camb
98B1 **Salal** Chad
81D4 **Şalālah** Oman
34A2 **Salamanca** Chile
23A1 **Salamanca** Mexico
50A1 **Salamanca** Spain
15C2 **Salamanca** USA
98B2 **Salamat** R Chad
71F4 **Salamaua** PNG
15C2 **Salamonica** USA
78D1 **Salang** Indon
38H5 **Salangen** Nor
30C3 **Salar de Arizaro** Arg
30C3 **Salar de Atacama** Salt Pan Chile
30C3 **Salar de Coipasa** Salt Pan Bol
30C3 **Salar de Uyuni** Salt Pan Bol
77F3 **Salasomaggiore** Italy
61J3 **Salavat** Russian Fed
70D4 **Salayar** Indon
105L5 **Sala y Gomez** I Pacific O
34C3 **Salazar** Arg
42C3 **Salfords** France
12E2 **Salcha** R USA
100A4 **Saldanha** S Africa
94C2 **Saldād** Syria
34C3 **Saldungaray** Arg
58C1 **Saldus** Latvia
109C3 **Sale** Aust
18C2 **Salem** Illinois, USA
87B2 **Salem** India

16D1 **Salem** Massachusetts, USA
16B3 **Salem** New Jersey, USA
20B2 **Salem** Oregon, USA
78C4 **Salembu Besar** I Indon
39G6 **Salen** Sweden
53B2 **Salerno** Italy
54A1 **Salford** Eng
59B3 **Salgótarján** Hung
31D3 **Salgueiro** Brazil
55C3 **Salihli** Turk
101C2 **Salima** Malawi
39K6 **Salimaa** L Fin
18A2 **Salina** Kansas, USA
53B3 **Salina** I Italy
30C3 **Salina Cruz** Mexico
30C3 **Salina de Arizato** Arg
34B3 **Salina Grande** Salt pan Arg
34B2 **Salina La Antigua** Salt pan Arg
35C1 **Salinas** Brazil
22B2 **Salinas** USA
22B2 **Salinas** R USA
34B3 **Salinas de Llancaneb** Salt Pan Arg
34B2 **Salinas Grandes** Salt Pan Arg
19B3 **Saline** R Arkansas, USA
27A2 **Salines,Pt** Grenada
31B2 **Salinópolis** Brazil
47A1 **Salins** France
  Salisbury = Harare
43D4 **Salisbury** Eng
15C3 **Salisbury** Maryland, USA
6C3 **Salisbury I** Can
43D4 **Salisbury Plain** Eng
38K5 **Salla** Fin
47B2 **Sallanches** France
48B2 **Sallisaw** USA
6C3 **Salluit** Can
86A1 **Sallyana** Nepal
93D2 **Salmas** Iran
38L6 **Salmi** Russian Fed
20C1 **Salmo** Can
8B2 **Salmon** USA
8B2 **Salmon Arm** Can
8B2 **Salmon River Mts** USA
39J6 **Salo** Fin
47D2 **Salò** Italy
49D3 **Salon-de-Provence** France
  Salonica = Thessalonika
54B1 **Salsette** India
38K6 **Salpausselka** Region, Fin
34B2 **Salsacate** Arg
61F4 **Sal'sk** Russian Fed
94B2 **Salt** Jordan
30C3 **Salta** Arg
30C3 **Salta** State, Arg
24B2 **Saltillo** Mexico
8B2 **Salt Lake City** USA
34C2 **Salto** Arg
34D2 **Salto** Urug
34B2 **Salto Angostura** Waterfall Colombia
35D1 **Salto da Divisa** Brazil
33E2 **Salto del Angel** Waterfall Ven
30E3 **Salto de Guaira** Waterfall Brazil
34B2 **Salto Grande** Waterfall Colombia
84C2 **Salt Range** Mts Pak
27H2 **Salt River** Jamaica
17B1 **Saluda** USA
47B2 **Saluzzo** Italy
31D4 **Salvador** Brazil
19B4 **Salvador,L** USA
23A1 **Salvatierra** Mexico
91B5 **Salwah** Qatar
76B1 **Salween** R Myan
93E2 **Sal'yany** Azerbaijan
57C3 **Salzburg** Austria
56C2 **Salzgitter** Germany
56C2 **Salzwedel** Germany

68B1	**Samagaltay** Russian Fed
79B4	**Samales Group** Is Phil
27D3	**Samaná** Dom Rep
92C2	**Samandaği** Turk
84B1	**Samangan** Afghan
79C3	**Samar** I Phil
6143	**Samara** Russian Fed
61G3	**Samara, Division,** Russian Fed
107E2	**Samarai** PNG
81D3	**Samarinda** Indon
80E2	**Samarkand** Uzbekistan
93D3	**Sāmarrā'** Iraq
79B3	**Samar S** Phil
86A2	**Sambalpur** India
78B2	**Sambas** Indon
101E2	**Sambava** Madag
84D3	**Sambhal** India
78D3	**Samboja** Indon
59C3	**Sambor** Ukraine
46B1	**Sambre** R France
74B3	**Samch'ŏk** S Korea
93D3	**Same** Tanz
47C1	**Samedan** Switz
46A1	**Samer** France
100B2	**Samfya** Zambia
76B1	**Samka** Myan
76C1	**Sam Neua** Laos
55C3	**Sámos** I Greece
55C2	**Samothráki** I Greece
34C2	**Sampacho** Arg
78D3	**Sampaga** Indon
78C3	**Sampit** Indon
78C3	**Sampit** R Indon
19B3	**Sam Rayburn Res** USA
76C3	**Samrong** Camb
56C1	**Samsø** I Den
92C1	**Samsun** Turk
97B3	**San** Mali
76D3	**San** R Camb
59C2	**San** R Pol
81C4	**San'a'** Yemen
98B2	**Sanaga** R Cam
27C4	**San Agustín** Arg
79C4	**San Agustin,C** Phil
90A2	**Sanandaj** Iran
22B1	**San Andreas** USA
25C3	**San Andrés Tuxtla** Mexico
9C3	**San Angelo** USA
53A3	**San Antioco** Sardegna
53A3	**San Antioco** I Medit S
34A2	**San Antonio** Chile
9C3	**San Antonio** New Mexico, USA
79B2	**San Antonio** Phil
9D4	**San Antonio** R Texas, USA
51C2	**San Antonio Abad** Spain
25D2	**San Antonio,C** Cuba
26A2	**San Antonio de los Banos** Cuba
22D3	**San Antonio,Mt** USA
29C4	**San Antonio Oeste** Arg
34D3	**San Agustin** Arg
34B2	**San Agustin de Valle Feríl** Arg
85D4	**Sanawad** India
23A1	**San Bartolo** Mexico
24A3	**San Benedicto** I Mexico
22B2	**San Benito** R USA
22B2	**San Benito Mt** USA
22D3	**San Bernardino** USA
34A2	**San Bernardo** Chile
17A2	**San Blas,C** USA
34A3	**San Carlos** Chile
32A1	**San Carlos** Nic
79B2	**San Carlos** Phil
29B4	**San Carlos de Bariloche** Arg
69E4	**San-chung** Taiwan
61G2	**Sanchursk** Russian Fed
34A3	**San Clemente** Chile
24D3	**San Clemente** USA
21B3	**San Clemente I** USA
34C2	**San Cristóbal** Arg
25C3	**San Cristóbal** Mexico
32C2	**San Cristóbal** Ven
34C2	**San Cristóbal** I Ecuador
107F2	**San Cristobal** I Solomon Is
25E2	**Sancti Spíritus** Cuba
78C3	**Sandai** Indon
70C3	**Sandakan** Malay
44C2	**Sanday** I Scot
9C3	**Sanderson** USA
13F1	**Sandfly L** Can
21B3	**San Diego** USA
92B2	**Sandikli** Turk
86A1	**Sandila** India
39F7	**Sandnes** Nor
38G5	**Sandnessjøen** Nor
98C3	**Sandoa** Zaïre
59C2	**Sandomierz** Pol
38D3	**Sandoy** Føroyar
20C1	**Sandpoint** USA
49D2	**Sandrio** Italy
18A2	**Sand Springs** USA
106A3	**Sandstone** Aust
73C4	**Sandu** China
14B2	**Sandusky** USA
39H6	**Sandviken** Sweden
7A4	**Sandy L** Can
34C2	**San Elcano** Arg
9B3	**San Felipe** Baja Cal, Mexico
34A2	**San Felipe** Chile
23A1	**San Felipe** Guanajuato, Mexico
27D4	**San Felipe** Ven
51C1	**San Feliu de Guixols** Spain
28A5	**San Félix** I Pacific O
34A2	**San Fernando** Chile
79B2	**San Fernando** Phil
79B2	**San Fernando** Phil
50A2	**San Fernando** Spain
27E4	**San Fernando** Trinidad
22C3	**San Fernando** USA
32D3	**San Fernando** Ven
17B2	**Sanford** Florida, USA
12F2	**Sanford,Mt** USA
34C2	**San Francisco** Arg
27C3	**San Francisco** Dom Rep
22A2	**San Francisco** USA
24B2	**San Francisco B** USA
24B2	**San Francisco del Oro** Mexico
23A1	**San Francisco del Rincon** Mexico
22D3	**San Gabriel Mts** USA
85C5	**Sangamner** India
18C2	**Sangamon** R USA
71F2	**Sangan C** Pacific O
87B1	**Sangäreddi** India
78D4	**Sangeang** I Indon
22C2	**Sanger** USA
72C2	**Sanggan He** R China
78C2	**Sanggau** Indon
98B2	**Sangha** R Congo
85B3	**Sanghar** Pak
76B2	**Sangkhla Buri** Thai
78D2	**Sangkulirang** Indon
87A1	**Sängli** India
98B2	**Sangmélima** Cam
9B3	**San Gorgonio Mt** USA
9C3	**Sangre de Cristo** Mts USA
34A3	**San Gregorio** Arg
22A2	**San Gregorio** USA
84D2	**Sangrür** India
79B3	**San Isidro** Phil
32B2	**San Jacinto** Colombia
21B3	**San Jacinto Peak** Mt USA
34A3	**San Javier** Chile
34D2	**San Javier** Sante Fe, Arg
74D3	**Sanjō** Japan
31C6	**São João del Rei** Brazil
22B3	**San Joaquin** R USA
22B2	**San Joaquin Valley** USA
32A1	**San José** Costa Rica
25C3	**San José** Guatemala
79B2	**San José** Luzon, Phil
79B3	**San José** Mindoro, Phil
22B2	**San Jose** USA
9B4	**San Jose I** Mexico
30D2	**San Jose de Chiquitos** Bol
34D2	**San José de Feliciano** Arg
34B2	**San José de Jachal** Arg
34C2	**San José de la Dormida** Arg
31B6	**San José do Rio Prêto** Brazil
24B2	**San José del Cabo** Mexico
34B2	**San Juan** Arg
27D3	**San Juan** Puerto Rico
34B2	**San Juan** State, Arg
27L1	**San Juan** Trinidad
32D2	**San Juan** Ven
26B2	**San Juan** Mt Cuba
8C3	**San Juan** Mts USA
34B2	**San Juan** R Arg
23B2	**San Juan** R Mexico
25D3	**San Juan** R Nic/Costa Rica
23A1	**San Juan Bautista** Mexico
30E4	**San Juan Bautista** Par
22B2	**San Juan Bautista** USA
25D3	**San Juan del Norte** Nic
27D4	**San Juan de los Cayos** Ven
23A1	**San Juan de loz Lagoz** Mexico
23A1	**San Juan del Rio** Mexico
25D3	**San Juan del Sur** Nic
20B1	**San Juan Is** USA
23B2	**San Juan Tepozcolula** Mexico
29C5	**San Julián** Arg
34C2	**San Justo** Arg
60D2	**Sankt-Peterburg** Russian Fed
98C3	**Sankuru** R Zaïre
92C2	**Şanliurfa** Turk
32B3	**San Lorenzo** Ecuador
34C2	**San Lorenzo** Arg
22B2	**San Lucas** USA
34B2	**San Luis** Arg
34B2	**San Luis** State, Arg
23A1	**San Luis de la Paz** Mexico
21A2	**San Luis Obispo** USA
23A1	**San Luis Potosi** Mexico
34B2	**San Luis Res** USA
53A3	**Sanluri** Sardegna
33D2	**San Maigualida** Mts Ven
34D3	**San Manuel** Arg
34A2	**San Marcos** Chile
23B2	**San Marcos** Mexico
52B2	**San Marino** Republic, Europe
34B2	**San Martín** Mendoza, Arg
112C3	**San Martín** Base Ant
47D1	**San Martino di Castroza** Italy
23B2	**San Martin Tuxmelucan** Mexico
22A2	**San Mateo** USA
30E2	**San Matias** Bol
72C3	**Sanmenxia** China
25D3	**San Miguel** El Salvador
22B3	**San Miguel** Arg
23A1	**San Miguel del Allende** Mexico
34D3	**San Miguel del Monte** Arg
30C4	**San Miguel de Tucumán** Arg
73D4	**Sanming** China
9B3	**San Nicolas I** USA
34C2	**San Nicolás de los Arroyos** Arg
101G1	**Sannieshof** S Africa
97B4	**Sanniquellie** Lib
59C3	**Sanok** Pol
26B5	**San Onofore** Colombia
22D4	**San Onofre** USA
79B3	**San Pablo** Phil
22A1	**San Pablo B** USA
34D2	**San Pedro** Buenos Aires, Arg
97B4	**San Pedro** Côte d'Ivoire
30D3	**San Pedro** Jujuy, Arg
30E3	**San Pedro** Par
22C4	**San Pedro Chan** USA
9C4	**San Pedro de los Colonias** Mexico
25D3	**San Pedro Sula** Honduras
53A3	**San Pietro** I Medit S
24A1	**San Quintin** Mexico
34B2	**San Rafael** Arg
22A2	**San Rafael** USA
22C3	**San Rafael Mts** USA
49D3	**San Remo** Italy
34D2	**San Salvador** Arg
26C2	**San Salvador** I Caribbean S
32J7	**San Salvador** I Ecuador
30C3	**San Salvador de Jujuy** Arg
97C3	**Sansanné - Mango** Togo
51B1	**San Sebastián** Spain
53C2	**San Severo** Italy
30C2	**Santa Ana** Bol
25C3	**Santa Ana** Guatemala
22D3	**Santa Ana** USA
22D4	**Santa Ana Mts** USA
34A3	**Santa Bárbara** Chile
24B2	**Santa Bárbara** Mexico
22C3	**Santa Barbara** USA
22C4	**Santa Barbara I** USA
22B3	**Santa Barbara Chan** USA
22C3	**Santa Barbara Res** USA
22C4	**Santa Catalina I** USA
22C4	**Santa Catalina,G of** USA
30F4	**Santa Catarina** State, Brazil
26B2	**Santa Clara** Cuba
22B2	**Santa Clara** USA
22C3	**Santa Clara** R USA
29C6	**Santa Cruz** Arg
30D2	**Santa Cruz** Bol
34A2	**Santa Cruz** Chile
79B3	**Santa Cruz** Phil
29B5	**Santa Cruz** State, Arg
22A2	**Santa Cruz** USA
22C4	**Santa Cruz I** USA
35D1	**Santa Cruz Cabrália** Brazil
22C3	**Santa Cruz Chan** USA
96A2	**Santa Cruz de la Palma** Canary Is
26B2	**Santa Cruz del Sur** Cuba
96A2	**Santa Cruz de Tenerife** Canary Is
100B2	**Santa Cruz do Cuando** Angola
35B2	**Santa Cruz do Rio Pardo** Brazil
22A2	**Santa Cruz Mts** USA
34D2	**Santa Elena** Arg
33E3	**Santa Elena** Ven
34C2	**Santa Fe** Arg
34C2	**Santa Fe** State, Arg
9C3	**Santa Fe** USA
35A1	**Santa Helena de Goiás** Brazil
73B3	**Santai** China

Santa Inés

29B6 Santa Inés I Chile
34B3 Santa Isabel La Pampa, Arg
34C2 Santa Isabel Santa Fe, Arg
107E1 Santa Isabel I Solomon Is
21A2 Santa Lucia Ra USA
21A2 Santa Lucia Range Mts USA
97A4 Santa Luzia I Cape Verde
9B4 Santa Margarita I Mexico
22D4 Santa Margarita R USA
26C4 Santa Maria Brazil
21A3 Santa Maria USA
96A1 Santa Maria I Açores
23B1 Santa Maria R Queretaro, Mexico
23A1 Santa Maria del Rio Mexico
32C1 Santa Marta Colombia
22C3 Santa Monica USA
22C4 Santa Monica B USA
29E2 Santana do Livramento Brazil
32B3 Santander Colombia
50B1 Santander Spain
52C3 Santanýy Spain
22C3 Santa Paula USA
31C2 Santa Quitéria Brazil
33G4 Santarem Brazil
50A2 Santarém Port
22A1 Santa Rosa California, USA
25D3 Santa Rosa Honduras
34C3 Santa Rosa La Pampa, Arg
34B2 Santa Rosa Mendoza, Arg
34B2 Santa Rosa San Luis, Arg
22B3 Santa Rosa I USA
24A2 Santa Rosalia Mexico
20C2 Santa Rosa Range Mts USA
31D3 Santa Talhada Brazil
35C1 Santa Teresa Brazil
53A2 Santa Teresa di Gallura Sardegna
22B3 Santa Ynez R USA
22B3 Santa Ynez Mts USA
17C1 Santee R USA
12C1 Santhia Italy
34A2 Santiago Chile
27C3 Santiago Dom Rep
32A2 Santiago Panama
79B2 Santiago Phil
32B4 Santiago R Peru
50A1 Santiago de Compostela Spain
26B2 Santiago de Cuba Cuba
30D4 Santiago del Estero Arg
30D4 Santiago del Estero State, Arg
22D4 Santiago Peak Mt USA
31C5 Santo State, Brazil
35A2 Santo Anastácio Brazil
30F4 Santo Ângelo Brazil
97A4 Santo Antão I Cape Verde
35A2 Santo Antonio da Platina Brazil
27D3 Santo Domingo Dom Rep
35B2 Santos Brazil
35C2 Santos Dumont Brazil
30E4 Santo Tomé Brazil
29B5 San Valentin Mt Chile
34A2 San Vicente Chile
98B3 Sanza Pomba Angola

30E4 São Borja Brazil
35B2 São Carlos Brazil
33G5 São Félix Mato Grosso, Brazil
35B2 São Fidelis Brazil
35C1 São Francisco R
31D3 São Francisco R
30G4 São Francisco do Sul Brazil
35B1 São Gotardo Brazil
99D3 São Hill Tanz
35C2 São João da Barra Brazil
35B2 São João da Boa Vista Brazil
35C1 São João da Ponte Brazil
35B2 São João del Rei Brazil
35B2 São Joaquim da Barra Brazil
96A1 São Jorge I Açores
35B2 São José do Rio Prêto Brazil
35B2 São José dos Campos Brazil
31C2 São Luis Brazil
35B1 São Marcos R Brazil
35C1 São Maria do Suaçui Brazil
35D1 São Mateus Brazil
35C1 São Mateus R Brazil
96A1 São Miguel I Açores
47C2 Saône R France
97A4 Saos Nicolau I Cape Verde
35B2 São Paulo Brazil
35B2 São Paulo State, Brazil
31C3 São Raimundo Nonato Brazil
35B1 São Romão Brazil
35B2 São Sebastio do Paraiso Brazil
35A1 São Simão Goias, Brazil
35B2 São Simão Sao Paulo, Brazil
97A4 São Tiago I Cape Verde
97C4 São Tomé I W Africa
97C4 São Tomé and Principe Republic, W Africa
96B2 Saoura Watercourse Alg
35B2 São Vicente Brazil
97A4 São Vicente I Cape Verde
55C2 Sápai Greece
78D4 Sape Indon
97C4 Sapele Nig
74E2 Sapporo Japan
53C2 Sapri Italy
18A2 Sapulpa USA
10C2 Saquenay R Can
90A2 Saráb Iran
54A2 Sarajevo Bosnia-Herzegovina
90D2 Sarakhs Iran
61J3 Saraktash Russian Fed
63A2 Sarala Russian Fed
15D2 Saranac L USA
15D2 Saranac Lake USA
55B3 Sarandë Alb
79A3 Sarangani Is Phil
61H2 Sarapul Russian Fed
17B2 Sarasota USA
54C1 Sarata Ukraine
15D2 Saratoga Springs USA
78C2 Saratok Malay
61G3 Saratov Division, Russian Fed
61G3 Saratov Russian Fed
61G3 Saratovskoye Vodokhranilishche Res Russian Fed
67F4 Sarawak State, Malay

92A2 Saraykoy Turk
90C3 Sarbisheh Iran
47D1 Sarca R Italy
95A2 Sardalas Libya
90A2 Sar Dasht Iran
52A2 Sardegna I Medit S
 Sardinia = Sardegna
33H5 Sarektjåkkå Mt Sweden
84C2 Sargodha Pak
98B2 Sarh Chad
90A2 Sāri Iran
94B2 Sarida R Isreal
93D1 Sarikamiş Turk
107D3 Sarina Aust
47B1 Sarine R Switz
84B1 Sar-i-Pul Afghan
95B2 Sarir Libya
95A2 Sarir Tibesti Desert Libya
74B3 Sariwŏn N Korea
48B2 Sark I UK
92C2 Sarkişla Turk
71E4 Sarmi Indon
29C5 Sarmiento Arg
39G4 Särna Sweden
47C1 Sarnen Switz
14B2 Sarnia Can
58D2 Sarny Ukraine
6E2 Saroaq Greenland
84B2 Sarobi Afghan
78A3 Sarolangun Indon
55B3 Saronikós Kólpos G Greece
47C2 Saronno Italy
55C2 Saros Körfezi B Turk
39G7 Sarpsborg Nor
46D2 Sarralbe France
46D2 Sarrebourg France
46D2 Sarreguemines France
46D2 Sarre-Union France
51B1 Sarrion Spain
85B3 Sartanahu Pak
53A2 Sartène Corse
48B2 Sarthe R France
61H4 Sarykamys Kazakhstan
65H5 Sarysu R Kazakhstan
86A2 Sasarām India
74B4 Sasebo Japan
5H4 Saskatchewan Province, Can
5H4 Saskatchewan R Can
13F2 Saskatoon Can
101G1 Sasolburg S Africa
61F3 Sasovo Russian Fed
97B4 Sassandra Côte d'Ivoire
97B4 Sassandra R Côte d'Ivoire
53A2 Sassari Sardegna
56C2 Sassnitz Germany
47D2 Sassuolo Italy
34C2 Sastre Arg
87A1 Sātāra India
4G2 Satellite B Can
78D4 Satengar Is Indon
38F1 Säter Sweden
17B1 Satilla R USA
61J2 Satka Russian Fed
84D2 Satluj R India
86A2 Satna India
85C4 Sātpura Range Mts India
54B1 Satu Mare Rom
34D2 Sauce Arg
39F7 Sauda Nor
80C3 Saudi Arabia Kingdom, Arabian Pen
46D2 Sauer R Germany/Lux
46D1 Sauerland Region, Germany
38B1 Sauðárkrókur Iceland
14A2 Saugatuck USA
16C1 Saugerties USA
13B2 Saugstad,Mt Can
7B5 Sault Ste Marie Can
14B1 Sault Ste Marie Can
14B1 Sault Ste Marie USA

71E4 Saumlaki Indon
48B2 Saumur France
98C3 Saurimo Angola
27M2 Sauteurs Grenada
54A2 Sava R Serbia, Yugos
97A4 Savalou Benin
17B1 Savannah Georgia, USA
17B1 Savannah R USA
76C2 Savannakhet Laos
26B3 Savanna la Mar Jamaica
7A4 Savant Lake Can
76D2 Savarane Laos
97C4 Savé Benin
101C3 Save R Mozam
90B3 Sāveh Iran
46D2 Saverne France
46B2 Savigliano Italy
46B2 Savigny France
49D2 Savoie Region France
49D3 Savona Italy
38K6 Savonlinna Fin
4A3 Savoonga USA
38K5 Savukoski Fin
71D4 Savu S Indon
76A1 Saw Myan
85D3 Sawai Mādhopur India
78A2 Sawang Indon
76B2 Sawankhalok Thai
75C1 Sawara Japan
12E1 Sawtooth Mt USA
106B2 Sawu I Indon
97C3 Say Niger
84B1 Sayghan Afghan
91B5 Sayhut Yemen
61G4 Saykhin Kazakhstan
68D2 Saynshand Mongolia
61H5 Say-Utes Kazakhstan
16C2 Sayville USA
13B2 Sayward Can
57C3 Sázava R Czech Republic
51C2 Sbisseb R Alg
42C2 Scafell Pike Mt Eng
44E1 Scalloway Scot
15C2 Scapa Flow Isl Scot
15C2 Scarborough Can
42D2 Scarborough Eng
27F4 Scarborough Tobago
44A2 Scarp I Scot
45B2 Scarriff Irish Rep
12C1 Schaffhausen Switz
57C3 Scharding Austria
46D1 Scharteberg Mt Germany
7D4 Schefferville Can
46B1 Schelde R Belg
10C2 Schenectady USA
47C2 Schio Italy
46D1 Schleiden Germany
56B2 Schleswig Germany
56B2 Schleswig Holstein State, Germany
16B1 Schoharie USA
71F4 Schouten Is PNG
7B5 Schreiber Can
21B2 Schurz USA
16A2 Schuylkill Haven USA
16A2 Schuylkill R USA
57B3 Schwabische Alb Upland Germany
57B3 Schwarzwald Upland Germany
12C1 Schwatka Mts USA
47D1 Schwaz Austria
57C2 Schweinfurt Germany
101G1 Schweizer Reneke S Africa
56C2 Schwerin Germany
47C1 Schwyz Switz
53B3 Sciacca Italy
14B3 Scioto R USA
109D2 Scone Aust
6D4 Scoresby Sd Greenland
103F7 Scotia Ridge Atlantic O
103F7 Scotia S Atlantic O

44B3 **Scotland** Country, UK
112B7 **Scott** Base Ant
13A2 **Scott,C** Can
9C2 **Scott City** USA
112C6 **Scott I** Ant
6C2 **Scott Inlet** B Can
42C2 **Scottish Borders** Division Scot
20B2 **Scott,Mt** USA
106B2 **Scott Reef** Timor Is
8C2 **Scottsbluff** USA
109C4 **Scottsdale** Aust
10C2 **Scranton** USA
47D1 **Scuol** Switz
Scutari = Shkodër
5J4 **Seal** R Can
108B3 **Sea Lake** Aust
18B2 **Searcy** USA
22B2 **Seaside** California, USA
20B1 **Seaside** Oregon, USA
20B1 **Seaside** USA
16B3 **Seaside Park** USA
20B1 **Seattle** USA
22A1 **Sebastopol** USA
58D1 **Sebez** Russian Fed
17B2 **Sebring** USA
111A3 **Secretary I** NZ
18B2 **Sedalia** USA
46C2 **Sedan** France
111B2 **Seddonville** NZ
94B3 **Sede Boqer** Israel
94B3 **Sederot** Israel
97A3 **Sédhiou** Sen
94B3 **Sedom** Israel
100A3 **Seeheim** Namibia
17B1 **Sefton,Mt** NZ
77C5 **Segamat** Malay
51B2 **Segorbe** Spain
97B3 **Ségou** Mali
Segovia = Coco
50B1 **Segovia** Spain
51C1 **Segre** R Spain
97B4 **Séguéla** Côte d'Ivoire
96A2 **Seguia el Hamra** Watercourse Mor
34C2 **Segundo** R Arg
78D2 **Seguntur** Indon
50B2 **Segura** R Spain
85B3 **Sehwan** Pak
46D2 **Seille** R France
38J6 **Seinäjoki** Fin
48C2 **Seine** R France
46B2 **Seine-et-Marne** Department, France
99D3 **Sekenke** Tanz
99D1 **Sek'ot'a** Eth
20B1 **Selah** USA
71E4 **Selaru** I Indon
78D4 **Selat Alas** Str Indon
78B3 **Selat Bangka** Str Indon
78A3 **Selat Berhala** Str Indon
71E4 **Selat Dampier** Str Indon
78B3 **Selat Gaspar** Str Indon
78D4 **Selat Lombok** Str Indon
78D4 **Selat Sape** Str Indon
78B4 **Selat Sunda** Str Indon
71D4 **Selat Wetar** Chan Indon
12B1 **Selawik** USA
12C1 **Selawik** R USA
12B1 **Selawik L** USA
42D3 **Selby** Eng
55C3 **Selçuk** Turk
12D3 **Seldovia** USA
100B3 **Selebi Pikwe** Botswana
6H3 **Selfoss** Iceland
95B2 **Selima Oasis** Sudan
5J4 **Selkirk** Can
42C2 **Selkirk** Scot
13D2 **Selkirk Mts** Can
22C2 **Selma** California, USA
50A1 **Selouane** Mor
12H2 **Selous,Mt** Can
78B3 **Selta Karimata** Str Indon
32C5 **Selvas** Region, Brazil
107D3 **Selwyn** Aust
4E3 **Selwyn** Mts Can
78C4 **Semarang** Indon
61E2 **Semenov** Russian Fed
12C3 **Semidi Is** USA
60E3 **Semiluki** Russian Fed
19A2 **Seminole** Oklahoma, USA
17B1 **Seminole,L** USA
65K4 **Semipalatinsk** Kazakhstan
79B3 **Semirara Is** Phil
90B3 **Semirom** Iran
78C2 **Semitau** Indon
90B2 **Semnan** Iran
46C2 **Semois** R Belg
23B2 **Sempoala** Hist Site, Mexico
32D5 **Sena Madureira** Brazil
100B2 **Senanga** Zambia
19C3 **Senatobia** USA
74E3 **Sendai** Honshū, Japan
74C4 **Sendai** Kyūshū, Japan
85D4 **Sendwha** India
15C2 **Seneca Falls** USA
97A3 **Senegal** Republic, Africa
97A3 **Sénégal** R Maur Sen
101G1 **Senekal** S Africa
31D4 **Senhor do Bonfim** Brazil
52B2 **Senigallia** Italy
52C2 **Senj** Croatia
69E4 **Senkaku Gunto** Is Japan
46C2 **Senlis** France
99D1 **Sennar** Sudan
7C5 **Senneterre** Can
49C2 **Sens** France
54A1 **Senta** Serbia, Yugos
98C3 **Sentery** Zaire
13C2 **Sentinel Peak** Mt Can
85D4 **Seoni** India
Seoul = Soul
110B2 **Separation Pt** NZ
76D2 **Sepone** Laos
7D4 **Sept-Iles** Can
95A2 **Séquédine** Niger
21B2 **Sequoia** Nat Pk, USA
71D4 **Seram** I Indon
78B4 **Serang** Indon
78B2 **Serasan** I Indon
54A2 **Serbia** Republic, Yugos
61F3 **Serdobsk** Russian Fed
77C5 **Seremban** Malay
99D3 **Serengeti Nat Pk** Tanz
100C2 **Serenje** Zambia
59D3 **Seret** R Ukraine
61G2 **Sergach** Russian Fed
31D4 **Sergipe** State, Brazil
60E2 **Sergiyev Posad** Russian Fed
78C2 **Seria** Brunei
78C2 **Serian** Malay
55B3 **Sérifos** I Greece
47C2 **Serio** R Italy
95B2 **Serir Calanscio** Desert Libya
46C2 **Sermaize-les-Bains** France
71D4 **Sermata** I Indon
61H3 **Sernovodsk** Russian Fed
65H4 **Serov** Russian Fed
100B3 **Serowe** Botswana
50A2 **Serpa** Port
60E3 **Serpukhov** Russian Fed
35B2 **Serra da Canastra** Mts Brazil
50A1 **Serra da Estrela** Mts Port
35B2 **Serra da Mantiqueira** Mts Brazil
35A1 **Serra da Mombuca** Brazil
35C1 **Serra do Cabral** Mt Brazil
33F5 **Serra do Cachimbo** Mts Brazil
35A1 **Serra do Caiapó** Mts Brazil
35A2 **Serra do Cantu** Mts Brazil
35C2 **Serra do Caparaó** Mts Brazil
31C5 **Serra do Chifre** Brazil
51C1 **Serra do Espinhaço** Mts Brazil
35B2 **Serra do Mar** Mts Brazil
35A2 **Serra do Mirante** Mts Brazil
33G3 **Serra do Navio** Brazil
35B2 **Serra do Paranapiacaba** Mts Brazil
35A6 **Serra dos Caiabis** Mts Brazil
35A2 **Serra dos Dourados** Mts Brazil
33E6 **Serra dos Parecis** Mts Brazil
35B1 **Serra dos Pilões** Mts Brazil
35A1 **Serra Dourada** Mts Brazil
33F6 **Serra Formosa** Brazil
55B2 **Sérrai** Greece
25D3 **Serrana Bank** Is Caribbean S
51B1 **Serrana de Cuenca** Mts Spain
35A1 **Serranópolis** Brazil
33E3 **Serra Pacaraima** Mts Brazil/Ven
33E3 **Serra Parima** Mts Brazil
33G3 **Serra Tumucumaque** Brazil
46B2 **Serre** R France
34B2 **Serrezuela** Arg
31D4 **Serrinha** Brazil
61G3 **Serrmilik** Greenland
35C1 **Serro** Brazil
35A2 **Sertãopolis** Brazil
72A3 **Sêrtar** China
78C3 **Seruyan** R Indon
100A2 **Sesfontein** Namibia
100B2 **Sesheke** Zambia
47B2 **Sestriere** Italy
74D2 **Setana** Japan
49C3 **Sète** France
50B1 **Sete Lagoas** Brazil
96C1 **Sétif** Alg
75B1 **Seto** Japan
75A2 **Seto Naikai** S Japan
96B1 **Settat** Mor
42C2 **Settle** Eng
5G4 **Settler** Can
50A2 **Setúbal** Port
93E1 **Sevan,Oz** L Armenia
60D5 **Sevastopol'** Ukraine
7B4 **Severn** R Can
43C3 **Severn** R Eng
61F5 **Severnaya Osetiya** Division Russian Fed
1B9 **Severnaya Zemlya** I Russian Fed
63C2 **Severo-Baykalskoye Nagorye** Mts Russian Fed
60E4 **Severo Donets** Ukraine
64E3 **Severodvinsk** Russian Fed
64H3 **Severo Sos'va** R Russian Fed
8B3 **Sevier** R USA
8B3 **Sevier L** USA
50A2 **Sevilla** Spain
Seville = Sevilla
54B2 **Sevlievo** Bulg
97A4 **Sewa** R Sierra Leone
12E2 **Seward** Alaska, USA
18A1 **Seward** Nebraska, USA
12A1 **Seward Pen** USA
13D1 **Sexsmith** Can
89K8 **Seychelles** Is Indian O
38C1 **Seyðisfjörður** Iceland
92C2 **Seyhan** Turk
91B9 **Seymour** R Russian Fed
100C3 **Seymour** Aust
16C2 **Seymour** Connecticut, USA
14A3 **Seymour** Indiana, USA
46B2 **Sézanne** France
96D1 **Sfax** Tunisia
54C1 **Sfîntu Gheorghe** Rom
56A2 **'s-Gravenhage** Neth
72B3 **Shaanxi** Province, China
98C3 **Shabunda** Zaire
82B2 **Shache** China
112C9 **Shackleton Ice Shelf** Ant
85B3 **Shadadkot** Pak
91B3 **Shādhām** R Iran
43C4 **Shaftesbury** Eng
29G8 **Shag Rocks** Is South Georgia
90A3 **Shahābād** Iran
94C2 **Shahba** Syria
91C3 **Shahdāp** Iran
86A2 **Shahdol** India
90A3 **Shāhīn Dezh** Iran
90C3 **Shāh Kūh** Iran
91C3 **Shahr-e Bābak** Iran
Shahresa = Qomisheh
90B3 **Shahr Kord** Iran
87B1 **Shājābād** India
84D3 **Shājahānpur** India
85D4 **Shājāpur** India
61F4 **Shakhun'ya** Russian Fed
61G2 **Shakhun'ya** Russian Fed
97C4 **Shaki** Nig
12B2 **Shaktoolik** USA
61J2 **Shamary** Russian Fed
99D2 **Shambe** Sudan
16A2 **Shamokin** USA
16B1 **Shandaken** USA
72D2 **Shandong** Province, China
73C5 **Shangchuan Dao** I China
72C1 **Shangdu** China
73E3 **Shanghai** China
72C3 **Shangnan** China
100B2 **Shangombo** Zambia
73D4 **Shangrao** China
73B5 **Shangsi** China
72C3 **Shang Xian** China
41B3 **Shannon** R Irish Rep
72D3 **Shanqiu** China
74B2 **Shansonggang** China
63F2 **Shantarskiye Ostrova** I Russian Fed
73D5 **Shantou** China
72C2 **Shanxi** Province, China
72D3 **Shan Xian** China
73C5 **Shaoguan** China
73E4 **Shaoxing** China
73C4 **Shaoyang** China
44C2 **Shapinsay** I Scot
94C2 **Shaqqā** Syria
72A1 **Sharhulsan** Mongolia
90C2 **Sharīfābād** Iran
91C4 **Shārjah** UAE
106A3 **Shark B** Aust
90C2 **Sharlauk** Turkmenistan
94B2 **Sharon,Plain of** Israel
61G2 **Sharya** Russian Fed
99D2 **Shashemenē** Eth
73C3 **Shashi** China
20B2 **Shasta L** USA
20B2 **Shasta,Mt** USA
93E3 **Shaṭṭ al Gharrāf** R Iraq
94B3 **Shaubak** Jordan
13F3 **Shaunavon** Can

Shaver L

22C2 Shaver L USA
16B2 Shawangunk Mt USA
15D1 Shawinigan Can
19A2 Shawnee Oklahoma, USA
73D4 Sha Xian China
106B3 Shay Gap Aust
94C2 Shaykh Miskin Syria
69E1 Shaykh 'Uthmān Yemen
60E1 Shchekino Russian Fed
60E3 Shchigry Russian Fed
60D3 Shchors Ukraine
65J4 Shchuchinsk Kazakhstan
99E2 Shebele R Eth
14A2 Sheboygan USA
98B2 Shebshi Mts Nig
12F1 Sheep R USA
45C1 Sheep Haven Estuary Irish Rep
43E4 Sheerness Eng
94B2 Shefar'am Israel
42D3 Sheffield Eng
84C2 Shekhupura Pak
13B1 Shelagyote Peak Mt Can
16C1 Shelburne Falls USA
14A2 Shelby Michigan, USA
8B2 Shelby Montana, USA
14A3 Shelbyville Indiana, USA
12H2 Sheldon,Mt Can
12D3 Shelikof Str USA
109D2 Shellharbour Aust
111A3 Shelter Pt NZ
20B1 Shelton USA
93E1 Shemakha Azerbaijan
18A1 Shenandoah USA
15C3 Shenandoah R USA
15C3 Shenandoah Nat Pk USA
97C4 Shendam USA
95C2 Shendi Sudan
72C2 Shenmu China
72E1 Shenyang China
73C5 Shenzhen China
85D3 Sheopur India
59D2 Shepetovka Ukraine
108C3 Shepparton Aust
6B2 Sherard,C Can
43C4 Sherborne Eng
97A4 Sherbro I Sierra Leone
15D1 Sherbrooke Can
85C3 Shergarh India
19B3 Sheridan Arkansas, USA
8C2 Sheridan Wyoming, USA
19A3 Sherman USA
56B2 s-Hertogenbosch Neth
12H3 Sheslay Can
40C1 Shetland Is Scot
93C2 Shevchenko = Aktau
91B4 Sheyk Sho'eyb I Iran
69H2 Shiashkotan I Russian Fed
84B1 Shibarghan Afghan
74D3 Shibata Japan
95C1 Shibin el Kom Egypt
75B1 Shibukawa Japan
72C2 Shijiazhuang China
84B3 Shikarpur Pak
67G3 Shikoku I Japan
75A2 Shikoku-sanchi Mts Japan
86B1 Shiliguri India
68D1 Shilka Russian Fed
68D1 Shilka R Russian Fed
16B2 Shillington USA
86C1 Shillong India
85E3 Shilovo Russian Fed
75A2 Shimabara Japan
75B2 Shimada Japan
69E1 Shimanovsk Russian Fed
74D3 Shimizu Japan

84D2 Shimla India
75B2 Shimoda Japan
87B2 Shimoga India
74C4 Shimonoseki Japan
75B1 Shinano R Japan
91C5 Shinas Oman
74D4 Shingū Japan
75C1 Shinjō Japan
74D3 Shinminato Japan
94C1 Shinshār Syria
99D3 Shinyanga Tanz
74E3 Shiogama Japan
75B2 Shiono-misaki C Japan
73A5 Shiping China
16A2 Shippensburg USA
72B3 Shiquan China
75C1 Shirakawa Japan
75B1 Shirane-san Mt Japan
75B1 Shirani-san Mt Japan
91B4 Shīrāz Iran
90B3 Shīr Kūh Iran
75B1 Shirotori Japan
90C2 Shīrvān Iran
12A1 Shishmaref USA
12A1 Shishmaref Inlet USA
4B3 Shishmaret USA
72B2 Shitanjing China
14A3 Shiveli USA
85D3 Shivpuri India
94B3 Shivta Hist Site Israel
101C2 Shiwa Ngandu Zambia
72C3 Shiyan China
72B2 Shizuishan China
54A2 Shkodër Alb
109D2 Shoalhaven R Aust
75A2 Shobara Japan
87B2 Shoranur India
87B1 Shorapur India
21B2 Shoshone Mts USA
60D3 Shostka Ukraine
19B3 Shreveport USA
43C3 Shrewsbury Eng
43C3 Shropshire County, Eng
72E1 Shuanglia China
69F2 Shuangyashan China
61J4 Shubar-Kuduk Kazakhstan
72D2 Shu He R China
73A4 Shuicheng China
84C3 Shujaabad Pak
85D4 Shujalpur India
68B2 Shule He China
54C2 Shumen Bulg
61G2 Shumerlya Russian Fed
73D4 Shuncheng China
12C1 Shungnak USA
72C2 Shuo Xian China
91C4 Shūr Gaz Iran
100B2 Shurugwi Zim
13D2 Shuswap L Can
61F2 Shuya Russian Fed
12D3 Shwebo Myan
82D3 Shwebo Myan
76B2 Shwegyin Myan
84A2 Siah Koh Mts Afghan
84C2 Sialkot Pak
79C4 Siarao I Phil
Sian = Xi'an
79B4 Siaton Phil
58C1 Šiauliai Lithuania
65G4 Sibay Russian Fed
101H1 Sibayi L S Africa
52C2 Šibenik Croatia
70A4 Siberut I Indon
84B3 Sibi Pak
68C1 Sibirskoye Russian Fed
98B3 Sibiti Congo
99D3 Sibiti R Tanz
54B1 Sibiu Rom
70A3 Sibolga Indon
86C1 Sibsagar India
78C2 Sibu Malay
79B4 Sibuguay B Phil

98B2 Sibut CAR
79B3 Sibuyan I Phil
79B3 Sibuyan S Phil
73A3 Sichuan Province, China
53B3 Sicilia I Medit S
53B3 Sicilian Chan Italy/Tunisia
Sicily = Sicilia
32C6 Sicuani Peru
85C4 Siddhapur India
87F1 Siddipet India
86A2 Sidhi India
95B1 Sidi Barrani Egypt
96B1 Sidi Bel Abbès Alg
96B1 Sidi Kacem Mor
42C3 Sidlaw Hills Scot
112B5 Sidley,Mt Ant
20B1 Sidney Can
8C2 Sidney Nebraska, USA
15C2 Sidney New York, USA
14B2 Sidney Ohio, USA
17B1 Sidney Lanier,L USA
Sidon = Saïda
52C2 Siedlce Pol
46D1 Sieg R Germany
46D1 Siegburg Germany
52B2 Siegen Germany
76C3 Siem Reap Camb
52B2 Siena Italy
58B2 Sierpc Pol
23B2 Sierra Andrés Tuxtla Mexico
34B3 Sierra Auca Mahuida Arg
9C3 Sierra Blanca USA
51B1 Sierra da Barracin Mts Spain
50B2 Sierra de Alcaraz Mts Spain
34B2 Sierra de Cordoba Mts Arg
50A1 Sierra de Gredos Mts Spain
50A2 Sierra de Guadalupe Mts Spain
50B1 Sierra de Guadarrama Mts Spain
51B1 Sierra de Guara Mts Spain
51B1 Sierra de Gudar Mts Spain
23B2 Sierra de Juárez Mexico
34C3 Sierra de la Ventana Mts Arg
51C1 Sierra del Codi Mts Spain
34B2 Sierra del Morro Mt Spain
34B3 Sierra del Nevado Mts Arg
24B2 Sierra de los Alamitos Mts Mexico
50B2 Sierra de los Filabres Spain
23A1 Sierra de los Huicholes Mexico
23A1 Sierra de Miahuatlán Mexico
23A1 Sierra de Morones Mts Mexico
50A2 Sierra de Ronda Mts Spain
34B2 Sierra de San Luis Mts Arg
50B2 Sierra de Segura Mts Spain
50B1 Sierra de Urbion Mts Spain
34B2 Sierra de Uspallata Mts Arg
34B2 Sierra de Valle Fértil Arg
23B2 Sierra de Zongolica Mexico
34C2 Sierra Grande Arg
97A4 Sierra Leone Republic, Africa

97A4 Sierra Leone,C Sierra Leone
79B2 Sierra Madre Mts Phil
23A2 Sierra Madre del Sur Mts Mexico
24B2 Sierra Madre Occidental Mts Mexico
24C2 Sierra Madre Oriental Mts Mexico
34B2 Sierra Malanzan Mts Arg
9C4 Sierra Mojada Mexico
50A2 Sierra Morena Spain
50B2 Sierra Nevada Spain
21A2 Sierra Nevada USA
32C1 Sierra Nevada de Santa Marta Colombia
34B2 Sierra Pié de Palo Mts Arg
47B1 Sierre Switz
55B3 Sifnos I Greece
59C3 Sighetu Marmaţiei Rom
54B1 Sighişoara Rom
38B1 Siglufjördur Iceland
50B1 Sigüenza Spain
97B3 Siguiri Guinea
Sihanoukville = Kompong Som
85E4 Sihora India
93D2 Siirt Turk
85D3 Sikai Hu L China
85D3 Sikar India
84B2 Sikaram Mt Afghan
97B3 Sikasso Mali
72E2 Sikeston USA
55C3 Sikinos I Greece
55B3 Sikionia Greece
86B1 Sikkim State, India
50A1 Sil R Spain
47C1 Silandro Italy
23A1 Silao Mexico
79B3 Silay Phil
86C2 Silchar India
96C2 Silet Alg
86A1 Silgarhi Nepal
92B2 Silifke Turk
82C2 Siling Co L China
54C2 Silistra Bulg
39F7 Silkeborg Den
47E1 Sillian Austria
18B2 Siloam Springs USA
19B3 Silsbee USA
95A3 Siltou Well Chad
58C1 Šilute Lithuania
93D2 Silvan Turk
35B1 Silvania Brazil
85C4 Silvassa India
21B2 Silver City Nevada, USA
9C3 Silver City New Mexico, USA
20B2 Silver Lake USA
16A3 Silver Spring USA
13B2 Silverthrone Mt Can
108B2 Silverton Aust
47C1 Silvretta Mts Austria/Switz
78C2 Simanggang Malay
76C1 Simao China
90A3 Simareh R Iran
55C3 Simav Turk
55C3 Simav R Turk
61G3 Simbirsk Russian Fed
15C2 Simcoe,L Can
70A3 Simeulue I Indon
60D5 Simferopol' Ukraine
55C3 Simi I Greece
46D1 Simmern Germany
13B2 Simoom Sound Can
49D2 Simplon Mt Switz
47C1 Simplon P Switz
4C2 Simpson,C USA
106C3 Simpson Desert Aust
6B3 Simpson Pen Can
39G7 Simrishamn Sweden

69H2 **Simushir** *I* Russian Fed
99E2 **Sina Dhaqa** Somalia
92B4 **Sinai** *Pen* Egypt
32B2 **Sincelejo** Colombia
17B1 **Sinclair,L** USA
85D3 **Sind** *R* India
85B3 **Sindh** Region, Pak
55C3 **Sindirgi** Turk
86B2 **Sindri** India
50A2 **Sines** Port
99D1 **Singa** Sudan
77C5 **Singapore** Republic, S E Asia
77C5 **Singapore,Str of** S E Asia
78D4 **Singaraja** Indon
99D3 **Singida** Tanz
78B2 **Singkawang** Indon
109D2 **Singleton** Aust
78A3 **Singtep** *I* Indon
76B1 **Singu** Myan
53A2 **Siniscola** Sardegna
93D2 **Sinjar** Iraq
84B2 **Sinkai Hills** *Mts* Afghan
95C3 **Sinkat** Sudan
82C1 **Sinkiang** Autonomous Region, China
33G2 **Sinnamary** French Guiana
92C1 **Sinop** Turk
54B1 **Sintana** Rom
78C2 **Sintang** Indon
50A2 **Sintra** Port
32B2 **Sinú** *R* Colombia
74A2 **Sinŭiju** N Korea
59B3 **Siófok** Hung
47B1 **Sion** Switz
8D2 **Sioux City** USA
8D2 **Sioux Falls** USA
10A2 **Sioux Lookout** Can
79B4 **Sipalay** Phil
27L1 **Siparia** Trinidad
69E2 **Siping** China
11283 **Siple** *Base* Ant
112B5 **Siple I** Ant
79B3 **Sipocot** Phil
70A4 **Sipora** Indon
79B4 **Siquijor** *I* Phil
87B2 **Sira** India
53C3 **Siracusa** Italy
86B2 **Sirajganj** Bang
13C2 **Sir Alexander,Mt** Can
84D1 **Sir Bani Yās** *I* UAE
106C2 **Sir Edward Pellew Group** *Is* Aust
54C1 **Siret** *R* Rom
12J2 **Sir James McBrien,Mt** Can
87B2 **Sir Kālahasti** India
13D2 **Sir Laurier,Mt** Can
93D2 **Şirnak** Turk
85C4 **Sirohi** India
87B1 **Sironcha** India
85D4 **Sironj** India
55B3 **Síros** *I* Greece
91B4 **Sirri** *I* Iran
84D3 **Sirsa** India
13D2 **Sir Sandford,Mt** Can
87A2 **Sirsi** India
95A1 **Sirte Desert** Libya
95A1 **Sirte,G of** Libya
52C1 **Sisak** Croatia
76C2 **Sisaket** Thai
76C3 **Sisophon** Camb
46B2 **Sissonne** France
90D3 **Sistan** Region, Iran/Afghan
49D3 **Sisteron** France
63B2 **Sistig Khem** Russian Fed
86A1 **Sītāpur** India
55C3 **Sitia** Greece
4E4 **Sitka** USA
12D3 **Sitkalidak I** USA
12D3 **Sitkinak I** USA
76B2 **Sittang** *R* Myan
46C1 **Sittard** Neth
86C2 **Sittwe** Myan
78C4 **Situbondo** Indon
92C2 **Sivas** Turk
93C2 **Siverek** Turk

92B2 **Sivrihisar** Turk
95B2 **Siwa** Egypt
84D2 **Siwalik Range** *Mts* India
86A1 **Siwalik Range** *Mts* Nepal
72D3 **Siyang** China
56C1 **Sjælland** *I* Den
39G7 **Skagen** Den
39F7 **Skagerrak** *Str* Nor/Den
20B1 **Skagit** *R* USA
20B1 **Skagit Mt** USA
4E4 **Skagway** USA
39G7 **Skara** Sweden
59C2 **Skarzysko-Kamlenna** Pol
5F4 **Skeena** *R* Can
13B1 **Skeena Mts** Can
4D3 **Skeenjek** *R* USA
42E3 **Skegness** Eng
38H5 **Skellefte** *R* Sweden
38J6 **Skellefteå** Sweden
45C3 **Skiathos** *I* Greece
45B3 **Skibbereen** Irish Rep
5E4 **Skidegate** Can
58C2 **Skiemiewice** Pol
39F7 **Skien** Nor
96C1 **Skikda** Alg
74C4 **Skikoku** *I* Japan
42D3 **Skipton** Eng
55B3 **Skíros** *I* Greece
39F7 **Skive** Den
56B1 **Skjern** Den
6F3 **Skjoldungen** Greenland
14A2 **Skokie** USA
55B3 **Skópelos** *I* Greece
54B2 **Skopje** Macedonia
39G7 **Skövde** Sweden
63E2 **Skovorodino** Russian Fed
4C3 **Skwentna** USA
58B2 **Skwierzyna** Pol
40B2 **Skye** *I* Scot
39G7 **Slagelse** Den
45C2 **Slaney** *R* Irish Rep
54B2 **Slatina** Rom
78C4 **Slaung** Indon
5G3 **Slave** *R* Can
13E1 **Slave Lake** Can
65J4 **Slavgorod** Russian Fed
59D2 **Slavuta** Ukraine
60E4 **Slavyansk** Ukraine
44B3 **Sleat,Sound of** *Chan* Scot
12C2 **Sleetmute** USA
45C2 **Sleeve Bloom** *Mts* Irish Rep
19C3 **Slidell** USA
16B2 **Slide Mt** USA
45B1 **Sligo** County, Irish Rep
41B3 **Sligo** Irish Rep
41B3 **Sligo B** Irish Rep
54C2 **Sliven** Bulg
54C2 **Slobozia** Rom
58D2 **Slonim** Belarus
43D4 **Slough** Eng
22B2 **Slough** *R* USA
59B3 **Slovakia** Republic, Europe
52B1 **Slovenia** Republic, Europe
56C2 **Slubice** Pol
59D2 **Sluch'** *R* Ukraine
58B2 **Słupsk** Pol
58D2 **Slutsk** Belarus
58D2 **Slutsk** *R* Belarus
41A3 **Slyne Head** *Pt* Irish Rep
63C2 **Slyudyanka** Russian Fed
7D4 **Smallwood Res** Can
54B2 **Smederevo** Serbia, Yugos
54B2 **Smederevska Palanka** Serbia, Yugos
60D4 **Smela** Ukraine
15C2 **Smethport** USA
13E1 **Smith** Can
4F3 **Smith Arm** *B* Can

13B2 **Smithers** Can
7C3 **Smith I** Can
13B2 **Smith Sd** Can
15C2 **Smiths Falls** Can
109C4 **Smithton** Aust
13D1 **Smoky** *R* Can
100D2 **Smoky C** Aust
13E2 **Smoky Lake** Can
38F6 **Smøla** *I* Nor
60D3 **Smolensk** Russian Fed
60D3 **Smolensk** Division, Russian Fed
55B2 **Smólikas** *Mt* Greece
54B2 **Smolyan** Bulg
58D2 **Smorgon'** Belarus
16B3 **Smyrna** Delaware, USA
17B1 **Smyrna** Georgia, USA
42B2 **Snaefell** *Mt* Eng
38B2 **Snafell** *Mt* Iceland
8B2 **Snake** *R* USA
8B2 **Snake River Canyon** USA
56B2 **Sneek** Neth
45B3 **Sneem** Irish Rep
59B2 **Sněžka** *Mt* Pol/Czech Republic
38F6 **Snohetta** *Mt* Nor
20B1 **Snohomish** USA
20B1 **Snoqualmie P** USA
76D3 **Snoul** Camb
43B3 **Snowdon** *Mt* Wales
43B3 **Snowdonia Nat Pk** Wales
4G3 **Snowdrift** Can
5H4 **Snow Lake** Can
108A2 **Snowtown** Aust
109C3 **Snowy Mts** Aust
9C3 **Snyder** USA
78A4 **Snan-kundo** *I* S Korea
99D2 **Sobat** *R* Sudan
31C2 **Sobral** Brazil
58C2 **Sochaczew** Pol
61E5 **Sochi** Russian Fed
9C3 **Socorro** USA
24A3 **Socorro** *I* Mexico
81D4 **Socotra** *I* Yemen
99C1 **Sodiri** Sudan
99D2 **Sodo** Eth
46E1 **Soest** Germany
101C2 **Sofala** Mozam
Sofia = **Sofiya**
54B2 **Sofiya** Bulg
69G4 **Sofu Gan** *I* Japan
32C2 **Sogamoso** Colombia
39F6 **Sognefjorden** *Inlet* Nor
82D2 **Sog Xian** China
95C2 **Sohâg** Egypt
82D3 **Sohipat** India
46B1 **Soignies** Belgium
46B2 **Soissons** France
85C3 **Sojat** India
74A3 **Sŏjosŏn-man** *B* N Korea
92A2 **Sŏke** Turk
97C4 **Sokodé** Togo
61E2 **Sokol** Russian Fed
97B3 **Sokolo** Mali
6H3 **Sokongens Øy** *I* Greenland
99D1 **Sokota** Eth
97G3 **Sokoto** *R* Nigeria
111A3 **Solander I** NZ
79B2 **Solano** Phil
47D1 **Solbad Hall** Austria
47D1 **Sölden** Austria
12D2 **Soldotna** USA
26C4 **Soledad** *Sd* Eng
46B1 **Solesmes** France
58D2 **Soligorsk** Belarus

61J2 **Solikamsk** Russian Fed
32C4 **Solimoes** *R* Peru
46D1 **Solingen** Germany
38H6 **Sollefteå** Sweden
61H3 **Sol'lletsk** Russian Fed
70B4 **Solok** Indon
105A4 **Solomon Is** Pacific O
47B1 **Solothurn** Switz
39F8 **Soltau** Germany
22B3 **Solvang** USA
42C2 **Solway Firth** *Estuary* Eng/Scot
100B2 **Solwezi** Zambia
72A4 **Sōma** Japan
55C3 **Soma** Turk
54A1 **Sombor** Serbia, Yugos
107D2 **Somerset** Aust
43C4 **Somerset** County, Eng
16D2 **Somerset** Massachusetts, USA
15C2 **Somerset** Pennsylvania, USA
100B4 **Somerset East** S Africa
6A2 **Somerset I**
16R3 **Somers Point** USA
16B2 **Somerville** USA
19A3 **Somerville** USA
54B1 **Someş** *R* Rom
46B2 **Somme** Department, France
46B2 **Somme** *R* France
46C2 **Sommesous** France
86A2 **Son** *R* India
74A3 **Sŏnch'ŏn** N Korea
39F8 **Sønderborg** Den
6E3 **Søndre Strømfjord** Greenland
47C1 **Sondrio** Italy
76D3 **Song Ba** *R* Viet
76D3 **Song Cau** Viet
101C2 **Songea** Tanz
73E3 **Songjiang** China
77C4 **Songkhla** Thai
74B3 **Songnim** N Korea
77C5 **Song Pahang** *R* Malay
72A3 **Songpan** China
72C1 **Sonid Youqi** China
76C1 **Son La** Viet
85B3 **Sonmiani** Pak
85B3 **Sonmiani Bay** Pak
22A1 **Sonoma** USA
22B2 **Sonora** California, USA
24A2 **Sonora** *R* Mexico
9B3 **Sonoran Desert** USA
22C1 **Sonora P** USA
25D3 **Sonsonate** El Salvador
71E3 **Sonsorol** *I* Pacific O
10B2 **Soo Canals** Can/USA
13C3 **Sooke** Can
58B2 **Sopot** Pol
59B3 **Sopron** Hung
22B2 **Soquel** USA
53B2 **Sora** Italy
14J3 **Sored** *R* Israel
15D1 **Sorel** Can
109C4 **Sorell** Aust
92C2 **Sorgun** Turk
50B1 **Soria** Spain
38J5 **Sørkjosen** Nor
64C2 **Sørksopp** *I* Barents S
61H4 **Sor Mertvyy Kultuk** *Plain* Kazakhstan
35B2 **Sorocaba** Brazil
61H3 **Sorochinsk** Russian Fed
99D2 **Soroti** Uganda
38J4 **Sereya** *I* Nor
53B2 **Sorrento** Italy
38K5 **Sorsatunturi** *Mt* Fin

Sorsele

38H5 **Sorsele** Sweden
79B3 **Sorsogon** Phil
38L6 **Sortavala** Russian Fed
74B3 **Sŏsan** S Korea
59B2 **Sosnowiec** Pol
65H4 **Sos'va** Russian Fed
98B2 **Souanké** Congo
97B4 **Soubré** Côte d'Ivoire
27F2 **Soufrière** St Lucia
27N2 **Soufrière** *Mt* St Vincent and the Grenadines
48C3 **Souillac** France
96C1 **Souk Ahras** Alg
74B3 **Soul** S Korea
51C2 **Soummam** *R* Alg
Sour = Tyr
101G1 **Sources,Mt aux** Lesotho
31D3 **Sousa** Brazil
96D1 **Sousse** Tunisia
100B4 **South Africa** Republic, Africa
16C1 **South Amboy** USA
42C4 **Southampton** Can
43D4 **Southampton** Eng
16C2 **Southampton** USA
6B3 **Southampton I** Can
28F6 **South Atlantic O**
7D4 **South Aulatsivik I** Can
106C3 **South Australia** State, Aust
104E5 **South Australian Basin** Indian O
42B2 **South Ayrshire** Division, Scot
19C3 **Southaven** USA
17B2 **South Bay** USA
 South Baymouth Can
14A2 **South Bend** Indiana, USA
20B1 **South Bend** Washington, USA
16D1 **Southbridge** USA
 South Cape = Ka Lae
11B3 **South Carolina** State, USA
70C2 **South China S** S E Asia
8C2 **South Dakota** State, USA
16C1 **South Deerfield** USA
43D4 **South Downs** Eng
109C4 **South East C** Aust
111A2 **Southen Alps** *Mts* NZ
5H4 **Southend** Can
43E4 **Southend-on-Sea** Eng
111A2 **Southern Alps** *Mts* NZ
106A4 **Southern Cross** Aust
5J4 **Southern Indian L** Can
27H2 **Southfield** Jamaica
105G5 **South Fiji Basin** Pacific O
12D2 **South Fork** *R* Alaska, USA
22B1 **South Fork** *R* California, USA
28F8 **South Georgia I** S Atlantic O
43C4 **South Gloucestershire** County Eng
14A2 **South Haven** USA
5J3 **South Henik L** Can
104F3 **South Honshu Ridge** Pacific O
111A2 **South I** NZ
16C2 **Southington** USA
74B3 **South Korea** Republic, S E Asia
21A2 **South Lake Tahoe** USA
42C2 **South Lanarkshire** Division, Scot
112C8 **South Magnetic Pole** Ant

17B2 **South Miami** USA
16A3 **South Mt** USA
4F3 **South Nahanni** *R* Can
26G1 **South Negril Pt** Jamaica
103F8 **South Orkney Is** Atlantic O
8C2 **South Platte** *R* USA
80E **South Pole** Ant
42C3 **Southport** Eng
27R3 **South Pt** Barbados
16B2 **South River** USA
44C2 **South Ronaldsay** *I* Scot
3C7 **South Sandwich Trench** Atlantic O
22A2 **South San Francisco** USA
5H4 **South Saskatchewan** *R* Can
42D2 **South Shields** Eng
110B1 **South Taranaki Bight** *B* NZ
44A3 **South Uist** *I* Scot
 South West Africa = Namibia
107D5 **South West C** Aust
105J5 **South West Pacific Basin** Pacific O
103D5 **South West Peru Ridge** Pacific O
43D3 **South Yorkshire** County, Eng
58C1 **Sovetsk** Russian Fed
61G2 **Sovetsk** Russian Fed
101G1 **Soweto** S Africa
98B3 **Soyo Congo** Angola
60D3 **Sozh** *R* Belarus
46C1 **Spa** Belg
50A1 **Spain** Kingdom Spain
 Spalato = Split
43D3 **Spalding** Eng
14B1 **Spanish** *R* Can
26B3 **Spanish Town** Jamaica
21B2 **Sparks** USA
11B3 **Spartanburg** USA
55B3 **Sparti** Greece
69F2 **Spassk Dal'niy** Russian Fed
27P2 **Speightstown** Barbados
12E2 **Spenard** USA
14A3 **Spencer** Indiana, USA
8D2 **Spencer** Iowa, USA
108A3 **Spencer,C** Aust
108A2 **Spencer G** Aust
6C3 **Spencer I** Can
111B2 **Spenser Mts** NZ
45C1 **Sperrin Mts** N Ire
44C3 **Spey** *R* Scot
57B3 **Speyer** Germany
27K1 **Speyside** Tobago
12F1 **Spike Mt** USA
20C1 **Spirit Lake** USA
5G4 **Spirit River** Can
 Spitsbergen = Svalbard
64C2 **Spitsbergen** *I* Barents S
57C3 **Spittal** Austria
38F6 **Spjelkavik** Nor
52C2 **Split** Croatia
47C1 **Splügen** Switz
20C1 **Spokane** USA
55C3 **Sporádhes** *Is* Greece
20C2 **Spray** USA
56C2 **Spree** *R* Germany
100A3 **Springbok** S Africa
18B2 **Springdale** USA
10B3 **Springfield** Illinois, USA
10C2 **Springfield** Massachusetts, USA
18B2 **Springfield** Missouri, USA
14B3 **Springfield** Ohio, USA
20B2 **Springfield** Oregon, USA

15D2 **Springfield** Vermont, USA
100B4 **Springfontein** S Africa
101G1 **Springs** S Africa
41D3 **Spurn Head** *Pt* Eng
13C3 **Squamish** Can
60E3 **Sredne-Russkaya Vozvyshennost** *Upland* Russian Fed
63B1 **Sredne Sibirskoye Ploskogorve** *Tableland* Russian Fed
61J2 **Sredniy Ural** *Mts* Russian Fed
76D3 **Srepok** *R* Camb
68D1 **Sretensk** Russian Fed
76C3 **Sre Umbell** Camb
83C5 **Sri Lanka** Republic, S Asia
84C2 **Srinagar** India
87A1 **Srivardhan** India
58B2 **Środa Wlk.** Pol
30H6 **Sta Clara** *I* Chile
32J7 **Sta Cruz** *I* Ecuador
56B2 **Stade** Germany
44A3 **Staffa** *I* Scot
43C3 **Stafford** County, Eng
43C3 **Stafford** Eng
16C2 **Stafford Springs** USA
 Stalingrad = Volgograd
6A1 **Stallworthy,C** Can
59C2 **Stalowa Wola** Pol
32J7 **Sta Maria** *I* Ecuador
16C2 **Stamford** Connecticut, USA
16B1 **Stamford** New York, USA
100A3 **Stampriet** Namibia
101G1 **Standerton** S Africa
14B2 **Standish** USA
101H1 **Stanger** S Africa
22B2 **Stanislaus** *R* USA
54B2 **Stanke Dimitrov** Bulg
109C4 **Stanley** Aust
29E6 **Stanley** Falkland Is
87B2 **Stanley Res** India
 Stanleyville = Kisangani
25D3 **Stann Creek** Belize
63E2 **Stanovoy Khrebet** *Mts* Russian Fed
47C1 **Stans** Switz
109D1 **Stanthorpe** Aust
59C2 **Starachowice** Pol
54B2 **Stara Planiná** *Mts* Bulg
60D2 **Staraya Russa** Russian Fed
54C2 **Stara Zagora** Bulg
58B2 **Stargard Szczecinski** Pol
19C3 **Starkville** USA
57C3 **Starnberg** Germany
58B2 **Starogard Gdanski** Pol
59D3 **Starokonstantinov** Ukraine
43C4 **Start Pt** Eng
60E3 **Staryy Oskol** Russian Fed
15C2 **State College** USA
16B2 **Staten I** USA
17B1 **Statesboro** USA
15C3 **Staunton** USA
39F7 **Stavanger** Nor
46C1 **Stavelot** Belg
61F4 **Stavropol'** Russian Fed
61F4 **Stavropol'** Division, Russian Fed
108A2 **Stawell** Aust
58B2 **Stawno** Pol
20B2 **Stayton** USA
17B2 **Stebbins** USA
12F2 **Steele,Mt** USA
16A2 **Steelton** USA
20C2 **Steens Mt** USA

6E2 **Steenstrups Gletscher** *Gl* Greenland
4H2 **Stefansson I** Can
101H1 **Stegi** Swaziland
47D1 **Steinach** Austria
8D2 **Steinbach** Can
38G6 **Steinkjer** Nor
12C2 **Stein Mt** Can
23B2 **Stemaco** Mexico
46C2 **Stenay** France
56C2 **Stendal** Germany
110B2 **Stephens,C** NZ
108D5 **Stephens Creek** Aust
14A1 **Stephenson** USA
12H3 **Stephens Pass** USA
7E5 **Stephenville** Can
100B4 **Sterkstroom** S Africa
8C2 **Sterling** Colorado, USA
14B2 **Sterling Heights** USA
61J3 **Sterlitamak** Russian Fed
13E2 **Stettler** Can
14B2 **Steubenville** USA
4D3 **Stevens Village** USA
13B1 **Stewart** Can
5H1 **Stewart** *R* Can
12G2 **Stewart** *R* Can
12G2 **Stewart Crossing** Can
111A3 **Stewart I** NZ
107F1 **Stewart Is** Solomon Is
5H1 **Stewart River** Can
16A3 **Stewartstown** USA
101G1 **Steyn** S Africa
57C3 **Steyr** Austria
12G3 **Stika** USA
12H3 **Stikine** *R* Can
12H3 **Stikine Ranges** *Mts* Can
18A2 **Stillwater** Oklahoma, USA
21B2 **Stillwater Range** *Mts* USA
108A2 **Stirling** Aust
44C3 **Stirling** Scot
44B3 **Stirling** Division Scot
16C1 **Stockbridge** USA
59B3 **Stockerau** Austria
39H7 **Stockholm** Sweden
42C3 **Stockport** Eng
22B2 **Stockton** California, USA
42D2 **Stockton L** USA
42D2 **Stockton-on-Tees** County Eng
43C3 **Stoke-on-Trent** Eng
38A2 **Stokkseyri** Iceland
38G5 **Stokmarknes** Nor
39K8 **Stolbtsy** Belarus
58D2 **Stolin** Belarus
16B3 **Stone Harbor** USA
44C3 **Stonehaven** Scot
19A3 **Stonewall** USA
12D2 **Stony** *R* USA
38H5 **Storavan** *L* Sweden
38G6 **Støren** Nor
44A2 **Stornoway** Scot
59D3 **Storozhinets** Ukraine
16C2 **Storrs** USA
38G6 **Storsjön** *L* Sweden
38H5 **Storuman** Sweden
16D1 **Stoughton** USA
43E3 **Stowmarket** Eng
45C1 **Strabane** N Ire
109C4 **Strahan** Aust
56C2 **Stralsund** Germany
38F6 **Stranda** Nor
39H7 **Strängnäs** Sweden
42B2 **Stranraer** Scot
49D2 **Strasbourg** France
15C3 **Strasburg** USA
14B2 **Stratford** Can
16C2 **Stratford** Connecticut, USA
110B1 **Stratford** NZ
43D3 **Stratford-on-Avon** Eng

108A3 Strathalbyn Aust
13E2 Strathmore Can
18C1 Streator USA
47C2 Stresa Italy
53C3 Stretto de Messina
  Str Italy/Sicily
38D3 Streymoy Føroyar
53C3 Stroboli I Italy
6E3 Strømfjord
  Greenland
44C2 Stromness Scot
18A1 Stromsburg USA
38H6 Stromsund Sweden
38G6 Ströms Vattudal L
  Sweden
44C2 Stronsay I Scot
43C4 Stroud Eng
16E2 Stroudsburg USA
54B2 Struma R Bulg
43B3 Strumble Head Pt
  Wales
55B2 Strumica Macedonia
59C3 Stryy Ukraine
59C3 Stryy R Ukraine
108B1 Strzelecki Creek R
  Aust
17B2 Stuart Florida, USA
13C2 Stuart R Can
12B2 Stuart I USA
13C2 Stuart L Can
47D1 Stubaier Alpen Mts
  Austria
76D3 Stung Sen Camb
76D3 Stung Treng Camb
52A2 Stura R Italy
112C7 Sturge I Ant
14A2 Sturgeon Bay USA
14C1 Sturgeon Falls Can
18C2 Sturgis Kentucky,
  USA
14A2 Sturgis Michigan,
  USA
106B2 Sturt Creek R Aust
108B1 Sturt Desert Aust
100B4 Stutterheim S Africa
19B3 Stuttgart USA
57B3 Stuttgart Germany
38A1 Stykkishólmur
  Iceland
59D2 Styr' R Ukraine
35C1 Suaçui Grande R
  Brazil
81B4 Suakin Sudan
73E5 Su-ao Taiwan
34C2 Suardi Arg
78B2 Subi I Indon
54A1 Subotica Serbia,
  Yugos
60C4 Suceava Rom
45B2 Suck R Irish Rep
30C2 Sucre Bol
35A1 Sucuriú R Brazil
98C1 Sudan Republic,
  Africa
14B1 Sudbury Can
43E3 Sudbury Eng
99C2 Sudd Swamp Sudan
33F2 Suddie Guyana
98C2 Sue R Sudan
4H2 Suerdrup Is Can
92A2 Suez Egypt
92B3 Suez Canal Egypt
92B4 Suez,G of Egypt
16B2 Suffern USA
43E3 Suffolk County, Eng
109D2 Sugarloaf Pt Aust
91C5 Suhār Oman
68C1 Sühbaatar Mongolia
84B3 Sui Pak
72C2 Suide China
69E2 Suihua China
73B3 Suining China
46C2 Suippes France
45B3 Suir R Irish Rep
73C3 Sui Xian China
72E1 Suizhong China
85C3 Sujāngarth India
78B4 Sukabumi Indon
78C3 Sukadana Borneo,
  Indon
78B4 Sukadana Sumatra,
  Indon
74E3 Sukagawa Japan
78C3 Sukaraya Indon

60E3 Sukhinichi
  Russian Fed
61F2 Sukhona R
  Russian Fed
61F5 Sukhumi Georgia
6E3 Sukkertoppen
  Greenland
6E3 Sukkertoppen L
  Greenland
38L6 Sukkozero
  Russian Fed
85B3 Sukkur Pak
67F1 Sukma India
95A2 Süknah Libya
100A3 Sukses Namibia
75A2 Sukumo Japan
13C1 Sukunka R Can
60E3 Sula R Russian Fed
84B3 Sulaiman Range Mts
  Pak
70C4 Sulawesi I Indon
54C1 Sulina Rom
38H5 Sulitjelma Nor
32A4 Sullana Peru
18B2 Sullivan USA
13B2 Sullivan Bay Can
18C2 Sullivan L Can
52B2 Sulmona Italy
19B3 Sulphur Louisiana,
  USA
19A3 Sulphur Oklahoma,
  USA
19A3 Sulphur Springs USA
86A1 Sultānpur India
79B4 Sulu Arch Phil
9D4 Sulu S Philip
30D4 Sumampa Arg
70C4 Sumatera I Indon
70C4 Sumba I Indon
78D4 Sumbawa I Indon
78D4 Sumbawa Besar
  Indon
99D3 Sumbawanga Tanz
100A2 Sumbe Angola
44E2 Sumburgh Head Pt
  Scot
78C4 Sumenep Indon
69G3 Sumisu I Japan
32D1 Summerland Can
5F4 Summit Lake Can
21B2 Summit Mt USA
111B2 Sumner,L NZ
75A2 Sumoto Japan
17B1 Sumter USA
60D3 Sumy Ukraine
16A2 Sunbury USA
34C2 Sunchales Arg
74B3 Sunch'ŏn N Korea
74B4 Sunch'ŏn S Korea
86A2 Sundargarh India
86B2 Sunderbans Swamp
  India
42D2 Sunderland Eng
13E2 Sundre Can
15C1 Sundridge Can
38H6 Sundsvall Sweden
38D3 Sunday Føroyar
78D3 Sungaianyar Indon
78A3 Sungaisalak Indon
20C1 Sunnyside USA
21A2 Sunnyvale USA
97B4 Sunyani Ghana
75A2 Suō-nada B Japan
38K6 Suonejoki Fin
61E3 Suoyarvi Russian Fed
91C5 Sür Oman
61E3 Sura R Russian Fed
78C4 Surabaya Indon
78C4 Surakarta Indon
109C1 Surat Aust
85C4 Sūrat India

84C3 Süratgarh India
77B4 Surat Thani Thai
85C4 Surendranagar India
16B3 Surf City USA
64J3 Surgut Russian Fed
87B1 Suriapet India
49D2 Sürich Switz
79C4 Surigao Phil
76C3 Surin Thai
33F3 Surinam Republic,
  S America
43D4 Surrey County, Eng
47C1 Sursee Switz
95A1 Surt Libya
38A2 Surtsey I Iceland
78A3 Surulangan Indon
47B2 Susa Italy
75A2 Susa Japan
75A2 Susaki Japan
21A1 Susanville USA
47D1 Süsch Switz
12E2 Susitna R USA
16A3 Susquehanna R USA
16B2 Sussex USA
43D4 Sussex West Eng
13B1 Sustut Peak Mt Can
100B4 Sutherland S Africa
84C2 Sutlej R Pak
21A2 Sutter Creek USA
14B3 Sutton USA
73C3 Sutwik I USA
74D3 Suwa Japan
58C2 Suwałki Pol
17B2 Suwannee R USA
94B2 Suweilih Jordan
74B3 Suwŏn S Korea
72D3 Su Xian China
75B1 Suzaka Japan
73E3 Suzhou China
75B2 Suzuka Japan
75B1 Suzu-misaki C
  Japan
64C2 Svalbard Is
  Barents S
59C3 Svalyava Ukraine
38G5 Svartisen Mt Nor
76D3 Svay Rieng Camb
38G6 Sveg Sweden
39G7 Svendborg Den
  Sverdlovsk =
  Yekaterinburg
61F4 Sverdlosk Division,
  Russian Fed
6A1 Sverdrup Chan Can
69F2 Svetlaya
  Russian Fed
58C2 Svetlogorsk
  Russian Fed
39K6 Svetogorsk
54B2 Svetozarevo Serbia,
  Yugos
54C2 Svilengrad Bulg
58D2 Svir' Belarus
59B3 Svitavy
  Czech Republic
69E1 Svobodnyy
  Russian Fed
38G5 Svolvaer Nor
107E3 Swain Reefs Aust
17B1 Swainsboro USA
100A3 Swakopmund
  Namibia
42D2 Swale R Eng
70C3 Swallow Reef I
  S E Asia
87B2 Swāmihalli India
25D3 Swan I Honduras
43C4 Swanage Eng
108B3 Swan Hill Aust
13D2 Swan Hills Can
13D2 Swan Hills Mts Can
26A3 Swan I Caribbean S
5H4 Swan River Can
43C4 Swansea Wales
43C4 Swansea County
  Wales
43C4 Swansea B Wales
101G1 Swartruggens
  S Africa
  Swatow = Shantou
101H1 Swaziland Kingdom,
  S Africa

39G7 Sweden Kingdom,
  N Europe
20B2 Sweet Home USA
9C3 Sweetwater USA
64J3 Swellendam S Africa
59B2 Świdnica Pol
58B2 Świdwin Pol
58B2 Świebodzin Pol
58B2 Świecie Pol
5H4 Swift Current Can
43D4 Swindon Eng
45B2 Swinford Irish Rep
56C2 Świnoujscie Pol
49D2 Switzerland Federal
  Republic, Europe
45C2 Swords Irish Rep
109D2 Sydney Aust
7D5 Sydney Can
64G3 Syktyvkar
  Russian Fed
17A1 Sylacauga USA
38G6 Sylarna Mt Sweden
86E2 Sylhet Bang
56B1 Sylt I Germany
14B2 Sylvania USA
112C11 Syowa Base Ant
  Syracuse = Siracusa
15C2 Syracuse USA
65H5 Syr Darya R
  Kazakhstan
93C2 Syria Republic, S W
  Asia
61J2 Sysert' Russian Fed
61G3 Syzran' Russian Fed
56C2 Szczecin Pol
58C2 Szczecinek Pol
58C2 Szczytno Pol
59C3 Szeged Hung
59B3 Székesfehérvár Hung
59B3 Szekszard Hung
59B3 Szolnok Hung
59B3 Szombathely Hung
58B2 Szprotaczk Pol

T

90C3 Tabas Iran
23A1 Tabasco Mexico
32D4 Tabatinga Brazil
96B2 Tabelbala Alg
76C2 Tabeng Camb
13E2 Taber Can
79B3 Tablas I Phil
100A4 Table Mt S Africa
12E1 Table Mt USA
18B2 Table Rock Res USA
78B3 Taboali Indon
57C3 Tábor
  Czech Republic
99D3 Tabora Tanz
97B4 Tabou Côte d'Ivoire
90A2 Tabriz Iran
92C4 Tabük S Arabia
23A2 Tacámbaro Mexico
82C1 Tacheng China
79C3 Tacloban Phil
30B2 Tacna Peru
8A2 Tacoma USA
99E1 Tadjoura Djibouti
87B2 Tādpatri India
74B3 Taebaek Sanmaek
  Mts S Korea
74B3 T'aebaek S Korea
74B4 Taehŭksan I S Korea
74B3 Taejŏn S Korea
51B1 Tafalla Spain
96C2 Tafassasset
  Watercourse Alg
43C4 Taff R Wales
94B3 Tafila Jordan
60E4 Taganrog Ukraine
97A3 Tagant Region, Maur
79B4 Tagbilaran Phil
96B2 Taguenout
  Haggueréte Well
  Maur
107E2 Tagula I Solomon Is
79C4 Tagum Phil
  Tagus = Tejo
96C2 Tahat Mt Alg
105J4 Tahiti I Pacific O
18A2 Tahlequah USA
21A2 Tahoe City USA
21A2 Tahoe,L USA
97C3 Tahoua Niger

71D3 Tahuna Indon
72D2 Tai'an China
72B3 Taibai Shan Mt China
72D1 Taibus Qi China
73E5 T'ai-chung Taiwan
111B3 Taieri R NZ
72C2 Taihang Shan China
110C1 Taihape NZ
72E3 Tai Hu, L China
108A3 Tailem Bend Aust
44B3 Tain Scot
73E5 T'ai-nan Taiwan
35C1 Taiobeiras Brazil
73E5 T'ai pei Taiwan
77C5 Taiping Malay
75A1 Taisha Japan
29B5 Taitao,Pen de Chile
73E5 T'ai-tung Taiwan
38K5 Taivelkoski Fin
69E4 Taiwan Republic, China
 Taiwan Haixia = Formosa Str
72C2 Taiyuan China
72D3 Taizhou China
81C4 Ta'izz Yemen
62A2 Tajikistan Republic, Asia
50B1 Tajo R Spain
76B2 Tak Thai
74D3 Takada Japan
75A2 Takahashi Japan
110B2 Takaka NZ
74C4 Takamatsu Japan
74C4 Takaoka Japan
110B1 Takapuna NZ
74D3 Takasaki Japan
75B1 Takayama Japan
74D3 Takefu Japan
70A3 Takengon Indon
76E3 Takeo Camb
75A2 Take-shima = Tok-do
90A2 Takestan Iran
75A2 Taketa Japan
4G3 Takjvik L Can
99D1 Takkaze R Eritrea/Eth
13B1 Takla L Can
13B1 Takla Landing Can
12B2 Takslesluk L USA
12H2 Taku Arn R Can
23A1 Tala Mexico
59B3 Talabanya Hung
64C2 Talagang Pak
34A2 Talagante Chile
87B3 Talaimannar Sri Lanka
97C3 Talak Desert Region, Niger
78A3 Talangbetutu Indon
32A4 Talara Peru
50B2 Talavera de la Reina Spain
34A3 Talca Chile
34A3 Talcahuano Chile
86B2 Tålcher India
82B1 Taldy Kurgan Kazakhstan
71D4 Taliabu Indon
84B1 Taligan Afghan
99D2 Tali Post Sudan
72D4 Taliwang Indon
12D2 Talkeetna USA
12E2 Talkeetna Mts USA
17A1 Talladega USA
93D2 Tall 'Afar Iraq
17B1 Tallahassee USA
94C1 Tall Bisah Syria
60B2 Tallinn Estonia
92C3 Tall Kalakh Syria
19B3 Tallulah USA
60D4 Tal'noye Ukraine
19E2 Talpaki Russian Fed
30B4 Taltal Chile
109C1 Talwood Aust
78D1 Tamabo Range Mts Malay
97B4 Tamale Ghana
96C2 Tamanrasset Alg
96C2 Tamanrasset Watercourse Alg

16B2 Tamaqua USA
 Tamatave = Toamasina
23A2 Tamazula Jalisco, Mexico
23B2 Tamazulapán Mexico
23B1 Tamazunchale Mexico
97A3 Tambacounda Sen
61F3 Tambov Division, Russian Fed
61F3 Tambov Russian Fed
74D1 Tambre R Spain
98C2 Tambura Sudan
97A3 Tamchaket Maur
50A1 Tamega R Port
23B1 Tamiahua Mexico
87B2 Tamil Nādu State, India
76D2 Tam Ky Viet
17B2 Tampa USA
17B2 Tampa B USA
39J6 Tampere Fin
23B1 Tampico Mexico
68D2 Tamsagbulag Mongolia
86C2 Tamu Myan
23B1 Tamuis Mexico
109D2 Tamworth Aust
43D3 Tamworth Eng
38K4 Tana Nor
99D1 Tana L Eth
99E3 Tana R Kenya
38K5 Tana R Nor/Fin
75B2 Tanabe Japan
38K4 Tanafjord Inlet Nor
78D3 Tanahgrogot Indon
71E4 Tanahmerah Indon
12D1 Tanana USA
12E2 Tanana R USA
 Tananarive = Antananarivo
47C2 Tanaro R Italy
74B2 Tanch'ŏn N Korea
34D3 Tandil Arg
78B2 Tandjong Datu Pt Indon
71E4 Tandjong d'Urville C Indon
78D3 Tandjong Layar C Indon
78B3 Tandjong Lumut C Indon
78D2 Tandjong Mangkalihet C Indon
78C3 Tandjong Sambar C Indon
78C2 Tandjong Sirik C Malay
71E4 Tandjong Vals C Indon
85B3 Tando Adam Pak
85B3 Tando Muhammad Khan Pak
108B2 Tandou L Aust
87B1 Tāndūr India
110C1 Taneatua NZ
76B2 Tanen Range Mts Myan/Than
96B2 Tanezrouft Desert Region Alg
91C4 Tang Iran
99D3 Tanga Tanz
60E4 Tanganrog Russian Fed
99C3 Tanganyika,L Tanz/ Zaire
96B1 Tanger Mor
82C2 Tanggula Shan Mts China
 Tangier = Tanger
78A2 Tangjungpinang Indon
82C2 Tangra Yumco L China
72D2 Tangshan China
79B4 Tangub Phil
63C2 Tanguy Russian Fed
 Taninthayri = Tenasserim
79B4 Tanjay Phil
101D3 Tanjona Ankaboa C Madag

101D2 Tanjona Babaomby C Madag
101D2 Tanjona Vilanandro C Madag
101D3 Tanjona Vohimena C Madag
78C4 Tanjong Bugel C Indon
78B4 Tanjong Cangkuang C Indon
78B4 Tanjong Puting C Indon
78C3 Tanjong Selatan C Indon
78D3 Tanjung Indon
70A3 Tanjungbalai Indon
78A3 Tanjung Jabung Pt Indon
78D3 Tanjungpandan Indon
78B4 Tanjung Priok Indon
78D2 Tanjungredeb Indon
78D3 Tanjungselor Indon
84C2 Tank Pak
68B1 Tannu Ola Mts Mongolia
97B4 Tano R Ghana
97C3 Tanout Niger
23B1 Tanquián Mexico
73E4 Tan-shui Taiwan
99D3 Tanzania Republic, Africa
72A3 Tao He R China
72B2 Taole China
96B1 Taourirt Mor
72B2 Tapa Estonia
25C3 Tapachula Mexico
33F4 Tapajós R Brazil
34C3 Tapalquén Arg
111A3 Tapanui NZ
32D5 Tapauá R Brazil
85D4 Tapi R India
86B1 Taplejung Nepal
111B2 Tapuaeenuku Mt NZ
35B2 Tapuaritinga Brazil
79B4 Tapul Group Is Phil
33E4 Tapurucuara Brazil
69U4 Tara Russian Fed
65J4 Tara R Russian Fed
54A2 Tara R Bosnia-Herzegovina/ Montenegro, Yugos
97D4 Taraba R Nig
30D2 Tarabuco Bol
 Tarābulus = Tripoli
50B1 Taracón Spain
110C1 Taradale NZ
78D2 Tarakan Indon
110B1 Taranaki, Mt NZ
44A5 Taransay I Scot
53C2 Táranto Italy
32B5 Tarapoto Peru
49C2 Tarare France
110C2 Tararua Range Mts NZ
96C2 Tarat Alg
110C1 Tarawera NZ
51B1 Tarazona Spain
44C3 Tarbat Ness Pen Scot
84C2 Tarbela Res Pak
42B2 Tarbert Strathclyde, Scot
44A3 Tarbert Western Isles, Scot
48C3 Tarbes France
106C4 Tarcoola Aust
109C2 Tarcoon Aust
109D2 Taree Aust
96A2 Tarfaya Mor
95A1 Tarhūnah Libya
91B5 Tarif UAE
30D3 Tarija Bol
81C4 Tarikere India
81C4 Tarim Yemen
99D3 Tarime Tanz
82C1 Tarim He R China
82C2 Tarim Pendi Basin China

84B2 Tarin Kut Afghan
18A1 Tarkio USA
79B2 Tarlac Phil
32B6 Tarma Peru
49C3 Tarn R France
59C2 Tarnobrzeg Pol
59C3 Tarnów Pol
107D3 Taroom Aust
51C1 Tarragona Spain
109C4 Tarraleah Aust
51C1 Tarrasa Spain
16C2 Tarrytown USA
92B2 Tarsus Turk
44D2 Tartan Oilfield N Sea
47D2 Tartaro R Italy
60C2 Tartu Estonia
92C3 Tartūs Syria
35C1 Tarumirim Brazil
70A3 Tarutung Indon
52B1 Tarvisio Italy
80D1 Tashauz Turkmenistan
78A4 Tashigang Bhutan
82A1 Tashkent Uzbekistan
65K4 Tashtagol Russian Fed
63A2 Tashtyp Russian Fed
78B4 Tasikmalaya Indon
94B2 Tasil Syria
6E2 Tasiussaq Greenland
95A3 Tasker Well Niger
110B2 Tasman B NZ
107D5 Tasmania I Aust
111B2 Tasman Mts NZ
109C4 Tasman Pen Aust
107E4 Tasman S NZ Aust
92C1 Taşova Turk
96C2 Tassili du Hoggar Desert Region, Alg
96C2 Tassili N'jjer Desert Region, Alg
96B2 Tata Mor
96D1 Tataouine Tunisia
65J4 Tatarsk Russian Fed
69G2 Tatarskiy Proliv Str Russian Fed
61G2 Tatarstan Russian Fed
75B1 Tateyama Japan
5G3 Tathlina L Can
12E2 Tatitlek USA
13C2 Tatla Lake Can
59B3 Tatry Mts Pol/ Slovakia
75A2 Tatsuno Japan
85B4 Tatta Pak
35B2 Tatui Brazil
93D2 Tatvan Turk
31C3 Tauá Brazil
35B2 Taubaté Brazil
110C1 Taumarunui NZ
101F1 Taung S Africa
76B2 Taungdwingyi Myan
76B2 Taung-gyi Myan
76A2 Taungup Myan
84C2 Taunsa Pak
43C4 Taunton Eng
16D2 Taunton USA
46E1 Taunus Region, Germany
110C1 Taupo NZ
110C1 Taupo,L NZ
52B2 Taurage Lithuania
110C1 Tauranga NZ
110C1 Tauranga Harbour B NZ
110B1 Tauroa Pt NZ
7A3 Tavani Can
7A3 Tavani Can
65H4 Tavda R Russian Fed
43B4 Tavistock Eng
76B3 Tavoy Myan
76B3 Tavoy Pt Myan
92A2 Tavşanli Turk
111B2 Tawa NZ
19A3 Tawakoni,L USA
14B2 Tawas City USA
70C3 Tawau Malay
98C1 Taweisha Sudan
79B4 Tawitawi I Phil
79B4 Tawitawi Group Is Phil
23B2 Taxco Mexico

23B2	Taxcoco Mexico
44C3	Tay R Scot
78C3	Tayan Indon
12B1	Taylor Alaska, USA
13C1	Taylor Can
14B2	Taylor Michigan, USA
19A3	Taylor Texas, USA
18C2	Taylorville USA
80B3	Taymā' S Arabia
76D3	Taymura R Russian Fed
76D3	Tay Ninh Viet
63B2	Tayshet Russian Fed
68B2	Tayshir Mongolia
79A3	Taytay Phil
90D3	Tayyebāt Iran
96B1	Taza Mor
95B2	Tāzirbū Libya
12E2	Tazlina L Can
64J3	Tazovskiy Russian Fed
65F5	Tbilisi Georgia
98B3	Tchibanga Gabon
95A2	Tchigaï,Plat du Niger
97C3	Tchin Tabaradene Niger
98B2	Tcholliré Cam
58B2	Tczew Pol
111A3	Te Anau NZ
111A3	Te Anau,L NZ
110C1	Te Aroha NZ
110C1	Te Awamutu NZ
96C1	Tébessa Alg
23A2	Teboman Mexico
23A2	Tecailtlán Mexico
23A2	Tecate Mexico
61K2	Techa R Russian Fed
23A1	Tecolotlán Mexico
23B2	Tecpan Mexico
54C1	Tecuci Rom
18A1	Tecumseh USA
80E2	Tedzhen Turkmenistan
65H6	Tedzhen R Turkmenistan
42D2	Tees R Eng
33E4	Tefé Brazil
23B2	Tegal Indon
78B4	Tegineneng Indon
25D3	Tegucigalpa Honduras
21B3	Tehachapi Mts USA
21B3	Tehachapi P USA
4J3	Tehek L Can
90B2	Tehrān Iran
23B2	Tehuacán Mexico
23B2	Tehuantepec Mexico
23B2	Tehuitzingo Mexico
43B3	Teifi R Wales
50A2	Tejo R Port
23A2	Tejupilco Mexico
111B2	Tekapo,L NZ
82B1	Tekeli Kazakhstan
32A1	Tekirdağ Turk
55C2	Tekir Dağlari Mts Turk
86C2	Teknaf Bang
110C1	Te Kuiti NZ
25D3	Tela Honduras
94B2	Tel Aviv Yafo Israel
34B3	Telen Indon
21E2	Telescope Peak Mt USA
33F5	Teles Pires R Brazil
47D1	Telfs Austria
63A2	Teli Russian Fed
94B3	Tell el Meise Mt Jordan
12A1	Teller USA
87E2	Tellicherry India
77C5	Telok Anson Malay
78D2	Télok Darvel Malay
71E4	Télok Flamingo R Indon
78C3	Télok Kumai R Indon
78B4	Télok Pelabuanratu R Indon
78D4	Télok Saleh R Indon
78C3	Télok Sampit R Indon
78B3	Télok Sukadona R Indon
23B2	Teloloapán Mexico
64G3	Tel'pos-iz Mt Russian Fed
58C1	Telšiai Lithuania
78C3	Telukbatang Indon
71E4	Teluk Berau R Indon
78B4	Telukbetung Indon
70D4	Teluk Bone R Indon
71E4	Teluk Cendrawasih R Indon
78D3	Teluk Mandar R Indon
71D4	Teluk Tolo R Indon
70D3	Teluk Tomini R Indon
71D3	Téluk Weda R Indon
14B1	Temagami,L Can
23B2	Temascal Mexico
78C3	Tembesi R Indon
78A3	Tembilahan Indon
27E5	Temblador Ven
77C5	Temerloh Malay
65G5	Temir Kazakhstan
65J4	Temirtau Kazakhstan
15C1	Temiscaming Can
109C2	Temora Aust
9B3	Tempe USA
19A3	Temple USA
43C2	Templemore Irish Rep
23B2	Tempoal Mexico
34A3	Temuco Chile
111B2	Temuka NZ
32B4	Tena Ecuador
87C1	Tenāli India
23B2	Tenancingo Mexico
65J4	Ténasserim Myan
43B4	Tenby Wales
99E1	Tendaho Eth
83D5	Ten Degree Chan Indian O
98B1	Ténéré Desert Region Niger
96A2	Tenerife I Canary Is
76B1	Teng R Myan
78D3	Tenggarong Indon
72A2	Tengger Shamo Desert China
112C2	Teniente Jubany Base Ant
112C2	Teniente Rodolfo Marsh Martin Base Ant
87B3	Tenkāsi India
100B2	Tenke Zaïre
97B3	Tenkodogo Burkina
106C2	Tennant Creek Aust
11B3	Tennessee State, USA
18C2	Tennessee R USA
34A2	Teno Chile
78D1	Tenom Malay
25C3	Tenosique Mexico
109D1	Tenterfield Aust
17B2	Ten Thousand Is USA
23A1	Teocaltiche Mexico
35C1	Teófilo Otóni Brazil
23B2	Teotihuacan Hist Site, Mexico
23B2	Teotitlán Mexico
24B2	Tepatepan Mexico
23A1	Tepeji Mexico
23A1	Tepic Mexico
57C2	Teplice Czech Republic
110C1	Te Puke NZ
23A1	Tequila Mexico
23B2	Tequistepec Mexico
51C1	Ter R Spain
97C3	Téra Niger
75B1	Teradomari Japan
52B2	Teramo Italy
96A1	Terceira I Açores
59D3	Terebovlya Ukraine
31C3	Teresina Brazil
35C2	Teresópolis Brazil
92C1	Terme Turk
80E2	Termez Uzbekistan
52B2	Termoli Italy
71D3	Ternate Indon
52B2	Terni Italy
59D3	Ternopol Ukraine
13B2	Terrace Can
53B2	Terracina Italy
100B3	Terrafirma S Africa
112C8	Terre Adélie Region, Ant
19B4	Terre Bonne B USA
14A3	Terre Haute USA
19A3	Terrell USA
56B2	Terschelling I Neth
12F1	Teruel Spain
4C2	Teshekpuk L USA
4C2	Teshekpuk L USA
74E2	Teshio R Japan
68B2	Tesiyn Gol Mts Mongolia
12H2	Teslin Can
12H2	Teslin R Can
12H2	Teslin L Can
63B3	Tesīyn Gol R Mongolia
96C2	Tessalit Mali
97C3	Tessaoua Niger
14C2	Tete Mozam
23A2	Tetela Mexico
96B1	Tetouan Mor
61G2	Tetyushi Russian Fed
30D3	Teuco R Arg
23A1	Teul de Gonzalez Ortega Mexico
77D4	Teun I Indon
52B2	Tevere R Italy
42C2	Teviot R Scot
62A4	Tevriz Russian Fed
111A3	Te Waewae B NZ
78C3	Tewah Indon
109D1	Tewantin Aust
109D1	Texas Aust
11A3	Texas State, USA
19A4	Texas City USA
19A3	Texoma,L USA
101G1	Teyateyaneng Lesotho
23B2	Teziutlán Mexico
86C1	Tezpur India
76C1	Tha Laos
101G1	Thabana Ntlenyana Mt Lesotho
101G1	Thaba Putsoa Mt Lesotho
101G1	Thaba 'Nchu S Africa
76B3	Thagyettaw Myan
76D1	Thai Binh Viet
76C2	Thailand Kingdom, S E Asia
76C3	Thailand,G of Thai
76D1	Thai Nguyen Viet
76C2	Thakhek Laos
84C2	Thal Pak
76C2	Thale Luang L Thai
109C1	Thallon Aust
110C1	Thames NZ
43E4	Thames R Eng
76D2	Thanh Hoah Viet
87B2	Thanjavur India
	Thanlwin = Salween
85C3	Thar Desert India
108B1	Thargomindah Aust
55B3	Thásos I Greece
76B2	Thaton Myan
76B2	Thayetmyo Myan
5F5	The Dalles USA
91B4	The Gulf S W Asia
4H3	Thelon R Can
107E3	Theodore Aust
9B3	Theodore Roosevelt L USA
55B3	Thermaïkós Kólpos G Greece
8C2	Thermopolis USA
4F2	Thesiger B Can
14B1	Thessalon Can
55B2	Thessaloníki Greece
43E3	Thetford Eng
15D1	Thetford Mines Can
101G1	Theunissen S Africa
19B4	Thibodaux USA
5J4	Thicket Portage Can
8D2	Thief River Falls USA
87D2	Thielsen,Mt USA
49C2	Thiers France
97A3	Thiès Sen
99D3	Thika Kenya
86B1	Thimphu Bhutan
49D2	Thionville France
55C3	Thíra I Greece
42D2	Thirsk Eng
	Thiruvananthapuram = Trivandrum
39F7	Thisted Den
55B3	Thívai Greece
48C2	Thiviers France
15C2	Thomaston Georgia, USA
	Thomastown Irish Rep
17B1	Thomasville Georgia, USA
6A2	Thom Bay Can
5J4	Thompson Can
18B1	Thompson R USA
4G3	Thompson Landing Can
13C2	Thompson R Can
18C2	Thompsonville USA
17B1	Thomson USA
107D3	Thomson R Aust
76C3	Thon Buri Thai
76B2	Thongwa Myan
47B1	Thonon-les-Bains France
22C2	Thornhill Scot
48B2	Thouars France
15C2	Thousand Is Can/ USA
13E2	Three Hills Can
7G4	Three Kings Is NZ
76B2	Three Pagodas P Thai
14A2	Three Rivers Michigan, USA
20B2	Three Sisters Mt USA
	Thrissur = Trichūr
6D2	Thule Greenland
47B1	Thun Switz
10B2	Thunder Bay Can
47B1	Thuner See L Switz
70B4	Thung Song Thai
47C1	Thur R Switz
57C2	Thüringen State, Germany
57C2	Thüringen Wald Upland Germany
45C2	Thurles Irish Rep
71F5	Thursday I Aust
44C2	Thurso Scot
112C4	Thurston I Ant
47C1	Thusis Switz
108B1	Thylungra Aust
73B5	Tiandong China
73B5	Tian'e China
73B5	Tianjin China
73B5	Tianlin China
73B5	Tian Shan Mts C Asia
72B3	Tianshui China
72A2	Tianzhu China
96C1	Tiaret Alg
35A2	Tibagi R Brazil
94B2	Tiberias Israel
94B2	Tiberias,L Israel
	Tiber,R = Tevere,R
95A2	Tibesti Mountain Region Chad
82C2	Tibet Autonomous Region, China
108B1	Tibooburra Aust
86A1	Tibrikot Nepal
24A2	Tiburón I Mexico
96A2	Tichit Mor
96A2	Tichla Mor
52A2	Ticino R Italy/Switz
15C2	Ticonderoga USA
25D2	Ticul Mexico
97A3	Tidjikja Maur
47C1	Tiefencastel Switz
46B1	Tielt Belg
46B1	Tienen Belg
65J5	Tien Shan Mts China/Kyrgyzstan
72D2	Tientsin China
39H6	Tierp Sweden
23B2	Tierra Blanca Mexico
23B2	Tierra Colorada Mexico

Tierra del Fuego

29C6 Tierra del Fuego Territory, Arg
28C8 Tierra del Fuego / Arg/Chile
35B2 Tietê Brazil
35A2 Tietê R Brazil
14B2 Tiffin USA
17B1 Tifton USA
32B4 Tigre R Peru
33E2 Tigre R Ven
93E3 Tigris R Iraq
23B1 Tihuatlán Mexico
21B3 Tijuana Mexico
85D4 Tikamgarh India
60D2 Tikhin Russian Fed
61F4 Tikhoretsk Russian Fed
93D3 Tikrit Iraq
1B8 Tiksi Russian Fed
46C1 Tilburg Neth
43E4 Tilbury Eng
30C3 Tilcara Arg
108B1 Tilê Aust
76A1 Tilin Myan
97C3 Tillabéri Niger
20B1 Tillamook USA
97C3 Tillia Niger
55C3 Tílos / Greece
108B2 Tilpa Aust
64G3 Tiluá Colombia
64G3 Timanskiy Kryazh Mts Russian Fed
111B2 Timaru NZ
60E4 Timashevsk Russian Fed
55B3 Timbákion Greece
19B4 Timbalier B USA
97B3 Timbédra Maur
Timbuktu = Tombouctou
97B3 Timétrine Monts Mts Mali
97C3 Timia Niger
96C2 Timis R Rom
54B1 Timişoara Rom
10B2 Timmins Can
106B1 Timor / Indon
27D5 Timaca Pr Phil
27D5 Tinaco Ven
87B2 Tindivanam India
96B2 Tindouf Alg
96C2 Tin Fouye Alg
6F3 Tingmiarmiut Greenland
32B5 Tingo Maria Peru
97B4 Tingréla Côte d'Ivoire
86B1 Tingri China
71F2 Tinian Pacific O
30C4 Tinogasta Arg
55C3 Tínos / Greece
43B4 Tintagel Head Pt Eng /
96C2 Tin Tarabine Watercourse Alg
108B3 Tintinara Aust
96C2 Tin Zaouaten Alg
22C2 Tioga P USA
77C5 Tioman / Malay
47D1 Tione Italy
45C2 Tipperary County, Irish Rep
41B3 Tipperary Irish Rep
18B2 Tipton Missouri, USA
87B2 Tiptūr India
23A2 Tiquicheo Mexico
55B2 Tiranë Alb
47D1 Tirano Italy
60C4 Tiraspol Moldova
87B2 Tirchchirāppalli India
55C3 Tire Turk
93C1 Tirebolu Turk
44A3 Tiree / Scot
54C2 Tîrgovişte Rom
54B1 Tîrgu Jiu Rom
54B1 Tîrgu Mureş Rom
84C1 Tirich Mir Mt Pak
96A2 Tiris Region, Mor
61J3 Tirlyanskiy Russian Fed
54B1 Tîrnăveni Rom

55B3 Tírnavos Greece
85D4 Tirodi India
47D1 Tirol Province, Austria
53A2 Tirso R Sardegna
87B3 Tiruchchendūr India
87B3 Tirunelveli India
87B2 Tirupati India
87B2 Tiruppattur India
87B2 Tiruppur India
87B2 Tiruvannamalai India
19A3 Tishomingo USA
94C2 Tisiyah Syria
59C3 Tisza R Hung
86A2 Titlagarh India
55B2 Titov Veles Macedonia
98C2 Titule Zaire
17B2 Titusville USA
13C4 Tiverton Eng
52B2 Tivoli Italy
23B2 Tixtla Mexico
99E2 Tiyeglow Somalia
25D2 Tizimín Mexico
96C1 Tizi Ouzou Alg
96B2 Tiznit Mor
23A1 Tizpan el Alto Mexico
23B2 Tlacolula Mexico
23B2 Tlacotalpan Mexico
23A2 Tlachuan Mexico
23B2 Tlalnepantla Mexico
23B2 Tlalpan Mexico
23B2 Tlaltenango Mexico
23B2 Tlancualpican Mexico
23B2 Tlapa Mexico
23B2 Tlapacoyan Mexico
23B2 Tlaquepaque Mexico
23B2 Tlaxcala Mexico
23B2 Tlaxcala State, Mexico
23B2 Tlaxiaco Mexico
96B1 Tlemcem Alg
101D2 Toamasina Madag
34C3 Toay Arg
75B2 Toba Japan
84B2 Toba and Kakar Ranges Mts Pak
27E4 Tobago / Caribbean S
13C2 Toba Inlet Sd Can
15D2 Tobermory USA
14B1 Tobermory Can
44A3 Tobermory Scot
71E3 Tobi / Pacific O
65H4 Tobol R Kazakhstan
70D4 Toboli Indon
65H4 Tobol'sk Russian Fed
Tobruk = Tubruq
31B2 Tocantíns R Brazil
31B3 Tocantins State, Brazil
17B1 Toccoa USA
47C1 Toce R Italy
30B3 Tocopilla Chile
30C3 Tocorpuri Mt Chile
32D1 Tocuyo R Ven
85D3 Toda India
47C1 Tödi Mt Switz
75A1 Todong S Korea
9B4 Todos Santos Mexico
13E2 Tofield Can
13B3 Tofino Can
12B3 Togiak USA
12B3 Togiak B USA
97C4 Togo Republic, Africa
72C1 Togtoh China
12F2 Tok USA
74E2 Tokachi R Japan
75B1 Tokamachi Japan
95C3 Tokar Sudan
69E4 Tokara Retto Arch Japan
93C1 Tokat Turk
74B3 Tokchok-kundo Arch S Korea
82B1 Tokmak Kyrgyzstan
110C1 Tokomaru Bay NZ
75A1 Tok-to / S Korea
12H3 Toku R Can/USA

78C3 Tokung Indon
69E4 Tokuno / Japan
74C4 Tokushima Japan
74D3 Tōkyō Japan
110C1 Tolaga Bay NZ
101D3 Tôlañaro Madag
50B3 Toledo Brazil
50B2 Toledo Spain
14B2 Toledo USA
19B3 Toledo Bend Res USA
101D3 Toliara Madag
23B1 Toliman Mexico
32B3 Tolima Mt Colombia
51B1 Tolosa Spain
29B3 Toltén Chile
23B2 Toluca Mexico
61G3 Tol'yatti Russian Fed
74E2 Tomakomai Japan
78D1 Tomani Malay
58C2 Tomaszów Mazowiecka Pol
11B3 Tombigbee R USA
98B3 Tomboco Angola
35C2 Tombos Brazil
97B3 Tombouctou Mali
100A2 Tomboua Angola
34A3 Tomé Chile
50B2 Tomelloso Spain
50A2 Tomer Port
106B3 Tomkinson Range Mts Aust
63E2 Tommot Russian Fed
55B2 Tomorrit Mt Alb
65K4 Tomsk Russian Fed
16B3 Toms River USA
23B2 Tonalá Mexico
20C1 Tonasket USA
15C2 Tonawanda USA
105H4 Tonga Is Pacific O
101H1 Tongaat S Africa
72A2 Tongde China
46C1 Tongeren Belg
76E2 Tonggu Jiao / China
73A5 Tonghai China
74B2 Tongiosong-man N Korea
76D1 Tongkin,G of China/Viet
72E1 Tonglia China
73D3 Tongling China
108B2 Tongo Aust
34A2 Tongoy Chile
73B4 Tongren Guizhou, China
72A2 Tongren Qinghai, China
75A2 Tonghua China
76B1 Tongsa Bhutan
76B1 Tongyu Myan
68B3 Tongtian He R China
44C2 Tongue Scot
72D2 Tong Xian China
72B2 Tongxin China
73B4 Tongzi China
9C4 Tónich Mexico
85D3 Tonk India
18A2 Tonkawa USA
76C3 Tonle Sap L Camb
21B2 Tonopah USA
12C2 Tonsina USA
8B2 Tooele USA
109D1 Toogoolawah Aust
108B1 Toompine Aust
109D1 Toowoomba Aust
22C1 Topaz L USA
18A2 Topeka USA
9C4 Topolobampo Mexico
20B1 Toppenish USA
99D2 Tor Eth
55C3 Torbali Turk
90C2 Torbat-e-Heydariyeh Iran
90D2 Torbat-e Jäm Iran
12D2 Torbert,Mt USA
50A1 Tordesillas Spain
43C4 Torfaen County Wales

56C2 Torgau Germany
46B1 Torhout Belg
69G3 Tori / Japan
47B2 Torino Italy
99D2 Torit Sudan
35A1 Torixoreu Brazil
50A1 Tormes R Spain
13E2 Tornado Mt Can
38J5 Torne L Sweden
38H5 Torneträsk Sweden
7D4 Torngat Mts Can
38J5 Tornio Fin
34C3 Tornquist Arg
70D3 Toroh Can
15C2 Toronto Can
Toropets Russian Fed
99D2 Tororo Uganda
92B2 Toros Dağlari Mts Turk
43C4 Torquay Eng
22C4 Torrance USA
50A2 Torrão Port
51C1 Torreblanca Spain
53B2 Torre del Greco Italy
50B1 Torrelavega Spain
50B1 Torremolinos Spain
108A2 Torrens,L Aust
24B2 Torreón Mexico
47B2 Torre Pellice Italy
107D2 Torres Str Aust
50A2 Torres Vedras Port
16C2 Torrington Connecticut, USA
8C2 Torrington Wyoming, USA
9C4 Torron USA
38D3 Tórshavn Faroyar
47C2 Tortona Italy
51C1 Tortosa Spain
90C2 Torud Iran
58B2 Toruń Pol
40B2 Tory / Irish Rep
60D2 Torzhok Russian Fed
75A2 Tosa Japan
74C4 Tosa-shimizu Japan
74C4 Tosa-wan B Japan
75B2 To-shima / Japan
Toshkent = Tashkent
60D2 Tosno Russian Fed
75A2 Toso Japan
92B1 Tosya Turk
61F1 Tot'ma Russian Fed
43C4 Totnes Eng
33F2 Totness Surinam
23B2 Totolapan Mexico
51B2 Totona Spain
109C2 Tottenham Aust
74C3 Tottori Japan
97B4 Touba Côte d'Ivoire
97A3 Touba Sen
96B1 Toubkal Mt Mor
97A3 Tougan Burkina
96C1 Touggourt Alg
97A3 Tougué Guinea
46C2 Toul France
49D3 Toulon France
48C3 Toulouse France
97B4 Toumodi Côte d'Ivoire
76B2 Toungoo Myan
46B1 Tourcoing France
96A2 Tourine Maur
46B1 Tournai Belg
48C2 Tours France
74E2 Towada Japan
74E2 Towada-ko L Japan
15C2 Towanda USA
107D2 Townsville Aust
16A3 Towson USA
43C4 Towy R Wales
74D3 Toyama Japan
75B1 Toyama-wan B Japan
75B2 Toyohashi Japan
75B2 Toyonaka Japan
75A1 Toyooka Japan
74D3 Toyota Japan
96C1 Tozeur Tunisia
46D2 Traben-Trarbach Germany
93C1 Trabzon Turk
22B2 Tracy California, USA
34A3 Traiguén Chile

13D3 Trail Can
41B3 Tralee Irish Rep
45B2 Tralee B Irish Rep
45C2 Tramore Irish Rep
39G7 Tranås Sweden
77B4 Trang Thai
71E4 Trangan I Indon
109C2 Trangie Aust
12E2 Transalaskan Pipeline USA
Transylvanian Alps = Munţii Carpaţii Meridionali
53B3 Trapani Italy
109C3 Traralgon Aust
97A3 Trarza Region, Maur
76C3 Trat Thai
108B2 Traveller's L Aust
56C2 Travemünde Germ
14A2 Traverse City USA
12C1 Traverse Peak Mt USA
111B2 Travers,Mt NZ
47C2 Trebbia R Italy
59B3 Trebič Czech Republic
54A2 Trebinje Bosnia-Herzegovina
57C3 Trebon Czech Republic
29F2 Treinta y Tres Urug
29C4 Trelew Arg
43B3 Trelleborg Sweden
43B3 Tremadog B Wales
15D1 Tremblant,Mt USA
13C2 Tremblay L Can
14A2 Tremont USA
59B3 Trenčin Slovakia
34C3 Trenque Lauquén Arg
43D3 Trent R Eng
47D1 Trentino Region, Italy
47D1 Trento Italy
15C2 Trenton USA
18B1 Trenton Missouri, USA
16B2 Trenton New Jersey, USA
7E5 Trepassey Can
34C3 Tres Arroyos Arg
35B2 Três Corações Brazil
30F3 Três Lagoas Brazil
34C3 Tres Lomas Arg
35C2 Três Pinos USA
35C2 Três Rios Brazil
47C2 Treviglio Italy
47E2 Treviso Italy
87B2 Trichūr India
108C2 Trida Aust
46D2 Trier Germany
52B1 Trieste Italy
45C2 Trim Irish Rep
87C3 Trincomalee Sri Lanka
33E6 Trinidad Brazil
29E2 Trinidad Urug
33C3 Trinidad I Arg
27E4 Trinidad I Caribbean S
103G6 Trinidade I Atlantic O
27E4 Trinidad & Tobago Republic Caribbean S
19A3 Trinity USA
9D3 Trinity R USA
7E5 Trinity B Can
12D3 Trinity Is USA
17A1 Trion USA
94B1 Tripoli Leb
95A1 Tripoli Libya
55B3 Trípolis Greece
86C2 Tripura State, India
103H6 Tristan da Cunha Is Atlantic O
87B3 Trivandrum India
59B3 Trnava Slovakia
107E1 Trobriand Is PNG
15D1 Trois-Rivières Can
61H4 Troitsk Russian Fed
39G7 Trollhättan Sweden
38F6 Trollheimen Mt Nor
9K9 Tromelin I Indian O

38H5 Tromsø Nor
38G6 Trondheim Nor
38G6 Trondheimfjord Inlet Nor
42B2 Troon Scot
102J3 Tropic of Cancer
103J6 Tropic of Capricorn
96B2 Troudenni Mali
7A4 Trout L Ontario, Can
17A1 Troy Alabama, USA
16C1 Troy New York, USA
14B2 Troy Ohio, USA
54B2 Troyan Bulg
49C2 Troyes France
91B5 Trucial Coast Region, UAE
21A2 Truckee R USA
25D3 Trujillo Honduras
32B5 Trujillo Peru
50A2 Trujillo Spain
32C2 Trujillo Ven
50A2 Trundle Aust
7D5 Truro Can
43B4 Truro Eng
68B2 Tsagaan Nuur L Mongolia
68B1 Tsagan-Tologoy Russian Fed
101D2 Tsaratanana Madag
100B3 Tsau Botswana
99D3 Tsavo Kenya
99D3 Tsavo Nat Pk Kenya
65J4 Tselinograd Kazakhstan
72B5 Tses Namibia
68C2 Tsetserleg Mongolia
97C4 Tsévié Togo
100B3 Tshabong Botswana
100B3 Tshane Botswana
98B3 Tshela Zaïre
98C3 Tshibala Zaïre
98C3 Tshikapa Zaïre
98C3 Tshuapa R Zaïre
101D3 Tsihombe Madag
61F4 Tsimlyanskoye Vodokhranilishche Res Russian Fed
Tsinan = Jinan
Tsingtao = Qingdao
101D2 Tsiroanomandidy Madag
13B2 Tsitsi Peak Mt Can
58D2 Tsna R Belarus
72B1 Tsogt Ovoo Mongolia
68C2 Tsomog Mongolia
75B2 Tsu Japan
75B1 Tsubata Japan
74E3 Tsuchira Japan
74E2 Tsugaru-kaikyō Str Japan
100A3 Tsumeb Namibia
100A3 Tsumis Namibia
75B1 Tsunugi Japan
74D3 Tsuruga Japan
74D3 Tsuruoka Japan
75B1 Tsushima Japan
74B4 Tsushima I Japan
74C3 Tsuyama Japan
50A1 Tua R Port
45B2 Tuam Irish Rep
60E5 Tuapse Russian Fed
111A3 Tuatapere NZ
30C4 Tubarão Brazil
94B2 Tubas Israel
79A4 Tubbataha Reefs Is Phil
57B3 Tübingen Germany
95B1 Tubruq Libya
16B3 Tuckerton USA
9B3 Tucson USA
30C4 Tucumán State, Arg
34B2 Tucumán Arg
33E2 Tucupita Ven
51B1 Tudela Spain
93C1 Tudmur Syria
101H1 Tugela R S Africa
109D2 Tuggerah L Aust
12D3 Tugidak I USA
79B2 Tuguegarao Phil
63F2 Tugur Russian Fed
72D2 Tuhai He R China
4E3 Tuktoyaktuk USA
58C1 Tukums Latvia

99D3 Tukuyu Tanz
84B2 Tukzar Afghan
60E3 Tula Russian Fed
60E3 Tula Division Russian Fed
23B1 Tulancingo Mexico
78A3 Tulangbawang R Indon
23B1 Tulcán Colombia
60C5 Tulcea Rom
5U1 Tuli Zim
94B2 Tulkarm Israel
48C2 Tulle France
19B3 Tullos USA
45C2 Tullow Irish Rep
18A2 Tulsa USA
93C3 Tulūl ash Shāmīyah Desert Region Syria/S Arabia
63C2 Tulun Russian Fed
78C4 Tulungagung Indon
32B3 Tumaco Colombia
109C3 Tumbarumba Aust
32A4 Tumbes Ecuador
108A2 Tumby Bay Aust
87B2 Tumkūr India
77C4 Tumpat Malay
85D4 Tumsar India
97B3 Tumu Ghana
109C3 Tumut Aust
109C3 Tumut R Aust
17C1 Tunapuna Trinidad
93C2 Tuncell Turk
99D3 Tunduma Zambia
101C2 Tunduru Tanz
54C2 Tundzha R Bulg
87B2 Tungabhadra R India
68D4 Tung-Chiang Taiwan
38B2 Tungnafellsjökull Mts Iceland
12J2 Tungsten Can
63B1 Tunguska R Russian Fed
76C1 Tuni India
96D1 Tunis Tunisia
88E4 Tunisia Republic, N Africa
32C2 Tunja Colombia
12B2 Tuntutuliak USA
12B2 Tununak USA
34B2 Tunuyán R Arg
34B2 Tunuyán Arg
22C2 Tuolumne Meadows USA
35A2 Tupã Brazil
35B1 Tupaciguara Brazil
19C3 Tupelo USA
30C3 Tupiza Bol
15D2 Tupper Lake USA
34B2 Tupungato Arg
29C2 Tupungato Mt Arg
86C1 Tura India
63C1 Tura Russian Fed
61K2 Tura R Russian Fed
90C2 Turān Iran
63B2 Turan Russian Fed
93A3 Turayf S Arabia
60D2 Turbat Pak
32B2 Turbo Colombia
54B1 Turda Rom
63A3 Turfan Depression China
65H4 Turgay Kazakhstan
63B3 Turgen Uul Mt Mongolia
54C2 Turgovishte Bulg
92A2 Turgutlu Turk
92C1 Turhal Turk
39K7 Türi Estonia
51B2 Turia R Spain
Turin = Torino
61K2 Turinsk Russian Fed
69F2 Turiy Rog Russian Fed
99D2 Turkana,L Kenya/Eth
80E1 Turkestan Region, C Asia
82A1 Turkestan Kazakhstan
92C2 Turkey Republic, W Asia
80D1 Turkmenistan Republic, Asia

90B2 Turkmenskiy Zaliv B Turkmenistan
27C2 Turks Is Caribbean S
39J6 Turku Fin
99D2 Turkwel R Kenya
22B2 Turlock USA
22B2 Turlock L USA
110C2 Turnagain,C NZ
25D3 Turneffe I Belize
16C1 Turners Falls USA
46C1 Turnhout Belg
13F1 Turnor L Can
54B2 Turnu Măgurele Rom
63A3 Turpan China
26B2 Turquino Mt Cuba
80E1 Turtkul' Uzbekistan
18A2 Turtle Creek Res USA
13F2 Turtle L Can
63A1 Turukhansk Russian Fed
63B3 Turuntayevo Russian Fed
35B2 Turvo R Goias, Brazil
35B2 Turvo R São Paulo, Brazil
58C2 Tur'ya R Ukraine
19C3 Tuscaloosa USA
18C2 Tuscola USA
90C3 Tusharik Iran
Tutera = Tudela
87B3 Tuticorin India
54C2 Tutrakan Bulg
57B3 Tuttlingen Germany
68C2 Tuul Gol R Mongolia
105G4 Tuvalu Is Pacific O
63B2 Tuvinskaya Respublika, Russian Fed
23A2 Tuxpan Jalisco, Mexico
24B2 Tuxpan Nayarit, Mexico
23C1 Tuxpan Veracruz, Mexico
23C2 Tuxtepec Mexico
25C3 Tuxtla Gutiérrez Mexico
50A1 Túy Spain
76D3 Tuy Hoa Viet
92B2 Tuz Gölü Salt L Turk
93D3 Tuz Khurmātū Iraq
54A2 Tuzla Bosnia-Herzegovina
60E2 Tver' Russian Fed
60D2 Tver' Division Russian Fed
42C2 Tweed R Eng/Scot
109D1 Tweed Heads Aust
42C2 Tweedsmuir Hills Scot
7E5 Twillingate Can
8B2 Twin Falls USA
111B2 Twins,The Mt NZ
14A2 Two Rivers USA
63E2 Tygda Russian Fed
19A3 Tyler USA
65K3 Tym R Russian Fed
69G1 Tymovskoye Russian Fed
42D2 Tyne R Eng
42D2 Tynemouth Eng
38G6 Tynset Nor
12D3 Tyonek USA
94B2 Tyr Leb
Tyre = Tyr
45C1 Tyrone County, N Ire
108B3 Tyrrell,L Aust
53B2 Tyrrhenian S Italy
65H4 Tyumen' Russian Fed
43B3 Tywyn Wales
55B3 Tzoumérka Mt Greece

U

99E2 Uarsciek Somalia
35C2 Ubá Brazil
35C1 Ubaí Brazil
98B2 Ubangi R CAR
47B2 Ubaye R France
75A2 Ube Japan
50B2 Ubeda Spain

Ubekendt Ejland

6E2 **Ubekendt Ejland** *I / Greenland*
35B1 **Uberaba** Brazil
35B1 **Uberlândia** Brazil
76C2 **Ubon Ratchathani** Thai
58D2 **Ubort** *R* Belarus
98C3 **Ubundi** Zaire
32C5 **Ucayali** *R* Peru
84C3 **Uch** Pak
63F2 **Uchar** *R* Russian Fed
74E2 **Uchiura-wan** *B* Japan
63B2 **Uda** *R* Russian Fed
85C4 **Udaipur** India
86B1 **Udaipur Garhi** Nepal
34D3 **Udaquoila** Arg
39G7 **Uddevalla** Sweden
38H5 **Udjaur** *L* Sweden
87B1 **Udgir** India
84D2 **Udhampur** India
61H2 **Udmurtia** Division, Russian Fed
76C2 **Udon Thani** Thai
63F2 **Udskaya Guba** *B* Russian Fed
87A2 **Udupi** India
75B1 **Ueda** Japan
99C2 **Uele** *R* Zaire
56C2 **Uelzen** Germany
98C2 **Uere** *R* Zaire
61J3 **Ufa** Russian Fed
61J2 **Ufa** *R* Russian Fed
100A3 **Ugab** *R* Namibia
99D3 **Ugaila** *R* Tanz
12D3 **Ugak** *B* USA
99D2 **Uganda** Republic, Africa
12C3 **Ugashik** *B* USA
12C3 **Ugashik** *L* USA
47B2 **Ugine** France
69G2 **Uglegorsk** Russian Fed
60E2 **Uglich** Russian Fed
60E3 **Ugra** *R* Russian Fed
44A3 **Uig** Scot
90B3 **Uige** Angola
61H4 **Uil** Kazakhstan
8B2 **Uinta Mts** USA
100B4 **Uitenhage** S Africa
59C3 **Ujfehértó** Hung
75B2 **Uji** Japan
99C3 **Ujiji** Tanz
30C3 **Ujina** Chile
85D4 **Ujjain** India
70C4 **Ujung Pandang** Indon
99D3 **Ukerewe** *I* Tanz
86C1 **Ukhrul** India
21A2 **Ukiah** California, USA
20C1 **Ukiah** Oregon, USA
58C1 **Ukmerge** Lithuania
60C4 **Ukraine** Republic, Europe
68C2 **Ulaanbaatar** Mongolia
68B2 **Ulaangom** Mongolia
72C1 **Ulaan Uul** Mongolia
82C1 **Ulangar Hu** *L* China
68C1 **Ulan Ude** Russian Fed
68B3 **Ulan Ul Hu** *L* China
34B2 **Ulapes** Arg
74B3 **Ulchin** S Korea
54A2 **Ulcinj** Montenegro, Yugos
68D2 **Uldz** Mongolia
68B2 **Uliastay** Mongolia
58D1 **Ulla** Lithuania
109D3 **Ulladulla** Aust
44B3 **Ullapool** Scot
38H5 **Ullsfjorden** Inlet Nor
42C2 **Ullswater** *L* Eng
74C3 **Ullung-do** *I* S Korea
57C3 **Ulm** Germany
108A1 **Uloowaranie,L** Aust
74B3 **Ulsan** S Korea
45C1 **Ulster** Region, N Ire
65K5 **Ulungur He** *R* China
65K5 **Ulungur Hu** *L* China
44A3 **Ulva** *I* Scot
42C2 **Ulverston** Eng

109C4 **Ulverstone** Aust
63G2 **Ulya** *R* Russian Fed
61G3 **Ul'yanovsk** Division, Russian Fed
60D4 **Uman** Ukraine
6E2 **Umanak** Greenland
86A2 **Umaria** India
85B3 **Umarkot** Pak
108A1 **Umaroona,L** Aust
20C1 **Umatilla** USA
38L5 **Umba** *R* Russian Fed
99D3 **Umba** *R* Tanz
38H6 **Ume** *R* Sweden
38J6 **Umea** Sweden
101H1 **Umfolozi** *R* S Africa
4C3 **Umiat** USA
91C4 **Umm al Qaiwain** UAE
91C5 **Umm as Samim** *Salt Marsh* Oman
99C1 **Umm Bell** Sudan
98C1 **Umm Keddada** Sudan
99D1 **Umm Ruwaba** Sudan
91B5 **Umm Sa'id** Qatar
20B2 **Umpqua** *R* USA
85D4 **Umred** India
100B4 **Umtata** S Africa
35A2 **Umuarama** Brazil
52C1 **Una** *R* Bosnia-Herzegovina/Croatia
35B1 **Unai** Brazil
12B2 **Unalakleet** USA
80C3 **Unayzah** S Arabia
16C2 **Uncasville** USA
101G1 **Underberg** S Africa
60D3 **Unecha** Russian Fed
94B3 **Uneisa** Jordan
7D4 **Ungava** *B* Can
30F4 **União de Vitória** Brazil
34B3 **Unión** Arg
18B2 **Union** Missouri, USA
17B1 **Union** S Carolina, USA
14C2 **Union City** Pennsylvania, USA
17A1 **Union Springs** USA
15C3 **Uniontown** USA
91B5 **United Arab Emirates** Arabian Pen
36C3 **United Kingdom** Kingdom, W Europe
2H4 **United States of America**
6B1 **United States Range** *Mts* Can
13F2 **Unity** Can
20C2 **Unity** USA
23A2 **Unna** Germany
86A1 **Unnao** India
44E1 **Unst** *I* Scot
13A1 **Unuk** *R* USA
92C1 **Unye** Turk
61F2 **Unzha** *R* Russian Fed
33E2 **Upata** Ven
98C3 **Upemba Nat Pk** Zaire
6E2 **Upernavik** Greenland
100A3 **Upington** S Africa
100B3 **Uplington** S Africa
14B2 **Upper Arlington** USA
13D2 **Upper Arrow L** Can
111C2 **Upper Hutt** NZ
20B2 **Upper Klamath L** USA
20B2 **Upper L** USA
45C1 **Upper Lough Erne** *L* N Ire
27L1 **Upper Manzanilla** Trinidad
39H7 **Uppsala** Sweden
72B1 **Urad Qianqi** China
91A4 **Urairah** S Arabia
61H3 **Ural** *R* Kazakhstan
109D2 **Uralla** Aust
61H3 **Ural'sk** Kazakhstan
65G4 **Uralskiy Khrebet** *Mts* Russian Fed
5H4 **Uranium City** Can
75B1 **Urawa** Japan
18C1 **Urbana** Illinois, USA
14B2 **Urbana** Ohio, USA
52B2 **Urbino** Italy
42C2 **Ure** *R* Eng
61G2 **Uren'** Russian Fed

80E1 **Urgench** Uzbekistan
84B2 **Urgun** Afghan
55C3 **Urla** Turk
54B2 **Uroševac** Serbia, Yugos
31B4 **Uruaçu** Brazil
23A2 **Uruapan** Mexico
35B1 **Urucuia** *R* Brazil
30E4 **Uruguaiana** Brazil
29E2 **Uruguay** Republic, S America
29E2 **Uruguay** *R* Urug
82C1 **Urümqi** China
69H2 **Urup** *R* Russian Fed
84B2 **Uruzgan** Afghan
61F3 **Uryupinsk** Russian Fed
61H2 **Urzhum** Russian Fed
54C2 **Urziceni** Rom
82C1 **Usa** China
75A2 **Usa** Japan
64G3 **Usa** *R* Russian Fed
92A2 **Uşak** Turk
100A3 **Usakos** Namibia
99D3 **Ushashi** Tanz
65J5 **Ush Tobe** Kazakhstan
29C6 **Ushuaia** Arg
63E2 **Ushumun** Russian Fed
43C4 **Usk** *R* Wales
92A1 **Üsküdar** Turk
63C2 **Usolye Sibirskoye** Russian Fed
34B2 **Uspallata** Arg
69F2 **Ussuriysk** Russian Fed
47C1 **Uster** Switz
53B3 **Ustica** *I* Italy
57C2 **Usti nad Labem** Czech Republic
65J4 **Ust'Ishim** Russian Fed
58B2 **Ustka** Pol
65K5 **Ust'-Kamenogorsk** Kazakhstan
63B2 **Ust'Kamo** Russian Fed
61J2 **Ust'Katav** Russian Fed
63C2 **Ust'-Kut** Russian Fed
61E4 **Ust Labinsk** Russian Fed
63F1 **Ust'Maya** Russian Fed
1C8 **Ust'Nera** Russian Fed
63E2 **Ust'Nyukzha** Russian Fed
63F2 **Ust'Ordynskiy** Russian Fed
64G3 **Ust'Tsil'ma** Russian Fed
63F2 **Ust'Umal'ta** Russian Fed
65G5 **Ustyurt Plateau** *Plat* Kazakhstan
75A2 **Usuki** Japan
25C3 **Usumacinta** *R* Guatemala/Mexico
101H1 **Usutu** *R* Swaziland
8B3 **Utah** State, USA
8B2 **Utah L** USA
58D1 **Utena** Russian Fed
85B3 **Uthal** Pak
10C2 **Utica** USA
51B2 **Utiel** Spain
12D1 **Utikuma L** Can
56B2 **Utrecht** Neth
101H1 **Utrecht** S Africa
50A2 **Utrera** Spain
38K5 **Utsjoki** Fin
74D3 **Utsunomiya** Japan
76C2 **Uttaradit** Thai
86A1 **Uttar Pradesh** State, India
65H4 **Uval** *R* Russian Fed
107F3 **Uvéa** *I* / Nouvelle Calédonie
99D3 **Uvinza** Tanz
99C3 **Uvira** Zaire
6E2 **Uvkusigssat** Greenland
39J6 **Uvsikaupunki** Fin
68B1 **Uvs Nuur** *L* China

74C4 **Uwajima** Japan
72B2 **Uxin Qi** China
63B2 **Uyar** Russian Fed
30C3 **Uyuni** Bol
80E1 **Uzbekistan** Republic, Asia
48C2 **Uzerche** France
59C3 **Uzhgorod** Ukraine
54A2 **Uzice** Serbia, Yugos
60E3 **Uzlovaya** Russian Fed
92A1 **Uzunköprü** Turk

V

101F1 **Vaal** *R* S Africa
101G1 **Vaal Dam** *Res* S Africa
100B3 **Vaalwater** S Africa
38J6 **Vaasa** Fin
59B3 **Vác** Hung
30F4 **Vacaria** Brazil
35C1 **Vacaria** *R* Minas Gerais, Brazil
21A2 **Vacaville** USA
85C4 **Vadodara** India
38K4 **Vadsø** Nor
47C1 **Vaduz** Leichtenstein
38D3 **Vágar** Faroyar
29E3 **Va Gesell** Arg
59B3 **Váh** *R* Slovakia
87B2 **Vaigai** *R* India
65K4 **Vakh** *R* Russian Fed
60B4 **Vălcea** Rom
29C4 **Valcheta** Arg
47D2 **Valdagno** Italy
60D2 **Valday** Russian Fed
60D2 **Valdayskaya Vozvyshennost'** *Upland* Russian Fed
32D2 **Val de la Pascua** Ven
50C2 **Valdepeñas** Spain
12E2 **Valdez** USA
29B3 **Valdivia** Chile
46B2 **Val d'Oise** *Department* France
17B1 **Valdosta** USA
20C2 **Vale** USA
31D4 **Valença** Bahia, Brazil
35C2 **Valença** Rio de Janeiro, Brazil
49C2 **Valence** France
51B2 **Valencia** Region, Spain
32D1 **Valencia** Ven
45A3 **Valencia** *I* / Irish Rep
50A3 **Valencia de Alcantara** Spain
46B1 **Valenciennes** France
47C2 **Valenza** Italy
43C4 **Vale of Glamorgan** County Wales
32C2 **Valera** Ven
54A2 **Valjevo** Serbia, Yugos
Valka = Valga
39J6 **Valkeakoski** Fin
25D2 **Valladolid** Mexico
50B1 **Valladolid** Spain
47B2 **Valle d'Aosta** Region, Italy
27D5 **Valle de la Pascua** Ven
23A1 **Valle de Santiago** Mexico
47B2 **Valle d'Isère** France
32C1 **Valledupar** Colombia
97C3 **Vallée de l'Azouak** *R* Niger
54A2 **Vallée Tilemis** *V* Mali
30D2 **Valle Grande** Bol
22A1 **Vallejo** USA
30B4 **Vallenar** Chile
53B3 **Valletta** Malta
8D2 **Valley City** USA
15D1 **Valleyfield** Can
13D1 **Valleyview** Can
47E2 **Valli di Comacchio** *Lg* Italy
51C1 **Valls** Spain

58D1 Valmiera Latvia
35A2 Valparaíso Brazil
34A2 Valparaíso Arg
23A1 Valparaíso Mexico
17A1 Valparaíso USA
101G1 Vals R S Africa
85C4 Valsâd India
60E3 Valukyl Russian Fed
50A2 Valverde del Camino Spain
38J6 Vammala Fin
93D2 Van Turk
63C1 Vanavara Russian Fed
18B2 Van Buren Arkansas, USA
13C3 Vancouver Can
20B1 Vancouver USA
5F5 Vancouver I Can
12G2 Vancouver,Mt Can
18C2 Vandalia Illinois, USA
14B3 Vandalia Ohio, USA
13C2 Vanderhoof Can
106C2 Van Diemen G Gulf Aust
39G7 Vänern L Sweden
39G7 Vänersborg Sweden
101D3 Vangaindrano Madag
93D2 Van Gölü Salt L Turk
76C2 Vang Vieng Laos
9C3 Van Horn USA
15C1 Vankarem Russian Fed
1C6 Vankarem Russian Fed
38H6 Vännäs Sweden
48B2 Vannes France
47B2 Vanoise Mts France
100A4 Vanrhynsdorp S Africa
6B3 Vansittart I Can
105G4 Vanuatu Is Pacific O
14B2 Van Wert USA
47C2 Varallo Italy
90B2 Varämin Iran
87A1 Vārānasi India
38K4 Varangerfjord Inlet Nor
38K4 Varangerhalvaya Pen Nor
52C1 Varazdin Croatia
39G7 Varberg Sweden
39F7 Varde Den
38L4 Vardo Nor
58C2 Varéna Lithuania
47C2 Varenna Italy
47C2 Varese Italy
35B2 Varginha Brazil
38K6 Varkaus Fin
54C2 Varna Bulg
39G7 Värnamo Sweden
17B1 Varnville USA
35C1 Várzea da Palma Brazil
47C2 Varzi Italy
50B1 Vascongadas Region, Spain
90B3 Vasil'kov Ukraine
14B2 Vassar USA
39H7 Västerås Sweden
39H7 Västervik Sweden
52B2 Vasto Italy
65J4 Vasyugan R Russian Fed
38B2 Vatnajökull Mts Iceland
38A1 Vatneyri Iceland
54C1 Vatra Dornei Rom
39G7 Vättern L Sweden
9C3 Vaughn USA
32C3 Vaupés R Colombia
13E2 Vauxhall Can
87C3 Vavuniya Sri Lanka
39G7 Växjö Sweden
64G2 Vaygach, Ostrov I Russian Fed
34C2 Vedia Arg
38G5 Vega I Nor
13E2 Vegreville Can
50A2 Vejer de la Frontera Spain
39F7 Vejle Den
52C2 Velebit Mts Croatia

52C1 Velenje Slovenia
35C1 Velhas R Brazil
39K7 Velikaya R Russian Fed
60D2 Velikiye Luki Russian Fed
61G1 Velikiy Ustyug Russian Fed
54C2 Veliko Tŭrnovo Bulg
97A3 Vélingara Sen
87B2 Vellore India
61F1 Vel'sk Russian Fed
87B3 Vembanad L India
34C2 Venado Tuerto Arg
35B2 Venceslau Braz Brazil
34C2 Vendôme France
12E1 Venetie USA
47D2 Veneto Region, Italy
47E2 Venezia Italy
32D2 Venezuela Republic, S America
87A1 Vengurla India
12C3 Veniaminof V USA
Venice = Venezia
87B2 Venkatagiri India
56B2 Venlo Neth
58C1 Venta R Latvia
101G1 Ventersburg S Africa
58C1 Ventspils Latvia
32D3 Ventuari R Ven
22C3 Ventura USA
60D1 Vepsovskaya Vozvyshennost' Upland Russian Fed
30D4 Vera Arg
51B2 Vera Spain
23B2 Veracruz Mexico
23B1 Veracruz State, Mexico
87B3 Verával India
47C2 Verbania Italy
47C2 Vercelli Italy
35A1 Verde R Goias, Brazil
23A1 Verde R Jalisco, Mexico
35A1 Verde R Mato Grosso do Sul, Brazil
23B2 Verde R Oaxaca, Mexico
Verde,C = Cap Vert
35C1 Verde Grande R Brazil
34C3 Verde,Pen Arg
49D3 Verdon R France
48C2 Verdun France
101G1 Vereeniging S Africa
61H2 Vereshchagino Russian Fed
97A3 Verga,C Guinea
34D3 Vergara Arg
50A1 Verín Spain
63D2 Verkh Angara R Russian Fed
61J3 Verkhneural'sk Russian Fed
63E1 Verkhnevilyuysk Russian Fed
1C6 Verkhoyansk Russian Fed
35A1 Vermelho R Brazil
13E2 Vermilion Can
10C2 Vermont State, USA
22B2 Vernalis USA
13D2 Vernon Can
46A2 Vernon France
90D3 Vernon USA
17E2 Vero Beach USA
54B2 Véroia Greece
47D2 Verolanuova Italy
47D2 Verona Italy
48B2 Versailles France
101H1 Verulam S Africa
46C1 Verviers Belg
46B2 Vervins France
46C2 Vesle R France
49D2 Vesoul France
38G5 Vesterâlen Is Nor
38G5 Vestfjorden Inlet Nor
38A2 Vestmannaeyjar Iceland
52B2 Vesuvio Mt Italy
59B3 Veszprém Hung
39H7 Vetlanda Sweden

61F2 Vetluga R Russian Fed
46B1 Veurne Belg
47B1 Vevey Switz
46A2 Vexin Region, France
47A2 Veynes France
50A1 Viana do Castelo Port
Viangchan = Vientiane
49E3 Viareggio Italy
39F7 Viborg Den
53C3 Vibo Valentia Italy
Vic = Vich
112C2 Vicecomodoro Marambio Base Ant
52B1 Vicenza Italy
51C1 Vich Spain
32D3 Vichada R Colombia
61F2 Vichuga Russian Fed
48C2 Vichy France
19B3 Vicksburg USA
35C2 Vicosa Brazil
106C4 Victor Harbour Aust
33C3 Victoria Can
34A3 Victoria Chile
108B3 Victoria State, Aust
51C1 Victoria R Aust
106C2 Victoria de las Tunas Cuba
100B2 Victoria Falls Zambia/Zim
4G2 Victoria I Can
108B2 Victoria,L Aust
99D3 Victoria,L C Africa
11287 Victoria Land Region, Ant
86C2 Victoria,Mt Myan
99D2 Victoria Nile R Uganda
111B2 Victoria Range Mts NZ
106C2 Victoria River Downs Aust
4H3 Victoria Str Can
15D1 Victoriaville Can
100B4 Victoria West S Africa
23B3 Victorica Arg
21B3 Victorville USA
34A2 Vicuña Chile
34C2 Vicuña Mackenna Arg
17B1 Vidalia USA
54C2 Videle Rom
54B2 Vidin Bulg
85D4 Vidisha India
58D1 Vidzy Belarus
29D4 Viedma Arg
26A4 Viejo Costa Rica
Vielha = Viella
51C1 Viella Spain
21B3 Vienna Georgia, USA
18C2 Vienna Illinois, USA
14B3 Vienna W Virginia, USA
Vienna = Wien
49C2 Vienne France
48C2 Vienne France
76C2 Vientiane Laos
47C1 Vierwaldstätter See L Switz
48C2 Vierzon France
53C2 Vieste Italy
70B2 Vietnam Republic, S E Asia
76D1 Vietri Viet
27P2 Vieux Fort St Lucia
79B2 Vigan Phil
47C2 Vigevano Italy
48B3 Vignemale Mt France
50A1 Vigo Spain
87C1 Vijayawāda India
55A2 Vijosë R Alb
38B2 Vik Iceland
52D2 Vikhren Mt Bulg
13E2 Viking Can
38G6 Vikna I Nor
101C2 Vila da Maganja Mozam
101C2 Vila Machado Mozam
101C3 Vilanculos Mozam

Vilanova i la Geltrú = Villanueva-y-Geltrú
50A1 Vila Real Port
101C2 Vila Vasco da Gama Mozam
35C2 Vila Velha Brazil
58D2 Vileyka Belarus
38H6 Vilhelmina Sweden
33E6 Vilhena Brazil
60C2 Viljandi Estonia
101G1 Viljoenskroon S Africa
9C3 Villa Ahumada Mexico
34B2 Villa Atuel Arg
50A1 Villaba Spain
23A2 Villa Carranza Mexico
52B1 Villach Austria
34B2 Villa Colon Arg
34C2 Villa Constitución Arg
34C1 Villa de Maria Arg
23A1 Villa de Reyes Mexico
34B2 Villa Dolores Arg
47D2 Villafranca di Verona Italy
34C2 Villa General Mitre Arg
34B2 Villa General Roca Arg
34D2 Villaguay Arg
25C3 Villahermosa Mexico
23A1 Villa Hidalgo Mexico
34C2 Villa Huidobro Arg
34C2 Villa Iris Arg
34C2 Villa Maria Arg
30D3 Villa Montes Bol
23A1 Villanueva Mexico
50A1 Villa Nova de Gaia Port
50A2 Villanueva de la Serena Spain
51C1 Villanueva-y-Geltrú Spain
34B3 Villa Regina Arg
51B2 Villarreal Spain
29B3 Villarrica Chile
30E4 Villarrica Par
50B2 Villarrobledo Spain
34D2 Villa San José Arg
51B2 Villa Valeria Arg
32C3 Villavicencio Colombia
49C2 Villefranche France
7C5 Ville-Marie Can
51B2 Villena Spain
46B2 Villeneuve-St-Georges France
48C3 Villeneuve-sur-Lot France
19B3 Ville Platte USA
46B2 Villers-Cotterêts France
49C2 Villeurbanne France
101G1 Villiers S Africa
87B2 Villupuram India
63D1 Vilyuy R Russian Fed
63E1 Vilyuysk Russian Fed
34A2 Viña del Mar Chile
51C1 Vinaroz Spain
14A3 Vincennes USA
38H5 Vindel R Sweden
85D4 Vindhya Range Mts India
16B3 Vineland USA
102B2 Vineyard Haven USA
76D2 Vinh Viet
76D3 Vinh Cam Ranh B Viet
77D4 Vinh Loi Viet
77D3 Vinh Long Viet
18A2 Vinita USA
54A1 Vinkovci Croatia
60C4 Vinnitsa Ukraine
112B3 Vinson Massif Ant
100A3 Vioolsdrift S Africa
47D1 Vipiteno Italy
79B3 Virac Phil
87B2 Virddhāchalam India

100A2 **Virei** Angola
35C1 **Virgem da Lapa** Brazil
101G1 **Virginia** S Africa
10C3 **Virginia** State, USA
10A2 **Virginia** USA
21D2 **Virginia City** USA
27E3 **Virgin Is** Caribbean S
52C1 **Virovitica** Croatia
46C2 **Virton** Belg
87B3 **Virudunagar** India
52C2 **Vis** I Croatia
21B2 **Visalia** USA
79B3 **Visayan S** Phil
39H7 **Visby** Sweden
4H2 **Viscount Melville Sd** Can
54A2 **Višegrad** Bosnia-Herzegovina
50A1 **Viseu** Port
83C4 **Vishākhapatnam** India
47B1 **Visp** Switz
49C1 **Vissingen** Neth
21B3 **Vista** USA
57C3 **Vitavia** R Czech Republic
87A1 **Vite** India
60D2 **Vitebsk** Belarus
52B2 **Viterbo** Italy
50A1 **Vitigudino** Spain
63D2 **Vitim** R Russian Fed
50B1 **Vitora** Spain
31C6 **Vitória** Brazil
31C4 **Vitória da Conquista** Brazil
48B2 **Vitré** France
46C2 **Vitry-le-Francois** France
38J5 **Vittangi** Sweden
53B3 **Vittoria** Italy
47E2 **Vittorio Veneto** Italy
69H2 **Vityaz Depth** Pacific O
50A1 **Vivero** Spain
63B1 **Vivi** R Russian Fed
34D3 **Vivorata** Arg
63C2 **Vizhne-Angarsk** Russian Fed
83C4 **Vizianagaram** India
54B1 **Vlădeasa** Mt Rom
61F5 **Vladikavkaz** Russian Fed
65F4 **Vladimir** Russian Fed
60E2 **Vladimir** Division, Russian Fed
59C2 **Vladimir Volynskiy** Ukraine
74C2 **Vladivostok** Russian Fed
56A2 **Vlieland** I Neth
46B1 **Vlissingen** Neth
55A2 **Vlorë** Alb
57C3 **Vöcklabruck** Austria
76D3 **Voeune Sai** Camb
47C2 **Voghera** Italy
101D2 **Vohibinany** Madag
101E2 **Vohimarina** Madag
99D3 **Voi** Kenya
97B4 **Voinjama** Lib
49D2 **Voiron** France
54A1 **Vojvodina** Aut Republic Serbia, Yugos
26A5 **Volcán Baru** Mt Panama
23B2 **Volcán Citlaltepetl** Mt Mexico
30C3 **Volcán Lullaillaco** Chile
34A3 **Volcáno Copahue** Mt Chile
34A3 **Volcáno Domuyo** Mt Arg
Volcáno Is = Kazan Retto
29B3 **Volcáno Lanin** Mt Arg
30C3 **Volcán Ollagüe** Mt Chile
34A3 **Volcáno Llaima** Mt Chile

34B2 **Volcáno Maipo** Mt Arg
34A3 **Volcáno Peteroa** Mt Chile
34B3 **Volcáno Tromen** V Arg
23A2 **Volcán Paracutín** Mt Mexico
32B3 **Volcán Puracé** Mt Colombia
34A2 **Volcán Tinguiririca** Mt Arg/Chile
61J2 **Volchansk** Russian Fed
61G4 **Volga** R Russian Fed
60E2 **Volgoda** Division, Russian Fed
61F4 **Volgodonsk** Russian Fed
61F4 **Volgograd** Russian Fed
61F4 **Volgograd** Division, Russian Fed
61G3 **Volgogradskoye Vodokhranilische** Res Russian Fed
60D2 **Volkhov** R Russian Fed
60D2 **Volkhov** R Russian Fed
58C2 **Volkovysk** Belarus
101G1 **Volksrust** S Africa
61F2 **Vologda** Russian Fed
48B2 **Volognes** France
55B3 **Vólos** Greece
61G3 **Vol'sk** Russian Fed
22B2 **Volta** USA
97B3 **Volta Blanche** R Burkina
97B4 **Volta,L** Ghana
97B3 **Volta Noire** R Burkina
35C2 **Volta Redonda** Brazil
97B3 **Volta Rouge** R Burkina
61F4 **Volzhskiy** Russian Fed
12D2 **Von Frank Mt** USA
6J3 **Vopnafjordur** Iceland
47C1 **Voralberg** Province, Austria
47C1 **Vorder Rhein** R Switz
56C1 **Vordingborg** Den
64H3 **Vorkuta** Russian Fed
39G6 **Vorma** R Nor
60E3 **Voronezh** Russian Fed
61F3 **Voronezh** Division, Russian Fed
38M5 **Voron'ya** R Russian Fed
39K7 **Võru** Estonia
49D2 **Vosges** Mt France
39F6 **Voss** Nor
63B2 **Vostochnyy Sayan** Russian Fed
112B9 **Vostok** Base Ant
61H2 **Votkinsk** Russian Fed
46C2 **Vouziers** France
60D4 **Voznesensk** Ukraine
54B2 **Vranje** Serbia, Yugos
54B2 **Vratsa** Bulg
54A1 **Vrbas** Serbia, Yugos
52C2 **Vrbas** R Serbia, Yugos
52B1 **Vrbovsko** Bosnia-Herzegovina
101G1 **Vrede** S Africa
33F2 **Vreed en Hoop** Guyana
54B1 **Vršac** Serbia, Yugos
52C2 **Vrtoče** Bosnia-Herzegovina
100B3 **Vryburg** S Africa
101H1 **Vryheid** S Africa
54A1 **Vukovar** Croatia
13E2 **Vulcan** Can
53B3 **Vulcano** I Italy
77D3 **Vung Tau** Viet
38J5 **Vuollerim** Sweden
38L6 **Vyartsilya** Russian Fed

61H2 **Vyatka** R Russian Fed
69F2 **Vyazemskiy** Russian Fed
60D2 **Vyaz'ma** Russian Fed
61F2 **Vyazniki** Russian Fed
60C1 **Vyborg** Russian Fed
64G3 **Vym'** R Russian Fed
43C3 **Vyrnwy** R Wales
60D2 **Vyshiy Volochek** Russian Fed
59B3 **Vyskov** Czech Republic
60E1 **Vytegra** Russian Fed

W

97B3 **Wa** Ghana
13E1 **Wabasca** R Can
5G4 **Wabasca** R Can
13E1 **Wabasca L** Can
14A2 **Wabash** USA
14A3 **Wabash** R USA
5J4 **Wabowden** Can
7D4 **Wabush** Can
17B2 **Waccasassa B** USA
16D1 **Wachusett Res** USA
19A3 **Waco** USA
85B3 **Wad** Pak
95A2 **Waddān** Libya
5G4 **Waddington,Mt** Can
93E4 **Wadi al Bātin** Watercourse Iraq
93D3 **Wadi al Ghudaf** Watercourse Iraq
94C2 **Wadi al Harir** V Syria
93D3 **Wadi al Mirah** Watercourse Iraq/S Arabia
93D3 **Wadi al Ubayyid** Watercourse Iraq
93D3 **Wadi Ar'ar** Watercourse S Arabia
91A5 **Wadi as Hasbā'** Watercourse S Arabia
92C3 **Wadi as Sirhān** V Jordan/S Arabia
94C2 **Wadi az Zaydi** V Syria
94C3 **Wadi edh Dhab'i** V Jordan
94A3 **Wadi el 'Arish** V Egypt
94C3 **Wadi el Ghadaf** V Jordan
94B3 **Wadi el Hasa** V Jordan
94C3 **Wadi el Janab** V Jordan
94B3 **Wadi el Jeib** V Israel/Jordan
95B3 **Wadi el Milk** Watercourse Sudan
92A3 **Wadi el Natrun** Watercourse Egypt
94B3 **Wadi es Sir** Jordan
94B3 **Wadi Fidan** V Jordan
94B3 **Wadi Hareidin** V Egypt
93D3 **Wadi Hawrān** R Iraq
95B3 **Wadi Howa** Watercourse Sudan
98C1 **Wadi Ibra** Watercourse Sudan
94C2 **Wadi Luhfi** Watercourse Jordan
94B3 **Wadi Mujib** V Jordan
94B3 **Wadi Qitaiya** V Egypt
80B3 **Wadi Sha'it** Watercourse Egypt
99D1 **Wad Medani** Sudan
93E4 **Wafra** Kuwait
6B3 **Wager B** Can
6A3 **Wager Bay** Can
109C3 **Wagga Wagga** Aust
106A4 **Wagin** Aust
95A2 **Wāha** Libya
21C4 **Wahaiwa** Hawaiian Is
18A1 **Wahoo** USA
8D2 **Wahpeton** USA

87A1 **Wai** India
111B2 **Waiau** NZ
111B2 **Waiau** R NZ
111B2 **Waiau** R NZ
71E3 **Waigeo** I Indon
110C1 **Waihi** NZ
111B2 **Waikaremoana,L** NZ
110C1 **Waikato** R NZ
108A2 **Waikerie** Aust
111B3 **Waikouaiti** NZ
21C4 **Wailuku** Hawaiian Is
111B2 **Waimakariri** R NZ
111B2 **Waimate** NZ
21C4 **Waimea** Hawaiian Is
106B1 **Waingapu** Indon
4B2 **Wainwright** Can
4B2 **Wainwright** USA
111B2 **Waipara** NZ
110C2 **Waipukurau** NZ
111C2 **Wairarapa,L** NZ
111B2 **Wairau** R NZ
110C1 **Wairoa** NZ
110C1 **Wairoa** R NZ
111B2 **Waitaki** R NZ
110C1 **Waitomo** NZ
110B1 **Waiuku** NZ
75B1 **Wajima** Japan
99E2 **Wajir** Kenya
75B1 **Wakasa-wan** B Japan
111A3 **Wakatipu,L** NZ
74D4 **Wakayama** Japan
42D3 **Wakefield** Eng
27H1 **Wakefield** Jamaica
16D2 **Wakefield** Rhode Island, USA
76B2 **Wakema** Myan
69G2 **Wakkanai** Japan
108B3 **Wakool** R Aust
59B2 **Wałbrzych** Pol
109D2 **Walcha** Aust
58B2 **Walez** Pol
46D1 **Waldbröl** Germany
16B2 **Walden** USA
43C3 **Wales** Country, UK
12A1 **Wales** USA
68B3 **Wales** I Can
109C2 **Walgett** Aust
112B4 **Walgreen Coast** Region, Ant
99C3 **Walikale** Zaire
21B2 **Walker L** USA
14B2 **Walkerton** Can
8B2 **Wallace** USA
108A2 **Wallaroo** Aust
20C1 **Walla Walla** Aust
20C1 **Walla Walla** USA
16C2 **Wallingford** USA
105H4 **Wallis and Futuna** Is Pacific O
20C1 **Wallowa** USA
20C1 **Wallowa Mts** Mts USA
109C1 **Wallumbilla** Aust
110B2 **Walouru** NZ
110C1 **Walouru** NZ
43D3 **Walsall** Eng
9C3 **Walsenburg** USA
78C1 **Walsenburgh** USA
17B1 **Walterboro** USA
17A1 **Walter F George Res** USA
16D1 **Waltham** USA
100A3 **Walvis Bay** Namibia
103J6 **Walvis Ridge** Atlantic O
97C4 **Wamba** Nig
98B3 **Wamba** R Zaire
18A2 **Wamego** USA
84B2 **Wana** Pak
108B1 **Wanaaring** Aust
111A2 **Wanaka** NZ
111A2 **Wanaka,L** NZ
14B1 **Wanapitei L** Can
109C1 **Wandoan** Aust
108B3 **Wanganella** Aust
110C1 **Wanganui** NZ
110C1 **Wanganui** R NZ
109C3 **Wangaratta** Aust
99E2 **Wanle Weyne** Somalia
76E2 **Wanning** China
87B1 **Wanparti** India

73B3 Wanxian China
73B3 Wanyuan China
13D2 Wapiti R Can
18B2 Wappapello,L USA
76C2 Wappingers Falls USA
87B1 Warangal India
109C4 Waratah Aust
108C3 Waratah B Aust
108C3 Warburton R Aust
108A1 Warburton R Aust
109C1 Ward R Aust
101G1 Warden S Africa
99E2 Warder Eth
85D4 Wardha India
111A3 Ware Can
15C2 Ware USA
16D2 Wareham Eng
109D1 Warialda Aust
76C2 Warin Chamrap Thai
100B3 Warmbad S Africa
16B2 Warminster Eng
21B2 Warm Springs USA
56C2 Warnemünde Germany
20B2 Warner Mts USA
17B1 Warner Robins USA
108B3 Warracknabeal Aust
108A1 Warrandirinna,L Aust
107D3 Warrego R Aust
19B3 Warren Arkansas, USA
109C2 Warren Aust
16D2 Warren Massachusetts, USA
14B2 Warren Ohio, USA
15C2 Warren Pennsylvania, USA
45C1 Warrenpoint N Ire
9C3 Warrenton S Africa
101F1 Warrenton S Africa
15C3 Warrenton USA
97C4 Warri Nig
108A1 Warrina Aust
42C3 Warrington Eng
108B3 Warrnambool Aust
Warsaw = Warszawa
58C2 Warszawa Pol
59B2 Warta R Pol
109D1 Warwick Aust
43D3 Warwick County, Eng
43D3 Warwick Eng
16B2 Warwick New York, USA
16D2 Warwick Rhode Island, USA
8B3 Wasatch Range Mts USA
101H1 Wasbank S Africa
21B2 Wasco USA
4H2 Washburn L Can
85D4 Washim India
10C3 Washington District of Columbia, USA
17B1 Washington Georgia, USA
14A3 Washington Indiana, USA
18B2 Washington USA
16B2 Washington New Jersey, USA
14B2 Washington Pennsylvania, USA
8A2 Washington State, USA
14B3 Washington Court House USA
6D1 Washington Land Can
15D2 Washington,Mt USA
43E3 Wash,The Eng
85A3 Washuk Pak
12E2 Wasilla USA
7C4 Waskaganish Can
26A4 Waspán Nic
70D4 Watampone Indon
16C2 Waterbury USA
45C2 Waterford County, Irish Rep
41B3 Waterford Irish Rep
45C2 Waterford Harbour Irish Rep

46C1 Waterloo Belg
10A2 Waterloo USA
15C2 Watertown New York, USA
101H1 Waterval-Boven S Africa
10D2 Waterville Maine, USA
16C1 Watervliet USA
5G4 Waterways Can
43D4 Watford Eng
15C2 Watkins Glen USA
8C1 Watrous Can
99C2 Watsa Eth
12J2 Watson Lake Can
22B2 Watsonville USA
71F4 Wau PNG
99C2 Wau Sudan
7B5 Waua Can
109D2 Wauchope Aust
17B2 Wauchula USA
14A2 Waukegan USA
14A2 Waukesha USA
14A2 Wauwatosa USA
106C2 Wave Hill Aust
14B3 Waveney R Eng
14B3 Waverly Ohio, USA
46C1 Wavre Belg
10B2 Wawa Can
95A2 Wāw Al Kabir Libya
95A2 Wāw an Nāmūs Well Libya
22C2 Wawona USA
19A3 Waxahachie USA
17B1 Waycross USA
17B1 Waynesboro Georgia, USA
19C3 Waynesboro Mississippi, USA
16A3 Waynesboro Pennsylvania, USA
15C3 Waynesboro Virginia, USA
18B2 Waynesville Missouri, USA
84B2 Wazi Khwa Afghan
43E4 Weald,The Upland Eng
42C2 Wear R Eng
19A3 Weatherford Texas, USA
20B2 Weaverville USA
14B1 Webbwood Can
16D1 Webster USA
18B2 Webster Groves USA
29D6 Weddell I Falkland Is
112C2 Weddell S Ant
13C2 Wedge Mt Can
20B2 Weed USA
101H1 Weenen S Africa
109C2 Wee Waa Aust
72D1 Weichang China
57C3 Weiden Germany
72D2 Weifang China
72E2 Weihai China
72C3 Wei He R Henan, China
72C2 Wei He R Shaanxi, China
109C1 Weilmoringle Aust
73A4 Weining China
107D2 Weipa Aust
14B2 Weirton USA
20C2 Weiser USA
72D3 Weishan Hu L China
57C2 Weissenfels Germ
17A1 Weiss L USA
99D1 Weldiya Eth
101G1 Welkom S Africa
15C2 Welland Can
43D3 Welland R Eng
106C2 Wellesley Is Aust
12G2 Wellesley L Can
43D3 Wellingborough Eng
109C2 Wellington Aust
18A2 Wellington Kansas, USA
111B2 Wellington NZ
6A2 Wellington Chan Can
13C2 Wells Can
43C4 Wells Eng
110B1 Wellsford NZ
106B3 Wells,L Aust
57C3 Wels Austria

43C3 Welshpool Wales
13D1 Wembley Can
7C4 Wemindji Can
20B1 Wenatchee USA
20C1 Wenatchee R USA
97B4 Wenchi Ghana
72E2 Wenden China
73E4 Wenling China
32J7 Wenman I Ecuador
73A5 Wenshan China
107D4 Wenthaggi Aust
108B2 Wentworth Aust
72A3 Wen Xian China
73E4 Wenzhou China
73C4 Wenzhu China
101C1 Wepener S Africa
100C2 Wessel Is Aust
14A2 West Allis USA
104C4 West Australian Basin Indian O
104C5 West Australian Ridge Indian O
94B2 West Bank Territory, S E Asia
19C3 West B USA
86B2 West Bengal State, India
43D3 West Bromwich Eng
16B3 West Chester USA
44B4 West Dunbartonshire Division, Scot
46D1 Westerburg Germ
56B2 Westerland Germany
16D2 Westerly USA
106A3 Western Australia State, Aust
39C4 Western Cape Province, S Africa
87A1 Western Ghats Mts India
44A3 Western Isles Division, Scot
96A2 Western Sahara Region, Mor
105H4 Western Samoa Is Pacific O
46B1 Westerschelde Estuary Neth
46D1 Westerwald Region, Germany
49D1 Westfalen Region, Germany
29D6 West Falkland I Falkland Is
16C1 Westfield Massachusetts, USA
15C2 Westfield New York, USA
18C2 West Frankfort USA
109C1 Westgate Aust
102E3 West Indies Is Caribbean S
13E2 Westlock Can
14B2 West Lorne Can
44C4 West Lothian Division, Scot
42C3 Westmorland County, Eng
18B2 West Memphis USA
43D3 West Midlands County, Eng
43D4 Westminster Eng
16A3 Westminster Maryland, USA
17B1 Westminster S Carolina, USA
100B3 West Nicholson Zim
78D1 Weston Malay
14B3 Weston USA
43C4 Weston-super-Mare Eng
17B2 West Palm Beach USA
18B2 West Plains USA
22B1 West Point California, USA
19C3 West Point Mississippi, USA

16C2 West Point New York, USA
12F2 West Point Mt USA
45B2 Westport Irish Rep
111B2 Westport NZ
40C2 Westray I Scot
13C2 West Road R Can
42E3 West Sole Oilfield N Sea
11B3 West Virginia State, USA
22C1 West Walker R USA
109C2 West Wyalong Aust
42D3 West Yorkshire County, Eng
71D4 Wetar I Indon
13E2 Wetaskiwin Can
99D3 Wete Tanz
46E1 Wetzlar Germany
Wevok = Cape Lisburne
71F4 Wewak PNG
19A2 Wewoka USA
45C2 Wexford County, Irish Rep
45C2 Wexford Irish Rep
54H5 Weyburn Can
43C4 Weymouth Eng
16D1 Weymouth USA
110C1 Whakatane NZ
110C1 Whakatane R NZ
44E1 Whalsay I Scot
110R1 Whangarei NZ
42D3 Wharfe R Eng
19A4 Wharton USA
111B2 Whataroa NZ
16A3 Wheaton Maryland, USA
8B3 Wheeler Peak Mt Nevada, USA
9C3 Wheeler Peak Mt New Mexico, USA
14B2 Wheeling USA
13C2 Whistler Can
15C2 Whitby Can
42D2 Whitby Eng
18B2 White R Arkansas, USA
12F2 White R Can
14A3 White R Indiana, USA
8C2 White R S Dakota, USA
7E4 White B Can
108B2 White Cliffs Aust
40C2 White Coomb Mt Scot
13D2 Whitecourt Can
14A1 Whitefish Pt USA
7D4 Whitegull L Can
15D2 Whitehall New York, USA
16B2 Whitehall Pennsylvania, USA
42C2 Whitehaven Eng
12G2 Whitehorse Can
10C1 White I NZ
19B4 White L USA
109C4 Whitemark Aust
16B2 White Mountain Peak Mt USA
12E1 White Mts Alaska, USA
15D2 White Mts New Hampshire, USA
99D1 White Nile R Sudan
16C2 White Plains USA
7B5 White River Can
15D2 White River Junction USA
White S = Beloye More
13B2 Whitesail L Can
20B1 White Salmon USA
17C1 Whiteville USA
97B4 White Volta R Ghana
42C2 Whithorn Scot
15C2 Whitney Can
21B2 Whitney,Mt USA
12E2 Whittier Alaska, USA
22C4 Whittier California, USA
5H3 Wholdia L Can

Whyalla

108A2 **Whyalla** Aust
14B2 **Wiarton** Can
18A2 **Wichita** USA
44C2 **Wick** Scot
45C2 **Wicklow** County, Irish Rep
45C2 **Wicklow** Irish Rep
45C2 **Wicklow** *Mts* Irish Rep
109C1 **Widgeegoara** *R* Aust
46D1 **Wied** *R* Germany
59B2 **Wielun** Pol
59B3 **Wien** Austria
59B3 **Wiener Neustadt** Austria
58C2 **Wieprz** *R* Pol
42C3 **Wigan** Eng
19C3 **Wiggins** USA
42B2 **Wigtown** Scot
42B2 **Wigtown B** Scot
47C1 **Wil** Switz
20C1 **Wilbur** USA
108B2 **Wilcannia** Aust
21B2 **Wildcat Peak** *Mt* USA
47B1 **Wildhorn** *Mt* Switz
13E2 **Wild Horse** Can
47D1 **Wildspitze** *Mt* Austria
17B2 **Wildwood** Florida, USA
16B3 **Wildwood** New Jersey, USA
101G1 **Wilge** *R* S Africa
56B2 **Wilhelmshaven** Germany
15C2 **Wilkes-Barre** USA
112B8 **Wilkes Land** Ant
42C2 **Wilkie** Can
20B2 **Willamette** *R* USA
108B2 **Willandra** *R* Aust
20B1 **Willapa B** USA
9C3 **Willcox** USA
27D4 **Willemstad** Curaçao
108A1 **William Creek** Aust
108B3 **William,Mt** Aust
21A2 **Williams** California, USA
13C2 **Williams Lake** Can
15C2 **Williamsport** USA
16C1 **Williamstown** Massachusetts, USA
14B3 **Williamstown** W Virginia, USA
16C2 **Willimantic** USA
16B2 **Willingboro** USA
13D2 **Willington,Mt** Can
107E2 **Willis Group** *Is* Aust
17B2 **Williston** Florida, USA
100B4 **Williston** S Africa
13C1 **Williston L** Can
8D2 **Willmar** USA
108A3 **Willoughby,C** Aust
13C2 **Willow** *R* Can
20B2 **Willow Ranch** USA
21A2 **Willows** USA
18B2 **Willow Springs** USA
108A2 **Wilmington** Aust
16B3 **Wilmington** Delaware, USA
17C1 **Wilmington** N Carolina, USA
7A5 **Wilmona** USA
11C3 **Wilson** USA
108B1 **Wilson** *R* Aust
6B3 **Wilson,C** USA
22C3 **Wilson,Mt** California, USA
20B1 **Wilson,Mt** Oregon, USA
109C3 **Wilsons Promontory** *Pen* Aust
43D4 **Wiltshire** County, Eng
46C2 **Wiltz** Lux
106B3 **Wiluna** Aust
14A2 **Winamac** USA
101G1 **Winburg** S Africa
16C1 **Winchendon** USA
15C1 **Winchester** Can
43D4 **Winchester** Eng

16C1 **Winchester** New Hampshire, USA
15C3 **Winchester** Virginia, USA
42C2 **Windermere** Eng
100A3 **Windhoek** Namibia
107D3 **Windorah** Aust
8C2 **Wind River Range** *Mts* USA
109D2 **Windsor** Aust
16C2 **Windsor** Connecticut, USA
43D4 **Windsor** Eng
7D5 **Windsor** Nova Scotia, Can
14B2 **Windsor** Ontario, Can
15D1 **Windsor** Quebec, Can
17B1 **Windsor Forest** USA
16C2 **Windsor Locks** USA
27E4 **Windward Is** Caribbean S
26C3 **Windward Pass** Caribbean S
13E1 **Winefred L** Can
18A2 **Winfield** Kansas, USA
109D2 **Wingham** Aust
34C3 **Winifreda** Arg
7B4 **Winisk** *R* Can
7B4 **Winisk L** Can
76B2 **Winkana** Myan
20B1 **Winlock** USA
97B4 **Winneba** Ghana
14A2 **Winnebago,L** USA
20C2 **Winnemucca** USA
19B3 **Winnfield** USA
5J4 **Winnipeg** Can
5J4 **Winnipeg,L** Can
5J4 **Winnipegosis** Can
4J4 **Winnipegosis,L** Can
15D2 **Winnipesaukee,L** USA
10A2 **Winona** Minnesota, USA
19C3 **Winona** Mississippi, USA
15D2 **Winooski** USA
9B3 **Winslow** USA
16C2 **Winsted** USA
11B3 **Winston-Salem** USA
46E1 **Winterberg** Germany
17B2 **Winter Garden** USA
17B2 **Winter Park** USA
22B1 **Winters** USA
47C1 **Winterthur** Switz
111A3 **Winton** NZ
43E3 **Wisbech** Eng
10B2 **Wisconsin** State, USA
7B5 **Wisconsin Rapids** USA
12D1 **Wiseman** USA
58B2 **Wisla** *R* Pol
56C2 **Wismar** Germany
33F2 **Witagron** Surinam
101G1 **Witbank** S Africa
9D3 **Witchita Falls** USA
43D3 **Witham** *R* Eng
42E3 **Withernsea** Eng
43D4 **Witney** Eng
46D1 **Witten** Germany
56C2 **Wittenberg** Germany
106A3 **Wittenoom** Aust
46D1 **Wittlich** Germany
58B2 **Wladyslawowo** Pol
58B2 **Wloclawek** Pol
58C2 **Wlodawa** Pol
109C3 **Wodonga** Aust
47C1 **Wohlen** Switz
71E4 **Wokam** Indon
43D4 **Woking** Eng
71F3 **Wokye** *I* Pacific O
20B2 **Wolf Creek** USA
8C2 **Wolf Point** USA
57C3 **Wolfsberg** Austria
56C2 **Wolfsburg** Germany
5H4 **Wollaston L** Can
5H4 **Wollaston Lake** Can
4G3 **Wollaston Pen** Can
109D2 **Wollongong** Aust

101G1 **Wolmaransstad** S Africa
59B2 **Wolow** Pol
43C3 **Wolseley** Aust
16A2 **Wolverhampton** Eng
109D1 **Wondai** Aust
74B3 **Wönju** S Korea
108B2 **Wonominta** *R* Aust
13C1 **Wonowon** Can
74B3 **Wönsan** N Korea
108C3 **Wonthaggi** Aust
108A2 **Woocalla** Aust
16B3 **Woodbine** USA
15C3 **Woodbridge** USA
5G4 **Wood Buffalo Nat Pk** Can
109D1 **Woodburn** Aust
20B1 **Woodburn** USA
16B3 **Woodbury** USA
12F1 **Woodchopper** USA
21A2 **Woodland** California, USA
20B1 **Woodland** Washington, USA
107D1 **Woodlark** *I* PNG
106C4 **Woodmera** Aust
106C3 **Woodroffe,Mt** Aust
14B2 **Woodstock** Ontario, Can
16B3 **Woodstown** USA
110C2 **Woodville** NZ
19B3 **Woodville** USA
108A2 **Woomera** Aust
15D2 **Woonsocket** USA
14B2 **Wooster** USA
43C3 **Worcester** Eng
100A4 **Worcester** S Africa
16D1 **Worcester** USA
47E1 **Wörgl** Austria
42C2 **Workington** Eng
8C2 **Worland** USA
46E2 **Worms** Germany
43B4 **Worms Head** *Pt* Wales
43D4 **Worthing** Eng
8D2 **Worthington** USA
71D4 **Wowoni** *I* Indon
12H3 **Wrangell** USA
12H3 **Wrangell I** USA
12F2 **Wrangell Mts** USA
40B2 **Wrath,C** Scot
43C3 **Wrexham** Wales
43C4 **Wrexham** County, Wales
17B1 **Wrightsville** USA
22D3 **Wrightwood** USA
4F3 **Wrigley** Can
59B2 **Wrocław** Pol
58B2 **Września** Pol
69E2 **Wuchang** China
76E1 **Wuchuan** China
72E2 **Wuda** China
72C2 **Wuding He** *R* China
72A3 **Wudu** China
73C4 **Wugang** China
72B2 **Wuhai** China
73C3 **Wuhan** China
73D3 **Wuhu** China
73D5 **Wuhua** China
84D2 **Wujang** China
72B1 **Wujia He** *R* China
73B4 **Wu Jiang** *R* China
97C4 **Wukari** Nig
73B4 **Wuling Shan** *Mts* China
97D4 **Wum** Cam
73A4 **Wumeng Shan** *Upland* China
72B2 **Wuqi** China
72D2 **Wuqing** China
57B3 **Würzburg** Germany
57B3 **Wurzen** Germany
72C2 **Wutai Shan** *Mt* China
71F4 **Wuvulu** *I* Pacific O
72A2 **Wuwei** China
73E3 **Wuxi** China
73E3 **Wuxing** China
72C2 **Wuyang** China
73D4 **Wuyi Shan** *Mts* China
72B1 **Wuyuan** China

76D2 **Wuzhi Shan** *Mts* China
72B2 **Wuzhong** China
73C5 **Wuzhou** China
14B2 **Wyandotte** USA
109C1 **Wyandra** Aust
43C4 **Wye** *R* Eng
43C4 **Wylye** *R* Eng
43E3 **Wymondham** Eng
108B2 **Wyndham** Aust
18B2 **Wynne** USA
4G2 **Wynniatt B** Can
109C4 **Wynyard** Aust
8C2 **Wyoming** State, USA
14A2 **Wyoming** USA
109D2 **Wyong** Aust

X

84D1 **Xaidulla** China
72D1 **Xai Moron He** *R* China
101C3 **Xai Xai** Mozam
23B2 **Xaltinguis** Mexico
100A2 **Xangongo** Angola
46D1 **Xanten** Germany
55B2 **Xanthi** Greece
100B3 **Xau,L** Botswana
14B3 **Xenia** USA
72A2 **Xiahe** China
73D5 **Xiamen** China
72B3 **Xi'an** China
73B4 **Xianfeng** China
73C3 **Xiangfan** China
73C4 **Xiang Jiang** *R* China
73C4 **Xiangtan** Province, China
73C4 **Xianning** China
72B3 **Xianyang** China
73C4 **Xiao Shui** *R* China
73A4 **Xiapu** China
73A4 **Xichang** China
23B1 **Xicotepec** Mexico
76C2 **Xieng Khouang** Laos
73B4 **Xifeng** China
86B1 **Xigazê** China
72A1 **Xi He** *R* China
72B2 **Xiji** China
73C5 **Xi Jiang** *R* China
72E1 **Xiliao He** *R* China
73B5 **Xilin** China
23B1 **Xilitla** Mexico
73D4 **Xinfeng** China
72C1 **Xinghe** China
73D5 **Xingning** China
73B4 **Xingren** China
72C2 **Xingtai** China
33G4 **Xingu** *R* Brazil
68B2 **Xingxingxia** China
73A4 **Xingyi** China
72A2 **Xining** China
72E2 **Xinjin** Liaoning, China
73A3 **Xinjin** Sichuan, China
72D2 **Xinwen** China
72C2 **Xin Xian** China
72C2 **Xinxiang** China
73C3 **Xinyang** China
73C5 **Xinyi** Guangdong, China
72D3 **Xinyi** Jiangsu, China
72E1 **Xi Ujimqin Qi** China
74A2 **Xiuyan** China
23B2 **Xochimilco** Mexico
73D3 **Xuancheng** China
73B3 **Xuanhan** China
72C1 **Xuanhua** China
73A4 **Xuanwei** China
72C3 **Xuchang** China
99E2 **Xuddur** Somalia
73C5 **Xun Jiang** *R* China
69E2 **Xunke** China
73D5 **Xunwu** China
73C4 **Xupu** China
76E1 **Xuwen** China
73B4 **Xuyong** China
72D3 **Xuzhou** China

Y

73A4 **Ya'an** China
108B3 **Yaapeet** Aust
98B2 **Yabassi** Cam
68C1 **Yablonovyy Khrebet** *Mts* Russian Fed

Zaliv Kara-Bogaz Gol

94C2 Yabrūd Syria
20B2 Yachats USA
30D3 Yacuiba Bol
87B1 Yādgir India
95A1 Yafran Libya
23A1 Yahualica Mexico
98C2 Yahuma Zaire
75B1 Yaita Japan
75B2 Yaizu Japan
73A4 Yajiang China
20B1 Yakima USA
20B1 Yakima R USA
97B3 Yako Burkina
98C2 Yakoma Zaire
74E2 Yakumo Japan
12G3 Yakutat USA
12G3 Yakutat B USA
63E1 Yakutsk Russian Fed
77C4 Yala Tha
23B2 Yalalag Mexico
98C2 Yalinga CAR
109C3 Yallourn Aust
68B3 Yalong R China
73A4 Yalong Jiang R China
54C2 Yalova Turk
60D5 Yalta Ukraine
74D3 Yalu Jiang R China
74C4 Yamaguchi Japan
68D1 Yamarovka Russian Fed
109D1 Yamba New S Wales, Aust
108B2 Yamba S Australia, Aust
99C2 Yambio Sudan
54C2 Yambol Bulg
71E4 Yamdena I Indon
 Yam Kinneret = Tiberias,L
108B1 Yamma Yamma,L Aust
97B4 Yamoussoukro Côte d'Ivoire
85D3 Yamuna R India
86C1 Yamzho Yumco L China
63F1 Yana R Russian Fed
108B3 Yanac Aust
75A2 Yanagawa Japan
87C1 Yanam India
72B2 Yan'an China
80B3 Yanbu'al Bahr S Arabia
108B2 Yancannia Aust
72E3 Yancheng Aust
72B2 Yanchi China
108B1 Yandama R Aust
98C2 Yangambi Zaire
72C1 Yang He R China
73C5 Yangjiang China
76B2 Yangon Myan
72C2 Yangquan China
73C5 Yangshan China
73C3 Yangtze Gorges China
72E3 Yangtze,Mouths of the China
72D3 Yangzhou China
73B4 Yanhe China
74E2 Yanji India
50D2 Yankton USA
68A2 Yanqqi China
72D1 Yan Shan Hills China
109D1 Yantabulla Aust
72E2 Yantai China
72D2 Yanzhou China
98B2 Yaoundé Cam
71E4 Yapen I Indon
71E3 Yap Is Pacific O
24B2 Yaqui R Mexico
61G2 Yaransk Russian Fed
32C3 Yari R Colombia
74D3 Yariga-dake Mt Japan
82B2 Yarkant He R China
86C1 Yarlung Zangbo Jiang R China
7D5 Yarmouth Can
94B2 Yarmūk R Syria/Jordan
61E2 Yaroslavl' Russian Fed

94B2 Yarqon R Israel
109C3 Yarram Aust
109D1 Yarraman Aust
109C3 Yarrawonga Aust
60D2 Yartsevo
63B1 Yartsevo Russian Fed
32B2 Yarumal Colombia
97C3 Yashi Nig
97C4 Yashikera Nig
61F4 Yashkul' Russian Fed
84C1 Yasin Pak
59C3 Yasinya Ukraine
109C3 Yass Aust
109C2 Yass R Aust
75A1 Yasugi Japan
18A2 Yates Center USA
98C2 Yatolema Zaire
74C4 Yatsushiro Japan
94B3 Yatta Israel
32C4 Yavari Peru
85D4 Yavatmāl India
74C4 Yawatahama Japan
76D2 Ya Xian China
92D2 Yazd Iran
90B3 Yazd-e Khvāst Iran
19B3 Yazoo R USA
19B3 Yazoo City USA
76B2 Ye Myan
59D3 Yedintsy Moldova
102A2 Yeelanna Aust
60E3 Yefremov Russian Fed
61F4 Yegorlyk R Russian Fed
99D2 Yei Sudan
65H4 Yekaterinburg Russian Fed
60E3 Yelets Russian Fed
44E1 Yell I Scot
87C1 Yellandu India
 Yellow = Huang He
8B1 Yellowhead P Can
4G3 Yellowknife Can
5G4 Yellowmead P Can
109C2 Yellow Mt aust
69E3 Yellow Sea China/Korea
8C2 Yellowstone R USA
8B2 Yellowstone L USA
6B1 Yelverton B Can
97C3 Yelwa Nig
81C4 Yemen Republic, Arabian Pen
76C1 Yen Bai Viet
97B4 Yendi Ghana
76B1 Yengan Myan
63B2 Yeniseysk
63B1 Yeniseysk Kryazh Ridge Russian Fed
64J2 Yeniseyskiy Zal B Russian Fed
12D2 Yentna R USA
43C4 Yeo R Eng
109C2 Yeoval Aust
43C4 Yeovil Eng
63C1 Yerbogachen Russian Fed
65F5 Yerevan Armenia
21B2 Yerington USA
21B3 Yermo USA
69E1 Yerofey-Pavlovich Russian Fed
94B3 Yeroham Israel
61G3 Yershov Russian Fed
 Yerushalayim = Jerusalem
92C1 Yeşil R Turk
94B2 Yesud Hama'ala Israel
109D1 Yetman Aust
96B2 Yetti Maur
93E1 Yevlakh Azerbaijan
60D4 Yevpatoriya Ukraine
72E2 Ye Xian China
60E4 Yeysk Russian Fed
52B2 Yiannitsa Greece
73A4 Yibin China
73C3 Yichang China
69E2 Yichun China
72B2 Yijun China

54C2 Yıldız Dağları Upland Turk
92C2 Yıldızeli Turk
73A5 Yiliang China
72B2 Yinchuan China
72D3 Ying He R China
72E1 Yingkou China
73D3 Yingshan Hubei, China
72B3 Yingshan Sichuan, China
73D4 Yingtan China
82C1 Yining China
72B1 Yin Shan Upland China
99D2 Yirga Alem Eth
99D2 Yirol Sudan
63D2 Yirshi China
73B5 Yishan China
72D2 Yishui China
55B3 Yithion Greece
38J6 Yivieska Fin
72D2 Yiyang China
38K5 Yli-Kitka L Fin
38J5 Ylilornio Sweden
19A4 Yoakum USA
23B2 Yogope Mexico
78C4 Yogyakarta Indon
13D2 Yoho Nat Pk Can
98B2 Yokadouma Cam
75B2 Yokkaichi Japan
75B1 Yokohama Japan
75B1 Yokosuka Japan
74C3 Yonago Japan
74E3 Yonezawa Japan
73D4 Yong'an China
72A2 Yongchang China
74B3 Yongch'on S Korea
73B4 Yongchuan China
72A2 Yongdeng China
73D5 Yongding China
72D2 Yongding He R China
74B3 Yöngdök S Korea
74B3 Yönghüng N Korea
74B3 Yongju S Korea
72B2 Yongning China
16C2 Yonkers USA
49C2 Yonne R France
42D3 York Eng
42D3 York County Eng
18A1 York Nebraska, USA
16A3 York Pennsylvania, USA
107D2 York,C Aust
108A2 Yorke Pen Aust
108A3 Yorketown Aust
7A4 York Factory Can
41C3 Yorkshire Moors Moorland Eng
42D2 Yorkshire Wolds Upland Eng
5H4 Yorkton Can
22B2 Yosemite L USA
22C1 Yosemite Nat Pk USA
75A2 Yoshii R Japan
75A2 Yoshino R Japan
61G2 Yoshkar Ola Russian Fed
74B4 Yösu S Korea
41B3 Youghal Irish Rep
45C3 Youghal Harb Irish Rep
73B5 You Jiang R China
109C2 Young Aust
25D2 Young Urug
111A2 Young Range Mts NZ
13E2 Youngstown Can
14B2 Youngstown Ohio, USA
22A1 Yountville USA
73B4 Youyang China
72B2 Yozgat Turk
92C1 Yozgat Turk
20B2 Yreka USA
39G7 Ystad Sweden
43C3 Ystwyth R Wales
44C3 Ythan R Scot
73C4 Yuan Jiang R Hunan, China
73A5 Yuan Jiang R Yunnan, China
73A4 Yuanmu China

72C2 Yuanping China
21A2 Yuba City USA
74E2 Yūbari Japan
25D3 Yucatán Pen Mexico
25D2 Yucatan Chan Mexico/Cuba
72C2 Yuci China
63F2 Yudoma R Russian Fed
73D4 Yudu China
73A4 Yuexi China
73C4 Yueyang China
54A2 Yugoslavia Republic, Europe
73B5 Yu Jiang R China
12C2 Yukon R Can/USA
4E3 Yukon Territory Can
76E1 Yulin Guangdong, China
73C5 Yulin Guangxi, China
72B2 Yulin Shaanxi, China
9B3 Yuma USA
68B3 Yumen China
72D2 Yunan China
34A3 Yungay Chile
73C5 Yunkai Dashan Hills China
108A2 Yunta Aust
72C3 Yunxi China
72C3 Yun Xian China
73B3 Yunyang China
32B5 Yurimaguas Peru
73E5 Yu Shan Mt Taiwan
38L6 Yushkozero Russian Fed
82D2 Yushu Tibet, China
73A5 Yuxi China
74F2 Yuzhno-Kuril'sk Russian Fed
69G2 Yuzhno-Sakhalinsk Russian Fed
61J3 Yuzh Ural Mts Russian Fed
46A2 Yvelines Department, France
47B1 Yverdon Switz

Z

56A2 Zaandam Neth
93D2 Zāb al Babir R Iraq
93D2 Zāb as Saghir R Iraq
68D2 Zabaykal'sk Russian Fed
59B3 Zabreh Czech Republic
59B2 Zabrze Pol
23A2 Zacapu Mexico
24B2 Zacatecas Mexico
23B2 Zacatecas Morelos, Mexico
23B2 Zacatepec Oaxaca, Mexico
23B2 Zacatlán Mexico
23A1 Zacoalco Mexico
23B1 Zacualtipan Mexico
52C2 Zadar Croatia
76B3 Zadetkyi I Myan
50A2 Zafra Spain
95C1 Zagazig Egypt
96B1 Zagora Mor
52C1 Zagreb Croatia
91B4 Zähedän Iran
94B2 Zahle Leb
51C2 Zahrez Chergui Marshland Alg
61H2 Zainsk Russian Fed
98C3 Zaire Republic, Africa
99B3 Zaire R Zaire/Congo
54B2 Zaječar Yugos
68C1 Zakamensk Russian Fed
93D2 Zakho Iraq
55B3 Zákinthos I Greece
59B3 Zakopane Pol
59B3 Zalaegerszeg Hung
54B1 Zalău Rom
56C2 Zalew Szczeciński Lg Pol
98C1 Zalingei Sudan
63F2 Zaliv Akademii R Russian Fed
65G5 Zaliv Kara-Bogaz Gol B Turkmenistan

Zyyi

74C2 Zaliv Petra Velikogo *B* Russian Fed
69G2 Zaliv Turpeniya *B* Russian Fed
95A2 Zaltan Libya
89H9 Zambesi *R* Mozam
100B2 Zambezi Zambia
100B2 Zambezi *R* Zambia
100B2 Zambia Republic, Africa
79B4 Zamboanga Phil
79A4 Zamboanga Pen Phil
58C2 Zambrów Pol
32B4 Zamora Ecuador
23A2 Zamora Mexico
50A1 Zamora Spain
59C2 Zamość Pol
72A3 Zamtang China
98B3 Zanaga Congo
50B2 Záncara *R* Spain
84D2 Zanda China
14B3 Zanesville USA
84D2 Zangla India
90A2 Zanjan Iran
34B2 Zanjitas Arg
34B2 Zanjon *R* Arg
99D3 Zanzibar *I* Tanz
99D3 Zanzibar *I* Tanz
96C2 Zaouatallaz Alg
72D3 Zaozhuang China
93D2 Zap *R* Turk
39K7 Zapadnaja Dvina *R* Russian Fed
65H3 Zapadno-Sibirskaya Nizmennost' *Lowland* Russian Fed
63B2 Zapadnyy Sayan *Mts* Russian Fed
34A3 Zapala Arg
60E4 Zaporozh'ye Ukraine
93C2 Zara Turk
23A1 Zaragoza Mexico
50B1 Zaragoza Spain
90B2 Zarand Iran
90C3 Zarand Iran
80E2 Zaranj Afghan
33D2 Zarara Ven
58D1 Zarasai Lithuania
34D2 Zárate Arg
90B3 Zard Kuh *Mt* Iran
12H3 Zaremba I USA
84B2 Zarghun Shahr Afghan
84B2 Zargun *Mt* Pak
97C3 Zaria Nig
92C3 Zarqa Jordan
94B2 Zarqa *R* Jordan

32B4 Zaruma Ecuador
58B2 Zary Pol
96D1 Zarzis Tunisia
84D2 Zäskär *Mts* India
84D2 Zäskär *R* India
94C2 Zatara *R* Jordan
Zatoka Gdańska = Gdańsk,G of
69E1 Zavitinsk Russian Fed
59B2 Zawiercie Pol
63C2 Zayarsk Russian Fed
65K5 Zaysan Kazakhstan
82D3 Zayü China
68B4 Zayü *Mt* China
58B2 Zduńska Wola Pol
46B1 Zeebrugge Belg
94B3 Zeelim Israel
101G1 Zeerust S Africa
94B2 Zefat Israel
97C3 Zegueren Watercourse Mali
99E1 Zeila Somalia
57C2 Zeitz Germany
72A2 Zekog China
61G2 Zelenodol'sk Russian Fed
39K6 Zelenogorsk Russian Fed
47D1 Zell Austria
98C2 Zemio CAR
64F1 Zemlya Aleksandry *I* Barents S
64F2 Zemlya Frantsa Iosifa *Is* Barents S
64F1 Zemlya Georga *I* Barents S
64H1 Zemlya Vil'cheka *I* Barents S
73B4 Zenning China
47B1 Zermatt Switz
63E2 Zeya Russian Fed
63E2 Zeya *Res* Russian Fed
50A1 Zézere *R* Port
94B1 Zghorta Leb
58B2 Zgierz Pol
72D1 Zhangjiakou China
73D4 Zhangping China
72D2 Zhangwei He *R* China
72E1 Zhangwu China
72A2 Zhangye China
73C5 Zhangzhou China
73A4 Zhanyi China
73C5 Zhaoqing China

73A4 Zhaotong China
72D2 Zhaoyang Hu *L* China
61J4 Zharkamys Russian Fed
63E1 Zhatay Russian Fed
73D4 Zhejiang Province, China
67F3 Zhengou China
72C3 Zhengzhou China
72D3 Zhenjiang China
73A4 Zhenxiong China
73B4 Zhenyuan China
61F3 Zherdevka Russian Fed
73C3 Zhicheng China
68C1 Zhigalovo Russian Fed
73B4 Zhijin China
58D2 Zhitkovichi Belarus
60C3 Zhitomir Ukraine
60D3 Zhlobin Belarus
60C4 Zhmerinka Ukraine
84B2 Zhob Pak
58D2 Zhodino Latvia
72B2 Zhongning China
112C10 Zhongshan *Base* Ant
73C5 Zhongshan China
72B2 Zhongwei China
68B4 Zhougdian China
73E3 Zhoushan Quandao *Arch* China
72E2 Zhuanghe China
72A3 Zhugqu China
73C3 Zhushan China
73C4 Zhuzhou China
72D2 Zibo China
106C3 Ziel,Mt Aust
58B2 Zielona Góra Pol
76A1 Zigaing Myan
73A4 Zigong China
97A3 Ziguinchor Sen
23A2 Zihuatanejo Mexico
94B2 Zikhron Ya'aqov Israel
59B3 Žilina Slovakia
95A2 Zillah Libya
47D1 Ziller *R* Austria
47D1 Zillertaler Alpen *Mts* Austria
58D1 Zilupe Russian Fed
63C2 Zima Russian Fed
23B1 Zimapan Mexico
23B2 Zimatlan Mexico
100B2 Zimbabwe Republic, Africa

94B3 Zin *R* Israel
23B2 Zinacatepec Mexico
23A2 Zinapécuaro Mexico
97C3 Zinder Niger
73C4 Zi Shui China
23A2 Zitácuaro Mexico
57C2 Zittau Germany
72D2 Ziya He *R* China
72A3 Ziyang China
61J2 Zlatoust Russian Fed
59B3 Zlin Czech Republic
65K4 Zmeinogorsk Russian Fed
58B2 Znin Pol
59B3 Znojmo Czech Republic
100B3 Zoekmekaar S Africa
47B1 Zofinger Switz
72A3 Zoigê China
59D3 Zolochev Ukraine
101C2 Zomba Malawi
98B2 Zongo Zaire
92B1 Zonguldak Turk
97B4 Zorzor Lib
96A2 Zouerate Maur
54B1 Zrenjanin Serbia, Yugos
47C1 Zug Switz
47D1 Zugspitze *Mt*
50A2 Zújar *R* Spain
100C2 Zumbo Mozam
23B2 Zumpango Mexico
97C4 Zungeru Nig
73B4 Zunyi China
76D1 Zuo *R* China
73B5 Zuo Jiang *R* China
47C1 Zürich Switz
47C1 Zürichsee *L* Switz
95A1 Zuwárah Libya
95A2 Zuwaylah Libya
61H2 Zuyevka Russian Fed
100B4 Zvishavane Zim
59B3 Zvolen Slovakia
54A2 Zvornik Bosnia-Herzegovina
97B4 Zwedru Lib
46D2 Zweibrücken Germany
47B1 Zweisimmen Switz
57C2 Zwickau Germany
56B2 Zwolle Neth
58C2 Zyrardów Pol
65K5 Zyryanovsk Kazakhstan
59B3 Żywiec Pol
94A1 Zyyi Cyprus